The Global Future

A Brief Introduction to World Politics

FOURTH EDITION

CHARLES W. KEGLEY, JR.
Carnegie Council for Ethics in International Affairs

GREGORY A. RAYMOND
Boise State University

 WADSWORTH
CENGAGE Learning™

Australia • Brazil • Japan • Korea • Mexico • Singapore • Spain • United Kingdom • United States

The Global Future: A Brief Introduction to World Politics, Fourth Edition
Charles W. Kegley, Jr.
Gregory A. Raymond

Publisher: Suzanne Jeans

Executive Editor: Carolyn Merrill

Development Editor: Kate Scheinman

Assistant Editor: Kate MacLean

Media Editor: Laura Hildebrand

Editorial Assistant: Angela Hodge

Marketing Manager: Lydia LeStar

Marketing Coordinator: Joshua Hendrick

Senior Marketing Communications Manager: Heather Baxley

Content Project Manager: Alison Eigel Zade

Art Director: Linda Helcher

Production Technology Analyst: Jeff Joubert

Print Buyer: Fola Orekoya

Rights Acquisition Specialist, Image: Mandy Groszko

Senior Rights Acquisition Specialist, Text: Katie Huha

Production Service: MPS Limited, a Macmillan Company

Cover Designer: Lou Ann Thesing

Cover Image: © Benjamin Rondel/CORBIS

Compositor: MPS Limited, a Macmillan Company

Indexer: Sonya Dintaman

For product information and technology assistance, contact us at
Cengage Learning Customer & Sales Support, 1-800-354-9706.

For permission to use material from this text or product, submit all requests online at **www.cengage.com/permissions**.
Further permissions questions can be emailed to
permissionrequest@cengage.com.

Library of Congress Control Number: 2010939139

Student Edition
ISBN 13: 978-0-495-89866-5
ISBN-10: 0-495-89866-X

Wadsworth
20 Channel Center Street
Boston, MA 02210
USA

Cengage Learning is a leading provider of customized learning solutions with office locations around the globe, including Singapore, the United Kingdom, Australia, Mexico, Brazil, and Japan. Locate your local office at **international.cengage.com/region**.

Cengage Learning products are represented in Canada by Nelson Education, Ltd.

For your course and learning solutions, visit
www.cengage.com.

Purchase any of our products at your local college store or at our preferred online store **www.cengagebrain.com**.

Instructors: Please visit **login.cengage.com** and log in to access instructor-specific resources.

Printed in the United States of America
1 2 3 4 5 6 7 14 13 12 11 10

To my loving wife, Debbie
—Charles W. Kegley, Jr.

To the public school teachers and college professors who
shaped my life through their encouragement and support
—Gregory A. Raymond

Brief Contents

Contents

PART IV   The Politics of Global Welfare   279

11   The Globalization of World Politics   280

12   The Political Economy of Trade and Monetary Relations   300

Maps

Preface

In all likelihood, you are enrolled in your first course on world politics (or international relations, as it is called in some college catalogs). Like most students in introductory courses, you probably have a few questions about the relevance of this subject for your education. In particular, you may be wondering why you should study world politics and when it became part of the typical college curriculum. Because we have written this textbook with students in mind, a good place to begin our exploration of world politics is by addressing these preliminary questions.

Why Should I Study World Politics?

World politics is an endless source of mystery and surprise. As you will see throughout this book, common sense is not sufficient for understanding international events. All too often, our intuition is wrong about why certain things happened. Albert Einstein once hinted at the challenge of explaining world politics when he was asked, "Why is it that when the mind of man has stretched so far as to discover the structure of the atom we have been unable to devise the political means to keep the atom from destroying us?" He replied, "This is simple, my friend, it is because politics is more difficult than physics."

In recent years, the world has experienced many unsettling changes that have made world politics even more difficult than in Einstein's day. The destructive power of military force has increased, terrorism has become a serious global threat, people across the planet continue to struggle through a protracted economic recession, and the global environment has suffered from the combined pressures of population growth, resource scarcities, and pollution. Further complicating matters is the interconnectedness of nations. Pressing military, social, economic, and environmental problems now spill across national borders, affecting the security and personal well-being of all of us. In more ways than we realize, our lives are affected by world politics.

Because events in distant parts of the world touch our daily lives, we should not leave crucial decisions about international issues to others. In a democracy, every citizen has an opportunity to influence policies on these issues by voting in elections, lobbying government officials, writing letters to newspapers, or joining protest demonstrations. To make the most of these opportunities, we need to understand world politics. This text introduces a set of concepts and analytic tools that will help you better understand the nature of world politics. The effort that you make in learning these concepts and tools will strengthen your ability to think critically about international issues and enhance your capability to advocate effectively for policies you believe will improve the human condition.

When Did World Politics Become an Academic Subject?

Although philosophers, theologians, historians, and statesmen have written about war and diplomacy since antiquity, the formal study of world politics began at the dawn of the twentieth century. Prior to the onset of World War I, many people believed that progress toward a more peaceful and prosperous world was inevitable. The great powers had not fought one another for decades, industrial development and international commerce were expanding at astonishing rates, and scientists seemed to be solving the deepest mysteries of the universe. By some accounts, it was the most optimistic period in history. Peace conferences held in The Hague during 1899 and 1907 inspired hope that future generations would settle their differences without resorting to arms. In 1910, the British writer Norman Angell declared that war had become obsolete because it was no longer profitable. Three years later, at the dedication of the building that would house the Permanent Court of Arbitration, the Scottish-American industrialist Andrew Carnegie wrote in his diary: "Looking back a hundred years, or less perchance, from today, the future historian is to pronounce the opening [of the Court] ... the greatest one step forward ever taken by man, in his long and checkered march upward from barbarism."

In those tranquil, confident times, students of world politics surveyed current events to glean insight on the international issues of the day. The study of world politics consisted mainly of commentary about personalities and interesting incidents, past and present. Rarely did scholars seek to generalize about patterns of behavior that might account for international events.

The gruesome toll extracted by World War I destroyed the sense of security that made this approach popular. However interesting descriptions of current events might be, they were of doubtful use to a world in search of ways to prevent future wars. International relations as a field of academic study emerged as scholars began searching for the underlying causes of the First World War. Not long after the guns had fallen silent, the Royal Institute of International Affairs was established in London, the Council of Foreign Relations was set up in New York, and the first university chair in International Relations was created at the University College of Wales, Aberystwyth. Soon institutions of higher learning throughout Britain and the United States began offering courses on world politics. Since then, the academic study of international affairs has spread to virtually every region of the world.

What Can We Learn about the Global Future?

Throughout history, people have tried to foresee the future. In many ancient cultures, natural phenomena from earthquakes to the alignment of celestial bodies were perceived as portents of important events, and oracles claiming an ability to communicate with a supernatural realm offered advice to those pondering momentous decisions. Although contemporary social scientists deny that anyone can predict exactly what will happen in the global future, they frequently project demographic, social, economic, political, military, and environmental trends to create scenarios depicting plausible alternative futures.

Systematic thinking about the global future began in earnest after the Second World War. During the 1950s, social scientists at the RAND Corporation, Hudson Institute, and other "think tanks" developed innovative forecasting techniques that stimulated broad academic and popular interest in anticipating and planning for the future. In 1967, the first World Future Research Conference was convened in Oslo, Norway. A few years later, Shell Oil incorporated future scenarios in its long-range strategic planning; the Club of Rome, a group of international business leaders, sponsored computer simulations of the likely impact of major trends; and the Rockefeller Foundation and the Carnegie Endowment for International Peace supported the World Order Models Project, which asked what choices could be made in the present to engender a more peaceful and just future. Meanwhile, government bodies, such as the Defense Advanced Research Projects Agency (DARPA) of the U.S. Department of Defense, funded work on early warning indicators, and the U.S. National Intelligence Council undertook a series of forward-looking studies that asked where the trajectory of international events was headed. Nowadays policy analysts in public agencies and the private sector regularly monitor global trends, examine how they may interact, and make contingency forecasts about the likelihood of alternative global futures. As such, they are heeding the wisdom of an old African proverb: "Tomorrow belongs to the people who prepare for it today."

OVERVIEW OF THE BOOK

Now that you have some idea about the relevance of studying world politics, let's briefly look at how *The Global Future* is organized and what you can do to take advantage of its features.

Organization and Content

To help you make sense of world politics, *The Global Future* is divided into five parts. Part I introduces the central issues and major theories in the study of international relations. Part II identifies the primary actors in the global arena and discusses the processes by which these actors make decisions. Part III looks at global security, focusing on the problems of war and terrorism as well as rival approaches to preserving peace. Part IV examines issues of global welfare. Following an analysis of the process of globalization, it addresses the topics of international economic relations, human rights, and the linkage between population dynamics and the environment. Finally, Part V explores alternative world futures by posing a set of questions that encourages you to consider what is possible in the decades ahead, what is probable, and what future you would most prefer.

Design and Pedagogy

The Global Future contains a variety of learning aids to help you understand the complexities of world politics.

- **Chapter outlines.** The first item in every chapter is an outline of the material that will be covered.

- **Introductory case studies.** To encourage you to think critically about the topics covered in the book, the narrative section of each chapter begins with a vignette that introduces its underlying theme.

- **Marginal glosses for all key terms.** Whenever we use a technical term for the first time, we highlight it in the text and define it in the margin. Pay close attention to these terms because they are part of the vocabulary scholars, journalists, and policymakers use when discussing world politics.

- **Controversy boxes presenting essential debates.** We use "controversy" boxes to portray ongoing debates within the field of international relations and to encourage you to weigh the arguments on each side as you develop your own opinion.

- **Application boxes highlighting the connection between theory and policy.** We also use box inserts to show how diplomats and world leaders applied the theoretical concepts covered in a particular chapter to policy problems that they faced.

- **Photographs.** To amplify the main points in the text, we have included photographs with captions that explain each image's relationship to key concepts and themes.

- **Tables, figures, and maps.** Visual aids are excellent tools for communicating complex material. When it would reinforce an explanation in the text, we have displayed important information in graphic form.

- **Chapter summaries, key terms, and critical thinking questions.** Each chapter concludes with a summary of its main themes, a list of the key terms, and a set of questions designed to help you think theoretically about some of the issues that were covered.

CHANGES TO THE FOURTH EDITION

Readers familiar with the previous edition of *The Global Future* will recognize that its underlying organizational structure remains intact, but the many changes that have taken place in world politics over the past few years have required us to revisit every chapter to integrate the latest international developments with the most current scholarship. The result is a text completely updated from beginning to end. Each chapter incorporates the most recent available data on global trends and the most recent research findings on their likely impact. In so doing, the fourth edition of *The Global Future* addresses the key issues on the world's agenda—ranging from terrorism and international hostilities to globalization and the world economy, and from the opportunities presented by the emergence of a global civil society to the challenges posed by global climate change. In addition, coverage has been expanded to take into account new departures in international relations theory that interpret these developments.

Beyond updating and refining each chapter, this edition contains the following new features:

- Part I, "Trend and Transformation in World Politics," has been revamped so that basic concepts, such as nation, state, nation-state, and nonstate actor, appear earlier in the book. The discussion in Chapter 1 on the role of perceptions in world politics has been streamlined, and new material on neo-classical realism and constructivism augments the presentation of theories of world politics in Chapter 2.

- Part II, "The Actors in World Politics," has been extensively reorganized. Chapter 3 on foreign policy decision making contains new coverage of rational political ambition theory and the friction between members of the Obama administration's policy-making team in Afghanistan. The discussion of historical great-power rivalries in Chapter 4 gives more attention to the Vietnam War. The analysis of the Global South in Chapter 5 now introduces the Beijing consensus and examines the impact of an emerging middle class on developing countries. Chapter 6, which describes nonstate actors in world politics, has been thoroughly revised to explore the political impact of the sovereign debt crisis in various European Union members, and to demonstrate how the web of interactions among state and nonstate actors affects what occurs in various issue-areas.

- Part III, "The Politics of Global Security," contains increased coverage of civil wars and insurgencies in the discussion patterns of armed conflict in Chapter 7. Expanded coverage is also given to counterinsurgency and counterterrorism policies in the presentation of strategies for the use of military force found in Chapter 8. Alliance politics receives more in-depth analysis in Chapter 9, as does the concept of *jus post bellum* in Chapter's 10 discussion of contemporary just war theory.

- Part IV, "The Politics of Global Welfare," takes a fresh look in Chapter 11 at the globalization of production and the prospects for deglobalization.

Chapter 12, which focuses on the political economy of trade and monetary relations, gives greater emphasis to the impact of the economic crisis of 2008 and to the growth of trade protectionism. The principle of responsibility to protect receives more attention in the discussion of human rights in Chapter 13, and the issue of aging populations in some Global East countries has been added to Chapter 14, along with a presentation of recent evidence on the unexpected rise in replacement fertility rates in some Global North countries.

- Part V, "Alternative World Futures," has been broadened to encourage students to think more deeply about what global futures are possible given current trends, what futures are probable, and what futures they would prefer. New material has been added to Chapter 15 on the economic problems that may reduce the role of the United States in world politics, relations between the United States and China, and the debate over whether diplomatic engagement with hostile states is prudent.

SUPPLEMENTS

To enhance teaching and learning, *The Global Future* is accompanied by an extensive, state-of-the-art ancillary package:

Online Instructor's Manual with Test Bank
ISBN-10: 0840066287 | ISBN-13: 9780840066282

A revised instructor's manual/test bank offers suggestions for class discussions, writing assignments, Internet and research projects, and exam questions.

Companion Website
ISBN-10: 0840066635 | ISBN-13: 9780840066633

The companion website features learning objectives, tutorial quizzes, glossary and flashcards, crossword puzzles, and Internet activities. It is available at www.cengage.com/politicalscience/kegley/globalfuture4e. Instructors also have access to the Instructor's Manual at this site.

ACKNOWLEDGMENTS

Countless friends and colleagues have helped us with their thoughts and suggestions. In particular, we are grateful to the scholars who provided meticulous critiques that guided our revisions for the fourth edition of *The Global Future*, including Jeneen Hobby, Cleveland State University; Raymond J. McCandless, University of Findlay; Stanley E. Spangler, Bentley University; as well as anonymous reviewers. We also appreciate the comments of past reviewers: Terrence Casey, Rose-Hulman Institute of Technology; Deborah Saunders Davenport,

University of Buckingham; Reggie Ecarma, North Greenville University; Richard Epps, San Diego State University; Damian Fernandez, Florida International University; Michael M. Gunter, Jr., Rollins College; William E. Hoehne, Jr., Georgia Institute of Technology; Ian Hurd, Northwestern University; George Kent, University of Hawaii; William W. Lamkin, Glendale Community College; John Mercurio, San Diego State University; Meike Mittelstadt, Spokane Falls Community College; John Thomas Preston, Washington State University; Bruce Sabin, Webber International University; David Schrupp, Montana State University; Vaughn Shannon, University of Northern Iowa; John F. Shively, Longview Community College; and Craig Warkentin, SUNY-Oswego.

We are deeply indebted as well to the skilled professionals at Cengage Learning, especially Executive Editor Carolyn Merrill and Developmental Editor Kate Scheinman, who carefully guided the process that brought the fourth edition into print. Others who made significant contributions at Cengage Learning include Angela Hodge, Editorial Assistant; and Alison Eigel Zade, Content Project Manager. In addition, we are grateful to Carly Bergey at PreMedia Global for assistance with photographs, and Charu Khanna from Macmillan Publishing Solutions for overseeing the book's production, as well as to Prashant Kumar Das at Macmillan Publishing Solutions; Margaret Berson, our copy editor; Lori Newhouse, our proofreader, our indexer, Sonya Dintaman and Lisa Huffstetler of the University of Memphis, who produced the test bank, web quizzes, and instructor's manual.

We also wish to acknowledge the encouragement that we have received from the Carnegie Council for Ethics in International Affairs and the Frank Church Institute. These outstanding institutions have made invaluable contributions to building a more secure and just global future through their exceptional educational programs.

Finally, as in the previous editions, we have benefited enormously from the patience and support of our wives, Debbie and Christine.

Charles W. Kegley, Jr.
Gregory A. Raymond

About the Authors

Charles W. Kegley, Jr. is the Vice Chair of the Board of Trustees of the Carnegie Council for Ethics in International Affairs and the Distinguished Pearce Professor of International Relations Emeritus at the University of South Carolina. A graduate of American University and Syracuse University, and a Pew Faculty Fellow at Harvard University, Kegley served as a past president of the International Studies Association (1993–1994), and has held faculty appointments at Georgetown University, the University of Texas, the People's University of China, and the Graduate Institute of International Studies, Geneva. A recipient of the Distinguished Scholar Award in Foreign Policy from the International Studies Association, Kegley's most recent of four dozen published books is *World Politics: Trend and Transformation* (coauthored with Shannon L. Blanton).

Gregory A. Raymond holds the Frank and Bethine Church Chair of Public Affairs at Boise State University. A graduate of Park College and the University of South Carolina, and a Pew Faculty Fellow at Harvard University, he was selected as the Idaho Professor of the Year (1994) by the Carnegie Foundation for the Advancement of Teaching. Raymond has been awarded nine teaching excellence awards from various faculty, student, and alumni organizations at Boise State University. The recipient of the university's outstanding researcher award, he has published numerous books and journal articles on foreign policy and world politics, and has lectured on international issues at universities and research institutes in 22 countries. He has been supported by travel and research grants from the United States Institute of Peace, the U.S. Department of State, the American Political Science Association, the Idaho Humanities Council, and the Idaho Higher Education Research Council.

Together, Kegley and Raymond have coauthored *The Multipolar Challenge* (2008), *After Iraq: The Imperiled American Imperium* (2007), *From War to Peace: Fateful Decisions in International Politics* (2002), *Exorcising the Ghost of Westphalia:*

Building International Peace in the New Millennium (2002), *How Nations Make Peace* (1999), *A Multipolar Peace? Great-Power Politics in the Twenty-First Century* (1994), and *When Trust Breaks Down: Alliance Norms and World Politics* (1990). They have also coedited *International Events and the Comparative Analysis of Foreign Policy* (1975) and coauthored over two dozen articles in such scholarly journals as the *International Studies Quarterly,* the *Journal of Conflict Resolution,* the *Journal of Politics,* the *Journal of Peace Research, International Interactions,* and the *Harvard International Review.*

PART I

Trend and Transformation in World Politics

S peaking to an audience of college students in Los Angeles during March 2010, United Nations (UN) Secretary-General Ban Ki-moon called on those in attendance to help transform the world. "We are living in an interconnected global society," he observed. "Never have the fates of the world's people been so closely linked," and never has the need for concerted action to deal with transnational threats such as political terrorism, economic recession, and climate change "been so crystal clear." Because many of these threats regularly intrude on our daily lives, a gnawing sense of insecurity torments many of us, regardless of gender, ethnicity, or nationality. Anxious about what might happen next, we struggle to divine our collective destiny. What lies ahead? Can we create a better world? How are we to think about the global future?

This book examines the impact of world politics on the global future. Of course, no one can foresee the future precisely. We can, however, identify emerging trends and imagine how they might coalesce in different ways to produce alternative global futures. According to engineer and social policy analyst Willis Harman (1976), thinking about trends is important because our expectations about the future shape the decisions we make today. Almost every action we take involves some view of the future—as we imagine it will be, as we hope it will be, or as we fear it will be. The objectives of Part I of this book are to encourage you to begin thinking about the integrative and disintegrative trends in world politics, and consider how the actions we take in response to our image of their impact will influence which alternative global future we will eventually inhabit.

A first step in thinking about the global future is to recognize that the events and trends we observe are not seen objectively. They are filtered through a lens of values and beliefs born from previous experiences. Chapter 1 shows how this lens can distort our perception of international affairs. It also demonstrates how viewing things from the individual, state, and systemic levels of analysis can help reduce distortions by providing an explicit, orderly way of examining world politics from multiple perspectives.

Chapter 2 introduces realism, liberalism, and constructivism, rival theories of world politics that emphasize causal factors operating at different levels of analysis. It also describes two powerful critiques of these mainstream theories: radicalism and feminism. As you will see in subsequent chapters, theories are important because they guide our search for answers to puzzling questions about the world. They help organize countless isolated observations into a coherent picture of reality. Yet no matter how compelling any particular theory may seem, its value hinges on whether it can provide us with a richer understanding of world politics than we would otherwise possess. In the remainder of the book, we will apply realism, liberalism, constructivism, radicalism, and feminism to various international security, economic, and environmental issues in order to assess their strengths and weaknesses, and therein sharpen our ability to evaluate competing visions of the global future.

1

Analyzing World Politics

CHAPTER OUTLINE

Today many things indicate that we are going through a transitional period, when it seems that something is on the way out and something else is painfully being born. It is as if something were crumbling, decaying, and exhausting itself, while something else, still indistinct, were arising from the rubble.

VÁCLAV HAVEL
DRAMATIST AND FORMER PRESIDENT OF THE CZECH REPUBLIC

state   an organized political entity with a permanent population, a well-defined territory, and a government; in everyday language, often used as synonymous with nation-state.

When people use the term *international relations*, they usually are referring to interactions among autonomous, territorial **states** that have no higher authority governing their behaviors. Our earliest records of such states come from ancient Mesopotamia, where some two dozen rival city-states flourished on the flood plains between the Tigris and Euphrates Rivers. Archaeologists believe that civilization began in Sumeria, the region's southern edge, which borders the coastline of what we now call the Persian Gulf. Here they find evidence of the first wheel and plow, the first extensive use of writing and metallurgy, the first legal codes and business contracts, as well as the first production of beer, of which there were nineteen varieties (Fields, Barber, and Riggs, 1998).

By roughly 2500 BCE, the typical Sumerian city-state possessed several thousand inhabitants, with most living within the city's high mud-brick walls. Fortifications were necessary because the flat terrain of southern Mesopotamia left city-states vulnerable to attack, and frequent conflict over water rights, grazing lands, and trade routes made war an ever-present threat. Sumerian armies were composed of an infantry supported by archers and four-wheeled war carts. Soldiers wore copper helmets and rudimentary armored kilts, carried large rectangular shields, and were armed with spears, swords, and axes (Keegan, 1993). Fighting occurred at close quarters. Victors in these brutal contests subjugated the defeated, plundering their land and enslaving their population.

The conflict between the city-states of Lagash and Umma exemplified the harsh nature of Sumerian warfare. After generations of sporadic hostilities, an army led by King Lugal-Zaggisi of Umma finally overwhelmed Lagash (circa 2350 BCE). He sacked the city, massacred many of its citizens, and, in a gesture of contempt, placed statues of their gods in bondage. In one of humanity's earliest works of literature, the poet Dingiraddamu mourned for the patron goddess of Lagash: "O Lady of my city, desolated, when wilt thou return?"

War continued to plague Mesopotamia long after the tragic clash between Lagash and Umma. Over the millennia, many armies marched into the region. When seen through the prism of history, the military campaign led by the United States during the spring of 2003 against Iraqi leader Saddam Hussein was simply the latest outbreak of war in this ancient land. Yet it was a war unlike any other. Touted as the world's first digital war, it used networked communications to merge data from multiple sources to coordinate precision air strikes with swarming ground attacks. Unlike the chaos that cloaked ancient battlefields, American commanders hundreds of miles from the fighting could monitor developments as they happened. Whereas scouts might relay sporadic reports on enemy defenses to Lugal-Zaggisi, Predator drones, Airborne Warning and Control System (AWACS) planes, and special operations units inserted behind enemy lines by helicopter fed General Tommy Franks a continual stream of intelligence. Whereas Sumerian warriors unleashed a volley of arrows and javelins before closing with the enemy, U.S. troops could expect a devastating barrage of cruise missile, stealth fighter, and heavy bomber strikes to begin

Werner Forman/Art Resource, NY

Courtesy of Staff Sgt. Klaus Baesu/U.S. Army

War in Human History "The story of the human race is War," British Prime Minister Winston Churchill once lamented. As shown in the depiction of an ancient Sumerian war cart and the photograph of a modern American M1–A1 Abrams tank, although war has been a constant feature of international relations, the means by which it has been waged has changed over time. Rapid advances in military technology during the past century and a half have made armed forces more lethal than ever before. A single American B-52 bomber, for example, can carry more explosive power than that used in all of the wars fought throughout recorded history.

a campaign. In short, speed and mobility now substitute for mass; information and firepower, for sheer numbers.

The military clash between Lagash and Umma is separated from us by over four millennia. What can we learn about contemporary world politics by comparing warfare in ancient Mesopotamia and modern Iraq? Quite simply, it reminds us that **politics** among territorial states is a mixture of *continuity* and *change*. On the one hand, states have lived under what political scientist Kenneth Waltz (1979) calls the "brooding shadow of violence" since antiquity. On the other hand, the way armed forces wield violence has changed profoundly. In a time of rapid advances in science and technology, it is easy for us to focus on the latest innovations and dismiss the past as irrelevant. Change is riveting; it captures our attention and stimulates our imagination. Still, we must be mindful that some features of world politics are relatively permanent. When considering how world politics might affect the global future, we need to be attentive to these entrenched continuities as well as to the sources of dramatic change. If the future seems uncertain to us, a mysterious place of endless surprises, it is often because we overlook how much of what lies ahead will be what economic historian Robert Heilbroner (1960: 15) calls the "culmination of the past" and "the growing edge of the present."

Looking beyond the confines of our immediate time is difficult. It requires an appreciation of the impact of yesterday's events on today's realities and how

politics the exercise of influence by competing individuals and groups to affect the allocation of values and distribution of resources; to political scientist Harold Lasswell, the process that determines "who gets what, when, how, and why."

current ideas and practices may shape tomorrow. Thus, to understand unfolding events and to forecast how they may shape the future, we will view them in the context of a long-term perspective that examines how some aspects of world politics have resisted change while other aspects have changed radically.

CONTINUITY AND CHANGE IN WORLD POLITICS

Imagine yourself returning home from a two-week vacation on a tropical island where you had no access to the news. The trip gave you a well-deserved break from school and allowed you to relax with a few friends at the end of the term. But now you are curious about what has happened while you were away. As you peek at a newspaper someone is reading in the airport's baggage claim area, headlines catch your eye. They indicate that the war in Afghanistan has taken the lives of more American soldiers, including a recent graduate from a local high school. While riding home from the airport, you listen to a radio program on the global economic recession. Glancing at a strip mall along the highway, you notice numerous commercial buildings for lease, including one that housed a business where you held a part-time job last year. Shortly after arriving at home, you connect to the Internet and find that the country is experiencing the worst labor market in a generation, and you begin to worry about career opportunities after graduation. While listening to the news on television later that evening, you hear several other reports: The International Monetary Fund warns that the debt many governments have incurred to fund economic recovery programs poses a risk to global financial stability; political unrest in some oil-producing countries may cause gasoline prices to rise in the United States; and complaints about the full-body scanning equipment that airports have installed to prevent terrorist attacks are mounting as people worry about privacy rights.

Although we have taken some literary license, the scenario just described is not completely hypothetical; it draws from various events that actually occurred during May 2010. Thinking about this rather typical month, one cannot help but be reminded that we are all affected by events that occur far from home and that we can all benefit by having a better grasp of their causes and consequences. But how can we best understand the political convulsions that confront the world's 6.8 billion people almost daily? Are the episodic shock waves throughout the world clearing the way for a truly new twenty-first-century world order? Or will many of today's dramatic disruptions ultimately prove temporary, mere spikes on the seismograph of history?

At the beginning of a new century, people often speculate about the global future. What will the new world be like? Will humanity be better off in the years ahead? Or will it suffer? Which international events will echo past patterns, and which will inaugurate revolutionary changes? We invite you to explore these questions with us. To begin our inquiry, let us introduce the *dramatis personae* on the global stage, those **actors** whose behavior affects world politics in important ways.

dual,
rganiza-
major role

The Emergence of the Nation-State System

Many actors (sometimes called *agents*) are players in the drama of world politics. The most fundamental, of course, are individual people. Every day, whether choosing to recycle waste, parent a child, or immigrate to another country, their behaviors affect in no small measure how trends in the world will unfold. People exert even more influence through organizations. As the philosopher Aristotle once remarked, human beings are political animals; they join groups to enhance their security and welfare. Throughout world history, people have belonged to many types of political organizations, including bands, tribes, chiefdoms, and states. When these organizations come into contact, they sometimes collaborate for mutual benefit; more often they compete over scarce resources.

Although nation-states are the preeminent political organizations on the world stage today, they did not achieve that position until the seventeenth century. The modern nation-state **system** was born with the Peace of Westphalia in 1648, which ended the Thirty Years' War. A complex, multidimensional conflict, the Thirty Years' War originated from a welter of cultural, political, and economic crosscurrents that swept through Europe following the Protestant Reformation. One dimension of the war was religious, involving a clash between Catholics and Protestants. Another dimension was governmental, consisting of a civil war over the issue of imperial authority within the Holy Roman Empire (a territory stretching from France to Poland, composed of numerous principalities united through marriages to the Catholic Hapsburg dynasty). A third dimension was geostrategic, pitting the Austrian and Spanish branches of the House of Hapsburg against the Danish, Swedish, Dutch, and French thrones (see Kegley and Raymond, 2002).

The incident that sparked the Thirty Years' War occurred in Prague on May 21, 1618, when members of a local assembly denounced the anti-Protestant policies of the Hapsburgs and threw two Hapsburg emissaries from a window in Hradčany Castle into a dungheap below. The Hapsburgs responded with force, igniting a war that drew participants from across Europe into the fray. By any measure, the fighting produced a tragedy of epic proportions. Much of central Europe lay desolate in its aftermath, stripped of resources and drained of population by massacre, pillage, famine, and disease. When the belligerents finally reached a peace agreement, they provided world politics with a new decentralized structure.

Although most Europeans prior to the Reformation lived in a galaxy of fiefdoms and principalities, they thought of themselves as belonging to a larger Christian commonwealth led by the Pope. Following the Thirty Years' War, this medieval vertical order was replaced by a horizontal system of autonomous states that recognized no higher authority. Under the terms of the Peace of Westphalia (so named because it was negotiated at concurrent conferences in the German cities of Münster and Osnabrück in Westphalia), all states possessed the same legal rights: sole jurisdiction over their territory, unrestricted control over domestic affairs, and the freedom to engage in foreign relations with other powers. The concept of **sovereignty** embodied the exclusive rights of states to

system a set of interconnected parts that function as a unitary whole. In world politics, the parts consist primarily of states that interact on a regular basis.

sovereignty under international law, the principle that no higher authority is above the state.

anarchy   the absence of a higher authority with the legitimacy and coercive capability to make and enforce rules that bind states.

make, enforce, and adjudicate laws within their domains. Because no overarching institution had the authority to regulate state conduct, **anarchy** rather than hierarchy became Westphalia's core organizing principle.

The Peace of Westphalia still colors nearly every aspect of world politics today and provides the terminology used to describe nation-states, the primary actors in international affairs over the past several centuries. Even though the term *nation-state* is often used interchangeably with "state" and "nation," technically the three are different. A state is a legal entity that possesses a permanent population, a well-defined territory, and a government capable of exercising sovereignty. A **nation** is a collection of people who, on the basis of ethnic, linguistic, or cultural affinity, perceive themselves to be members of the same group. The term **nation-state** implies a convergence between territorial states and the psychological identification of people within them. However, in employing this terminology, we must be cautious. Whereas a few nation-states like Japan and Iceland are ethnically homogeneous, most states contain many ethnic groups that consider themselves as nations, and some nations overlap the borders between different states. For example, Nigeria is a *multination state*, with a population composed of the Yoruba, Ibo (Igbo), and Hausa-Fulani nations, as well as dozens of smaller ethnic groups. The Kurds, on the other hand, exemplify a *multistate nation*, with members of this ethnic group living in Iran, Iraq, and Turkey.

nation   a group of people who feel a common identity due to a shared language, culture, and history.

nation-state   a specific geographic area containing a sovereign polity whose population identifies with that polity.

The Rise of Nonstate Actors

Because the history of world politics since 1648 has largely been a chronicle of the interactions among nation-states, some scholars and diplomats conceptualize the world in state-centric terms. Their vision is often metaphorically represented by a game of billiards, with impervious states colliding like balls on a pool table. From this perspective, action–reaction principles explain how world politics works. Just as knowing the location of the billiard balls, the direction of their movement, and the force with which they strike one another allows us to predict the outcome of each collision, the geographic location, policy direction, and amount of force brought to bear by one state against another is said to give us insight into international outcomes.

billiard-ball model   a conception of world politics that envisions states as the sole movers of global affairs, explains their behavior as unitary responses to external threats, and attributes little importance to domestic sources of foreign policy.

nonstate actors   all transnationally active groups other than states, such as international organizations whose members are states (IGOs) and non- 'organiza-
        ose
        lividuals
        ıps from
        state.

Though embraced by various students and practitioners of world politics, the **billiard-ball model** provides an inadequate basis for understanding today's world. Not only does it gloss over socio-economic conditions and political dynamics within nation-states that affect foreign policy, but it disregards the influence of **nonstate actors** on global affairs. Nation-states are no longer the only significant actors on the world stage. According to Richard Haass (2008: 45), a former senior staff member of the U.S. National Security Council, "states are being challenged from above, by regional and global organizations; from below, by militias; and from the side, by a variety of nongovernmental organizations." Many of these entities conduct independent foreign policies and thus can be thought of as global actors in their own right. For example, the World Trade Organization and the International Monetary Fund sometimes flex their political muscles in contests with individual states, as do groups ranging from Hezbullah and the Taliban to Greenpeace and Doctors Without Borders. Today's international system, in other words, includes more than sovereign, territorial states; it consists of a complex web of interactions among nation-states, international institutions, multinational corporations, transnational religious movements, and a host of other entities that operate across frontiers. Nation-states may receive top billing, but they are not the sole performers in the drama of world politics.

In our exploration of world politics and its future, we shall analyze both state and nonstate actors. The emphasis and coverage will vary, depending on the topics under examination in each chapter. But you should keep in mind that *all* actors are simultaneously active today, and their importance depends on the issue under consideration.

The growth in the importance of nonstate actors on a stage where nation-states continue to command the spotlight underscores how change occurs in world politics alongside continuity. Whereas some features of world politics vary over time, others are deeply entrenched. Moreover, as the state-centric assumptions underpinning the billiard-ball model illustrate, it is easy to mistake familiar features for permanent ones. Our challenge, then, is to observe developing events and deep-seated patterns carefully, and to recognize how our images of reality shape what we see. This requires a set of tools to help us think systematically about world politics in order to avoid overlooking significant aspects of the international scene. Hence, the remainder of this chapter will briefly examine the impact that images of reality have on our understanding of world politics, and then will describe some of the tools we will use in this book to interpret global trends and transformations.

HOW PERCEPTIONS SHAPE OUR INTERPRETATION OF WORLD POLITICS

We all hold mental images of world politics—explicit or implicit, conscious or subconscious. But whatever our level of self-awareness, our images simplify "reality" by exaggerating some features of our environment while ignoring others. Thus, we live in a world defined by our expectations and images.

These mental pictures, or perceptions, are inevitably distortions, as they cannot fully capture the complexity and configurations of even physical objects, such as the globe itself (see CONTROVERSY: Should We Believe What We See?).

Many of our images of world politics are built on illusions and misconceptions. And even images that are now accurate can easily become outdated if we fail to recognize changes in the world. Indeed, the world's future will be determined not only by changes in the "objective" facts of world politics but also by the meaning that people ascribe to those facts, the assumptions on which they base their interpretations, and the actions that flow from these assumptions and interpretations—however accurate or inaccurate they might be.

The effort to simplify one's view of the world is inevitable and even necessary. Just as cartographers' projections simplify complex geophysical space so we can better understand the world, each of us inevitably creates a "mental map"—a habitual way of organizing information—to make sense of a confusing abundance of information. Although mental maps are neither inherently right nor wrong, they are important because we tend to react according to the way the world appears to us rather than the way it is.

CONTROVERSY   Should We Believe What We See?

Many people assume that "seeing is believing" without questioning whether their perceptions are accurate. But is there more to seeing than meets the eye? When looking at the world, do we perceive it in ways that produce distortions? Students of perceptual psychology think so. They maintain that seeing is not a strictly passive act: What we observe is partially influenced by our preexisting values and expectations. Two observers looking at the same object might easily perceive different realities. To illustrate this, psychologists are fond of displaying the following drawing, which, depending on how the viewer looks at it, can be seen as either a goblet or two faces opposing each other.

is principle has great importance for students of
ics. Depending on one's perspective, people
on how they view international
d issues. To appreciate the disagree-
sult from the fact that different peo-

ple can easily see different realities when they look at the same thing, consider something as basic as viewing the location and size of the continents in the world. There exists a long-standing controversy among cartographers about the "right" way to map the globe, that is, how to make an accurate projection of the Earth's surface. All maps of the globe are distorted, because it is impossible to perfectly represent the three-dimensional globe on a two-dimensional piece of paper. The difficulty that cartographers face can be appreciated by trying to flatten an orange peel. You can only flatten it by separating pieces of the peel that were joined when it was spherical. Cartographers who try to flatten the globe on paper, without "ripping it" into separate pieces, face the same problem. Although there are a variety of ways to represent the three-dimensional object on paper, all of them involve some kind of distortion. Thus cartographers must choose among the imperfect ways of representing the globe by selecting those aspects of the world's geography that they consider most important to describe accurately, while making adjustments to other parts.

Cartographers' ideas of what is most important in world geography have varied according to their own global perspectives, or according to those of the person or organization for which a particular map was created (see Klinghoffer, 2006). These three maps (Maps 1.1, 1.2, and 1.3) depict the distribution of the earth's land surfaces, but each portrays a different image. Each is a model of reality, an abstraction that highlights some features of the globe while ignoring others. What a map highlights is significant politically because it shapes how people view what is important. In examining these three ways of viewing and interpreting the globe, evaluate which projection you think is best. Which features of global reality are most worthy of emphasizing to capture an accurate picture? What does your answer reveal about your values and view of the world?

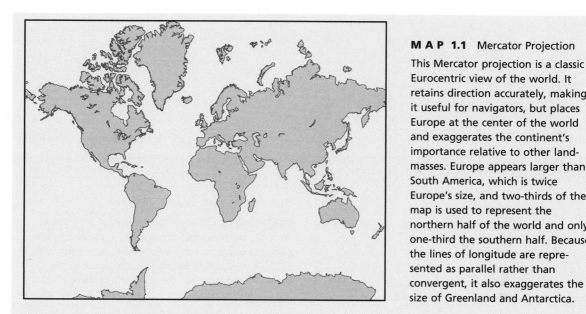

M A P 1.1 Mercator Projection

This Mercator projection is a classic Eurocentric view of the world. It retains direction accurately, making it useful for navigators, but places Europe at the center of the world and exaggerates the continent's importance relative to other land-masses. Europe appears larger than South America, which is twice Europe's size, and two-thirds of the map is used to represent the northern half of the world and only one-third the southern half. Because the lines of longitude are repre-sented as parallel rather than convergent, it also exaggerates the size of Greenland and Antarctica.

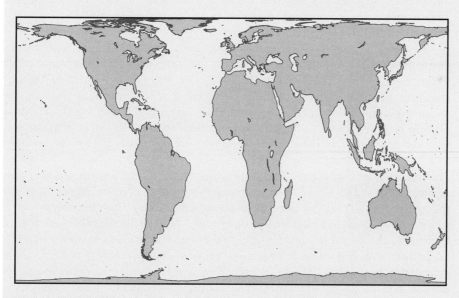

M A P 1.2 Peter's Projection

In a Peter's projection, each landmass appears in correct proportion in relation to all others, but it distorts the shape and position of landmasses. Unlike most geographic representations, it draws attention to the countries of Africa, Asia, and Latin America, where more than three-quarters of the world's population live today.

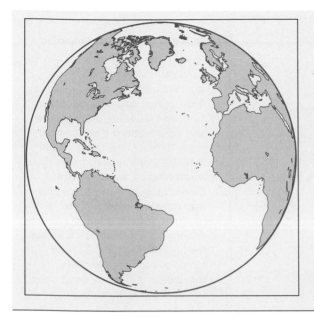

M A P 1.3 Orthographic Projection

The orthographic projection, centering on the mid-Atlantic, conveys some sense of the curvature of the Earth by using rounded edges. The size and shapes of the continents toward the outer edges of the circle are distorted to give a sense of spherical perspective.

Most of us—policymakers included—look for information that reinforces our preexisting beliefs about the world; we assimilate new data into familiar images, and deny information that contradicts our expectations. Let us briefly examine each of these tendencies.

Research in cognitive psychology suggests that human beings employ mental shortcuts known as **heuristics** to cope with the complexity and uncertainty of life (Kahneman, Slovic, and Tversky, 1982). These unconscious "rules of thumb" enable us to make decisions quickly when faced with limited information and looming deadlines. However, they also create biases in the way we think. Many of these cognitive biases foster selective attention—the tendency to focus on only a limited amount of available information. For instance, most people are attentive to things that confirm their preconceived beliefs, they are prone to rely on readily available data, and they give disproportionate weight to the first information they receive. What makes these biases so troublesome is that they are ingrained in our thought processes; they are not simply due to ignorance or indifference.

Research also indicates that humans are "categorizers" who attempt to understand the world by matching what they see with images in their memories of prototypical people and events—a process that psychologists refer to as **schematic reasoning** (Larson, 1994). The absentminded professor, the shady lawyer, and the kindly grandmother are examples of "stock" images that many of us have of certain types of people. Although the professors, lawyers, and grandmothers that we meet may bear only a superficial resemblance to these stereotypes, when we know little about someone our expectations will be shaped by presumed similarities to these characters. Similarly, when we are unfamiliar with an emerging situation, we look for parallels with earlier experiences that we imagine typify these events.

heuristics judgmental shortcuts used to compensate for limited information about complicated problems.

schematic reasoning the process by which new ~nation is interpreted ~ring it to generic ~ed in memory ~reotypical ~ of

Many factors shape our images, including how we were socialized as children, vivid experiences from our past, and exposure to the ideas of people whose expertise we respect (Jervis, 1976). Once we have acquired an image, it seems self-evident. Accordingly, we try to keep it consistent with our other beliefs and, through a psychological process known as **cognitive dissonance** (Festinger, 1957), reject information that contradicts how it portrays the world. In short, our mind selects, screens, and filters information; consequently, our perceptions depend not only on what happens in daily life but also on how we interpret and internalize those events.

Of course, cognitive biases vary among individuals. Some people are more open than others to new information that clashes with their preconceptions. Nonetheless, to some extent, we are all prisoners of our perceptions, which makes it difficult to identify the myriad causes of international events.

As we speculate about the global future, we need to think critically about the foundations on which our perceptions rest. Questioning our images is one of the most important challenges we face in analyzing world politics. One of the purposes of this book is to help you cultivate a critical perspective on your beliefs regarding international relations. To that end, we will ask you to evaluate rival perspectives on global issues, even if they differ from your standpoint. Indeed, we will expose you to schools of thought prevailing today that you may find unconvincing, and possibly repugnant. Why are they included? Because many other people make these views the bedrock of their outlooks on the world. Critical thinking within the field of international relations entails confronting one's own assumptions and biases, as well as recognizing that the perceptual predispositions held by others may lead them to interpret events in ways that may be at odds with our own points of view. The ability to see things from someone else's perspective is a valuable skill (see APPLICATION: Seeing the World through Foreign Eyes). Drawing on years of experience in international negotiations, U.S. diplomat Dennis Ross (2007) concludes that the more one can put himself or herself in another person's shoes, the greater his or her facility to comprehend the perplexing behavior often found on the world stage.

cognitive dissonance
the psychological tendency to deny or rationalize away discrepancies between one's preexisting beliefs and new information.

A FRAMEWORK FOR ANALYZING WORLD POLITICS

If people seek information that confirms what they already believe, and they exaggerate the accuracy of their perceptions, how can we avoid seeing world events through a distorted lens? What can we do to bring to light evidence that runs counter to our intuition? There are no sure-fire solutions to the problem of making accurate observations, no way to guarantee that we possess an objective view of international relations. However, there are a number of tools available that can improve our ability to analyze world affairs. One approach is to use an analytical framework to discipline our observations. Analytic frameworks suggest where to look for information pertinent to some puzzling phenomenon, and how to organize it in an inventory of possible causes. Although no analytical framework can ensure that we will have an impartial view of world politics, social scientists

A perennial issue within the field of international relations concerns the relationship between theory and practice. To what extent are theories of world politics relevant to the practice of statecraft? How can the theories produced by the academic community assist practitioners who formulate and conduct foreign policy?

In this chapter we have introduced you to some of the theoretical concepts that scholars use to describe the role of perceptions in world politics. According to Dennis Ross, a diplomatic envoy in the administrations of Bill Clinton, George H.W. Bush, and Barack Obama, understanding the perceptions held by the other side is crucial for conducting successful negotiations. It is important, he argues, to know what others value as well as what they fear, what pressures will harden their bargaining position as well as what may soften it. In the following excerpt, Ross describes how asking probing questions and carefully listening to the other side's responses helped him during arms control negotiations with the Soviet Union and the Russian Federation.

> With first the Soviets and then the Russians, I would have long conversations with Sergei Tarasenko and Yuri Mamedov, key aids to then-foreign ministers Eduard Shevardnadze and Andrei Kosyrev. Conversations with them revealed a great deal about what was and wasn't possible on arms control—not necessarily because I was pumping them for information, but because I

asked questions that conveyed an interest in trying to understand the broader circumstances in which they had to operate.

For example, sometimes I would ask questions about how much reform was really possible. Frequently, this led to discussions about decline and malaise in the Soviet Union, the advocates and opponents of varying degrees of reform, their arguments, where arms-control agreements fit in, and their views about where we and others could either help or harm the reform process.

One essential attribute for any negotiator is to be a good listener. It's crucial to know when to talk but, more important, when to listen. You won't be learning when you are talking. You may be shaping or conditioning attitudes, but you will not be learning. You learn when you listen. Being a good listener conveys a level of interest and respect. It shows that you take seriously those with whom you are dealing. You are likely to elicit more when you convey such respect and listen actively (D. Ross, 2007: 191–192).

Theory and research on the perceptual outlooks of political leaders indicates that each actor on the international stage sees the world somewhat differently. Policymakers who ignore these differences can easily overlook meaningful signals from their adversaries and fail to capitalize on fleeting opportunities for diplomatic breakthroughs.

frequently build *levels of analysis* and *time sequences* in the frameworks they use in an effort to illuminate causal factors that they might otherwise neglect.

Levels of Analysis

At the heart of almost every international event lies a puzzle. Someone is mystified why a particular event happened, or is curious about what would have happened if a different action had been taken by one of the participants. The first step in solving the puzzle is to ask: "Of what larger pattern is this event an instance?" (Rosenau and Durfee, 1995; Lave and March, 1975). Visualizing an event as part of a larger pattern invites us to imagine that the pattern is the end result of some unknown process, and encourages us to think about the causal mechanisms that might have produced the pattern.

When trying to solve a complex puzzle, it is helpful to group similar pieces together before attempting to combine them into a larger pattern. Scholars often

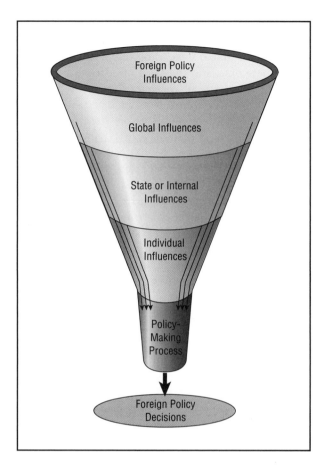

FIGURE 1.1 Explaining International Events: Influences at Three Levels

The factors that shape international events can be categorized according to three levels of analysis. At the systemic level are features of the global system, such as the prevalence of alliances and the extent of trade. At the state level are domestic influences, such as the type of government and form of economy. At the individual level are the characteristics of a country's political leader—his or her personal beliefs, values, and personality. Factors from all three levels may affect any given event, but their relative importance will vary depending on prevailing circumstances and the issues involved.

follow a similar strategy when trying to explain a puzzling international event. Rather than jumping to a hasty conclusion, they classify all of the possible causes for the event according to three *levels of analysis*: the individual, the state, and the entire global system (see Figure 1.1). The **individual level of analysis** refers to the distinctive personality traits, experiences, and behavior of those responsible for making decisions on behalf of state and nonstate actors, as well as ordinary citizens whose behavior has important political consequences. Here, for example, we may properly locate the impact of a leader's political beliefs, attitudes, and opinions on his or her behavior, and explore questions such as why presidents Bill Clinton and George W. Bush dealt with Saddam Hussein in different ways.

The **state level of analysis** consists of the domestic attributes of nation-states, including their types of government, levels of economic development, characteristics of their societies, and so on. The processes by which governments make decisions regarding war and peace, for instance, fall within the state level of analysis. A common example can be found in the argument that authoritarian governments are more bellicose than democracies because their leaders are not constrained by competitive elections or political cultures grounded in norms of tolerance and compromise.

individual level of analysis an analytical approach to the study of world politics that emphasizes the psychological factors motivating people who make foreign policy decisions on behalf of states and other global actors.

state level of analysis an analytical approach to the study of world politics that emphasizes how the internal attributes of states influence their foreign policy behavior.

systemic level of analysis an analytical approach to the study of world politics that emphasizes the impact of international structures and processes on the behavior of global actors.

The **systemic level of analysis** provides the most comprehensive view of world politics, focusing on the distribution of resources and the pattern of interaction among the political actors on the global stage. The dispersion of military capabilities, the density of alliance networks, and the level of economic interdependence among state and nonstate actors are all characteristics of the international system as a whole. Explanations of international events that are framed at the systemic level contend that the behavior of global actors stems from their placement within the international system. Different actors behave similarly when they have similar positions of power and wealth within the system.

In summary, categorizing possible causes of an event according to levels of analysis is useful because it encourages us to look beyond our preconceived images. It helps guard against single-factor explanations that hinge on one decisive cause. Like a telescopic camera lens, it allows us to zoom in and examine fine-grained details at the individual level, and then move back to the state and systemic levels to see things from a broader perspective. Shifting from one level to another, looking at parts as well as the whole, suggests different questions to ask and what kinds of evidence would be necessary to arrive at meaningful answers.

Time Sequences

Once we have identified factors from different levels of analysis that may combine to produce some outcome, it is useful to place them in a sequence that specifies the order in which they occurred. Anyone who owns a combination lock knows that the correct numbers must be entered in their proper order to open the lock. Similarly, to explain why something happened in world politics, we must determine how various individual, state, and systemic-level factors fit together in a process that unfolds over time.

remote causes phenomena that are removed in time from the effects that they produce or help to produce.

proximate causes phenomena occurring close in time to the effects that they produce or help to produce.

One way to build time sequences into our analytic framework is to consider how close each individual, state, or systemic factor was to the occurrence of the event in question. We could do this in several different ways, but for illustrative purposes we will simply distinguish between remote and proximate causes. **Remote causes** are deep, underlying factors that set off a train of events. **Proximate causes** are those with more immediate effects. Consider, for example, the outbreak of a forest fire following a brief thunderstorm over parched mountainous terrain. The remote cause was a prolonged draught that desiccated the region; the proximate cause, a lightning strike that ignited a dry pine tree.

By searching for remote and proximate causes across multiple levels of analysis, we guard against having our perceptual biases unnecessarily constrict our frame of reference, which can lead us to hastily embrace enticing but incomplete explanations for the phenomena we hope to understand. To illustrate, let us apply our analytical framework to the puzzle of why the Cold War ended peacefully.

Applying the Framework to the Cold War's End

During the Second World War, the United States and the Soviet Union aligned against Nazi Germany. In the waning months of the conflict, mutual suspicions in Moscow and Washington hardened into policy disagreements over the future of the postwar world. The day before his suicide, Adolf Hitler predicted that the "laws of both history and geography" would compel the Soviet Union and the United States to engage in "a trial of strength" (Bullock, 1962: 772–773). As Soviet-American relations plummeted in a downward spiral of charges and countercharges, it seemed as if Hitler's ominous prediction would come to pass.

But fighting did not ensue. Despite over forty years of intense rivalry in what was called the Cold War, the Soviet Union and the United States avoided a trial of strength. Had they not, the results would have been catastrophic. By 1983, when President Ronald Reagan referred to the Soviet Union as an "evil empire," the two superpowers had amassed such enormous nuclear arsenals that if their combined explosive power had been converted to an equivalent amount of TNT and loaded into boxcars on a freight train, the train would have stretched from the earth to the moon and back at least a half dozen times. Thus it came as a great relief when the Cold War ended without bloodshed following the collapse of the Soviet Union in 1991.

Some people argue that the American military buildup during the Reagan administration drove the Soviet Union into submission. The Cold War ended due to "the Reagan policy of firmness," insisted Richard Perle, one of the former president's advisors. Our policy was "peace through strength," added George H. W. Bush, Reagan's vice president and immediate successor in the White House. "It worked" (see Kegley, 1994).

This argument sounds persuasive because the disintegration of the Soviet Union occurred alongside a massive weapons-building program in the United States. Furthermore, the argument fit a set of preconceptions derived from America's experience with Nazi Germany: Dictators cannot be appeased; the language of military might is the only language they understand. Soviet leaders, many Americans believed, were demagogic and rapacious like Hitler. Whereas British and French vacillation in the 1930s emboldened Hitler, Reagan's steadfastness allegedly brought the Soviets to heel.

Vivid historical images are seductive. They frame how we see the present, often in ways that inhibit dissecting analogies to past events. Rather than patiently examining an issue from every angle, we draw parallels with a memorable incident and stop searching for additional information. For example, the assertion that "Ronald Reagan won the Cold War by being tough on the communists" (Glynn, 1993: 172) animates such powerful imagery that seeking other explanations might seem unnecessary. But by not evaluating plausible, rival explanations, we can be misled. The prominent Russian scholar Georgi Arbatov contends that rather than convincing Kremlin hardliners to give up, Reagan's "tough" policy actually stiffened their resolve, thereby prolonging the Cold War (Kegley and Raymond, 1994: 29).

Analytical frameworks help prevent us from giving easily recalled analogies more weight than they deserve by widening the search for additional insights and information. Table 1.1 shows how looking at different levels of analysis and time sequences can assist in identifying alternative explanations of why the Cold War ended peacefully. At the individual level, a strong case could be made that

TABLE 1.1   Contending Images of the Cold War's End

Level of Analysis	Time Sequence	
Individual	**Remote Causes**	**Proximate Causes**
	Leaders as moral exemplars "The pope [John Paul II] started this chain of events that led to the end of communism." —Lech Walesa	*Leaders as movers of history* "Ronald Reagan won the Cold War by being tough on the communists." —Patrick Glynn "[The end of the Cold War was possible] primarily because of one man—Mikhail Gorbachev. The transformations we are dealing with now would not have begun were it not for him." —James A. Baker III
State		
	Political inertia "Given communism's inherent unworkability … the Soviet empire was doomed in the long run." —Arthur Schlesinger, Jr. *Economic mismanagement* "No other industrialized state [than the Soviet Union] in the world for so long spent so much of its national wealth on armaments and military forces. Soviet militarism, in harness with communism, destroyed the Soviet economy and thus hastened the self-destruction of the Soviet empire." —Fred Charles Iklé	*Media attention* "It was the moral reassessment of the seventy-odd years of this socialist experiment that shook the nation…. It was the flood of publications of the Soviet Union's human rights record and its tremendous distortions of moral and ethical principles that discredited the system, especially when introduced into the everyday lives of its individual citizens through the popular media." —Vladimir Benevolenski and Andrei Kortunov *Grassroots movements* "The changes wrought by thousands of people serving in the trenches [were] essential to events in recent years and at least partially responsible for [ending the Cold War]." —David Cortright *Ethnonationalism* "In less than two years, communism collapsed everywhere…. The causes [were] the national communities." —Hélène Carrère d'Encausse
Systemic		
	Containment "The U.S. and our allies deserve great credit for maintaining the military and economic power to resist and turn back the Soviet aggression." —Richard Nixon	*Imperial overstretch* "The acute phase of the fall of communism started outside of the Soviet Union and spread to the Soviet Union itself. By 1987, Gorbachev made it clear that he would not interfere with internal experiments in Soviet bloc countries … Once communism fell in Eastern Europe, the alternative in the Soviet Union became civil war or dissolution." —Daniel Klenbort

SOURCES: Kegley (1994), Kegley and Raymond (1994: 42–44).

Mikhail Gorbachev's sweeping reforms, not Ronald Reagan's toughness, played the key role (A. Brown, 2009: 602; S. Cohen, 2009: 160). Another possibility is that both leaders played important roles (Matlock, 2010: 67; Leffler, 2007). Still another possibility is that Pope John Paul II's visits to his native Poland had already begun eroding communism in Eastern Europe before Gorbachev came to power. At the state level of analysis, political inertia and economic mismanagement may have gradually weakened the Soviet Union, while social discontent, grassroots protest movements, and the explosive growth of **nationalism** among non-Russian ethnic groups in the Baltic republics and elsewhere accelerated the downfall of the communist regime. Finally, at the systemic level, the long-term U.S. policy of **containment**, the spread of human rights norms following the signing of the 1975 Helsinki Accords (Thomas, 2001), and the eventual dissolution of the Soviet position in Eastern Europe may have been critical to ending the Cold War.

It is also useful to examine *chains of causation* that run between levels over time. For example, political inertia and economic deterioration within the Soviet Union (state level) may have been remote causes of Gorbachev's reforms (individual level), which became a proximate cause of the collapse of the network of Soviet military alliances (systemic level) by providing an opportunity for Eastern Europeans to chart a new course in the foreign affairs. Yet another possibility is that Gorbachev's political reforms gave non-Russian ethnic groups in various Soviet republics (state level) the opportunity to express nationalist sentiments and break away from the Soviet Union. We could hypothesize other chains of cause and effect. Determining which ones best account for the collapse of the Soviet Union and the end of the Cold War is a task for subsequent research. Our purpose here is merely to demonstrate how preconceived mental images limit a person's field of vision. We get a richer, more nuanced perspective by studying world politics from multiple levels of analysis across time.

nationalism the belief that political loyalty lies with a body of people who share ethnicity, linguistic, or cultural affinity, and perceive themselves to be members of the same group.

containment a term coined by U.S. policymaker George Kennan for deterring expansion by the Soviet Union, which has since been used to describe a strategy aimed at preventing a state from using force to increase its territory or sphere of influence.

THINKING ABOUT THE GLOBAL FUTURE

Throughout history people have tried to predict the future. To be sure, many of these efforts are more noteworthy today for their absurdity than for their accuracy. Early in the nineteenth century, for example, the *Quarterly Review* asserted that it would be foolish to expect locomotives to travel twice as fast as stagecoaches. High-speed rail travel was simply not possible, added British writer Dionysius Larder, because passengers would be unable to breathe (Lee, 2000). Although these and other equally amusing examples of erroneous predictions remind us that we cannot know the distant future with certainty, many theorists argue that events in the near future lie on a continuum of predictability, with some being foreseeable if a systematic effort is made to consider how social, economic, political, and technological trends may combine in different ways to yield alternative potential futures (Bazerman and Watkins, 2004). As you investigate various aspects of world politics in the chapters ahead, we encourage you to reflect on the global future. Think about what is possible, evaluate what is probable, and advocate for what is preferable. "We are not prisoners of fate," writes futurist Edward Cornish (2004: 210). Rather we have extraordinary power to assess past events and weigh current trends, responding to what we learn in ways that can improve the human prospect.

The Investigative Challenge

Because world politics is complex and our images of it are often discordant, scholars differ in their approaches to understanding world politics. Some take a *macropolitical* perspective that focuses on the global system as a totality and explains the behavior of the actors within it by emphasizing how they are positioned. Accentuating the individual and state levels of analysis, other scholars adopt a *micropolitical* perspective that focuses on the actors and extrapolates from their behavior to describe the global system as an aggregate whole. Both approaches make important contributions to understanding world politics: The former reveals how the external environment sets limits on political choice; the latter draws attention to how an actor's preferences, capabilities, and strategic calculations account for the choices it makes from the options that are available. By looking at world politics from a macropolitical perspective, we can see why actors who are similarly situated within the system may behave alike, despite their internal differences. By taking a micropolitical perspective, we can appreciate why some actors behave differently, despite their similar placement within the global system (Waltz, 1988: 43).

What happens in world politics thus depends on the constraining and enabling forces of the global system that establish the range of political choice (macropolitics), as well as on the perceptions and motives that influence the foreign policy decisions made by discrete actors (micropolitics). We get a richer, more comprehensive picture of world politics when we draw insights from both vantage points and explore how systemic structures influence the behavior of international actors, whose interactions in turn have an impact on the system's structure. Consequently, in the chapters that follow, we adopt an analytical approach that looks at (1) the key macro *trends* in world politics that set the parameters for action, (2) the preferences, capabilities, and strategic calculations of the *actors* affected by these trends, and (3) the *interactions* among actors on security and welfare issues that ultimately shape the trajectories of global trends.

Examining patterns of interaction among actors is important because many of the patterns that characterize world politics are the result of **contingent behavior**. According to political economist Thomas Schelling (1978: 13–17), sometimes the aggregate patterns we see can be easily projected from the individual actors. For example, if we know that every state increases its military budget annually by a certain amount due to internal bureaucratic demands for more funding, we can make a simple persistence forecast to project the trend in global military spending over time. But if some states increase their budgets when neighboring states have increased theirs, estimating the trend is more complicated. Here national leaders are *responding* to each other's behavior as well as

contingent behavior
actions that depend on
what others are doing.

influencing each other's behavior. Sometimes the resulting pattern may be sequential: If your expenditures induce me to increase my expenditures, mine may encourage someone else to spend more, and so on. Sometimes the pattern may be reciprocal: Apprehensive about your expenditures, I spend more, which prompts you to raise your expenditures even further. When, as in these two cases, state behavior is contingent on the behavior of other states, the results usually do not allow a simple summation to the aggregate. To forecast the global future under these circumstances, we have to look at the dynamic interaction between actors and their environment, which includes other actors responding to one another's behavior.

The analytical approach outlined here has the advantage of taking into account the interplay of proximate and remote explanatory factors at the individual, state, and systemic levels of analysis while not dwelling on particular people, countries, or incidents whose long-term significance is likely to diminish. Instead, it places historical and contemporary events into a broader theoretical context, highlighting the general patterns that will shape the future and providing you with the conceptual tools to interpret the implications of those patterns.

An Overview of the Book

Our journey begins in Chapter 2 with an overview of the realist, liberal, and constructivist theoretical traditions that scholars and policymakers use most often to interpret world politics. Next we consider radicalism and feminism, which offer powerful critiques of these mainstream traditions. The comparison of these contending theories provides the intellectual background for the description and explanation of the issues and developments that are treated in the remaining chapters.

Chapter 3 begins the analysis of actors, issues, and their interactions with a close examination of foreign policy decision-making processes *within* nation-states, which remain the principal actors in world politics. It also considers the role of leaders in making foreign policy, and how various external and domestic forces can constrain the impact of political leaders.

We will then turn our attention to each of the types of actors in world politics and examine how their characteristics and capabilities affect their interests and influence in the world. Great powers (those wealthy countries with the most powerful militaries) are the focus of attention in Chapter 4. In Chapter 5, we turn our attention to the weaker, less economically developed countries, explaining how the fate of this group of states is shaped by their relations with great powers. Then, in Chapter 6, we cover two groups of nonstate actors, intergovernmental organizations (IGOs) and nongovernmental organizations (NGOs), and demonstrate how they interact with nation-states and increasingly challenge even the great powers.

The next group of chapters shifts attention to how the preferences, capabilities, and strategic calculations of the principal actors in world politics affect security and welfare issues on the global agenda. Security issues are addressed in Chapters 7 through 10. Finally, in Chapters 11 through 14, we examine problems relating to globalization, international political economy, human rights, and the environment.

In the concluding section, we revisit the major trends in world politics surveyed throughout the book. Chapter 15 draws on the theories and evidence presented in earlier chapters, and presents alternative views of the global future by focusing on some of the most hotly debated questions most likely to dominate political discussion during the next decade.

Understanding today's world requires a willingness to confront complexity. The challenge is difficult, but the payoff warrants the effort. Humankind's ability to chart a more rewarding future hinges on its ability to entertain complex ideas, to free itself from the sometimes paralyzing grip of prevailing orthodoxies, and to develop a healthy, questioning attitude about rival perspectives on international realities. On that hopeful yet introspective note, we begin our exploration of world politics.

CHAPTER SUMMARY

- To understand the global future, one must examine the ways in which the contemporary international system has changed and the ways in which its fundamental characteristics have resisted change.

- Trends in world politics rarely unfold in a constant, linear direction. Moreover, no trend stands alone. The path to the future is influenced by multiple determinants, some integrative and others disintegrative.

- Following the Peace of Westphalia, the nation-state became the primary actor in world politics. It was never the sole actor, however. Many types of nonstate actors play significant roles on the world stage.

- Everyone has some kind of "mental model" of world politics that simplifies reality by exaggerating some features of international affairs and ignoring others.

- The shape of the world's future will be determined not only by changes in the objective conditions of world politics, but also by the meanings that people ascribe to those conditions.

- Although most people are prone to look for information that reinforces their beliefs and give disproportionate weight to initial impressions and information they can easily recall, dramatic events can alter an individual's mental model of world politics.

- An adequate account of continuities and changes in world politics requires examining a variety of causal factors flowing from the individual, state, and systemic levels of analysis. Whereas some factors are remote from the effects they help produce, others have an impact that is more proximate in time.

- Causal factors operating at the individual level of analysis explain international events by focusing on the personal characteristics of humans; those at the state level, by looking at the national attributes of states; and those at the systemic level, by concentrating on the structure and processes of the global system as a whole.

KEY TERMS

actor

anarchy

billiard-ball model

cognitive dissonance

containment

contingent behavior

heuristics

individual level of
    analysis

nation

nation–state

nationalism

nonstate actors

politics

proximate causes

remote causes

schematic reasoning

sovereignty

state

state level of analysis

system

systemic level of analysis

SUGGESTED READINGS

Ferguson, Yale H., and Richard W. Mansbach. *Remapping Global Politics: History's Revenge and Future Shock.* New York: Columbia University Press, 2004.

Hughes, Barry B., and Evan E. Hillebrand. *Exploring and Shaping International Futures.* Boulder, CO: Paradigm Publishers, 2006.

Kegley, Charles W., Jr., and Gregory A. Raymond. *Exorcising the Ghost of Westphalia: Building World Order in the New Millennium.* Upper Saddle River, NJ: Prentice-Hall, 2002.

Thompson, William R. (ed.). *Systemic Transitions: Past, Present, Future.* New York: Palgrave Macmillan, 2008.

Tickner, Arlene B., and Ole Wæver. (eds.). *International Relations Scholarship Around the World.* New York: Routledge, 2009.

CRITICAL THINKING QUESTIONS

Why did the United States invade Iraq in 2003? When weapons of mass destruction (WMD) were not found after Saddam Hussein was ousted, the most common argument was that the war was "largely about oil" (Greenspan, 2007: 463). Facing rising energy demands and insecure supplies, the Bush administration sought access to Iraq's vast petroleum reserves (Hart, 2004: 98–99). While seductive, this single-factor explanation overlooks other plausible causes of the Iraq War. Wars, according to most scholars, have multiple causes that can be found at different levels of analysis. What follows is a nonexhaustive inventory of other factors that may have caused the war to occur.

- Due to unipolarity, there was no countervailing power to deter an American attack (Keegan, 2005: 98).

- The terrorist attacks of 9/11 shifted the Bush administration's attention to the problem of state-sponsored terrorism (Allawi, 2007: 80; Aldonsi, 2006: 408; Nuechterlein, 2005: 39).

- The success in ousting the Taliban from power in Afghanistan boosted the confidence of the Bush administration, leading it to conclude that regime change in Iraq would be relatively easy (F. Kaplan, 2008: 39–40; Steinberg, 2008: 156).

- The decision-making process within the Bush administration was flawed; intelligence was "cherry picked," a wide range of policy options were not examined, and criticism of the favored course of action was not encouraged (McClelland, 2008; Dobbins, 2007: 64; Pillar, 2006).

- Congress failed to provide sufficient oversight of administration actions (Ricks, 2006: 4).

- Neoconservatives (for example, Paul Wolfowitz, John Bolton, Douglas Feith) were a vocal pressure group insisting for years that Saddam Hussein was an evil leader who should have been removed from power during the 1991 Persian Gulf War; if his regime was replaced by a democratic government, they predicted that democracy would spread throughout the region (Stoessinger, 2011: 329–330; Galbraith, 2006: 9).

- Powerful, assertive members of the administration, such as Vice President Dick Cheney, believed in the importance of taking preventive military actions against perceived threats (Woodward, 2004: 4).

- President Bush was an intuitive, risk-acceptant decision maker who saw the world as a moral struggle between the forces of good versus evil, with no neutral ground between them (Cashman and Robinson, 2007: 336).

How would you classify these possible causes by level of analysis and time sequence? Which factors operated at the individual, state, and systemic levels? Which factors were remote and which might have been proximate causes of the war? How might certain specific factors from different levels of analysis have interacted with one another over time in a chain of causation to increase the probability of the Iraq War?

2

Theories of World Politics

CHAPTER OUTLINE

There is an inescapable link between the abstract world of theory and the real world of policy. We need theories to make sense of the blizzard of information that bombards us daily. Even policymakers who are contemptuous of "theory" must rely on their own (often unstated) ideas about how the world works in order to decide what to do. ... Everyone uses theories—whether he or she knows it or not.

STEPHEN M. WALT
POLITICAL SCIENTIST

Although the academic study of international relations is relatively new, attempts to theorize about state behavior date back to antiquity. Perhaps the best example can be found in Thucydides, the Greek historian who analyzed the Peloponnesian War (431–404 BCE) between ancient Sparta and Athens. Thucydides (1951: 14–15) believed "knowledge of the past" would be "an aid to the interpretation of the future" and therefore wrote a history of the war, not to win the applause of the moment, but as "a possession for all time." Examining the hostilities like a physician diagnosing a patient, his detailed clinical observations were recorded as a case study that described the symptoms of war-prone periods and offered a prognosis of the probable consequences of different foreign policy actions.

Greece in Thucydides' day was not unified; it contained a welter of small, autonomous city-states scattered throughout the Balkan Peninsula, the Aegean Archipelago, and what is today western Turkey. Sparta and Athens were the strongest of these fiercely independent states. The former was a cautious, conservative land power; the latter, a bold, innovative sea power. Relations between them were contentious. When their rivalry eventually escalated to war in 431 BCE, they became trapped in a long, debilitating military stalemate.

Stung by mounting losses during a decade of fruitless combat, in 421 BCE Sparta and Athens agreed to a cessation of hostilities. Neither side expected it to last, however. The two rivals refrained from attacking one another over the next few years, but each side maneuvered to gain an advantage over the other in anticipation of the next round of fighting. A strong, reliable network of allies, the Athenians thought, might provide a decisive edge when the war resumed. To consolidate their position among Greeks living on islands throughout the Aegean Sea, in 416 BCE Athens sent an expedition of thirty-eight ships and approximately 3,000 soldiers to Melos, a city-state that wished to remain nonaligned during the war. The Athenians declared that if Melos did not agree to become their ally, it would be obliterated. The Melians argued that such a brutal attack would be unjust since they had not harmed Athens. Moreover, it was in Athens's self-interest to show restraint: destroying Melos would drive other neutral city-states into the Spartan camp. Finally, the Melians pointed out that it would be unreasonable to surrender while there was still hope of being rescued by the Spartans. Scornful of these appeals to justice, expedience, and reasonableness, the Athenians proclaimed that in interstate relations "the strong do what they can and the weak suffer what they must" (Thucydides, 1951: 331). Regardless of the merits of the Melian argument, Athens had the strength to subjugate Melos if it so desired. Resistance was futile; nevertheless, the Melians refused to submit. The Athenian troops promptly besieged the city, forcing it to capitulate shortly thereafter. Following the city's surrender, they killed all adult men and sold the women and children into slavery.

The Athenian practice of raw power politics raises timeless questions about world affairs. How can states achieve security in an anarchic international system? In the absence of a central authority to resolve the disputes among states, are there limits to the use of military power? What role should ethical considerations play in the conduct of foreign policy? This chapter will focus on the three schools of thought that have most influenced how policymakers and scholars think about these kinds of questions: realism, liberalism, and constructivism.

CONTENDING THEORIES OF WORLD POLITICS

Imagine yourself the newly elected president of the United States. You are scheduled to deliver the State of the Union address on your views of the current world situation. Your task is to identify those international issues most worthy of attention and explain how you plan to deal with them. To convince citizens these issues are important, you must present them as part of a larger picture of the world, showing how the situation you face may be part of a pattern. You must, in short, think *theoretically*. The success of your effort to explain the causes of current problems, predict their long-term consequences, and persuade others that you have a viable policy to address them will hinge on how well you understand the way the world works.

When leaders face these kinds of intellectual challenges, they fortunately benefit from the existence of several theories of world politics from which they can draw guidance. A **theory** is a set of statements that purports to explain a particular phenomenon. In essence, it provides a map, or frame of reference, that makes the complex, puzzling world around us intelligible. Choosing which theory to heed is an important decision, because each rests on different assumptions about the nature of international politics, each advances different causal claims, and each offers a different set of foreign policy recommendations. Our aim in this chapter is to compare the assumptions, causal claims, and policy prescriptions of realism, liberalism, and constructivism, the most common theoretical perspectives policymakers and scholars use to interpret international relations. We begin with realism, the oldest of these contending schools of thought.

theory a set of interrelated propositions that explains an observed regularity.

REALIST THEORY

Political realism has a long, distinguished history that dates back to the writings of Thucydides about the Peloponnesian War. Other influential figures that contributed to realist thought include the sixteenth-century Italian philosopher Niccolò Machiavelli and the seventeenth-century English philosopher Thomas Hobbes. Realism deserves careful examination because its worldview continues to guide much thought about international politics.

The Realist Worldview

Realism, as applied to contemporary international politics, views the nation-state as the most important actor on the world stage since it answers to no higher

Tito, Santi di (1536-1603) Portrait of Niccolo' Machiavelli (1469-1527)/ Palazzo Vecchio, Florence, Italy/ Scala / Art Resource, NY

Thomas Hobbes (1588-1679), Fuller, Isaac (1606-72)/©Burghley House Collection, Lincolnshire, UK/Bridgeman Art Library

Realist Pioneers of Power Politics In *The Prince* (1532) and *The Leviathan* (1651), Niccolò Machiavelli and Thomas Hobbes, respectively, emphasized a political calculus based on interest, prudence, power, and expediency above all other considerations. This formed the foundation of what became a growing body of modern realist thinking that accepts the drive for power over others as necessary and wise statecraft.

power the ability to make someone continue a course of action, change what he or she is doing, or refrain from acting.

self-help the principle that in anarchy actors must rely on themselves.

relative gains a measure of how much one side in an agreement benefits in comparison with the other's side.

political authority. States are sovereign: They have supreme power over their territory and populace, and no one stands above them wielding the legitimacy and coercive capability to govern the international system. Given the absence of a higher authority to which states can turn for protection and to resolve disputes, realists depict world politics as a ceaseless, repetitive struggle for **power** where, as in the Melian episode described by Thucydides, the strong dominate the weak. Because each state is ultimately responsible for its own survival and feels uncertain about its neighbors' intentions, realism claims that prudent political leaders seek arms and allies to enhance national security. In other words, the anarchic structure of the international system leads even well-intentioned leaders to practice **self-help**, increasing military strength and aligning with others to deter potential threats. Realist theory does not preclude the possibility that rival powers will cooperate on arms control or on other security issues of common interest. Rather it asserts that cooperation will be rare because states worry about the distribution of **relative gains** emanating from cooperation and the possibility that the other side will cheat on agreements.

Realists, with their emphasis on the ruthless nature of international life, tend to be skeptical about the role of ethical considerations in foreign policy deliberations. As they see it, some policies are driven by strategic imperatives that may require national leaders to contravene moral norms. Embedded in this "philosophy of necessity" is a distinction between private morality, which guides the behavior of ordinary people in their daily lives, and reason of state *(raison d'état)*, which governs the conduct of leaders responsible for the security and survival of the state. Whatever actions that are in the interest of state security must be carried out no matter how repugnant they might seem in the light of private morality. "Ignoring one's interests, squandering one's resources in fits of altruism," so this line of argument goes, "is the fastest road to national disaster." For a national leader, "thinking with one's heart is a serious offense. Foreign policy is not social work" (Krauthammer, 1993: 74).

The Evolution of Realist Thought

We have seen how the intellectual roots of political realism reach back to ancient Greece. They also extend beyond the western world to India and China. Discussions of "power politics" abound in the *Arthashastra*, an Indian treatise on statecraft written during the fourth century BCE by Kautilya, as well as in works written by Han Fei and Shang Yang in ancient China.

Modern realism emerged on the eve of the Second World War, when the prevailing belief in a natural harmony of interests among nations came under attack. Just a decade earlier, this belief had led numerous countries to sign the 1928 Kellogg-Briand Pact, which renounced war as an instrument of national policy. Now, with Nazi Germany, Fascist Italy, and Imperial Japan all violating the treaty, British historian and diplomat E. H. Carr (1939: 53) complained that the assumption of a universal interest in peace had allowed too many people to "evade the unpalatable fact of a fundamental divergence of interest between nations desirous of maintaining the *status quo* and nations desirous of changing it."

In an effort to counter what they saw as a utopian, legalistic approach to foreign affairs, Reinhold Niebuhr (1947), Hans J. Morgenthau (1948), and other realists articulated a pessimistic view of human nature. Echoing the seventeenth-century philosopher Baruch Spinoza, many of them pointed to an innate conflict between passion and reason; furthermore, in the tradition of St. Augustine, they stressed that material appetites enabled passion to overwhelm reason. For them, the human condition was such that the forces of light and darkness would perpetually vie for control.

The realists' picture of international life appeared particularly persuasive after World War II. The onset of rivalry between the United States and the Soviet Union, the expansion of the Cold War into a wider struggle between East and West, and the periodic crises that threatened to erupt into global violence seemed to support the realists' emphasis on the inevitability of conflict, the poor prospects for cooperation, and the divergence of national interests among incorrigibly selfish, power-seeking states.

Whereas these so-called "classical" realists sought to explain state behavior by drawing on explanatory factors located at the individual level of analysis, *neorealism* (sometimes labeled structural realism), the next wave of realist theorizing, emphasized the systemic level of analysis. Kenneth Waltz (1979), the leading proponent of what has come to be called "defensive" realism, proposed that international anarchy—not some allegedly evil side of human nature—explained why states were locked in fierce competition with one another. The absence of a central arbiter was the defining structural feature of the international system. Vulnerable and insecure, states behaved defensively by forming alliances against looming threats. According to Waltz, balances of power form automatically in anarchic environments. Even when they are disrupted, they are soon restored.

A more recent variant of realist theory also resides at the systemic level of analysis, but asserts that the ultimate aim of states is to achieve military supremacy, not merely a balance of power. For John Mearsheimer (2001) and other exponents of "offensive" realism, the anarchic structure of the international system encourages states to maximize their shares of world power in order to improve the odds of surviving the competition for relative advantage. A state with an edge over everyone else has insurance against the possibility that a predatory state might someday pose a grave threat. To quote the old cliché: The best defense is a good offense.

Finally, scholars known as "neoclassical" realists advocate combining system-level accounts of state behavior with factors drawn from other levels of analysis (see Schweller, 2006). Renewed attention, they insist, should be devoted to variations in the ambitions of political leaders and the goals of different types of governments. From their vantage point, whether a state seeks to revise the prevailing distribution of world power or is content to work within the status quo is as significant in explaining the dynamics of world politics as the effects of international anarchy.

The Limitations of Realism

However persuasive the realists' image of the essential properties of international politics, their policy recommendations suffered from a lack of precision in the way they used such key terms as *power* and *national interest*. Thus, once analysis moved beyond the assertion that national leaders should acquire power to serve the national interest, important questions remained: What were the key elements of national power? What uses of power best served the national interest? Did arms furnish protection or provoke costly arms races? Did alliances enhance one's defenses or encourage threatening counteralliances? From the perspective of realism's critics, seeking security by amassing power was self-defeating. The quest for absolute security by one state would be perceived as creating absolute insecurity for other members of the system, with the result that everyone would become locked in an upward spiral of countermeasures that jeopardized the security of all (Vasquez, 1993; 1998).

Because much of realist theorizing was vague, it began to be questioned. Realism offered no criteria for determining what historical data were significant in evaluating its claims and what epistemological rules to follow when interpreting relevant information (Vasquez and Elman, 2003). Even the policy recommendations that purportedly flowed from its logic were often divergent. Realists themselves, for example, were sharply divided as to whether U.S. intervention in Vietnam served American national interests and whether nuclear weapons contributed to international security. Similarly, whereas some observers used realism to explain the 2003 U.S. invasion of Iraq (Gvosdev, 2005), others drew on realist arguments to criticize the invasion (Mansfield and Snyder, 2005; Mearsheimer and Walt, 2003).

A growing number of critics also pointed out that realism did not account for significant developments in world politics. For instance, it could not explain the creation of new commercial and political institutions in Western Europe in the 1950s and 1960s, where the cooperative pursuit of mutual advantage led Europeans away from the unbridled power politics that brought them incessant warfare since the birth of the nation-state some three centuries earlier. Other critics began to worry about realism's tendency to disregard ethical principles and about the material and social costs that some of its policy prescriptions seemed to impose, such as retarded economic growth resulting from unrestrained military expenditures.

Despite realism's shortcomings, many people continue to think about world politics in the language constructed by realists, especially in times of global tension. An example can be found in the comments by former Bush administration adviser Michael Gerson (2006: 59–60) about how the United States should deal with Iran's nuclear ambitions. Arguing from the realist assumption that "peace is not a natural state," he has called for a robust American response based on a steely-eyed focus on the country's national security interest in preventing the proliferation of weapons of mass destruction in the Middle East. "There must be someone in the world capable of drawing a line—someone who says, 'This much and no further.'" Peace, he concludes, cannot be achieved by "a timid foreign policy that allows terrible threats to emerge." Unless those who threaten others pay a price, "aggression will be universal."

LIBERAL THEORY

Liberalism has been called the "strongest contemporary challenge to realism" (Caporaso, 1993: 465). Like realism, it has a distinguished pedigree, with philosophical roots extending back to the political thought of John Locke, Immanuel Kant, and Adam Smith. Liberalism warrants our attention because it speaks to issues that realism disregards, including the impact of domestic politics on state behavior, the implications of economic interdependence, and the role of international norms and institutions in facilitating international cooperation.

The Liberal Worldview

There are several distinct schools of thought within the liberal tradition. Drawing broad conclusions from such a diverse body of theory risks misrepresenting the

Kean Collection/Hulton Archive/Getty Images

The Print Collector/Alamy Limited

Pioneers in the Liberal Quest for World Order Immanuel Kant (left) in *Perpetual Peace* (1795) helped to redefine modern liberal theory by advocating global (not state) citizenship, free trade, and a federation of democracies as a means of achieving world peace. Richard Cobden (right) believed that if contact and communication among people could expand through free trade, so too would prosperity and, in turn, peace.

position of any given author. Nevertheless, there are sufficient commonalities to abstract some general themes.

Liberals differ from realists in several important ways. At the core of liberalism is a belief in reason and the possibility of progress. Liberals view the individual as the seat of moral value and assert that human beings should be treated as ends rather than means. Whereas realists counsel decision makers to seek the lesser evil rather than the absolute good, liberals emphasize ethical principle over the pursuit of power, and institutions over military capabilities (see Doyle, 1997; Zacher and Matthew, 1995). Politics at the international level is more of a struggle for consensus and mutual gain than a struggle for power and prestige.

Instead of blaming international conflict on an inherent lust for power, liberals fault the conditions that people live under. Reforming those conditions, they argue, will enhance the prospects for peace. The first element common to various strands of liberal thought is an emphasis on undertaking political reforms to establish stable democracies. U.S. President Woodrow Wilson (1992: 268), for example, proclaimed that "democratic government will make wars less likely." President Franklin Roosevelt later reflected this view when he asserted "the continued maintenance and improvement of democracy constitute the most important guarantee of international peace" (cited in Talbott, 1996: 40). Based on tolerance, accommodation, and procedural rights, democratic political cultures are said to shun lethal force as a means of settling disagreements. Politics is not seen as a **zero-sum game**, so that the use of persuasion rather than coercion and a reliance on judicial avenues to settle rival claims are the primary means of dealing with conflict.

According to liberal theory, conflict resolution practices used at home are also employed when dealing with international disputes. Leaders socialized within democratic cultures share a common outlook. Viewing international politics as an extension of domestic politics, they externalize their norms of regulated competition. Disputes with kindred governments rarely escalate to war because each side accepts the other's legitimacy and expects it to rely on peaceful means of conflict resolution. These expectations are reinforced by the transparent nature of democracies. The inner workings of open polities can be scrutinized by anyone; hence, it is difficult to demonize them as scheming adversaries.

The second thrust common to liberal theorizing is an emphasis on free trade. The idea that commerce helps promote conflict resolution has roots in the work of Montesquieu, Adam Smith, and various Enlightenment thinkers. "Nothing is more favourable to the rise of politeness and learning," noted the philosopher David Hume (1817: 138), "than a number of neighboring and independent states, connected by commerce." This view was later embraced by the Manchester School of political economy and formed the basis for Norman Angell's (1910) famous rebuttal of the assertion that military conquest yields economic prosperity.

The doctrine that unfettered trade helps prevent disputes from escalating to wars rests on several propositions. First, commercial intercourse creates a material incentive to resolve disputes peacefully: War reduces profits by interrupting vital economic exchanges. Second, cosmopolitan business elites who benefit most from these exchanges comprise a powerful transnational interest group with a stake in promoting amicable solutions to festering disagreements. Finally, the web of trade between nations increases communication, erodes parochialism, and encourages both sides to avoid ruinous clashes. In the words of Richard Cobden, an opponent of the protectionist Corn Laws that once regulated British international grain trade: "Free Trade! What is it? Why, breaking down the barriers that separate nations; those barriers, behind which nestle the feelings of pride, revenge, hatred, and jealousy, which every now and then burst their bounds, and deluge whole countries with blood" (cited in Wolfers and Martin, 1956: 193).

Finally, the third commonality in liberal theorizing is an advocacy of international institutions. Liberals recommend replacing cutthroat, balance-of-power politics with organizations based on the principle that a threat to peace anywhere is a common concern to everyone. They see foreign policy as unfolding in a nascent global society populated by actors who recognize the cost of conflict, share significant interests, and can realize those interests by using institutions to mediate disputes whenever misconceptions, wounded sensibilities, or aroused national passions threaten their relations.

The Evolution of Liberal Thought

Contemporary liberal theory rose to prominence in the wake of the First World War. Not only had the war involved more participants over a wider geographic

zero-sum game a situation in which what one side wins, the other side loses.

area than any previous war, but modern science and technology made it a war of machinery: Old weapons were improved and produced in great quantities, new and far more deadly weapons were rapidly developed and deployed. By the time the carnage was over, nearly 20 million people were dead.

For liberals like Woodrow Wilson, World War I was "the war to end all wars." Convinced that another horrific war would erupt if states resumed practicing power politics, liberals set out to reform the international system. These "idealists," as they were called by hard-boiled realists, generally fell into one of three groups (Herz, 1951). The first group advocated creating international institutions to mitigate the raw struggle for power between egoistic, mutually suspicious states. The League of Nations was the embodiment of this strain of liberal thought. Its founders hoped to prevent future wars by organizing a system of **collective security** that would mobilize the entire international community against would-be aggressors. Peace, they declared, was indivisible: An attack on one member of the League would be considered an attack on all. Since no state was more powerful than the combination of all other states, aggressors would be deterred and war averted.

A second group called for the use of legal procedures to adjudicate disputes before they escalated to armed conflict. Adjudication is a judicial procedure for resolving conflicts by referring them to a standing court for a binding decision. Immediately after the war, several governments drafted a statute to establish a Permanent Court of International Justice (PCIJ). Hailed by Bernard C. J. Loder, the court's first president, as the harbinger of a new era of civilization, the PCIJ held its inaugural public meeting in early 1922 and rendered its first judgment on a contentious case the following year. Liberal champions of the court insisted that the PCIJ would replace military retaliation with a judicial body capable of bringing the facts of a dispute to light and issuing a just verdict.

A third group of liberal thinkers followed the biblical injunction that states should beat their swords into plowshares and sought disarmament as a means of avoiding war. Their efforts were exemplified between 1921 and 1922 by the Washington Naval Conference, which tried to curtail maritime competition among the United States, Great Britain, Japan, France, and Italy by placing limits on battleships. The ultimate goal of this group was to reduce international tensions by promoting general disarmament, which led them to convene the Geneva Disarmament Conference in 1932.

Although a tone of idealism dominated policy rhetoric and academic discussions during the interwar period, little of the liberal reform program was ever seriously attempted, and even less of it was achieved. The League of Nations failed to prevent the Japanese invasion of Manchuria (1931) or the Italian invasion of Ethiopia (1935); major disputes were rarely submitted to the Permanent Court of International Justice; and the 1932 Geneva Disarmament Conference ended in failure. When the threat of war began gathering over Europe and Asia in the late 1930s, enthusiasm for liberal idealism receded.

The next surge in liberal theorizing arose decades later in response to realism's neglect of **transnational relations** (Keohane and Nye, 1971). Although

collective security a security regime based on the principle that an act of aggression by any state will be met by a collective response from the rest.

transnational relations interactions across state boundaries that involve at least one actor that is not the agent of a government or intergovernmental organization.

realists continued to focus on the state, the events surrounding the 1973 oil crisis revealed that nonstate actors could affect the course of international events, and occasionally compete with states. This insight led to the realization that **complex interdependence** (Keohane and Nye, 1977) sometimes offered a better description of world politics than realism, especially on international economic and environmental matters. Rather than contacts between countries being limited to high-level governmental officials, multiple communication channels connected societies. Rather than security dominating foreign policy considerations, issues on national agendas did not always have a fixed priority. Rather than military force serving as the primary instrument of statecraft, other means frequently were more effective when bargaining occurred between economically interconnected nations. In short, the realist preoccupation with government-to-government relations ignored the complex network of public and private exchanges crisscrossing national boundaries. States were becoming increasingly interdependent; that is, mutually dependent on, sensitive about, and vulnerable to one another in ways that were not captured by realist theory.

While interdependence was not new, its growth during the last quarter of the twentieth century led many liberal theorists to challenge the realist conception of anarchy. Although agreeing that the international system was anarchic, they suggested that it was more properly conceptualized as an "ordered" anarchy because most states followed commonly acknowledged normative standards, even in the absence of hierarchical enforcement. When a body of norms fosters shared expectations that guide a regularized pattern of cooperation on a specific issue, we call it an **international regime**. Various types of regimes have been devised to govern behavior in trade and monetary affairs, as well as to manage access to common resources like fisheries and river water. By the turn of the century, as pressing economic and environmental issues crowded national agendas, a large body of liberal scholarship delved into how regimes developed and what led states to follow their injunctions.

Fueled by a belief that increased interdependence can lead to higher levels of cooperation, this new wave of liberal theorizing, known as *neoliberalism* (also called neoliberal institutionalism), mounted a serious challenge to realism and neorealism during the last decade of the twentieth century. Neoliberals argued that states attempt to maximize **absolute gains** by cooperating to advance mutual interests, and that international institutions provide a mechanism for coordinating multilateral action and reducing the odds of anyone reneging on their commitments. On the one hand, institutions strengthen cooperative arrangements by providing information on the preferences of others; on the other, they dampen the incentive to cheat by monitoring compliance with agreements.

More recently, neoliberals have explored **moral hazard** dilemmas that can arise when states behave in ways that exacerbate a pressing problem because they expect international institutions to bail them out. For example, a country that is unable to make payments on its outstanding debts may continue borrowing under the assumption that an institution such as the International Monetary Fund will provide it with financial backing (Martin, 2007: 118–124). Research

complex interdependence a model of world politics based on the assumptions that states are not the only important actors, security is not the dominant national goal, and military force is not the only significant instrument of foreign policy.

international regime a set of principles, norms, and rules governing behavior within a specified issue area.

absolute gains conditions in which all participants in exchanges become better off.

moral hazard a situation in which international institutions create incentives for states to behave recklessly.

into dilemmas of this kind have led neoliberals to gain insights into how international institutions occasionally carve out enough autonomy to pursue their own agendas despite pressure to respond to the desires of their most powerful members.

The Limitations of Liberalism

Liberal theorists share an interest in probing the conditions under which the convergent and overlapping interests among otherwise sovereign political actors may result in cooperation. Taking heart in the international prohibition, through community consensus, of such previously entrenched practices as slavery, piracy, dueling, and colonialism, they emphasize the prospects for progress through institutional reform. Studies of European integration during the 1950s and 1960s paved the way for the liberal institutionalist theories that emerged in the 1990s. The expansion of trade, communication, information, technology, and immigrant labor propelled Europeans to sacrifice portions of their sovereign independence to create a new political and economic union out of previously separate units. These developments were outside of realism's worldview, creating conditions that made the call for a theory grounded in the liberal tradition convincing to many who had previously questioned realism.

Yet as compelling as contemporary liberal institutionalism may seem in the early twenty-first century, many realists complain that it has not transcended its idealist heritage (see APPLICATION: Steel and Good Intentions). They charge that just like the League of Nations and the Permanent Court of International Justice, institutions today exert minimal influence on state behavior. International organizations cannot stop states from behaving according to balance-of-power logic, calculating how each move they make affects their relative position in a world of relentless competition (Mearsheimer, 1994/1995).

low politics the category of global issues related to the economic, social, and environmental aspects of relations between governments and people.

high politics the category of global issues related to military and security aspects of relations between governments and people.

Critics of liberalism further contend that most studies supportive of international institutions appear in the **low politics** arena of commercial, financial, and environmental affairs, not in the **high politics** arena of national defense. While it may be difficult to draw a clear line between economic and security issues, some scholars note that different institutional arrangements exist in each realm, with the prospects for cooperation among self-interested states greater in the former than the latter (Lipson, 1984). National survival hinges on the effective management of security issues, insist realists. Collective security organizations naively assume that all members perceive threats in the same way, and are willing to run the risks and pay the costs of countering those threats. Because avaricious states are unlikely to see their vital interests in this light, international institutions cannot provide timely, muscular responses to aggression. On security issues, conclude realists, states will trust in their own power, not in the promises of international institutions.

A final realist complaint lodged against liberalism is an alleged tendency to turn foreign policy into a moral crusade. Whereas realists claim that heads of state are driven by strategic necessities, many liberals believe moral necessities impose categorical imperatives on leaders. Consider the 1999 war in Kosovo, which pitted the North Atlantic Treaty Organization (NATO) against the Federal

---

APPLICATION Steel and Good Intentions

Political realists frequently refer to those who believe that international morality can contribute to fostering peaceful relations among states as "idealists" or "utopians." Asking us to look at the world with candor, they insist that politics is a struggle for power that cannot be eliminated from the international scene. In the words of Otto von Bismarck, German chancellor during the late nineteenth century and the foremost realist of his day, conducting foreign policy with moral principles would be like walking along a narrow forest path while carrying a long pole in one's mouth.

Although the prevailing caricature of realists depicts them as ruthless practitioners of guileful tactics, many policymakers who subscribe to realism aver that prudence requires raw power to be restrained by moral limitations. In the passage that follows, Margaret Thatcher, who served as prime minister of the United Kingdom from 1979 to 1990, discusses how realist prescriptions about the use of power as well as moral principles informed her foreign policy decisions.

> Above all, foreign and security policy is about the use of power in order to achieve a state's goals in its relations with other states. As a conservative, I have no squeamishness about stating this. I leave it to others to try to achieve the results they seek in international affairs without reference to

power. They always fail. And their failures often lead to outcomes more damaging than pursuit of national interest through the normal means of the balance of power and resolute defense would ever have done.

> It is sometimes suggested, or at least implied, that the only alternative … [to idealism] is the total abandonment of moral standards. … Yet I am not one of those who believe that statecraft should concern power without principle. For a start, pure Realpolitik—that is, foreign policy based on calculations of power and the national interest—is a concept which blurs at the edges the more closely it is examined. … [T]he pursuit of statecraft without regard for moral principles is all but impossible, and it makes little sense for even the most hard-nosed statesman to ignore this fact.

> … For my part, I favor an approach to statecraft that embraces principles, as long as it is not stifled by them; and I prefer such principles to be accompanied by steel along with good intentions (Thatcher, 2002: xix–xxii).

For Thatcher, who dealt with issues ranging from confrontations with the Soviet Union to war with Argentina during her tenure in office, moral posturing was no substitute for a muscular foreign policy. However, effective policy required a moral vision.

Republic of Yugoslavia. Pointing to Yugoslav leader Slobodan Milosevic's repression of ethnic Albanians living in the province of Kosovo, NATO Secretary General Javier Solana, British Prime Minister Tony Blair, and U.S. President Bill Clinton all argued that humanitarian intervention was a moral imperative. Although nonintervention into the internal affairs of other states had long been a cardinal principle of international law, they saw military action against Yugoslavia as a duty because human rights were an international entitlement and governments that violated them forfeited the protection of international law. Sovereignty, according to many liberal thinkers, is not sacrosanct. The international community has an obligation to use armed force to stop flagrant violations of human rights.

Realists remain skeptical about liberal claims of moral necessity. On the one hand, they deny the universal applicability of any single moral standard in a culturally pluralistic world. On the other hand, they worry that adopting such a standard will breed a self-righteous, messianic foreign policy. Realists embrace **consequentialism**. If there are no universal standards covering the many situations in which moral choice must occur, then policy decisions can only be judged in terms of their consequences in particular circumstances. Prudent

consequentialism an approach to evaluating moral choices on the basis of the results of the action taken.

leaders recognize that competing moral values may be at stake in any given situation, and they must weigh the trade-offs among these values, as well as how pursuing them might impinge on national security and other important interests. As the former U.S. diplomat and celebrated realist scholar George Kennan (1951: 60) once put it, the primary obligation of government "is to the interests of the national society it represents, not to the moral impulses that individual elements of that society may experience."

CONSTRUCTIVIST THEORY

Since the end of the Cold War, many students of international relations have turned to social constructivism in order to understand world politics. In contrast to realism and liberalism, which emphasize how material factors such as military power and economic wealth affect the relations among states, constructivism focuses on the impact of ideas. As discussed in the previous chapter, international reality is defined by our images of the world. Constructivists emphasize the inter-subjective quality of these images. We are all influenced by collective conceptions of world politics that are reinforced by social pressures from the reference groups to which we belong. Awareness of how our understandings of the world are socially constructed, and of how prevailing ideas mold our beliefs about what is immutable and what can be reformed, allows us to see world politics in a new, critical light.

The Constructivist Worldview

As shown in Table 2.1, constructivists differ from realists and liberals most fundamentally by insisting that world politics is socially constructed. That is to say, material resources, such as those contributing to brute military and economic power, only acquire meaning for human action through the structure of shared knowledge in which they are embedded. The social structure of a system makes actions possible by constituting actors with certain identities and interests, and material capabilities with certain meanings (Onuf, 1989; 2002). Hence the meaning of a concept such as "anarchy" depends on the underlying structure of shared knowledge. An anarchy among allies, for example, entails a different meaning for the states in question than an anarchy composed of bitter rivals. Thus, British nuclear weapons are less threatening to the United States than the same weapons in North Korean hands, because shared Anglo-American expectations about one another differ from those between Washington and Pyongyang. The nature of international life within an anarchy, in other words, is not a given. Anarchy and other socially constructed concepts like "sovereignty" and "power" are simply what states make of them (Wendt, 1995).

The Evolution of Constructivist Thought

The intellectual roots of constructivism extend from the work of the early twentieth-century Frankfurt School of critical social theory to more recent research by Peter Berger and Thomas Luckmann (1967) on the sociology of

T A B L E 2.1   A Comparison of Realist, Liberal, and Constructivist Theories

Feature	Realism	Liberalism	Constructivism
Core concern	How vulnerable, self-interested states survive in an environment where they are uncertain about the intentions and capabilities of others	How rational egoists coordinate their behaviors through rules and organizations in order to achieve collective gains	How ideas and identities shape world politics
Key actors	States	States, international institutions, global corporations	Individuals, nongovernmental organizations, transnational networks
Central concepts	Anarchy, self-help, national interest, relative gains, balance of power	Collective security, international regimes, complex interdependence, transnational relations	Ideas, shared knowledge, identities, discourses
Approach to peace	Protect sovereign autonomy and deter rivals through military preparedness	Democratization, open markets, and international law and organization	Activists who promote progressive ideas and encourage states to adhere to norms of appropriate behavior
Global outlook	Pessimistic: great powers locked in relentless security competition	Optimistic: cooperative view of human nature and a belief in progress	Agnostic: global prospect hinges on the content of prevailing ideas and values

knowledge and by Anthony Giddens (1984) on the relationship between agency and social structure. Sometimes described as more of a philosophically informed perspective than a fully fledged general theory, constructivism includes a diverse group of scholars who by and large agree that the international institutions most people take for granted as the natural and inevitable result of world politics need not exist (Hacking, 1999). Like the institution of slavery, they are social constructs that depend upon human agreement for their existence and are therefore changeable.

The unraveling of the Warsaw Pact and subsequent disintegration of the Soviet Union stimulated scholarly interest during the 1990s in constructivist interpretations of world politics. Neither realism nor liberalism foresaw the peaceful end to the Cold War, and both theories had difficulty explaining why it occurred when it did. Constructivists pointed to the challenge that Mikhail Gorbechev's "new thinking" posed to traditional ideas about national security (Koslowski and Kratochwil, 1994). New thinking, they suggested, led to the rise of new **norms** governing the relations between Moscow and Washington.

Norms can be the sources of action in three ways: they may be *constitutive* in the sense that they define what counts as a certain activity; they may be *constraining* in that they enjoin an actor from behaving in a particular way; or they may be *enabling* by allowing specific actions (Raymond, 1997). In American football,

norms generalized standards of behavior that embody collective expectations about appropriate conduct.

Pioneering Influences on Constructivist Thought Many constructivists have been influenced by critical theory, especially as it was developed by Max Horkheimer (1947) and Jürgen Habermas (1984). The roots of critical theory can be traced to the Institute for Social Research, which was founded in Frankfurt, Germany, during the 1920s. According to the so-called "Frankfurt School" of philosophical thought, the aims of critical theory were to critique and change society, not merely understand it. Rather than viewing the world as a set of neutral, objective "facts" that could be perceived apart from the situation in which observation occurred, critical theorists saw things as embedded within a specific socio-historical context (Price and Reus-Smit, 1998; Cox, 1996).

for instance, there are constitutive rules that give meaning to action on the field by defining what counts as a touchdown, a field goal, or a safety. There also are two kinds of regulative rules that guide play: constraining rules prohibit things like clipping and holding, while enabling rules permit players to throw laterals and forward passes. Similarly, in the modern world system, constitutive norms of sovereignty define what counts as statehood, while regulative norms that either constrain or enable specify how sovereign states ought to conduct themselves. Rather than simply following a *logic of consequences*, where the anticipatory costs and benefits of alternative actions are weighed to ascertain what will maximize one's interests, states take into account a *logic of appropriateness*, where behavior is guided by norms that define what consists of legitimate conduct given one's identity.

For constructivists, the game of power in international relations revolves around actors' abilities through debate about values to persuade others to accept their ideas. People and groups become powerful when their efforts to proselytize succeed in winning converts to those ideas and norms they advocate, and a culture of shared understandings emerges. The capacity of some activist transnational nongovernmental organizations, such as Human Rights Watch or

Greenpeace, to promote global change by convincing many people to accept their ideas about political liberties and environmental protection are examples of how shared conceptions of moral and legal norms can change the world. Shared understandings of interests, identities, and images of the world—how people think of themselves, who they are, and what others in the world are like—demonstrably can alter the world when these social constructions of international realties change (M. Barnet, 2005; Adler, 2002).

The Limitations of Constructivism

The most common criticism of constructivism concerns its explanation of change. If changes in ideas and discourses lead to behavioral changes within the state system, what accounts for the rise and fall of different ideas and discourses over time? How, when, and why do social structures of shared knowledge emerge? "Constructivists are good at describing change," writes political scientist Jack Snyder (2004: 61), "but they are weak on the material and institutional circumstances necessary to support the emergence of consensus about new values and ideas." Moreover, even if new values and ideas are not reflections of developments in the material world, critics charge that constructivists remain unclear about what nonmaterial factors lead certain ideas and discourses to become dominant while others fall by the wayside (Mearsheimer, 1994/95: 42–43). In particular, they "downplay the individual psychological needs" that "shape the social construction of identities" (Levy, 2003b: 273). "What is crucial," asserts Robert Jervis (2005: 18), "is not people's thinking, but the factors that drive it." Constructivists, he continues, have excessive faith in the ability of ideas that seem self-evident today to replicate and sustain themselves; however, future generations who live under different circumstances and who may think differently could easily reject these ideas. For constructivists, socially accepted ideas, norms, and values are linked to collective identities—stable, role-specific understandings and expectations about self. Although constructivists recognize that shared identities are not pre-given and can change over time, critics submit that constructivists cannot explain why and when they dissolve.

A related concern about constructivism is that it overemphasizes the role of social structures at the expense of the purposeful agents whose practices help create and change these structures (Checkel, 1998: 340–342). According to Cynthia Weber (2010: 79–80), constructivism as exemplified in the work of Alexander Wendt (1999) reifies states as the authors or producers of international life; that is, it treats them as objects that already exist and says little about the "practices that produce states as producers." Although Wendtian constructivism calls our attention to the importance of the intersubjectively constituted structure of identities and interests that influence how states see themselves and behave, it does not offer an account of the practices that construct states themselves as producers of international anarchy and other features of world politics.

Finally, a third criticism of constructivism maintains that it says little about what is morally right in world politics. Notwithstanding constructivism's emphasis on the role of norms in explaining why actors behave in a particular way on the global stage, it offers scant guidance on how they ought to behave. Constructivist theory provides an account for why prevailing moral norms have come to be intersubjectively held, and it offers insight into how things might be different if other norms took root; however, it does not stipulate a priori what generalized standards of behavior are good or ethical (M. Hoffmann, 2009).

Despite these criticisms, constructivism remains a popular approach to the study of world politics. By highlighting the influence that socially constructed images of the world have on our interpretations of international events, and by making us aware of their inherent subjectivity, constructivism reminds us of the contingent nature of all knowledge and the inability of any theory of world politics to fully capture global complexities.

WHAT'S MISSING IN THEORIES OF WORLD POLITICS?

Although realism, liberalism, and constructivism dominate thinking about international relations in today's academic and policy communities, these schools of thought have been challenged. Two of the most significant critiques have come from radicalism and feminism.

The Radical Critique

For much of the twentieth century, socialism was the primary radical alternative to mainstream international relations theorizing. Although there are many strands of socialist thought, most have been influenced by Karl Marx's (1818–1883) argument that explaining events in contemporary world affairs requires understanding capitalism as a global phenomenon. Whereas realists emphasize state security, liberals accentuate individual freedom, and constructivists highlight ideas and identities, socialists focus on class conflict and the material interests embodied by each class (Doyle, 1997).

"The history of all hitherto existing society," proclaim Marx and his coauthor Friedrich Engels (1820–1895) in the *Communist Manifesto*, "is the history of class struggles." Capitalism, they argue, has given rise to two antagonistic classes: a ruling class (bourgeoisie) who owns the means of production, and a subordinate class (proletariat) who sells its labor but receives little compensation. According to Marx and Engels, "The need of a constantly expanding market for its products chases the bourgeoisie over the whole surface of the globe." By expanding worldwide, the bourgeoisie gives "a cosmopolitan character to production and consumption in every country" (Marx and Engels, 1948: 9, 12).

Vladimir Ilyich Lenin (1870–1924) extended Marx's analysis to the study of imperialism, which he interpreted as a stage in the development of capitalism where monopolies supplant free-market competition. Drawing from the work of British economist John Hobson (1858–1940), Lenin maintained that advanced capitalist states eventually face the twin problems of overproduction and

INTERFOTO Pressbildagentur/Alamy Limited

Marxism and Radical Political Thought Pictured here is the German philosopher Karl Marx (1818–1883), who focused attention on the relationship between the economic means of production and political power.

underconsumption. They respond by seeking foreign markets and investments for their surplus goods and capital, and by dividing the world into spheres of influence that they can exploit. While his assertions have been heavily criticized on conceptual and empirical grounds (see Dougherty and Pfaltzgraff, 2001: 437–442), the attention given to social classes and uneven development engendered several new waves of theorizing about capitalism as a global phenomenon.

One prominent example is dependency theory. As expressed in the writings of André Gunder Frank (1969), Amir Samin (1976), and others (see Dos Santos, 1970; Cardoso and Faletto, 1979), dependency theorists claimed that much of the poverty in Asia, Africa, and Latin America stemmed from the exploitative structure of the capitalist world economy. As they saw it, the economies of less-developed countries had become dependent on exporting inexpensive raw materials and agricultural commodities to advanced industrial states, while simultaneously importing expensive manufactured goods from them. Raúl Prebisch, an Argentinian economist who directed the United Nations Economic Commission for Latin America, feared that these producers of primary products would find it difficult to develop, because the price of their products would fall over time relative to the price of manufactured goods. Dependency theory was criticized for recommending withdrawal from the world economy (T. Shannon,

1989; Packenham, 1992), and was eventually superseded by efforts to trace the economic ascent and decline of individual countries as part of long-run, system-wide change.

World-system theory, which was influenced by both Marxist and dependency theorists, represents the most recent effort to interpret world politics in terms of an integrated capitalist division of labor (see Wallerstein, 2005; Chase-Dunn, 1989). The capitalist world economy, which emerged in sixteenth-century Europe and ultimately expanded to encompass the entire globe, is viewed as containing three structural positions: a *core* (strong, well-integrated states whose economic activities are diversified and capital-intensive), a *periphery* (areas lacking strong state machinery and engaged in producing relatively few unfinished goods by unskilled, low-wage labor), and a *semi-periphery* (states embodying elements of both core and peripheral production). Within the core, a state may gain economic primacy by achieving productive, commercial, and financial superiority over its rivals. Primacy is difficult to sustain, however. The diffusion of technological innovations and the flow of capital to competitors, plus the massive costs of maintaining global order, all erode the dominant state's economic advantage. Thus in addition to underscoring the exploitation of the periphery by the core, world-system theory calls attention to the cyclical rise and fall of hegemonic core powers.

Whereas the various radical challenges to mainstream theorizing enhance our understanding of world politics by highlighting the roles played by corporations, transnational movements, and other nonstate actors, they overemphasize economic interpretations of international events and consequently omit other potentially important explanatory factors. According to feminist theorists, one such factor is gender.

The Feminist Critique

During the last quarter of the twentieth century, feminism began challenging conventional international relations theory. In particular, feminist theory attacked the exclusion of women in discussions about international affairs as well as the injustice and unequal treatment of women this prejudice caused. The mainstream literature on world politics dismissed the plight and contributions of women, treating differences in men's and women's status, beliefs, and behaviors as unimportant. As feminist theory evolved over time, it moved away from focusing on a history of discrimination and began to explore how gender identity shapes foreign policy decision making and how gendered hierarchies reinforced practices that perpetuated inequalities between men and women (see Peterson and Runyan, 2009; Tickner, 2005; and Enloe, 2004).

Rather than conceiving of gender as the biological differences between men and women, feminists see gender as socially defined expectations regarding what it means to be masculine or feminine. Even though not all men and women fit these expectations, feminists assert that higher value is attributed in the political sphere to idealized masculine characteristics like domination, autonomy, and competition, which are then erroneously depicted as reflecting objective laws

Women Leaders and World Politics Although world politics has been male dominated, some women have held important leadership positions. Their paths to power have varied. For example, Argentine President Christina Fernández de Kirchner (left) put gender at the forefront of her 2007 campaign, while German Chancellor Angela Merkel (right) chose to minimize the issue in her campaign.

rooted in human nature (Tickner, 1988). By treating this idealization as if it were grounded in universal laws of behavior, feminists insist that conventional international relations theories provide only a partial understanding of world politics.

Although all feminists stress the importance of gender in studying international relations, there are several contending schools of thought within feminist scholarship. Some feminists assert that on average there are no significant differences in the capabilities of men and women; others claim differences exist, with each gender being more capable than the other in certain endeavors; still others insist that the meaning ascribed to a person's gender is an arbitrary cultural construct that varies from one time or place to another (Goldstein, 2002). Regardless of the position taken on the issue of gender differences, feminist scholars emphasize the relevance of women's experiences in international affairs and the contributions they have made. More than simply acknowledging the impact of female leaders such as Margaret Thatcher of Great Britain, Megawati Sukarnoputri of Indonesia, Golda Meir of Israel, Corazón Aquino of the Philippines, Ellen Johnson-Sirleaf of Liberia, Angela Merkel of Germany, Christina Fernández de Kirchner of Argentina, Michelle Bachelet of Chile, or Laura Chinchilla of Costa Rica, they urge us to examine events from the personal perspectives of the countless women who have been involved in international affairs as caregivers, grassroots activists, and participants in the informal labor force. "Women have never been *absent* in world politics," writes Franke Wilmer (2000: 390). They have, for the most part, remained "*invisible* within the discourse conducted by men" about world politics.

One result of the feminist critique of conventional international relations theorizing has been a surge in research that uses gender as an explanatory variable when analyzing world politics. For example, recent studies have found that high levels of gender equality within countries are associated with low levels of interstate and intrastate armed conflict (Caprioli, 2005; Melander, 2005; Regan and Pasevicute, 2003; Caprioli and Boyer, 2001). Pointing to the results from these and other studies, feminists recommend that everyone who studies international politics "ask gender questions and be more aware of the gendered implications of global politics" (Tickner and Sjoberg, 2007: 199).

FORECASTING THE GLOBAL FUTURE WITH THEORIES OF WORLD POLITICS

As we seek to understand the global future, we must recognize the limitations of our knowledge of world politics. The world is complex, and our understanding of its workings remains incomplete. Nor is there a scholarly consensus on what research methods we should use to fill the gaps in our knowledge (see CONTROVERSY: Can Behavioral Science Advance the Study of World Politics?). As suggested in the previous chapter, comprehending world politics is like trying to make sense of a disassembled jigsaw puzzle. Each piece shows a part of the whole picture, but it's unclear how they fit together. Some pieces depict a struggle for power among self-interested states; others reveal countries pooling their sovereignty to create a supranational union. Some pieces portray wrenching ethnonationalist conflicts; others reveal an absence of war between democracies. Some pieces show an upsurge in parochialism; others describe an emerging global civil society (see Puchala, 1994). Disintegrative trends are splintering the political landscape at the very time that integrative trends are shrinking the planet. Whereas some countries seem mired in a dog-eat-dog world of international anarchy and self-help, others appear to live in a world of international institutions and interdependence.

Theories are like maps. They guide us in fitting the seemingly incompatible pieces of complex puzzles together to reveal the complete picture. But just as some maps are more accurate than others, some theories are more useful than others. "There is nothing so practical as a good theory," psychologist Kurt Lewin once remarked (cited in Myers, 1990: 17). But what makes a "good" theory? The following are some of the criteria that social scientists use when judging the quality of a theory (see Van Evera, 1997):

- *Clarity*. A good theory is clearly framed: Its concepts are precisely defined, cause-and-effect relationships governing observed patterns are adequately specified, and the argument underpinning those hypothesized relationships is logically coherent.

- *Parsimony*. A good theory simplifies reality: It focuses on an important phenomenon and contains all of the factors relevant for explaining it without becoming excessively complex.

- *Explanatory power*. A good theory has empirical support: It deepens our understanding of a phenomenon, and explains things about it that are not accounted for by rival theories.

CONTROVERSY   Can Behavioral Science Advance the Study of World Politics?

How should scholars analyze world politics? Unfortunately, there is no simple answer to this question. The field of international relations is torn between differing conceptions of what the study of world politics should encompass and how its subject matter should be investigated. Traditionally, scholars tried to understand some unique political event or sequence of events by submerging themselves in archival records, legal documents, or field work related to the phenomenon under investigation. Relying on experience and wisdom to evaluate this material, they typically presented their insights in a narrative that asserted: "Based on *my judgment* of the information that I have examined, I conclude X, Y, and Z."

Dissatisfied with the reliability of a research methodology that depended so heavily on the personal judgment and intuitive information-gathering procedures of a single individual, various scholars in the 1960s promoted a movement known as **behavioralism**, which had as its goals the application of the scientific method and rigorous quantitative techniques to the study of world politics (see J.D. Singer, 1968). Behavioralists assumed that a world exists independent of our minds; this world has an order that is open to human understanding; recurring patterns within it can be discovered; and reproducible evidence about these patterns can be acquired by carefully formulating and stringently testing **hypotheses** inferred from theories devised to explain how the world works. What made behavioralism innovative was its systematic, empirical approach to the process of inquiry, replacing ad hoc, idiosyncratic procedures for information gathering with explicit, replicable procedures for data making, and supplanting the appeal to the "expert" opinion of authorities with a deliberate, controlled method of data analysis. Behavioralism attempted to overcome the tendency of many traditional researchers to select historical facts and cases to fit their preexisting conceptions about international behavior. Instead, all available data were examined. By being as clear and precise as possible, behavioralists asserted that other researchers could determine how a given study was conducted, evaluate the significance of its findings, and gradually build a cumulative body of intersubjectively transmissible knowledge.

A variety of criticisms have been leveled against behavioralism over the past few decades. One of the most common draws from the work of the German sociologist Max Weber (1864–1920), who believed that the mode of explanation used in the social sciences was different from that in the physical sciences. Many people influenced by Weber contend that unlike physicists, who do not analyze sentient beings engaged in

purposeful behavior, social scientists face perplexing questions about why their subjects chose to act in a certain way and what meaning they ascribed to their actions. Not burdened with the need to consider how molecules may or may not choose to respond to external stimuli, physicists appeal to causal laws that hold true across time and space in order to explain such things as why gases become liquids at certain temperatures. But to explain things like why a national leader chooses to respond in a particular way to some external stimulus, social scientists must understand the reasons behind the actions that were taken. This difference between the physical and social sciences, so the argument goes, makes it difficult for the student of world politics to emulate the physicist when conducting empirical research. Instead of using quantitative techniques to search for law-like regularities that span the universe of international phenomena, this school of thought urges the social scientist to employ qualitative, interpretative methods to figure out the intentions of particular actors at specific moments in time.

Another prominent criticism of applying the scientific method to world politics comes from postmodernism, a label commonly given to a diverse group of thinkers influenced by French philosophers Jean-Francois Lyotard (1924–1998), Michel Foucault (1926–1984), and Jacques Derrida (1930–2004), among others. Premised on the belief that knowledge is only true relative to some situation or historical condition, postmodernists contend that it is impossible to analyze world politics from an objective, value-free point of view. Because no one can discover transcendent truths, scholars are exhorted to unmask the hidden meanings in prevailing texts and discourses, question the adequacy of the worldviews they espouse, and examine how these accounts of world politics are able to dominate and silence others.

Most scholars today remain motivated by the quest to build theories of world politics that can be used to describe, explain, and predict occurrences in world politics. What do you think about how they should go about this task? Is the scientific analysis of international behavior a reasonable undertaking? If so, can the research techniques of the physical sciences be applied to the study of world politics? Or do the social sciences require a different approach to inquiry that gives more weight to the intentions of human agents? Alternatively, are both causal and interpretative explanations of world politics impossible? Do you concur with postmodernists who argue that any attempt to apply the scientific method to international behavior is misguided because there is no singular, objective reality to study?

behavioralism an approach to the study of world politics that emphasizes the application of the scientific method.

hypotheses conjectural statements that describe the relationship between an independent variable (the presumed cause) and a dependent variable (the effect).

- *Prescriptive richness.* A good theory provides policy recommendations: It describes how problems can be avoided or mitigated through timely countermeasures.

- *Falsifiability.* A good theory can be proven wrong: It indicates what evidence would refute its claims.

Although realism, liberalism, and constructivism are the dominant ways of thinking about world politics today, none of these theories completely satisfies all of the criteria in the preceding list. Recall that realism is frequently criticized for relying on ambiguous concepts, liberalism is often derided for making naive policy recommendations based on idealistic assumptions, and constructivism is charged with an inability to explain change. Moreover, as the challenges mounted by radicalism and feminism suggest, these three mainstream theories overlook seemingly important aspects of world politics, which limits their explanatory power.

Despite these drawbacks, each theory has strengths in highlighting certain kinds of international events and foreign policy behaviors. As international relations scholar and former U.S. policymaker Joseph Nye (2005: 8) notes, "When I was working in Washington and helping formulate American foreign policies as an assistant secretary in the State Department and the Pentagon, I found myself borrowing from all three types of thinking: realism, liberalism, and constructivism. I found them all helpful, though in different ways and in different circumstances." Because we lack a single overarching theory able to account for all facets of world politics, we will draw on realist, liberal, and constructivist thought in subsequent chapters. Moreover, we will supplement them with insights from radicalism and feminism, where these theoretical traditions can best help to interpret the topic covered.

CHAPTER SUMMARY

- A theory is a set of interrelated propositions that explains why certain events occurred. Three overarching theories have dominated the study of world politics: realism, liberalism, and constructivism.

- Several strains of realist theory exist. At the risk of oversimplification, the realist worldview can be summarized as follows:

    1. People are by nature selfish, competitive, and domineering. Changing human nature is a utopian aspiration.

    2. The international system is anarchic. Without the support and protection of a higher authority, states strive for autarchy and engage in self-help.

    3. Under such conditions, international politics is a struggle for power, "a war of all against all," as the sixteenth-century English philosopher Thomas Hobbes put it. The primary obligation of every state in this

environment—the goal to which all other objectives should be subordinated—is to follow its "national interest" defined in terms of acquiring power.

4. Security is a function of power, and power is a function of military capability. States should procure the military capability to deter or subdue any potential rival. They should not entrust their security to the good will of allies or to the promises of international law and organizations.

5. International stability results from maintaining a balance of power among contending states.

- Various forms of liberal theory also exist. The liberal worldview can be summarized as follows:

1. People are capable of collaboration and mutual aid. Malicious behavior is the product of an environment that encourages people to act selfishly.

2. Reason enables people to change the conditions they live under, and therefore makes progress possible.

3. The first important change needed to reduce the probability of war is to promote national self-determination and democratic governance. The domestic characteristics of states vary, and these variations affect state behavior. Democracies are more peaceful than autocratic governments.

4. The second important change is to promote international commerce. Economic interdependence leads states to develop mechanisms to resolve conflict, which reinforces the material incentive to avoid wars that inhibit business opportunities.

5. The third change is to replace secret diplomacy and the shifting, rival military alliances characteristic of balance-of-power politics with international institutions based on collective security. Competitive, self-interested behavior need not be arbitrary and disorderly. By encouraging reciprocity, reducing uncertainty, and shaping expectations, international institutions help states coordinate their behavior and achieve collective gains.

6. World politics is increasingly shaped by transnational networks, in which states are enmeshed in complex webs that include multinational corporations, international organizations, and nongovernmental organizations.

- Constructivist theories of world politics are united by a common focus on the importance of ideas and discourse. Their worldview can be summarized as follows:

1. The fundamental structures of world politics are social; they acquire meaning through shared human understandings and expectations, and are sustained by recurrent social practices.

2. These collective, intersubjective structures define the identities of international actors.

3. Social identities constitute actors' interests and shape their actions by stipulating what behavior is appropriate in a given situation.

4. International actors acquire agency through language; rules and other forms of discourse make the world what it is.

5. Agents and structures are mutually constituted: Agents shape society, and society shapes agents through reciprocal interaction.

■ The explanation of world politics cannot be reduced to any one simple yet compelling account. While realism, liberalism, and constructivism each explain certain types of international phenomena well, none of them adequately captures all facets of world politics. As a result, rival interpretations of world politics have periodically challenged these mainstream theories. In recent years, theorists belonging to the radical and feminist schools of thought have voiced some of the most prominent criticisms of conventional international relations theory.

KEY TERMS

absolute gains

behavioralism

collective security

complex
   interdependence

consequentialism

high politics

hypotheses

international regime

low politics

moral hazard

norms

power

relative gains

self-help

theory

transnational relations

zero-sum game

SUGGESTED READINGS

Acharya, Amitav, and Barry Buzan, (eds.). *Non-Western International Relations Theory.* London: Routledge, 2009.

Baldwin, David A., (ed.). *Theories of International Relations.* Burlington, VT: Ashgate, 2008.

Dunne, Tim, Milja Kurki, and Steve Smith, (eds.). *International Relations Theories: Discipline and Diversity*, 2nd ed. Oxford: Oxford University Press, 2010.

Freyberg-Inan, Annette, Ewan Harrison, and Patrick James, eds. *Rethinking Realism in International Relations.* Baltimore: Johns Hopkins University Press, 2009.

Telo, Mario. *International Relations: A European Perspective.* Farnham, UK: Ashgate, 2009.

CRITICAL THINKING QUESTIONS

A vigorous debate between neorealists and neoliberals has dominated mainstream international relations scholarship for the past quarter century (Lamy, 2008). The issues dividing the two camps center on the different assumptions they make about the following topics (Baldwin, 1993: 4–8):

- *The nature and consequences of anarchy.* Whereas everyone recognizes that the international system is anarchical because effective institutions for global governance are lacking, neorealists argue that anarchy may be preferable to the restraints of world government. Neoliberals see anarchy as a big problem that can be reformed through the creation of strong global institutions.

- *International cooperation.* Although neorealists and neoliberals agree that cooperation is possible, neorealists think it is difficult to sustain, while neo–liberals believe it can be expected because collaboration yields rewards that reduce the temptation to compete.

- *Relative versus absolute gains.* Neorealists believe that the desire to get ahead of competitors by obtaining relative gains is the primary motive behind state behavior, whereas neoliberals believe that states are motivated by the search for opportunities that will produce absolute gains for all parties.

- *Priority of state goals.* Neorealists stress national security as the most important goal pursued by states. Neoliberals think states place a greater priority on economic welfare.

- *Intentions versus capabilities.* Neorealists maintain that the distribution of states' capabilities is the primary determinant of their behavior and international outcomes. Neoliberals maintain that states' intentions, information, and ideals are more influential than the distribution of capabilities.

- *Institutions and regimes.* Neorealists argue that institutions such as the United Nations are arenas where states carry out their competition for influence. Neoliberals believe that international institutions create norms that are binding on their members and that change patterns of international politics.

How significant are these differences between neorealists and neoliberals? Which assumptions do you think are the most accurate for interpreting twenty-first-century world politics? Are there any important issues that are left out of this debate?

The Actors in World Politics

In studying world politics we typically use the term *actor* to refer to the agents who participate in world politics. They include countries (for example, United States and Japan), international organizations (the United Nations and the Nordic Council), multinational corporations (Wal-Mart and Sony), nongovernmental organizations (Greenpeace and the World Wildlife Federation), indigenous nationalities (the Kurds in Iran, Iraq, and Turkey), and terrorist networks (Al Qaeda).

Part II identifies the major actors in world politics today and describes the roles they perform and the policies they pursue. We begin in Chapter 3 with an analysis of nation-states. In Chapter 4 special attention is given to states with the greatest military and economic capabilities—the great powers. Next, in Chapter 5, we examine the weaker, economically less-developed countries known collectively as the Global South, because the majority of them are located along the equator or in the earth's southern hemisphere. Finally, Chapter 6 deals with the growing role of nonstate actors, which include intergovernmental organizations such as the European Union as well as nongovernmental organizations ranging from multinational corporations to transnational religious movements.

3

Foreign Policy Decision Making

CHAPTER OUTLINE

> Policy faces inward as much as outward, seeking to reconcile conflicting goals, to adjust aspirations to available means, and to accommodate the different advocates of these competing goals and aspirations to one another. It is here that the essence of policy making seems to lie, in a process that is in its deepest sense political.
>
> ROGER HILSMAN
> FORMER U.S. ASSISTANT SECRETARY OF STATE

Following the attacks of September 11, 2001, on the World Trade Center and the Pentagon, U.S. President George W. Bush and his national security advisers began formulating a new strategy for striking terrorist organizations and the states that harbor them. "We face a threat with no precedent," the president insisted during a commencement speech at West Point in June 2002. Imploring Americans to be forward-looking and resolute, he declared that the country's military "must take the battle to the enemy, disrupt his plans, and confront the worst threats before they emerge." Bush promised that his administration would be patient, focused, and methodical in choosing where and when to apply this strategy. As he explained in an interview with journalist Bob Woodward (2002), teamwork within his cabinet was necessary for the decision-making process to operate effectively.

By the fall of 2002, however, the national security decision-making process looked more messy than methodical, as serious divisions emerged within the Bush administration over whether to wage war against Saddam Hussein's regime in Iraq. On one side stood Vice President Dick Cheney; Secretary of Defense Donald Rumsfeld, and his Deputy Paul Wolfowitz; Chair of the Pentagon Defense Policy Board, Richard Perle; as well as House Majority Whip Tom Delay, a conservative Republican congressman. Arguing that Saddam Hussein possessed weapons of mass destruction that could be used against the United States, they urged the president to invade Iraq, even if America had little international support for launching a preventive war.

Opposing an invasion were Secretary of State Colin Powell and an unlikely coalition of officials from the first Bush administration, including trusted national

Mai/Mai/Time Life Pictures/Getty Images

Collective Decision Making During crises that threaten a country's national security, decisions usually are made by the head of state and a small group of advisers rather than by large-scale bureaucracies. George W. Bush and advisers in the White House Situation Room during October 2002 make plans for war against Iraq.

security advisers Brent Scowcroft and James A. Baker III, as well as former secretary of state Larry Eagleburger. In one way or another, those questioning a military strike all reflected Powell's qualms about the costs of undertaking such a war with few allies and uncertain domestic support. Although they agreed that Saddam Hussein was a menace, they counseled against military action until it could be proved that the Iraqi dictator possessed weapons of mass destruction. A retired general and the only combat veteran among Bush's senior aides, Powell wrote in *My American Journey*, "Many of my generation, the career captains, majors, and lieutenant colonels seasoned in … [the Vietnam War], vowed that when our turn came to call the shots, we would not acquiesce in half-hearted warfare for half-baked reasons that the American people could not understand or support."

As rumors of war spread and the debate between these two groups intensified, the national security policy-making process fell into disarray. Treasury Secretary Paul O'Neill likened it to "June bugs hopping around on a lake" (quoted in Suskind, 2004: 306). While the president had promised to craft a clear, coherent strategy for dealing with Iraq, discord among the members of his foreign policy team suggested otherwise. The fissures within the administration widened as key advisers quarreled over whether they should obtain United Nations backing for an American attack. Whereas one side stressed the immediate threat posed by Saddam Hussein and advocated acting unilaterally if necessary, the other side emphasized the long-term risks of removing him by force without UN Security Council approval and multilateral assistance. Disagreement over this issue so strained relations between Vice President Cheney and Secretary of State Powell that it unraveled the many ties that had connected them for so many years (Woodward, 2004).

The battle among Bush's advisers soon dominated Washington's headlines, leading many people to ask whether the administration was following a deliberate, methodical policy-making process as the president had promised. Republican Senator Chuck Hagel, for instance, worried that the White House had not explored all of the possible ramifications that might result from a military intervention. "If we invade Iraq," he asked, "what allies would we have? Who governs after Saddam? What is the objective? Have we calculated the consequences, particularly the unintended consequences? What does [a war with Iraq] mean for the unfinished work with Afghanistan? For the Israeli-Palestinian conflict?" (cited in Broder, 2002: 15). Looking askance at the administration's behavior, Fareed Zakaria (2002), former editor of the influential journal *Foreign Affairs*, criticized the way in which a major decision about war was unfolding when he claimed that "parlor politics" had trumped power politics in the Bush administration. Cheney, Rumsfeld, and their allies, he suggested, were as interested in marginalizing Powell's influence as they were in ousting Iraq's dictator. Rather than through judicious steps, the Bush administration's foreign policy toward Iraq emerged from an intensely political process where, according to Richard Haass (2009), director of policy planning at the State Department, the president seemed more attracted to doing something bold than acting prudently.

The division among senior officials within the Bush administration led to infighting among their deputies and undersecretaries at lower levels of the bureaucracy. Deputy Secretary of State Richard Armitage, for example, clashed with Cheney's Chief of Staff, I. Lewis Libby; and Undersecretary of State for Political Affairs Marc Grossman struggled with Undersecretary of Defense for Policy Douglas J. Feith. Unable to manage the growing conflict, National Security Adviser Condoleeza Rice tended to paper over these disagreements and presented Bush with policy recommendations that she thought would fit with his preexisting beliefs (Mitchell and Massoud, 2009).

What explains the disarray in the Bush policy-making process? National leaders often describe their foreign policies as the result of neat, orderly, and rational procedures. By their account, they carefully define emerging problems; specify the goals they wish to achieve; identify all the alternative ways of attaining these goals; weigh the costs, benefits, and risks associated with each alternative; and then select the option with the best chance of attaining the desired goals. Yet, promises to the contrary, the Bush policy-making process hardly followed these procedures. Despite the president's desire to have his administration function as a unified body, the process of deciding how to deal with Iraq was contentious and turbulent. Was this turmoil unique to the Bush administration's handling of the Iraq situation? Or, was it typical of how foreign policy is made generally? To put it another way, is **rational choice** more an idealized standard than an accurate description of real-world behavior?

rational choice decision-making procedures guided by careful definition of problems, specification of goals, weighing the costs, risks, and benefits of all alternatives, and selection of the optimal alternative.

To answer these questions, this chapter will investigate how states make foreign policy. Drawing on the levels of analysis framework introduced in Chapter 1, we will examine how the properties of the international system, various national attributes, and the personal characteristics of political leaders combine to shape foreign policy. After considering factors at the systemic, state, and individual levels of analysis that influence foreign policy, we will conclude by exploring how they create impediments to rational decision making.

EXPLAINING FOREIGN POLICY

When we speak about foreign policy and the decision-making processes that produce it, we mean the goals that officials heading nation-states (or other non-state actors) seek abroad, the values that underlie those goals, and the means or instruments used to pursue them. Although nation-states are not the only actors on the world stage, due to their preeminence we begin our examination of foreign policy making by looking at the many factors affecting the opportunity, capacity, and willingness of state and nonstate actors to make foreign policy choices.

Due to the diversity of international actors, as well as their different positions within the contemporary global system, it is difficult to generalize about the influence of any one factor or combination of factors. To determine the relative impact of specific factors under different circumstances, we must first distinguish between different types of influences on policy choices. Figure 3.1 draws on the levels-of-analysis framework introduced in Chapter 1 to describe the multiple influences on states' foreign policy-making processes. Recall that the systemic

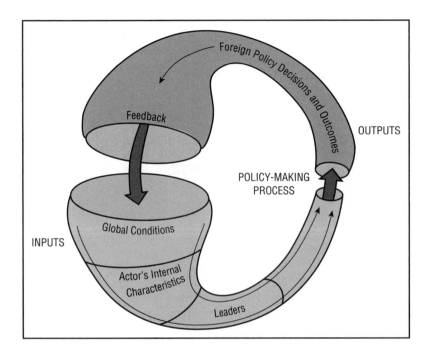

FIGURE 3.1 The Dynamics of Foreign Policy Making

The factors that influence foreign policy choices are depicted here as layers of a "causal funnel." Global conditions, characteristics of the state or nonstate actor in question, and the skills, personalities, and beliefs of the leaders who make key decisions can be thought of as *inputs* into a policy-making process that produces *outputs* in the form of actions. These actions yield results or *outcomes*, which eventually serve as *feedback* that has consequences for the input factors themselves at a later time.

or global influences on foreign policy include all activities occurring beyond a state's borders that structure the choices its officials make. Such factors as the number of great powers and the pattern of alliances sometimes profoundly affect the choices of decision makers. State-level influences focus on the internal characteristics of states, including variations in military capabilities, level of economic development, type of government, and organizational processes. Finally, individual-level influences give attention to the personal characteristics of the leaders who govern different states. Let us examine each of these three types of foreign policy determinants in turn.

INTERNATIONAL SOURCES OF FOREIGN POLICY

The international environment within which states and nonstate actors operate shapes *opportunities* for action. It sets a context that limits some foreign policy choices but facilitates others (Sprout and Sprout, 1965; Starr, 1978). Among the most significant facets of the international environment that make possible certain courses of action but not others are the distribution of power among states and the pattern of the alliances around the most powerful.

Polarity and Polarization

Power can be distributed in many ways. It can be concentrated in the hands of one preponderant state, as in the ancient Mediterranean world at the zenith of the Roman Empire, or it may be diffused among several rival states, as it was during the Italian Renaissance when Venice, Florence, Milan, Naples, and the papal states possessed approximately equal strength. Scholars use the term **polarity** to describe the distribution of power among members of the state system. *Unipolar* systems have one dominant power center, *bipolar* systems contain two centers of power, and *multipolar* systems possess more than two such centers.

Closely related to the distribution of power is the pattern of alignments among states. The term **polarization** refers to the degree to which states cluster around the powerful. For instance, a highly polarized system is one in which small- and medium-sized states align tightly with the dominant powers. The network of alliances around the United States and Soviet Union during the Cold War exemplified such a system.

Polarity and alliance polarization influence foreign policy by affecting the decision latitude possessed by states. Imagine, for instance, the opportunities for action in a unipolar versus a multipolar system. When power is concentrated in the hands of a single state, it has more latitude to use military force and intervene in the affairs of others than it would in a system characterized by a diffuse distribution of power, where rivals might obstruct its actions. Now imagine how decision latitude changes as a diffuse distribution of power becomes less polarized over time. When alliances are tight military blocs, the members of each alliance feel compelled to conform with the dictates of the alliance's leader. Conversely, when alliances are loosely structured and their membership is fluid, smaller states have greater latitude to craft foreign policies that are independent of the wishes of the powerful. Of course, we could think of other examples to show how the structural properties of the international system affect decision latitude. What they would show is that the foreign policy impact of polarity and polarization hinges on the geostrategic position of a given state.

> **polarity** the degree to which military and economic capabilities are concentrated among the major powers in the state system.
>
> **polarization** the degree to which states cluster in alliances around the most powerful members of the state system.

Geostrategic Position

Some of the most important influences on a state's foreign policy behavior are its location and physical terrain. The presence of natural frontiers, for example, may profoundly guide policy makers' choices. Consider the United States, which was secure throughout most of its early history because vast oceans separate it from potential threats in Europe and Asia. The advantage of having oceans as barriers to foreign intervention, combined with the absence of militarily powerful neighbors, permitted the United States to develop into an industrial giant and to practice an isolationist foreign policy for over 150 years. Consider also mountainous Switzerland, whose easily defended topography has made neutrality a viable foreign policy option.

Similarly, maintaining autonomy from continental politics has been an enduring theme in the foreign policy of Great Britain, an island country whose physical detachment from Europe long served as a buffer separating it from entanglement in major power disputes on the Continent. Preserving this protective shield has been a priority for Britain throughout its history, and helps to explain why London has been so hesitant to accept full integration into the European Union (EU).

Most countries are not insular, however. They have many states on their borders, denying them the option of noninvolvement in world affairs. Germany, which sits in the geographic center of Europe, historically has found its domestic political system and foreign policy preferences shaped by its geostrategic position. In the twentieth century, for example, Germany struggled through no less than six major radical changes in governing institutions, each of which pursued very different foreign policies: (1) the empire of Kaiser Wilhelm II; (2) the Weimar Republic; (3) Adolf Hitler's dictatorship; its two post–World War II successors, (4) the capitalist Federal Republic in West Germany, (5) the communist German Democratic Republic in East Germany; and, finally, (6) a reunited Germany after the end of the Cold War, now committed to liberal democracy and full integration in the European Union. Each of these governments was preoccupied with its relations with neighbors, but responded to the opportunities and challenges presented by Germany's position in the middle of the European continent with very different foreign policy goals. In no case, however, was isolationistic withdrawal from involvement in continental affairs a practical geostrategic option.

History is replete with other examples of geography's influence on states' foreign policy goals, which is why geopolitical theories have a venerable place in the field of international relations. **Geopolitics** stresses the influence of geographic factors on state power and international conduct. Illustrative of early geopolitical thinking is Alfred Thayer Mahan's (1890) *The Influence of Sea Power in History*, which maintained that control of the seas shaped national power. According to Mahan, states with extensive coastlines and ports enjoyed a competitive advantage. Later geopoliticians, such as Sir Halford Mackinder (1919) and Nicholas Spykman (1944), stressed that not only location but also topography, size (territory and population), climate, and distance between states are powerful determinants of the foreign policies of individual countries. The underlying principle behind the geopolitical perspective is self-evident: Leaders' perceptions of available foreign policy options are influenced by the geopolitical circumstances that define their states' places on the world stage.

System structure and geostrategic position are only two aspects of the global environment that may influence foreign policy. In other chapters we will discuss additional factors. But next, we comment briefly on the main internal attributes of states that influence their foreign policies.

geopolitics   a school of thought claiming that a state's foreign policies is determined by its location, natural resources, and physical environment.

DOMESTIC SOURCES OF FOREIGN POLICY

Whereas the structure of the international system and a state's geostrategic position within it influence the opportunities for state action, various domestic factors affect the *capacity* of states to act when opportunities arise. While scholars have investigated many national attributes that determine the amount of resources available to states and the ability to use them, we will concentrate on four prominent factors: military capability, level of economic development, type of government, and organizational structures and processes.

Military Capabilities

The proposition that states' internal capabilities shape their foreign policy priorities is supported by the fact that states' preparations for war strongly influence their later use of force (Levy, 2001). Thus, while most states may seek similar goals, their ability to realize them will vary according to their military capabilities.

Because military capabilities limit a state's range of prudent policy choices, they act as a mediating factor on leaders' national security decisions. For instance, in the 1980s, Libyan leader Muammar Qaddafi repeatedly provoked the United States through anti-American rhetoric and by supporting various terrorist activities. Qaddafi was able to act as he did largely because neither bureaucratic organizations nor a mobilized public existed in Libya to constrain his personal whims. However, Qaddafi was doubtlessly more highly constrained by the outside world than were the leaders in the more militarily capable countries toward whom his anger was directed. Limited military muscle compared with the United States precluded the kinds of belligerent behaviors that he threatened to practice.

Conversely, Saddam Hussein made strenuous efforts to build Iraq's military might (partly with the help of U.S. arms sales) and by 1990 had built the fourth-largest army in the world. Thus, invading Kuwait to seize its oil fields became a feasible foreign policy option. In the end, however, even Iraq's impressive military power proved ineffective against a vastly superior coalition of military forces, headed by the United States. The 1991 Persian Gulf War forced Saddam Hussein to capitulate and withdraw from the conquered territory. Twelve years thereafter, the United States invaded Iraq and finally ousted Saddam Hussein from office.

Economic Conditions

The level of economic and industrial development that a state enjoys also affects the foreign policy goals it can pursue. Generally, the more economically developed a state, the more likely it is to play an activist role in the global political economy. Rich states have interests that extend far beyond their borders and typically possess the means to pursue and protect them. Not coincidentally, states that enjoy industrial capabilities and extensive involvement in international trade also tend to be militarily powerful—in part because military might is a function of economic capabilities.

Although economically advanced states are more active globally, this does not mean that their privileged circumstances dictate adventuresome policies. Rich states frequently conclude that they have much to lose from revolutionary change and global instability. Seeing the status quo as serving their interests, they tend to forge international economic policies aimed at protecting their position at the pinnacle of the global hierarchy.

Levels of productivity and prosperity also affect the foreign policies of the poor states at the bottom of the hierarchy. Some economically weak states respond to their situation by complying with the wishes of the rich on whom they depend. Others rebel, sometimes succeeding (despite their disadvantaged bargaining position) in resisting the efforts by great powers and powerful international organizations to control their behaviors.

Thus, generalizations about the economic foundations of states' international political behavior often prove inaccurate. Although levels of economic development vary widely among states in the global system, they alone do not determine foreign policies. Instead, leaders' perceptions of the opportunities and constraints that their states' economic resources provide may more powerfully influence their foreign policy choices.

Type of Government

A third important attribute that affects states' international behaviors is their political system. Although realism predicts that all states will act similarly to protect their interests, a state's type of government demonstrably constrains important choices, including whether threats to use military force are carried out. Here the important distinction is between **constitutional democracy** (representative government) on one end of the spectrum and **autocratic rule** (authoritarian or totalitarian) on the other.

According to **rational political ambition theory**, the leaders of all types of governments seek to stay in power (Ray, 2008: 51). In neither democratic (sometimes called "open") nor autocratic ("closed") political systems can they survive long without the support of organized domestic political interests. But in democratic systems those interests are likely to spread beyond the government itself. Public opinion, interest groups, and the mass media are a more visible part of the policy-making process in democratic systems. Similarly, the electoral process in democratic societies more meaningfully frames choices and produces results about who will lead than the process used in authoritarian regimes, where the real choices are made by a few elites behind closed doors. With a multitude of competing individuals and organizations involved in the political processes of democratic countries, like-minded people form coalitions to get their proposals adopted. Logrolling, promising to support someone on an issue he or she favors in exchange for his or her backing on an issue important to you, is often used to enhance the political leverage of these coalitions. In this environment of wheeling and dealing, the ultimate test of a foreign policy proposal is not whether it is the most rational means for achieving some end, "but rather whether enough people and organizations having a stake in the policy and holding power agree to the policy" (Hilsman, 1993: 72).

The proposition that domestic political considerations, and not simply international stimuli, are a source of foreign policy is not novel. Many scholars have observed that national leaders sometimes make foreign policy decisions for domestic purposes—as, for example, when bold or aggressive acts abroad are intended to influence election outcomes at home or to divert public attention from economic woes. This is sometimes called the "scapegoat" phenomenon or the **diversionary theory of war** (Levy, 1989).

Some see the intrusion of domestic politics into foreign policy making as a disadvantage of democratic political systems that undermines their ability to deal

constitutional democracy a governmental system in which political leaders' power is limited by a body of fundamental principles, and leaders are held accountable to citizens through regular, fair, and competitive elections.

autocratic rule a governmental system where unlimited power is concentrated in the hands of a single person.

rational political ambition theory an approach to the study of foreign policy that assumes that state leaders want to maintain power and make decisions with that goal in mind.

diversionary theory of war the contention that leaders initiate conflict abroad as a way of steering public opinion at home away from controversial domestic issues.

decisively with crises or to bargain effectively with less democratic adversaries and allies. Democracies are subject to inertia. They move slowly on issues, because so many disparate elements are involved in decision making and because officials in democracies are accountable to public opinion and must respond to pressure from a variety of domestic interest groups. A crisis sufficient to arouse the attention and activity of a large proportion of the population may need to erupt in order for large changes in policy to come about. In contrast, authoritarian governments can make decisions more rapidly, and they have mechanisms to ensure domestic compliance with the policies they choose. But there is a cost: fear of retribution may lead advisers to avoid making policy proposals and to withhold criticism of ideas proposed by the leadership. Over time, these forms of self-censorship often make authoritarian governments less effective than democracies in developing foreign policy innovations.

The impact of government type on foreign policy choice has taken on great significance following the conversion of many dictatorships to democratic rule. These liberal government conversions have occurred in three successive "waves" since the 1800s (Huntington, 1991). The first wave occurred between 1878 and 1926; the second between 1943 and 1962; and the third began in the 1970s and continued through 1998. According to Freedom House, the percentage of countries designated as free has not changed significantly since the turn of the century, but many countries that had been making progress toward democracy have regressed. By their count, 46 percent of the world's population lived in free countries in 2010, 20 percent lived in partially free countries, and 34 percent lived in countries not judged to be free.

The growth of democracy during the last decades of the twentieth century emboldened many liberals to predict that the twenty-first century will be safer than its predecessor. Their reasons for predicting the onset of a **democratic peace** vary, but rely on the logic that Immanuel Kant outlined in his 1795 treatise *Perpetual Peace*. Kant believed that because democratic leaders are accountable to the public, and because ordinary citizens have to supply the soldiers and bear the human and financial cost of aggressive policies, they would constrain leaders from initiating foreign wars (especially against other liberal democracies similarly constrained by norms and institutions that respect peaceful methods of conflict resolution).

democratic peace the theory that although democratic states sometimes wage wars against other states, they do not fight each other.

A considerable body of empirical evidence supports the proposition that democracies do not wage war against each other (Rasler and Thompson, 2005; Russett and Oneal, 2001; Ray, 1995). The type of government and, more specifically, whether leaders are accountable to opposition groups through multiparty elections, strongly influence foreign policy goals. Although liberals generally emphasize the pacifying effects of democracy, research findings on the democratic peace have led some political conservatives to advocate a policy called "democratic realism" (Yang, 2005; Krauthammer, 2004), which would promote democracy through targeted interventions into regions where the advance of freedom is deemed critical in the struggle against Al Qaeda and other radical groups that pose existential threats to the United States. However, the difficulties faced by the Bush and Obama administrations in their attempts to create stable democracies in Afghanistan and Iraq have led many people to question the wisdom of such interventions.

Organizational Processes and Politics

In today's world, leaders turn to large-scale organizations for information and advice when they face critical foreign policy choices. Although this is more true of major powers than of small states, even those without large budgets and complex foreign policy bureaucracies seldom make decisions without the advice and assistance of many individuals and administrative agencies. Bureaucratic organizations perform vital services, enhancing the state's capacity to cope with changing global circumstances.

Bureaucracies increase efficiency by assigning responsibility for different tasks to different people. They define **standard operating procedures (SOPs)** that specify how tasks are to be performed; they rely on record systems to gather and store information; and they engage in forward planning to anticipate long-term needs and prepare the means to attain them. Because they assiduously follow set routines, improvisation is rare. Although major shifts in organizational behavior may occur following a policy fiasco, change tends to occur incrementally. The best predictor of a government agency's behavior is what it did in the recent past. Owing to inertia, what it does tomorrow will likely be only marginally different from what it is doing today (Allison and Zelikow, 1999).

Before jumping to the conclusion that bureaucracies are neutral instruments that merely implement what government leaders ordain, we should emphasize that decision making by and within large organizations sometimes compromises rather than facilitates rational choice. According to what is commonly called **bureaucratic politics** (Halperin, Clapp, and Kanter, 2006), government agencies tend to see each other as rivals. Every administrative unit within a state's foreign policy-making bureaucracy seeks to promote its own purposes and power. Organizational needs, such as larger staffs and budgets, sometimes become equated with the nation's needs, as bureaucrats come to see their own interests as the national interest. Bureaucracies fight for survival, even when their usefulness has vanished. Rather than thinning and cutting back, governments usually propose adding new layers of bureaucracy, a phenomenon known as the "thickening of government" (Shane, 2005). Far from being impartial managers, desiring only to carry out orders from the head of state, bureaucratic organizations frequently take policy positions designed to increase their own influence relative to that of other agencies. "Where you stand depends on where you sit" is an aphorism that reflects the nature of bureaucratic politics. Where someone stands on a policy issue may depend on which department he or she sits within.

Fighting among insiders within an administration and the formation of factions to carry on battles over the direction of foreign policy decisions are chronic in nearly every country (but especially in democracies accepting of participation by many people in the policy-making process). Consider the United States. Splits among key advisers over important foreign policy choices have been frequent.

standard operating procedures (SOPs) rules for reaching decisions about particular types of situations.

bureaucratic politics a description of decision making that sees foreign policy choices as based on bargaining and compromises among government agencies.

For example, under presidents Nixon and Ford, Secretary of State Henry Kissinger fought often with James Schlesinger and Donald Rumsfeld, who headed the Department of Defense, over strategy regarding the Vietnam War; Jimmy Carter's national security adviser, Zbigniew Brzezinski, repeatedly engaged in conflicts with Secretary of State Cyrus Vance over the Iran hostage crisis; and under Ronald Reagan, Caspar Weinberger at Defense and George Shultz at State were famous for butting heads on most policy issues. Such conflicts are not necessarily bad, because they force each side to better explain its viewpoint, and this allows heads of state the opportunity to weigh their competing advice before making decisions. However, battles among advisers can lead to paralysis and to rash decisions that produce poor results (see APPLICATION: Bureaucratic Games). As Morton Abramowitz (2002), a former assistant secretary of state in the Reagan administration, summarized the problem: Internal wars pervade the making of American foreign policy in every administration; however, when bureaucratic infighting becomes excessive, it can lead to policy inconsistencies and short-term concerns taking precedence over long-run goals.

The events of September 11, 2001, provide a telling example of what can go wrong when bureaucratic politics contaminate the policy-making process. The terrorist attacks on the World Trade Center and the Pentagon were regarded by many as the worst intelligence failure since Pearl Harbor. U.S. intelligence agencies, it was later discovered, received information beforehand that terrorists were likely to attack the United States with hijacked airliners as weapons. Why weren't the warnings acted on in time to prevent the disaster? Why weren't the dots connected? One answer accepted by many analysts was that America's system of intelligence was hampered by turf-protecting bureaucracies that did not share the vital information with each other. More than fifty units of government are involved with national security policy, and agencies like the CIA, the FBI, and the INS in the State Department are habitually loath to share information with each other for fear of compromising "sources and methods." As the bipartisan National Commission on Terrorist Attacks Upon the United States (2004: 353) concluded, these agencies "are like a set of specialists in a hospital, each ordering tests, looking for symptoms, and prescribing medications. What is missing is the attending physician who makes sure they work as a team." Moreover, as FBI Special Agent Coleen Rowley testified in June 2002, "There's a mutual-protection pact in bureaucracies. Mid-level managers avoid decisions out of fear a mistake will sidetrack their careers while a rigid hierarchy discourages agents from challenging superiors. There is a saying: 'Big cases, big problems; little cases, little problems; no cases, no problems.' The idea that inaction is the key to success manifests itself repeatedly" (Toner, 2002). These types of problems are difficult to control, and few students of organizational behavior believe that they can automatically be overcome through massive reorganization and restructuring. Bureaucratic routines "favor continuity over change," notes political scientist Jean Garrison (2006: 291), "because information is processed in certain ways and certain sources of information are privileged." Indeed, as Ronald Reagan once commented, "a government bureau is the nearest thing to eternal life we'll ever see on this earth."

APPLICATION Bureaucratic Games

When attempting to explain a foreign policy undertaking, most people assume that the agent was a national government engaged in purposeful, goal-directed behavior. It is in this sense that journalists report "Argentina decided to do X" or that scholars write "Chile responded to Argentina by doing Y." National governments are treated as if they were individuals with a single set of preferences who respond to strategic problems through deliberate choice.

In this chapter we have introduced another way of thinking about happenings in world politics. Rather than emanating from the carefully calibrated calculations of a single-minded entity, foreign policy may be the result of bargaining and infighting among a wide variety of organizations, each with competing preferences and unequal influence. An example of a statesman who understood how bureaucratic politics could affect his country's policies was Richard Holbrooke, who currently serves as special envoy for the Obama administration to Afghanistan and Pakistan. In 1995, when working for the Clinton administration on European affairs, he was assigned the task of negotiating an end to a war in Bosnia that had been raging among Serbs, Croats, and Muslims for several years. Holbrooke was an experienced, pragmatic, and assertive negotiator, known by his peers as "the Muhammad Ali of diplomacy" because of his ability to wear down even the most difficult opponent (Traub, 2000). In the following excerpt, he describes how various bureaucratic agencies began lobbying for roles in the peace process once his small negotiation team had begun to make headway.

> When we returned [to Washington], we found that interest in our activities had increased substantially. Agencies and individuals that had paid us little attention now wanted to be part of the process. For example, the Agency for International Development (AID), asserting that it would have to carry out the reconstruction program, sought a major role in the negotiations. Some agencies or bureaus wanted to place representatives on the delegation; we fended them off on the grounds that our plane was too small.
>
> ... We were concerned that if the unprecedented degree of flexibility and autonomy we had been given by Washington were reduced, and we were subjected to the normal Washington decision-making process, the negotiations would become bogged down.
>
> ... Faced with similar challenges in earlier crises, some administrations had created secret bypass mechanisms that kept information and authority within a small group—but also deceived or cut out everyone else. Most famously, when [Henry] Kissinger was National Security Advisor, he had frequently ignored the entire State Department—once making a secret trip to Moscow without the knowledge of the American Ambassador, and regularly withholding almost all information about his secret discussions with China from the Secretary of State. We did not want to arouse the kind of distrust and intrigue that, as a result, had marred the Nixon-Kissinger period... .
>
> To avoid this classic bureaucratic dilemma, [Deputy Assistant Secretary of State] John Kornblum set up a small, informal team to support our efforts. As we envisioned it, the group would be, in effect, an extension of the negotiating team, but located in Washington... . [Its members] would have to agree not to process drafts through the regular interagency "clearance process" which... was too cumbersome and time-consuming for a fast-moving negotiation (Holbrooke, 1998: 170–171).

Holbrooke's approach to sidestepping potential bureaucratic roadblocks was, in his words, "highly unusual." Rarely do foreign service officers have such free rein. But he maintained that it was crucial to minimize interference in his team's activities by holding off efforts by outsiders to get involved in the negotiation process.

INDIVIDUAL SOURCES OF FOREIGN POLICY

In addition to examining the opportunities for state action presented by the international environment and the capacity of states to act based on their national attributes, it is also necessary to consider the *willingness* of political leaders to act when they have the opportunity and capacity. Ultimately, leaders and the kind of leadership that they exert shape the way in which foreign policies are made and the consequent behavior of states in world politics. "There is properly no history, only biography" is the way Ralph Waldo Emerson expressed the view that individual leaders move history.

Leaders as the Makers of the Global Future

We expect leaders to lead, and we assume new leaders will make a difference. Journalists and scholars reinforce this image when they attach the names of leaders to policies, such as the "Brezhnev Doctrine" used to justify the 1968 Soviet military intervention into Czechoslovakia. Moreover, leaders themselves seek to create impressions of their own self-importance while attributing extraordinary powers to other leaders. The assumptions they make about the personalities of their counterparts, consciously or unconsciously, in turn influence their own behavior, as political psychologists who study the impact of leaders' perceptions and personalities on their foreign policy preferences demonstrate (Hermann and Hagan, 2004).

Nevertheless, we must be wary of ascribing too much importance to individual leaders. Their influence is likely to be subtler, as U.S. President Bill Clinton suggested in 1998 when he observed, "Great presidents don't do great things. Great presidents get a lot of other people to do great things." Most leaders operate under a variety of pressures that limit what they can accomplish. The question at issue is not whether political elites lead or whether they can make a difference. They clearly do both. The relevant question is under what conditions leaders' personal characteristics are influential.

Factors That Affect the Capacity to Lead

The impact of leaders' personal characteristics on their state's foreign policy generally increases when their authority and legitimacy are widely accepted by citizens or, in authoritarian regimes, when leaders are protected from broad public criticism. Moreover, certain circumstances enhance individuals' potential influence. Among them are new situations that free leaders from conventional approaches to defining the situation; complex situations involving many different factors; and situations without social sanctions, which permit freedom of choice because norms defining the range of permissible options are unclear (Hermann, 1988).

A leader's **political efficacy**, or self-image, combined with the citizenry's relative desire for leadership, will also influence the degree to which personal values and psychological needs govern decision making. For example, when public opinion strongly favors a powerful leader, and when the head of state has an exceptional need for admiration, foreign policy will more likely reflect that leader's inner needs. Thus, Kaiser Wilhelm II's narcissistic personality

political efficacy the extent to which a policy maker believes in his or her ability to control events politically.

allegedly met the German people's desire for a symbolically powerful leader, and German public preferences in turn influenced the foreign policy that Germany pursued during Wilhelm's reign, ending in World War I (Baron and Pletsch, 1985).

Other factors undoubtedly influence how much leaders can shape their states' choices. For instance, when leaders believe that their own political survival is at stake, they tend to respond by making decisions in a two-stage process (Mintz, 2004). In the first phase, leaders reject policy options that appear too costly politically; in the second, they evaluate the remaining options analytically, gauging the costs and benefits of each in terms of its relation to their country's interests.

The amount of information available about a particular situation is also important. Without pertinent information, policy is likely to be based on leaders' personal likes or dislikes. Conversely, the more information leaders have about international affairs, the more likely they are to engage in rational decision making.

Similarly, the timing of a leader's assumption of power is significant. When an individual first assumes a leadership position, the formal requirements of that role are least likely to restrict what he or she can do. That is especially true throughout the "honeymoon" period routinely given to new heads of state, during which time they are relatively free of criticism and excessive pressure. Moreover, when a leader assumes office following a dramatic event (a landslide election, for example, or the assassination of a predecessor), he or she can institute policies almost with a free hand (Hermann, 1976).

A national crisis is a potent circumstance that increases a leader's control over foreign policy making. Decision making during crises is typically centralized and handled exclusively by the top leadership. Crucial information is often unavailable, and leaders see themselves as responsible for outcomes. Not surprisingly, great leaders (for example, Napoleon Bonaparte, Winston Churchill, and Franklin D. Roosevelt) customarily emerge during periods of extreme tumult. A crisis can liberate a leader from the constraints that normally would inhibit his or her capacity to control events or engineer foreign policy change.

History abounds with examples of the importance of political leaders who emerge in different times and places and under different circumstances to play critical roles in shaping world history. Mikhail Gorbachev dramatically illustrates an individual's capacity to change the course of history. As noted in Chapter 1, many scholars believe that the Cold War could not have been brought to an end had it not been for Gorbachev's vision, courage, and commitment to engineering revolutionary changes. Ironically, those reforms led to his loss of power when the Soviet Union imploded in 1991.

Having said that the influence of individual leaders can sometimes be significant, we must be cautious and remember that leaders are not all-powerful determinants of states' foreign policy behavior. Rather, their personal influence varies with the context, and often the context is more influential than the leader (see CONTROVERSY: Policy and Personality: Do Leaders Make a Difference?). Of course, this ultimately leaves us with the question of whether famous leaders

CONTROVERSY	Policy and Personality: Do Leaders Make a Difference?

Some theorists assume that any leader will respond to a choice in the same way, given the same costs and benefits. But does this assumption square with the facts? What do we know about the impact of people's perceptions and values on the way they view choices? Political psychology tells us that the same option is likely to have different values to different leaders. Does this mean that different leaders would respond differently to similar situations?

Consider the example of Richard Nixon. In 1971, Americans took to the streets outside the White House to protest Nixon's massive bombing of Vietnam. His reaction was to shield himself from the voice of the people, without success, as it happened. Nixon complained that "nobody can know what it means for a president to be sitting in that White House working late at night and to have hundreds of thousands of demonstrators charging through the streets. Not even earplugs could block the noise." Earlier, on a rainy afternoon in 1962, John F. Kennedy faced a similar citizen protest. Americans had gathered in front of the White House for a Ban the Bomb demonstration. His response was to send out urns of coffee and dough-nuts and invite the leaders of the protest to come inside to state their case, believing that a democracy should encourage dissent and debate.

Nixon saw protesters as a threat; Kennedy saw them as an opportunity. This comparison suggests that the type of leader can make a difference in determin-ing the kinds of choices likely to be made in response to similar situations. More important than each president's treatment of the protesters, however, was whether he actually changed his policy decisions based on the protests. Although Kennedy was hospitable to protesters, he did not ban nuclear weapons; in fact, military spending under Kennedy grew to consume half of the federal budget. Many would insist that Kennedy alone could not be expected to eliminate nuclear weapons—that this period of history was dominated by fear of the Soviet Union and intense concern for national security. The protesters in 1971, however, were more in keeping with the spirit of the times. Although they alone may not have persuaded Nixon to alter his policies in Vietnam, widespread pro-test and discontentment with the war, as well as America's inability to win, eventually prompted Nixon to order the gradual withdrawal of U.S. troops, ending American participation in the Vietnam War. These outcomes suggest that leaders are captive to the larger forces that drive international relations in their times.

What do you think? Did Kennedy and Nixon choose courses of action that reflected who they were as individuals? Or would any president in their respective eras have made similar choices?

would have an impact whenever and wherever they lived. That question may be unanswerable, but it reminds us at least that multiple factors affect states' foreign policy decisions.

CONSTRAINTS ON THE FOREIGN POLICY–MAKING PROCESS

We began this chapter by looking at the political competition within the Bush administration with regard to Iraq, and by asking whether the struggle among the participants reflected how foreign policy making generally transpires. People like to think that those who make decisions in the name of the state agree on what strategic goals to pursue, assess the alternative means of attaining them through deliberate, exacting procedures, and ultimately select the approach that is most effective and efficient. Yet, as we have seen, despite the image of **procedural rationality** that policy makers seek to project, the actual practice of foreign policy decision making contains many impediments to rational choice.

procedural rationality
a method of decision making based on having perfect information with which all possible courses of action are carefully evaluated.

Consider the formulation of American foreign policy toward Afghanistan during the first year of the Obama presidency. Although the process was touted by the White House as methodical, bitter personality conflicts and cutthroat bureaucratic infighting marred the policy's development and implementation (Alter, 2010). Friction existed among the three principal U.S. officials in Afghanistan: U.S. Ambassador Karl W. Eikenberry, Special Envoy Richard C. Holbrooke, and General Stanley A. McChrystal, Obama's top military commander in the country. It also arose between McChrystal and Vice President Joseph R. Biden, Jr., as well as between members of McChrystal's staff and National Security Adviser General James L. Jones. The political backbiting eventually grew to the point that General McChrystal was fired in June 2010 for derisive comments that he and his staff had made about nearly every senior civilian official on the president's national security team.

As Bush's Iraq policy and Obama's Afghanistan policy suggest, foreign policy is not made by **unitary actors**—monolithic decision-making units whose behavior reflects the value-maximizing calculations of a central decision maker who possesses a clear definition of the national interest, is supported by a cohesive team of advisors who share the leader's definition, and has access to accurate, comprehensive information from dutiful government agencies about threats and opportunities within the strategic environment. Instead, as Robert Putnam (1988) argues, national leaders actually play **two-level games**. Besides making moves on an international game board, they also maneuver on a domestic board to obtain support at home for their initiatives abroad. Because moves on one game board affect play on the other, neither level can be ignored. Indeed, astute players recognize that the right move on one level can affect the outcome on the other level. Foreign policies, in other words, have domestic consequences, and actions aimed at domestic constituencies frequently reverberate beyond national borders. As a result, it is often difficult to know where foreign policy ends and domestic policy begins.

Putnam's two-level game metaphor reminds us that foreign policy making occurs in an environment of multiple, competing international and domestic interests. On occasion, it also occurs in situations when national values are threatened, policy makers are caught by surprise, and a quick decision is needed. The stress produced by these factors impairs leaders' cognitive abilities and may cause them to rely on various psychological coping techniques. First, owing to the process of cognitive dissonance described in Chapter 1, policy makers may try to cope with stress by denying that a problem exists, blocking out negative information, and looking instead for data that justifies their optimistic viewpoint. A second common coping technique is procrastination. Here they recognize that a problem exists, but hope that it will go away by itself. Finally, a third technique for dealing with stress is **satisficing** (Simon, 1957). Because policy makers work in an environment of uncertainty, incomplete information, and short deadlines, their evaluation of alternative policy options is seldom exhaustive. Rather than finding the option with the best chance of success, they may end their evaluation as soon as an alternative appears that seems superior to those already considered. Moreover, according to **prospect theory**, the alternative that they perceive as superior will often be colored by a concern over relative losses. Experimental

unitary actor   an agent in world politics (usually a sovereign state) assumed to be internally united, so that changes in its internal circumstances do not influence its foreign policy as much as do the decisions that actor's leaders make to cope with changes in its global environment.

two-level games   a concept that refers to the interaction between international bargaining and domestic politics.

satisficing   the tendency for decision makers to choose the first available alternative that meets minimally acceptable standards.

prospect theory   a behavioral decision theory that contends decision makers assess policy options in comparison to a reference point and that they take greater risks to prevent losses than to achieve gains.

evidence suggests that policy makers tend to be risk averse in choices among gains but risk acceptant with respect to losses. Fearing potential losses more than they value potential gains, they frequently are willing to take risks in the hope of avoiding loss, even though their actions may yield a far greater loss (Levy, 2003a).

Compounding the cognitive constraints just mentioned are emotional constraints. For example, when frustrated with a seemingly intractable problem and a looming deadline, impatient policy makers may "shoot from the hip" rather than carefully review a range of options, trusting that sheer boldness will yield good results. Furthermore, once they have invested resources in a particular course of action that is failing, powerful emotions involving self-esteem and guilt may lead them to try to rescue their ill-advised policy by allocating more resources to the enterprise, thus falling into what economists call the **sunk costs** trap. Reflecting on how these psychological constraints can cause leaders to commit *errors of commission* (selecting a perilous course of action when better options were available) and *errors of omission* (overlooking something important), Brent Scowcroft, President George H. W. Bush's national security adviser, lamented: "We continuously step on our best aspirations. We're humans. Given a chance to screw up, we will" (quoted in George, 2006: 63).

Finally, in addition to cognitive and emotional constraints on rational decision making, affiliative constraints also breed potential problems. During a crisis, national leaders typically bypass the standard operating procedures of their foreign affairs bureaucracies and rely on a small, ad hoc group of advisers. There is some evidence that when these groups contain people with similar backgrounds who are insulated from outside opinions and surmise their leader's preferred course of action, they may exhibit excessive concurrence-seeking, or what Irving Janis (1982) calls **groupthink**. In the interest of group cohesion, they place extraordinarily high values on conformity and consensus. In addition to stifling dissent, group members adopt stereotypes of their opponents, ignore the full range of possible options, suppress personal reservations about the moral consequences of their recommendations, and fail to develop contingency plans to deal with potential setbacks.

Studies of policy making suggest that groupthink is but one type of interaction pattern that may occur within small, high-level groups and therefore should not be thought of as a general propensity of their dynamics (Stern and Sundelius, 1997; 't Hart, 1990). Another pattern associated with excessive conformity is the **newgroup syndrome**. Rather than being triggered by crisis-induced stress, concurrence-seeking can arise in newly formed policy groups that lack well-developed decision-making procedures. Anxious and insecure about their roles, members may engage in self-censorship, avoid critiquing one another's ideas, and conform with the positions staked out by the most assertive individuals (Stern, 1997), which leads to premature closure of the decision process.

The quality of decisions made by small advisory groups is also affected by the leadership style of those in charge (Preston, 2001; Garrison, 1999). Personality, level of expertise in foreign affairs, and prior management experience all have a bearing on leadership style, which varies according to the degree of control these

sunk costs   a concept that refers to costs that have already been incurred and cannot be recovered.

groupthink   the propensity for members of small, cohesive groups to accept the group's prevailing attitudes in the interest of group harmony, rather than speak out for what they believe.

newgroup syndrome   the propensity of members of newly formed groups to conform with the opinions expressed by powerful, assertive peers or the group's leader due to a lack of well-developed procedural norms.

individuals desire over the policy process, the extent to which they seek to manage the flow of information, their preferences regarding how interpersonal relations are conducted, their tolerance for conflict among advisers, and their openness to divergent viewpoints (Preston, 1997: 201; Preston and Hermann, 2004). The kinds of advisers that a leader chooses and how they are organized are influenced by these variables. For example, leaders with a need for control and a desire to manage information gravitate toward formal, hierarchical advisory structures with clear chains of command. On the other hand, leaders comfortable with face-to-face interaction, vigorous argumentation, and political infighting generally favor structures based on competition and multiple channels of information. Each advisory system has its advantages and drawbacks. What matters most for the quality of decisions is having a system that fits the personal characteristics of the leader.

To sum up, although policy makers can sometimes absorb new information quickly under great pressure and launch creative policy initiatives based on careful planning, the cognitive, emotional, and affiliative impediments to procedural rationality in foreign policy making are substantial (see Tetlock, 2006; Janis, 1989). An effective decision-making process, insists former U.S. Secretary of State Henry Kissinger (1999: 1067), must address the following questions: "What are we trying to achieve, or what are we trying to prevent? What consequences do we expect from this decision, and what steps do we have in mind for dealing with them? What is the cost of the proposed action? Are we willing to pay that price, and for what length of time?" Answering these questions is never easy, notes another former government official: "The facts may be in doubt or dispute. Several policies, all good, may conflict. Several means, all bad, may be all that are open … [and] there may be many interpretations of what is right, what is possible, and what is in the national interest" (Sorensen, 1963: 19–20).

Table 3.1 compares how the decision process *should* work with how it usually works. Most theorists consider a foreign policy choice to be rational if it is consistent with the decision maker's preferences, and is based on a thorough assessment of the costs, risks, and benefits associated with alternative ways of attaining what he or she prefers. Ideally, the process would be governed by the following sequential steps:

1. *Problem recognition and definition.* Policy makers identify the essential elements of an emerging problem as well as the severity and imminence of the risks they face. They have full information about the situation due to an exhaustive search for all the relevant facts.

2. *Goal selection and prioritization.* Next, those responsible for making foreign policy choices must determine what they want to accomplish. This requires clarifying the values that underpin one's interests, establishing feasible objectives that capture these interests, and ranking them from most to least preferred.

3. *Development and assessment of alternatives.* Once policy objectives have been specified and ranked, a broad range of options is created, each representing a

T A B L E   3.1   Foreign Policy Decision Making in Theory and Practice

Ideal Process	Actual Practice
Accurate, comprehensive information	Distorted, incomplete information
Clear definition of national interests and goals	Personal motivations and organizational interests bias national goals
Exhaustive analysis of all options	Limited number of options considered; none thoroughly analyzed
Selection of optimal course of action for producing desired results	Course of action selected by political bargaining and compromise
Effective statement of decision and its rationale to mobilize domestic support	Confusing and contradictory statements of decision, often framed for media consumption
Careful monitoring of the decision's implementation by foreign affairs bureaucracies	Neglect of the tedious task of managing the decision's implementation by foreign affairs bureaucracies
Instantaneous evaluation of consequences followed by correction of errors	Superficial policy evaluation, imperfect detection of errors, and delayed correction

different course of action for attaining desired objectives. In addition, the costs, benefits, uncertainties, and tradeoffs of each option are estimated.

4. *Choice and evaluation.* Finally, following a rigorous means-ends, cost-benefit analysis, the option with the best prospects for success is selected. Implementation is monitored to determine whether adjustments are needed in the course of action that has been chosen.

Although policy makers often describe their deliberations in these terms, research suggests otherwise. Many policy makers just muddle through; rather than formulating policies with bold, innovative strokes, they make policy changes through trial-and-error adjustments (Lindblom, 1979). As one former U.S. official put it, rather than through "grand decisions on grand alternatives," policy changes seem to come through a series of "slight modifications of existing policy," with new policy emerging "slowly and haltingly, by small and usually tentative steps. It is a process of trial and error in which policy zigs and zags, reverses itself, and then moves forward" (Hilsman, 1993: 68).

The trends currently unfolding in world politics are the products of countless decisions made daily throughout the world. Some decisions are more consequential than others, and some actors are more important than others. Throughout history, great powers such as the United States have at times stood at the center of the world political stage, possessing the combination of natural resources, military might, and the means to project power worldwide that earned them their lofty status. How great powers have responded to one another has had profound consequences throughout international history. To better understand this, we turn our attention next to the dynamics of great-power rivalry.

CHAPTER SUMMARY

- Actors on the world stage are many and varied. States demand special attention because they are the principal repositories of economic and military capabilities in world affairs, and they alone possess the legal right to use force.

- The foreign policies of states consist of purposeful acts aimed at achieving international goals. Foreign policy making is a complex process that occurs in an environment of multiple, competing international and domestic interests.

- Foreign policy behavior is shaped by a combination of factors operating at different levels of analysis. At the systemic level, polarity, alliance polarization, and geostrategic position influence the opportunity for states to act in certain ways. At the state level, military might, economic strength, the type of government, and its organizational processes influence the capacity to act on available opportunities. At the individual level, a leader's personality and the situation surrounding his or her ascension to power influence the willingness or motivation to act.

- Scholars describe rationality as a sequence of decision-making activities involving the following intellectual steps: (1) problem recognition and definition; (2) goal specification; (3) identification and evaluation of alternatives for attaining the desired goals; and (4) selection of the option that maximizes benefits and minimizes costs and risks.

- Although national leaders often claim that they follow procedural rationality when formulating their foreign policies, rational choice is more of an idealized standard than an accurate description of real-world behavior. Many cognitive and organizational factors interfere with effective problem solving. Rather than choosing the course of action with the best chance of success, decision makers may end their analysis of policy options as soon as an alternative appears that seems better than those already considered.

KEY TERMS

autocratic rule

bureaucratic politics

constitutional democracy

democratic peace

diversionary theory of war

geopolitics

groupthink

newgroup syndrome

polarity

polarization

political efficacy

procedural rationality

prospect theory

rational choice

rational political ambition theory

satisficing

standard operating procedures (SOPs)

sunk costs

two-level games

unitary actor

SUGGESTED READINGS

Breuning, Marijke. *Foreign Policy Analysis*. New York: Palgrave Macmillan, 2007.

Deibel, Terry L. *Foreign Affairs Strategy*. New York: Cambridge University Press, 2007.

Mintz, Alex, and Karl DeRouen, Jr. *Understanding Foreign Policy Decision Making*. New York: Cambridge University Press, 2010.

Neack, Laura. *The New Foreign Policy: Power Seeking in a Globalized Era*, 2nd ed. Lanham, MD: Rowman & Littlefield, 2008.

Smith, Steve, Amelia Hadfield, and Tim Dunne. *Foreign Policy: Theories, Actors, Cases*. Oxford: Oxford University Press, 2008.

CRITICAL THINKING QUESTIONS

Although research suggests that democracies lose fewer wars than nondemocracies (Reiter and Stam, 2002), some analysts worry that they are slow to recognize emerging threats and mobilize the resources needed to counter them. The American diplomat George Kennan (1951: 59), likened democracy to "one of those prehistoric monsters with a body as long as this room and a brain the size of a pin." Because he pays little attention to his environment, said Kennan, "you practically have to whack off his tail to make him aware that his interests are being disturbed." Once aroused, however, he marshals the wherewithal to defeat his adversary.

A question that has intrigued some scholars is whether Kennan's observation is restricted to the American presidential system, or whether it also pertains to parliamentary systems, which place responsibility in a cabinet led by a prime minister, who obtains his or her position by being the leader of the party with the most seats in the legislature, not through a direct popular vote. A corollary question is whether the type of cabinet matters, because some have members from the same political party but others are coalitions composed of members from two or more parties (see Kesgin and Kaarbo, 2010; Kaarbo, 2008).

Do these institutional differences affect how different kinds of democracies formulate and conduct foreign policy? Are certain forms of democracy better at recognizing and responding to emerging foreign policy problems? Are presidential democracies, with their single dominant leaders who are directly elected by the public, able to respond more quickly and flexibly than parliamentary democracies? Among parliamentary systems, can we expect variation in the performance of single-party versus multiparty coalition cabinets that are attributable to differences in their structures?

4

Great-Power Politics in Historical Perspective

CHAPTER OUTLINE

Great powers fear each other. They regard each other with suspicion, and they worry that war may be in the offing. They anticipate danger. There is little room for trust…. From the perspective of any one great power, all other great powers are potential enemies…. The basis of this fear is that in a world where great powers have the capability to attack each other and might have the motive to do so, any state bent on survival must be at least suspicious of other states and reluctant to trust them.

JOHN MEARSHEIMER
REALIST POLITICAL THEORIST

On November 9, 1799, a young, ambitious general named Napoleon Bonaparte rose to power in France after leading a military coup against the ruling government. A man with remarkable persuasive and intellectual abilities, he described his mind as an ordered chest of drawers: Each drawer contained a vast amount of information on a particular topic, and he could open any of them whenever necessary to inspect their contents without missing a single detail. Napoleon was brilliant, but he was also coarse, temperamental, and unscrupulous. Claiming to be following a star of destiny, he gradually turned the French Republic into a personal dictatorship.

In foreign affairs, Napoleon's strategy was to win quick, decisive military victories in an incessant pursuit of territorial gain. He combined speed, artillery, and flanking maneuvers, deftly massing his forces against the weakest point in an opponent's lines. In 1805, he defeated the Austrians at Ulm and Austerlitz; in 1806, he routed the Prussians at Jena and Auerstädt; and in 1807, he overpowered the Russians in the Battle of Friedland. His triumphs gave him dominion over most of Europe and the opportunity to redraw its political boundaries. Beyond France (which included Belgium and lands on the left bank of the Rhine) were rings of dependent states and political allies. The former encompassed what today is the Netherlands, Spain, Switzerland, western and southern Germany, most of Italy, and part of Poland. The latter included Austria, Prussia, Denmark, Sweden, and Russia. His ultimate objective was to establish a new, vertical international order, one that would replace the horizontal Westphalian system of sovereign autonomous states with a hierarchy of subservient territories presided over by the French emperor.

Napoleon's quest for hegemony stalled after 1811. British naval power thwarted his forays beyond the Continent, an interminable guerrilla war in Spain drained precious resources, and an invasion of Russia ended in disaster, with roughly two-thirds of his forces succumbing in the cold darkness of the Russian winter. Heartened by Napoleon's setbacks, a coalition consisting of Great Britain, Russia, Prussia, and Austria moved against France. Napoleon's dream of "universal monarchy" was finally crushed at Waterloo in 1815. His defeat concluded a period that had battered Europe for almost a quarter century and left 2.5 million combatants dead. When measured by battle deaths per population, the toll exceeded all previous wars fought during the preceding three centuries. The carnage galvanized a consensus among the victors who met at the Congress of Vienna to forge a peace settlement that would restore the decentralized Westphalian system of sovereign equals, and prevent any single great power from again becoming strong enough to threaten the others.

The Napoleonic Wars and the Congress of Vienna highlight a common pattern in world politics. The ascendancy of one great power relative to its principal rivals eventually prompts opposition from the rest. If this hegemonic struggle escalates to global war, the victors will try to design a security regime aimed at preventing the recurrence of such a catastrophic conflict by staving off future challenges to the new international order they have constructed.

Classic Image/Alamy

Choosing Between Reconciliation and Retribution
A key part of the peace settlement crafted at the
Congress of Vienna (1814–1815) was its resuscitative
policy toward France. Although Napoleon was sent
into exile and France was divested of territories he
had conquered, the French were included in the
newly created Concert of Europe, a system of great-
power consultation and policy coordination. The
Vienna settlement suggests that the prospects for a
durable peace can be enhanced by giving defeated
states a stake in the post-war order.

This general pattern has colored twentieth-century world politics, with three
global conflicts breaking out. World Wars I and II were fought with fire and
blood; the Cold War was fought by less destructive means but with equal inten-
sity. Like the Napoleonic Wars, each of these conflicts triggered major transformations in world politics. In this chapter we explore their causes and
consequences in order to uncover the dynamics of great-power rivalries. By
understanding the origins and impact of these struggles over world leadership,
we will be in a better position to anticipate whether in the twenty-first century
the great powers will be able to avoid yet another global war.

LONG CYCLES OF WORLD LEADERSHIP

"All history shows," political scientist Hans J. Morgenthau (1985: 52) once
remarked, "that nations active in international politics are continuously preparing
for, actively involved in, or recovering from organized violence in the form of
war." Recently, many scholars have become intrigued with the possibility that

this process is cyclical and unfolds through a series of distinct phases. According to **long-cycle theory**, over the past five centuries periods of global war have been followed by periods of international rule-making and institution-building, with shifts in the cycle usually occurring in tandem with changes in the major states' relative power (Modelski and Thompson, 1999). Each global war led to the emergence of a **hegemon**, a preponderant state capable of dominating the conduct of international political and economic relations. With its unrivaled power, the hegemon reshapes the rules and institutions of the state system to preserve its preeminent position.

Hegemony imposes an extraordinary burden on the world leader, which must bear the costs of maintaining political and economic order while protecting its position and upholding its dominion. Over time, as the weight of global engagement takes its toll, the hegemon overextends itself, challengers arise, and the security regime so carefully crafted after the last global war comes under attack. Historically, this struggle for power has set the stage for another global war, the demise of one hegemon and the ascent of another. Table 4.1 summarizes 500 years of the cyclical rise and fall of great powers, their global wars, and their subsequent efforts to restore order.

Critics note that long-cycle theorists disagree on whether economic, military, or domestic factors produce these cycles. They also express frustration with the deterministic tone of the theory, which to them implies that global destiny is beyond policy makers' control. Still, long-cycle theory invites us to consider how shifts in the relative strength of great powers affect world politics. It rivets our attention on hegemonic transitions, the rise and fall of leading states in the international system. To underscore the importance of struggles over world leadership in understanding world politics, this chapter inspects the three global great-power conflicts of the twentieth century, as well as the lessons these clashes suggest for the twenty-first century.

long-cycle theory a theory that focuses on the rise and fall of the leading global power as the central political process of the modern world system.

hegemon a single, overwhelmingly powerful state that exercises predominate influence over the global system.

THE FIRST WORLD WAR

World War I profoundly altered the world's geopolitical map. By the time it ended, nearly 10 million people had died, three empires had crumbled, and a generation of Europeans had become disillusioned with foreign policies grounded in political realism. How can such a catastrophic war be explained? Many scholars believe that World War I was inadvertent, not the result of anyone's master plan. It was a war bred by uncertainty and circumstances beyond the control of those involved, one that people neither wanted nor expected. Other scholars regard the war as a product of calculated choices. It was "a tragic and unnecessary conflict ... because the train of events that led to its outbreak might have been broken at any point during the five weeks of crisis that preceded the first clash of arms, had prudence or common goodwill found a voice" (Keegan, 1999: 3). As we shall see, each of these interpretations captures a different dimension of the war's origins. Although none of Europe's great

TABLE 4.1   The Evolution of Great-Power Rivalry for World Leadership, 1495–2025

Dates	Preponderant State(s) Seeking Hegemony	Other Powers Resisting Domination	Global War	New Order after Global War
1495–1540	Portugal	Spain, Valois, France, Burgundy, England, Venice	Wars of Italy and the Indian Ocean, 1494–1517	Treaty of Tordesillas, 1517
1560–1609	Spain	The Netherlands, France, England	Spanish-Dutch Wars, 1580–1608	Truce of 1609; Evangelical Union and the Catholic League formed
1610–1648	Holy Roman Empire (Hapsburg dynasty in Spain and Austria-Hungary)	Shifting ad hoc coalitions of mostly Protestant states (Sweden, Holland) and German principalities as well as Catholic France against remnants of papal rule	Thirty Years' War 1618–1648	Peace of Westphalia, 1648
1650–1713	France (Louis XIV)	The United Provinces, England, the Hapsburg Empire, Spain, major German states, Russia	Wars of the Grand Alliance, 1688–1713	Treaty of Utrecht, 1713
1792–1815	France (Napoleon)	Great Britain, Prussia, Austria, Russia	Napoleonic Wars, 1792–1815	Congress of Vienna and Concert of Europe, 1815
1871–1914	Germany, Austria-Hungary, Turkey	Great Britain, France, Russia, United States	World War I, 1914–1918	Treaty of Versailles creating League of Nations, 1919
1933–1945	Germany, Japan, Italy	Great Britain, France, Soviet Union, United States	World War II, 1939–1945	Bretton Woods, 1944; United Nations, 1945; Potsdam, 1945
1945–1991	United States, Soviet Union	Great Britain, France, China, Japan	Cold War, 1945–1991	NATO/Partnerships for Peace, 1995; World Trade Organization, 1995
1991–?	United States	China, European Union, Japan, Russia, India, Brazil	A cold peace or hegemonic war, 2015–2025?	A new security regime to preserve world order?

powers deliberately sought a general war, prevailing conditions made such an outcome highly probable, though not inevitable.

To explain how this long, grueling war happened, let us return to the analytic framework introduced in Chapter 1. We can piece together an understanding of the war's origins by looking for causal mechanisms operating at different levels of analysis, and placing them in a time sequence. By examining World War I from multiple levels across time, we can inoculate ourselves against naive, single-factor explanations of this complex event.

The Causes of World War I

The proximate causes of World War I can be found at the individual level of analysis. A Serbian nationalist seeking to free Slavs in the Balkans from Austrian rule assassinated Archduke Franz Ferdinand, heir to the Hapsburg throne of the Austrian-Hungarian Empire, at Sarajevo on June 28, 1914. This incident sparked a series of moves and countermoves by political leaders in Austria, Germany, and Russia, who held virtuous images of themselves and diabolical images of their adversaries. Rather than take the time to carefully craft policies that did not risk war, they made reactive, fatalistic decisions that seized upon the first suitable option (Williamson, 1988). Their impulsive behavior over the next few weeks turned what had been a local dispute between Austria and Serbia into a horrific conflagration.

The archduke's assassination offered Austria an opportunity to weaken Serbia, which Vienna perceived as the source of separatist agitation that was undermining Hapsburg authority within the empire's large Slavic population. On July 25, Serbia rejected an Austrian ultimatum that demanded its officials be allowed to participate in Serbia's investigation of the assassination plot, as well as in the punishment of the perpetrators. Serbia's refusal prompted the Austrians to declare war and bombard Belgrade. Responding to Serbian pleas for help, Russia mobilized its forces along the Austrian and German frontiers. In turn, Germany declared war on Russia and its ally, France. When German troops swept into Belgium on August 4 in order to outflank France, Britain declared war on Germany. Eventually, thirty-two countries on six continents became enmeshed in the conflict.

As this rapid, almost mechanical sequence of moves suggests, a combination of deeper, more remote causes had created an explosive situation that the clumsy statesmen in Vienna, Berlin, and St. Petersburg ignited. At the state level of analysis, many historians view the growth of nationalism, especially in southeastern Europe, as having created a climate of opinion that made war likely. Groups that glorified the distinctiveness of their national heritage began championing their own country above all others. Long-suppressed ethnic prejudices soon emerged, even among political leaders. Russian foreign minister Sergei Sazonov, for example, claimed to "despise" Austria, and Kaiser Wilhelm II of Germany asserted: "I hate the Slavs" (Tuchman, 1962).

Domestic unrest inflamed these passions, making it hard to see things from another point of view. Believing that they were upholding their national honor, the Austrians could not comprehend why Russians labeled them the aggressors. German insensitivity to others' feelings prevented them from understanding Russia's feelings of pride and anger, and their fear of humiliation if they allowed Germany and Austria-Hungary to destroy their protégé, Serbia (R. White, 1990). With each side denigrating the character of the other, diplomatic alternatives to war evaporated.

At the systemic level of analysis, a web of rigid alliances and interlocking war plans quickly spread the fighting from one end of the Continent to the other. During the decade before Franz Ferdinand's assassination, European military alignments had become polarized, pitting the Triple Alliance of Germany, Austria-Hungary, and the Ottoman Empire against the Triple Entente of France, Britain, and Russia. Once Russia mobilized in response to Austria's attack on Serbia, alliance commitments pulled one European great power after another into the war.

Another factor underlying the outbreak of the First World War was the rise of German power and the challenge it posed to the British. Although Germany did not become a unified country until 1871, it prospered and used its growing wealth to create an awesome military machine. As the leader of the Continent's foremost industrial and military power, Kaiser Wilhelm II proclaimed in 1898 that Germany had "great tasks outside the narrow boundaries of old Europe." Under the concept of *weltpolitik* (world policy), Germany began building a strong navy to command respect around the globe. Britain, alarmed by the threat this might present to its maritime interests, established formal ties with France and Russia. Convinced that the British, French, and Russians were trying to encircle Germany, Wilhelm sought more armaments and closer relations with Austria-Hungary.

Germany was not the only rising great power at the turn of the century. Russia was also expanding, and becoming a threat to Germany. The decline in power of the Austrian-Hungarian Empire, Germany's only ally, heightened Berlin's anxieties. Hence, Germany reacted strongly to Archduke Ferdinand's assassination. Confident that a short, localized, and victorious Balkan war would shore up Austria-Hungary and weaken Russia's influence in Europe, Wilhelm gave the Austrians a "blank check" to crush Serbia.

Germany's unconditional support for Austria-Hungary proved to be a serious miscalculation, as it solidified the bonds between France and Russia, the two allied powers on Germany's western and eastern borders. Under the so-called Schlieffen Plan, Germany's generals had long based their military preparations on the premise that in the event of war with both France and Russia, German troops would first defeat the French and then turn against the larger but slower-moving Russian army. The quickest way to crush the French, they reasoned, was to swing through neutral Belgium in a vast arcing movement and attack France from the north, where its defenses were the weakest. But when the Germans stormed through Belgium, Britain entered the war on the side of France and Russia. Recognizing the magnitude of the unfolding catastrophe, British foreign secretary Sir Edward Grey lamented: "The lamps are going out all over Europe; we shall not see them lit again in our lifetime."

The Consequences of World War I

World War I transformed the face of Europe. In its wake, three empires—the Austrian-Hungarian, Russian, and Ottoman (Turkish)—collapsed, and in their place the independent states of Poland, Czechoslovakia, and Yugoslavia emerged. In addition, the countries of Finland, Estonia, Latvia, and Lithuania were born (see Map 4.1). The war also contributed to the overthrow of the

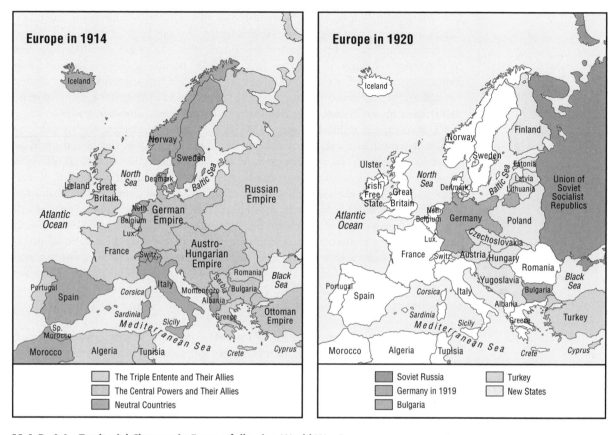

M A P 4.1 Territorial Changes in Europe following World War I

World War I redrew the boundaries of Europe. The map on the left shows state boundaries on the eve of the war in 1914, as well as the members of the two major opposing coalitions that formed. The map on the right shows the new borders in 1920, with the nine new states that emerged from the war.

SOURCE: From *Strategic Atlas, Comparative Geopolitics of the World's Powers*, revised edition, by Gerard Chaliand and Jean-Pierre Rageau. Copyright © 1990 by Gerard Chaliand and Jean-Pierre Rageau. Reprinted by permission of HarperCollins, Inc.

Russian czar in 1917 by the Bolsheviks, a change in government and ideology that would have consequences for another seventy years.

World War I evoked revulsion for war and theories of political realism that justified armaments, secret alliances, and power politics. The staggering human and material costs of the previous four years led many of the delegates to the 1919 peace conference convened at Versailles, outside Paris, to reevaluate their convictions about statecraft. The time was ripe for a new approach to building world order. Disillusioned with realism, many turned to liberalism for guidance on how to manage the global future.

The decade following World War I was the high point of liberal idealism. Woodrow Wilson's ideas about world order, as expressed in his January 1917

"Fourteen Points" speech, were anchored in a belief that by reordering the international system according to liberal principles, the Great War (as World War I was then called) would be "the war to end all wars." Wilson's chief proposal was to construct a League of Nations that allegedly would guarantee the independence and territorial integrity of all states. His other recommendations included strengthening international law, settling territorial claims on the basis of self-determination, and promoting democracy, disarmament, and free trade.

However, once the delegates to the peace conference began their work, the knives of parochial national interest began whittling away at the liberal philosophy underpinning Wilson's proposals. Many European leaders had been offended by the pontificating American president. "God was content with Ten Commandments," growled Georges Clemenceau, the cynical French prime minister. "Wilson must have fourteen." As negotiations at the conference proceeded, hard-boiled power politics prevailed. Ultimately, the delegates were only willing to support those elements in the Fourteen Points that served their national interests. After considerable wrangling, Wilson's League of Nations was written into the peace treaty with Germany as the first of 440 articles. The rest of the treaty was punitive, aimed at stripping the country of its great-power status. Similar treaties were later forced on Austria-Hungary and Germany's other wartime allies.

The Treaty of Versailles grew out of a desire for retribution. In brief, Germany's military was drastically cut; it was forbidden to possess heavy artillery, military aircraft, or submarines, and its forces were banned from the Rhineland. Germany also lost territory in the west to France and Belgium, in the south to the new state of Czechoslovakia, and in the east to the new states of Poland and Lithuania. Overseas, Germany lost all its colonies. Finally, in the most humiliating clause of the treaty, Germany was assigned responsibility for the war and charged with paying reparations for the damages. On learning of the treaty's harsh provisions, the exiled German Kaiser is said to have declared that "the war to end wars has resulted in a peace to end peace."

THE SECOND WORLD WAR

Germany's defeat in the First World War and its humiliation under the Treaty of Versailles did not extinguish its hegemonic aspirations. On the contrary, they intensified them. Thus, conditions were ripe for the second great-power war of the twentieth century, which pitted the Axis trio of Germany, Japan, and Italy against an unlikely "grand alliance" of four great powers who united despite their incompatible ideologies—communism in the case of the Soviet Union and democratic capitalism in the case of Britain, France, and the United States.

The world's fate hinged on the outcome of this massive effort to defeat the Axis. The Allied powers achieved success but at a terrible cost: 53 million people died during six years of fighting. To understand the origins of this devastating conflict, we will once again examine how causal factors operating at different levels of analysis fit into a time sequence.

The Causes of World War II

Following Germany's capitulation in 1918, a democratic constitution was drafted by a constituent assembly meeting in the city of Weimar. Many Germans had little enthusiasm for the Weimar Republic. Not only was the new government linked in their minds to the humiliating Versailles Treaty, but it also suffered from the 1923 French occupation of the industrial Ruhr district, various political rebellions, and the ruinous economic collapse of 1929. By the parliamentary elections of 1932, over half of the electorate supported extremist parties that disdained democratic governance. The largest of these was the Nazi, or National Socialist German Workers, party.

On January 30, 1933, the Nazi leader, Adolf Hitler, was appointed chancellor of Germany. Less than a month later, the Reichstag (Parliament) building burned down under mysterious circumstances. Hitler used the fire to justify an emergency edict allowing him to suspend civil liberties and move against communists and other political adversaries. Once all meaningful parliamentary opposition had been eliminated, Nazi legislators passed an enabling act that suspended the constitution and granted Hitler dictatorial power.

In his 1924 book *Mein Kampf* ("My Struggle"), Hitler urged Germany to recover territories taken by the Treaty of Versailles, absorb Germans living in neighboring lands, and colonize Eastern Europe. During his first year in power, however, he cultivated a pacific image, signing a nonaggression pact with Poland in 1934. The following year, the goals originally outlined in *Mein Kampf* climbed to the top of Hitler's foreign policy agenda: In 1935, he repudiated the military clauses of the Versailles Treaty; in 1936, he ordered troops into the demilitarized Rhineland; in March 1938, he annexed Austria; and in September 1938, he demanded control over the Sudetenland, a region of Czechoslovakia containing ethnic Germans (see Map 4.2). To address the Sudeten German question, a conference was convened in Munich, attended by Hitler, British Prime Minister Neville Chamberlain, and leaders of France and Italy (ironically, Czechoslovakia was not invited). Convinced that **appeasement** would halt further German expansionism, Chamberlain and the others agreed to Hitler's demands.

Instead of satisfying Germany, appeasement encouraged Hitler to press for further revisions in the international status quo. He was joined in this effort by Japan and Italy. The former invaded Manchuria in 1931 and China proper in 1937; the latter attacked Ethiopia in 1935 and Albania in 1939. Furthermore, both Germany and Italy intervened in the Spanish civil war on the side of the fascists, headed by General Francisco Franco.

These acts of aggression paved the way for the century's second massive war. After Germany occupied the rest of Czechoslovakia in March 1939, Britain and France formed an alliance to protect the next likely victim, Poland. They also opened negotiations with Moscow in hopes of enticing the Soviet Union to join the alliance. Then, on August 23, 1939, Hitler and the Soviet leader Joseph Stalin stunned the world by signing a nonaggression pact. Certain that the Western democracies would not intervene without Soviet assistance, Hitler invaded

appeasement a strategy of making concessions to another state in the hope that, satisfied, it will not make additional claims.

M A P 4.2   World War II Redraws the Map of Europe

The map on the left shows the height of German expansion in 1943, when it occupied Europe from the Atlantic Ocean and Baltic Sea to the gates of Moscow in the Soviet Union. The map on the right shows the new configuration of Europe after the "Grand Coalition" of Allied forces—Great Britain, the United States, and the Soviet Union—defeated the Axis' bid for supremacy.

SOURCE: Europe in 1945 from *Strategic Atlas, Comparative Geopolitics of the World's Powers,* revised edition, by Gerard Chaliand and Jean-Pierre Rageau. Copyright © 1990 by Gerard Chaliand and Jean-Pierre Rageau. Reprinted by permission of HarperCollins, Inc.

Poland on September 1, 1939. Britain and France, honoring their pledge to defend the Poles, declared war on Germany two days later.

The war expanded rapidly. Hitler next turned his forces loose on the Balkans, North Africa, and westward. Powerful mechanized German units invaded Norway and marched through Denmark, Belgium, Luxembourg, and the Netherlands. They swept around France's defensive barrier, the Maginot line, and forced the British to evacuate an expeditionary force from the French beaches at Dunkirk. Paris itself fell in June 1940, and in the months that followed, the German air force pounded Britain in an attempt to force it into submission. Instead of invading Britain, in June 1941, Nazi troops attacked the Soviet Union, Hitler's former ally.

Germany's military successes provided an opportunity for Japan to move against British, French, and Dutch colonies in Asia, with the aim of replacing Western influence with a Greater East Asian Co-Prosperity Sphere under Tokyo's leadership. Japan followed its earlier conquests of Manchuria and eastern China with pressure on the Vichy French government to allow Japanese military bases in Indochina (now Vietnam, Laos, and Cambodia), from which the vital petroleum and mineral resources of Southeast Asia could be threatened. Concerned that the United States would try to thwart its ambitions, Japan launched a surprise attack on the U.S. naval base at Pearl Harbor, Hawaii, on December 7, 1941. Almost immediately, Germany declared war on the United States. Over the next six months, Japan occupied the Philippines, Malaya, Burma, and the Dutch East Indies (now Indonesia). The military challenges posed by the Japanese and Germans ended U.S. **isolationism**, enabling President Franklin Roosevelt to forge a coalition with Britain and the Soviet Union to oppose the Axis powers.

The proximate cause of the war lies at the individual level of analysis. Adolf Hitler's truculent personality and aggressive schemes triggered the Second World War. Other more remote factors exerted significant impacts as well. At the state level of analysis, hypernationalism, domestic economic crises, and the demise of democratic governance in Germany provided an environment in which Hitler could rise to power. In addition, a belief in the dominance of defense over offense held by military establishments that had experienced the First World War made some states complacent in the face of German rearmament. Governments who remembered the rapid escalation of events during the summer of 1914 were also hesitant to respond to German actions in ways that might precipitate an upward spiral of conflict. Recalling the trauma produced by World War I, appeasement seemed preferable to confrontation.

Finally, at the systemic level of analysis, the vindictive peace settlement constructed at Versailles, the collapse of the global economic system, U.S. isolationism, and the failure of the League of Nations were crucial factors in explaining the outbreak of the Second World War. Unlike in the aftermath of the Napoleonic Wars, when delegates to the Congress of Vienna gave France a stake in the new world order, the Versailles Treaty aggravated relations between victor and vanquished. The potential for conflict accelerated as the world sank into the Great Depression of 1929–1931. With the United States retreating into isolationism and the League of Nations unable to deter aggression, France and Britain had difficulty coordinating their approaches to Germany. While France wanted to restrain Germany, it was unwilling to act without British support. Britain, in contrast, saw appeasement as the way to prevent a new round of bloodshed with Germany. Meanwhile, Japan saw in Germany's initial military victories an opportunity to expand its control over Chinese territory and move against British, French, and Dutch colonies in Southeast Asia. As the fighting gradually spread across the globe, liberal faith in the capacity of international law and organization to prevent great-power warfare seemed as naïve as political realists had suggested.

isolationism a policy of withdrawing from active participation with other actors in world affairs and instead concentrating state efforts on managing internal affairs.

The Consequences of World War II

By May 1945, Germany lay in ruins. Three months later, the U.S. atomic bombing of Hiroshima and Nagasaki forced Japan to surrender. The Allied victory over the Axis redistributed power and reordered borders. The Soviet Union absorbed nearly 600,000 square kilometers of territory from the Baltic states of Estonia, Latvia, and Lithuania, and from Finland, Czechoslovakia, Poland, and Romania—recovering what Russia had lost in the 1918 Treaty of Brest-Litovsk. Poland, a victim of Soviet expansionism, was compensated with land taken from Germany. Meanwhile, Germany was divided into occupation zones that eventually provided the basis for its partition into East and West Germany. Finally, pro-Soviet regimes assumed power throughout Eastern Europe (see Map 4.2). In the Far East, the Soviet Union took the four Kurile Islands (or Northern Territories) from Japan, and Korea was divided into Soviet and U.S. occupation zones at the thirty-eighth parallel.

With the defeat of the Axis, one global system ended, but the defining characteristics of the new system had not yet become clear. Although the United Nations was created to replace the old, discredited League of Nations, the management of world affairs still rested in the hands of the victors. Yet victory only magnified their distrust of one another's intentions. The "Big Three" leaders—Winston Churchill, Franklin Roosevelt, and Joseph Stalin—had met at the Yalta Conference in February 1945 to design a new world order, but the vague compromises they reached concealed political differences percolating below the surface. Following Germany's unconditional surrender, the Big Three (with the United States now represented by Harry Truman) met again in July 1945 at Potsdam. The meeting ended without agreement, and the façade of Allied unity began to crumble.

multipolar an international system with more than two dominant power centers.

Perhaps the most important change in the structure of the international system engendered by the war was the shift from a **multipolar** to a **bipolar** distribution of power. Whereas significant military capabilities previously were spread among several great powers, now they were concentrated in the hands of two superpowers, the United States and the Soviet Union. Great Britain and France, exhausted by the war, fell from the apex of world power. Germany, Italy, and Japan, defeated in war, also slipped from the ranks of the great powers. Thus, as the French political sociologist Alexis de Tocqueville had foreseen over a century earlier, the Americans and Russians would hold sway over the destinies of half of mankind. In what eventually became known as the Cold War, the two giants began the third and last hegemonic struggle of the twentieth century.

bipolar an international system with two dominant power centers.

THE COLD WAR

Unparalleled in scope and unprecedented in destructiveness, the second great war of the twentieth century brought into being a system dominated by two superpowers, whose nuclear might far surpassed the military capabilities of the rest of the world. Out of these circumstances grew the conflict known as the Cold War, a competition between Washington and Moscow for hegemonic leadership.

The Causes and Evolutionary Course of the Cold War

The origins of the twentieth century's third struggle for world leadership are debated to this day because the historical evidence lends itself to different interpretations (see Gaddis, 1997). Several possible causes stand out. The first is advanced by realism: The Cold War stemmed from discordant geostrategic interests. The preeminent status of the United States and the Soviet Union at the top of the international hierarchy made their rivalry inescapable. As direct competitors for global influence who presumed that gains by one side would yield losses for the other, they were mutually suspicious and relentlessly contentious.

A second interpretation holds that the Cold War was simply an extension of the superpowers' mutual disdain for each other's economic beliefs and political system. American animosity toward the Soviet Union arose during the 1917 Bolshevik revolution in Russia, which brought to power a government that embraced the radical ideas of Karl Marx. U.S. fears of Marxism led it to adopt an ideology of anticommunism and embark on a crusade to contain Soviet influence. Under what was popularly known as the **domino theory**, U.S. policy makers assumed that the fall of one country to communism would trigger the fall of its neighbors, and in turn still other countries, until the entire world came under Soviet domination.

Soviet leaders were equally hostile to the United States. Believing that communism could not coexist with capitalism, they tried to stoke revolutionary fires around the world in an effort to encourage communist insurgencies. Thus, when viewed through the lens of ideology, diametrically opposed systems of belief precluded compromise between the superpowers, locking them into a long, bitter struggle (see Controversy: Was Ideology the Primary Source of East–West Conflict?).

A third explanation sees the Cold War rooted in psychological factors, particularly in the superpowers' misperceptions of each other's motives. Mistrustful actors are prone to see virtue in their own behavior and malice in those of their adversaries. When such **mirror images** exist, hostility becomes more likely as each side sees its own actions as constructive, but its adversary's responses as obstinate (Bronfenbrenner, 1961). Moreover, as perceptions of an adversary's duplicity become accepted, **self-fulfilling prophecies** can arise. Suspicious of the other side, national leaders become fixated on alleged intrigues, exaggerate the susceptibility of their opponent to coercion, and assume that decisive action will yield a **bandwagon** of support. From this perspective, the Cold War was not simply a product of divergent interests. Nor was it merely attributable to incompatible ideologies. Instead, it was a conflict steeped in reciprocal anxieties bred by the way policy makers on both sides misinterpreted each other's intentions.

Additional factors beyond those rooted in conflicting interests, ideologies, and images contributed to the Soviet-American rivalry. To sort out their relative causal influence, scholars have found it useful to trace how the Cold War changed over its forty-two-year history. We can highlight these changes by dividing the Cold War into the three chronological phases shown in Figure 4.1.

domino theory   a metaphor popular during the Cold War, which predicted that if one state fell to communism, its neighbors would also fall in a chain reaction, like a row of falling dominoes.

mirror images   the tendency of people in competitive interaction to perceive each other similarly—to see an adversary the same way as an adversary sees them.

self-fulfilling prophecies   the tendency for one's expectations to evoke behavior that helps to make the expectations become true.

bandwagon   the tendency for weak states to seek alliance with the strongest power, regardless of that power's ideology or form of government, in order to increase security.

Cold War America was gripped by a "Great Fear" not simply of the Soviet Union but of communism. Senator Joseph McCarthy led an infamous hunt for communist sympathizers in government, Hollywood production companies blacklisted supposed communist sympathizers, and average American citizens were often required to take loyalty oaths at their offices. Everywhere communism became synonymous with treasonous, un-American activity. As the nuclear arms race escalated and the U.S. government took military action to contain the Soviet Union, its justification was almost always expressed in terms of ideology. The threat, it claimed, was that of an atheistic, inherently expansionistic communist system that challenged America's democratic freedoms. The Soviet Union also couched its Cold War rhetoric in terms of ideology, objecting to the imperialistic, capitalist system that Washington allegedly planned to impose on the whole world. Indeed, many Soviets echoed former leader Vladimir Lenin's prediction: "As long as capitalism and socialism exist, we cannot live in peace; in the end, either one or the other will triumph—a funeral dirge will be sung either over the Soviet Republic or over world capitalism." Some would argue that fear of the other side's world dominance may have been more important in the Cold War than pure ideology. Both

the American and the Soviet governments may have entered the Cold War to secure their relative power in the world order as much as to protect pure principles. After all, the United States and the Soviet Union had managed to transcend differing ideologies when they allied against the Axis powers in World War II. Following the war, a power vacuum created by the decline of Europe's traditional great powers drew them into conflict with each other, and as they competed, ideological justifications surfaced.

Ideologies fulfill a common human need to simplify and explain a complex and confusing world. But commitment to an ideology may at times cause hatred and hostility. Fervent believers in a particular ideology are prone to perceive other ideologies competitively—as challenges to the truth of their own core beliefs. Ideology can thus become an excuse for violence. Although scholars are still debating the causes of the Cold War, we need to ask whether it was, in fact, an ideological contest over ideas or a more general contest for power.

What do you think? Was the Cold War really an ideological contest between communism and democratic capitalism? Or was it an intense geostrategic rivalry that would have occurred even in the absence of contending ideologies?

Confrontation, 1945–1962.   A brief period of wary friendship preceded the mutual antagonism that developed between the United States and the Soviet Union. In February 1946, Stalin gave a speech in which he spoke of "the inevitability of conflict with the capitalist powers." Shortly thereafter, George F. Kennan, then a diplomat in the American embassy in Moscow, sent to Washington his famous "long telegram" assessing the sources of Soviet conduct. Kennan's ideas were circulated widely in 1947, when the journal *Foreign Affairs* published his views in an article signed simply "X." In it, Kennan argued that Soviet leaders forever would feel insecure about their political ability to maintain power against forces both within Soviet society and in the outside world. Their insecurity would lead to an activist—and perhaps aggressive—Soviet foreign policy. However, the United States had the power to increase the strains under which the Soviet leadership would have to operate, which could lead to a gradual mellowing or final end of Soviet power. Hence, Kennan concluded that in these circumstances the cornerstone of American policy toward the Soviet Union should be "a long-term, patient but firm and vigilant containment of Russian expansive tendencies."

containment a strategy to prevent another state from using force to expand its sphere of influence.

Soon thereafter, President Harry S. Truman made **containment** the central element of American postwar foreign policy. Alarmed by domestic turmoil in

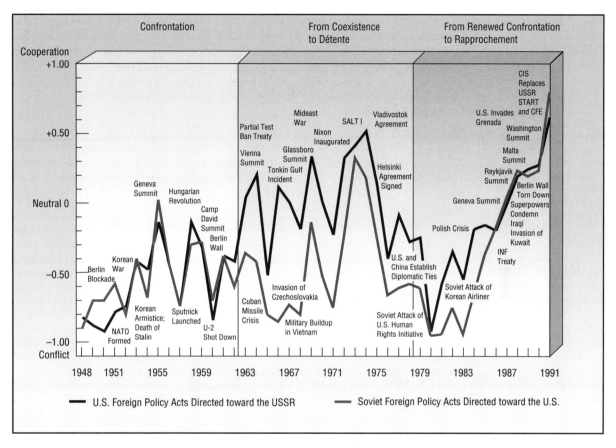

FIGURE 4.1 Key Events in the Evolution of U.S.–Soviet Relations, 1948–1991

The evolution of U.S.–Soviet relations during the Cold War displays a series of shifts between periods of conflict and cooperation. As this figure shows, each superpower's behavior toward the other tended to be reciprocal, and, for most periods prior to 1983, confrontation prevailed over cooperation.

Turkey and Greece, which he asserted was communist inspired, Truman declared, "I believe that it must be the policy of the United States to support free peoples who are resisting attempted subjugation by armed minorities or by outside pressures." Eventually known as the **Truman Doctrine**, this statement defined the grand strategy that the United States would pursue for the next forty years, over Kennan's objections that it did not adequately discriminate between vital and peripheral security interests, between different levels of threats, and between different types of response (Gaddis, 1982: 238–239). The grand strategy of containment sought to prevent the expansion of Soviet influence by encircling the Soviet Union with military alliances backed with the threat of nuclear retaliation.

A seemingly endless series of Cold War crises soon followed. They included the communist coup d'état in Czechoslovakia in 1948; the Soviet blockade of

Truman Doctrine the declaration by President Harry S. Truman that U.S. foreign policy would use intervention to support peoples who allied with the United States against external subjugation.

West Berlin in June of that year; the communist acquisition of power on the Chinese mainland in 1949; the outbreak of the Korean War in 1950; the Chinese invasion of Tibet in 1950; and a series of on-again, off-again Taiwan Straits crises. The Soviets finally broke the U.S. atomic monopoly in 1949. Thereafter, the risks of massive destruction of each side necessitated restraint and changed the terms of their rivalry.

peaceful coexistence Soviet leader Nikita Khrushchev's 1956 doctrine that war between capitalist and communist states is not inevitable and that interbloc competition could be peaceful.

Because the Soviet Union remained strategically inferior to the United States, Nikita Khrushchev (who succeeded Stalin upon his death in 1953) pursued a policy of **peaceful coexistence** with capitalism. Nonetheless, the Soviet Union at times cautiously sought to increase its power in places where opportunities appeared to exist. As a result, the period following Stalin's death saw many Cold War confrontations, with Hungary, Cuba, Egypt, and Berlin becoming flash points.

In 1962, the surreptitious placement of Soviet missiles in Cuba set the stage for the greatest test of the superpowers' capacity to manage their disputes—the Cuban Missile Crisis. The superpowers stood eyeball to eyeball. Fortunately, a political solution to the standoff was reached, and the crisis ended. This experience expanded both sides' awareness of the suicidal consequences of a nuclear war, and transformed the way that Washington and Moscow would henceforth think about how the Cold War should be waged.

From Coexistence to Détente, 1963–1978. The looming threat of mutual destruction, in conjunction with the growing parity of American and Soviet military capabilities, made coexistence or nonexistence appear to be the only alternatives for political leaders in Washington and Moscow. At the American University commencement exercises in 1963, U.S. president John F. Kennedy warned that the superpowers were "caught up in a vicious and dangerous cycle in which suspicion on one side breeds suspicion of the other and new weapons beget counterweapons." He went on to signal a shift in how the United States hoped thereafter to interact with the Soviet Union, which elicited a positive response from the Kremlin.

Nevertheless, the superpowers intervened throughout Asia, Africa, and Latin America in the hope of curbing each other's influence. The foremost example occurred during the early 1960s when President Kennedy dispatched military advisers to South Vietnam in an attempt to support Saigon against a communist insurgency. Following Kennedy's assassination, President Lyndon Johnson expanded American involvement by sending increasing numbers of U.S. troops, which created deep divisions within domestic public opinion that contributed to the decision to withdraw American combat forces from the country under the 1973 Paris Peace Accords.

détente a strategy of relaxing tensions between adversaries to reduce the possibility of war.

Following Richard Nixon's election in 1968, the United States initiated a new approach to dealing with the Soviet Union that he labeled **détente**. The Soviets also adopted this term to describe their policies toward the United States, and relations between the two countries moved in a more constructive direction. Arms control stood at the center of their activities. The Strategic Arms Limitation Talks (SALT), initiated in 1969, sought to restrain the threatening, expensive, and spiraling arms race by limiting the deployment of antiballistic missiles. As Figure 4.1 shows, cooperative interaction became more commonplace than hostile relations. Visits, cultural exchanges, trade agreements, and joint technological ventures replaced threats, warnings, and confrontations.

From Renewed Confrontation to Rapprochement, 1979–1991. Despite the careful nurturing of détente, it did not endure. When the Soviet Union invaded Afghanistan in 1979, President Jimmy Carter defined the situation as "the most serious strategic challenge since the Cold War began." He promptly declared America's willingness to use military force to protect its access to oil supplies from the Persian Gulf. In addition, he suspended grain exports to the Soviet Union, and attempted to organize a worldwide boycott of the 1980 Moscow Olympics.

Relations deteriorated dramatically thereafter. Carter's successor in the White House, Ronald Reagan, described the Soviet Union as "the focus of evil in the modern world." His counterparts in the Kremlin (first Yuri Andropov and then Konstantin Chernenko) responded with equally scathing criticisms of the United States. As the rhetorical salvos became increasingly harsh, the arms race resumed. Some American leaders hinted that a nuclear war could be "winnable," and advocated a military strategy that included the threat of a "first use" of nuclear weapons in the event of a conventional attack by the Soviets. Under the **Reagan Doctrine** the United States pledged support for anticommunist insurgents who sought to overthrow Soviet-supported governments in Afghanistan, Angola, and Nicaragua.

By 1985, superpower relations had deteriorated to the point that Mikhail Gorbachev, the new Soviet leader, characterized the situation as "explosive." Further complicating matters for the Soviet Union, its economy was buckling under the weight of exorbitant military expenditures, estimated at roughly a quarter of the country's gross domestic product. Faced with economic stagnation and declining civic morale, Gorbachev implemented a series of far-reaching domestic reforms to promote democratization and a market system. Meanwhile, in an effort to reduce the suffocating level of military expenditures, he sought a **rapprochement** or reconciliation with the West, and proclaimed his desire to end the Cold War. "We realize that we are divided by profound historical, ideological, socioeconomic, and cultural differences," he noted in 1987 during his first visit to the United States. "But the wisdom of politics today lies in not using those differences as a pretext for confrontation, enmity, and the arms race." Soviet spokesperson Georgi Arbatov elaborated, informing the United States that "we are going to do a terrible thing to you—we are going to deprive you of an enemy." Surprisingly, the Soviets ended their aid to Cuba, withdrew from Afghanistan, and announced unilateral reductions in military spending. Gorbachev also agreed to two new disarmament agreements: the Strategic Arms Reduction Treaty (START) for deep cuts in strategic arsenals, and the Conventional Forces in Europe (CFE) Treaty to reduce the Soviet presence in Europe. Finally, to nearly everyone's astonishment, Moscow acquiesced to the disbanding of the Warsaw Pact and the reunification of Germany. In 1989, the

Reagan Doctrine a pledge of U.S. backing for anticommunist insurgents who sought to overthrow Soviet-supported governments.

rapprochement in diplomacy, a policy seeking to reestablish normal relations between enemies.

Berlin Wall was dismantled. Long a stark, frightening symbol of the division between East and West, its removal heralded the end of the Cold War. Its peaceful conclusion suggested something quite different from the twentieth century's two world wars: Hegemonic struggles are not doomed to end in violence; sometimes great-power rivals can reconcile their differences without resorting to global war.

The Consequences of the Cold War

Though locked in a geostrategic rivalry exacerbated by antagonistic ideologies and mutual misperceptions, the United States and the Soviet Union avoided a fatal showdown. In accepting the devolution of their empire, Soviet leaders made the most dramatic peaceful retreat from power in history. The end of the Cold War altered the face of world affairs in profound and diverse ways. With the dissolution of the Soviet Union in 1991, no immediate great-power challenger confronted American hegemonic leadership. However, a host of new security threats emerged, ranging from aspiring nuclear powers such as North Korea and Iran to terrorist networks such as Al Qaeda. As the turbulent twentieth century wound down, the simple Cold War world of clearly defined adversaries gave way to a shadowy world of elusive foes.

THE FUTURE OF GREAT-POWER POLITICS

Rapid, unanticipated changes in world politics often create uncertainty about the global future. To optimists, the tides of change that swept across the world following the collapse of communism signified "the universalization of Western liberal democracy as the final form of government" (Fukuyama, 1989). To pessimists, these sea changes suggested not history's end, but its resumption (Kagan, 2008). Both groups recognized that Cold War bipolarity had been superseded by a **unipolar** configuration of power that presented new and difficult challenges.

unipolar an international system with one dominant power center.

America's Unipolar Moment

Unipolarity refers to the concentration of power in a single preponderant state. Following the collapse of the Soviet Union, the United States stood alone at the summit of the international hierarchy. It was the only country with the military, economic, and cultural assets to be a decisive player in any part of the world it chose (Krauthammer, 1991). Its military was not just stronger than anybody's—it was stronger than everybody's, with defense expenditures eventually exceeding all other countries combined.

Complementing America's military might was its economic strength. With less than 5 percent of the global population, the United States accounted for almost a third of the global gross domestic product and two-fifths of the entire world's spending on research and development (Emmott, 2002: 4). Furthermore, America wielded enormous **soft power** as a source of popular culture and the hub of global communications, through which its values spread all over the

soft power the ability of a country to get what it wants in international affairs through the attractiveness of its culture, political ideals, and policies.

world (Nye, 2004). In the words of former French Foreign Minister Hubart Védrine, the United States was not simply a superpower; it was a hyperpower.

The United States began the new millennium with hopes of peace and prosperity. From Washington's perspective, a safe, prosperous world was emerging under its leadership. When Al Qaeda operatives crashed hijacked airliners into the World Trade Center and the Pentagon, they shattered widespread optimism about the prospects for the twenty-first century. In U.S. president George W. Bush's words, "Night fell on a different world." Progress no longer seemed inevitable, a matter of steady, predictable advances toward a bright, promising future. Humanity, as UN Secretary-General Kofi Annan observed, had "entered the third millennium through a gate of fire."

The confluence of enormous military, economic, and cultural power on American soil after the Cold War gave the United States the ability to launch its so-called "global war on terror" following the Al Qaeda attack on September 11, 2001 (9/11). Overwhelming power can easily tempt national leaders to act in a **unilateral** manner. Rather than working with others, independent action may seem attractive to a strong, self-confident nation worried about being hamstrung

unilateral a strategy that relies on independent, self-help behavior in foreign policy.

Carmen Taylor/AP Photo

9/11 and American Foreign Policy
The terrorist attack on the World Trade Center's twin towers on 9/11 is widely regarded as having a significant impact on U.S. foreign policy during its so-called "unipolar moment." Overnight, writes columnist Anne Applebaum (2005: 14), "America's military objectives changed, [and] America's diplomatic priorities were transformed."

by quibbling lesser powers. Unilateralism has costs, however. Going it alone erodes international support on issues, such as combating global terrorism, where the United States needs cooperation from others. American power, argues political scientist Stephen Walt (2005: 229) "is most effective when it is seen as *legitimate*, and when other societies believe it is being used to serve their interests as well as those of the United States." But, as former Reagan administration official Clyde Prestowitz (2003) lamented, Washington's neglect of the politics of consensus building when it expanded military operations from Afghanistan to Iraq in 2003 led many countries to question the legitimacy of U.S. foreign policy.

With the unraveling of its financial system in the fall of 2008, many analysts have concluded that America's unipolar moment is ending. As Figure 4.2 shows, long-term economic trajectories based on differential national growth rates point to a world in which other great powers will challenge American economic preeminence within the next two decades. At the same time, the United States will find it costly to maintain military dominance. Aside from major deployments in Afghanistan and Iraq, U.S. forces are positioned in 737 military bases spread throughout 132 foreign countries reaching from the Korean Peninsula to the Gulf of Aden to Latin America (Freeland, 2007: 18). **Imperial overstretch**, the gap between internal resources and external commitments, has bedeviled every leading great power (Kennedy, 1987). Throughout history, hegemons

imperial overstretch
the historical tendency of hegemons to weaken themselves through costly foreign pursuits that drain their resources.

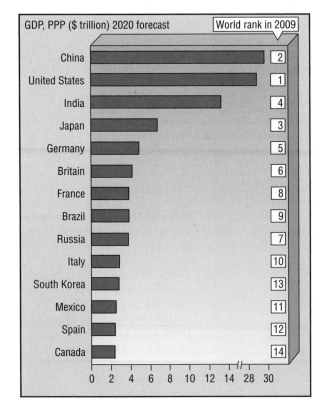

FIGURE 4.2 Emerging Centers of Power

Using purchasing power parities (PPP) to remove differences in countries' price levels, this figure presents a forecast of the largest economies in 2020.

SOURCES: *Economist*, April 1, 2006; *World Factbook* (2009).

repeatedly have defined their security interests more broadly than other states only to slip from the pinnacle of power by reaching beyond their grasp. The characteristic error for a unipole, writes Robert Jervis (2009: 197–200), is excessive expansion. Given the absence of countervailing power, unipolarity offers the dominant state an opportunity to pursue grandiose goals that can push the cost of maintaining preeminence above its economic capacity.

From Unipolarity to Multipolarity?

Speaking to the nation from the United States Military Academy at West Point on December 1, 2009, President Barack Obama acknowledged the connection between economic capacity and national security. "Our prosperity provides a foundation for our power," he asserted. "It pays for our military. It underwrites our diplomacy." Suggesting that America's foreign policy commitments must be brought into balance with its resources, Obama insisted that he would refuse to set goals that lie beyond the country's means.

Does the Obama administration's suggestion of scaling back U.S. overseas commitments reflect a deeper shift in the global distribution of power? Some analysts are skeptical. Relative power shifts slowly, they contend. The United States "remains first on any scale of power that matters—economic, military, diplomatic, or cultural—despite being embroiled in two wars and beset with the worst economic crisis since the Great Depression" (Joffe, 2009: 24). Furthermore, its lead on each of these scales over would-be challengers is too large to be overcome in the next few decades. The United States, they conclude, will remain the world's sole superpower for years to come, although it will share the world stage with several regional great powers of varying strength.

Other analysts doubt that unipolarity will remain intact (National Intelligence Council, 2010). Owing to profligacy at home, overstretch abroad, and the growing strength of other states, they expect America's power to decline in relative terms, thus ushering in a period of multipolarity. The shift will be gradual; the world will not be unipolar one day and multipolar the next. New centers of meaningful power will arise over ensuing decades, making the United States one major power among many. Some of the rising powers frequently mentioned as possible peer competitors include China, the European Union, Japan, India, Russia, and Brazil. Commentators disagree, however, over which ones will eventually summit the global hierarchy.

Because it is common to hear forecasts of a multipolar future, let us briefly explore what such a world might look like. As a state system composed of several comparatively equal great powers vying for influence and advantage, multipolarity would be complex, fluid, and fraught with uncertainty. Predicting what cleavages would develop among the great powers will be difficult insofar as allies in military affairs may be rivals in trade relationships. Conflict could emerge between any pair of great powers, but it may be restricted to one sphere of activity. For example, the United States and Japan exhibit conflict in their commercial relations but nevertheless also display continuing efforts to manage their security relations collaboratively. Such crosscutting axes of conflict and cooperation will affect global stability. Throughout history different types of multipolar systems have existed, some of which have exhibited more stability than others. The most unstable have possessed rigid, polarized alignments, such as during the period prior to the outbreak of World War I (Kegley and Raymond, 1994). Polarized systems are dangerous because they focus adversaries' attention on a single threat, thus making it more likely that minor disagreements will become magnified into larger tests of will. A system where great powers compete in one sphere of activity but cooperate elsewhere has the potential to prevent any given issue from polarizing the members of the state system. Great-power conflict would be frequent, but as long as security and economic disputes do not overlap, they would not necessarily divide the system into two antagonistic camps. Under these circumstances, the danger of polarization could be managed if the great powers developed international rules and institutions to manage their fluid, mixed-motive relationships.

Establishing rules to manage potential great-power conflicts will also be important because the transition to multipolarity is unlikely to be smooth. Scholars have found that the combination of a declining hegemon and an unstable hierarchy among the major powers are related to increases in the occurrence of warfare (Geller and Singer, 1998). Historically, interstate hostilities have tended to flare up when the principal defender of the status quo loses its relative advantage over other major powers.

APPLICATION   **Integrate, But Hedge**

One of the main foreign policy problems facing the United States today is how to reconcile itself to ascending powers that are becoming formidable competitors. Joseph S. Nye, Jr. served as U.S. assistant secretary of defense during the 1990s, with responsibility for developing an East Asian security strategy. In the following passage, he describes how he drew on international relations theory to develop a strategy for responding to China's growing strength.

There was a great deal of concern [among policy makers] about the rise of Chinese power; indeed, some voices advocated a policy of containment before China became too strong. In my view, such an approach would guarantee Chinese enmity and unnecessarily discount possible benign futures. Yet treating China as a friend would not guarantee friendship. We designed a strategy that drew upon both realism and liberalism. From a realist perspective, the three key powers in East Asia were the United States, Japan, and China. We first reinforced the U.S.-Japan security relationship which was then in disrepair because many analysts

regarded it as a Cold War relic and saw Japan as a "geo-economic" threat. By reestablishing the security relationship with Japan, we insured that China could not play a Japan card against us. The second part of the strategy relied on liberalism. We eschewed the language of containment, opened markets with China, and supported its accession to the World Trade Organization. I have termed the policy "integrate, but hedge." If China becomes aggressive as its strength increases, Japan will be a key partner in organizing a policy of containment, but if China mellows as it prospers and its ties of interdependence deepen, the world may see a more benign outcome. There are always uncertainties about the future, but the policy is robust against failure (Nye, 2008: 159).

Nye uses this episode to point out that the theories produced in a university setting were valuable in making foreign policy in Washington. "Political science theory," he maintains, "was crucial to the way in which I framed and crafted solutions to practical policy issues."

Of course, we have no way of knowing whether the future will resemble the past history of multipolar systems. Patterns and practices can change, and it is possible for policy makers to learn from previous mistakes and avoid repeating them (see Application: Integrate, But Hedge). However, we can anticipate that the future will be largely in the hands of the great powers, because "powerful states make the rules" (Keohane and Nye, 2001a). What kinds of rules and institutions will they create, and what impact will they have on other states? To explore these questions, in Chapter 5, we will turn our attention from the rich, powerful, and commercially active great powers at the center of the world system and examine the poorer, weaker, and economically dependent states that lie along its periphery.

CHAPTER SUMMARY

- Great powers possess enormous military and economic capabilities relative to other states. As a result, they play a leading role in world politics, particularly on international security issues.

- Change is endemic to world politics, but one constant stands out: great-power rivalry. World politics tends to be reordered following hegemonic wars among the great powers. In their aftermath, the victors tend to create new international rules and institutions in an effort to prevent a repetition of these horrific conflicts.

- Single-factor theories are inadequate for explaining great-power war. Such conflicts involve causal mechanisms operating on multiple levels of analysis, and a fusion of proximate causes with deeper, more remote structural causes.

- The twentieth century experienced three great-power struggles for world leadership: World Wars I and II, and the Cold War.

- The proximate causes of World War I were the assassination of Franz Ferdinand, and the series of reactive, fatalistic decisions made by political leaders of Austria, Germany, and Russia. Deeper underlying causes included the rise of nationalism in southeastern Europe, the growth of German power, the creation of rigid mobilization plans, and the development of a polarized system of military alliances.

- The proximate causes of World War II can be found in Adolf Hitler's voracious appetite for conquest and domination, and the failed efforts by the internally divided Western democracies to appease the Nazi dictator. The remote causes included German resentment over the Treaty of Versailles, the rise of hypernationalistic ideologies within the Axis countries, the collapse of the international economic system, and the U.S. foreign policy of isolationism.

- The advent of nuclear weapons transformed world politics by radically changing the role that threats of force would henceforth play in international bargaining.

- Scholars disagree about the causes of the Cold War. Some of them see it as the result of a conflict of interests between the United States and the Soviet Union, others point to ideological incompatibilities, and still others emphasize the superpowers' misperceptions of each other's motives.

- Several conspicuous patterns existed throughout the Cold War. While periods of intense conflict alternated with periods of relative cooperation, the United States and the Soviet Union consistently made avoidance of all-out war their highest priority. Reciprocal, action–reaction exchanges were also evident (friendly U.S. initiatives toward the Soviet Union were reciprocated in kind). Both rivals were also willing to disregard their respective ideologies whenever their perceived national interests rationalized such inconsistencies; for example, each backed allies with political systems antithetical to its own when the necessities of power politics seemed to justify doing so.

- Following the collapse of the Soviet Union in 1991, the United States emerged as the preponderant global power. However, many scholars believe that the current unipolar system will not persist. Factors such as uneven economic growth and imperial overstretch will alter the relative positions of the great powers and bring about a multipolar structure.

KEY TERMS

appeasement	imperial overstretch	Reagan Doctrine
bandwagon	isolationism	self-fulfilling prophecies
bipolar	long-cycle theory	soft power
containment	mirror images	Truman Doctrine
détente	multipolar	unilateral
domino theory	peaceful coexistence	unipolar
hegemon	rapprochement	

SUGGESTED READINGS

Kegley, Charles W., Jr., and Gregory A. Raymond. *After Iraq: The Imperiled American Imperium*. New York: Oxford University Press, 2007.

Senese, Paul D., and John A. Vasquez. *The Steps to War: An Empirical Study*. Princeton: Princeton University Press, 2008.

Sutter, Robert G. *U.S.-Chinese Relations: Perilous Past, Pragmatic Future*. Lanham, MD: Rowman & Littlefield, 2010.

Tsygankov, Andrei P. *Russia's Foreign Policy: Change and Continuity in National Identity*. Lanham, MD: Rowman & Littlefield, 2010.

Zakaria, Fareed. *The Post-American World*. New York: Norton, 2009.

CRITICAL THINKING QUESTIONS

What are the root causes of great-power war? For some scholars, the question can be answered only if the effects of international anarchy are recognized. To illustrate their point, they ask us to consider the "parable of the tribes." Imagine a remote island populated by several tribes living within reach of one another. If they all choose to behave peacefully, they all will enjoy security. But if all but one tribe choose peace, what will be the consequences for the others? What will happen if a single power-maximizing tribe embarks on a campaign of conquest?

Suppose their campaign begins with an attack on a peaceful neighboring tribe, which results in its inhabitants being exterminated and the territory seized. Shortly thereafter, another peaceful tribe is attacked, and its surviving members are forced to serve their conqueror. Fearing they will suffer a similar fate, a third peaceful tribe leaves the island, and its former homeland becomes part of the growing empire of the power-maximizing tribe. By this time, the remaining peaceful tribes learn of these alarming events and, wishing to preserve their independence and autonomy, arm and begin training for war. Ironically, defending themselves against a power-maximizing aggressor requires that they become more like their foe.

According to Andrew Schmookler (1984), the parable's author, the underlying lesson is that anarchy makes an intense competitive struggle for power inevitable. Given the existence of one ambitious, self-interested tribe, the peaceful tribes have few options: destruction, absorption, withdrawal (if physically possible), or imitation. In each case, he concludes, the ways of power spread. Power-maximizing behavior, once introduced, inexorably diffuses throughout a system of regularly interacting political entities.

Do you find this argument persuasive? Does anarchy constitute a sufficient cause of great-power war in the absence of any other? How would realists, liberals, and constructivists respond to the parable?

5

The Global South in a World of Powers

CHAPTER OUTLINE

A global human society based on poverty for many and prosperity for a few, characterized by islands of wealth surrounded by a sea of poverty, is unsustainable.

THABO MBEKI
FORMER PRESIDENT OF SOUTH AFRICA

On February 4, 1992, Hugo Chávez Frías, a flamboyant and charismatic lieutenant colonel, led a military coup against the Venezuelan government. When his outnumbered forces failed to take control of Caracas and capture President Carlos Andrés Pérez, he surrendered and was taken into custody. In a televised statement, Chávez grudgingly admitted that the rebellion was over but only "*por ahora*" (for now).

Three years earlier, the army had been used by President Pérez to suppress riots that erupted when he implemented economic austerity measures called for by the International Monetary Fund. Angered by what they saw as a weak government ceding control over the country's economy to foreign interests, Chávez and other junior officers began plotting their rebellion. Two figures provided inspiration. The first, Simón Bolívar, organized a movement to liberate much of South America from Spanish colonial rule and established a country that briefly included present-day Columbia, Panama, Venezuela, and Ecuador. The second, Fidel Castro, engineered a socialist revolution in Cuba and worked assiduously to undermine U.S. influence in Latin America. Animated by the dream of sparking a socialist revolution in Venezuela and constructing a large bloc of Latin American countries to challenge the United States, the officers launched their ill-fated coup.

During the next two years, while Chávez and his co-conspirators were incarcerated, President Pérez was impeached for corruption. Chávez subsequently received a pardon and, upon his release from prison, began campaigning for the presidency on a populist platform. Elected in 1998 (and reelected in 2000 and 2006), he promised to root out Venezuela's "predatory oligarchs" who served international capital. As he told his followers in a March 1, 2004 speech, he sought to end the oppressive system whereby rich countries kept poor countries in the role of "producers of wealth and recipients of leftovers." Capitalism, he reiterated in a speech to the World Social Forum the following year, "is savagery"; it causes misery and poverty.

Throughout his tenure in office, Chávez has unveiled numerous reforms, insisting that they would help Venezuela transcend capitalism. With great fanfare, socialist-inspired programs to reduce illiteracy, improve health care, and redistribute land have been initiated. The key to implementing them lay in the country's petroleum vast resources. Venezuela possesses the world's sixth-largest proven oil reserves and ranks eighth worldwide in the number of barrels produced per day. To harness that potential wealth, Chávez exerted control over Petróleos de Venezuela (the state oil company), demanded an increase in royalty percentages on joint extraction contracts with foreign oil companies, and nationalized the pumping and refining facilities of those companies that refused to accept his terms. Whereas when Chávez came to power the price of oil was $10 a barrel and the government budget was 7 billion dollars, by June 2008 oil had risen to over 140 dollars a barrel, which translated into a government budget exceeding 54 billion dollars (Anderson, 2008: 48). As oil revenues soared, Chávez allocated larger amounts to his social welfare programs, which buttressed his position among the country's impoverished masses.

Chávez's public policies are hotly debated. Observers disagree passionately over whether they have eroded or enhanced the country's quality of life. Venezuela's crime rate is high, its infrastructure remains in disrepair, shortages persist in staple goods, and inflation has climbed to over 30 percent (*Economist*, May 15, 2010: 28). With his approval rate falling below 50 percent in public opinion polls, rumors of plots against him regularly swirl through the capital, fueled by memories of an unsuccessful coup that briefly removed him from power in April 2002. Although his current term ends in 2013, he has hinted that he would like to remain in office longer, although a referendum to amend the constitution to allow him to run again was defeated in 2007.

"I always think like a subversive," Chávez boasted in a March 2007 interview with journalist José Vicente Rangel. Perhaps nowhere is this more apparent than in his efforts to subvert U.S. foreign policy in Latin America, which he characterized in an address to the United Nations on September 20, 2006, as a "scheme of domination, exploitation and pillage." On the one hand, he has tried to forge strong bilateral relations with anti-U.S. leaders ranging from Iran's Mahmoud Ahmadinejad to the guerrillas heading the Colombian Revolutionary Armed Forces (FARC). On the other hand, he has attempted to cobble together multilateral organizations such as his Bolivian Alternative for the Americas

Hugo Chávez and Twenty-First-Century Socialism Criticizing what he calls the "siren song of capitalism," President Hugo Chávez of Venezuela campaigns against the privatization of state-owned enterprises and policies aimed at increasing the role of the market in Global South countries' economies.

(ALBA) to counter Washington's support for a regional trade agreement known as the Free Trade Area of the Americas (FTAA). In Chávez's mind, confrontation with imperial powers is inevitable. Venezuela, he vowed in a January 27, 2006 speech, will never be "a colony of the United States" or a pawn of international financial institutions run by wealthy industrialized countries.

Chávez's fiery rhetoric frustrates U.S. policy makers, who generally try to ignore what they see as his annoying provocations. Yet his depiction of a global capitalist system that benefits some states and limits others resonates elsewhere in the Western Hemisphere, especially among people who take a Marxist approach to understanding world poverty. Regardless of one's opinion about *Chavismo*, it is a political ideology that highlights the ways in which many people in developing countries interpret world politics differently than their counterparts in more powerful, prosperous countries.

In the previous chapter we examined the strongest states within the international system, those with the economic and military capabilities to dominate everyone else. The experience of Venezuela during the Chávez years raises important questions about those states that are not great powers. Does being a less wealthy and militarily mighty country place one's future in the hands of others? What accounts for the inequalities that currently divide humanity? Can anything be done to close the gap between the world's rich and poor?

GLOBAL INEQUALITIES

Earth is divided into two hemispheres, north and south, at the equator. This artificial line of demarcation is, of course, meaningless except for use by cartographers to chart distance and location on maps. However, this divide also represents a popular way of describing the inequalities that separate rich and poor states. By and large, these two groups are located on either side of the equator (see Map 5.1).

Life for most people in the Northern Hemisphere is very different from that in the Southern Hemisphere. The disparities are profound, and in many places appear to be growing. The division in power and wealth between the states comprising the **Global North** and **Global South** poses both moral and security problems. Poverty and inequality have existed throughout most periods of recorded history. But today the levels have reached unprecedented proportions. The states in the less-developed Global South find themselves marginalized, with even their very identities shaped by a subordinate position in the global hierarchy. The purpose of this chapter is to examine the causes and consequences of the inequality among the more than two hundred states in the global system. Why is it that the great powers experience abundance while many other countries seem trapped in poverty? What has bred such inequality?

Many analysts begin addressing these questions at the systemic level of analysis. They believe that the interstate system has properties built into it that account for the inability of most poor countries to close the gap with the wealthy countries. From their perspective, current inequalities are part of a

Global North   a term used to refer to the world's wealthy, industrialized countries located primarily in the Northern Hemisphere.

Global South   a term used to designate the less-developed countries located primarily in the Southern Hemisphere.

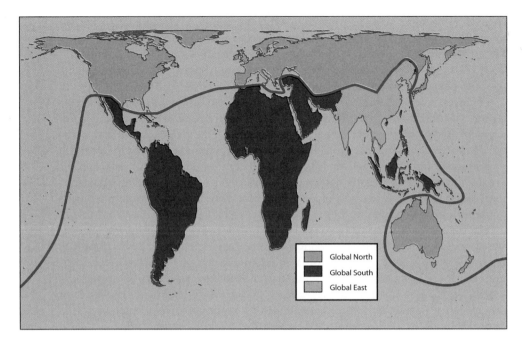

M A P 5.1 The Global North, Global South (and Global East)

The countries of the Global North are those that are wealthy, democratic, and technologically innovative, with declining birth rates and aging populations. In contrast, the countries of the Global South tend to be poorer and have higher birth rates and younger populations. Some scholars also refer to a "Global East," countries that have arisen from the Global South and are now positioned to rival the levels of prosperity in the Global North.

colonialism   the rule of a region by an external sovereign power.

Third World   a Cold War term to describe the developing countries of Africa, Asia, and Latin America.

First World   the relatively wealthy industrialized countries that share a commitment to varying forms of democratic political institutions and developed market economies.

Second World   during the Cold War, the group of countries, including the Soviet Union and its then–Eastern European allies, that shared a commitment to centrally planned economies.

much longer historical pattern. To understand the Global South today, they recommend we take into consideration the legacy of **colonialism**. Almost all the now-independent sovereign states in the Southern Hemisphere were at one time colonies, subjugated by far more powerful states.

THE COLONIAL EXPERIENCE OF THE GLOBAL SOUTH

During the Cold War, the French demographer Alfred Sauvy coined the term **Third World** to describe the economically less-developed states that tended to share a colonial past. They were contrasted with the so-called **First World**, composed of the industrialized democracies in western Europe, North America, and Japan, and the **Second World**, which consisted of the Soviet Union and its allies. Today the communist countries comprising the former Second World have almost totally vanished, thus making the term *Third World* obsolete. Now the terms *Global North* (the wealthy countries previously known as the First World) and *Global South* (the less-developed countries along the equator and in the Southern Hemisphere) are popular.

Although journalists, policy makers, and scholars frequently generalize about the Global South, considerable diversity exists within this group of states. For example, it includes low-income countries such as Ghana and Haiti, where a majority of the population works in subsistence agriculture; middle-income countries like Mexico and Malaysia, which produce manufactured goods; and a few countries like Kuwait and Qatar, where petroleum exports have generated incomes rivaling those of Global North countries.

Global South countries are diverse in other ways as well. Included among their ranks is Indonesia, an archipelago of more than 17,000 islands scattered throughout an oceanic expanse larger than the United States, and Burundi, a landlocked state slightly smaller than Maryland. Also included are Nigeria, with some 152 million inhabitants, and Belize, with approximately 315,000 people. Aside from these geographic and demographic differences, Global South countries also vary politically and culturally, ranging from democratic Costa Rica to autocratic Myanmar (Burma).

Despite this diversity, most Global South countries in Africa, Asia, and Latin America share a set of common problems, which allow us to differentiate them from the countries in the Global North. Although the Global South is home to 84 percent of the world's people, it commands less than 30 percent of its wealth (WDI, 2010: 64, 232). Many of these countries are characterized by low productivity, high rates of population growth, and skewed patterns of income distribution, with large segments of their populations suffering from poverty, illiteracy, and ill health. Indeed, the world's three richest people—Mexican businessman Carlos Slim Helú, Microsoft co-founder Bill Gates, and investor Warren Buffet—possess more wealth than the poorest forty Global South countries combined (see Map 5.2).

The emergence of the Global South as an identifiable group of states is a distinctly contemporary phenomenon. Although most Latin American countries were independent before World War II, not until then did other countries of the Global South gain that status. In 1947, Great Britain granted independence to India and Pakistan, after which **decolonization**—the freeing of colonial peoples from their dependent status—gathered speed. Since then, a profusion of new sovereign states has joined the global community, nearly all carved from the British, Spanish, Portuguese, Dutch, and French empires built under colonialism 400 years ago.

decolonization the achievement of independence by countries that were once colonies of other states.

Today, the decolonization process is almost complete. However, the effects persist. Many of the ethnic conflicts now so prevalent in the Global South have colonial roots, as the imperial powers drew borders with little regard for the identities of the indigenous peoples. In addition, the poverty facing most Global South countries is partly a product of their imperial pasts, when they were exploited by European powers. Given colonialism's impact, let us briefly examine how it evolved over the course of the past six centuries.

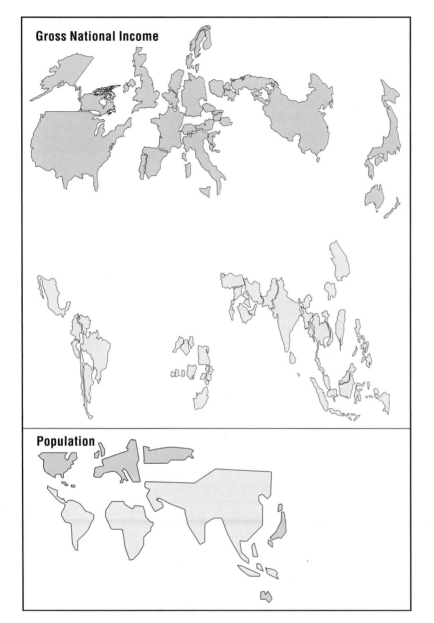

M A P   5.2 The North–South Divide in Wealth and Population

If the countries of the world were redrawn to reflect the size of their economies, as shown here, huge differences would be visible. Small, wealthy countries such as Belgium or the Netherlands would be depicted as bigger than poorer African countries such as Nigeria or Sudan, whose area in square miles is actually far larger than either European state.

SOURCE: Adapted from data in WDR (2010).

The First Wave of European Imperialism

The first wave of European empire building began in the late fifteenth century, as the Dutch, English, French, Portuguese, and Spanish used their military power to conquer territories for commercial gain. As scientific innovations made the European explorers' adventures possible, merchants followed in their wake, seizing the opportunity to expand their business and increase their profits. Europe's governments, in turn, "perceived the possibilities for increasing their own power and wealth. Commercial companies were chartered and financed, with military and naval expeditions frequently sent out after them to ensure political control of overseas territories" (B. Cohen, 1973: 20).

The economic strategy underlying the relationship between colonies and colonizers during this era is known as **mercantilism**: an economic philosophy advocating government regulation of economic life to increase state power and security. Early mercantilists believed acquiring gold and silver increased power. Later mercantilists shifted their emphasis to building strong, self-sufficient economies by using royal decrees to launch new industries, subsidize strategically targeted enterprises, protect domestic producers from foreign competition through tariff barriers, and maintain a "favorable" balance of trade by increasing exports and curbing imports.

To maximize national power and wealth, European leaders saw the conquest of foreign territory as a natural by-product of active government management of the economy. In addition to providing them with precious metals and other raw materials, colonies were untapped markets, which could be closed to commercial competition from other powers. By selling finished goods to their colonies under monopolistic conditions, it was thought that imperial powers could boost domestic employment and keep the profits from these sales at home.

By the end of the eighteenth century, the European powers had spread themselves, although thinly, throughout virtually the entire world, but the colonial empires they had built now began to crumble. Britain's thirteen North American colonies declared their independence in 1776, and most of Spain's possessions in South America won their freedom in the early nineteenth century. Nearly 100 colonial relationships worldwide were terminated in the half-century ending in 1825.

As the first wave of European colonization waned, belief in the mercantilist philosophy also declined. In 1776, the Scottish political economist Adam Smith published *The Wealth of Nations,* a vigorous critique of mercantilism that called for free trade. While Smith acknowledged that the state should be involved in defending the nation against external aggression, enforcing property rights, upholding contracts, and the like, he denied that it could be more efficient or innovative than an unregulated market. His arguments laid much of the intellectual foundation for **laissez-faire economics**. Henceforth, European powers would continue to seek colonies, but the rationale for their imperial policies began to change.

> **mercantilism** an economic strategy for accumulating state wealth and power by using governmental regulation to encourage exports and curtail imports.

> **laissez-faire economics** a body of thought emphasizing free markets with little governmental regulation.

The Second Wave of European Imperialism

Beginning in the 1870s and extending until the outbreak of World War I, a new wave of imperialism washed over the world as Europe, joined later by the United States and Japan, aggressively colonized new territories. The portion of the globe that Europeans controlled was one-third in 1800, two-thirds by 1878, and four-fifths by 1914 (Fieldhouse, 1973: 3). In the last twenty years of the nineteenth century, Africa fell under the control of seven European powers (Belgium, Britain, France, Germany, Italy, Portugal, and Spain), and in all of

sphere of influence
the area dominated by a great power.

the Far East and the Pacific, only China, Japan, and Siam (Thailand) were not conquered. China, however, was divided into **spheres of influence** by the foreign great powers, and Japan itself occupied Korea and Formosa (Taiwan). Elsewhere, the United States acquired Puerto Rico and the Philippines in the 1898 Spanish-American War, extended its colonial reach westward to Hawaii, leased the Panama Canal Zone "in perpetuity" from the new state of Panama (an American creation), and exercised considerable control over several Caribbean islands, notably Cuba. The preeminent imperial power, Great Britain, in a single generation expanded its empire to cover one-fifth of the earth's land area. As British imperialists were proud to proclaim, it was an empire on which the sun never set.

Why did most of the great powers—and those that aspired to great-power status—engage in this expensive and often vicious competition to control other peoples and territories? What explains the second wave of imperialism? The answers are rooted in economics and politics.

Economic Explanations for the Second Wave of Imperialism. With the Industrial Revolution, capitalism grew, emphasizing the free market, private ownership of the means of production, and the accumulation of wealth. Radical theorists, following Karl Marx, saw imperialism as the result of competition among capitalists for profitable overseas outlets for their surplus capital. One of them was the Soviet leader Vladimir Lenin. In his famous 1916 monograph *Imperialism, The Highest Stage of Capitalism,* Lenin argued that military expansion abroad was produced by the "monopoly stage of capitalism." He concluded that the only way to end imperialism was to abolish capitalism. Liberal economists, on the other hand, regarded the new imperialism not as a product of capitalism as such but rather as a result of maladjustments within the capitalist system, which could be corrected. What the two perspectives shared was the belief that economics explained the new wave of imperialism: the demands in advanced capitalist societies for cheap raw materials, markets to consume their growing production, and places to invest their accumulating capital. Thus, from both the Marxist and classical liberal perspectives, the material needs of capitalist societies explained their imperial drive.

Political Explanations for the Second Wave of Imperialism. Not everyone agreed that economic motives underpinned the second wave of imperial expansion. Political factors were also identified. For example, in his influential 1902 book, *Imperialism,* J. A. Hobson argued that the jockeying for power and prestige between competitive empires had always characterized the great powers' behavior in the European balance-of-power system, and that imperialism through overseas expansion was simply a global extension of this inter-European competition for dominance.

Self-Determination and Decolonization

self-determination
the doctrine that people should be able to determine the government that will manage their affairs.

Regardless of the causes underlying the second wave of imperialism, world opinion took an anti-imperial turn when the Versailles peace settlement that ended World War I embraced the principle of national **self-determination** advocated by U.S. President Woodrow Wilson. Self-determination meant that each distinct people would have the right to decide which authority would represent and rule them. Wilson and others who shared his liberal convictions believed that freedom of choice would lead to the creation of states and governments content with their territorial boundaries and therefore less inclined to make war. In practice, however, the attempt to redraw states' borders to separate nationality groups was applied almost exclusively to war-torn Europe, where six new states were created from the territory of the former Austrian-Hungarian Empire (Austria, Czechoslovakia, Hungary, Poland, Romania, and the ethnically divided Yugoslavia). Other territorial adjustments were also made in Europe, but the proposition that self-determination should be extended to Europe's overseas empires did not receive serious support.

Still, the colonial territories of the powers defeated in World War I were not simply parceled out among the victorious allies, as had typically happened in the past. Instead, the territories controlled by Germany and the Ottoman Empire were transferred under League of Nations auspices to countries that would govern them as "mandates" pending their eventual self-rule. The principle implicit in the mandate system was that colonies were a trust, not something to be exploited. This set an important precedent for the negotiations after World War II, when territories of the defeated powers placed under the United Nations trusteeship system were not absorbed by others but were promised eventual self-rule, and support for self-determination gained momentum. The decolonization process accelerated in 1947, when the British relinquished political control of India and Pakistan. War eventually erupted between these newly independent states as each sought to gain control over disputed territory in Kashmir. Violence also broke out in Indochina and Algeria in the 1950s and early 1960s as the French sought to regain control over colonial territories they had held before World War II. Similarly, bloodshed followed closely on the heels of independence in the Congo when the Belgians granted their African colony independence in 1960, and it dogged the unsuccessful efforts of Portugal to battle the winds of decolonization that swept over Africa as the 1960s wore on.

Despite these conflicts, decolonization for the most part was not only extraordinarily rapid but remarkably peaceful. Not only had World War II sapped the economic and military vitality of many of the colonial powers, but colonialism became morally less acceptable. In 1960, Global South states took advantage of their growing numbers in the UN General Assembly to secure passage of the historic *Declaration on the Granting of Independence to Colonial Countries and Peoples*. It held that the subjection of people to foreign domination was a denial of their human rights and an impediment to international peace.

As the old colonial order crumbled—and as the leaders in the newly emancipated territories discovered that freedom did not translate automatically into autonomy, economic independence, and domestic prosperity—the conflict between the rich Global North and the emerging states of the Global South began.

NORTH AND SOUTH TODAY: WORLDS APART

The Global South is sometimes described today as a "zone of turmoil" in large measure because, in contrast with the democratic and peaceful Global North, many of the people in the Global South face poverty, war, and tyranny. Although democracy has spread to much of the Global South since the 1980s, the commitments of some of these governments to regular elections and human rights are fragile. Furthermore, many Global South countries lack well-developed domestic market economies based on entrepreneurship and private enterprise. Differences in technological capabilities also separate North and South. Typically, Global South countries have been unable to evolve an indigenous technology appropriate to their own resources and have been dependent on powerful Global North **multinational corporations (MNCs)** to transfer technical know-how. This means that research and development expenditures are directed toward solutions of the Global North's problems, with technological advances seldom meeting the needs of the Global South.

Life is a constant struggle for those who live in extreme poverty. One former resident of the Tangra slum in Kolkata, India, describes it as a force that "robs you of confidence…steals your pride, deadens your ambition, limits your imagination and psychologically cripples" (Mazumdar, 2009: 34). The data reported in Table 5.1 reflect some of the brutal disparities between Global North and Global South countries. This picture darkens even more when focus is shifted to the plight of the poorest in the low-income developing countries. According to criteria used by the UN Economic and Social Council, forty-nine countries currently comprise the **least developed countries (LDCs)** of the Global South. They have gross national incomes (GNI) per capita of under $900 per year, and their overwhelmingly rural populations depend on agriculture for subsistence and frequently rely on **barter** in their economic exchanges. These low-income countries are not significant participants in the global market. Their meager exports are largely confined to inexpensive primary products, including foodstuffs (cocoa, coffee, and tea), minerals, hides, and timber. Because they consume most of what they produce, theirs is typically a subsistence economy, and the prospects for change are dim, because most of these countries have been bypassed by direct foreign investment and ignored by foreign aid donors.

Geographic location also hampers the economic development in Global South countries. Landlocked developing countries that lack navigable rivers or efficient road and rail networks are highly disadvantaged due to the expenses they face in accessing world markets. The "median landlocked country pays up to 50 percent more in transportation costs than the median coastal nation," points out Ricardo Hausmann (2001: 47), former chief economist of the Inter-American Development Bank. Some small island developing states are burdened with high transportation costs as well, largely due to their remoteness from major global markets. Moreover, because many of these landlocked and island countries are located in tropical areas, their economies are further strained by the ravages of diseases such as malaria. According to recent statistical estimates, when controlling for other factors, the per capita economic growth in countries with malaria is more than 1 percent lower than in countries without malaria (Sachs, 2002).

multinational corporations (MNCs) business enterprises headquartered in one state that invest and operate extensively in other states.

least-developed countries (LDCs) the most impoverished states in the Global South.

barter the exchange of one good for another rather than the use of currency to buy and sell items.

T A B L E 5.1   Global South and North: An International Class Divide

Characteristic	Developing Global South	Developed Global North
Number of countries	144	66
Population (millions)	5,629	1,069
Land area (thousands of sq. km)	98,797	35,299
GNI ($ billions)	$15,649	$42,415
Gross national income for each person	$2,780	$42,415
Imports ($ billions)	$5,503	$13,741
Exports ($ billions)	$5,938	$13,710
Women holding seats in parliament (%)	18%	22%
Life expectancy at birth	67	80
Infant mortality rate per 1,000 births	50	6
Access to improved sanitation (% of population)	55%	100%
Paved roads (%)	24%	87%
Personal computers for each 100 people	5	68
Internet users for each 100 people	15	69
Population covered by cellular networks (%)	76%	99%
Daily newspapers for each 1,000 people	59	261
Electric power consumption for each person (kwh)	1,478	9,753

SOURCES: WDR (2010); WDI (2010).

For many people living in the Global South, the future is bleak. The aggregate pattern underlying global trends in the last twenty years shows that more than sixty countries today are worse off than they were and are falling ever further behind the levels achieved by the countries in the Global North. This tragic situation raises a basic theoretical question: Why does so much of the Global South suffer from such destitution?

Why Do North–South Disparities Persist?

Why has the Global South lagged so far behind the Global North in its comparative level of well-being and **development**? And why, as shown in Table 5.2, have the development experiences even within the Global South differed so

development the processes through which a country increases its capacity to meet its citizens' basic human needs and raise their standard of living.

T A B L E 5.2   **Global South Progress in Attaining Development Goals**

	North Africa	Sub-Saharan Africa	Western Asia	South Asia	South-eastern Asia	Latin America & Caribbean
Reduce extreme poverty by half	+	–	– –	–	++	–
Reduce hunger by half	++	–	––	––	+	–
Improve the lives of slum-dwellers	++	–	––	++	+	–
Reduce mortality of under-five-year olds by two-thirds	+	–	–	–	–	+
Increase productive and decent employment	– –	– –	– –	–	–	–
Halt and reverse spread of HIV/AIDS	– –	–	+	–	–	–
Halt and reverse spread of tuberculosis	+	– –	–	+	++	++
Halve proportion without improved drinking water	+	–	+	++	++	++
Halve proportion without sanitation	++	–	–	–	+	–
Universal primary schooling	+	–	–	+	–	–
Equal girls' enrollment in primary schools	+	+	+	++	++	++

While meeting at the United Nations in 2000, 189 countries signed the Millennium Declaration, which outlined a set of developmental goals to be attained by 2015. This chart shows the progress as of 2010 that different regions within the Global South have made toward reaching some of the key targets for the health, education, and economic welfare goals.
– – No progress or a deterioration or reversal
– Target not expected to be met if current trends persist
+ Target expected to be met if current trends persist
++ Target already met or very close to being met
SOURCE: The Millennium Development Goals Report (2010).

widely? A generation ago, for example, Nigeria's gross national product (GNP) per capita exceeded those of Thailand, Malaysia, and Indonesia. By the 1990s, however, Nigeria lagged far behind its Asian counterparts. Nor was Nigeria's experience atypical. The economic fortunes of various other African countries declined precipitously as the twentieth century drew to a close, just as several East Asian countries enjoyed significant economic growth (Landes, 1998). What accounts for these stark differences? Will they continue?

The diversity evident in the Global South invites the conclusion that under-development is explained by a combination of factors. Some theorists explain underdevelopment by looking primarily at internal causes. Other theorists focus on the position of developing countries in the global political economy. We shall briefly discuss each of these schools of thought, beginning with the interpretation proposed by classical economic development theory.

Internal Factors: Classical Economic Development Theory's Interpretation

Liberal economic development theories of **modernization** emerged in the early post–World War II era. They argued that the major barriers to development were posed by the Global South countries' own internal characteristics. Productivity remained low due to managerial inefficiency, a lack of modern technology, and inadequate transportation and communication infrastructures. To overcome these barriers, most classical theorists recommended that the wealthy countries supply various "missing components" of development, such as investment capital through foreign aid or private foreign direct investment.

Once sufficient capital was accumulated to promote economic growth, these theorists predicted that its benefits would eventually "trickle down" to broad segments of society. In this way, everyone, not just a privileged few, would enjoy the benefits of rising affluence. Walt W. Rostow, an economic historian and U.S. policy maker, formalized this theory in his influential book *The Stages of Economic Growth* (1960). He predicted that traditional societies beginning the path to development would inevitably pass through various stages by means of the free market and would eventually "take off" to become similar to the mass-consumption societies of the capitalist Global North. Even though the rich are likely to get richer, it was argued, as incomes in the world as a whole grow, the odds increase that a preindustrialized economy will grow faster and eventually reduce the gap between it and richer countries.

That prognosis and the policies on which it was based were ultimately rejected by the Global South. Leaders there did not accept the classical liberal argument that Global North countries became prosperous because they concentrated on work, invention, and skill. Instead, they were persuaded by a rival theory that attributed the Global South's plight to the structure of the global political economy.

modernization a view of development that argues that self-sustaining economic growth is created through technological innovation, efficient production, and investments from capital accumulation.

External Factors: Dependency Theory's Interpretation

Whereas classical developmental theory pointed to internal factors to explain the plight of the Global South, **dependency theory** emphasized external factors. Although the dependency literature is large and diverse (see Packenham, 1992), all dependency theorists reject Rostow's stages-of-growth thesis, arguing that development is not a linear process that all societies uniformly follow. As noted in Chapter 2, dependency theory builds on Lenin's critique of imperialism, but goes beyond it to account for changes that have occurred in recent decades. Its central proposition is that the structure of the capitalist world economy is based on a division of labor between a dominant core and a subordinate periphery. As a result of colonialism, the Global South countries that make up the periphery have been forced into an economic role whereby they export raw materials and

dependency theory a view of development asserting that the leading capitalist states dominate and exploit the poorer countries on the periphery of the world economy.

import finished goods. While classical liberal theorists submit that specialization according to comparative advantage will increase income in an unfettered market and therein help close the gap between the world's haves and have-nots, dependency theorists maintain that global inequalities cannot be reduced so long as developing countries continue to specialize in primary products for which there are often numerous competing suppliers and limited demand.

Dependency theorists also argue that countries in the Global South are vulnerable to cultural penetration by outside forces, which saturate them with values from other societies. The Nigerian author Chimamanda Ngozi Adichie (2010), for instance, recalls the difficulty finding her voice as a young writer because most of the children's literature that she read as an elementary school student dealt with British life and was written in English, rather than in her native tongue.

dualism   the existence of a rural, impoverished, and neglected sector of society alongside an urban, developing, or modernizing sector, with little interaction between the two.

Once cultural penetration occurs, locals who embrace foreign values may gain economically from the ties that they forge with the governments and corporations doing business in their country. The argument that a privileged few benefit from dependency underscores the dual nature of many developing countries. **Dualism** refers to the existence of two separate economic and social sectors operating side by side. Dual societies typically have a rural, impoverished, and neglected sector operating alongside an urban, developing, or advanced sector—but with little interaction between the two. Thus whatever growth occurs in the industrial sector does not trigger a corresponding growth process in the rural sector. MNCs contribute to dualism by locating primarily in urban centers and widening the wage differentials between the small number of modern-sector workers they employ and the larger rural workforce (Todaro, 2000).

newly industrialized countries (NICs)   prosperous members of the Global South, which have become important exporters of manufactured goods.

Although dependency theory has great appeal within the Global South, it cannot easily explain the emergence of what many people call **newly industrialized countries (NICs)**, members of the Global South that have begun exporting manufactured goods to the Global North. To explain this phenomenon, they sometimes use the term **dependent development** to describe the industrialization of peripheral areas in a system otherwise dominated by the Global North. The term suggests the possibility of either growing or declining prosperity, but not outside the confines of a continuing dominance–dependence relationship between North and South.

dependent development   the industrialization of areas outside of the leading capitalist states within confines set by the dominant capitalist states, which enables the poor to become wealthier without ever catching up to the core Global North countries.

Can the Economic Gap Be Closed?

Is it possible for the Global South to escape the vicious cycle of poverty? When we look at the situation from the perspective of the poorest of the poor countries, the prospects appear dismal. However, a basis for optimism can be found if you broaden the picture and see the conspicuous exceptions to the general pattern of persistent poverty. Although many Global South countries appear to be mired in inexorable poverty, some have managed to break the chains of underdevelopment. By pursuing bold paths for growth, they have seen their fortunes rise and are poised to enter the ranks of the advanced industrial economies. The ability of some developing countries to escape the syndrome that still affects the rest of the Global South suggests that others can succeed as well.

Consider the example of the newly industrialized countries, which have moved beyond the export of primary products to the export of manufactured goods. Today the NICs are among the largest exporters of manufactured goods. Because of the economic success of several NICs located in East and South Asia, they sometimes are distinguished from the rest of the Global South and referred to as the **Global East** (recall Map 5.1). In particular, the so-called "Asian Tigers" (South Korea, Singapore, Taiwan, and Hong Kong) have taken advantage of comparatively low wage rates to promote export-led economic growth through "neomercantilist" practices such as protecting infant industries from foreign competition with tariff and nontariff barriers and providing financial incentives for manufacturing industries. Spectacular economic growth has followed. With their population growth generally in check, the Asian Tigers have joined the ranks of the world's wealthiest states, and still other "new tigers" such as India have emerged as exports and foreign investment have stimulated a booming economy.

Global East   the rapidly growing economies of East and South Asia that have made their countries competitors with the traditionally dominant members of the Global North.

The achievements of the Asian NICs alongside the plummeting financial fate of the poorest Global South countries provoke policy questions: Despite these differences and the inequalities between Global South states, is there a commonality that unites them as a group? What strategies have they forged to deal with their position of weakness in a world of powers?

THE GLOBAL SOUTH'S FOREIGN POLICY RESPONSE

The vast political, economic, and social differences separating the Global North (and East) from the Global South indicate that the remaining countries in the South are vulnerable and insecure, and that these conditions are products of both domestic and international factors. Coping with this insecurity has long been a primary foreign policy goal of Global South states, and efforts to overcome it have often brought the Global South into contention with the Global North. Ironically, the end of the Cold War reduced the great powers' security interest in providing economic aid to Global South countries. However, with the Global South now experiencing a burst of new armed conflicts, aid from the advanced industrialized countries has recently begun to increase.

Given the myriad problems confronting the Global South, crafting foreign policy strategies to maximize security and prosperity preoccupy its leaders. Different states have taken different approaches. Let us examine how the Global South countries are pursuing their objectives, particularly in their relationships with the Global North.

In Search of Security

The Global South countries emerging after World War II struggled on separate tracks to find a foreign policy approach that could provide them with the security they lacked. Some states aligned themselves with either the United States or Soviet Union; others avoided taking sides in the Cold War. The latter approach gathered momentum in 1955, when twenty-nine Asian and African countries met in Bandung, Indonesia, to devise a strategy to combat colonialism. Six years later, leaders from twenty-five countries, mostly former colonies, met in Belgrade, Yugoslavia, where they created the Nonaligned Movement (NAM), a political coalition whose membership would later grow to more than 100 countries.

nonalignment   a foreign policy posture that rejects participating in military alliances with rival blocs for fear that formal alignment will entangle the state in an unnecessary war.

Nonalignment.   Because many Global South countries feared becoming entrapped in the Cold War, they adopted foreign policies based on **nonalignment**. The strategy energized both the United States and the Soviet Union to renew their efforts to woo the uncommitted Global South countries to their own network of allies, often offering economic and military aid as an inducement. The Cold War's end eroded the bargaining leverage nonalignment had provided the Global South. As a strategy, nonalignment "died" with the Cold War. But the passion of Global South leaders to eradicate global inequalities lives on, as can be seen in the 2003 *Non-Aligned Kuala Lumpur Summit Declaration*, which raised questions about the inability of many Global South countries to benefit from globalization.

The challenge facing the nonaligned states today is how to promote their interests in a world where few listen to their voices. The nonaligned Global South can complain, but its bargaining power to engineer institutional reforms is limited. This weakness is displayed in the UN, where the most influence the Global South has mustered has symbolically been to delay serious proposals to make Germany and Japan permanent members of the Security Council by insisting that one of the larger developing countries (such as Brazil, Indonesia, Mexico, or South Africa) also be given a seat among the mighty. Weak states have some vocal power in numbers but no clout or control. Thus, the Global South worries that in the future even newer forms of imperialism might continue to erode any Global South hopes for progress.

failed states   countries whose governments have little or no control over their territory and population.

Arms Acquisitions.   During the Cold War, many developing countries became battlegrounds on which the superpowers conducted covert activities, paramilitary operations, and proxy wars. The vast majority of the inter- and intrastate conflicts during the past half-century occurred within the Global South (Hewitt, Wilkenfeld, and Gurr, 2010). Today, the danger of anarchy and violence has reached epidemic proportions, as the Global South contains numerous **failed states** that do not have governments strong enough to preserve domestic order.

Faced with seemingly endless conflict at home or abroad, it is not surprising that the Global South has joined the rest of the world's quest to acquire modern weapons of war—including in some cases (China, India, North Korea, Pakistan) nuclear weapons. As a result, the burden of military spending (measured by the ratio of military expenditures to GNP) is highest among those least able to bear it. In the Global South, military spending typically exceeds expenditures on health and education; impoverished states enmeshed in ethnic or religious strife at home are quite prepared to sacrifice expenditures for economic development in order to acquire weapons.

Few Global South states produce their own weapons. Weak governments, anxious over the possibility of separatist revolts and other forms of civil strife, have invested large proportions of their country's modest national budgets in arms rather than allocating these scarce revenues to social and economic programs aimed at reducing poverty. Ironically, many Global South countries have raised their military spending to purchase arms produced in the Global North at higher rates than their wealthy Global North counterparts do (Grimmett, 2009). Thus, in responding to its security concerns, the Global South appears to be increasing its dependence for arms purchases on the very same rich states whose military and economic domination they historically have most feared and resented.

Reducing Vulnerability to Natural Disasters.   Adding to the Global South's problems is still another source of turmoil. The widespread death and disease that resulted from the 2005 tsunami in the Indian Ocean, the 2008 cyclone that devastated Myanmar (Burma), and the 2010 earthquake in Haiti underscore the magnitude of the threat posed by recurring natural disasters. Although the scale of tragedies such as these can be reduced with effective warning and response systems, the economic struggle for survival within the world's poorest countries leaves few resources for investing in the technology needed for disaster

THONY BELIZAIRE/AFP/Getty Images

Haiti Suffers from a Massive Earthquake Haitians inspect the remains of a six-story building that collapsed during the magnitude 7.0 earthquake of January 12, 2010. Much of Port-au-Prince, the capital city, was reduced to rubble. The poorest country in the Western Hemisphere, Haiti will need a significant amount of international assistance to rebuild.

preparedness. As a result, the Global South is petitioning the Global North for help, to expand its global network of seismometer and tidal monitoring instruments, and to share data from weather satellites that can be used to chart dangerous storms and reduce their risks.

In Search of Prosperity

import-substitution industrialization a strategy for economic development that involves encouraging domestic entrepreneurs to manufacture products traditionally imported from abroad.

Breaking out of their dependent status and pursuing their own industrial development remains the greatest foreign policy priority for countries in the Global South. To this end, some of them (particularly those in Latin America) have pursued development through an **import–substitution industrialization** strategy designed to encourage domestic entrepreneurs to manufacture products traditionally imported from abroad. Governments (often dictatorships) have been heavily involved in managing their economies and in some cases became the owners and operators of industry.

export-led industrialization a growth strategy that concentrates on developing domestic export industries capable of competing in overseas markets.

Import-substitution industrialization eventually fell from favor, in part because manufacturers often found that they still had to rely on Global North technology to produce goods for their domestic markets. The preference now is for **export-led industrialization**, based on the realization that what boosted the Global North's economic fortunes was not national autonomy and self-sufficiency, but exporting manufactured goods, which commanded higher prices than raw materials. As exemplified by the NICs, the shift toward export-led growth strategies has transformed some Global South countries from being suppliers of raw materials into manufacturers of products already available in the Global North.

Although the Asian Tigers of the Global East have some of the world's most dynamic economies, the global recession of 2008–2009 has revealed a danger in relying too heavily on exports to a limited number of countries. As consumer spending plummeted in Global North countries, the tigers, whose exports amount on average to 47 percent of their GDP, were left with excess manufacturing capacity and unemployed workers. The remedy, many economists believe, will be to rely more on domestic consumption and expand export markets beyond the Global North. According to a recent forecast by the OECD Development Centre, Global South countries now make up 37 percent of world trade, with South–South exchanges representing half of that total. If current trends continue, today's emerging economies will account for almost 60 percent of world GDP in **purchasing power parity (PPP)** terms by 2030 (OECD, 2010).

purchasing power parity (PPP) a model of calculating the relative purchasing power of different countries' currencies for an equal basket of commodities.

Not all Global South economies are positioned to survive in this highly competitive globalized market, where skilled labor, capital, technology, and production are increasingly integrated worldwide. Many of the least-developed countries are heavily dependent on the sale of raw materials and other primary products for their export earnings. Malawi, for example, relies on tobacco for nearly 60 percent of its exports. Thus, while some gain from economic globalization and prosper, others are not able to take advantage of its benefits, and they remain vulnerable to downturns in the market for the resources they mine or the crops they grow.

How to cope with dominance and dependence thus remains a key Global South concern. As they search for status and economic security, let us next evaluate the Global South's key strategies in their relations with the Global North.

A New International Economic Order?   The emerging Global South countries were born into an international economic order with rules they had no voice in creating. In order to gain control over their economic futures, they began coordinating their efforts within the United Nations, where their growing numbers and voting power gave them greater influence than they could otherwise command. In the 1960s, they formed a coalition of the world's poor, the **Group of 77** (known in diplomatic circles simply as the G-77) and used their voting power to convene the UN Conference on Trade and Development (UNCTAD). UNCTAD later became a permanent UN organization through which the Global South would express its interests concerning development issues.

A decade later, the G-77 (then numbering more than 120 countries) again used its UN numerical majority to push for a **New International Economic Order (NIEO)** to replace the international economic regime championed by the United States and the other capitalist powers since World War II. Motivated by the oil-exporting countries' rising bargaining power, the Global South sought to compel the Global North to abandon practices perceived as perpetuating their dependence. More specifically, the proposals advanced under the banner of the NIEO included:

- Giving preferential, nonreciprocal treatment to Global South exports to industrialized countries;

- Establishing commodity agreements to regulate and stabilize the world market for primary commodities;

- Linking the price of Global South exports to the price of imports from industrialized states;

- Increasing financial resource transfers to Global South countries;

- Reducing the burden of Global South debt through rescheduling, interest subsidization, or cancellation;

- Increasing the participation and voting power of Global South countries in international financial institutions;

- Regulating the activities of multinational corporations in the Global South to promote the reinvestment of profits earned by MNCs in host country economies; and

- Expanding technical assistance programs and reducing the cost of transferring technology to the Global South.

Not surprisingly, the Global North rebuffed many of the South's proposals, although some of the issues that were raised (such as debt relief) remain on the global agenda. At the 2003 World Trade Organization meeting in Cancún, Mexico, for example, the poor countries united to demand major concessions

Group of 77 (G-77)   the coalition of Third World countries that sponsored the 1963 Joint Declaration of Developing Countries calling for reforms to allow greater equity in North–South trade.

New International Economic Order (NIEO)   the 1974 policy resolution in the UN that called for a North–South dialogue to open the way for the less-developed countries of the Global South to participate more fully in the making of international economic policy.

from the wealthy countries, especially with regard to foreign subsidies. In 2008, another step was taken when *Banco del Sur* (Bank of the South) was launched in Latin America to go around financial institutions dominated by Global North countries and fund large infrastructure projects with the region's oil wealth.

Regional Trade Regimes.   With the failure of reform envisioned by the NIEO, the integration of Global South countries into the globalization process will occur according to the rules dictated by the Global North. Are there alternatives? Can regional arrangements enable Global South states to take advantage of growing economic interdependence to achieve their development goals?

To promote growth through regional economic agreements, in the 1990s the global economy began to subdivide into three "trade blocs"—one in Europe, with the European Union (EU) as its hub; a second in the Americas, with the United States at the center; and a third in the Global East, with Japan and China dominant. Consider some recent developments:

- *In the Americas:* The North American Free Trade Agreement (NAFTA), formalized in 1994, brought Canada, Mexico, and the United States into a single free-trade area, in which tariffs among member countries are eliminated. In addition, the Mercosur agreement, which links Argentina, Brazil, Paraguay, Uruguay, and Venezuela in Latin America's largest trade bloc, has incorporated Bolivia, Colombia, Ecuador, and Peru as associate members. Furthermore, the 2005 Central American Free Trade Agreement (CAFTA) to reduce trade barriers between the United States and Costa Rica, El Salvador, Guatemala, Honduras, Nicaragua, and the Dominican Republic has been ratified.

- *In Asia:* The association of Asia-Pacific Economic Cooperation (APEC), an informal forum created in 1989 that has committed itself to creating a free-trade zone during the next twenty-five years. In addition, the members of the Association of Southeast Asian Nations (ASEAN), first established in 1967 by Brunei, Indonesia, Malaysia, the Philippines, Singapore, and Thailand and now including Vietnam, agreed to set up a free-trade area.

- *In Africa:* The Southern African Development Community (SADC) formed in 1980 is the largest of twelve free-trade areas in the region.

Will the lofty expectations of these regional politico-economic groups be realized? In the past, political will and shared visions have proven to be indispensable elements in successful regional trade regimes. Economic complementarity is another essential component, as the goal is to stimulate greater trade among the members of the free-trade area, not simply between it and others. If one or more members export products that each of the others wants, the chances of the regime's success are greater; if, on the other hand, they all tend to export the same products or to have virtually no trade with one another, failure is more likely.

Foreign Aid, Investment, and Debt Relief.   The developing countries have long pleaded for greater access to the Global North's markets in order to fuel their economic growth. These pleas have meet with success in recent years, with the number of free-trade agreements between Global South and Global North countries increasing to 109, from only 23 in 1990 (*Harper's*, February 2005: 13). But many Global South countries have not improved their lot, often for two major reasons. First, market access has become increasingly difficult because domestic pressure groups in Global North countries have lobbied their governments to reduce the imports of other countries' products that compete with their own industries. Trade may be desired by the Global South, but political barriers often interfere with free trade. Second, the character and distribution of foreign aid have changed as criticism of its effectiveness and effects has risen. Consequently, levels of aid have remained moderate.

Foreign aid comes in a variety of forms and is used for a variety of purposes. Some aid consists of outright grants of money, some of loans at concessional rates, and some of shared technical expertise. Although most foreign aid is bilateral and is termed **official development assistance (ODA)**—meaning the money flows directly from one country to another—an increasing portion is now channeled through global institutions such as the World Bank, and hence is known as "multilateral aid." Moreover, the purposes of aid are as varied as its forms. Commonly stated foreign aid goals include not only the reduction of poverty through economic development, but also human development, environmental protection, the development of private enterprise, increased power for women, the promotion of democratic governance and human rights, humanitarian disaster relief, and assistance to refugees. However, security objectives traditionally have figured prominently as motives of donors in the allocation of both economic aid and military assistance, and still do. For example, the United States continues to target Israel and Egypt as major recipients to symbolize friendship, maintain a balance of power, and tilt the scales toward peace in the Middle East. Also, security was the primary motive behind the doubling of the U.S. foreign assistance budget following 9/11, to provide funds for allies' use in the war on global terrorism.

According to the OECD's Development Assistance Committee, Global North donors gave $119 billion to poor countries in 2009, with an average contribution of 0.48 percent of gross national income, which is below the 0.7 percent target set by the United Nations (see Figure 5.1). The commitment to fostering economic development has waivered in certain Global North countries due to doubts over the effectiveness of aid programs, despite evidence that foreign aid has made a positive difference in the Global South (Easterbrook, 2002). Critics particularly resent what they perceive to be a state of mind in some Global South cultures that stands in the way of development, which—while bemoaning poverty—at the same time condemns competition, the profit motive, and individual entrepreneurial activity. Most bothersome to these critics are the failures to deal with what they see as endemic corruption.

Some donors have ultimately concluded that long-term foreign aid may be detrimental to Global South countries, an opinion echoed by Zambian economist Dambisa Moyo (2010). Roughly a dozen African countries depend on aid for a fifth or more of their national incomes. This climate of opinion has

official development assistance (ODA) grants or loans to countries from other countries, usually channeled through multilateral aid organizations, for the primary purpose of promoting economic development and welfare.

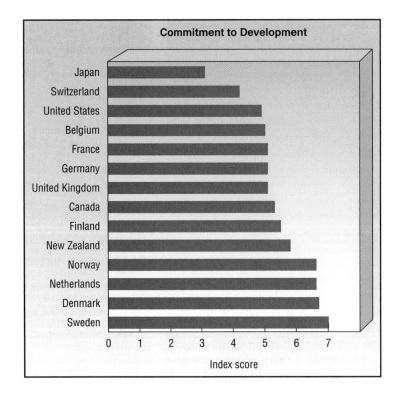

FIGURE 5.1 Commitment to Development

The Commitment to Development Index rates selected Global North countries on how much they help Global South countries in seven policy areas: aid, trade, investment, migration, environment, security, and technology. Based on its performance in 2009, each country received a rating for each policy area, and the ratings were then averaged to create the index score. Sweden, Denmark, the Netherlands, and Norway ranked the highest on the index in their commitment to assist development in the Global South. Each state exceeded the UN target of providing at least 0.7 percent of GDP in official development assistance.

spawned more "conditionality," or demands that recipient countries must meet to receive aid. Almost one-fourth of official development assistance is tied to purchasing goods and services from the donor country. It has been estimated that tying aid reduces its value by 15 to 30 percent.

On top of this practice of tying aid, donors are highly selective in choosing the countries they target for assistance, especially when they treat foreign aid as a subsidy for their domestic corporations producing exports. Although most donors distribute aid to the poorer countries, almost 40 percent of aid goes to middle- and high-income countries. In fact, far more money is funneled into Global South economies through the **remittances** that migrant laborers working in the Global North send home to their families. Global remittances have steadily climbed since the 1970s to reach $316 billion in 2009—more than two and a half times the amount of all ODA. To cite one example, nearly 10 percent of the population of the Philippines lives abroad, sending home $15 billion a year, a seventh of the country's gross domestic product. The figures are even higher in other countries, reaching 18 percent of GDP in El Salvador, 30 percent in Haiti, and 32 percent in Tonga (*USA Today*, July 10–12, 2009: 2; *International Herald Tribune*, April 21–22, 2007: 2).

Another indicator of the modest level of Global North support for Global South development assistance is seen in charitable contributions from private

remittances the money earned by immigrants working in wealthy countries that they send to family members still living in their home country.

CONTROVERSY   Multinational Corporations in the Global South: Do They Help or Hurt?

Within the Global South, there is widespread concern about the impact of multinational corporations (MNCs) on the economies and societies of the countries in which they operate. Because their record can be evaluated on different criteria, MNCs are praised by some people and condemned by others. The following is a "balance sheet" summarizing the major arguments for and against MNCs. Using this summary of contending interpretations, you can easily see why the role of MNCs is so controversial. What do you think? On balance, do MNCs help or harm the Global South's ability to close the gap in wealth with the Global North? How do you assess their relative benefits and costs for Global South countries?

Positive

- Increase the volume of trade.
- Assist the aggregation of investment capital that can fund development.
- Finance loans and service international debt.
- Lobby for free trade and the removal of barriers to trade, such as tariffs.
- Underwrite research and development that allows technological innovation.
- Introduce and dispense advanced technology to less-developed countries.
- Reduce the costs of goods by encouraging their production according to the principle of comparative advantage.
- Generate employment.
- Encourage the training of workers.
- Produce new goods and expand opportunities for their purchase through the internationalization of production.
- Disseminate marketing expertise and mass advertising methods worldwide.
- Provide investment income to facilitate the modernization of less-developed countries.
- Generate income and wealth.
- Advocate peaceful relations between and among states in order to preserve an orderly environment conducive to trade and profits.

- Break down national barriers and accelerate the globalization of the international economy and culture and the rules that govern international commerce.

Negative

- Give rise to huge conglomerations that reduce competition and free enterprise.
- Raise capital in host countries (thereby depriving local industries of investment capital) but export profits to home countries.
- Limit the availability of commodities by monopolizing their production and controlling their distribution in the world marketplace.
- Create "sanctuary markets" that restrict and channel other investments to give MNCs an unfair advantage.
- Export technology ill-suited to underdeveloped economies.
- Inhibit the growth of infant industries and local technological expertise in less-developed countries while making Global South countries dependent on Global North technology.
- Conspire to create monopolies that contribute to inflation.
- Contribute to environmental degradation by extracting natural resources from host countries through methods that contain costs but compromise safety.
- Limit workers' wages.
- Erode traditional cultures and national differences, leaving in their place a homogenized world culture dominated by consumer-oriented values.
- Widen the gap between rich and poor countries.
- Increase the wealth of local elites at the expense of the poor.
- Support and rationalize repressive regimes in the name of stability and order.
- Challenge national sovereignty and jeopardize the autonomy of the states.

citizens to humanitarian aid agencies such as CARE. Although some $11.1 billion a year is funneled to Global South countries through charities, official developmental assistance dwarfs private giving, even though in most donor countries charitable gifts are income tax write-offs (*Economist*, March 4, 2006: 96).

Recently, some Global South leaders have criticized the various conditions that donors attach to foreign aid, calling the practice an instrument of neocolonialism imposed by the International Monetary Fund and other multilateral economic institutions. They have joined the chorus of developmental economists who advocate increases in **foreign direct investment (FDI)**. Of course, this strategy for economic growth is criticized by those who question whether the investment of capital by multinational corporations (and, to a lesser extent, private investors) into local or domestic business ventures is really a financial remedy. The strategy has always been controversial, because there are many hidden costs, or **externalities**, associated with permitting corporations controlled from abroad to set up business within the host state for the purpose of making a profit. What share of the benefits will foreign investors and host countries get from the investments that are made? Considerable risks are entailed, as are a number of trade-offs among competing values (see CONTROVERSY: Multinational Corporations in the Global South: Do They Help or Hurt?).

foreign direct investment (FDI) an investment in a country involving a long-term relationship and control of an enterprise by nonresidents and including equity capital, reinvestment of earnings, other long-term capital, and short-term capital as shown in balance of payments accounts.

externalities the unintended side effects of choices that reduce the true value of the original decision.

Vigorous debates about these trade-offs have erupted in the last few years over foreign investment in Global South agriculture. Various governments have purchased or leased poor countries' farmland, where they grow crops to ship home, thus bypassing the need to buy food on the world market. Since 2006, the amount of farmland involved in these deals has roughly equaled the size of the combined acreage of France's agricultural land, an area worth about $30 billion (*Economist*, May 23, 2009: 61). Whereas foreign investment in farming previously tended to involve private investors acquiring land from private owners, most of these transactions involve government buyers and sellers. Angola, Cameroon, Kenya, Mali, Tanzania, and other states that have participated in these arrangements assert that they earn revenue from the lease or sale and benefit from the introduction of new agricultural technology into their countries. Critics retort that the land often is not state-owned property, the investors rarely pay its true cost, and the revenues benefit government officials rather than the local population.

The primary dangers with activities of this type are their potential to erode the host government's capacity to regulate its economy, and the possibility that foreign business interests will not reinvest their profits locally but channel them abroad for new investments or disburse them as dividends for their shareholders. However, despite the risks, many developing countries have relaxed restrictions in order to attract foreign investors, with emphasis placed less on liberalizing investment restrictions and encouraging open domestic economic competition than on offering tax and cash enticements and opportunities for joint ventures. This has stimulated a recent surge in the inflow of FDI to the Global South, reaching over $620 billion in 2008. Due to the global recession, FDI inflows dropped 31 percent the following year, but they are projected to increase gradually (see Figure 5.2).

The prospects for either foreign aid or for foreign direct investments to contribute to the future development of, and relief of poverty in, the Global South will depend on a number of other factors. Foremost is the extent to which the staggering level of debt facing many Global South countries can be

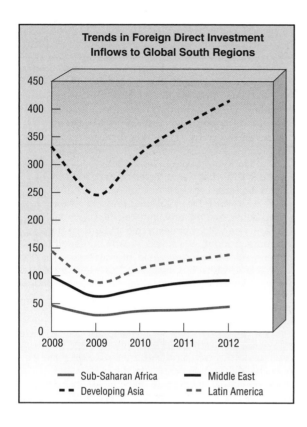

FIGURE 5.2 Trends in Foreign Direct Investment Inflows to Global South Regions

The amount of FDI inflows to the Global South vary by region, with Sub-Saharan countries receiving the lowest volume and Asian countries the highest. Inflows declined significantly in every region between 2008 and 2009. Economic forecasts through 2012 project upswings, especially in Asia.

SOURCES: *World Investment Report* (2010); Economist Intelligence Unit (2010).

managed (see APPLICATION: Development, Democracy, and Debt). The International Monetary Fund (2010: 30, 36) estimates that Global South debt now exceeds $5,054 billion and that its debt-service payments are equivalent to over 25 percent of their gross domestic product. Most developmental economists see this situation as unsustainable and threatening to future growth. Worse off are the forty **Heavily Indebted Poor Countries (HIPCs)** that are eligible or potentially eligible for relief through debt rescheduling or cancellation under a joint program of the International Monetary Fund and the World Bank. The financial dilemmas faced by Zambia illustrate the problem. According to the World Bank, Zambia began the new millennium with $5.2 billion in public external debt (net present value), which was roughly equivalent to 60 percent of its GDP and 500 percent of Zambia's exports of goods and nonfactor services. Merely servicing this debt (paying the interest and principal) amounted to 24.5 percent of the central government's revenues. Obviously, such a staggering amount of debt poses an enormous constraint on the government's ability to improve the quality of life of the 68 percent of its citizens who live in poverty.

Heavily Indebted Poor Countries (HIPCs) the subset of countries identified by the World Bank's Debtor Reporting System whose ratios of government debt to gross national product are so substantial that they cannot meet their payment obligations without experiencing political instability and economic collapse.

APPLICATION   Development, Democracy, and Debt

What determines whether a country is able to make the transition from authoritarian to democratic government? Benazir Bhutto, who twice served as the prime minister of Pakistan (1988–1990; 1993–1996) before her assassination in December 2007, gave considerable thought to this question. She wrote fondly in her autobiography about the time that she devoted to studying Locke, Mill, and other democratic theorists during her university years (Bhutto, 1988). As the following passage describes, once in office she tried to apply what she studied but found herself constrained by the country's debt and pressures from international financial institutions to cut spending on programs that she saw as the foundation for building democracy in Pakistan.

> Democracy cannot be sustained around the world in the absence of a stable and growing middle class. Huge economic disparities between social classes in a society strain national unity, creating a gap between the rich and the poor.
>
> … But how can a nation build a middle class? The first step is to build an education system that allows children to rise to a higher social and economic status than their parents—in other words, an educational system that delivers hope and real opportunity is a prerequisite for democracy. Good public educational opportunity is the key to the economic and political progress of nations… .
>
> As prime minister, I attempted to put as much funding into the social sector and education as I could. Overburdened with the debts run up by

[the previous] dictatorship, my government still built almost fifty thousand elementary and secondary schools around the country, and especially in the rural areas. I wish our debts had been rescheduled so we could have done more. The fundamental constraint upon my government in prioritizing our budget was the enormous percent of our GNP that was directed to debt repayment and defense.

> … I was under enormous pressure—from the public, the military, and key international players—all of whom expected a chunk of the federal budget, which was already burdened by debt. All this occurred while international financial institutions, including the International Monetary Fund, were pressing me to cut national expenditure to reduce the budget deficit. This undermined my ability to govern effectively (Bhutto, 2008: 284–286).

Making the transition from authoritarian to democratic rule is difficult. Since Aristotle, political philosophers have linked democracy to the presence of a vibrant, influential middle class. Experts disagree about what factors are necessary for democracy-building, but many concur that when a country's middle class is "small, weak, or politically dependent on authoritarian elements in society…, democratic development is less likely" (Handelman, 2009: 41). However, finding the funds for programs that can promote democratic development in a country saddled with debt can frustrate even the most energetic political leader.

---

structural adjustment reforms aimed at reducing the role of the state while increasing the role of the market in Global South countries' economies.

Washington consensus the view that Global South countries can best achieve sustained economic growth through democratic governance, fiscal discipline, free markets, a reliance on private enterprise, and trade liberalization.

Debt relief—slashing the amount owed by Zambia and the other heavily indebted poor countries—is reflective of the changing attitudes toward the Global South by the great powers and multilateral institutions. The World Bank's "Enhanced HIPC Initiative" and the International Monetary Fund's "Enhanced **Structural Adjustment** Facility," are the primary products of this attempt to reduce the widening disparities between the Global North and Global South. As of 2010, debt reduction packages that provide $51 billion of relief had been approved for Zambia and 34 other countries. Whether these programs will succeed in the long run, argue their sponsors, will depend on the degree to which developing countries can undertake often painful liberalizing political and economic reforms (see Kim and Wolfensohn, 1999). This argument embodies what is known as the "**Washington consensus**," the view held by numerous U.S. government, World Bank, and IMF officials (all headquartered in Washington, D.C.)

that balanced government budgets, the privatization of state-owned enterprises, the reduction of barriers to trade and foreign investment, and the elimination of subsidies to domestic producers are prerequisites for economic growth.

Yet these reforms may not be as successful as their advocates claim. On the one hand, China and Singapore have enjoyed rapid economic growth without undertaking significant political liberalization. On the other hand, many Global South countries that have implemented economic liberalizing reforms have not experienced growth (Vreeland, 2003). The September 2008 collapse of Lehman Brothers Holdings, Inc., America's fourth-largest financial-services firm, together with the demise of the investment bank Bear Stearns, the Federal Reserve bailout of insurance giant AIG, and the government seizures of the Federal National Mortgage Association (Fannie Mae) and the Federal Home Loan Mortgage Corporation (Freddie Mac), revealed the fragility of America's financial industry and eroded the mystique of the Washington consensus. Many Global South leaders began looking for an alternative economic development model. China's resilience during the global recession that followed in the wake of the Lehman Brothers bankruptcy led some of them to talk about a "Beijing consensus." While defined in different ways by different people, it is generally thought of as a pragmatic process of experimentation and innovation characterized by high levels of state involvement in economic management. Whether this constitutes a model for others to emulate, avers Leo Horn-Phathanothai (2010) of the United Nations Development Programme, is unclear. Given China's unique culture, history, and size, its developmental experience may not be replicable.

Any developmental strategy that ignores the sociocultural contexts of the countries where they are applied is likely to yield disappointing results. Indeed, some of the most successful programs have taken a local, grassroots approach to development. **Microfinance**, pioneered by Bangladeshi economist Muhammad Yunus through his Grameen Bank, has helped many people climb out of poverty. It entails loaning as little as a hundred dollars to poor, budding entrepreneurs who lack the incomes or collateral typically required of borrowers. Rural women, who tend to be ignored by lending institutions when they seek credit to start small businesses, have been major beneficiaries of these community-based programs. Although most microfinance institutions focus on lending, some have expanded their services to include savings, agreeing to handle small deposits at low transaction costs.

microfinance providing small loans to poor entrepreneurs, usually to help start or expand a small business.

In summary, an unqualified free-market approach to development that minimizes the role of the state may not be sufficient by itself to create rapid economic growth. Other factors, such as fair, effective systems of property and regulatory law, and honest, responsive political institutions, are needed to augment trade openness. Moreover, under certain circumstances, a stronger role for the state is advantageous, especially in providing a safety net for the most vulnerable members of society and in addressing distributional inequities related to ethnicity, gender, or geographic region. Given the diversity of the Global South, development strategies for the future should avoid grandiose claims of universality and one-size-fits-all policies. What works in one country may be impractical or undesirable in another (Cohn, 2005: 399, 427–429).

Karen Kasmauski/Getty Images

A Beneficiary of Microfinance A Bangladeshi woman uses a sewing machine that she purchased with a loan from the Grameen Bank. Her daughters watch as she operates her small business.

THE NEW MIDDLE CLASS
AND THE FUTURE OF THE GLOBAL SOUTH

It is useful to remember the historic trends underlying the problems faced by the countries of the Global South. Most were colonized by people of another race, experienced varying degrees of poverty, and felt powerless in a world system dominated by the affluent countries that once controlled them and perhaps still do. Considerable change occurred as post–World War II decolonization proceeded but much also remained the same.

According to the World Bank, 1.4 billion people endure extreme poverty, defined as living on less than $1.25 a day at purchasing power parity. Sub-Saharan Africa has the highest proportion of very poor people within any region of the Global South, containing just under 51 percent living in extreme poverty. Fortunately, the amount of extreme poverty has been declining throughout the Global South for the past two decades and is expected to fall to 900 million by 2015 (WDI, 2010: 4, 91). Global East countries have experienced the most dramatic decreases, with the percentage of very poor people in China dropping from 60.2 percent to 15.9 percent between 1990 and 2005.

Declines in poverty across the Global South have been accompanied by the emergence of a new middle class. Consisting of approximately 2.5 billion people who retain about one-third of their incomes for discretionary spending after paying for food and housing, their numbers are expected to double by 2030. Members of this group come from a variety of backgrounds and occupations; nevertheless, they share certain attitudes and behaviors. In general, they are committed to educating the next generation, supportive of increased government accountability, and inclined toward entrepreneurship (*Economist*, February 14, 2009: 6–7, 12–17). Confident about their prospects yet vulnerable to a prolonged global downturn, it is difficult to foresee how they would respond if their expectations are frustrated. Barring an acute economic crisis that pushes the lower tier of the new middle class back into poverty, their consumption patterns over the next two decades will very likely transform the way we think about the Global South. Preliminary evidence indicates that cycles of output, consumption, and investment within Global South countries have begun to decouple from business cycles in the Global North (Kose, Otrok, and Prasad, 2008).

As poverty rates change, the relationships between the world's developed and developing countries will no doubt continue to change, but exactly how remains uncertain. Although the fate of the Global South remains to be determined, it is clear that, for the time being, the choices of the great powers will strongly influence its future. That influence is often funneled through international organizations like the United Nations and the World Bank, which the great powers have created. To fully understand world politics, we need to inspect the roles played by these intergovernmental organizations, or IGOs, as actors in the global arena. And to complete the picture, we also need to examine nongovernmental organizations, or NGOs, whose roles are important as well. We turn to these nonstate actors in Chapter 6.

CHAPTER SUMMARY

- The term *Global South* refers to the world's poorer, economically less-developed countries, most of which lie along the equator or in the Southern Hemisphere and were once colonies of other states. Significant inequalities exist between these countries and those industrialized states that comprise the Global North. Whereas the Global South contains 84 percent of the world's population, it commands less than 30 percent of its wealth.

- Considerable diversity exists among Global South countries: some are big, others are small; some possess vast quantities of oil and natural gas; others lack significant natural resources; some have subsistence economies, others export manufactured goods; some are democracies, others are autocracies. Despite these and other differences, most Global South countries share a set of common problems related to their poverty and vulnerability.

- Between the fifteenth and twentieth centuries, two waves of European imperialism resulted in the colonization of the Global South. Decolonization began in earnest after World War II and is now complete. For the most part, it was not only extraordinarily rapid but also remarkably peaceful. Still, the vestiges of colonialism remain, and they have important consequences for the shape of the global future.

- Although the debate over how to eliminate the disparities between the Global North and South focuses on the economic development of impoverished countries, these issues are intensely political. They derive from the struggle by those at the bottom of the international hierarchy to improve their position in the global pecking order.

- The development process is complex because the problems faced by the Global South are characterized by a series of intertwined vicious circles, none of which seems capable of being broken without addressing the others.

- Classical economic development theory claims that the causes of underdevelopment are internal. Among the factors it identifies are low rates of productivity, a lack of sufficient investment capital, and inadequate communication and transportation systems.

- Dependency theory holds that the causes of underdevelopment are external. Less-developed countries are vulnerable to penetration by outside forces. According to dependency theory, the Global South has been exploited by wealthier, more powerful members of the world capitalist system.

- Global South states have tried various strategies to overcome their weakness and insecurity. To cope with the threat of separatist movements, many of them have sought to acquire modern weaponry, even if that meant sacrificing funds for health, education, and welfare programs. To promote economic growth, many have tried to forge regional free-trade groups, encourage foreign direct investment, and seek relief from staggering levels of debt.

KEY TERMS

barter
colonialism
decolonization
dependency theory
dependent development
development
dualism
export-led industrialization
externalities
failed states

First World
foreign direct investment (FDI)
Global East
Global North
Global South
Group of 77 (G-77)
Heavily Indebted Poor Countries (HIPCs)
import-substitution industrialization

laissez-faire economics
least-developed countries (LDCs)
mercantilism
microfinance
modernization
multinational corporations (MNCs)
New International Economic Order (NIEO)

newly industrialized countries (NICs)

nonalignment

official development assistance (ODA)

purchasing power parity (PPP)

remittances

Second World

self-determination

sphere of influence

structural adjustment

Third World

Washington consensus

SUGGESTED READINGS

Cohen, Jessica, and William Easterly (eds.). *What Works in Development?* Washington, DC: Brookings, 2009.

Collier, Paul. *The Bottom Billion*. New York: Oxford University Press, 2007.

Goldin, Ian, and Kenneth Reinert. *Globalization for Development*. London: Palgrave Macmillan, 2006.

Seddon, David. *Theories of Development*. New York: Routledge, 2009.

Yunus, Muhammad. *Creating a World Without Poverty*. New York: Public Affairs, 2008.

CRITICAL THINKING QUESTIONS

Recently, large deposits of petroleum were found in Ghana. Based on current estimates, the country could earn at least $1 billion a year through 2029 from its newly discovered oil reserves, which would add more than 25 percent to government revenues (Perry, 2010: 6). Whereas some observers see this as a boon, others remain skeptical that this small West African land will benefit from a flourishing extractive industry. Pointing to the conflict and corruption associated with oil in Nigeria and diamonds in Sierra Leone, they fear that the discovery of abundant natural resources can flood poor countries in a sea of trouble.

Are large endowments of petroleum, natural gas, gold, diamonds, or other valuable natural resources a blessing or a potential source of trouble? According to what has been called the "resource curse," resource-abundant countries often grow more slowly than less well-endowed countries. Although the harmful effects of export booms in oil and minerals can be counteracted in various ways, such as setting aside some revenue in a "rainy day" fund for future use, sharp increases in the returns from the sale of these commodities can breed inflation and an appreciation in the domestic currency. With a stronger currency, imported goods become cheaper and possibly less expensive than products produced domestically, which makes the agricultural and manufacturing sectors of the economy less competitive on the world market and thus less profitable. Under these conditions, foreign investment tends to go into oilfields and mines, which employ few unskilled people and yield cash windfalls that are concentrated in the hands of a few powerful individuals, who can use these revenues to ease social pressures that might otherwise lead to demands for economic diversification, political accountability, and higher levels of education (M. Ross, 2001; Friedman, 2006).

(Continued)

Beyond the economic impacts of windfall profits from natural resources, are there significant political impacts? If a country lacks well-established, transparent governmental institutions and it suddenly becomes flush with cash due to skyrocketing prices for its resources (or the discovery of valuable resources within its borders), will the political system be skewed in an authoritarian direction? Can civil liberties and political freedoms be jeopardized by a sudden influx of wealth from oil or mineral exports? If so, what causal processes do you think impede democracy?

Nonstate Actors and the Challenge of Global Governance

A novel redistribution of power among states, markets, and civil society is underway, ending the steady accumulation of power in the hands of states that began with the Peace of Westphalia in 1648.

JESSICA T. MATHEWS
PRESIDENT OF THE CARNEGIE ENDOWMENT FOR INTERNATIONAL PEACE

On July 12, 2006, guerrillas from Lebanon's Islamist movement, Hezbollah, ambushed an Israeli army patrol along the border, killing several soldiers and taking two hostages. When the Israelis pursued them in an unsuccessful rescue attempt, they lost several more soldiers. Coming on the heels of the abduction of an Israeli corporal by Hamas, the primary Islamist group in the Palestinian territories, the incident prompted Israeli Prime Minister Ehud Olmert to order ferocious artillery and air assaults against suspected Hezbollah strongholds in Beirut and southern Lebanon, an action some of his military advisors had been long advocating. According to Israeli Defense Minister Amir Peretz, the goal was for this to end with Hezbollah "so badly beaten that not a man in it does not regret having launched the incident" (*Time*, July 24, 2006: 28).

As the Israelis blockaded Lebanon and pummeled its transportation infrastructure in hopes of isolating Hezbollah militants, Hezbollah retaliated by firing salvos of Katyusha rockets into northern Israel, paralyzing Haifa, the country's third-largest city and one of its busiest ports. "Our homes will not be the only one's destroyed," declared Hezbollah leader Sheikh Hassan Nasrallah. "You don't know who you're fighting" (*Newsweek*, July 24, 2006: 24).

Hezbollah (or the "Party of God") was formed in 1982 after Israel invaded Lebanon to drive out the Palestinian Liberation Organization (PLO), which had been using Lebanon as a base for harassing northern Israeli settlements with small arms and mortar fire. An extremist Shiite Muslim organization with close ties to Iran, Hezbollah's members have been blamed for the 1983 bombing of the U.S. Marine barracks in Beirut, the 1985 hijacking of TWA Flight 847, and numerous kidnappings. Operating within a weak and fractious nation-state, Hezbollah has had virtually free reign over parts of Lebanon.

During the 1990s, Hezbollah evolved beyond a simple paramilitary organization, developing extensive social welfare programs, which included operating several schools and health clinics within the Shiite parts of Lebanon. It also began participating in Lebanese elections, winning 14 seats of 128 parliamentary seats in 2005. Despite these changes, Hezbollah continued to view Israel as an illegal entity and vowed to pressure the Israelis into releasing imprisoned Lebanese and withdrawing from the disputed Shebaa region.

Israel's foremost concern about Hezbollah centered on its growing arsenal of Iranian-supplied weaponry. While the inaccurate Katyusha rocket has a range of between 10 and 20 miles, the Israelis worried that Iran had provided Hezbollah with an unknown quantity of more sophisticated missiles, which could target all of Israel's population centers with warheads capable of carrying chemical or biological agents. Their anxiety increased a few days into the conflict when a C–802 radar-guided missile disabled an Israeli warship off the coast of Lebanon. Fearing that Hezbollah might also possess the longer-range Zelzal-2 missile, the Israelis continued pounding Lebanon despite calls from UN Secretary-General Kofi Annan for a cease-fire. Hezbollah, in turn, maintained its constant barrage against northern Israel. As the grim toll of civilian casualties mounted on both sides,

Lebanese Prime Minister Fouad Siniora lamented that his country was being torn to shreds.

Over the ensuing weeks, three contending explanations for why Hezbollah initiated hostilities circulated among journalists, diplomats, and world leaders. The first claimed that the July 12 attack was a miscalculation: Hezbollah had undertaken similar cross-border raids in recent years without triggering a major Israeli response, so its commanders presumably thought they could do it again with impunity. The second argued that it was a diversion: Iran, which had trained and supplied Hezbollah, allegedly encouraged the attack to draw international attention away from its budding nuclear weapons program. Finally, the third explanation proposed that the attack was a provocation: After Israel ended its occupation of southern Lebanon in 2000, Hezbollah fortified the area and acquired thousands of short- and medium-range rockets. With the United States bogged down in Iraq and the Israelis preoccupied with unrest in the Palestinian territories, Hezbollah's leadership may have concluded that Israel was vulnerable; bold action would allow Hezbollah to demonstrate its military prowess to the Arab world while dealing Israel a crippling blow.

Although long-time observers of the Middle East disagree over what weight to give any of these explanations, they concur that the political dynamics of the region involve more than the interactions of nation-states. Any analysis that concentrated on Israel, Lebanon, Iran, and other states to the neglect of Hezbollah, Hamas, the PLO, and other nonstate actors would be woefully incomplete. Nonstate entities ranging from global and regional intergovernmental organizations (IGOs) to ethnic and religious nongovernmental organizations (NGOs) are important actors that must be taken into account when examining world politics. Indeed, as the Lebanese conflict demonstrates, it would be impossible to make sense of contemporary international affairs without devoting attention to them. In view of their importance, the aims of this chapter are to describe the various types of nonstate actors and to explain when and how they exert their influence.

TYPES OF NONSTATE ACTORS

The history of world politics for the past 350 years has largely been a chronicle of interactions among sovereign, territorial states. Today, however, world affairs are also being shaped by organizations that transcend national boundaries. In addition to the United Nations and regional bodies such as the European Union, the course of world affairs is affected by groups of people who band together for ethnic, religious, or other reasons. Diverse in scope and purpose, these nonstate actors push their own agendas and increasingly exert international influence.

There are two principal types of nonstate actors: **intergovernmental organizations (IGOs)**, whose members are states, and **nongovernmental organizations (NGOs)**, whose members are private individuals and groups. The Union of International Organizations, which maintains comprehensive, up-to-date information on these organizations, records that their numbers increased sharply during the

intergovernmental organizations (IGOs) institutions created and joined by states' governments, which give them authority to make collective decisions to manage particular problem(s) on the global agenda.

nongovernmental organizations (NGOs) transnational organizations of private citizens that include foundations, professional associations, multinational corporations, or groups in different countries joined together to work toward common interests.

T A B L E 6.1   A Simple Classification of Intergovernmental Organizations (IGOs)

Geographic Scope of Membership	Range of Stated Purpose	
	Multiple Purposes	**Single Purpose**
Global	United Nations	World Health Organization
	World Trade Organization	International Labor Organization
	UNESCO	International Monetary Fund
	Organization of the Islamic Conference	Universal Postal Union
Interregional, regional, subregional	European Union	European Space Agency
	Organization for Security and Cooperation in Europe	Nordic Council
	Organization of American States	North Atlantic Treaty Organization
	Organization of African Unity	International Olive Oil Council
	League of Arab States	International North Pacific Coffee Organization
	Association of Southeast Asian Nations	African Groundnut Council

nineteenth century, as international commerce and communications grew alongside industrialization. In 1909, there were 37 IGOs and 176 NGOs. According to data collected by the Union of International Associations, by 1960 there were 154 IGOs and 1,255 NGOs, and by 2009, these numbers had risen to 240 and 7,628, though some analysts using other measures and data sources place the current number of NGOs significantly higher (see *Yearbook of International Organizations*, 2008–2009).

IGOs are created by states to solve shared problems. As shown in Table 6.1, they vary widely in size and purpose. The North Atlantic Treaty Organization (NATO), for example, is primarily a military alliance, while others, such as the Organization of American States (OAS), promote economic development. Most IGOs concentrate their activities on specific economic or social issues of special concern to them, such as the management of trade, or of transportation.

NGOs also differ widely. They span virtually every facet of political, social, and economic activity, including science, health care, culture, theology, law, security, and defense. As organizations that are independent of governments, NGOs link people from different societies in transnational networks in order to advocate specific policies. For this purpose, many NGOs interact formally with IGOs. More than 1,000 NGOs actively consult with various agencies of the extensive UN system, maintain offices in hundreds of cities, and hold parallel conferences with IGO meetings to which states send representatives. Such partnerships between NGOs and IGOs enable both types of organizations to work (and lobby) together in pursuit of common policies and programs.

In this chapter, we will begin our analysis of nonstate actors by discussing some prominent and representative IGOs, including the United Nations (UN) and the European Union (EU). Next, we will turn our attention to NGOs, examining the impact of ethnopolitical groups, religious movements, multi-national corporations and transnational banks, and issue-advocacy groups. Finally, we will ask whether the activities of nonstate actors are undermining the position of the nation-state in world politics.

GLOBAL INTERGOVERNMENTAL ORGANIZATIONS

The United Nations

The United Nations is the best-known global organization. What distinguishes it from most other IGOs is its nearly universal membership, including today 192 independent states from every region of the world (see Figure 6.1). The UN's nearly fourfold growth from the fifty-one states that joined it in 1945 has

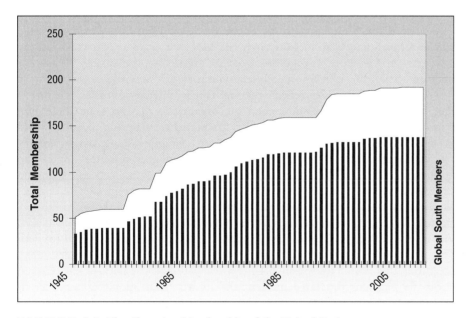

FIGURE 6.1 The Changing Membership of the United Nations

The UN's membership has seen episodic bursts of growth from 51 states in 1945 to 192 in 2010. Over its history, the United Nations has added countries as they became independent from colonial control. This shift has influenced the kinds of issues the UN has confronted, expanding the global agenda to include priorities important to the developing states in the Global South.

SOURCE: United Nations.

been spectacular, but the admission process has from the start been governed by political conflicts that show the extent to which the organization reflects the relationships of the five great powers that shape its direction through their veto authority in the Security Council.

Purposes and Agenda.   In addition to possessing nearly universal membership, the UN is also a multipurpose organization. As Article 1 of the UN Charter states, its objectives are to:

- Maintain international peace and security

- Develop friendly relations among nations based on respect for the principle of equal rights and self determination of peoples

- Achieve international cooperation in solving international problems of an economic, social, cultural, or humanitarian character and in promoting and encouraging respect for human rights and for fundamental freedoms for all

- Function as a center for harmonizing the actions of nations in the attainment of these common ends

Peace and security figured prominently in the thinking of those responsible for creating the United Nations at the end of the Second World War to replace the League of Nations. However, the ambitions that the UN's founders had in the security realm were soon frustrated by the Cold War between the United States and the Soviet Union. Although the UN was unable to make headway on security issues, work toward the goal of improving the quality of life for humanity carried the UN into nearly every corner of the world.

The history of the UN reflects the fact that both rich countries and developing countries have successfully used the organization to promote their own foreign policy objectives, and this record has bred hopes throughout the world that the UN will be able to manage an ever-changing and growing agenda. However, ambitions for the UN may exceed its meager resources. Since the end of the Cold War, the organization has been asked to address an expanding set of global problems, including AIDS, economic development, climate change, energy shortages, dwindling fresh water supplies, human rights abuses, and internationally organized crime. In response to the demands that have been placed upon it, the United Nations has developed an administrative structure with offices not only in the UN headquarters in New York but also in centers spread throughout the world (see Map 6.1). To evaluate the capacity of the United Nations to shoulder the huge burdens that it has been asked to carry, let us examine how it is organized.

Organizational Structure.   The UN's limitations are perhaps rooted in the ways it is organized for its wide-ranging purposes. According to the Charter, the UN structure contains the following six principal organs:

- *General Assembly*. Established as the main deliberative body of the United Nations, all members are equally represented according to a

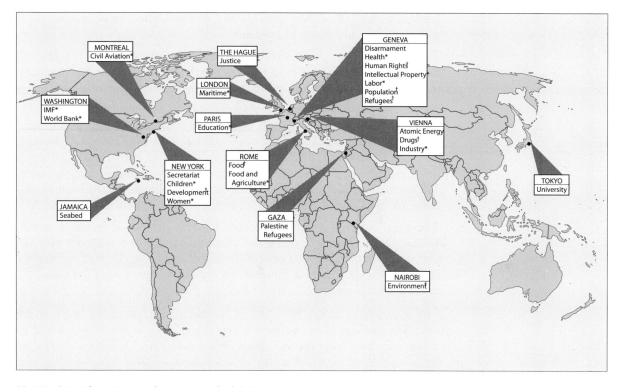

MAP 6.1 The UN's Headquarters and Global Network

The United Nations has sought, since its creation, to address the continuously expanding problems on the global agenda. As shown in this map, the United Nations has spread its administrative arm to every corner of the globe to fulfill its primary purpose of spearheading international cooperation.

* Specialized agencies.

† Funds and programs.

SOURCE: *The UN Handbook.*

one-state/one-vote formula. Decisions are reached by a simple majority vote, except on so-called "important questions," which require a two-thirds majority. The resolutions it passes, however, are only recommendations.

- *Security Council.* Given primary responsibility by the Charter for dealing with threats to international peace and security, the Security Council consists of five permanent members with the power to veto substantive decisions (the United States, the United Kingdom, France, Russia, and the People's Republic of China), and ten nonpermanent members elected by the General Assembly for staggered two-year terms.

- *Economic and Social Council.* Responsible for coordinating the UN's social and economic programs, functional commissions, and specialized agencies, its 54 members are elected by the General Assembly for staggered three-year terms. This body has been particularly active by addressing economic development and human rights issues.

- *Trusteeship Council.* Charged with supervising the administration of territories that had not achieved self-rule, the Trusteeship Council suspended operation in 1994, when the last remaining trust territory gained independence.

- *International Court of Justice.* The principal judicial organ of the United Nations, the International Court of Justice is composed of fifteen independent judges who are elected for nine-year terms by the General Assembly and Security Council. The competence of the Court is restricted to disputes between states, and its jurisdiction is based on the consent of the disputants. The Court may also give nonbinding advisory opinions on legal questions raised by the General Assembly, Security Council, or other UN agencies.

- *Secretariat.* Led by the secretary-general (currently, Ban Kai-moon of South Korea), the Secretariat contains the international civil servants who perform the administrative and secretarial functions of the UN. The staff numbers over 8,000 under the core budget, and almost as many people working under special funding.

The founders of the UN expected the Security Council to become the organization's primary body, because it was designed to maintain peace and its permanent members were the victorious great powers who had been allied during the Second World War. With the onset of the Cold War, however, frequent use of the veto power—initially by the Soviet Union and later by the United States—prevented the Council from acting on many security problems, with the result that the General Assembly gradually assumed wider responsibilities.

Beyond the six principal organs, the UN system also contains numerous programs and funds, research and training institutes, and functional and regional commissions (see Figure 6.2). In addition, it is affiliated with a host of autonomous specialized agencies that have their own charters, budgets, and staffs. They include the World Health Organization (WHO), the International Labor Organization (ILO), and the UN Educational, Scientific, and Cultural Organization (UNESCO).

The United Nations has changed in many ways not envisioned by its founders, evolving into an extraordinarily complex network of overlapping institutions, some of which (the UN Children's Fund or the United Nations University, for example) fulfill their mission in part through NGOs. The UN has also increasingly come to rely on the many NGOs that are not under its formal authority. This collaboration blurs the line between governmental and nongovernmental functions, but UN–NGO cooperation helps the UN's mission. In the process, the UN has become not one organization but a decentralized conglomerate of countless committees, bureaus, boards, commissions, centers, institutes, offices, and agencies scattered around the globe, with each of its many specialized activities managed from offices in various cities.

Many of the UN's changes have come in response to concerns voiced by Global South countries, who seized the advantage of their growing numbers

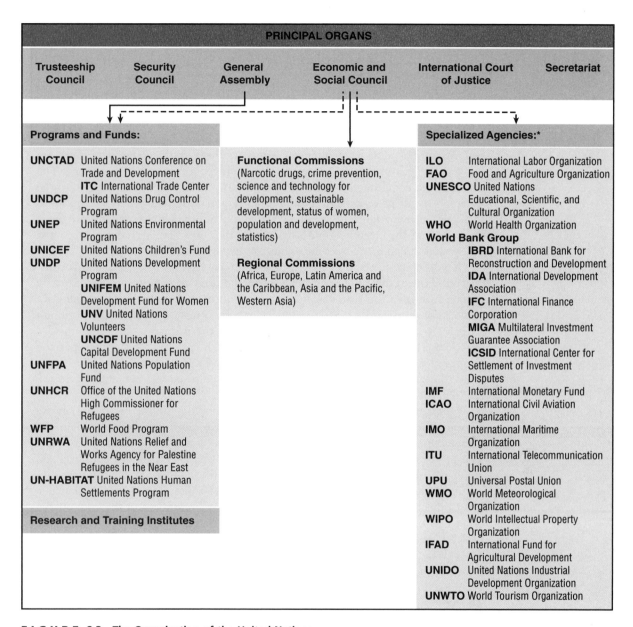

FIGURE 6.2 The Organization of the United Nations

NOTE: Solid lines from the principal organs indicate a direct reporting relationship; --- dashed lines indicate a nonsubsidiary relationship.

*Specialized agencies are autonomous organizations working with the UN through the coordination of the Economic and Social Council.

SOURCE: Abridged organizational chart from the United Nations Department of Public Information.

under the one-state/one-vote rules of the General Assembly to push the UN in new directions. Today, a coalition of Global South countries comprised of three-fourths of the UN membership and led by the Group of 77 attempt to steer the organization's programs toward the needs of its poorer members.

North–South differences over perceived priorities are most clearly exhibited in the heated debate over the UN's budget. This controversy centers on how members should interpret the organization's charter, which states that "expenses of the Organization shall be borne by the members as apportioned by the General Assembly." The UN budget consists of three distinct elements: the core budget, the peacekeeping budget, and the budget for voluntary programs. The core budget covering the years 2010 and 2011 is $5.16 billion, with the total spending by all UN agencies, peacekeeping operations, and programs and funds totaling approximately $13.9 billion. States contribute to the voluntary programs and some of the peacekeeping activities as they see fit. The core budget and other peacekeeping activities are subject to assessments.

The precise mechanism by which assessments have been determined is complicated, but, historically, assessments were allocated according to states' capacity to pay. Although this formula is under attack in many wealthy states, it still governs. Thus, the United States, which has the greatest resources, contributes 22 percent of the core UN budget (and is also the primary contributor to UN peacekeeping and voluntary programs), whereas the poorest 54 members pay the minimum (0.001 percent) and contribute only $24,363 annually. By this agreement, the richest 28 percent of states were assessed to pay 97 percent toward the last biennial UN budget.

Resistance to this budgetary formula for funding UN activities has always existed. But it has grown progressively worse, in large part because when the General Assembly apportions expenses, it does so according to majority rule. The problem is that those with the most votes (the Global South countries) do not have the money, and the most prosperous (the Global North countries) do not have the votes. Wide disparities have grown so that the ten largest contributors to the UN command only ten votes, but pay 76 percent of the cost. At the other end of the spectrum, the remaining members paid only 24 percent of the UN budget but commanded 182 votes. This deep imbalance has led to many fierce disputes over the kinds of issues on which the UN's attention and resources should be focused. The wealthy members charge that the existing budget procedures institutionalize a system of taxation without fair representation. The critics counter with the argument that the great-power members should bear financial responsibilities commensurate with their wealth and influence.

At issue, of course, is not simply money. Differences in images of what is important and which states should have political influence are the real issues. Poor states argue that needs should determine expenditure levels. Major contributors, sensitive to the amounts asked of them and the purposes to which the funds are put, do not want to pay for programs they oppose. The United States in particular was historically the most vocal about its dissatisfaction, and since 2000 has been in arrears an average of $1.35 billion each year.

In response to persisting cash flow problems and rising complaints about the UN's inefficient administration, efforts were begun in 2005 to consolidate programs, reduce costs, eliminate waste, and reassign administrative responsibilities in order to make the UN more efficient. These massive reforms cut the Secretariat's administrative costs by one-third, from 38 percent of the core budget to 25 percent, and put the savings into a development fund for poor countries. The assessments of some Global North members were also adjusted: The United States in 2008 was paying 22 percent of the core budget, and the four other permanent members of the Security Council were scheduled to pay proportionally less (Britain, 6.6 percent; France, 6.3 percent; China, 2.7 percent; and Russia, 1.2 percent). This formula understandably upsets the other major contributors who pay large sums but are still excluded from Security Council participation as permanent members. Consider Japan, which pays 16.6 percent of the core budget (second only to the United States) while holding fewer key posts in the organization than states paying far less. Frustrated by what it considers an unreasonably high assessment and over a decade of unsuccessful efforts to obtain a permanent seat on the Security Council, Japan has considered cutting its annual contributions to voluntary programs.

Japan's interest in joining the Security Council as a permanent member is shared by several other states, most notably Germany, India, and Brazil. They contend that the current makeup of the council does not reflect the political and economic changes that have occurred in the world since 1945. Opponents of adding new permanent members assert that enlargement would make the council unwieldy. The United States has resisted proposals to expand the Security Council because they would dilute the American influence within the UN, adding that those states campaigning for permanent seats would only be supported by Washington if they agreed not to request the veto power. For now, the great-power victors in World War II hold privileged positions within the organization; however, the debate over enlargement continues as South Africa, Nigeria, and various Middle Eastern states have also called for reforms that would make the Security Council more representative culturally and geographically.

The future of shape and direction of the UN is uncertain. Concerns about the organization have been compounded by a string of scandals, including charges of mismanagement in the 1990s Iraqi "Oil-for-Food" program, sexual abuse of women in the Congo by UN peacekeepers, and inaction until late 2007 in the face of genocide in the Darfur region of Sudan. John Bolton, a former U.S. ambassador to the UN, exemplified those who are frustrated with the organization when he once quipped that if the top ten floors of the UN headquarters building were eliminated, it wouldn't make a difference. Nevertheless, many of the UN's supporters feel optimistic about the organization's reforms to strengthen accountability and management performance. These reforms include protection for "whistle-blowers," an anti-fraud and corruption policy, a unified standard of conduct for peacekeepers, and expanded financial disclosure requirements for senior officials. Still, with less money than the annual budget for New York City's police department, the UN will be challenged to serve the needs of the world's 6.8 billion people.

In the final analysis, the UN can be no more than the mandates and power that the member states give to it. The English poet Alfred Tennyson "dreamed of a parliament of man" and through the United Nations "we have now lived it," observes essayist Charles Krauthammer (2006: 39). Because of what realists would describe as the diverging interests and priorities of the great powers, he adds that the UN "has not worked. It never will." The United Nations may be maligned, but according to liberals it is still needed. The organization has participated in 63 peacekeeping missions since 1948 and currently has deployed roughly 113,000 personnel to trouble spots around the world, a five-fold increase since 1999. Of course, the presence of peacekeepers does not guarantee an end to armed conflict, either within or between states. But according to recent statistical studies of peacekeeping operations (Fortna, 2004; 2008), peacekeepers reduce the probability of renewed fighting by around 60 percent in civil wars and 85 percent in interstate wars. Despite its shortcomings, the evidence suggests that the UN has made a modest though meaningful contribution promoting peace and human security. As former Secretary-General Dag Hammarskjöld is said to have explained: "The purpose of the UN is not to get us to heaven but to save us from hell."

Other Prominent Global IGOs

Beyond the UN, literally hundreds of other IGOs are active internationally. To round out our examples of global IGOs, we look briefly at three of the most significant: the World Trade Organization, the World Bank, and the International Monetary Fund.

The World Trade Organization. Remembering the hardships caused by the Great Depression of 1929, the United States sought to create international economic institutions after World War II that would prevent another depression by facilitating the expansion of world trade. One proposed institution was the International Trade Organization (ITO), first conceived as a specialized agency within the overall framework of the UN. While negotiations for the anticipated ITO were dragging on, many people urged immediate action. Meeting in Geneva in 1947, 23 states agreed to a number of **bilateral** tariff concessions that were written into a final act called the General Agreement on Tariffs and Trade (GATT), which originally was thought of as a temporary arrangement until the ITO came into operation.

When a final agreement on the ITO proved elusive, GATT provided a mechanism for continued multilateral negotiations on reducing tariffs and other barriers to trade. Over the next several decades, eight rounds of negotiations were held to liberalize trade. Under the principle of nondiscrimination, GATT members were to give the same treatment to each other as they gave to their "most favored" trading partners.

On January 1, 1995, GATT was superseded by the World Trade Organization (WTO). Although not exactly the ITO envisaged immediately following World War II, it nevertheless represented the most ambitious undertaking yet

bilateral relationships or agreements between two states.

launched to regulate world trade. Unlike GATT, which functioned more as a coordinating secretariat, the World Trade Organization is a full-fledged intergovernmental organization with a formal decision-making structure at the ministerial level. Mandated to manage trade conflicts among members, the WTO was given authority for enforcing trading rules and adjudicating trade disputes among its 153 members. During the past decade, an average of over twenty disputes per year have been brought to the WTO for resolution.

The present goal of the WTO is to transcend the existing matrix of free-trade agreements between pairs of countries and within particular regions or free-trade blocs, and replace them with an integrated and comprehensive world-wide system of liberal or free trade. This liberal agenda poses a threat to some states. At the heart of their complaint is the charge that the WTO undermines the traditional rule of law that prohibits interference in sovereign states' domestic affairs, including management of economic practices *within* the states' territorial jurisdiction. However, the WTO, it should be kept in mind, developed as a result of agreements states reached to voluntarily surrender some of their sovereign decision-making freedom, under the conviction that this pooling of sovereignty would produce greater gains than losses. Nonetheless, the WTO seems destined to remain a target for criticism because many of its policies are orchestrated by its most powerful members during informal meetings that do not include the full WTO membership.

The World Bank.   Created in July 1944 at the United Nations Monetary and Financial Conference held in Bretton Woods, New Hampshire, attended by 44 countries, the World Bank (or International Bank for Reconstruction and Development) was originally established to support reconstruction efforts in Europe after the Second World War. Over the next decade, the Bank shifted its attention from reconstruction to developmental assistance. Because Global South countries often have difficulty borrowing money to finance projects aimed at promoting economic growth, the Bank offers them loans with lower interest rates and longer repayment plans than they could typically obtain from commercial banks. By 2009, the Bank had provided loans of more than $639 billion, making it the most influential IGO for combating poverty in the Global South.

Administratively, ultimate decision-making authority in the World Bank is vested in a board of governors, consisting of a governor and an alternate appointed by each of the Bank's 185 member countries. A governor customarily is a member country's minister of finance, or an equivalent official. The board meets annually in the Bank's Washington, DC headquarters to set policy directions, and choose delegates responsible for the routine operations of the Bank to the twenty-four directors of its executive board. The five countries with the largest number of shares in the World Bank's capital stock (the United States, Germany, Japan, France, and the United Kingdom) appoint their own executive directors, and the remaining executive directors are either appointed (Saudi Arabia), elected by their states (China, Russia, and Switzerland), or elected by groups of countries. Votes are tallied according to a weighted system that is intended to protect the interests of the great powers that make the most substantial contributions to the World Bank's resources. As a result, the president of the Bank has always been an American, and the United States together with Western Europe possesses majority control over the board of governors.

Over the years, both the self-image and operations of the World Bank have changed—from a strictly financial IGO passing judgment on loan applications to that of a development agency assisting states with planning and training. The World Bank also has promoted democratic governance, by its recent insistence on political reforms as a condition for economic assistance. Additionally, with charges of bribery, kickbacks, and embezzlement being leveled against World Bank projects from road building in Kenya to dam construction in Lesotho, the Bank has insisted on anticorruption reforms as well.

Despite its increased pace of activity, the World Bank has never been able to meet all the needs for financial assistance of the developing states and has been criticized for focusing on middle-income rather than the most impoverished countries. The deficiencies of the World Bank, however, have been partly offset by the establishment of another lending IGO, the International Monetary Fund.

The International Monetary Fund.   Prior to World War II, the international community lacked institutional mechanisms to manage the exchange of money across borders. At the 1944 Bretton Woods Conference, the United States was a prime mover in creating the International Monetary Fund (IMF), a global institution designed to maintain currency-exchange stability by promoting international monetary cooperation and orderly exchange arrangements, and by functioning as a lender of last resort for countries experiencing financial crises.

The IMF is now one of the 16 specialized agencies within the UN system. Each IMF member is represented on its governing board, which meets annually to fix general policy. Day-to-day business is conducted by a twenty-four-member executive board chaired by a managing director, who is also the administrative head of a staff of approximately 2,000 employees.

The operating funds for the IMF come from its 187 member states. Contributions are based on a quota system set according to a state's national income, monetary reserves, and other factors that affect each member's ability to contribute. In this way, the IMF operates like a credit union that requires each participant to contribute to a common pool of funds from which it can borrow when the need arises. The IMF's voting is weighted according to a state's monetary contribution, giving a larger voice to the wealthier states.

The IMF attaches strict conditions to its loans, which has led to considerable criticism. Some people charge that the IMF imposes austerity measures on countries in financial crises, forcing them to cut government spending on social programs when they are most needed. Others complain that the IMF makes political demands regarding democratization and privatization that exceed the institution's original mandate. Many theorists from radical branches of the socialist tradition argue that IMF conditions are tools for weakening domestic groups opposing the spread of international capitalism. Responding to these criticisms, the IMF's director, Dominique Strauss-Kahn, has championed reforms that will allow it to distribute loans

AP Photo/Jose Luis Magana

Protests against Global IGO Policies Both the World Trade Organization and the International Monetary Fund have come under heavy grassroots criticism lately. Protesters at recent meetings of the WTO (left) and IMF (right) expressed outrage at economic policies that they believed adversely affected some countries.

faster with fewer conditions. In addition, he has secured promises of $500 billion from member countries that would triple the institution's lending capacity.

REGIONAL INTERGOVERNMENTAL ORGANIZATIONS

The tug-of-war between states within global IGOs like the UN, WTO, World Bank, and IMF is a reminder that these organizations are run by the states that join them. This severely inhibits the IGOs' ability to rise above interstate competition and pursue their own purposes. Because they cannot act autonomously, global IGOs are often viewed more as instruments of their state members' foreign policies and arenas for debate than as independent nonstate actors.

When certain powerful states dominate global IGOs, the prospects for international cooperation decline because, as realist theorists emphasize, national leaders fear multilateral organizations that may compromise their country's vital interests. Yet, as liberal theorists argue, *regional* cooperation among powerful states is possible, as evidenced by the evolution of the European Union (EU). In many respects, the EU is unique, if for no other reason than that it stands as the world's greatest example of peaceful international cooperation, producing an integrated **security community** with a single economy and a common currency.

security community a group of states whose high level of noninstitutionalized collaboration results in the settlement of disputes by compromise rather than by force.

The European Union

Europe emerged from the Second World War a devastated continent with a demoralized population. Over 35 million Europeans perished during the fighting. Much of the urban landscape was reduced to bomb craters and rubble. Countless buildings were uninhabitable, the transportation infrastructure lay in ruins, and food was scarce. Some Europeans felt that the only way to prevent their countries from squaring off on the battlefield in a generation was through political and economic unification.

The process of European unification began with the creation of the European Coal and Steel Community (ECSC) in 1951. A year earlier, French Foreign Minister Robert Schuman had proposed placing all French and German coal and steel resources under a joint authority, and allowing other European states to take part in the new organization. As part of the ECSC, Germany could revive its heavy industry after the war without alarming its neighbors, who would now possess some degree of control over key German resources by virtue of their representation in the joint authority. Ultimately, France and Germany were joined in the ECSC by Belgium, Luxembourg, the Netherlands, and Italy.

The drive toward further European unity gathered momentum in 1957 with the creation of the European Atomic Energy Community (Euratom), patterned after the ECSC, and the European Economic Community (EEC), a fledgling common market that provides for the free movement of goods, people, and capital among member states. These three communities were collectively recognized in the 1992 Maastricht Treaty as the first "pillar" of the EU structure. Two additional pillars have since been under construction: a Common Foreign and Security Policy pillar and a Justice and Homeland Affairs pillar. The former is an attempt to create a single European foreign and defense policy; the latter, common policies on immigration and criminal justice.

During this process of regional institution-building, membership grew in a series of waves to encompass twenty-seven countries by 2010: Belgium, France, Germany, Italy, Luxembourg, and the Netherlands (the original "six"); Denmark, Ireland, and the United Kingdom (which joined in 1973); Greece (1981); Portugal and Spain (1986); Austria, Finland, and Sweden (1995); Poland, the Czech Republic, Slovakia, Hungary, Slovenia, Latvia, Lithuania, Estonia, Malta, and Cyprus (2004); and Bulgaria and Romania (2007). These sequential enlargements have created the world's biggest free-trade bloc, with over half a billion citizens and an economy that exceeds $16 trillion.

Further expansion is also conceivable, with Iceland applying for membership in 2009, the procedures for possible membership currently underway for Croatia and Turkey, and with various political leaders from countries in the western Balkans expressing interest in future membership. Expansion remains controversial, however. In particular, the prospect of a populous Muslim Turkey joining the EU raises fundamental questions about Europe's identity. As constructivists point out, identities shape how agents envision their interests and, in turn, how they act. The possible entry of Turkey and perhaps countries even farther afield would have major implications for the way many people, especially within the six western founders of the EU, conceive of Europe. Nevertheless, the idea of a single, integrated Europe is compelling for those who are haunted by the specter of European nationalities and states that have been fighting each other ever since the Pax Romana collapsed 1,800 years ago.

The enlargement of the European Union through eastward expansion has thus presented the organization with a host of troublesome questions, compounded by the fact that citizens in the members added since 2004 earn far less than people living elsewhere in the EU. These new members have different needs and interests that can make reaching agreement on policy decisions difficult. Some of the EU's original members, suffering from unemployment and sluggish economic growth, worry about competition from cheaper labor from the east and chafe over paying subsidies to these poorer but faster-growing countries. Furthermore, because the new eastern members tended to support the American war in Iraq while the older western members, with the exception of Great Britain, generally opposed the invasion, some observers fear that the EU could fracture into two opposed coalitions, which would immeasurably complicate collective policy making.

The principal institutions for EU governance and policy making include the Council of the European Union, the European Commission, a European Parliament, a Court of Justice, and the European Central Bank. The EU's key policy-making unit, the Council of the European Union (formerly the Council of Ministers), consists of cabinet ministers drawn from the EU's member states, whose participation depends on the specific issue being considered. For example, agriculture ministers attend when farm policies are discussed; environmental ministers, when pollution control is on the agenda. Most decisions are made by a complex weighted system called "qualified majority voting," designed to give more votes to larger countries while simultaneously preventing them from dominating smaller ones. Highly sensitive issues, such as tax or security policy, require unanimity, however.

The council also sets general guidelines for the European Commission, which consists of twenty-seven commissioners, nominated by EU member governments and approved by the European Parliament. Headquartered in Brussels, the primary functions of the European Commission are to propose new laws for the EU, oversee EU treaties, and execute the decrees of the European Council. A professional staff of over 18,000 civil-service "Eurocrats" assist the commission in proposing legislation and implementing EU policies. It also manages the EU's budget, which, in contrast with most international organizations, derives part of its revenues from sources not under the control of member states.

The European Parliament represents the political parties and public opinion within Europe. It has existed from the beginning of Europe's journey toward political unification, although at its creation this legislative body was appointed rather than elected and had very little power. That is no longer the case. The European Parliament is now chosen in a direct election by the citizens of the EU's member states. Its 736 deputies debate issues at the monumental glass headquarters in Brussels and at a lavish Strasbourg palace in the same way that democratic national legislative bodies do. The European Parliament shares authority with the Council of the European Union, but the Parliament's influence has increased over time. The deputies elected through universal suffrage pass laws with the council, approve the EU's budget, oversee the European Commission, and can overturn its acts.

The European Court of Justice in Luxembourg has also grown in prominence and power as European integration has gathered depth and breadth. From the start, the court was given responsibility for adjudicating claims and conflicts among EU governments as well as between those governments and the new institutions the EU created. Comprising twenty-seven judges, the court interprets EU law for national courts, rules on legal questions that arise within the EU's institutions, and hears and rules on cases concerning individual citizens. The fact that its decisions are binding distinguishes the European Court of Justice from most other international tribunals.

Finally, the European Central Bank was established to manage the common monetary policy that emerged when the euro replaced the national currencies of twelve member states in 2002 (since 2007, Slovenia, Cyprus, Malta, and Slovakia joined the Euro zone, bringing the total to sixteen). Its responsibilities include setting interest rates and controlling the money supply. Having a common currency facilitates commerce by eliminating the transaction costs involved when one currency is converted to another. It also makes it easier to compare commodity prices in different countries. However, eliminating German marks, French francs, and other national currencies entails a loss of sovereignty to a supranational authority.

The political unification of Europe has been built step-by-step as the EU has marched toward ever greater unity. Moving beyond the nation-state toward a single integrated European federation has not been smooth, and disagreement persists over the extent to which the EU should become a single, truly united superstate, a "United States of Europe." Some people complain that the only democratically elected institution in the EU is the European Parliament. Debate continues also over how far and how fast such a process of **pooled sovereignty** should proceed, and about the natural geographical limits of the EU's membership and boundaries. These concerns are reflected in the difficulty of implementing a European Constitutional Treaty. Following a set of general principles sketched out at a December 2001 leadership summit in Laeken, Belgium, representatives from EU countries drafted a document, which was approved in modified form by an Intergovernmental Conference in 2004, but required ratification by all member countries in order to go into effect. During the following year, however, French and Dutch voters rejected the draft constitution. By 2007, EU leaders agreed on a new treaty (known as the European Reform Treaty, or Lisbon Treaty), which sought to add accountability to EU decision-making procedures and establish a permanent presidency of the European Council to replace the six-month rotating position. Irish voters initially rejected it, but reversed themselves in an October 2009 referendum.

Another challenge for the European Union arose with the Greek sovereign-debt crisis. In 2009, Greece's budget *deficit* stood at 127 percent of GDP and its public *debt* (the sum of past annual deficits minus accumulated surpluses) had reached 113 percent of GDP, far exceeding the fiscal rules of the EU's Stability and Growth Pact, which stipulated that deficits should be less than three percent

pooled sovereignty
legal authority granted to an IGO by its members to make collective decisions regarding specified aspects of public policy heretofore made exclusively by each sovereign government.

of GDP and debt below 60 percent. Alarm soon spread over how a revenue-strapped Greece would cope with some $23 billion of government bonds that were maturing. If they could not be refinanced, Greece would default on its bonds, which would raise fears about defaults by Portugal, Ireland, Italy, and Spain, other euro-zone countries with high budget deficits and public debt. Anxiety over these governments' capabilities to repay creditors spread across the Continent because a large proportion of the bonds were held by banks elsewhere in Europe, most notably in France and Germany (*Economist*, May 1, 2010: 64).

To restore investor confidence, the EU unveiled a nearly $1 trillion bailout plan for deeply indebted members. Having averted financial panic, the EU now must wrestle with the deeper, more complex questions of how to improve fiscal discipline among deficit-plagued members, and whether it is possible to have a monetary union without a full-fledged political union. One school of thought, voiced by the French, sees the answer in establishing a "council of the euro zone," a new economic decision-making body composed of the sixteen countries using the euro. A second school, led by the Germans who prize the European Central Bank's political independence, worries that such a council would pressure the ECB into more rescue packages, treating sovereign-debt problems as if they were due to **illiquidity** rather than insolvency (*Economist*, May 22, 2010: 12).

As a result of the sovereign-debt crisis, pessimists grouse that the EU's future is in limbo. "The European whole," reportedly quipped a British diplomat, "is less than the sum of its parts." Optimists, however, proclaim that the EU represents a remarkable success story in the history of international relations, one whose final chapter has yet to be written. Who, after all, would have expected competitive states, which have spent most of their national experiences waging war against one another, to put their clashing ambitions aside, and construct a new European identity built on confederated decision making?

illiquidity   an inability to convert assets into cash quickly.

Other Regional IGOs

Since Europe's move toward economic and political integration, more than a dozen regional IGOs have been created in various other parts of the world, notably among states in the Global South. Most seek to stimulate regional economic growth, but many have drifted from that original purpose to pursue multiple political and military purposes as well. The major regional IGOs include:

- The North Atlantic Treaty Organization (NATO), a military alliance created in 1949 primarily to deter the Soviet Union in Western Europe, has expanded its membership to 28 countries and broadened its mission to promote democratization and combat terrorism outside its traditional territory within Europe.

- The Council of Arab Economic Unity (CAEU), established in 1964 to promote trade and economic integration among its 10 members.

- The Association of Southeast Asian Nations (ASEAN), established in 1967 to promote regional economic, social, and cultural cooperation, created a free-trade zone among its 10 members in 1999 and focuses today on political, economic, and environmental problems that beset the region.

- The Caribbean Community (CARICOM), established in 1973 as a common market to promote economic development among its 15 country and territory members.

- The Economic Community of West African States (ECOWAS), established in 1975 to promote regional trade and economic cooperation among its 15 members.

- The Latin American Integration Association (LAIA), established in 1980 to promote and regulate free trade among its 12 members.

- The South Asian Association for Regional Cooperation (SAARC), established in 1985 to promote economic, social, and cultural cooperation among its seven members.

- The Asia Pacific Economic Cooperation (APEC) forum, established in 1989 and with a current membership of 21, plans to establish free and open trade in the region for developing countries by 2020.

- The Southern African Development Community (SADC), established in 1992 to promote regional economic development among its 14 members.

As these examples illustrate, most IGOs are organized on a regional rather than global basis. The governments creating them usually concentrate on one or two major goals instead of attempting to address at once the complete range of issues that they face in common. Africa illustrates this tendency, possessing a complex network of regional IGOs with multiple crosscutting memberships. Some are large multipurpose groups such as the Economic Community of Western African States (ECOWAS) and the Southern African Development Community (SADC). Alongside these are many smaller organizations such as the Economic Community of the Great Lakes Countries, the Mano River Union, and the East African Community (EAC).

While it is hazardous to generalize about organizations so widely divergent in membership and purpose, we can say that none of the regional IGOs outside of Europe have managed to collaborate at a level that begins to match the institutionalized collective decision making achieved by the EU. The reasons vary, but in general these regional IGOs are limited by national leaders' reluctance to make politically costly choices that would undermine their personal popularity at home and their governments' sovereignty. The obstacles to creating new political communities out of previously divided ones are enormous; nonetheless, these attempts at regional cooperation demonstrate many states' acceptance of the fact that they cannot individually resolve many of the problems that confront them collectively.

IGOs are not the only nonstate actors on the world stage. Another set of agents are nongovernmental organizations (NGOs), such as ethnopolitical groups, religious movements, multinational corporations, transnational banks, and issue-advocacy groups. NGOs are growing in number and voice, making them increasingly influential in world politics. We now turn our attention to their behavior and impact.

NONGOVERNMENTAL ORGANIZATIONS

If you are like most people, there is at least one problem of concern to you that crosses national borders. You would like to see it resolved, but you probably realize that you cannot engineer global changes all by yourself. Recognizing that collective voices are more likely to be heard, many people have found that by joining nongovernmental organizations (NGOs), they can lobby more effectively for causes they support. NGOs are international actors whose members are not states, but instead are people drawn from the populations of two or more societies who have come together to promote their shared interests. There are almost 30,000 NGOs in existence worldwide, and they tackle global issues ranging from environmental protection to human rights. Most of them pursue objectives that are highly respected and constructive, and therefore do not arouse much opposition. For example, NGOs such as the International Chamber of Commerce, the Red Cross, Save the Children, and the World Wildlife Federation enjoy widespread popular support. Others, like Hezbollah, are more controversial.

What makes NGOs increasingly prominent on the world stage is that their activities are now shaping responses to issues that once were determined exclusively by governments. Greenpeace, Amnesty International, and other global issue-advocacy groups have used their technical expertise, organizational flexibility, and grassroots connections to affect every stage of the development of **international regimes**, from problem recognition through policy implementation. As constructivists point out, NGOs matter because of the power of ideas: They help set political agendas, promote normative change, and energize constituencies to support the policies they back. Their influence demonstrates that world politics is not merely the interaction of sovereign, territorial states. It also involves complex networks of people, who coalesce in myriad combinations at different times for various purposes.

As NGOs rise in numbers and influence, it is important to consider how they may transform world politics. Although NGOs comprise a large, heterogeneous group of nonstate actors, a small subset of them receive the most attention. Within this subset, NGOs based on ethnic identity are particularly noteworthy.

international regimes sets of principles, norms, rules, and decision-making procedures agreed to by global actors to guide their behavior in particular issue-areas.

Ethnopolitical Movements

Although the state remains the most visible actor in world affairs, some people pledge their primary allegiance not to the government that rules them, but rather to an **ethnopolitical group**, whose members share a common nationality, language, cultural tradition, and kinship ties. They view themselves as members of their ethnic group first and of their state only secondarily. Many states are

ethnopolitical group people whose identity is primarily defined by their sense of sharing a common ancestral nationality, language, cultural heritage, and kinship ties.

divided, multiethnic societies made up of a variety of politically active groups that seek, if not outright independence, a greater level of regional autonomy and a greater voice in the domestic and foreign policies of the state. Roughly three-quarters of the world's large countries have significant minority groups, and some, such as the Kurds in Iraq, Turkey, and Iran, spill across several countries. Thus, images of the state as a unitary actor and of governments as autonomous rulers of integrated nations are not very accurate. These ethnic divisions and the NGOs that often develop around them make thinking of international relations as exclusively interactions between homogeneous states with impermeable, hard-shell boundaries—the realist "billiard ball model"—dubious.

Indigenous peoples are the ethnic and cultural groups that were native to a geographic location now controlled by another state or political group. The world is populated by an estimated 6,800 separate indigenous nations, each of which has a unique language and culture and strong, often spiritual, ties to an ancestral homeland. In most cases, indigenous people were at one time politically sovereign and economically self-sufficient. As shown in Map 6.2, today an estimated 650 million indigenous people, or about one-tenth of the world's population, are scattered in more than seventy countries (Center for World Indigenous Studies, http://www.cwis.org).

indigenous peoples
the native ethnic and cultural inhabitant populations within countries ruled by a government controlled by others, referred to as the "Fourth World."

Religious Movements

Religion is another force that can create identities and loyalties that transcend national boundaries. In theory, religion would seem a natural force for global harmony. Yet millions have died in the name of religion. The Crusades between the eleventh and fourteenth centuries left countless Christians and Muslims dead. Similarly, the religious conflicts during the Thirty Years' War (1618–1648) between Catholics and Protestants killed nearly one-fourth of all Europeans.

Many of the world's more than 6.8 billion people are affiliated in some form with a religious movement—a politically active organization based on strong religious convictions. At the most abstract level, a religion is a system of thought shared by a group that provides its members with an object of devotion and a code of behavior by which they can ethically judge their actions. This definition points to commonalities across the great diversity of organized religions in the world, but it fails to capture that diversity. The world's principal religions vary greatly in the theological doctrines they embrace. They also differ widely in the size of their followings, in the geographical locations where they are most prevalent, and in the extent to which they engage in political efforts to influence international affairs.

These differences make it risky to generalize about the impact of religious movements on world affairs. Those who study religious movements comparatively note that a system of beliefs provides followers with their main source of identity, and that this identification with and devotion to their religion springs from the natural human need to find a set of values with which to evaluate the meaning of life. Sometimes this need leads believers to perceive the values of their own creed as superior to those of others. Members of many religious movements

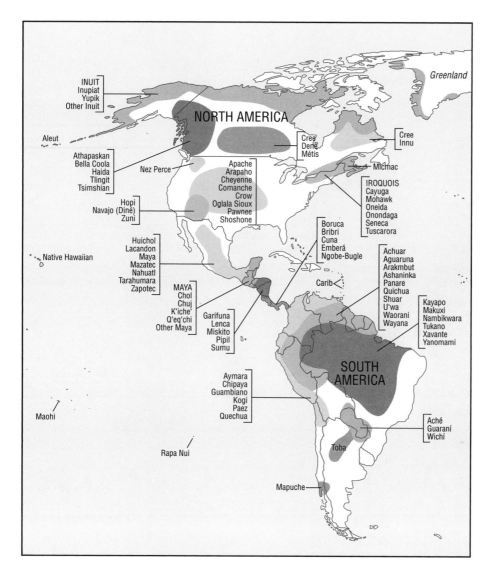

MAP 6.2 The Indigenous Cultures of the World

Indigenous peoples live in many countries. As the UN's Office of the High Commissioner for Human Rights has noted, "All over the world indigenous peoples are asserting their cultural identity, claiming their right to control their futures, and struggling to regain their ancestral lands." To accomplish these aims, many of these people have begun to organize in NGOs to lobby for their human rights.

believe that their religion should be universal, and actively proselytize to convert nonbelievers to their faith. Although conversion is usually sought through persuasion, at times it has been achieved by the sword (see CONTROVERSY: Are Religious Movements Causes of War or Sources of Transnational Harmony?).

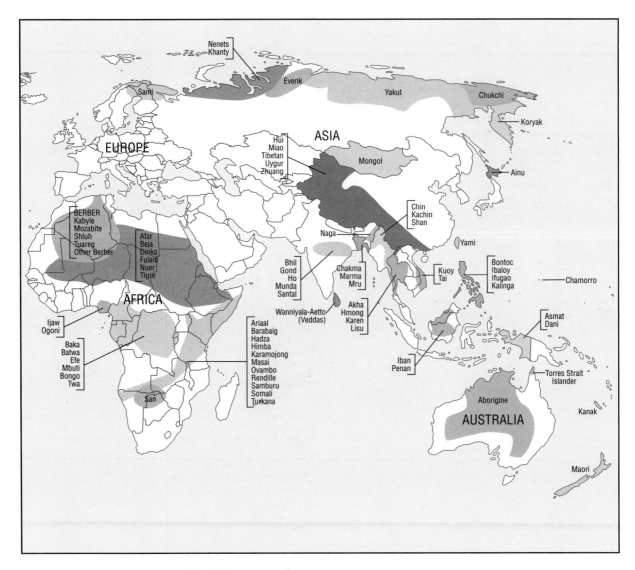

M A P   6.2   Continued

In evaluating the impact of religious movements, it is important to distinguish carefully the high ideals of doctrines from the activities of the people who head these religious bodies. The two realms are not the same, and each can be judged fairly only against the standards they set for themselves. To condemn what large-scale religious movements sometimes do when they abuse the principles of the religions they manage does not mean that the principles themselves deserve condemnation. Still, many observers maintain that otherwise humanitarian religions sometimes oppose each other violently, despite their professed doctrines of tolerance. When they do, religious movements become sources of international tension.

Along with ethnopolitical groups, militant religious movements may contribute to five types of transnational activities. The first is **irredentism**—the attempt by a dominant religion or ethnic group to reclaim previously possessed territory in an adjacent region from a foreign state that now controls it. The second is **secession**—the attempt by a religious (or ethnic) minority to break away from an internationally recognized state in a separatist revolt. Third, militant religions tend to incite migration, the departure of religious minorities from their countries of origin to escape persecution. Whether they move by force or by choice, the result—a fourth consequence of militant religion—is the same: The emigrants create **diasporas**, or communities that live abroad in host countries but maintain economic, political, and emotional ties with their homelands. Finally, a fifth effect of militant religions is international terrorism in the form of support for radical coreligionists abroad.

irredentism   efforts by an ethnonational or religious group to regain control of territory by force so that existing state boundaries will no longer separate the group.

secession   the attempt by a religious or ethnic minority to break away from an internationally recognized state.

diasporas   the migration of religious or ethnic groups to foreign lands despite their continued affiliation with the land and customs of their origin.

CONTROVERSY   **Are Religious Movements Causes of War or Sources of Transnational Harmony?**

After September 11, 2001, debate about the impact of religion on international conflict intensified, because many believed that the terrorist attacks on the World Trade Center and the Pentagon were motivated by religious fanatics within the Al Qaeda organization. As a result, the religious sources of political violence have received considerable attention, as have religious NGOs more generally (Haynes, 2004).

It is difficult to understand the religious origins of violence because most people equate religion with compassion and forgiveness, not hatred and intolerance. Indeed, many of the principles that the world's major religious movements espouse would seem conducive to peace. They all voice respect and reverence for the sanctity of life and acceptance of all people as equal creations of a deity, regardless of race or ethnicity. These are noble ideals. Religions speak to universal principles, across time and place—to enduring values in changing times.

If all the world's great religious movements espouse pacific ideals, why are those same religions increasingly criticized as sources of international conflict—of hatred, terror, and war?

In evaluating the role of religious NGOs in international affairs, consider first the view of sociologists of religion who contend that religious hostility results from the fact that universalistic religions are managed by organizations that often adopt a particularistic and dogmatic outlook (see Juergensmeyer, 2003).

Fundamentalist followers of a religion may conceive the world through a lens that sees outsiders as rivals and other creeds as challenges to their own faith. In a word, religious movements often practice intolerance—disrespect for diversity and the right of people to freely embrace another religion's beliefs. Sometimes the next step is for fanatics to portray these outsiders as evil and call for violence against them. "If you want war," sociologist William Graham Sumner once remarked, "nourish a doctrine." Does this argument hold up under careful examination? Those who think it doesn't point out that societies recognizing no higher deity also have waged war against others. Meanwhile, many religions perform ably the mission of peace making.

It is important for you to weigh the evidence about the impact of religious NGOs on international affairs. Observing that many wars have been fought in the name of religion, some people argue that religion can be a serious danger to world order, because it may foster zealotry and a crusading spirit that transforms international disputes into prolonged wars for total stakes. Compromise, the mutual accommodation of conflicting claims, is difficult when disputants are the standard-bearers of rival faiths. Others, however, insist that the moral precepts in religious belief have worked for the betterment of world affairs by promoting fellowship and harmony among diverse people. What do you think?

Multinational Corporations

In an age of porous borders and growing interdependence, we need to look beyond ethnopolitical groups and religious movements to consider the role of multinational corporations as nonstate actors, even though some people only apply the designation "NGO" to nonprofit organizations. **Multinational corporations (MNCs)** have grown dramatically in scope and influence since World War II. Wal-Mart exemplifies the impact that these giants have over global trade. With annual revenues of more than $408 billion and 2 million employees, Wal-Mart attracts over 100 million customers every week to its stores worldwide. According to recent statistics, the combined sales of the top 100 MNCs were the equivalent of roughly one-fifth of the world's gross domestic product. The UN estimates that MNCs account for approximately two-thirds of the world's exports and one-third of the stock of all foreign direct investment (FDI).

In the past, MNCs were headquartered almost exclusively in the United States, Europe, and Japan, and their common practice was to make short-term investments in the Global South's plants, sales corporations, and mining operations. At the end of the twentieth century, about 80 percent of all MNCs' employees worked in developing countries, where wages were lower, to bolster corporate profits at the parent headquarters where key business functions remained. But this is no longer true; aided by the spread of digital information technology, a growing number of companies are now shifting many of these headquarter functions away from their home offices, with a quarter of them being relocated to the Global South. For example, Thomson, a Canadian media company, has 97.8 percent of its assets, 96.6 percent of its sales, and 97.3 percent of its jobs outside of Canada. Other MNCs that rank almost as high include Roche and Nestlé, based in Switzerland, and Phillips, based in the Netherlands.

Another new trend is the rise of MNCs from the Global South, which are investing in Global North countries as well as in the developing world. Whereas in 1990 foreign direct investment from companies in these countries accounted for 5 percent of the world's total, by 2006 it had reached 14 percent. Brazil's Embraer, which specializes in regional jets, has become the world's third-largest aircraft company, with over 95 percent of its sales outside Brazil. Four-fifths of the revenues earned by Mexico's Cemex, one of the world's largest producers of ready-mixed concrete, comes from outside Mexico. Similarly, China's Hisense Electronic and India's Tata Motors have fanned out across the world (*Economist*, January 12, 2008: 62–64).

MNC expansion has been facilitated by **transnational banks (TNBs)**, another type of global NGO whose revenues and assets are primarily generated by financial transactions in the international economy. TNBs help to reduce the meaning of political borders by transferring capital through international loans and investments, thus increasing global economic interdependence. Through their loans to the private sector, TNBs have made capital highly mobile and

multinational corporations (MNCs) business enterprises headquartered in one state that invest and operate extensively in other states.

transnational banks (TNBs) the world's top banking firms, whose financial activities are concentrated in transactions that cross state borders.

expanded the capacity of MNCs to function as the primary agents in the globalization of production. During the recession of 2008–2009, TNBs outside of Global North countries experienced rapid growth. By 2010 they accounted for roughly one-third of the industry's global revenues and ranked among the world's largest and best-funded banks. As measured by market capitalization, four of the top ten banks are Chinese, with ICBC and China Construction Bank holding the top two positions (*Economist*, July 10, 2010: 69; May 15, 2010: 4, special report). Other major banks in the Global South are located in Brazil and India, including Itaú Unibanco, Banco do Brasil, the State Bank of India, and ICICI Bank.

Table 6.2 captures the importance of MNCs in world politics, ranking firms by annual sales and states by GNI. The profile shows that of the world's top 100 economic entities, multinationals account for only 9 of the top 50, but in the next 50, they account for 40. MNCs' financial clout thus rivals or exceeds that of most countries, with the result that many people worry that these corporate giants are undermining the ability of national governments to control their own economies and therefore their own fates.

Because of their financial strength and global reach, it is tempting to conclude that MNCs are a threat to state power. Their ability to make decisions on many issues over which national political leaders have little control appears to be eroding state sovereignty, the international system's major organizing principle. However, this interpretation overlooks the fact that at the same time MNCs have grown in size, the regulatory power of states has increased. Corporations must deal with governments on a host of matters, ranging from opening banks to establishing aviation routes.

Still, controlling intricate webs of corporate interrelationships, joint ventures, and shared ownership for any particular national purpose is nearly impossible. Part of the reason is that about 30 to 40 percent of world trade in goods and services occurs *within* multinationals, from one branch to another (Oatley, 2008: 170). Joint production and **strategic corporate alliances** to create temporary phantom "virtual corporations" undermine states' ability to identify the MNCs they seek to control. This changing business environment is so dramatic, argues IBM CEO Samuel Palmisano, that the very term "multinational" no longer adequately describes the major companies of the twenty-first century. He prefers to call them "globally integrated enterprises" to reflect how "their many components, from back office to manufacturing to product development, ... [are] dispersed around the planet in a vast network" (Pethokoukis, 2006: 42). Roughly half of Xerox's employees, for example, "work on foreign soil, and less than half of Sony's employees are Japanese. More than 50 percent of IBM's revenues originate overseas; the same is true for Citigroup, ExxonMobil, DuPont, Procter & Gamble, and many other corporate giants" (Weidenbaum, 2004: 26). The question raised by this blurring of the boundaries between foreign and domestic enterprise is how any single state can manage MNCs when no country can claim that any of them is "one of ours."

strategic corporate alliances cooperation between multinational corporations and foreign companies in the same industry, driven by the movement of MNC manufacturing overseas.

T A B L E   6.2   **Countries and Corporations: A Ranking by Size of Economy and Revenues**

Rank	Country/Corporation	GNI/Revenues (Millions of Dollars)	Rank	Country/Corporation	GNI/Revenues (Millions of Dollars)
1	United States	14,573,576	31	EXXON MOBIL	284,650
2	Japan	4,869,121	32	South Africa	283,194
3	China*	3,888,082	33	Venezuela	257,865
4	Germany	3,506,923	34	Finland	252,902
5	United Kingdom	2,827,343	35	Thailand	247,171
6	France	2,695,615	36	BP	246,138
7	Italy	2,121,598	37	Ireland	220,281
8	Spain	1,454,803	38	Portugal	219,627
9	Canada	1,453,773	39	Colombia	207,935
10	Brazil	1,401,333	40	TOYOTA MOTOR	204,106
11	Russian Federation	1,371,173	41	JAPAN POST HOLDINGS	202,196
12	India	1,186,664	42	Malaysia	195,955
13	Mexico	1,062,405	43	SINOPEC	187,518
14	South Korea	1,046,285	44	STATE GRID	184,496
15	Australia	862,461	45	Israel	180,641
16	Netherlands	811,350	46	Romania	178,142
17	Turkey	666,593	47	Nigeria	177,398
18	Belgium	477,257	48	AXA	175,257
19	Sweden	469,417	49	Czech Republic	173,605
20	Poland	447,094	50	Philippines	170,410
21	Saudi Arabia	440,456	51	Singapore	168,227
22	Indonesia	426,789	52	CHINA NATIONAL PETROLEUM	165,497
23	Switzerland	424,524	53	CHEVRON	163,527
24	Norway	416,438	54	ING GROUP	163,204
25	WAL-MART STORES	408,214	55	Chile	157,460
26	Austria	382,669	56	Pakistan	157,341
27	Denmark	323,020	57	GENERAL ELECTRIC	156,779
28	Greece	319,179	58	TOTAL	155,887
29	Argentina	286,606	59	BANK OF AMERICA	150,450
30	ROYAL DUTCH SHELL	285,129	60	Ukraine	148,643

T A B L E   6.2   Countries and Corporations: A Ranking by Size of Economy and Revenues (Continued)

Rank	Country/Corporation	GNI/Revenues (Millions of Dollars)	Rank	Country/Corporation	GNI/Revenues (Millions of Dollars)
61	Egypt	146,774	81	NIPPON TELEGRAPH & TELEPHONE	109,656
62	VOLKSWAGEN	146,205	82	SAMSUNG ELECTRONICS	108,927
63	Algeria	144,149	83	CITIGROUP	108,785
64	CONOCO PHILLIPS	139,515	84	MCKESSON	108,702
65	PNB PARIBAS	130,708	85	VERIZON COMMUNICATIONS	107,808
66	Hungary	128,581	86	CRÉDIT AGRICOLE	106,538
67	ASSICURAZIONI GENERALI	126,013	87	BANCO SANTENDER	106,345
68	ALLIANZ	125,999	88	GENERAL MOTORS	104,589
69	AT&T	123,018	89	HSBC HOLDINGS	103,736
70	CARREFOUR	121,453	90	SIEMENS	103,605
71	New Zealand	118,821	91	AMERICAN INTERNATIONAL GROUP	103,189
72	FORD MOTOR	118,308	92	LLOYDS BANKING GROUP	102,967
73	ENI	117,235	93	CARDINAL HEALTH	99,613
74	J.P. MORGAN CHASE	115,632	94	NESTLÉ	99,115
75	Peru	115,064	95	CVS CAREMARK	98,729
76	HEWLETT-PACKARD	114,552	96	WELLS FARGO	98,636
77	E.ON	113,849	97	Kazakhstan	96,635
78	BERKSHIRE HATHAWAY	112,493	98	HITACHI	96,593
79	GDF SUEZ	111,069	99	IBM	95,758
80	DAIMLER	109,700	100	DEXIA GROUP	95,144

By integrating production and marketing their products worldwide, MNCs rival many countries in wealth, which they are translating into political influence.
Note: MNCs listed in capital letters. Current data on Iran and Kuwait not available.
*Based on seasonally unadjusted second-quarter economic statistics released in August 2010, China is projected to move ahead of Japan by 2011.
SOURCES: MNC revenues, *Fortune* (July 26, 2010), p. F-1; countries' gross national income (GNI), WDI (2010).

Issue-Advocacy Groups and Global Civil Society

A final type of NGO that we will examine is composed of associational interest groups organized around special policy interests, such as environmental protection or upholding human rights. Greenpeace, for example, focuses much of its

attention on preventing pollution and maintaining biodiversity through education programs, lobbying, and nonviolent protest demonstrations. Boasting a
worldwide membership of 2.9 million and offices in forty countries, Greenpeace
has a total income of approximately $250 million, derived largely from individual
donations and foundation grants. Included among what it claims as its successes
are international prohibitions on large-scale driftnet fishing, dumping of radioactive wastes at sea, and mining in Antarctica.

Issue-oriented NGOs like Greenpeace flourish when governments permit
freedom of expression and association, and thus have increased exponentially as
the number of democracies worldwide has risen over the past two decades. Their
increase has led some scholars to observe that NGOs are empowering ordinary
people, giving them a voice and a means of political leverage. In effect, the proliferation of NGOs is "creating an incipient, albeit imperfect, civil society at the
global level" (Keohane and Nye, 2001a).

However, not everyone believes that we are witnessing the formation of a
global civil society. Skeptics claim that NGOs have tended to reinforce existing
power structures, having members and headquarters primarily in Global North
countries and making decisions with scant democratic representation or accountability (Stephenson, 2000). According to this account, world politics is still controlled by states—especially the great powers.

How influential and effective are grassroots NGOs? Research on this question suggests the following conclusions, which reduce confidence in the expectation that pressure from NGOs can lead to far-reaching reforms in the conduct
of international relations:

- Interest group activity operates as an ever-present, if limited, constraint on
  global policy making, but the impact varies with the issue.

- As a general rule, NGOs are relatively weak in the high politics of international security, because states remain in control of defense policy.

- Conversely, the NGOs' clout is highest with respect to issues in low politics,
  such as protecting endangered species.

- The influence between states and NGOs is reciprocal, but it is more probable that government officials exercise somewhat greater influence over
  transnational interest groups. When NGO interests parallel those of states,
  government officials often channel funds through NGOs in order to allow
  them to bring their expertise to bear on a given policy problem.

- Single-issue NGO interest groups have more influence than large general-
  purpose organizations.

- NGOs sometimes seek inaction from governments and maintenance of the
  status quo; such efforts are generally more successful than efforts to bring
  about major changes in international relations.

To sum up, the mere presence of issue-advocacy NGOs, and the mere fact
that they are organized with the intent of persuasion, does not guarantee their penetration of the global policy-making process. On the whole, NGOs have

participation without significant power and involvement without substantial influence, given that most have limited economic resources and the ability of any *one* to exert influence is offset by the tendency for countervailing powers to materialize over the disposition of major issues. That is, as any particular coalition of issue-advocacy NGOs combine in a caucus to work together on a common cause, other groups threatened by the changes advocated spring up to balance it. When an interest group seeks vigorously to push policy in one direction, other NGOs—aroused that their interests are being disturbed—are stimulated to push policy in the opposite direction. Global policy making consequently resembles a taffy pull: Every NGO attempts to yank policy in its own direction, with the result that movement on many global problems fails to proceed consistently in any single direction.

This balance between opposing actors helps to account for the reason why so few global issues are resolved. Competition stands in the way of consensus, and contests of will over international issues are seldom settled. No side can ever claim permanent victory, for each decision that takes international policy in one direction merely sets the stage for the next round of the contest, with the possibility that the losers of the moment will be winners tomorrow. The struggle between those wishing to make protection of the environment a global priority and those placing economic growth ahead of environmental preservation provides one among many examples.

NONSTATE ACTORS IN THE WEB OF WORLD POLITICS

Political realists generally discount IGOs and NGOs as important actors on the global stage. From their perspective, some of these organizations simply serve the interests of states, whereas others are marginal players in the drama of world politics. Liberals and constructivists disagree. They believe that as people, products, and information increasingly move across the planet, IGOs and NGOs will play ever-larger roles in the world, multiplying channels of access to international affairs for concerned citizens everywhere. More than at any time since the Peace of Westphalia in 1648, nonstate actors are challenging sovereign, territorial states in the management of international affairs. Not only are they challenged from above by multinational corporations, transnational banks, and global economic IGOs, but they are also being challenged from below by the grassroots NGOs of an emerging global civil society (see APPLICATION: Mixed-Actor Approaches to Global Diplomacy).

After three and a half centuries, it is sometimes difficult to think about world politics as involving anything beyond the interaction of sovereign, territorial nation-states. Yet in a world characterized by ever-increasing ties among individuals and organizations who see territorial boundaries as anachronisms, nation-states are not the Leviathans described by the seventeenth-century philosopher Thomas Hobbes. Rather than being autonomous entities, they are enmeshed with nonstate actors in complex webs that obscure the distinction between foreign and domestic affairs. If the traditional Westphalian worldview could be symbolized by a static two-dimensional map depicting discrete territorial states

World politics is increasingly shaped by advocacy groups whose influence transcends national boundaries. Many of these NGOs interact with IGOs and attend conferences to which states send representatives (Tarrow, 2006). A prominent example can be seen in the diplomatic process that led to a 1997 treaty that banned antipersonnel landmines, which was signed by 155 countries. Lloyd Axworthy, Canada's foreign minister from 1996 to 2000, sees that process as an alternative to the traditional "top down," great-power approach to diplomacy. Called the "Ottawa Process" because the key meetings occurred in the Canadian capital, it involved a close working relationship among officials from like-minded middle powers, IGOs, and NGOs. In the following excerpt, Axworthy describes its origins at a 1996 meeting attended by representatives from over seventy countries, UN officials, and a large delegation of NGOs. Many attendees were frustrated by the insistence of the great powers that future discussions of landmines be confined to established channels, which would allow them to control the pace of negotiations and exclude NGOs.

> As the conference began to wind down, I assembled a group of senior officials and staff .... The next afternoon was to be the wrap-up to the meeting and I was scheduled to give the benediction. What should I say?
>
>   It was then that a senior official—Paul Heinbecker, then the new Canadian Assistant Deputy Minister for Global Affairs—mentioned ... the possibility of short-circuiting the conventional process and setting up a separate track leading to a treaty banning landmines.
>
>   ... There was no one else to pass the decision to. I said, "It's the right thing. Let's do it." As the

> Saturday session drew to a close, with delegates voting on a declaration and an action plan, I waited in the wings to deliver the closing remarks with more than a twinge of nervousness. I knew I would be committing Canada to a course of action that defied diplomatic niceties and procedures and challenged the positions of the permanent members of the Security Council.
>
>   ... [At the podium] I went through the normal list of thank-yous and words of appreciation, and then concluded: "The challenge is to see a treaty signed no later than the end of 1997 ...." I then issued an invitation for all the delegates (and their friends) to come to Ottawa a year hence to sign the treaty.
>
>   The reaction in the hall was a mixture of surprise, applause, and incredulity. The NGO contingents rose to their feet, the representatives of many governments sat in their seats, too stunned to react, several barely suppressing their anger and opposition.
>
>   ... [We] had just stepped out of the accustomed protocol of diplomatic deference to the powerful, and launched forth on an uncharted course of action (Axworthy, 2008: 237–238).

Established diplomatic channels, argues Axworthy, were a recipe for stalemate, because some of the great powers were reluctant to forego controlling the negotiations. The "bottom-up" mixed-actor approach pioneered through the Ottawa Process enabled a coordinated network of NGOs and sympathetic officials from IGOs and middle-power countries to create an alternative to the state-centric way of conducting diplomacy.

on a grid of longitude and latitude, then a post-Westphalian worldview might be represented by a dynamic holographic projection of a vast, multilayered network linking states with many other types of actors (see Figure 6.3). When seen from this perspective, global governance will involve a complex, interlocking mix of supranational, national, and subnational actors, with international regimes playing an ever greater role in world politics.

To sum up, IGOs and NGOs are changing the face of international affairs as they seek to reshape the global agenda. Of course, this does not mean that the era of state dominance is over. States retain a near-monopoly on the use of coercive force in the world, and they mold the activities of nonstate actors more than

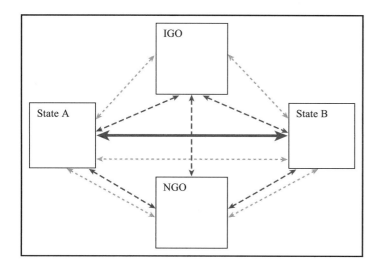

FIGURE 6.3 **The Web of World Politics**

World politics is more than government-to-government relations among sovereign, territorial states (depicted by the solid line between States A and B). As shown here, it also includes relations among states and IGOs, states and NGOs, IGOs and NGOs (all depicted with dashed lines), as well as among the private citizens within the societies of different states who may interact with each other and with IGOs and NGOs (depicted by the dotted lines).

their behavior is molded by them. It is also true that increases in political influence by nonstate actors do not necessarily translate into reductions in state power (see Paul, Ikenberry, and Hall, 2003). Nevertheless, we must conclude that whereas it would be premature to abandon the focus on the state in world politics, it would be equally mistaken to exaggerate the state's power as a determinant of the world's fate and dismiss the expanding role of nonstate actors in shaping the global future.

CHAPTER SUMMARY

- Despite states having an enormous capacity to influence national and global welfare, the state is ill-suited for managing many transnational policy problems; consequently no analysis of world politics would be complete without a treatment of the role played by nonstate actors.

- There are two principal types of nonstate actors in world politics, intergovernmental organizations (IGOs) and nongovernmental organizations (NGOs). Even though the vast majority of nonstate actors are NGOs, IGOs generally wield more influence because their members are states.

- Most IGOs engage in a comparatively narrow range of activities. Given its global membership and purposes, the United Nations (UN) differs from other IGOs. Because the UN is a mirror of world politics, not an alternative to it, the UN reflects the forces outside the organization that have animated world politics since the end of World War II.

- Although the European Union (EU) has some supranational elements, the term *pooled sovereignty* captures its essence, because states remain paramount in its institutional structures and decision-making processes. Regional IGOs outside of Europe have not approached the same level of institution-building because of the reluctance of national leaders to make political choices that would undermine their state's sovereignty.

- Many people do not pledge their primary allegiance to the state. Rather, they think of themselves primarily as members of an ethnic nation group and the cultural values it represents. Ethnopolitical groups based on these feelings are among the most important NGOs in contemporary world politics.

- As a force in world politics, religious movements not only bring people together but also divide them. While not all extremist religious NGOs are alike, many of them incite irredentist claims, separatist revolts, migration, and political violence.

- Since World War II, MNCs have grown dramatically in scope and power. To some observers, this growth has undermined the ability of sovereign states to control their own economies; to others, this growth is helping to create a more prosperous world.

- Issue-advocacy NGOs have become influential in the fields of economic development, human rights, and the environment. Although some people see these groups as rabble-rousers, others contend that they provide an avenue for citizens of different countries who have shared interests to associate with one another, lobby collectively, and exert leverage over state policies. Moreover, they believe that these kinds of interactions are creating a rudimentary global civil society.

- The dramatic growth of nonstate actors challenges the traditional state-centric view of world politics. Although some nonstate actors are capable of advancing their interests largely outside the direct control of states, the state still molds the activities of nonstate actors more than its behavior is molded by them.

KEY TERMS

bilateral

diasporas

ethnopolitical group

illiquidity

indigenous peoples

intergovernmental
    organizations (IGOs)

international regimes

irredentism

multinational
    corporations (MNCs)

nongovernmental
    organizations
    (NGOs)

pooled sovereignty

secession

security community

strategic corporate
    alliances

transnational banks
    (TNBs)

SUGGESTED READINGS

Heins, Volker. *Nongovernmental Organizations in International Society*. New York: Palgrave Macmillan, 2008.

Joachim, Jutta M. *Agenda Setting, the UN and NGOs*. Washington, DC: Georgetown University Press, 2007.

Kennedy, Paul. *The Parliament of Man: The Past, Present, and Future of the United Nations*. New York: Random House, 2006.

Milner, Helen V., and Andrew Moravcsik. *Power, Interdependence, and Nonstate Actors in World Politics*. Princeton, NJ: Princeton University Press, 2009.

Weiss, Thomas G., David P. Forsythe, Roger A. Coate, and Kelly-Kate Pease. *The United Nations and Changing World Politics*, 6th edition. Boulder, CO: Westview.

CRITICAL THINKING QUESTIONS

Is it time to replace the global intergovernmental organizations that were established at the end of World War II? Are they too old to meet the challenges of a rapidly changing world? Recently, various scholars and politicians in the United States have called for the creation of a "League of Democracies" (Lindsay, 2009; see also Carothers, 2008). By most accounts, it would be an exclusive club, composed of countries with democratic political systems. One conception of such an organization is that it would focus on security, leaving issues of health, development, and the like to a truncated United Nations. Another conception would eliminate the UN and have the democratic league absorb its main features. What do you think? Is a League of Democracies a viable alternative to the UN? Would its smaller size, shared values, and political commonalities make it more effective than the UN in addressing global security problems? How would it fare in dealing with global health, economic development, or environmental problems? What organizational difficulties might arise when designing its charter? Would it alienate autocratic governments with whom cooperation is necessary to solve pressing global problems?

PART III

The Politics of Global Security

The threat of violence casts a dark cloud over much of the world. Many people live in fear of terrorist attacks, invasion by neighboring states, or repression by their own government, bent on persecuting its citizens because of their ethnicity or religion. Even though the Cold War is long over, global security remains precarious. Millions of people are the victims of aggression, and millions more have had to flee their homelands to seek sanctuary from the ravages of war. Armed conflict "promises human tragedy," U.S. President Barack Obama noted during his acceptance speech at the December 11, 2009 Nobel Peace Prize ceremony in Oslo, Norway. But, he continued, the "hard truth" is that we "will not eradicate violent conflict in our lifetimes."

Part III of *The Global Future* examines the quest for security in the twenty-first century. Chapter 7 begins our examination by looking at trends in the incidence of armed conflict since the birth of the modern world system. In addition to analyzing what scholars and policy makers believe are the major causes of interstate and intrastate war, it traces the evolution of political terrorism into a worldwide threat. Chapter 8 addresses the national security strategies national leaders use to cope with the dangers posed by rival states and global terrorists. Finally, in the last two chapters of Part III, we consider the alternative paths to peace prescribed by the realist theoretical tradition and its liberal and constructivist critics. Whereas Chapter 9 assesses the use of military alliances to prevent war by creating a balance of power among rival states, Chapter 10 evaluates the use of international law, organization, and integration.

7

Patterns of Armed Conflict

CHAPTER OUTLINE

Trends in Armed Conflict

What Causes Armed Conflict?

The First Level of Analysis: Human Nature

APPLICATION: When Is It Worth Going To War?

The Second Level of Analysis: Internal Characteristics of States

CONTROVERSY: Does Love of Country Cause War with Foreign Nations?

The Third Level of Analysis: System Structure and Processes

The Future of Armed Conflict

Terrorism and Asymmetric Warfare

The Changing Nature of Terrorism

> War is a matter of vital importance to the state: the province of life or death; the road to survival or ruin.
>
> SUN TZU
> ANCIENT CHINESE MILITARY STRATEGIST

On July 8, 2008, a combined United Nations and African Union peacekeeping force was ambushed while on patrol sixty miles east of Al Fāshir in the Sudanese province of Darfur. Approximately 200 heavily armed men in trucks and on horseback attacked the peacekeepers, killing seven and wounding twenty-two in a battle that raged for over two hours.

The peacekeeping force had been deployed to protect civilians from a series of complex, overlapping armed conflicts involving the central government in Khartoum, neighboring countries, and a galaxy of rival militias. The UN estimates that roughly 300,000 people have died in Darfur since 2003 due to political violence, starvation, and disease, and another 2.7 million have fled to refugee camps. According to one respected African diplomat, if the fighting in Sudan escalates further, "it will unlock the gates of hell" (cited in Natsios, 2008: 81).

Preventing Sudan from collapsing into chaos is complicated by the multidimensional nature of the conflict. One dimension is a long-standing dispute between the politically dominant Arab Muslims living in the northern Nile River valley and the more numerous non-Arab Christians and animists residing in the south. Hostilities between the two sides were temporarily extinguished by a 1972 peace agreement but reignited eleven years later, resulting in bitter fighting that claimed the lives of 2.5 million southerners and displaced 4.6 million people. After slow, painstaking negotiations, a new peace agreement was reached in 2005, based on a political power-sharing arrangement between the Arab National Congress Party (NCP) and the southern rebel group, the Sudan People's Liberation Movement (SPLM). Additionally, a semiautonomous Government of Southern Sudan (GOSS) was established for six years, after which a referendum would be held on secession. Despite this agreement, relations between the NCP and SPLM remain strained over the status of Abyei, an area rich in petroleum resources that each side covets. Other problems that could undermine the stability of South Sudan as a new country are the widespread charges of corruption made against GOSS officials over their squandering of oil revenues and the flare-ups of ethnic violence, which killed more than 2,000 people in 2009.

A second dimension of the political violence plaguing Sudan is an armed conflict between the Arab-dominated central government and black, non-Arab Muslim rebels in the western region of Darfur, who seek a power-sharing agreement with Khartoum similar to the one obtained by the SPLM. In 2003, against the backdrop of growing tensions over water and grazing rights between the region's Arab herdsmen and black African subsistence farmers, two rebel groups, the Sudanese Liberation Army (SLA) and the Justice and Equality Movement (JEM), began attacking government offices and military outposts. Khartoum responded with a brutal campaign against the African population, orchestrated by the Sudanese military and the pro-government Janjaweed militia. Over the next five years, some 2,700 villages were destroyed, leading to charges of genocide being brought against President Omar al-Bashir by the chief prosecutor of the International Criminal Court. Meanwhile, Darfur's rebel groups have splintered into over twenty competing factions, further complicating efforts to bring the fighting to a halt. In early 2010, a cease-fire was negotiated with JEM based on a tentative agreement to include its representatives within the government. Even though armed bandits continued to roam Darfur, the level of violence dropped significantly. But because other rebel groups were not parties to the peace agreement, Darfur's future remains unpredictable.

The third dimension of the ongoing violence is a proxy war pitting Sudan against Chad. Friction between these neighboring countries has increased in recent years as refugees from Darfur began pouring across the border into Chad, with the Janjaweed militia on their heels. Relations deteriorated rapidly in early 2008 when the Sudanese government backed Chadian guerrillas who assaulted N'Djamena, Chad's capital, in the hope of toppling President Idriss Déby, whose Zaghawa tribe has links to leaders of some Darfur rebel groups. Chad retaliated three months later by supporting a JEM offensive that reached

SALAH OMAR/AFP/Getty Images

Refugees in Search of Sanctuary Beginning in 2003, the Janjaweed, a paramilitary group supported by the Sudanese government, attacked the country's non-Arab population in the Darfur region. Shown here is the Kalma refugee camp filled with 150,000 people from Darfur.

the outskirts of Khartoum. Sudanese troops, in turn, attacked a Chadian border garrison at Ade, raising fears that the cold war between the two countries could escalate to a military showdown.

Finally, the last dimension of political violence in Sudan concerns the possible erosion of a 2006 peace accord between the central government and the Beja and Rashida peoples in the east. Backed by the neighboring country of Eritrea, a rebel group known as the Eastern Front has engaged in sporadic skirmishing with government troops. Given the multifaceted problems facing Khartoum, with each capable of igniting a new round of armed conflict, it is not surprising that Sudan ranks third worldwide in vulnerability to state collapse ("Failed State Index," 2010: 76).

In international relations, conflict regularly occurs when actors on the world stage have disputes that arise out of incompatible interests. However, the costs can become staggering when disputants take up arms to settle their differences. Most people conceive of armed conflict as conventional war—sustained fighting between the regular military units of sovereign states undertaken to coerce adversaries into submission. But as the fighting in Sudan illustrates, this conception is too narrow. The belligerents may include a kaleidoscope of state and nonstate actors that wage war through both conventional and unconventional means. This chapter explores the challenge that these multidimensional armed conflicts pose in world politics, examining their trends, causes, and changing form since the end of the Second World War.

TRENDS IN ARMED CONFLICT

Throughout history, war has caused untold human misery. By one account, in the past 3,400 years, "humans have been entirely at peace for 268 of them, or just eight percent of recorded history" (Hedges, 2003). Social scientists have attempted to measure the frequency of military conflict in an effort to ascertain if the level of international violence has been increasing, decreasing, or holding steady over time. According to one such study (Brecke, 1999: 10), the frequency of military conflict has risen significantly during the last 300 years, with the twentieth century being extraordinarily violent.

Several patterns in the incidence of armed conflict have emerged since the end of World War II with implications for the global future. A total of 240 armed conflicts occurred between 1946 and 2008. The trend in battle deaths during this period has been downward, although the number of fatalities spiked during the Korean, Vietnam, and Iran-Iraq wars. As 2009 began, there were thirty-six armed conflicts underway in twenty-six locations throughout the world (Harbom and Wallersteen, 2009: 577; Gleditsch, 2008: 693). Figure 7.1 provides a closer look at the frequency of armed conflict within and between states since the end of the Cold War. Behind these frequency counts are the following general trends:

- The proportion of countries throughout the world engaged in **interstate wars** has declined in recent years.

- In particular, wars between the great powers have decreased; since 1945 the world has experienced a long peace—the most prolonged period in modern history in which no wars occurred between the most powerful countries.

- Most armed conflicts now occur in the Global South, which is home to the highest number of states, with the largest populations, the least income, and the least stable governments.

- The majority of these armed conflicts are **civil wars** and insurgencies within countries, which on average last four times as long as interstate wars (Levy and Thompson, 2010: 186).

- Civil wars pose a higher risk than interstate wars of relapsing into violence after being terminated, though democracies experience fewer conflict recurrences than other types of regimes (Hewitt, Wilkenfeld, and Gurr, 2010).

These trends, together with the wars in Afghanistan and Iraq, hint that the character of armed conflict is changing. In the past, when people thought about armed conflicts, they focused on wars between states and only secondarily on

interstate war sustained armed conflict between two or more sovereign states.

civil war armed conflict within a country between the central government and one or more insurgent groups, sometimes referred to as internal war.

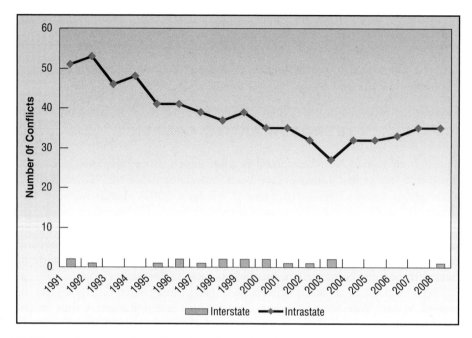

FIGURE 7.1   **Armed Conflicts since the End of the Cold War**

This figure shows the trends in interstate and intrastate armed conflicts from 1991 through 2008. Compared to armed conflicts within states, those that occur between states have been infrequent since the end of the Cold War. Although the number of insurgencies and civil wars has declined, intrastate armed conflicts continue to pose serious security problems. Note: The intrastate data include those wars that became internationalized due to the government or opposition receiving external military support.

SOURCE: Lotta Harbom and Peter Wallensteen, "Armed Conflicts, 1946-2008," Journal of Peace Research 46, no. 4 (2009): 577–587, p. 578

internationalized civil war   an armed conflict between the central government of a country and insurgents with outside intervention by at least one other state in support of the insurgents.

civil wars within states. Now military planners expect to face a more complex security environment that includes **internationalized civil wars**. Between 1989 and 2009, 29 percent of intrastate wars involved troops from outside powers in support of the government in power, the opposition, or both sides (Harbom and Wallersteen, 2009: 578).

Further complicating matters, old security threats have reappeared in new form. Pirates armed with assault rifles and rocket-propelled grenades have used high-speed motorboats to attack commercial vessels in some of the world's major shipping lanes. With insufficient resources to patrol their coastal waters, African countries such as Somalia, Tanzania, and Nigeria have been unable to stop pirates from hijacking ships and kidnapping the crews for ransom. According to the International Maritime Organization, between 2001 and 2009, 2,966 pirate attacks occurred worldwide, resulting in some 3,200 seafarers being kidnapped, 500 injured, and 160 killed. Because 64 percent of these attacks were successful (Coggins, 2010: 86–87; *New York Times*, April 20, 2008: 12), some shipping companies have turned for help to mercenaries and private armed escort vessels to augment the naval patrols now conducted by more than two dozen countries in the world's most perilous waters.

Trends such as these raise several questions about the nature of contemporary war. Why do certain states and nonstate actors resort to violence? What causal factors increase the probability of war? Do they interact with one another in a dynamic sequence of steps that unfold over time? To seek answers, let's examine a few of the most common theories about the sources from which wars originate.

WHAT CAUSES ARMED CONFLICT?

Throughout history, efforts have been made to explain why people engage in organized violence. Inventories of war's origins (see Levy and Thompson, 2010; Cashman, 2000; Vasquez, 2000; Geller and Singer, 1998) generally agree that hostilities are rooted in multiple sources found at various levels of analysis. Some are proximate causes that directly influence the odds of war; others are remote and indirect, creating explosive background conditions that enable any one of a number of more immediate factors to trigger violence. The most commonly cited sources of war can be classified into three broad categories: (1) aggressive traits found in the human species; (2) pernicious national attributes that beget conflict-prone states; and (3) unstable structures and volatile processes within the international system that encourage disputes to become militarized.

The First Level of Analysis: Human Nature

In a sense, all wars between states originate from the decisions of national leaders, whose choices ultimately determine whether armed conflict will occur (see Chapter 3). We must therefore begin looking for the causes of war at the individual level of analysis, where questions about human nature are central.

The repeated outbreak of war has led some, such as psychologist Sigmund Freud (1968), to conclude that aggression is an instinctive part of human nature that stems from humans' genetic programming and psychological makeup. Identifying *Homo sapiens* as the deadliest species, ethologists (those who study animal behavior in order to understand human behavior) such as Konrad Lorenz (1963) similarly argue that humankind is one of the few species practicing intraspecific aggression (routine killing of its own kind), in comparison with most other species, which practice interspecific aggression (killing only other species, except in the most unusual circumstances—cannibalism in certain tropical fishes being one exception). Like humans, chimpanzees also engage in intraspecific aggression. Primatologists have documented organized raids and ambushes directed against chimps in adjacent territories. Their skirmishes resemble the kind of warfare waged by humans who live in hunting and gathering societies (Mitani, Watts, and Amsler, 2010).

Robert Ardrey (1966) proposes a "territorial imperative" to account for intraspecific violence. Humans instinctively defend territory they believe belongs to them. Occasionally, they also fight to annex land, and its associated resources, from neighboring groups. Ethologists are joined in this interpretation by those political realists who assume that the drive for power is innate and cannot be eliminated. Some of them even apply Charles Darwin's ideas about evolution to world politics. For these so-called "social" Darwinists, international life is a struggle for survival of the fittest, where natural selection eliminates traits that interfere with successful competition.

Many scholars question these views on both empirical and logical grounds. If aggression is a deep-seated drive emanating from human nature, then shouldn't all people exhibit this behavior? Most people, of course, do not; they reject killing as evil and neither murder nor excuse homicide committed by others. At some fundamental level, argues Francis Fukuyama (1999; see also Gazzaniga, 2005), human beings are built for consensus, not for conflict: People prefer to live in societies that have moral rules. Even accepting natural selection as an explanation of human evolution need not lead to the conclusion that aggression is ordained by heredity. As James Q. Wilson (1993: 23) argues, "the moral sense must have adaptive value; if it did not, natural selection would have worked against people who had such useless traits as sympathy, self-control, or a desire for fairness in favor of those with the opposite tendencies."

Most social scientists now strongly disagree with the premise that humans fight wars because of innate genetic drives. Although conflict among humans is ubiquitous, a compelling body of anthropological evidence indicates that various societies have avoided outright warfare. Some, like the Semi of the Central Malay Peninsula, have accomplished this through internalized psychological restraints; others, like the Mehinaku of the Xingu River in Brazil, have done it through external sociocultural constraints (Gregor and Robarchek, 1996). For these reasons, the 1986 *Seville Statement,* endorsed by more than a dozen professional scholarly associations, maintains that "it is scientifically incorrect" to say that "we have inherited a tendency to make war from our animal ancestors," or that war is "genetically programmed into our human nature."

If the origins of war do not lie in elemental instincts, are there other factors at the individual level of analysis that may increase the probability of disputes escalating to war? In Chapter 3, we saw how the idiosyncrasies, perceptions, and beliefs of political leaders can, on occasion, impair rational decision making, which may lead to hard-line behavior even when political differences between rivals are bridgeable. To be sure, some military conflicts are consciously sought by their initiators. But this does not mean that war is a product of violent instincts deeply engrained within the human species. On the contrary, the origins of many wars are traceable to certain psychological processes experienced by specific leaders at certain points in time. Under stress, for example, leaders are more sensitive to the hostile acts they perceive. In a crisis atmosphere, they tend to draw superficial lessons from the immediate past, inflating the meaning of recent successes and ignoring information that contradicts their convictions. Believing that their adversaries have more options than they have themselves, force may be seen as a simple way of resolving problems (Vasquez, 1993: 205). Yet, as the eighteenth-century Prussian general Karl von Clausewitz stressed, "war is a continuation of policy by other means." As an instrument of statecraft, it should not be wielded without a thorough analysis of political aims, possible side effects, and

Early on the morning of August 2, 1990, columns of T-72 tanks from Iraq's elite Republican Guard crossed the country's southern border with Kuwait and raced down a six-lane highway toward its capital city. Within hours, resistance to the invasion collapsed. Saddam Hussein, the Iraqi leader who ordered the attack, announced that the tiny, oil-rich emirate would be annexed. If he followed up his conquest of Kuwait by overrunning Saudi Arabia, Hussein would control almost half of the world's proven petroleum reserves.

In the following passage, General Colin Powell, then-chairman of the Joint Chiefs of Staff, describes a meeting of the National Security Council convened by President George H.W. Bush to discuss what posture the United States should take regarding the potential Iraqi threat to Saudi Arabia. Echoing Clausewitz, he asked the group to weigh the strategic value of a war with Iraq before concentrating on logistics and tactics.

> [Secretary of Defense] Cheney turned to me to review military options. Again, I went over the ... plan for defending Saudi Arabia. I described the units we could put into the Gulf region in a hurry. I was reasonably sure that the Iraqis had not yet decided to invade Saudi Arabia. I was also confident that they did not relish a war with the United States. "But it's important," I said, "to plant the American flag in the Saudi desert as soon as possible, assuming we can get their okay." We did not want our inaction to embolden Saddam further.
>
> ... I then asked if it was worth going to war to liberate Kuwait. It was a Clausewitzian question which I posed so that the military would know what preparations it might have to make. I detected a chill in the room. The question ...

should not have come from me. I had overstepped. I was not the National Security Advisor now; I was only supposed to give military advice. Nevertheless,... as a midlevel career officer, I had been appalled at the docility of the Joint Chiefs of Staff, fighting the war in Vietnam without ever pressing the political leaders to lay out clear objectives for them. Before we started talking about how many divisions, carriers, and fighter wings we need, I said we have to ask, to achieve what end?

... [Later] Cheney brought up our earlier meeting with the President. "Colin," he said. "you're Chairman of the Joint Chiefs. You're not Secretary of State. You're not the National Security Advisor any more. And you're not Secretary of Defense. So stick to military matters." ... I was not sorry, however, that I had spoken out in the White House. What I had said about giving the military clear objectives had to be said (Powell, 1995: 464–466).

On August 7, Saudi Arabia requested American help in deterring a possible Iraqi attack, and the next day President Bush ordered the deployment of U.S. troops to the Persian Gulf. In November, UN Resolution 678 authorized member states to use all necessary means to evict Iraq from Kuwait. On January 17, 1991, the United States began a relentless air assault on Iraqi positions, followed a few weeks later by a devastating ground attack. Kuwait was liberated on February 26. Two days later, the president ended offensive military operations. It was an impressive military victory. However, little thought had gone into analyzing the long-term strategic consequences of a postwar Iraq still ruled by Saddam Hussein.

long-term repercussions. In an early expression of this admonition, the Athenians told the Spartans on the eve of the Peloponnesian War that it is a common mistake to go into war the wrong way around, starting with action and only later turning to a discussion of the costs, risks, and trade-offs (see APPLICATION: When Is It Worth Going To War?).

The Second Level of Analysis: Internal Characteristics of States

Do different types of states exhibit different amounts of war involvement? Conventional wisdom holds that variations in the geography, culture, society, economy, and government of states influence whether their leaders will initiate war. To evaluate this claim, we need to examine research findings on how the internal characteristics of states affect leaders' choices regarding the use of force.

Geographic Location.   Natural resources, transportation routes, strategic borders, and other factors related to a country's territory have long been recognized as important sources of international friction. Following the end of the Cold War, competitions over access to valuable commodities ranging from oil to water produced a "new geography of conflict," a reconfigured cartography in which resource flows traced the major fault lines (Klare, 2001). Territorial issues can be thought of as remote, underlying causes of war. That is to say, depending on how they are handled, they can set off a chain of events that increases the probability of war. Researchers have found that contiguous states are more likely than geographically distant states to have their disputes escalate to full-scale war (Gibler, 2007), especially when they involve territorial issues. Furthermore, states involved in territorial disputes tend to experience recurrent conflict (Hensel, 2000).

Geographic factors affect the prospects for civil war as well. Mountainous countries with a lightly populated hinterland, for example, have been found to face an enhanced risk of rebellion when valuable natural resources are discovered because the people living in such localities suddenly have an enormous incentive to secede. Additionally, rebels can extort funds from the trade in these resources to finance their operations (Collier, 2005).

Finally, geography influences civil war through a neighborhood effect. The likelihood of domestic political instability increases when a neighboring state is experiencing armed conflict, especially when there are ethnic ties to groups in that conflict (Buhaug and Gleditsch, 2008).

Demographic Stress.   A number of demographic factors contribute to the onset of armed conflict. Research shows that the risk of civil war is the greatest in those countries where population dynamics impact heavily on living conditions. Population size and density have been found to be associated with the onset of civil war (J. Dixon, 2009: 709–710). Particularly influential is the presence of a large proportion of young, unemployed males in the population who are concentrated in cities (Urdal, 2006). "Countries with a high proportion of adults under thirty have two and a half times the probability of experiencing a new outbreak of civil conflict as do those more mature age structures relative to population size" (Cincotta and Engleman, 2004: 18).

Cultural Values.   Human behavior is strongly influenced by culture. Some governments promote political cultures that encourage citizens to accept whatever their leaders declare is necessary for national security, including using military force to resolve international disagreements. The risk of war increases whenever values that sustain **xenophobia** and blind obedience gain wide acceptance.

xenophobia   a fear of foreigners.

Nationalism can become a caldron within which these self-glorifying and other-maligning values simmer (Van Evera, 1994). The tendency of people to seek their identity and fulfillment through the nation-state, Jack Levy (2001)

CONTROVERSY Does Love of Country Cause War with Foreign Nations?

What does *patriotism* mean? The most familiar definition is popularly expressed as "love for one's country." Often, it involves "love for the nation or nationality of the people living in a particular state," especially when the population of that state primarily consists of a single ethnonational racial or linguistic group.

Because "love" for valued objects of affection, such as a person's homeland, is widely seen as a virtue, it is understandable why governments everywhere teach young citizens that love for country is a moral duty. Nationalism fosters a sense of political community, and thereby contributes to civic solidarity. On these grounds, nationalism is not controversial.

However, some people find nationalism to be potentially dangerous in its extreme form. Hypernationalists, these critics warn, measure their patriotism by the degree of opposition exhibited toward foreign nations and by the blind approval of every policy and practice of their own nation. They allegedly ignore transcendent moral principles such as the love for all humanity (Etzioni, 2005), and are skeptical about cosmopolitan values that put the interests of all above those of a specific national group (O'Sullivan, 2005). Given these criticisms, is nationalism sometimes a cause of war between nations? What do you think?

In thinking about this controversial issue—about whether nationalism and internationalism are mutually exclusive—consider the view of Karl Deutsch, a German-born immigrant and famous scholar who taught for many years at Harvard University. Deutsch, an authority on nationalism, described nationalism's linkage to armed conflict in these moving words:

> Nationalism is an attitude of mind, a pattern of attention and desires. It arises in response to a condition of society and to a particular stage in its development. It is a predisposition to pay far more attention to messages about one's own people, or to messages from its members, than to messages

from or about any other people. At the same time, it is a desire to have one's own people get any and all values that are available. The extreme nationalist wants his people to have all the power, all the wealth, and all the well-being for which there is any competition. He wants his people to command all the respect and deference from others; he tends to claim all rectitude and virtue for it, as well as all enlightenment and skill; and he gives it a monopoly of his affection. In short, he totally identifies himself with his nation. Though he may be willing to sacrifice himself for it, his nationalism is a form of egotism written large … .

> Even if most people are not extreme nationalists, nationalism has altered the world in many ways. Nationalism has not only increased the number of countries on the face of the earth, it has helped to diminish the number of its inhabitants. All major wars in the twentieth century have been fought in its name … .

> Nationalism is in potential conflict with all philosophies or religions—such as Christianity—which teach universal standards of truth and of right and wrong, regardless of nation, race, or tribe. Early in the nineteenth century a gallant American naval officer, Stephen Decatur, proposed the toast, "Our country! In her intercourse with foreign nations, may she be always in the right, but our country, right or wrong." Nearly 150 years later the United States Third Army, marching into Germany following the collapse of the Nazi regime, liberated the huge concentration camp at Buchenwald. Over the main entrance to that place of torture and death, the Nazi elite guard had thoughtfully written, "My Country, Right or Wrong." (K. Deutsch, 1974: 124–125)

explains, is a powerful catalyst to war. When people acquire an intense loyalty to the state and this commitment is bolstered by national myths emphasizing the moral and physical strength of the state and by individuals' feelings of powerlessness, nationalism contributes to the onset of war. The connection between nationalism and war has a long history and provokes much debate (see CONTROVERSY: Does Love of Country Cause War with Foreign Nations?). Critiques of nationalism were especially pronounced in the last century. The English essayist Aldous Huxley once termed nationalism "the religion of the twentieth century."

Today nationalist feelings remain intense in many parts of the world, and continue to arouse violence among stateless nations seeking their own independent states. Intrastate armed conflicts in which the rebels mobilize along ethnonationalist lines are 92 percent more likely to experience intensified violence in the first year or two of fighting than are those that do not mobilize along ethnic lines (Eck, 2009: 384).

While not denying the power of nationalism, feminist theory points to another set of cultural values that may lead to war. As pointed out in Chapter 2, some feminists believe that aggression is rooted in the masculine ethos that prepares people to accept war and to respect the warrior as a hero (Tickner, 2002; Enloe, 2000). Celebrating certain gender roles and marginalizing others contributes to society's militarization, they argue. The penchant for warfare does not breed in a vacuum; it is produced by **socialization**. When powerful social institutions promote values that condone organized violence, disputes within and between states are more likely to be resolved through force than amicable procedures (Lind, 1993). Furthermore, as feminist scholars maintain, civil strife is more common when cultural norms condone gender repression (Caprioli, 2005; Melander, 2005).

socialization the processes by which people learn the beliefs, values, and behaviors that are acceptable in a given society.

Economic Conditions.   Does a state's economic system affect the probability that it will initiate a war or suffer from civil strife? The question has provoked controversy for centuries. Marxists, for example, claim that capitalism is the primary cause of war. Recall from Chapter 5 that according to Vladimir Lenin's theory of imperialism, the need for capitalist states to export surplus capital spurs military efforts to capture and protect foreign markets. For Marxists, the only way to end war is to end capitalism.

Contrary to Marxist theory is liberalism's conviction that free-market systems promote peace, not war. The reasons are multiple, but they center on the premise that commercial enterprises are natural lobbyists for world peace because their profits depend on it. War interferes with trade, destroys property, causes inflation, consumes scarce resources, and encourages big government and counterproductive controls over business activity. By extension, this reasoning continues, as government regulation of internal markets declines, prosperity will increase and fewer wars will occur.

The debate between Marxists and liberals was at the heart of the ideological contest between East and West during the Cold War, when the relative virtues and vices of socialism and capitalism were uppermost in people's minds. At the time, Marxists cited the record of European colonial wars to support their claim that capitalist states were war-prone. However, they generally omitted references to communist uses of military force, including the Soviet invasion of Finland in 1939, North Korea's attack on South Korea in 1950, and the People's Republic of China's occupation of Tibet in 1959. Nor did they explain the repeated military clashes between communist states, such the Soviet Union with Hungary (1956), Czechoslovakia (1968), and China (1969), and China with Vietnam (1979 and 1987). Simply put, the proposition that communist states were inherently peaceful failed to stand up to empirical evidence.

The end of the Cold War did not end the debate about the relationship between economics and war. It simply moved the discussion away from a preoccupation with capitalism versus communism and riveted people's attention on whether economic interdependence promoted peace. The widening and deepening economic connections among wealthy countries in the Global North led scholars to ask whether market freedom, openness to the global economy, high amounts of bilateral trade, and economic development reduce the probability of war (Gartzke, 2007; McDonald, 2007; Weede, 2005). The evidence to date supports the liberals' belief that economic openness and high levels of economically important trade are significant constraints on the use of force (Russett and Oneal, 2001). In addition, states with highly advanced economies appear less likely to fight one another than pairs of states with less developed economies, or pairs with one advanced and one less developed economy (Bremer, 1992; Lemke, 2003).

Aside from affecting the probability of interstate war, a country's level of economic development is related to the incidence of intrastate violence. Poor countries experiencing newly imposed economic liberalization policies can experience violent protests and civil strife (Bussmann and Schneider, 2007). The probability of a country undergoing civil strife also is affected by a feeling of **relative deprivation**. When people perceive that they are unfairly deprived of the wealth, status, or opportunities that they deserve in comparison with advantaged others, their frustration and anger often explodes into violence (Gurr, 1970). These feelings can be particularly pronounced in countries experiencing rapid, unequal economic growth (Murdoch and Sandler, 2004), and in those with significant inequalities between different geographic regions (Østby, Nordås, and Rød, 2009).

relative deprivation
people's perceptions that they are unfairly deprived of wealth and status in comparison to others who are advantaged but not more deserving.

Many analysts believe that internal economic strife is linked to interstate war because leaders who experience acute opposition at home provoke crises abroad to divert attention from their domestic failures. As mentioned in Chapter 3, this diversionary theory of war stems from sociological research that shows in-group bonds tighten when faced with an out-group threat. War, according to this theory, gives a leader the opportunity to introduce ruthless forms of domestic political control while simultaneously being hailed as a protector. The evidence does not point to a clear, direct connection between civil strife and interstate war initiation, however. Perhaps the most compelling reason for these results is that when domestic conflict becomes severe, there is a greater likelihood that a state will reduce its foreign engagements in order to handle the situation at home.

Before drawing any final conclusions about the impact of poverty on war, we must note that the *most* impoverished countries have been the least prone to start wars with their neighbors. The poorest countries cannot vent their frustrations aggressively because they lack the military or economic resources to do so. This does not mean that the poorest countries will always remain peaceful. If the past is a guide to the future, then the impoverished countries that develop economically will be those most likely to acquire arms and eventually go to war. In particular, many studies suggest that states are likely to initiate foreign wars *after* sustained periods of economic growth—that is, during periods of rising prosperity, when they can most afford them (Cashman, 2000). This signals danger if rapidly developing countries in the Global South direct their new resources toward armament rather than invest in sustained development.

Political Institutions.   As discussed in Chapter 2, liberal theory assigns great weight to the kinds of political institutions that states possess. Furthermore, as pointed out in Chapter 3, researchers have found that although democratic governments use force against nondemocracies, they rarely make war on other democracies. In fact, they hardly ever skirmish. "Pairs of democratic states have been only one-eighth as likely as other kinds of states to threaten to use force against each other, and only one-tenth as likely actually to do so" (Russett, 2001: 235; see also Sobek, 2005).

The capacity of democracies to manage conflict with one another has led scholars to speculate about the consequences of having democratic institutions diffuse around the world. As the proportion of democracies grows, will norms and practices of nonviolent conflict resolution cascade throughout the state system? Some scholars imagine that once a critical mass of democratic states is reached, many other states would be persuaded to adopt democratic institutions, which would prompt another round of adoptions, and so on. A world populated by stable democracies, they predict, would be freed from the curse of war.

Although the community of liberal democracies has grown over the past two centuries, the euphoria surrounding democraticization has given way to the realization that there is no certainty that liberal democracy will become universal. Nor will halting, erratic moves toward liberalization by the world's remaining autocracies automatically produce a more peaceful global order. Democratizing countries pass through an unstable transition period (Bremmer, 2007), and unlike their older, constitutionally secure brethren, fledgling democracies occasionally resort to force (Mansfield and Snyder, 2005). Illiberal democracies, those which conduct elections but lack a supporting infrastructure of civil liberties, a functioning rule of law, and separation of powers, are particularly prone to domestic strife (Collier, 2010; Zakaria, 2003). Finally, the fact that leaders in established democracies are accountable to electoral approval does not guarantee that they will moderate the use of force when it is applied. The sensitivity of democratic leaders to casualties sometimes leads to greater uses of firepower to end wars quickly (E. Cohen, 1998).

The preceding discussion of the characteristics of states that influence their proclivity for armed conflict does not exhaust the subject. Many other state-level causes have been hypothesized. But, however important domestic influences might be, many believe that the nature of the international system is even more critical.

The Third Level of Analysis: System Structure and Processes

As we saw in Chapter 2, some political realists see war as a product of the decentralized character of the international system that encourages self-help rather than teamwork. To illustrate how the absence of a central authority affects behavior, the philosopher Jean-Jacques Rousseau suggests we imagine a group of primitive hunters tracking a stag (male deer). The hunters are hungry, and must all cooperate in order to have a chance of trapping an animal large enough to feed the entire group. While stalking the creature, one hunter spots a hare. If he leaves the group to pursue the hare, he would almost certainly bag it and feed himself. But without his help, the remaining hunters could not catch the stag and would go hungry. Rousseau uses this allegory to show how egoistic actors in an anarchic environment are tempted to follow their own short-term interests, which undercuts the opportunity to attain larger goals that benefit everyone. Applying this reasoning to the outbreak of the First World War, the British scholar G. Lowes Dickinson (1926) claimed that war was inevitable whenever an anarchy of armed states existed.

International anarchy may make war likely, but as a constant condition of modern international life, it doesn't explain why some periods erupt in violence, while others remain tranquil. As discussed in Chapter 2, constructivists point out that international anarchy is what states make of it: Anarchies of distrustful actors are different from anarchies of friends. To account for variation in the amount of interstate war and internationalized civil war over time, we need to look at changes in the structure and processes operating within the anarchic international system. More specifically, we need to consider how the distribution of power among the members of the state system, as well as shifts in that distribution, may affect the outbreak of armed conflict.

Power Distributions.   Theories of world politics are abstract, conjectural representations of the world. Thus far we have examined theories that attempt to explain the outbreak of armed conflict by concentrating on human nature and the internal makeup of states. An alternative approach focuses on the structure of the state system; that is, how states are positioned or arranged according to the distribution of power among the system's members. In Chapter 3, we introduced the concept of polarity to describe the distribution of material capabilities. Unipolar systems contain a structure with one dominant power center, bipolar systems have two centers of power, and multipolar systems possess more than two such centers. Although civil wars have become internationalized under each type of structure, preliminary research indicates that unipolar periods characterized by the concentration of power in the hands of a single preponderant state are highly intervention-prone (Raymond and Kegley, 1987). When it comes to predicting interstate war, however, the evidence is less clear, with scholars debating whether bipolar or multipolar systems are more likely to experience war.

Advocates of bipolarity assert that a world containing two centers of power that are significantly stronger than the next tier of states will be stable because the dire consequences of war between these giants encourages them to exercise caution when dealing with one another, and to prevent conflicts among their allies from engulfing them in a military maelstrom. Conversely, those favoring multipolarity believe that situations of rough parity among several great powers will be peaceful because a rise in interaction opportunities and a diminution in the share of attention that can be allocated among many potential adversaries reduce the rigidity of conflicts. In rebuttal, the former submit that because of its ambiguous nature, multipolarity will promote war through miscalculation. The latter retort that bipolarity, lacking flexibility and suppleness, will deteriorate into a struggle for supremacy (see Christensen and Snyder, 1990; Midlarsky, 1988; Deutsch and Singer, 1964).

Research into the relative merits of bipolar versus multipolar structures suggests that the distribution of material capabilities within the state system is not related to the onset of war (Kegley and Raymond, 1994; Bueno de Mesquita, 1981; Ostrom and Aldrich, 1978); nevertheless it affects the *amount* of war should armed conflict occur (Levy, 1985; Wayman, 1985). Wars occur in both bipolar and multipolar systems, but multipolar systems experience larger, more severe wars (Vasquez, 1986).

Although different polarity configurations do not raise or lower the probability of war, alliance polarization makes war more likely. Recall that polarity differs from polarization. As discussed in Chapter 3, polarity concerns the distribution of power; alliance polarization refers to the propensity of lesser powers to cluster around the strongest states. The interstate system can be said to be moving toward greater polarization if its members align in two hostile blocs.

Alliance polarization is hazardous because the structural rigidity it fosters reduces the opportunities for a wide array of multifaceted interactions among states, therein decreasing the chances for **crosscutting cleavages** to emerge. Crosscutting reduces the odds of war, because opponents on one issue may be partners on another. They are not implacable enemies confined to an endless zero-sum struggle. In an international environment of **overlapping cleavages**, adversaries have few interests in common, and thus become fixated on the things that divide them. Under these circumstances, minor disagreements are magnified into bigger tests of will where reputations are thought to be at stake. Tight, polarized blocs of states are thus war-prone; peace is best preserved when there is a moderate amount of flexibility in the structure of alliances (Kim, 1989; Kegley and Raymond, 1982; Wallace, 1973).

Power Trajectories and Transitions. Although the international system is anarchic, possessing no higher authority above the sovereign state, it is nonetheless stratified due to variations in the relative power of its members. If the international pecking order is clear, with the dominant state holding a substantial advantage over its nearest potential rival, then efforts to alter the rank order of states by force are unlikely (Mowle and Sacko, 2007). Conversely, if the capability advantage of the dominant state is minimal or eroding due to the growth of a challenger, the probability of war increases (Geller, 2000).

According to what has been dubbed **power transition theory**, peace is most likely to be preserved when there is an marked imbalance of capabilities between dissatisfied and satisfied nations that favors the latter (Organski and Kugler, 1980). War, it is argued, often involves "rear-end" collisions between a rapidly rising dissatisfied state and the dominant state, which wishes to preserve the status quo. When the relative strength of the revisionist challenger and the dominant state converge toward rough parity, armed conflict can erupt in two

crosscutting cleavages   a situation where politically relevant divisions between international actors are contradictory, with their interests pulling them together on some issues and separating them on others.

overlapping cleavages   a situation where politically relevant divisions between international actors are complementary; interests pulling them apart on one issue are reinforced by interests that also separate them on other issues.

power transition theory   the contention that war is likely when a dominant great power is threatened by the rapid growth of a rival's capabilities, which reduces the difference in their relative power.

Carlos Humberto/LatinContent/Getty Images

Rising Powers on the Global Landscape Brazil and India are widely viewed as rising international powers. Here Brazilian President Luis Inacio Lula da Silva (left) and Indian Prime Minister Manmohan Singh (right) meet at an April 2010 summit conference to discuss mutual cooperation.

different ways. First, the dominant state may initiate a preventive war so as not to be overtaken by the challenger. Second, and more commonly, the challenger may strike first, confident that it can accelerate its climb to the apex of international power. Research suggests that these patterns also hold within regional subsystems, where the confluence of parity among small state rivals and dissatisfaction with the status quo increase the probability of minor-power wars (Lemke, 2002).

Some scholars believe that the trajectory of state power follows a cycle of ascendance, maturation, and decline, based on the ratio of its strength relative to others within the system (Doran, 2000; Doran and Parsons, 1980). According to **power cycle theory**, war is most likely at certain critical points along this cycle; namely, when shifts in the rate of growth or decline in a state's relative power create discontinuities between prior foreign policy expectations and future realities. Whenever "these states encounter an unexpected reversal in the direction or rate of change in their power trajectories, they are subject to various psychological impulses or judgmental challenges that increase the danger of extensive wars" (Tessman and Chan, 2004: 131). Preliminary research indicates that when numerous great powers pass through these critical points at the same time, massive wars ensue (Doran, 1989).

Cyclical theories have always provoked discussion. Years ago, for example, Italian historian Luigi da Porto received considerable attention by asserting: "Peace brings riches; riches bring pride; pride brings anger; anger brings war;

power cycle theory
the contention that armed conflict is probable when a state passes through certain critical points along a generalized curve of relative power, and wars of enormous magnitude are likely when several great powers pass through critical points at approximately the same time.

war brings poverty; poverty brings humanity; humanity brings peace; peace, as I have said, brings riches, and so the world's affairs go round." For many people, assertions like this make it seem plausible that certain rhythms characterize the tides of history.

As discussed in Chapter 4, various scholars have looked for long cycles in the rise and fall of hegemonic leaders over the past five centuries (see Hopkins and Wallerstein, 1996; Modelski and Thompson, 1996; Goldstein, 1988). However, they have failed to reach a consensus about the existence of periodicities in global war. Their findings diverge, because different definitions of hegemonic leadership and different measures of global war lead to different estimates of the duration of periods of peace and war. Another problem with theories of war that emphasize power transition dynamics is the tendency to assume that dominant states are satisfied with the status quo. Rather than being content to maintain things as they are, some dominant states in unipolar systems have actively sought to move the world in new directions. Hence the debate continues as to whether the onset of war follows a repeating sequence driven by underlying structural dynamics within the global system.

THE FUTURE OF ARMED CONFLICT

Since the birth of the modern world system some three and a half centuries ago, national leaders have prepared for wars against other countries. Throughout this period, war has been conceived as large-scale organized violence between the regular armies of sovereign states, or between the army of a state and the conventional army of a rebel province or region, as in the case of the American Civil War. Although leaders today still ready their nations for such clashes, increasingly they are faced with the prospect of **asymmetric warfare**—armed conflict between conventional military forces and transnational terrorist networks.

asymmetric warfare armed conflict between belligerents of vastly unequal military strength, in which the weaker side is often a nonstate actor that relies on unconventional tactics.

Terrorism and Asymmetric Warfare

Terrorism was well known even in ancient times, as evident in the campaign of assassinations conducted by the Sicarii (named after a short dagger, or *sica*) in Judea during the first century CE. Today it is practiced by a diverse group of movements scattered throughout the world. Political terrorism is the deliberate use or threat of violence against noncombatants, calculated to instill fear, alarm, and ultimately a feeling of helplessness in an audience beyond the immediate victims. Because perpetrators of terrorism often strike symbolic targets in a horrific manner, the psychological impact of an attack can exceed the physical damage. A mixture of drama and dread, political terrorism is not senseless violence; it is a premeditated strategy of extortion that presents people with a danger that seems ubiquitous, unavoidable, and unpredictable.

Terrorism can be employed to support or change the political status quo. Repressive terror, which is wielded to sustain an existing political order, has

terrorism the premeditated use or threat of violence perpetrated against noncombatants, usually intended to induce fear in a wider audience.

been utilized by governments as well as by vigilantes. From the Gestapo (secret state police) in Nazi Germany to the "death squads" in various countries, establishment violence attempts to defend the prevailing political order by eliminating opposition leaders and by intimidating virtually everyone else.

Dissidents who use terrorism to change the political status quo vary considerably. Some groups, like the MPLA (Popular Movement for the Liberation of Angola), used terrorism to expel colonial rulers; others, such as ETA (Basque Homeland and Liberty), adopted terrorism as part of an ethnonational separatist struggle; still others, including the Islamic Jihad, the Christian Identity Movement, the Sikh group Babbar Khalsa, and Jewish militants belonging to Kach, placed terror in the service of what they saw as religious imperatives; finally, groups such as the Japanese Red Army and Italian Black Order, turned to terrorism for left- or right-wing ideological reasons. In short, dissident terror may be grounded in anticolonialism, separatism, religion, or secular ideology.

Although the ultimate goals of individuals and groups that employ terrorism differ, they seek similar intermediate objectives as a means of attaining their goals. The following objectives are the most common:

- The *agitational* objectives of terrorism include promoting the dissident group, advertising its agenda, and discrediting rivals. Shocking behavior makes people take heed, especially when performed at a time and place imbued with symbolism. Nineteenth-century anarchists were among the first to emphasize the propaganda value of terrorism. One stunning act, they believed, would draw more attention than a thousand leaflets.

- The *coercive* objectives of terrorism include disorienting a target population, inflating the perceived power of the dissident group, wringing concessions from authorities, and provoking a heavy-handed overreaction from the police and military. Launching vicious, indiscriminate attacks at markets, cafes, and other normally tranquil locations can create a paralyzing sense of foreboding within the general public and goad political leaders into adopting repressive policies, which terrorists hope will drive the population to their side of the struggle.

- The *organizational* objectives of terrorism include acquiring resources, forging group cohesion, and maintaining an underground network of supporters. Robbing banks, obtaining ransom for hostages, and collecting protection money from businesses can finance training and logistical support for field operations. Moreover, because high initiation costs tend to lower group defections, these activities can increase allegiance when recruits are required to participate in violent acts.

To accomplish these objectives, terrorists use a variety of tactics, including bombing, assault, hijacking, and taking hostages. Hijacking and hostage-taking generally involve more complex operations than planting a bomb in a crowded department store or gunning down travelers in an airport lounge. An example of such careful planning can be seen in the coordinated hijacking of five airliners by Palestinians during September 1970, which eventually led to one airliner being blown up in Cairo and three others at Dawson Field in Jordan. To be successful, these kinds of seizures require detailed preparation, vigorous bargaining, and the capacity to guard captives for long periods of time. Among the payoffs of such efforts is the opportunity to articulate the group's grievances. The Lebanese group behind the 1985 hijacking of TWA flight 847, for instance, excelled at using U.S. television networks to articulate their grievances to the American public, which had the effect of circumscribing the options that the Reagan administration entertained while searching for a solution to the crisis.

Beyond bombings, assaults, hijacking, and hostage-taking, two other threats could become part of the terrorist repertoire. First, terrorists may acquire weapons of mass destruction to deliver a mortal blow against their enemies. Nuclear armaments are the ultimate terror weapons, but radiological, chemical, and biological weapons also pose extraordinary dangers. Crude radiological weapons can be fabricated by combining ordinary explosives with nuclear waste or radioactive isotopes, which could be stolen from hospitals, industrial facilities, or research laboratories. Rudimentary chemical weapons can be made from herbicides, pesticides, and other toxic substances that are available commercially. Biological weapons based on viral agents are more difficult to produce, though the dispersal of anthrax spores through the mail during the fall of 2001 illustrated that low-technology attacks with bacterial agents in powder form are a frightening possibility.

The second tactical innovation on the horizon is cyberterrorism. Not only can the Internet be used by extremists as a recruiting tool and a means of coordinating their activities with like-minded groups, but it allows them to case potential targets by hacking into a foe's computer system. Viruses and other weapons of **information warfare** could cause havoc if they disabled financial institutions, power grids, air traffic control systems, and other key elements in a country's communication infrastructure.

information warfare
attacks on an adversary's telecommunications and computer networks to degrade the technological systems vital to its defense and economic well-being.

Efforts to measure the frequency and severity of terrorism began in earnest during the 1960s. According to the U.S. Department of State's Office of Counterterrorism, global terrorist activity increased nearly threefold between 1968 and 1987, after which the number of incidents gradually but erratically declined—until 2004 when the new National Counter-Terrorism Center (NCTC) took over responsibility for counting the number of terrorist incidents and broadened the definitional criteria to include civilian casualties from the war in Iraq. Figure 7.2 shows that as measured by these new criteria, 11,770 terrorist attacks occurred in 2008, claiming 15,765 lives.

The Changing Nature of Terrorism

The traditional view of terrorism as a rare and relatively remote threat was challenged by the events of September 11, 2001. The horrors visited upon the World Trade Center and the Pentagon forced the world to confront a grim new reality: Terrorists were capable of executing catastrophic attacks almost anywhere, even without an arsenal of sophisticated weapons. Not only did groups like Al Qaeda have global reach, but stealth, ingenuity, and meticulous planning could compensate for their lack of firepower.

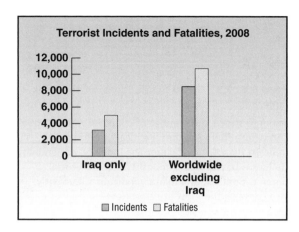

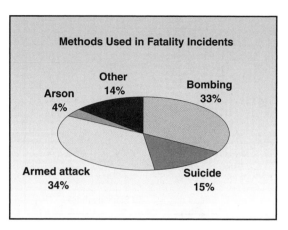

F I G U R E 7.2 **The Threat of Global Terrorism**

The figure on the left shows the number of terrorist incidents and fatalities during 2008, both in Iraq and throughout the rest of the world. The figure on the right records the percentage of the 15,765 fatalities that were caused by each major method used in the 11,770 terrorist incidents that occurred in 2008.

SOURCE: NCTC (2009: 21, 34).

What arguably made September 11 a symbolic watershed was that it epitomized a deadly new strain of terrorism. During the Cold War, those who used terrorist tactics tended to be localized subnational groups. Some, like the Tupamaros in Uruguay, were self-sufficient. Others, like the Abu Nidal Group in the Middle East, received weapons and rudimentary training from foreign powers, and thus exemplified what came to be known as **state-sponsored terrorism**. Virtually all of these groups saw terrorism as political theater, a frightening drama where the perpetrators wanted a lot of people watching, not a lot of people dead. Today's groups, however, seem to have a desire to kill as many people as possible. Driven by searing hatred, annihilating enemies appears more important to post–Cold War terrorists than winning sympathy for their cause.

state-sponsored terrorism   formal assistance, training, and arming of foreign terrorists by a state in order to achieve foreign policy goals.

Another feature of this new strain of terrorism is its organizational form. Instead of having a hierarchical command structure, Al Qaeda, for example, possesses a decentralized, horizontal structure. Loosely tied together by the Internet, e-mail, and cellular telephones, Al Qaeda originally resembled a hub-and-spoke organization: Osama bin Laden and a small core of loyalists provided strategic direction, training, and aid to a franchise of affiliated terrorist cells. Rather than serving as a commander, bin Laden functioned as a coordinator who, in addition to planning dramatic, high-casualty attacks, provided financial and logistical support to extremist groups fighting those whom he perceived as archenemies.

Following the ouster of the Taliban regime in Afghanistan by the American military and its partners from the Northern Alliance, Al Qaeda underwent a structural change. Combined with its loss of a sanctuary in Afghanistan, the killing or capture of roughly one-third of Al Qaeda's leadership transformed the organization into an entity that resembled a chain. Bin Laden and his close

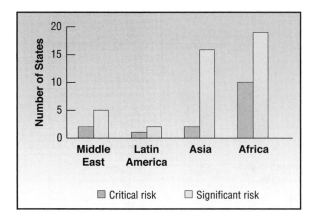

F I G U R E 7.3 Global South States on the Brink of Failure

This figure shows the number of countries in the Global South where there is either a critical or a lower but still significant risk of state failure. The index of vulnerability to failure is based on a composite of twelve social, economic, political, and military indicators. Currently, Africa contains the most at-risk states.

SOURCE: "The Failed State Index" (2010: 76)

associates regrouped in Pakistan's mountainous tribal areas along the frontier with Afghanistan, and continued broadcasting ideological inspiration to small, disparate cells around the world, but they no longer were directly involved in the planning and execution of most of the attacks undertaken in Al Qaeda's name. Operating independently, without the training, financing, and logistical infrastructure previously available through a central headquarters, Al Qaeda's diffuse underground cells have concentrated on "soft" targets, sometimes attacking in conjunction with sympathetic local forces. The July 2005 resort bombings in Sharm el Sheikh, Egypt, and the November 2005 hotel bombings in Amman, Jordan, illustrate this pattern of activity.

What makes the new breed of terrorists who belong to organizations such as Al Qaeda more lethal than previous terrorists is their religious fanaticism, which allows them to envision acts of terror on two levels. At one level, terrorism is a means to change the political status quo by punishing those culpable for felt wrongs. At another level, terrorism is an end in itself, a sacrament performed for its own sake in an eschatological confrontation between good and evil (Juergensmeyer, 2003). Functioning only on the first level, most secular terrorist groups rarely employ suicide missions. Operating on both levels, religious terrorist groups see worldly gain as well as transcendent importance in a martyr's death (Bloom, 2005; Pape, 2005).

Today's relatively open, borderless world makes it easy for transnational networks of like-minded militants to use terrorist tactics. Many **failing states** in the Global South offer out-of-the-way places for them to relocate and train (see Figure 7.3). Weak, failing states lack the capacity and often the willingness to provide physical security and socioeconomic welfare for their populations. Unable to control their borders or regulate their territory, failing states are enticing to terrorist groups for several reasons. First, they offer a refuge where members can plan and train for future operations. Second, the wrenching economic conditions in failing states provide terrorist groups with a pool of potential recruits. Finally, failing states furnish a safe haven for smuggling and other revenue-generating illicit activities, as well as a place where front organizations can be established to launder money (Takeyh and Gvosdev, 2009: 80–82).

failing states states in danger of political collapse due to overwhelming internal strife.

The future course of terrorism cannot be easily foreseen. There is no terrorist orthodoxy among its practitioners on strategic questions, no canon on how to conduct asymmetric warfare. Rather, terrorism has evolved in response to new technologies, new targets of opportunity, and new counterterrorist policies. The perpetrators of political terrorism are not mindless; they have long-term aims and they carefully consider how different operations may facilitate accomplishing their purposes. Indeed, it is their ability to plan, execute, and learn from these operations that makes them so dangerous.

Armed conflict in all its forms extracts a terrible toll on human life. In this chapter, we have briefly examined trends in its frequency and changing character, as well as several prominent theories about its causes. We have seen that interstate and civil wars are not the legacy of what Sigmund Freud once called a "death instinct" embedded within human nature. Neither are they the product of a single cause, whether at the state or systemic levels of analysis. Both intrastate and interstate wars can be brought on by various causal sequences, each involving a complex combination of factors. In the next chapter, we will explore the national security policies that states use to advance their interests in a world where the threat of war abounds.

CHAPTER SUMMARY

- Force is an instrument that states often use to resolve their conflicts. However, war is not inevitable: Some societies have never known the outbreak of war, and some historical periods have not experienced warfare.

- Since the end of World War II, most wars have been between countries in the Global South or have entailed military action by great powers against them. None have occurred between the great powers. Civil wars have become more common than interstate wars.

- War is best explained by multiple factors operating at various levels of analysis.

- There is little evidence that human nature is a direct cause of war.

- Evidence pertaining to state-level explanations of interstate war suggests that the probability of militarized conflict is increased by hypernationalism and territorial disputes among contiguous countries. Its probability declines significantly when both parties to a dispute are stable democracies, and they possess open, advanced economies linked by commerce. The likelihood of civil wars increases when countries experience demographic stress, relative deprivation, and border other states undergoing civil strife.

- Evidence pertaining to system-level explanations of war suggest that the following conditions increase the probability of militarized conflict: polarized alliances, an unstable hierarchy of states, and the existence of several great powers simultaneously passing through critical points in their cycle of relative power. Whether a system is bipolar or multipolar in structure does not affect the occurrence of war; however, it influences the magnitude and severity of any wars that break out, with multipolarity suffering from larger wars that involve more casualties.

- The global future is likely to experience an increasing amount of asymmetric warfare between sovereign states and terrorist networks.

- Political terrorism is the purposeful use or threat of violence against noncombatants, undertaken to intimidate a wider audience. The ultimate goals of those who employ terrorism vary: Some groups employ it to support the political status quo; others, to overthrow the status quo. For both types of groups, terror is used to accomplish agitational, coercive, and organizational objectives.

- Traditionally, terrorist groups have relied on bombing, assault, hijacking, and hostage-taking to intimidate their target audience. Two emerging threats are the use of weapons of mass destruction (nuclear, radiological, chemical, and biological weapons) and cyberterrorism—attacks on an opponent's computer systems.

KEY TERMS

asymmetric warfare

civil war

crosscutting cleavages

failing states

information warfare

internationalized civil
   war

interstate war

overlapping cleavages

power cycle theory

power transition theory

relative deprivation

socialization

state-sponsored
  terrorism

terrorism

xenophobia

SUGGESTED READINGS

Cashman, Greg, and Leonard C. Robinson. *An Introduction to the Causes of War: Patterns of Interstate Conflict from World War I to Iraq.* Lanham, MD: Rowman & Littlefield, 2007.

Colaresi, Michael P., Karen Rasler, and William R. Thompson. *Strategic Rivalries in World Politics.* New York: Cambridge University Press, 2007.

Levy, Jack S., and William R. Thompson. *Causes of War.* Malden, MA: Wiley-Blackwell, 2010.

Midlarsky, Manus I. (ed.). *Handbook of War Studies III: The Intrastate Dimension.* Ann Arbor, MI: University of Michigan Press, 2009.

Vasquez, John A., and Marie T. Henehan. *Territory, War and Peace: An Empirical and Theoretical Analysis.* New York: Routledge, 2009.

CRITICAL THINKING QUESTIONS

Game theory is a branch of mathematics used to analyze the strategic interaction of two or more actors. One of the most widely known game-theoretic approaches to the study of conflict dynamics is the Prisoner's Dilemma game. Imagine that two suspects following an armed robbery are taken into police custody and placed in separate cells by the district attorney, who is certain that they are guilty but only has sufficient evidence to convict them on an illegal weapons charge. The district attorney tells prisoner A and prisoner B that there are two choices: confess to the robbery, or remain silent. If one prisoner confesses and the other doesn't, he will be given immunity from prosecution for turning state's evidence while his accomplice will get a sentence of ten years in the state penitentiary. If both confess, they will be given a reduced sentence of five years in the penitentiary. If neither confesses, they will be convicted on the weapons charge and serve only six months in the county jail. Because both prisoners want to spend as little time incarcerated as possible, their preferences are rank-ordered from the best to the worst outcomes as follows: (1) immunity from prosecution; (2) six months in the county jail; (3) five years in the state penitentiary; and (4) ten years in the penitentiary. The following matrix depicts the results that will occur depending on whether each prisoner chooses to cooperate with his accomplice by remaining silent or defect by confessing to the district attorney.

Note: The first number in each cell of the matrix is A's payoff; the second number is B's payoff. The number 1 represents the most preferred outcome, whereas 4 represents the least preferred outcome.

Faced with this situation, what should each prisoner do? Remember that they both want as little time behind bars as possible, and they are being interrogated separately so they cannot communicate. Furthermore, neither prisoner is sure that he can trust the other. Although the optimal strategy for both prisoners would be to tacitly cooperate with each other and keep quiet so each receives only a six-month sentence (the payoff of 2,2 in the matrix), the structural properties of this situation are such that there are powerful incentives to defect from your partner and give state's evidence to the district attorney. First, there is an offensive incentive to defect based on the prospect of getting immunity by confessing. Second, there is a defensive incentive to defect, grounded in the fear of being double-crossed by an accomplice who squeals. If one prisoner refuses to talk but the other confesses, the one who tried to cooperate with his accomplice to get a mutually beneficial result would receive the worst possible payoff (4, or ten years in the penitentiary), while the prisoner who defected to the district attorney would receive the best payoff (1, or immunity). Not wanting to be a "sucker" who spends a decade incarcerated while his partner in crime goes free, both prisoners conclude that it is in their self-interests to defect and testify against one another; consequently, they both receive a worse result (the payoff 3, 3 in the matrix, or five years in prison) than if they had tacitly cooperated by remaining silent. The dilemma is that seemingly rational calculations by each individual actor can yield collectively worse results for both than had they chosen other strategies.

Many theorists liken various aspects of world politics to the Prisoner's Dilemma game. Consider two countries (A and B) that are approximately equal in military capability, are uncertain of whether they can trust one another, and currently face two choices: cooperate in lowering arms spending or defect by increasing arms spending. Suppose that each country prefers to have a military advantage over the other and fears being at a serious disadvantage, which would happen if one increased arms spending while the other reduced expenditures (the payoffs 1, 4 and 4, 1 in the matrix). By cooperating to lower arms spending, they could devote more resources to other national needs such as education and health care (the payoff 2, 2), but given offensive and defensive incentives that are similar to those tempting the two prisoners in our earlier example, they both conclude that it is in their individual self-interests to play it safe and arm. As a result of their joint defection (payoff 3, 3), they end up worse off by locking themselves into an expensive arms race that may destabilize the prevailing balance of power.

The Prisoner's Dilemma game highlights some of the difficulties in reaching mutually beneficial agreements among self-interested actors who distrust their peers. Beyond the study of arms races, do you see any other possible applications of this game in world politics? What strategies might help the players escape the dilemma they portrayed in the game?

8

Military Power
and the Use of Force

> If you want peace, prepare for war.
> FLAVIUS VEGETIUS RENATUS
> ROMAN GENERAL

On September 30, 1862, Count Otto von Bismarck, the chief minister of Prussia, addressed a legislative budget committee on the need to expand the country's military. It was a difficult task for the tall, broad-shouldered, and often abrasive minister. Many members of parliament had been resisting tax increases for some time, even to fund reforms of the armed forces.

Prussia was one of 38 Germanic states scattered across central Europe in the mid-nineteenth century. According to German nationalists, the division of the German people into numerous small- and medium-sized states kept them at the mercy of larger neighbors. Many Germans supported unification but were leery of Prussian ambitions to lead a united Germany. Austria and France were worried as well. A united Germany under Prussian leadership would pose an enormous security threat. With skilled labor, an educated population, and unparalleled electrical, chemical, and steel industries, German unification would create an economic and military powerhouse. Consequently, political leaders in Vienna and Paris preferred to leave the Germans divided among several dozen innocuous states.

Bismarck recognized these barriers to Prussian aspirations, and feared they might not be overcome without a modern military. "The position of Prussia in Germany," he told the legislative budget committee, "will be determined not by its liberalism but by its power." Prussia must strengthen its military. "Not through speeches and majority decisions are the great questions of the day decided," he thundered, "but through iron and blood." During the next decade, Bismarck's policy of iron and blood led to wars against Denmark (1864), Austria (1866), and France (1870–1871). Collectively known as the Wars of German Unification, they were won by a combination of Bismarck's uncanny ability to isolate his international opponents, and the training, firepower, and mobility of Prussia's modernized military. Together, they transformed the fragmented German lands into a strong centralized state. Before these wars, Prussia was the smallest of Europe's great powers; afterward, it had a near-hegemony over the continent.

Bismarck's genius resided in his ability to entertain multiple courses of action, explore all of their permutations, and move on several fronts simultaneously. No single move was an end in itself; each positioned him to advance in another direction. "One cannot play chess," he insisted, "if from the outset sixteen of the sixty-four squares are out of bounds." A tenacious advocate of Prussian interests and a master of intrigue, he could see opportunities presented by different political configurations on the diplomatic chessboard. To exploit them, he was willing to be disingenuous and, at times, even ruthless. "If it hadn't been for me, there wouldn't have been three great wars, 80,000 men would not have died, and parents, brothers, sisters, and widows would not be in mourning," he once admitted. "But that I have to settle with God." Like Karl von Clausewitz, the Prussian general who had fought against Napoleon half a century earlier, Bismarck saw war as an extension of foreign policy by other means, a political instrument for attaining one's goals when diplomacy fails to resolve a stalemate. To Bismarck, conflict was normal, and war was a way to resolve it by compelling an adversary to do one's will. Success hinged on military power. As Frederick the Great, King of Prussia during the eighteenth century, put it: "Diplomacy without an army is like music without instruments." This chapter examines the role of power in world politics. It begins by analyzing the ambiguous concept of "power." After reviewing the difficulties in measuring a country's power potential, it evaluates states' efforts to amass military capabilities by exploring trends in military spending, the arms trade, and weapons technology. Finally, the chapter concludes by discussing how states use their military and economic resources to exercise influence over other international actors.

POWER IN WORLD POLITICS

Throughout history, many leaders have seen the acquisition of power as their primary objective. In their eyes, security is a function of power; therefore, increasing power is in the national interest. Yet the meaning of "power" is not self-evident. It is used in different ways by different people. Most scholars define power in relational terms, as the ability of one state to make another continue a course of action, change what it is doing, or refrain from acting. A powerful state, in other words, has the capacity to control others. By exercising power, it can reduce the probability of something it does not want to happen and increase the probability of a preferred outcome.

The Elements of State Power

Having defined power in terms of control, the question remains as to how we might measure the potential of one international actor to make another do what it otherwise would not. As David Baldwin (1989: 26) points out, "the problem of measuring political power is like the problem of measuring purchasing power in an economy without money." In the absence of a standard unit of account, it is difficult to create a precise ranking of states that would predict who would prevail in a political conflict. Our intuition may suggest that larger countries are more powerful than smaller ones, but size alone does not always determine the outcome of political conflicts. France and, later, the United States were unable to exercise control over Vietnam. Similarly, the Soviet Union could not control Afghanistan. Indeed, history is replete with examples of small countries that won wars or defended their independence against much larger states.

Because we lack a single measuring rod for assessing **power potential**, scholars and policy makers alike try to rank order states according to a combination of capabilities or resources presumed necessary to influence others. Like chefs at a chili cook-off, everyone has his or her own list of ingredients. Usually, some combination of geographic, demographic, economic, and other tangible factors are mixed with intangible factors like leadership and public morale. Though the recipes may differ, the results are usually the same: Power is equated with those capabilities that enhance a country's war-making ability.

The importance customarily accorded to military prowess arises from the tendency to regard force as the ultimate arbiter of serious international disputes. Recall from earlier chapters that the anarchical environment of world politics requires states to rely on self-help for protection. No higher authority safeguards their interests. Under such conditions, military strength is seen as the primary source of national security and international influence.

power potential the relative capabilities or resources held by a state that are considered necessary to its asserting influence over others.

While military strength may be effective in controlling the behavior of friends and foes in some contexts, it is ineffective in others. Power is situationally specific: The capabilities that allow an actor to influence one set of countries on a certain issue may be useless in influencing other countries on a different matter. A state's overall power, therefore, is defined in terms of the kinds of actors that it can control and the types of issues over which it has influence. As discussed in Chapter 4, a great power is a state that is able to exercise control over a wide domain of targets and an extensive scope of issues, usually by having a broad range of rewards and punishments at its disposal.

Power and Influence

Although military capability is central to most realist conceptions of power and security, some liberal theorists argue that the sources of state power today depend less on military strength than on factors such as information, technology, and trade competitiveness (Nye, 1990). Since the end of World War II, a handful of states have increased their relative power by investing their resources in civilian rather than military technology. Whereas the United States spends most of its research and development budget on military programs, Japan and many European countries invest heavily in developing new technologies related to consumer goods. If we are entering a world based on education and human capital, one where creative ideas, product design, financing, and marketing will increasingly become major sources of wealth and power as political scientist Richard Rosecrance (1999) suggests, then the United States is not keeping up with its competitors, even though it accounts for almost half of the world's military expenditures.

opportunity costs the concept in decision-making theories that when the occasion arises to use resources, what is gained for one purpose is lost for other purposes, so that every choice entails the cost of some lost opportunity.

Critics of the realist emphasis on continually preparing for war also claim that military expenditures extract high **opportunity costs** (see CONTROVERSY: Does High Military Spending Lower Human Security?). Military spending, they assert, crowds out private and public investment. Had U.S. military outlays remained at the 1990 level, the peace dividend from the end of the Cold War would have exceeded $700 billion in the next fifteen years and potentially could have been made available for other purposes. In addition to sacrificing other economic opportunities, this argument continues, military spending has direct costs, because expensive equipment quickly becomes outdated in the face of rapid technological innovations. This creates the need for even more sophisticated new weapons, the costs of which are staggering.

Finally, critics of realism submit that less tangible sources of national power now figure more prominently in calculations regarding national defense. Sometimes, it is possible for political leaders to exert influence by setting the agenda and determining the framework of a debate, instead of relying on inducements and threats to coerce people. The ability to get others to embrace your values, to see your objectives as legitimate, tends to be associated with intangible power resources such as the attractiveness of your country's ideals and the seductiveness of its culture. These intangible resources constitute *soft power,* in contrast with the *hard power* usually associated with tangible resources like military and economic strength (Nye, 2004). Soft power is the ability to achieve one's objectives through

---

CONTROVERSY Does High Military Spending Lower Human Security?

Politics requires making hard choices about how public funds should be spent. One such choice is between "guns versus butter"—how much of a country's budget should be allocated to military preparedness as opposed to social welfare programs. The former emphasizes *state security*; the latter, *human security*. Neither goal can be pursued without making some sacrifice for the realization of the other.

The guns-versus-butter trade-off is significant in every country, and different leaders deal with it in different ways. One way to picture these differences is to group states according to how much of their gross domestic product (GDP) they devote to the military. There are wide variations in military spending, with many countries allocating high proportions of their GDP to defense and other countries choosing to use their wealth to enhance human security. Indeed, some comparatively wealthy states (Kuwait, Israel, and Brunei) bear a heavy defense burden, whereas other states whose citizens have high average incomes (Japan, Austria, and Luxembourg) have a low defense burden. Likewise, the citizens of some very poor countries (Burundi, Madagascar, and Zimbabwe) are heavily burdened, whereas those of others (Bhutan and Gambia) are not. Thus, it is difficult to generalize about the precise relationship between a country's defense burden and its citizens' standard of living, human development, or stage of development.

"The problem in defense spending," as former U.S. President Dwight D. Eisenhower once observed, "is to figure out how far you should go without destroying from within what you are trying to defend from without." How much should a country spend on national security? To some, the price is never too high. However, others argue that high levels of military spending reduce a state's ability to provide for its citizens. This view was expressed by Oscar Arias, the 1987 Nobel Peace laureate and former president of Costa Rica, who argued that "World leaders must stop viewing militaristic investment as a measure of national well-being. The sad fact is that half the world's governments invest more in defense than in health programs. If we channelled just $40 billion each year away from armies and into antipoverty programs, in ten years all of the world's population would enjoy basic social services—education, health care and nutrition, potable water, and sanitation. Another $40 billion each year over ten years would provide each person on this planet with an income level above the poverty line for his or her country."

If you were a head of state, what budget priorities would you propose for your country's national security and your citizens' human security? How would you reconcile the need for defense with the need to provide for the common welfare? The choices you would make would be difficult, because they entail trade-offs between competing values.

---

attraction rather than coercion, often by convincing others to follow norms and institutions that elicit the desired behavior (Keohane and Nye, 2001b). If soft power grows in relative importance in today's so-called information age, military force ratios will no longer translate into power potential in the way they once did. Of course, military capability will remain important. While it would be simplistic to assume that political influence is proportional to military strength, it would be a more serious error to deny any connection between the two (Majeed, 1991).

THE PURSUIT OF MILITARY CAPABILITY

How people spend their money reveals their values. Similarly, how governments allocate their revenues reveals their priorities. An examination of national budgets discloses an unmistakable pattern: Although the sources of global political power may be changing, many states continue to seek security by spending substantial portions of their national treasures on arms.

Trends in Military Spending

The weapons that governments believe they require for national security are costly. World military expenditures by the beginning of 2010, for example, reached $1,531 billion, at current prices (SIPRI, 2010: 214–215). When measured in constant dollars adjusted for inflation, this level of military spending shows an increase over past levels: three times that spent in 1960, twice that of the 1970 total, and above the 1980 Cold War peak. Compared to the mid-1930s, world military spending has increased over seventeen-fold, a growth rate exceeding that of world population, the rate of expansion of global economic output, and expenditures for public health.

These aggregate figures do not tell the entire story, because the global total spent for arms conceals widely varying trends for particular groups of countries. Historically, the rich countries have spent the most money on arms acquisitions, a pattern that has continued. In 2009, the Global North spent $1,167 billion for defense, in contrast with the Global South's $365 billion, which amounts to only 24 percent of the world total. However, military spending by the Global South has been increasing (see Figure 8.1). Its military expenditure in 1961 was about 7 percent of the world total, but by 2009, it had more than tripled. In short, poor states are copying the costly, military budgetary habits of the wealthiest states.

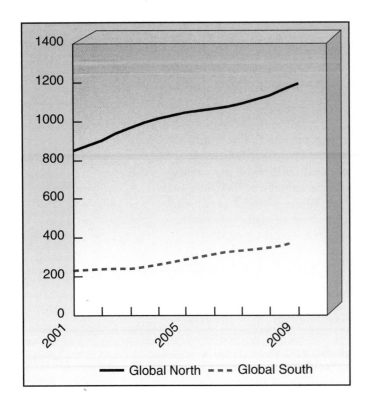

FIGURE 8.1 Changes in Military Expenditure Since 2001, Global North and Global South

Although military expenditures by Global South countries have gradually increased since the turn of the century, spending by Global North countries far exceeds the spending of Global South countries.

SOURCE: SIPRI (2010: 214–215).

Trends in the Weapons Trade

During the Cold War, many states sought to increase their security by purchasing weapons. The Cold War's end did not slow the arms trade, however. The total value of all international arms deliveries since 1991 exceeded $551 billion (Grimmett, 2009: 4), of which the majority were exported to developing countries, primarily in Asia and the Middle East. The weapons delivered by major suppliers to developing countries between 2005 and 2008 alone included 1,411 tanks and self-propelled cannons, 1,840 artillery pieces, 360 supersonic combat aircraft, 6,869 surface-to-air missiles, and other technologically advanced weapons systems (Grimmett, 2009: 63).

Besides looking at arms importers, it is also important to observe the activities of arms suppliers. By the end of the Cold War, more than sixty states were selling weapons abroad, with the United States dominating the arms export market. Since the turn of the century, the United States accounted for a higher proportion of worldwide contracts to sell arms than any other supplier (see Figure 8.2). Economic gain was an important rationale for these contracts, as the United States used arms exports to offset its chronic balance-of-trade deficits. To cement its share of the arms trade, one-quarter "of all U.S. foreign aid goes to helping the recipients by U.S.-produced weapons, equipment, or services" (*Harper's*, October 2005: 11). Because the sale of weapons is big business, arms manufacturers constitute a powerful domestic lobby. A highly organized **military-industrial complex** is believed by many to exercise enormous power over defense budgets and arms sales agreements in the United States as well as in many other Global North countries (Fallows, 2002).

In addition to reaping economic benefits, states sell weapons for various political reasons, including to support friendly governments and to cultivate new allies. Whether arming other countries has accomplished all of its intended

military-industrial complex a term coined by U.S. President Eisenhower to describe the coalition among arms manufacturers, military bureaucracies, and top government officials that promotes defense expenditures for its own profit and power.

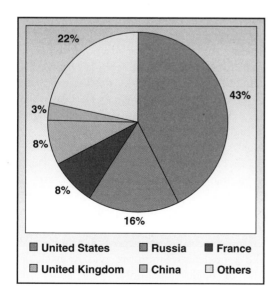

FIGURE 8.2 Percentage Value of Arms Transfer Agreements, 2005–2008

Global arms sales are dominated by a few countries. Between 2005 and 2008, the United States had the highest percentage of value in arms transfer agreements worldwide, worth $94 billion in constant 2008 U.S. dollars. Roughly 60 percent of the agreements were with Global South countries.

SOURCE: Grimmett (2009: 23)

political goals is open to question, however. During the Cold War, for example, the United States and the Soviet Union thought they could maintain peace by spreading arms to politically pivotal recipients. Between 1983 and 1987, the United States provided arms to fifty-nine less-developed countries while the Soviet Union supplied forty-two (Klare, 1990: 12). Yet many of the recipients engaged in war with their neighbors or experienced internal rebellion. Of the top twenty arms importers in 1988, more than half "had governments noted for the frequent use of violence" (Sivard, 1991: 17).

The inability of arms suppliers to control the uses to which their military hardware will be put is troubling. Friends can become foes, and supplying weapons to other states can backfire, as the United States discovered when the weapons it sold to Iraq were used against U.S. forces by Saddam Hussein in the Persian Gulf War (Timmerman, 1991), and when the Stinger missiles the United States supplied to mujahideen forces resisting the Soviet Union's 1979 invasion in Afghanistan fell into the hands of terrorists later opposing the United States. Likewise, in 1982, Great Britain found itself shipping military equipment to Argentina just eight days before Argentina's attack on the British-controlled Falkland Islands. Nevertheless, suppliers seem eager to sell to any purchaser, and they continue to sell weapons to both sides of a number of international disputes.

Trends in Weapons Technology

The widespread quest for armaments has created a potentially "explosive" global environment. This description is especially apt when we consider not only trends in defense expenditures and the arms trade but also the destructiveness of modern weapons.

Nuclear Weapons. Technological research and development has radically expanded the destructiveness of national arsenals. The largest "blockbuster" bombs of World War II delivered the power of 10 tons of TNT. The atomic bomb that leveled Hiroshima had the power of over 15,000 tons of TNT. Less than twenty years later, the former Soviet Union built a nuclear bomb with the explosive force of 57 megatons (million tons) of TNT. Since 1945, more than 130,000 nuclear warheads had been built, all but 2 percent by the United States (55 percent) and the Soviet Union (43 percent). Most have been dismantled since the 1986 peak, but more than 8,392 remain operational, with roughly one-quarter of them maintained on a high state of alert (SIPRI, 2010).

At the start of 2010, there were nine "official" members of the nuclear club—the United States, Russia, Great Britain, France, China, India, Pakistan, Israel, and North Korea. In addition, Iran and as many as twenty other states or terrorist organizations were believed to be seeking nuclear capability. Obstacles to nuclear **proliferation** are weak. First, the expertise necessary for weapons development has spread with the globalization of advanced scientific training. Second, export controls designed to stop technology transfer for military purposes are ineffectual. Finally, the materials needed to make a nuclear weapon are widely available, primarily due to the widespread use of nuclear technology for generating

proliferation the spread of weapon capabilities throughout the state system.

electricity. Today, almost 450 nuclear power reactors are in operation throughout the world, with over 70 new reactors either under construction or planned. States could reprocess the uranium and plutonium that power plants produce as waste for clandestine nuclear weapons production. Current estimates suggest that commercial reprocessing reactors are producing enough plutonium to make as many as 40,000 nuclear weapons.

Nuclear weapons serve as a symbol of status and power. Because of the widespread conviction rooted in realism that military might confers political stature, some countries regard the **Nuclear Nonproliferation Treaty (NPT)** as hypocrisy because it provides a seal of approval to those who first acquired nuclear weapons while denying it to all others. The belief held by some leaders that it is acceptable to develop a nuclear capacity for deterrence, influence, and prestige makes it difficult to imagine eliminating nuclear weapons, which U.S. President Barack Obama proposed during an April 2009 speech in Prague. "There's not a snowball's chance in hell we'll eliminate all nuclear weapons from the face of the earth," explains Matthew Bunn, editor of *Arms Control Today*. "That genie is long since out of the bottle and there's no chance of ever getting him back in" (cited in Kegley and Wittkopf, 2004: 471).

Nuclear Nonproliferation Treaty (NPT) an international agreement that seeks to prevent the spread of nuclear weapons by prohibiting further nuclear weapons sales, acquisitions, or production.

Biological and Chemical Weapons.   Despite the 1972 Biological Weapons Convention that prohibited the development, production, and stockpiling of biological weapons, many people fear that some states and terrorist organizations are trying to "weaponize" bacteria, viruses, and toxins. Similarly, although the 1925 Geneva Protocol banned the use of chemical weapons in warfare, and the Chemical Weapons Convention (CWC), now signed by 97 percent of the world's countries, required the destruction of existing stocks of nerve, blood, blister, and choking agents, roughly a dozen states are suspected of producing chemical weapons. As realists note, Iran's and Iraq's use of gas in their war against one another in the 1980s, and Iraq's use of chemical weapons in 1989 against its own Kurdish people demonstrate the weakness of these legal barriers.

Because biological and chemical weapons are lethal, they can be produced at comparatively low costs, and are easy to manufacture, transport, and deliver, their acquisition by state and nonstate actors may be unavoidable. On the one hand, weak states that acquire such weapons may see in them a way to deter great powers by threatening to inflict significant damage on anyone who dares attack them. On the other hand, extremist groups, often operating beyond the control of failing states, may find these weapons of mass destruction to be an effective means of promoting global terror.

From the perspective of the user, biological weapons have fewer disadvantages than chemical weapons, whose effectiveness is limited by wind, temperature, and other environmental conditions. For example, many pathogens are highly contagious and have a substantial incubation period. Consequently, an attack would not have to target a large number of people to produce mass casualties, and the perpetrators would have time to go into hiding before authorities realized that an attack had occurred. Although the dangers of nuclear proliferation are widely recognized, less attention has been given to the strategic consequences emanating from the development and diffusion of modern biological weaponry (Preston, 2007).

Weapons Delivery Systems.   Advances in weapons technology have been rapid and extraordinary. Particularly deadly have been the technological refinements in ballistic missiles that enable states to deliver weapons from as far away as 11,000 miles to within 100 feet of their targets in less than 30 minutes. During the Cold War, the United States and Soviet Union equipped their ballistic missiles with **multiple independently targetable reentry vehicles (MIRVs)**, which enable a single missile to launch several warheads toward different targets simultaneously. One U.S. MX (Peacekeeper) missile equipped with MIRV could carry ten nuclear warheads—enough to wipe out a city and everything else within a 50-mile radius.

Other technological improvements have led to steady increases in the speed, accuracy, range, and effectiveness of weapons. **Smart bombs** have become a part of the weapons inventory, as the recent wars in Kosovo, Afghanistan, and Iraq have shown. New anti-ship weapons, such as supersonic cruise missiles and high-speed cavitating torpedoes, like the Russian-made Sizzler and Shkval, have prompted research into exotic seaborne defensive systems. Furthermore, remote-controlled aircraft such as the Predator drone are widely used for surveillance, force protection, and close air support. Linked by satellites to pilots thousands of miles away from the war zone, Predators are armed with two Hellfire missiles that can be launched at targets on the ground. Newer drones, such as the Reaper, carry more ordinance, and Northrop-Grumman is developing an unmanned bomber that would operate from an aircraft carrier. The main drawback of drones resides in the vulnerability of the military reconnaissance and communication satellites upon which they rely. On January 11, 2007, China used a medium-range ballistic missile to destroy one of its own weather satellites orbiting about 530 miles above Earth, thereby demonstrating that control of space cannot be taken for granted by the United States. Another problem with remote-controlled weaponry emerged in 2009, when militants in Iraq were able to intercept live video feeds from Predator drones, thus alerting them to what targets were under surveillance.

Military strategists expect future wars to include even more innovative weapons technologies. They foresee the development of beamed energy and acoustic weapons that can take down enemies without necessarily killing them; electromagnetic pulse bombs, which can be hand delivered in a suitcase and can immobilize an entire city's computer and communications systems; and logic bombs that can confuse and redirect traffic on the target country's air and rail system. Finally, within the next decade or so, robots, which already are used in bomb disposal, may begin replacing soldiers for certain missions. Many of these technological advances in warfare are likely to make orthodox ways of classifying weapons systems as well as prior equations for measuring power ratios obsolete.

For decades, a **firebreak** has separated conventional wars from nuclear wars. The term comes from the barriers of cleared land that firefighters use to keep forest fires from racing out of control. In the context of modern weaponry, it

---

multiple independently targetable reentry vehicles (MIRVs)   a technological innovation permitting many nuclear warheads to be delivered from a single missile.

smart bombs   precision-guided military technology that enables a bomb to search for its target and detonate at the precise time it can do the most damage.

firebreak   the psychological barrier between conventional and nuclear war.

Remote-Controlled Warfare Unmanned aerial vehicles (UAVs) are playing a major role in counterterrorism operations. Shown here is the Predator. With a wingspan of almost 50 feet and weighing only 1,130 pounds, it can loiter over a target area for hours at an altitude where it cannot be easily seen or heard. At least forty countries have begun to develop different types of UAVs.

is a psychological barrier whose purpose is to prevent even the most intensive forms of conventional combat from escalating into nuclear war. As both nuclear and conventional weapons technologies advance, there is danger that the firebreak is being crossed from both directions—by a new generation of "near-nuclear" conventional weapons capable of levels of violence approximating those of a limited nuclear strike, and by a new generation of "near-conventional" nuclear weapons capable of causing destruction similar to that of the most powerful conventional weapons. For example, the United States is hoping to deploy a system called Prompt Global Strike by 2020, which would generate the destructive power of a nuclear weapon by hurling a massive conventional warhead on a maneuverable missile at high speed at a target with pinpoint accuracy. Once the firebreak has been crossed by deploying weapons of this type, many people fear that a major restraint on the conduct of modern warfare will disappear.

In sum, a pervasive sense of insecurity haunts much of the world. The danger of nuclear annihilation has not disappeared with the end of the Cold War. Nor are there effective controls over the proliferation of biological and chemical weapons. The twenty-first century has not become the peaceful and prosperous period many people expected. In response, many national leaders today echo the recommendation of the Roman general, Flavius Vegetius Renatus: "If you want peace, prepare for war." Security, as realists insist, requires military capability. But because the possession of military capability does not automatically result in its wise use, we turn now to look at how it is employed as an instrument of statecraft. We begin with an examination of nuclear weapons.

STRATEGIES FOR THE USE OF FORCE

The dropping of the atomic bomb on Japan on August 6, 1945, is the most important event distinguishing pre– from post–World War II international politics. In a blinding flash, the world was transformed. Once the devastating power of nuclear weapons became clear, policy makers in those states that acquired these weapons had to grapple with two central policy issues: (1) whether they should use them; and (2) how to prevent others from using them. The search for answers to these questions has been critical, for the immediate and delayed effects of an all-out nuclear war are terrifying to contemplate. Simply put, life as we know it would cease. The planet would be uninhabitable, because a **nuclear winter** would result, with devastating consequences: "Fires ignited in such a war could generate enough smoke to obscure the sun and perturb the atmosphere over large areas … [lowering] average planetary temperatures … [and darkening] the skies sufficiently to compromise green plant photosynthesis" (Sagan and Turco, 1993: 369). It has been estimated that the twenty-four Trident II missiles on board a single U.S. submarine, each carrying an average of six 455-kiloton W88 warheads, may be enough to initiate nuclear winter—enough to end human existence.

nuclear winter   the expected freeze that would occur in the earth's climate from the fallout of smoke and dust in the event nuclear weapons were used, blocking out sunlight and destroying plant and animal life that survived the original blast.

Although weapons of mass destruction have existed since World War II, the postures of the nuclear-armed powers toward them evolved as technologies, defense needs, capabilities, and global conditions changed. For analytical convenience, we can treat those postures in terms of three periods: compellence, deterrence, and preemption. The first began at the end of World War II and lasted until the Cuban missile crisis. U.S. nuclear superiority was the dominant characteristic of this period. The second began in 1962 and lasted until the breakup of the Soviet Union in 1991. Growing Soviet military capability was the dominant characteristic of this period, which meant that the United States no longer stood alone in its ability to annihilate another country without fear of its own destruction. The third phase began after the end of the Cold War, taking shape as the great powers began revising their strategic doctrines in the light of new global threats.

Compellence

Countries that possess military preeminence often think of weapons as instruments in diplomatic bargaining. The United States, the world's first and, for many years, unchallenged nuclear power, adopted the strategic doctrine of **compellence** (Schelling, 1966) when it enjoyed a clear-cut superiority over the Soviet Union. Nuclear capabilities do not have to be used for them to be useful; a state may exercise influence over others simply by demonstrating its awesome power and suggesting it may be used under certain circumstances. The U.S. doctrine of compellence made nuclear weapons tools of political influence, employed not for fighting but to convince others to do what they might not otherwise do.

compellence   a threat of force aimed at making an adversary grant concessions against its will.

The United States sought to gain bargaining leverage by conveying the impression that it would actually use nuclear weapons. This posture was especially evident during the Eisenhower administration, when Secretary of State John Foster Dulles practiced **brinkmanship**, deliberately threatening U.S. adversaries with nuclear destruction so that, at the brink of war, they would concede to U.S. demands. Brinkmanship was part of the overall U.S. strategic doctrine known as **massive retaliation**. To contain communism and Soviet

brinkmanship   intentionally taking enormous risks in bargaining with an adversary in order to compel submission.

massive retaliation   a policy of responding to any act of aggression with the most destructive capabilities available, including nuclear weapons.

expansionism, it called for a **countervalue targeting strategy**, that is, aiming U.S. nuclear weapons at what the Soviets valued most—their population and industrial centers. Some strategists, however, argued that it would be sufficient to adopt a **counterforce targeting strategy**, which would aim at military installations, thus presumably sparing civilian lives.

The threat of massive retaliation heightened fears in the Kremlin that a nuclear exchange would destroy the Soviet Union but permit the survival of the United States. Thus, in addition to augmenting their nuclear capabilities, Soviet leaders accelerated their missile program and successfully launched the world's first satellite (*Sputnik*), therein demonstrating Moscow's ability to deliver nuclear weapons beyond the Eurasian landmass. As Soviet leader Nikita Khrushchev put it in a July 1957 interview: "If you live among dogs, keep a stick." The superpowers' strategic competition now took a new turn, as the United States for the first time faced a nuclear threat to its homeland.

Deterrence

As U.S. strategic superiority eroded, American policy makers began to question the usefulness of weapons of mass destruction as tools in political bargaining. They were horrified by the destruction that could result if compellence provoked a nuclear exchange. The nearly suicidal Cuban missile crisis of 1962 brought about a major change in American strategic thought, shifting strategic policy from compellence to **deterrence**.

Whereas compellence contains an offensive coercive threat aimed at persuading an adversary to relinquish something without resistance, deterrence seeks to dissuade an adversary from undertaking some future action against one's homeland (direct deterrence) or against an ally (extended deterrence). Strategists often distinguish between two variants of deterrence. The first, *deterrence by denial*, is based on the assumption that opponents can be convinced to forego an attack if they are shown that their efforts would be futile. The second, *deterrence by punishment*, rests on the assumption that the deterrer has the ability to punish an adversary with unacceptably high costs if an attack is launched. This latter variant informed most of the theorizing about how the United States and Soviet Union would deter one another. The key elements of a deterrence strategy based on punitive threats are: (1) *capabilities*—the possession of military resources that can make threats of military retaliation plausible; (2) *credibility*—the belief that the target of an attack will actually follow through on its threats; and (3) *communication*—the facility to send a potential aggressor the clear message that the deterrer has both the ability and willingness to strike back. Advocates of deterrence by punishment argue that it "will succeed if threatened costs can be communicated to the challenger, assessed by the challenger, and believed by the challenger" (Harknett, 1994).

Ironically, the shift from compellence to deterrence stimulated rather than inhibited the U.S.–Soviet arms race. A deterrent strategy that depends on the unquestionable ability to inflict intolerable damage on an opponent requires a **second-strike capability**, which would enable a country to withstand an

countervalue targeting strategy targeting strategic nuclear weapons against an enemy's most valued nonmilitary resources, such as the people and industries located in its cities (sometimes known as countercity targeting).

counterforce targeting strategy targeting nuclear weapons on the military capabilities of an opponent.

deterrence a strategy designed to dissuade an adversary from doing what it would otherwise do.

second-strike capability a state's capacity to retaliate after absorbing a first-strike attack with weapons of mass destruction.

triad the combination of ICBMs, SLBMs, and long-range bombers in a second-strike nuclear force.

adversary's first strike and still retain the ability to retaliate with a devastating counterattack. To ensure a second-strike capability and an adversary's awareness of it, deterrence rationalized an unrestrained search for sophisticated retaliatory capabilities. Any system that could be built was built because, as President Kennedy explained in 1961, "only when arms are sufficient beyond doubt can we be certain without doubt that they will never be employed." Both superpowers ultimately deployed a **triad** of land-based intercontinental ballistic missiles (ICBMs), submarine-launched ballistic missiles (SLBMs), and long-range bombers, believing that all three could not be destroyed simultaneously in a first-strike attack.

mutual assured destruction (MAD) a system of deterrence in which both sides possess the ability to survive a first strike and launch a devastating retaliatory attack.

Policy makers coined the phrase **mutual assured destruction (MAD)** to describe the strategic balance that emerged between the United States and the Soviet Union after the Cuban missile crisis. Regardless of who struck first, the other side could destroy the attacker. Under these circumstances, initiating a nuclear war was irrational; the frightening costs outweighed any conceivable benefits. As Soviet Premier Nikita Khrushchev warned: "If you reach for the push button, you reach for suicide." Safety, in former British prime minister Winston Churchill's words, was "the sturdy child of terror and survival the twin brother of annihilation."

nuclear utilization theory (NUTs) a body of strategic thought that claimed deterrent threats would be more credible if nuclear weapons were made more usable.

As U.S.–Soviet relations evolved, strategic thinking in the United States split into rival positions. Although MAD continued to dominate the policy recommendations of some, others in the 1980s called for what became known as **nuclear utilization theory (NUTS)**, an approach whereby nuclear weapons would not simply play a deterrent role but also could be used in war. Advocates of this position argued that the use of nuclear weapons would not necessarily escalate to an all-out exchange; instead, they reasoned, it was possible to fight a "limited" nuclear war. By making nuclear weapons more usable, the United States allegedly could make its threats more credible. Proponents of MAD, on the other hand, held that deterrence remained the only sane purpose for nuclear weapons. They contended that any use of nuclear weapons, however limited initially, would surely escalate to an unrestrained exchange.

Strategic Defense Initiative (SDI) a plan conceived by the Reagan administration to deploy an antiballistic missile system using space-based lasers that would destroy enemy nuclear missiles.

Yet another shift in strategic thinking occurred in 1983, when U.S. President Reagan proposed building a space-based defensive shield against ballistic missiles. The **Strategic Defense Initiative (SDI)**, or "Star Wars" as critics labeled it, called for the development of a defense against Soviet ballistic missiles, using orbiting laser-based weapons to destroy missiles launched in fear, anger, or by accident. The goal, as President Reagan defined it, was to make nuclear weapons impotent and obsolete. Thus, SDI sought to shift U.S. nuclear strategy away from mutual assured destruction, which President Reagan deemed morally unacceptable. However, despite spending over $170 billion by 2010, the United States still remains far away from a reliable ballistic missile defense. But with North Korea and Iran testing ballistic missiles, the American effort to construct such a system, now with ground- and sea-based interceptors rather than space-based lasers, continues.

Preemption

The end of the Cold War has not brought strategic planning to a conclusion. New dangers appeared on the horizon, dangers that some strategists believe can only be addressed through a new strategy of **preemption**. "We face a threat with no precedent," President George W. Bush insisted during his commencement address at West Point on June 1, 2002. On the one hand, modern technology allows shadowy terrorist networks to launch catastrophic attacks against the United States. On the other hand, these networks cannot be dissuaded by the threat of punishment because they have no fixed territory or populace to protect. "We must take the battle to the enemy," he exhorted, "and confront the worst threats before they emerge."

Bush's call for acting preemptively against terrorists and the states that harbored them was reiterated in his September 17, 2002, report, *The National Security Strategy of the United States of America* (NSS), and reaffirmed in a subsequent document published in March 2006. Building on the proposition that "nations need not suffer an attack before they can lawfully take action to defend themselves against forces that present an imminent danger," the report argued that the acquisition of weapons of mass destruction by terrorists and rogue states provided the United States with a compelling case for engaging in anticipatory self-defense. Preemption rather than deterrence was required for national security.

Although under international law states have a legal right to defend themselves against imminent attacks, critics charge that beneath the language of military preemption lies a more radical policy of **preventive war**. In brief, a *preemptive* military attack entails the use of force to quell or mitigate an impending strike by an adversary. A *preventive* attack entails the use of force to eliminate any possible future strike, even if there is no reason to believe that the capacity to launch an attack is operational. Whereas the grounds for preemption lie in evidence of a credible, imminent threat, the basis for prevention rests on the suspicion of an incipient, contingent threat (Kegley and Raymond, 2007).

To illustrate the differences between military actions grounded in preemptive versus preventive motivations, let us briefly compare two historical cases. The Six-Day War between Israel and an alliance of Egypt, Syria, Jordan, and Iraq was an example of preemption. Tensions between Israel and its Arab neighbors had been growing throughout the spring of 1967 and reached their zenith in May, when Egyptian President Gamal Abdel Nasser undertook a series of steps that raised fears in Tel Aviv of an imminent attack. Besides mobilizing his troops and cementing military ties with Syria, Jordan, and Iraq, Nasser ordered the UN Emergency Force to leave the Sinai, where they had been deployed since the 1956 Suez War as a buffer between Egypt and Israel. Furthermore, he announced a blockade of the Straits of Tiran, Israel's vital waterway to the Red Sea and Indian Ocean, and proclaimed that his goal in any future war with Israel would be the destruction of the Jewish state. Assuming that an invasion was forthcoming and survival was doubtful if Egypt landed the first blow, the Israelis launched a surprise attack on June 5, which enabled them to win a decisive victory.

Whereas the Six-Day War exemplifies preemption, Israel's June 1981 raid on Iraq's Osiraq nuclear reactor illustrates preventive military action. From the Israeli perspective, the type of reactor Baghdad had acquired, its purchase of fuel that could be used in weapons manufacturing, and the termination of

preemption a quick first-strike attack that seeks to defeat an adversary before it can organize a retaliatory response.

preventive war a war undertaken to preclude an adversary from acquiring the capability to attack sometime in the future.

inspections by the International Atomic Energy Agency provided circumstantial evidence that Iraq was seeking a military nuclear capability. Given the vehement hostility expressed by Iraqi leaders toward Israel, as well as the vulnerability of Israel's population centers and nuclear arsenal to a first strike, Israeli leaders concluded that Saddam Hussein could not be deterred; Iraq's reactor had to be destroyed before it became operational. In contrast to 1967, when Israeli leaders saw an immediate threat from Egypt, they attacked in 1981 on the chance that someday Iraq might become a nuclear threat. It was better, they reasoned, to take preventive action straightaway in order to avoid the risk of fighting under less favorable circumstances later.

It is tempting for national leaders to order a swift, decisive attack against a budding threat, especially when they believe that the cost of inaction today may be devastation tomorrow. Yet critics maintain that the preventive use of military force sets a dangerous precedent. Pointing to America's failure to accurately assess Iraq's weapons programs, they argue that preventive wars may be triggered by unreliable intelligence about an adversary's aims and capabilities. Predicting another state's future behavior is difficult because leadership intentions are hard to discern, information on long-term goals may be shrouded in secrecy, and signals of its policy direction may be distorted by background noise. If mere suspicions about an adversary become a justifiable cause for military action, critics continue, every truculent leader will have a rough-and-ready pretext for ordering first strikes against prospective foes. A major policy dilemma facing political leaders contemplating preventive military action is the ratio of "false positives" to "false negatives." How can leaders avoid launching preventive wars against states that are wrongly believed to be planning aggression without foregoing action against states that are indeed planning aggression?

The strategy of anticipatory self-defense thus raises anew timeless questions about the conditions under which, and the purposes for which, military force is justifiable. How can threats and force be used to influence an adversary's decision-making calculus? What are the conditions that affect the success of coercive diplomacy?

THE LIMITS OF FORCEFUL PERSUASION

Since the end of the Second World War, strategists have debated the relative merits of two approaches to the use of military force (Gacek, 1994). The first would apply force decisively, employing every possible means to win a swift, unequivocal victory whenever vital interests are at stake. Operation Desert Storm, the U.S. plan for liberating Kuwait from Iraqi control in 1991, exemplified this approach. It centered on what then–Chairman of the Joint Chiefs of Staff Colin Powell called the "doctrine of invincible force." Powell advocated using all of the resources available to overwhelm the Iraqis in a massive, fast-and-furious campaign. In his words, it was the mindset of a New York street fighter: "Here's my bat, here's my gun, here's my knife, I'm wearing armor.

I'm going to kick your ass." The second approach contends that limits on the use of force may be necessary depending on one's political objectives. Rather than going all out or doing nothing, members of this school of thought recommend widening the array of policy options by applying military force in a flexible, discriminating manner calibrated to the type of threat one faces. Power and diplomacy, they maintain, must work in tandem when dealing with security challenges that are significant but do not demand full-scale war.

Wielding Power against Rivals

The strategy of **coercive diplomacy** exemplifies a flexible, discriminating approach to the use of force. It employs threats or limited force to persuade an opponent to change its behavior, sometimes supplementing the "stick" of punishment with the "carrot" of positive inducements. The goal is to alter the target state's calculation of costs and benefits, so it is convinced that acceding to one's demands will be better than defying them. This may be accomplished by delivering an **ultimatum** that promises an immediate and significant escalation in the conflict, or by issuing a warning and gradually increasing pressure on the target. Although coercive diplomacy's reliance on a mix threats, exemplary uses of force, and accommodations is designed to avoid the bloodshed and expenses associated with all-out military campaigns, it still carries some risk of war.

Correlates of Effective Military Coercion. Orchestrating the mix of threats and armed force can be done in various ways. One method involves military intimidation, which can range from traditional "gunboat diplomacy" (threatening an adversary with a show of naval force) to "tomahawk diplomacy" (striking it with cruise missiles). Another method entails **military intervention**. States can intervene physically through direct entry into another country or indirectly through **covert operations**. When resorting to any of these measures, states can act alone or in league with others.

Policy makers today disagree about the appropriate use of military coercion. Research on coercive diplomacy suggests that its success depends on the context of each specific situation. The following conditions are thought to favor the effective use of coercive diplomacy (Pape, 1996; George, 1991):

- *Clarity of user objectives.* The coercing power's demands must be clearly understood by the target state. Having the target refrain from taking an action is considered less difficult than demanding the target do something it otherwise would not do.

- *Asymmetry of motivation favoring the user.* Military superiority does not guarantee success. The coercing power must be more highly motivated than the target by what is at stake. Timing is critical. Military coercion tends to be effective when it occurs prior to the target making a firm commitment on the issue at hand, and when factions exist within the target state's government. It is far more difficult for a coercing power to undo something that has already been accomplished by the target state.

coercive diplomacy the use of threats or limited armed force to persuade an adversary to alter its foreign and/or domestic policies.

ultimatum a demand that contains a time limit for compliance and a threat of punishment for resistance.

military intervention overt or covert use of force by one or more countries that cross the border of another country in order to affect the target country's government and policies.

covert operations secret activities undertaken by a state outside its borders through clandestine means to achieve specific political or military goals.

- *Opponent's fear of escalation and belief in the urgency for compliance.* The coercing power must create in the adversary's mind a sense of urgency for compliance with its demand. Two factors are important in affecting an adversary's perceptions: (1) the coercing power's reputation for successfully using armed force in the past, and (2) its capability to increase pressure to a level that the target would find intolerable. Coercion generally fails when the target has the ability to absorb the punishment delivered by the coercing state.

- *Adequate domestic and international support for the user.* In addition to having political support at home, the coercing power is helped when it also can count on support from key states and international organizations.

- *Clarity on the precise terms of settlement.* The coercing power must be able to articulate the specific conditions for ending the crisis, as well as give assurances that it will not formulate new demands for greater concessions once the target capitulates. Offering positive inducements to the target state can lower its cost of acquiescence. Rewards improve the chances of success when made after a threat of demonstrative use of force, not before. Coercive diplomacy is more potent when the target state understands that you are seeking policy change rather than regime change.

Although these conditions improve the odds of coercive diplomacy being effective, they do not guarantee a favorable outcome. Historically, coercive diplomacy has a success rate of 32 percent (Art, 2003: 387). National leaders who resort to forceful persuasion start a process over which they have imperfect control.

Given the uncertainties surrounding the use of armed force, states often employ nonmilitary methods to alter an opponent's behavior. Recalling an ambassador and terminating cultural or scientific exchanges are some of the ways that states signal their displeasure. Economic sanctions also figure prominently in this regard, being widely thought of as a proportional response to threats to interests that are less than vital.

Correlates of Effective Economic Coercion. When the Arab members of the Organization of Petroleum Exporting Countries (OPEC) placed an embargo on the shipment of oil to the United States and the Netherlands in 1973, their purpose was to alter these countries' policies toward the Arab-Israeli conflict. When the UN Security Council decided in August 1990 that the world organization should cease trade with Iraq, its purpose was to accomplish the immediate and unconditional withdrawal of Iraqi forces from Kuwait. Both are examples of the use of **economic sanctions**—deliberate actions to penalize a target state by imposing trade or financial restrictions on normal economic relations.

economic sanctions
the punitive use of trade or monetary measures, such as an embargo, to harm the economy of an enemy state in order to exercise influence over its policies.

Economic sanctions are an increasingly popular approach to convincing another state to desist from some unacceptable behavior. They include a broad array of instruments: withholding foreign aid, placing tariffs and quotas on imports from a targeted state, boycotting its products, declaring an embargo on the sale of goods to the target, and freezing assets it may have in local banks. The rationale for employing sanctions as instruments of influence stems largely from the fact that they avoid the dangers of using armed force. Military coercion can easily backfire, draining government budgets, producing undue casualties, and provoking widespread criticism at home and abroad. In comparison, economic sanctions appear less risky and far less costly.

Research on the effectiveness of economic sanctions indicates that financial restrictions on assets and investment have a higher success rate than trade restrictions (Cortright and Lopez, 1995). The latter, which generally attempt to pressure a country by depriving it of certain imports, tend to be more effective when there is (1) an **inelastic demand** for the commodity in the target country, (2) inadequate supply of the commodity in the target country, (3) no inexpensive substitutes for the commodity, and (4) multilateral support for the restrictions. However, the more trade sanctions cost domestic economic interests in the country applying the sanctions (for example, due to lost sales), the less likely they will be imposed decisively and kept in place long enough for them to succeed (see APPLICATION: Who Is Penalizing Whom?).

Critics of economic sanctions argue that they do not work because they can easily be circumvented. Even worse, they can be counterproductive, triggering rally-around-the-flag support for the target state's government while hurting disenfranchised groups rather than ruling elites (Pape, 1997). To be sure, sanctions

inelastic demand a condition under which the quantity demanded of a good does not decrease as its price increases.

| APPLICATION | Who Is Penalizing Whom? |

Economic sanctions often promise more than they produce because the target state's government can take countermeasures to blunt their impact. Madeleine Albright served as the U.S. secretary of state from 1997 to 2001. In the following excerpt, she describes the domestic repercussions in the coercing country that can weaken the effectiveness of sanctions on a target country.

> When I was secretary of state, President Clinton issued an executive order imposing sanctions on Sudan, whose government was violating human rights, bombing school children, and giving aid and comfort to terrorists. This seemed a simple step, and I supported it; and yet it was not simple—the reason was sap. Gum Arabic, which is derived from the acacia tree, is a natural emulsifier used in such products as candy bars, colas, cosmetics, and fireworks. The two leading American processors are located in New Jersey, while 80 percent of the world's supply comes from Sudan. I soon received a phone call from New Jersey congressman Robert Menendez demanding that we exempt gum Arabic from the sanctions. I asked him, "How can you ask for an exemption to sanctions for Sudan

> while you oppose so vehemently any exceptions to our embargo of Cuba?" His answer: "jobs." Over my objections, Menendez won his exemption for gum Arabic, which remains the law. In 2007, the Bush administration announced plans to seek UN sanctions against Sudan in connection with the genocide in Darfur. Sudan's ambassador to Washington responded by calling a press conference. Standing surrounded by a display of soft drink products, he warned that his country would retaliate against UN sanctions by halting shipments of gum Arabic to the United States—thereby threatening to hit us with the same club we had intended to use against Sudan. That's the problem with sanctions: it is often unclear who is penalizing whom (Albright, 2008: 96–97).

Foreign policy, observes Albright, is "not like tennis practice, where you bang the ball against a concrete barrier and the ball bounces back straight and true. It's more like Wimbledon, where your opponent has his own tricks." As such, she concludes, "the use of economic sanctions is no more amenable to a rigid set of rules than the use of military force. Each situation has unique aspects."

have a checkered history. At times they have succeeded, as in the case of Libya, where after a decade of international pressure, Libyan dictator Muammar Qaddafi finally turned over to Western powers for trial two Libyans alleged to have blown up Pan Am Flight 103 over Scotland in 1988, which killed all of its 280 passengers. Despite this and a few other successes, the historical record casts great doubt on the capacity of sanctions to work, even when used by the world's foremost powerful economic power, the United States. Conspicuous in the many cases where U.S. economic coercion failed is the experience with Cuba. The United States placed sanctions on the Castro regime shortly after it came to power in 1959 and forged an alliance with the Soviet Union. In response, Washington banned all trade with Cuba and pressured other countries to do the same, hoping to overthrow the Castro regime. This goal was not realized, as the regime has survived even after Fidel Castro stepped down due to illness almost a half century after his rise to power.

Sanctions are seldom effective in bringing about major changes in the policies of a target country. According to one statistical survey, they only work about a third of the time and require an almost 2.5 percent impact on the target's GNP for three years (Hufbauer, Schott, and Elliott, 1990). Furthermore, sanctions are rarely successful in preventing war. A study of 200 cases found that when economic sanctions were used to punish a government, military conflict actually became "as much as six times more likely to occur between two countries than if sanctions had not been imposed" (*Foreign Policy*, July/August 2007: 19). Rather than inducing a target country to comply with the initiator's preferences, economic sanctions mainly serve a symbolic function by publicizing unacceptable behavior by other states to foreign and domestic audiences.

The limitations of economic sanctions as a tool of coercive diplomacy can be seen in the unsuccessful efforts to topple the Iraqi dictator Saddam Hussein after the Persian Gulf War ended in 1991. Despite a UN embargo, Hussein was able to continue exporting oil on the black market through dummy corporations and purchase weapons from foreign manufacturers. Meanwhile, ordinary Iraqis suffered, leading the UN to begin experimenting with so-called "smart" sanctions (Cortright and Lopez, 2002), which would target governmental elites, not innocent citizens.

The choice between the options of military force and economic sanctions is always a difficult one when national leaders face situations that seem to demand coercive measures. Reliance on economic sanctions is likely to remain high because they enable leaders to take action without bearing the costs and risks of military operations.

COPING WITH TERRORISM AND INSURGENCY

As we saw in the previous chapter, intrastate wars have become the most widespread form of armed conflict today. In asymmetric conflicts between regular government forces and irregular insurgent forces, the latter have enjoyed surprising success in recent decades. Whereas before World War II, the materially weaker sides in asymmetric conflicts usually lost, during the last half of the twentieth century that winning percentage soared to 51 percent, up from just over 20 percent for the previous century and a half (Arreguín-Toft, 2005: 4, 228–232). In powerful states accustomed to prevailing on the battlefield, this trend has stimulated lively debates over how to fight asymmetric wars. To round out our analysis of the limits of military force, we turn to a consideration of counterterrorism and counterinsurgency policies.

Counterterrorism. As noted in Chapters 6 and 7, terrorist groups are nonstate actors distinguished by their use of violence as the primary method of exercising influence. Disagreement among policy makers in most countries over the character and causes of political terrorism is pronounced, and, without agreement on these preliminaries, a consensus on the best response remains elusive. Those persuaded by one image of terrorism are drawn to certain counterterrorism policies, while those holding a different image recommend contrary policies.

Consider the diametrically opposed opinions on whether military repression or political conciliation is the most effective counterterrorism policy. Those advocating repression see terrorism springing from the cold calculations of incorrigible fanatics who should be tracked down and eliminated by special operations forces and air strikes. In a series of speeches that collectively were called the **Bush Doctrine**, former U.S. President George W. Bush vowed that efforts to combat terrorism would continue until every terrorist group with global reach had been found and destroyed. Since 2008, the United States has launched more than 100 drone strikes against suspected Al Qaeda and Taliban members hiding in Pakistan's remote tribal areas, killing an estimated 400 militants (*The Atlantic*, July/August, 2010: 42). Intelligence officers in the Obama administration believe that the Predator program is the single most effective tool against Al Qaeda. Unnerved by these attacks, surviving militants allegedly have curtailed some of their overt activities out of security concerns (Mayer, 2009: 40–42).

Bush Doctrine a policy that singles out states that support terrorist groups and advocates military strikes against them to prevent a future attack on the United States.

In contrast to this approach to counterterrorism, those who see terrorism anchored in deeper political and socioeconomic grievances and view the perpetrators of terrorism as criminals, propose policies built around interdiction, conciliation, and remediation. More specifically, they back freezing the financial assets of front groups linked to terrorism, disrupting terrorist networks, apprehending their leaders, and engaging in efforts to reduce terrorism's appeal to potential sympathizers and reintegrate rank-and-file members back into society. Believing that terrorism cannot be eradicated by military means, they stress the importance of incident management—mitigating the effects of terrorist attacks after they occur.

The debate over counterterrorism policy revolves around a series of interconnected issues. Are special operations and drone strikes a form of targeted assassination? If so, are they legal? What are the moral implications of attacks that may kill innocent people due to mistaken identity or collateral damage? Are serious negotiations with violent extremists possible? Is terrorism primarily a law enforcement problem? Questions about coping with terrorism have ramifications for dealing with larger insurgencies. Although counterterrorism and counterinsurgency are not identical, they frequently overlap and, when properly conducted, are complementary (Cavoli, 2011).

Counterinsurgency.   Insurgency is typically defined as an organized movement aimed at overthrowing an established government through subversion and armed conflict. Whereas some perpetrators of terrorism do not espouse insurgent aims, others imagine themselves to be part of a wider insurgent movement. As in the case of counterterrorism, there are different opinions on how to conduct counterinsurgency campaigns.

One method of trying to defeat insurgencies is enemy-focused. Epitomized by U.S. General William Westmoreland's search-and-destroy strategy during the Vietnam War, it involves hunting down rebel units and then overwhelming them with superior firepower. Attrition grinds down the insurgency. The drawbacks of this approach, observes David Kilcullen (2010: 9), a senior counterinsurgency advisor to American commanders in Afghanistan and Iraq, center on its impact on the civilian noncombatant population. Chasing rebel units all across the countryside requires enormous resources, is exhausting, and can harm ordinary people, thus strengthening their support for the insurgency.

An alternative method is population-focused. Associated today with U.S. General David Petraeus, it is rooted in a clear-and-hold strategy that rests on the proposition that providing for the security and well-being of civilian noncombatants within territories liberated from rebel control is critical for winning their "hearts and minds," and gaining their assistance against the insurgents. Rather than operating out of remote, fortress-like compounds, counterinsurgency troops live in the neighborhoods they wish to secure, building relationships with locals that allow them to discriminate between those rebels who can be won over and those who are irreconcilable. Successful counterinsurgency, according to this approach, demands political acumen and military patience. It is nation-building in the midst of armed opposition (Nagl, 2002).

Fighting insurgencies, T. E. Lawrence (better known as "Lawrence of Arabia") once concluded is "messy and slow, like eating soup with a knife." By one account, no successful counterinsurgency in the twentieth century took less than a decade (Ricks, 2009: 315). States that have lost to insurgencies have tended to suffer from some combination of inferior political will, an ill-suited military strategy, and an inability to choke off external support for the insurgents (Record, 2009: 132–133). Because counterinsurgency operations do not yield quick, definitive victories, arguments about the proper use of military force in these asymmetric wars appear destined to continue alongside the ongoing debates over how to wield power in symmetrical conflicts with rival states.

FORCE AND STATECRAFT

Since antiquity, preparation for war has often been seen as a prerequisite for security. Calls for a policy of "peace through strength" are understandable in a world where states alone remain responsible for their own self-defense. As former U.S. President Dwight Eisenhower once noted, "until war is eliminated from international relations, unpreparedness for it is well nigh as criminal as war itself." Fear of national vulnerability in an anarchic, self-help environment induces defense planners to assume the worst about other states' capabilities and intentions. Even if the military capabilities accumulated by a neighbor are defensively motivated, they may trigger a strong reaction. The state "always feels itself weak if there is another that is stronger," observed the eighteenth-century political philosopher Jean-Jacques Rousseau (1971: 56). "Its security and preservation demand that it make itself more powerful than its neighbors."

State power, Rousseau reminds us, is relative. Efforts to obtain absolute security by one state tend to be perceived as creating absolute insecurity for others, with the result that everyone becomes locked into an upward spiral of countermeasures that diminishes the security of all. Scholars refer to this as a **security dilemma**, a condition that results when each state's increase in military capabilities is matched by the others, and all wind up with no more security than when they began arming (Snyder, 1984; Jervis, 1976). "Security based on strength is a mirage," concluded French theorist Raymond Aron (1965: 212) as he observed the United States and Soviet Union during the Cold War. "If one side feels safe from attack, the other will feel at the mercy of the enemy."

Asking whether preparing for war endangers, rather than ensures, national security raises an uncomfortable question that challenges the prevailing approach to national security throughout much of the world's history. Yet many experts believe such questioning is justified. To their way of thinking, security in the twenty-first century must be defined more broadly so as to include nonmilitary, transnational threats, including environmental, economic, and epidemiological hazards that can jeopardize the global future. At issue is whether this new way of thinking about security will gain wider acceptance, or whether traditional realist approaches to national security will continue to resonate in the world's capitals. The next chapter examines the ways in which arms, alliances, and the balance of power are pursued by national leaders who believe that political realism provides the safest path to peace.

> **security dilemma**   the propensity of armaments undertaken by one state for ostensibly defensive purposes to threaten other states, which arm in reaction, with the result that their national security declines as their arms increase.

CHAPTER SUMMARY

- In world politics, power refers to the ability of one international actor to control the behavior of another actor, making it continue some course of action, change what it is doing, or refrain from acting.

- Although most scholars agree that states are not equal in their ability to influence one another, there is little consensus on how to best weigh the various factors that contribute to state power. Their impact depends on the circumstances in a bargaining situation between states, and especially on how leaders perceive them.

- National leaders tend to assume that security is a function of power, and power is a function of military capabilities.

- As states spend increasing amounts of national wealth on arms, war-making capabilities have become more widespread than ever. Those countries least able to afford the broad spectrum of available weapons have made the greatest sacrifices to get them, often reducing the quality of their citizens' lives by retarding social welfare programs and economic development.

- Advances in military technology have increased the destructive capacity of weapons and improved their range and precision.

- Although states ostensibly arm for defensive purposes, neighboring countries frequently perceive their military acquisitions as threatening. When one state's armaments increases are matched by others, everyone winds up paying higher costs with no more security than they had before this vicious cycle began.

- States that enjoy military superiority over their adversaries often think of their weapons as instruments for coercive bargaining. Threats of military force are used for both compellence and deterrence. Deterrence requires three ingredients: (1) capabilities—the possession of military resources to make threats of retaliation plausible; (2) credibility—the belief by others that a state is willing to carry out its threats; and (3) communication—the ability to send an opponent a clear message about one's capabilities and intentions.

- Preemptive military attacks entail the use of force against imminent threats; preventive attacks are aimed at threats that might possibly emerge in the future.

- Coercive diplomacy uses a mix of threats, limited exemplary uses of force, and positive inducements to affect the behavior of other states.

- International interdependence multiplies the opportunities to use economic instruments for coercive purposes, though they often fall short of their objectives. Nonetheless, economic sanctions serve an important symbolic function, providing a policy alternative to the use of military force and a way to publicize unacceptable behavior by other states.

- Some contemporary terrorist groups have acquired the means to strike targets almost anywhere in the world. This threat has led to a vigorous debate over counterterrorism policies. Those who see the roots of terrorism in an inextinguishable hatred by extremists generally favor repressing terrorist networks through air strikes and covert special operations attacks. In contrast, those who attribute terrorism to larger underlying grievances tend to advocate more conciliatory policies.

- Terrorism and insurgency are different phenomena. Debates over counter-insurgency policy revolve around enemy-centered versus population-centered strategies.

KEY TERMS

brinkmanship

Bush Doctrine

coercive diplomacy

compellence

counterforce targeting strategy

countervalue targeting strategy

covert operations

deterrence

economic sanctions

firebreak

inelastic demand

massive retaliation

military-industrial complex

military intervention

multiple independently targetable reentry vehicles (MIRVs)

mutual assured destruction (MAD)

Nuclear Nonproliferation Treaty (NPT)

nuclear utilization theory (NUTs)

nuclear winter

opportunity costs

power potential

preemption

preventive war

proliferation

second-strike capability

security dilemma

smart bombs

Strategic Defense Initiative (SDI)

triad

ultimatum

SUGGESTED READINGS

Caldwell, Dan, and Robert E. Williams. *Seeking Security in an Insecure World*. Lanham, MD: Rowman & Littlefield, 2006.

Howard, Russell D., and James J. F. Forest (eds.). *Weapons of Mass Destruction and Terrorism*. New York: McGraw-Hill, 2008.

Kilcullen, David. *Counterinsurgency*. New York: Oxford University Press, 2010.

Preston, Thomas. *From Lambs to Lions: Future Security Relationships in a World of Biological and Nuclear Weapons*. Lanham, MD: Rowman & Littlefield, 2007.

Singer, P. W. *Wired for War: The Robotics Revolution and Conflict in the 21st Century*. New York: Penguin, 2009.

CRITICAL THINKING QUESTIONS

As the discussion of compellence in this chapter notes, brinkmanship is a bargaining strategy in which rival states threaten mutual disaster in an effort to make the other side capitulate. The game of Chicken often is used to analyze crises where brinkmanship may be attempted. The game originates from the 1950s story of rival teenagers (A and B) who want to demonstrate their fortitude to peers by racing their cars toward one another on a narrow road. If one driver doesn't swerve and the other does, the former gains a reputation for courage while the latter is disgraced. If both swerve, each loses some prestige. If neither swerves, they both die in a head-on collision. Because both drivers want to live and earn as much status as possible, their preferences can be rank ordered from best to worst as follows: (1) win a reputation for fearlessness; (2) suffer a slight loss in prestige; (3) suffer a significant loss in prestige; and (4) die in a collision. The matrix shown in the illustration on the next page depicts the results that will occur depending on whether each driver swerves or doesn't.

(Continued)

	B	
	Swerve	Not Swerve
Swerve	2, 2	3, 1
Not Swerve	1, 3	4, 4

A

Note: The first number in each cell of the matrix is A's payoff, the second number is B's payoff. The number 1 represents the most preferred outcome, whereas 4 represents the least preferred outcome.

Now imagine that players A and B in the matrix are heavily armed states, not teenage drivers; furthermore, assume that swerving represents backing down in a confrontation and not swerving represents standing firm. In this representation, the lower right cell shows the outcome when neither side gives way (collision/war, or payoff 4, 4), the upper left cell displays the outcome when both sides flinch (de-escalation, or payoff 2, 2), and the remaining cells (payoffs 3,1 and 1, 3) signify one side's victory and the other's capitulation.

Given the payoff structure of this game, what would you expect a player to do when he or she must act without knowing what the other player will do? Is it "irrational" to commit to a strategy of standing firm in a crisis regardless of the costs? What incentives are there to manipulate shared risk, acting provocatively to induce the other side to accommodate? How important is credibility to the outcome of this game? Beyond armed confrontations such as the Cuban missile crisis, is the game of Chicken a good analogue for other bargaining situations in world politics where mutual intransigence would be catastrophic for both sides?

Alliances, Arms Control, and the Balance of Power

CHAPTER OUTLINE

As nature abhors a vacuum, so international politics abhors unbalanced power. Faced by unbalanced power, states try to increase their own strength or they ally with others to bring the international distribution of power into balance.

KENNETH N. WALTZ
POLITICAL SCIENTIST

The specter of a world teeming with nuclear-armed states has haunted many people for decades. Although some scholars contend that the spread of nuclear weapons would make war more dangerous and therefore less likely, most people fear that an increase in the number of fingers on nuclear triggers would raise the probability of one being pulled, whether by accident or by design.

As mentioned in the previous chapter, the 1968 Nuclear Nonproliferation Treaty (NPT) sought to control the diffusion of nuclear weapons by requiring those who possessed them to pledge not to share the technology with others, and by stipulating that those without these weapons promise not to acquire them. Under the terms of the treaty, which eventually was ratified by 189 countries (North Korea withdrew in 2003, however), all parties could develop civilian nuclear power for peaceful purposes, although non-nuclear-weapons states were required to accept safeguards over their activities as set forth in an agreement negotiated with the UN's International Atomic Energy Agency (IAEA).

India, which had not signed the NPT, possessed an active program for developing nuclear power to meet its enormous energy needs. On May 18, 1974, India exploded a nuclear device made from its reactor in Trombay, demonstrating that given sufficient scientific expertise and technological skill, nations seeking to join the nuclear club could use fuel from civilian power plants to fabricate weapons.

In response, Pakistan, which had fought bitter wars against India in 1947–1948, 1965, and 1971, began working covertly to build nuclear weapons. Concerned that Chinese military assistance to the Pakistanis might embolden them, the Indians decided to demonstrate their strength by conducting a series of nuclear weapons tests in 1998. Pakistan, however, followed suit with its own tests. The United Nations condemned both sides, and the United States underscored the UN reprimand by imposing sanctions against New Delhi and Islamabad.

India strongly objected to the criticism. In the aftermath of the tests, it accelerated the modernization of its air and naval power-projection capabilities, announcing that it expected to deploy at least three aircraft carriers by 2020. From roughly $11 billion for 1999–2000, India's defense budget climbed to $32 billion by 2010–2011. With its economy growing at 7 percent a year, India also embarked on an ambitious space program, launching 21 satellites between 2000 and 2010, an unmanned lunar mission in 2008, and announcing plans to put astronauts in space by 2016. Like other up-and-coming powers, India's continued economic growth is not assured. Widespread poverty, water shortages, and a problematic infrastructure could stall the country's drive to be accepted on an equal footing with other great powers. Nevertheless, projections by many analysts suggest that India's percentage share of the world's gross domestic product will rank third by mid-century, behind only the United States and China.

Despite international pressure on India to halt its weapons program and become a party to the NPT, it has continued to complain that the nonproliferation regime arbitrarily defines the possession of nuclear weapons by the United States, Russia, Britain, France, and China as legitimate while outlawing them to everyone else. Given the history of friction between New Delhi and Washington over nuclear weapons, many observers were shocked when Prime Minister Manmohan Singh and President George W. Bush announced at a 2006 meeting that they had reached an agreement that would treat India as an exception to the rules of the nonproliferation regime. In exchange for obtaining nuclear fuel and sensitive technology from the United States, India would open its civilian reactors to IAEA inspectors. With limited supplies of domestic uranium, the agreement would allow India to use imports to cover nonmilitary needs. Critics grumbled that this would undermine the NPT. Prime Minister Singh countered by saying that India was willing to join the NPT as a nuclear-weapons state.

Why did the United States abruptly change its position regarding India and the NPT? Democratic India, the Bush administration professed, had been a responsible custodian of its nuclear facilities; New Delhi had not transferred nuclear weapons or technology to others. Although there would be no surveillance over India's military reactors and no limits would be placed on the number of nuclear weapons that India could produce, supporters of the agreement maintained that placing the country's civil nuclear programs under permanent inspections was a significant step forward.

Political realists expressed skepticism over this explanation. They believed that America's policy shift was a product of balance-of-power politics, not India's probity. With China emerging as a near-peer competitor, the United States wanted to augment its longstanding ties to Japan with new ties to India, which it viewed as a "swing state" in the Asian balance of power (Mohan, 2006). By making a deal favorable to New Delhi, America would have an opportunity to build a strategic partnership with India, adding its weight to Japan's in counterbalancing China. Mired in territorial disputes with Beijing over the border of the Arunachal Pradesh region in the east and the Aksai Chin border in the west, India could use such a partnership as a hedge against possible armed clashes with China. Joint naval exercises held in the Bay of Bengal during the summer of 2007 by the United States, Japan, and India accentuated the converging security policies.

From Beijing's perspective, this triangular arrangement is aimed at containing China's influence, denying the country its rightful status in the world. Leery of American motives, Japanese ambitions, and Indian assertiveness, China has looked for countervailing alliances. In 2010, it revealed a proposed sale of two civilian nuclear reactors to Pakistan, who had responded to the U.S.-Indian nuclear agreement by building a plant to salvage plutonium from old reactor fuel. In addition to its traditional ties with Pakistan on India's western border, China also worked to build relationships with several of India's eastern neighbors, including Bangladesh and Myanmar. More importantly, it has established the Shanghai Cooperation Organization (SCO). Although not a collective defense pact like NATO, the SCO has brought together China, Russia,

Manish Swarup/AP Photos

Wary Neighbors Despite the efforts of Prime Ministers Wen Jiabao of China and Manmohan Singh of India to establish friendly relations between their countries, unresolved territorial disputes, divergent interests, and mutual suspicions have complicated their interaction.

Kazakhstan, Kyrgyzstan, Tajikistan, and Uzbekistan for joint military exercises, such as those conducted in 2007 and 2009.

Realists submit that this geopolitical maneuvering reflects an age-old process of balancing against potential threats. The United States may support the principle of nonproliferation, but it was willing to carve out an exception to the NPT for India to enlist New Delhi's help in balancing against an ascending China. New Delhi may have been frustrated with America's nuclear policies, but the Indians also had apprehensions about China. Although the United States and India were at loggerheads for years, they shared a common interest in preserving a balance of power in Asia.

REALISM AND THE BALANCING OF POWER

Our discussion of conflict and its management in Part III of *The Global Future* has followed a logical progression. Chapter 7 began by exploring why the frequency of war makes preparations for it so necessary. Chapter 8 examined the search for national security through the acquisition of military capabilities. We now take up the question of how to sustain peace in a world populated by armed, egoistic states that frequently practice coercive diplomacy.

balance of power the theory that national survival in an anarchic world is most likely when military power is distributed to prevent a single hegemon or bloc from dominating the state system.

Realists, liberals, and constructivists offer different answers to this question. In this chapter, we will concentrate on the realist response: maintaining a **balance of power** by forming alliances with other countries to offset the military might of an adversary, and negotiating arms control agreements to maintain strategic parity.

Assumptions of Balance-of-Power Theory

The concept of a balance of power has a long and controversial history. Although the practice of balance-of-power politics can be traced back to antiquity, its modern usage in theorizing about state behavior begins in 1561 with Francesco Guicciardini's history of the Renaissance Italian city-state system. Early in the fifteenth century, when Milan was growing in power, Florence aligned with Venice to restrain Milan. Later, as Venice grew in strength, Florence joined with Milan to counterbalance the Venetians. For the next five centuries in Europe, great powers tended to balance against hegemonic threats. According to one statistical study of this period, when the leading state possessed a disproportionate and growing share of power, counterbalancing alliances formed against it nearly two-thirds of the time (Levy and Thompson, 2005: 28).

Proponents envision balancing as an equilibrating process that maintains peace by offsetting the military might of any state that seeks preponderance. They also believe that by checking hegemonic ambitions and promoting restraint, a balance of power fosters conditions conducive to the development of international law. Critics scoff at these claims, arguing that balance-of-power politics breeds jealousy, intrigue, and antagonism. Part of the difficulty in evaluating rival claims about power balancing lies in the different meanings attributed to the concept (Claude, 1962; Haas, 1953). Although "balance of power" may be widely used in everyday discourse, there is confusion over precisely what it entails.

At the core of nearly all of the various meanings of "balance of power" is the idea that national security is enhanced when military capabilities are distributed so that no one state is strong enough to dominate everyone else. If one state gains inordinate power, balance-of-power theory predicts that it will take advantage of its strength and attack weaker neighbors; therefore, compelling incentives exist for those threatened to unite in a defensive coalition. According to the theory, their combined military might would deter (or, if need be, defeat) the state harboring expansionist aims. Thus for realists, laissez-faire competition among states striving to maximize their national power yields an international equilibrium, which ensures everyone's survival by checking hegemonic ambitions.

The Balancing Process. Although balancing is occasionally described as an automatic, self-adjusting process, most realists see it as the result of deliberate actions undertaken by national leaders to maintain an equilibrium among contending states. Some actions, like augmenting military capabilities through armaments and alliances, attempt to add weight to the lighter side of the international balance. Others, such as negotiating limits on weaponry and spheres of influence, attempt to decrease the weight of the heavier side. Only by constantly monitoring shifts in relative strength can leaders calibrate their policies to rectify imbalances of power.

Various theorists have attempted to specify a set of rules that must be heeded in order for the balancing process to function effectively. What follows is a brief synthesis of these rules:

1. *Stay vigilant.* Constantly watch foreign developments in order to identify emerging threats and opportunities. Because international anarchy makes each state responsible for its own security, and states can never be sure of one another's intentions, self-interest encourages them to maximize their relative power. As Morton Kaplan (1957: 23) writes: "Act to increase capabilities but negotiate rather than fight." [However] "Fight rather than pass up an opportunity to increase capabilities."

2. *Seek allies whenever you cannot match the armaments of your adversaries.* States align with each other when they adopt a common stance toward some shared security problem. An **alliance** is produced when they formally agree to coordinate their behavior under certain specified circumstances. The degree of coordination may range from a detailed list of military forces that will be furnished by each party in the event of war to the more modest requirement that they will consult with one another should hostilities erupt. According to balance-of-power theory, alliances are the primary means of compensating for an inability to keep up with a rival's arms acquisitions.

alliance   a formal agreement among sovereign states for the purpose of coordinating their behavior to increase mutual security.

3. *Alliances should remain flexible.* Formed and dissolved according to the strategic needs of the moment, alliances must be made without regard to cultural or ideological affinities (Owen, 2005). Because alliances are instrumental, short-term adjustments aimed at rectifying imbalances in the distribution of military capabilities, past experiences should not predispose states to accept or reject any potential partner. Nowhere is this better seen than in the **balancer** role Great Britain once played in European diplomacy (see Figure 9.1). From the sixteenth through the early twentieth centuries, the British shifted their weight from one side of the Continental balance to the other, arguing that they had no permanent friends and no permanent enemies, just a permanent interest in preventing the balance from tipping either way (Dehio, 1962). As described by Winston Churchill (1948: 207–208), Britain's goal was "to oppose the strongest, most aggressive, most dominating Power on the Continent. ... [It] joined with the less strong Powers, made a combination among them, and thus defeated and frustrated the Continental military tyrant whoever he was, whatever nation he led." Indeed, when Churchill faced Nazi Germany in the early days of World War II, he indicated that Britain would be flexible enough to make common cause with anyone, regardless of their political ideology. "If Hitler invaded Hell," he once quipped, "I would at least make a favorable reference to the Devil in the House of Commons."

balancer   an influential global or regional state that throws its support in decisive fashion to the weaker side of the balance of power.

4. *Oppose any state that seeks hegemony.* The purpose of engaging in balance-of-power politics is to survive in a world of potentially dangerous neighbors. If any state achieves absolute mastery over everyone else, it will be able to act with impunity. Under such circumstances, the territorial integrity and political autonomy of other states will be in jeopardy. By joining forces with the weaker side to prevent the stronger side from reaching preponderance, states can preserve their independence. In short, power balancing is a strategy of "helping the underdog because if you help the top dog, it may eventually turn around and eat you" (Nye and Welch, 2011: 76).

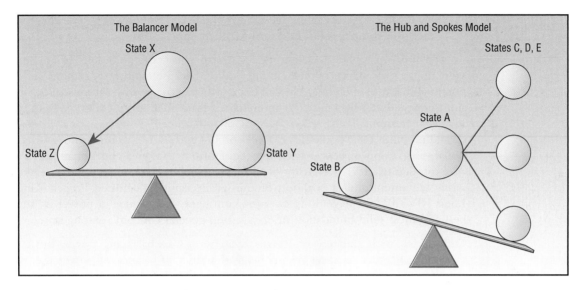

FIGURE 9.1 **Two Models of Alliance Statecraft**

Alliances are a method of aggregating power. They allow vulnerable states to compensate for their military weakness by partnering with others. As illustrated on the left, State **X** can attempt to preserve the status quo by maintaining a balance of power between rivals **Y** and **Z** by aligning with the weaker party (in this case, State **Z**) whenever revisionist threats are voiced by the stronger side. British foreign policy from the rule of Henry VIII (1509–1547) until the early twentieth century exemplified this "balancer" strategy.

Military alliances can also be used to immobilize power (Joffe, 1995). Imagine State **A** in the illustration on the right is strong enough to defeat any other great power but not all of them together. Further imagine that State **B** is hostile toward **A** but lacks the capability to take military action alone. To forestall the possibility of **B** getting help from any of the great powers, **A** forges alliances with **C**, **D**, and **E**, entangling them in a web of commitments. This "hub-and-spokes" strategy attempts to preserve the status quo by isolating the revisionist state. German foreign policy under Otto von Bismarck exemplified this approach to statecraft. To isolate a hostile France after the Franco-Prussian War, Germany established ties with Austria (1873, 1881, 1879), Russia (1873, 1881, 1887), and Italy (1883). Thus, the balancer model tries to preserve peace through equilibrium; the hub-and-spokes model, through a disequilibrium that is disadvantageous to the revisionist state. Theorists today continue to debate the relative merits of these two models of alliance statecraft.

5. *Be moderate in victory.* "An equilibrium," argues Edward Gulick (1955: 72), "cannot perpetuate itself unless the major components of that equilibrium are preserved." In the event of war, the winning side should not eliminate the defeated. Looking forward rather than backward, it should do as little damage as possible to those it has vanquished because yesterday's enemy may be needed as tomorrow's ally. Victors who couple firmness regarding their own interests with fairness toward the interests of others encourage defeated powers to work within the postwar balance of power. Similarly, states who

win at the bargaining table can stabilize the balance of power by granting the other side compensation in return for their concessions.

To sum up, political realists urge states to check the ambitions of anyone who threatens to amass overwhelming power, because aspiring hegemons are a potential threat to everyone. Human beings, they argue, are by nature selfish and shortsighted, but balancing rival interests stabilizes their interactions. Weakness invites aggression. Thus, when faced with unbalanced power, national leaders should mobilize their domestic resources or ally with others to bring the international distribution of power back into equilibrium (Vasquez and Elman, 2003). As expressed in the 1713 Treaty of Utrecht, which spelled out the terms of the peace settlement after a coalition of European countries defeated French King Louis XIV's bid for hegemony over the continent, the balance of power is "the best and most solid foundation of ... a lasting general concord" among states.

Difficulties with Balance-of-Power Systems. Can balancing power further international order, as most realists believe? Critics of balance-of-power theory raise several objections about the proposition that balancing promotes peace. First, some scholars argue that the theory's rules for behavior are contradictory (Riker, 1962). On the one hand, states are urged to increase their power. On the other hand, they are told to oppose anyone seeking preponderance. Yet sometimes **bandwagoning** with (rather than balancing against) the dominant state can increase a weaker country's capabilities by allowing it to share in the spoils of a future victory. Preliminary research on this issue suggests that states that are content with the status quo tend to balance against rising powers more than states that are dissatisfied.

bandwagoning
the strategy of seeking national security by aligning with the strongest state, regardless of its ideology or form of government.

A second objection to balance-of-power theory is that it assumes policy makers possess accurate, timely information about other states. As we have discussed in the previous chapter, "power" is an ambiguous concept. Tangible factors, such as the performance capabilities of the different types of weapons found in an adversary's inventory, are hard to compare. Intangible factors, such as leadership skills and troop morale, are even more difficult to gauge. Without a precise measure of relative strength, how can policy makers know when power is becoming unbalanced? Moreover, in an environment of secret alliances, how can they be sure who is really in league with whom? An ally who is being counted on to balance the power of an opponent may have secretly agreed to remain neutral in the event of a showdown; consequently, the actual distribution of power may not resemble the distribution that one side or the other expects.

Problems in determining the strength of adversaries and the trustworthiness of allies lead to a third objection to balance-of-power theory: The uncertainty of power balances frequently causes defense planners to engage in worst-case analysis, which can spark an **arms race**. The intense, reciprocal anxiety that shrouds balance-of-power politics fuels exaggerated estimates of an adversary's strength, which prompts one side, and then the other, to expand the quantity and enhance the quality of their weaponry. Critics of realism warn that if a serious dispute occurs between states locked in relentless arms competition, the probability of war increases.

arms race an action-reaction process in which rival states rapidly increase their military capabilities in response to one another.

Paul Popper/Popperfoto/Getty Images

Anti-hegemonic Alliance Balance-of-power theory counsels national leaders to put aside their ideological differences and align together against common threats. Shown here are the "Big Three" (Joseph Stalin, Franklin Roosevelt, and Winston Churchill), who fought together against Nazi Germany in World War II despite having significant political differences among themselves.

A fourth objection is that balance-of-power theory assumes that decision makers are risk averse. When confronted with countervailing power, they refrain from fighting because the dangers of taking on an equal are too great. Yet national leaders assess risk differently. Some are risk acceptant and believe that with a little luck they can prevail. Thus, rather than being deterred by equivalent power, they prefer gambling on the chance of winning, even if the odds are long. Marshaling comparable power against adversaries with a high tolerance for risk will not have the same effect as it would on those who avoid risks.

Although states with awesome military capabilities can pose potential security dangers, a fifth objection to balance-of-power theory is that perceptions of intent are more important when determining whom to balance against. "Even states with rather modest capabilities may prompt others to balance if they are perceived as especially aggressive," writes political scientist Stephen Walt (1987: 264). He theorizes that national leaders form counterbalancing alliances against the most threatening state on the horizon, not necessarily against the most powerful.

Finally, many people object to the balance-of-power theory because it has not been effective. If the theory's assumptions are correct, historical periods during which its rules were followed should also have been periods in which war was less frequent. Yet, a striking feature of those periods is their record of warfare. Researchers have found that a balance of capabilities between opposing alliances increases the probability of war (Kim, 1989). From the Thirty Years' War through World War II, the great powers participated in a series of increasingly destructive general wars that threatened to engulf and destroy the multistate system. As Inis L. Claude (1989: 78) soberly concludes, it is difficult to consider these wars "as anything other than catastrophic failures, total collapses, of the balance-of-power system. They are hardly to be classed as stabilizing maneuvers or equilibrating processes, and one cannot take seriously any claim of maintaining international stability that does not entail the prevention of such disasters. ..." Indeed, the historical record has led some theorists to offer **hegemonic stability theory** as an alternative to the balance of power, which postulates that a single, dominant state can guarantee peace better than military parity among contending great powers (Ferguson, 2004; Wohlforth, 1999; Organski, 1968).

hegemonic stability theory the argument that a single dominant state is necessary to enforce international cooperation, maintain international rules and regimes, and keep the peace.

Managing the Balance through a Concert of Great Powers

A significant problem with the balance-of-power system is its haphazard character. To bring order to the system, occasionally the great powers have tried to institutionalize channels of communication. The Concert of Europe that commenced with the Congress of Vienna in 1815 exemplified this strategy. In essence, it was "an exclusive club for the great powers" (Claude, 1971: 21).

The idea behind a **concert** is rule by a coalition of great powers (see Figure 9.2). It is predicated on the belief that these leading powers will see their interests advanced by collaborating to contain conflict in those regions under their mutual jurisdiction. Although it is assumed that the great powers share a common outlook, concerts still allow "for subtle jockeying and competition to take place among them. Power politics is not completely eliminated; members may turn to internal mobilization and coalition formation to pursue divergent interests. But the cooperative framework of a concert, and its members' concern about preserving peace, prevent such balancing from escalating to overt hostility and conflict" (Kupchan and Kupchan, 1992: 253).

concert a cooperative agreement among great powers to jointly manage international relations.

A common sense of duty is the glue that holds great-power concerts together. When a belief in mutual self-restraint dissipates, concerts unravel. "Friction tends to build as each state believes that it is sacrificing more for unity than are others," notes Robert Jervis (1985: 61). "Each will remember the cases in which it has been restrained, and ignore or interpret differently cases in which others believe they acted for the common good." Overcoming this friction requires continuous consultation in order to reinforce expectations of joint responsibilities. Concert members should not be challenged over their vital interests, nor should they suffer an affront to their national dignity or prestige.

While a concert framework can help manage relations among counterposed great powers, the normative consensus underpinning this arrangement is fragile

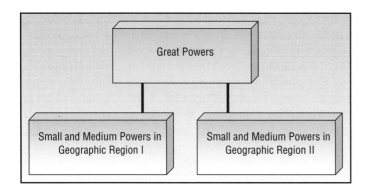

FIGURE 9.2 A Great-Power Concert

The idea of a great-power concert has a long history. As early as the fourteenth century, the French writer Pierre Dubois proposed that an organization of reigning princes in Europe manage political affairs on the continent. As depicted in this figure, the great powers in a concert agree to consult with each other regularly, coordinate their policies toward one or more geographic regions, and, if necessary, intervene militarily to manage the affairs of the small-and medium-sized states within those regions.

and easily eroded. As a result, realists have looked beyond concerts for other ways to steady vacillating power balances. One approach is to limit everyone's arsenals, especially with regard to those weapons that are seen as provocative and thus destabilizing.

STABILIZING POWER BALANCES
THROUGH ARMS CONTROL

Liberal reformers have often questioned the theory that power can be balanced to preserve world order. They have advocated instead the biblical prescription that states should beat their swords into plowshares. The destructiveness of today's weapons has inspired many people once again to take this tenet of liberal theory seriously. But this approach is not solely a liberal preserve. Many realists also see utility in arms limitation, primarily as a way of stabilizing the balance of power by dampening arms races. In fact, most policy makers who have negotiated such agreements have been realists who perceived these treaties as a prudent tool to maintain military parity with rivals.

Despite renewed interest in arms control, military competition is difficult to curb because states acting in what they perceive as their rational self-interest can become trapped in self-defeating behavior, rejecting efforts to restrain arms buildups despite the fact that all parties could benefit by cooperating. As a first step toward determining why it is hard to rein in arms races, let us draw a distinction between arms control and disarmament.

Arms Control versus Disarmament

Although the terms *arms control* and *disarmament* are often used interchangeably, they are not synonymous. **Arms control** refers to agreements designed to regulate arms levels either by limiting their growth or by restricting how they may be used. This is a far more common and less ambitious endeavor than

arms control bilateral or multilateral agreements to contain arms buildups by setting limits on the number and types of weapons that states are permitted.

disarmament agreements to reduce or eliminate weapons or other means of attack.

disarmament, which is the reduction or elimination of weapons. Controlling war by reducing weapons inventories is hardly a novel idea. Yet until very recently, states have generally failed to negotiate disarmament agreements. True, some countries in the past did reduce their armaments. For example, the Chinese states in 600 BCE formed a disarmament league that produced a peaceful century for the league's members, and Canada and the United States disarmed the Great Lakes through the 1817 Rush–Bagot Agreement. Nonetheless, these kinds of achievements have been relatively rare in history. Most disarmament has been involuntary, the product of reductions imposed by the victors in the immediate aftermath of a war, as when the Allied powers attempted to disarm a defeated Germany after World War I.

In addition to differentiating between arms control and disarmament, we should also distinguish between bilateral and multilateral approaches to limiting weaponry. Because the former involve only two countries, they are often easier to negotiate and to enforce than are the latter, which are agreements among three or more countries. As a result, bilateral arms agreements tend to be more successful than multilateral agreements. By far the most revealing examples are the superpower agreements to control nuclear weapons. Let us briefly look at the record of Soviet-American negotiations before examining the checkered history of multilateral arms control and disarmament.

Bilateral Arms Control and Disarmament

The Cold War between the Soviet Union and the United States never degenerated into open warfare. One of the reasons was the series of more than twenty-five arms control agreements Moscow and Washington negotiated in the wake of the Cuban missile crisis. Prior to their nuclear face-off in October 1962, the superpowers seemed trapped in a self-reinforcing cycle of hostilities and armaments (see APPLICATION: Conflict Spirals and Self-Defeating Behavior). Beginning with the 1963 Hot Line Agreement, which established a direct radio and telegraph communication system between the two governments, Soviet and American leaders reached a series of modest agreements aimed at stabilizing the military balance and reducing the risk of war. Each of these bilateral treaties lowered tensions and helped build a climate of trust that encouraged efforts to negotiate further agreements.

Perhaps the most important agreements were the Strategic Arms Limitation Talks (SALT) of 1972 and 1979; the Strategic Arms Reduction Treaties (START) of 1991, 1993, and 2010; and the Strategic Offensive Reductions Treaty (SORT) of 2002. The first two agreements stabilized the nuclear arms race, while the remaining ones reduced the weapons in each side's inventory (see Figure 9.3). When the Cold War ended in 1991, the United States had more than 9,500 nuclear warheads and Russia had about 8,000. However, the 1993 START agreement pledged to cut their combined arsenals to about 6,500 by the year 2003. Even more dramatically, this agreement also affected the kinds of weapons each country could possess. Under its terms, Russia and the United States gave up all the multiple independently targetable reentry vehicles (MIRVs)

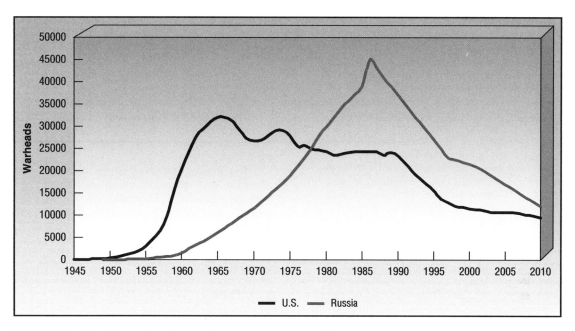

FIGURE 9.3   **U.S. and Russian Nuclear Weapons Inventories, 1945–2010**

After decades of adding to their nuclear arsenals, the United States and Russia, through a series of arms control agreements, have cut the number of warheads in their stockpiles. Shown here are trends in their nuclear inventories between 1945 and 2010.

SOURCE: Data reported in Norris and Kristensen (2010: 81–82).

on their land-based intercontinental ballistic missiles (ICBMs) and reduced submarine-launched ballistic missile (SLBM) warheads to no more than 1,750.

The next major step occurred during May 2002 when presidents George W. Bush and Vladimir Putin signed the Strategic Offensive Reductions Treaty (SORT). This brief document called for the two countries to cut their combined number of strategic nuclear warheads by two-thirds over the next ten years but contained no requirement to destroy warheads taken out of service, and permitted either side to withdraw from the agreement with three months' notice by citing "a supreme national interest." In April 2010, presidents Barack Obama and Dmitri Medvedev signed a treaty that would further reduce each country's strategic arsenal. If ratified by the U.S. Senate and the Russian parliament, the number of strategic warheads would be cut from the 2,200 allowed under the 2002 SORT agreement to 1,550. Additionally, each side agreed to on-site inspections and to a limit of 800 launchers, down from the 1,600 permitted under the 1991 START agreement. Although the treaty does not deal with lower-yield tactical nuclear warheads, it inspires some hope that negotiations can be expanded to cover more types of weapons and other states. The history of multilateral arms control and disarmament speaks to this aspiration.

Many scholars have described the dynamics of arms competition between states as a conflict spiral (Jervis, 1976: 62–113). The imagery highlights the tendency of military preparations by one state to exacerbate the insecurities of its rival, engendering confrontational policies that raise tensions, the perceived stakes of the conflict, and the level of preparations by both sides to new heights. In a speech to the editors of United Press International in San Francisco on September 18, 1967, U.S. Secretary of Defense Robert S. McNamara drew upon the spiral model when reflecting on the irony that decisions made by the United States and Soviet Union for the sake of security actually resulted in greater insecurity.

> In 1961, when I became Secretary of Defense, the Soviet Union possessed a very small operational arsenal of intercontinental missiles. However, they did possess the technological and industrial capacity to enlarge that arsenal very substantially over succeeding years.
>
> Now we had no evidence that the Soviets did in fact plan to fully use that capacity. But ... a strategic planner must be "conservative" in his calculations; that is, he must prepare for the worst plausible case and not be content to hope and prepare merely for the most probable.
>
> Since we could not be certain of Soviet intentions—since we could not be sure that they would not undertake a massive buildup—we had to insure against such an eventuality by undertaking ourselves a major buildup ... .

> Clearly, the Soviet buildup [was] in part a reaction to our buildup since the beginning of the decade. Soviet strategic planners undoubtedly reasoned that if our buildup were to continue at its accelerated pace, we might conceivably reach, in time, a credible first-strike capability against the Soviet Union.
>
> This was not in fact our intention. Our intention was to assure that they—with their theoretical capacity to reach such a first-strike capability—would not in fact outdistance us.
>
> But they could not read our intentions with any greater accuracy than we could read theirs. And thus the result has been that we both built up our forces to a point that far exceeds a credible second-strike capability against the forces we each started with ... .
>
> It is futile for each of us ... at the end of all the spending, and at the end of all the deployment, and at the end of all that effort, to be relatively at the same point of balance on the security scale (cited in G. Snyder, 1971: 72–73).

Whereas McNamara and others use the spiral model to draw attention to self-amplifying and destabilizing pressures, the model also offers a policy recommendation: "If you seek security, cut your arms and make your adversary more secure" (Jervis, 1997: 287n). Realists who subscribe to balance-of-power theory caution that any cuts should be mutual, verifiable, and result in parity.

Multilateral Arms Control and Disarmament

There are many historical examples of multilateral arms control and disarmament efforts. As early as the eleventh century, the Second Lateran Council prohibited the use of crossbows in fighting. The 1868 St. Petersburg Declaration prohibited the use of explosive bullets. In 1899 and 1907, International Peace Conferences at the Hague restricted the use of some weapons and prohibited others. The leaders of the United States, Britain, Japan, France, and Italy signed treaties at the Washington Naval Conferences (1921–1922) agreeing to adjust the relative tonnage of their fleets.

Nearly 30 major multilateral agreements have been signed since the Second World War. Of these, the 1968 Nuclear Nonproliferation Treaty (NPT), which prohibited the transfer of nuclear weapons and production technologies to non-nuclear-weapons states, stands out as the most symbolic multilateral agreement with 189 signatory parties. While adherence to the treaty has been widespread, India, Pakistan, and North Korea have broken the NPT's barriers to become nuclear-weapons states. In addition, Israel is believed to have clandestinely produced nuclear weapons, and Iran remains outside the NPT and is seeking to become a nuclear-weapons state. The forty-six countries that launched the International Nuclear Fuel Cycle Evaluation negotiations in 2005 to sever the link between nuclear energy and nuclear proliferation was a step forward; however, some of the signatory parties complain that the pledge by the original nuclear powers to disarm has gone unheeded.

Similar problems plague other multilateral agreements. The 1993 Chemical Weapons Convention (CWC), for example, required all stockpiles of chemical weapons to be destroyed. However, the agreement lost some of its authority in 2001 when the Bush administration refused to accept the enforcement measures. This erosion of support for multilateral arms control and disarmament led U.S. President Barack Obama to warn during a 2009 speech in Prague that complacency in the face of weapons proliferation is tantamount to accepting that the use of these weapons is inevitable.

The Problematic Future of Arms Control and Disarmament

The obstacles to arms control and disarmament treaties are formidable. Critics complain that these agreements frequently regulate obsolete armaments or ones that the parties to the agreement have little incentive for developing in the first place. Even when agreements are reached on modern, sophisticated weapons, the parties often set ceilings higher than the number of weapons currently deployed, so they do not have to slash their inventories.

A second pitfall is the propensity of limits on one type of weapon system to prompt developments in another system. Like a balloon that is squeezed at one end but expands at the other, constraints on certain parts of a country's arsenal can lead to enhancements elsewhere. An example can be seen in the 1972 SALT I agreement, which limited the number of intercontinental ballistic missiles possessed by the United States and the Soviet Union. Although the number of missiles was restricted, no limits were placed on the number of nuclear warheads that could be placed on each missile; consequently, both sides began developing multiple independently targetable reentry vehicles. The quantitative freeze on launchers led to qualitative improvements in their warhead delivery systems.

Also reducing faith in the future of meaningful arms control is the slow, weak, and ineffective ability of the international community to ban some of the most dangerous and counterproductive weapons. Consider the case of antipersonnel landmines (APLs). Between 100 and 300 million landmines are believed to be scattered on the territory of more than 70 countries (with another 100 million in stockpiles). In the mid-1990s, there was about one mine for every 50 humans on earth, and each year they killed or maimed more than 26,000 people—almost all of them civilians. Yet, not a single state would endorse a prohibition on these deadly weapons. It took a peace activist, Jody Williams, to organize the International Campaign to Ban Landmines that produced the

Convention on the Prohibition of the Use, Stockpiling, Production, and Transfer of Antipersonnel Mines and Their Destruction, which was opened for signature in December 1997. For her efforts, she was awarded the Nobel Peace Prize. Still, the challenge of enforcing the ban now signed by 155 states, and the task of removing APLs, remains staggering.

A final problem facing those advocating arms control and disarmament is continuous innovation. By the time limits are negotiated on one type of weapon, a new generation of weapons has emerged. Further complicating matters, modern technology is creating an ever-widening range of novel weapons—increasingly smaller, deadlier, and easier to conceal.

Why do states often make decisions to arm that apparently imprison them in the grip of insecurity? On the surface, the incentives for meaningful arms control seem numerous. Significant controls would save money, reduce tension, reduce the environmental hazards, and diminish the potential destructiveness of war. However, most countries are reluctant to limit their armaments in a self-help system that requires each state to protect itself. Thus, states find themselves caught in a vicious cycle summarized by two basic principles: (1) "Don't negotiate when you are behind. Why accept a permanent position of number two?" and (2) "Don't negotiate when you are ahead. Why accept a freeze in an area of military competition when the other side has not kept up with you?" (R. Barnet, 1977: 100).

The tendency of states to make improving their weapons a priority over controlling them is illustrated by the example of nuclear testing. The nine known nuclear-weapons states conducted a total of 2,056 nuclear explosions in twenty-four different locations since 1945—an average of one test every ten days. The Partial Test Ban Treaty of 1963, which prohibited atmospheric and underwater testing but not underground explosions, did not slow the pace of testing. Three-fourths of all nuclear tests took place after the ban went into effect in 1963. Today, both China and the United States regularly conduct so-called zero-yield nuclear experiments and are suspected of conducting explosive tests so small that they can't be detected.

To sum up, arms control remains a murky policy area, and the past record suggests that we should not exaggerate its potential. As long as aggressive national leaders exist, it would be imprudent to disarm. Limits on weapons may confine the rivalry between states, but they do not remove the underlying source of the conflict. Arms, after all, are less the causes of war than the symptoms of political tension: People do not fight because they have weapons; they have weapons because they fear that they must fight to preserve their security.

BALANCING POWER IN THE CONTEMPORARY INTERNATIONAL SYSTEM

The use of alliances and arms control to balance power typically follows one of two distinct patterns. In the pattern of "direct opposition," one powerful state tries to prevail over another powerful state, which raises arms or seeks allies to offset its adversary's strength. Over time, each increase in military capabilities by one side calls forth an increase by the other. If neither side yields, they may negotiate arms control agreements to stabilize their competition and avoid waging war.

In the more fluid pattern of "competition," encroachment by one state against another also precipitates a quest for arms and allies. But rather than resulting in the formation of rigid, counterbalanced blocs, it triggers shifts in a kaleidoscope of overlapping alliances. The diplomatic checkerboard of eighteenth-century Europe illustrates this second pattern of balance-of-power politics. As described by Michael Doyle (1997: 177), France was sandwiched between its rivals, Britain and Austria (Austria possessed what today is Belgium); consequently, France established ties with Prussia, an enemy of the British and Austrians. Simultaneously, Holland balanced against France with British support, Saxony balanced against Prussia with Austrian support, and Bavaria leaned toward France and Prussia in an effort to balance against Austria. Owing to a desire to offset what he saw as an alarming increase in Prussian power ever since it seized the province of Silesia from his country in 1740, Austrian foreign minister Wenzel Kaunitz forged an alliance with France, Austria's longstanding foe and heretofore Prussia's ally. Britain, Austria's former ally, responded by concluding an alliance with Prussia. In what is known as the "Diplomatic Revolution of 1756," the configuration of great-power alliances was completely reversed in response to growing Prussian power.

According to the eminent realist Hans J. Morgenthau (1985), if no state possesses overwhelming military superiority, world politics follows either the pattern of direct opposition or the more complex pattern of ever-shifting competition. Having examined the theory of how the balance of power is supposed to operate, let us consider how it actually functioned in world politics since the end of the Second World War.

The Cold War Pattern of Direct Opposition

Most countries were devastated by World War II. The United States, however, was left in a dominant position, its economy accounting for about half the world's combined gross national product (GNP). The United States was also the only country with the atomic bomb, and had demonstrated its willingness to use the new weapon. American hegemony was short-lived, however, as the recovery of the Soviet economy and the growth of its military capabilities eroded U.S. supremacy and gave rise to a new distribution of world power. The Soviets broke the U.S. monopoly on atomic weapons in 1949 and exploded a thermonuclear device in 1953, less than a year after the United States. This achievement symbolized the creation of a bipolar system of direct opposition. Military capabilities were now concentrated in the hands of two rival "superpowers," each heading its own bloc of allies.

The formation of the North Atlantic Treaty Organization (NATO), linking the United States to the defense of Western Europe, and the Warsaw Pact, linking the former Soviet Union in an alliance with its Eastern European clients, reinforced this bipolar structure. The opposing blocs formed in part because the superpowers competed for allies and in part because the less powerful states looked to one super-power or the other for protection. Correspondingly, each superpower's allies gave it forward bases from which to carry on the competition.

By grouping the system's states into two blocs, each led by a superpower, the Cold War's bipolar structure bred insecurity among all. The balance was constantly at stake. Each bloc leader, worrying that its adversary would attain primacy, viewed every move, however defensive, as the first step toward world conquest. Both superpowers attached great importance to recruiting new allies. Fear that an old ally might desert the fold was ever-present. Nonalignment was viewed with suspicion. Bipolarity left little room for compromise or maneuver and worked against the normalization of superpower relations.

The major Cold War coalitions associated with bipolarity began to disinte-grate in the 1960s and early 1970s. As their internal cohesion eroded, new cen-ters of power emerged. At the same time, weaker alliance partners were afforded more room for maneuvering. Diverse relationships among the states subordinate to the superpowers developed, such as the friendly relations between the United States and Romania, and between France and the Soviet Union. The super-powers remained dominant militarily, but this less rigid system allowed other states to perform more independent foreign policy roles.

Rapid technological innovation in the superpowers' major weapons systems was a catalyst in the dissolving of the Cold War blocs. Intercontinental ballistic missiles, capable of delivering nuclear weapons from one continent to another, lessened the importance of forward bases on allies' territory. Furthermore, the narrowed differences in the superpowers' arsenals loosened the ties that had pre-viously bound allies to one another. The European members of NATO in par-ticular began to question whether the United States would, as it had pledged, protect Paris or Bonn by sacrificing New York. Under what conditions might Washington or Moscow be willing to risk a nuclear holocaust? The uncertainty became pronounced while the pledge to protect allies through **extended deter-rence** seemed increasingly insincere.

extended deterrence
the use of military threats by a great power to deter an attack on its allies.

The movement toward democracy and market economies by some commu-nist states in the late 1980s further eroded the bonds of ideology that had for-merly helped these countries face their security problems from a common posture. The 1989 dismantling of the Berlin Wall tore apart the Cold War archi-tecture of competing blocs. With the end of this division, and without a Soviet threat, the consistency of outlook and singularity of purpose that once bound NATO members together disappeared. Many perceived the need to replace NATO and the defunct Warsaw Pact with a new security arrangement. How-ever, most leaders maintained that some configuration of a European defense architecture was still necessary to cement relationships and stabilize the rush of cascading events.

A Future of Balance-of-Power Competition?

Following the dissolution of the Soviet Union in 1991, a new era of unipolarity arose, with the United States emerging as the world's only superpower.

Columnist Charles Krauthammer proclaimed that no country had been as dominant militarily, economically, and culturally since the Roman Empire. For hegemonic stability theorists, this was beneficial. As they saw it, a unipolar concentration of power would allow the global leader to police chaos and maintain international peace.

Against this optimistic view ran a strong suspicion about the future stability of a unipolar world under U.S. management. Critics warned that whenever countries became hegemons in the past, they tended to want everything their own way. American leaders, they believed, would behave in a similar fashion, ultimately measuring their foreign policy undertakings according to whether they helped preserve the country's position as top dog.

Regardless of whether the optimists or pessimists are correct, many scholars believe that U.S. preponderance will not last far into the twenty-first century. Unipolarity, they argue, is giving way to a new configuration of power whose probable consequences are not clear. Some forecast the return of a bipolar pattern of direct opposition, with the United States facing off against China (see CONTROVERSY: How Should the United States Respond to China's Growing Power?). Others see the emergence of a more complex pattern of balance-of-power competition, where the United States, China, Japan, India, Russia, the European Union, and possibly Brazil would constitute multiple centers of global power. According to this image of the future, as power becomes more equally distributed, each player will be increasingly assertive, independent, and competitive, leading to confusion about the identity of friends and foes. Finally, still others speculate that the erosion of unipolarity will begin a descent into apolarity—a fragmented world characterized by dozens of regional power centers, with no one exercising global leadership (Haass, 2008).

CONTROVERSY   How Should the United States Respond to China's Growing Power?

In explaining the origins of the twenty-seven-year Peloponnesian War between Athens and Sparta, the historian Thucydides pointed to the growth of Athenian power and the alarm that it caused in Sparta, the dominant state in Greece during the fifth century BCE. As noted in the discussion of power transition theory in Chapter 7 and depicted in the figure on the next page, we can categorize states according to where they stand on the international hierarchy of power and how satisfied they are with the status quo. The likelihood of war increases, argue some theorists, when the power of states lower on the hierarchy that are dissatisfied with the international status quo grows to the point of overtaking the dominant state, which supports the status quo (Kugler, Tammen, and Efired, 2004: 164). Just as Sparta faced the challenge of an ascending Athens, throughout history, states at the apex of power have wrestled with the question of how to respond to rising competitors.

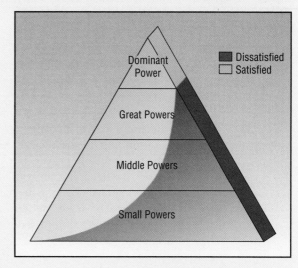

One of the principal foreign policy challenges for contemporary American foreign policy, suggests historian John Lewis Gaddis (2005: 9), is not to make the Middle East the single lens through which the United States views the world. Iraq is a serious problem today and a nuclear-armed Iran may be the "wild card" of the next decade or so, but what happens in China "may well be as important for the future of the international system as what transpires in the Middle East." The question is no longer whether China will become strong but how the United States will respond to the growth of Chinese power.

When China began its market reforms in 1978, it accounted for less than 1 percent of the world's economy, and its foreign trade totalled $20.6 billion. Since then, China has averaged 9.5 percent annual GDP growth and by 2009 accounted for 8 percent of the world economy, with foreign trade increasing to $2.21 trillion. Today, China is the world's largest producer of steel, the largest exporter of information technology goods, the second largest consumer of energy, and its GDP is projected by the U.S. National Intelligence Council to equal the United States' in 2042. These resources position China, formerly regarded as a sleeping giant, to awaken and play an active role on the world stage commensurate with its power. Having spent an estimated $115 billion in foreign investments over the past decade and possessing some $2.1 trillion in foreign exchange wealth, China could become the world's leading exporter of capital (*Fortune*, October 26, 2009: 88–89).

Still, China has far to go in order to become a military superpower. Its annual defense spending has been growing at a double-digit rate for the past decade, but most estimates place total expenditures somewhere between 14 and 19 percent of those of the United States. Over the next several decades, however, China's defense budget could triple as the country upgrades its antiquated ground, air, and maritime forces, and deploys a credible, second-strike nuclear arsenal. Currently, China is constructing its first aircraft carrier, which to some military analysts indicates that Beijing is redefining its naval interests beyond coastal defense.

A future U.S. confrontation with a more muscular China is, of course, not preordained. Yet some people in the United States are alarmed about China's growing economic power, which they worry will be translated into a robust military capability. They recommend that America craft a foreign policy that contains China, just as the country did when addressing the challenge posed by the Soviet Union after World War II. Others are concerned that a new containment policy will eventually lead Washington and Beijing to square off against one another. From their perspective, the United States will have to accommodate itself to peer competitors. Rather than attempt to block China's rise, they recommend making room for an ascending China, giving it a stake in the existing international order, and enmeshing it in a web of international institutions that smooth any future power transitions.

The United States and China are at a crossroads. America's bombing of the Chinese embassy during the war with Serbia in 1999, the collision of an American EP-3 spy plane with a Chinese interceptor in 2001, China's harassment of an American surveillance ship in 2009, and continued friction over human rights, intellectual property rights, and the attempt by the Chinese National Offshore Oil Corporation to acquire Unocal, a California-based oil company, have sparked lively discussions across the United States over what policy that Washington should adopt toward China. What do you think? How should the United States respond to China's growing power?

Although those who see a gradual passing of America's unipolar moment disagree on what will come next, they concur that U.S. security commitments have stretched the country's military capabilities thin. Further complicating matters, the United States is suffering under a staggering debt burden and the worst financial crisis since the Great Depression. America may still be the home of astonishing creativity and a vibrant entrepreneurial spirit, and it will continue to be a formidable power, but these analysts conclude that the combination of military overreaching abroad, domestic economic problems, and the rise of fast-growing challengers will shape the contours of global future. "The international landscape of a few decades hence," writes one scholar, "may resemble that of Easter Island: dominated by giants, and battered by tempestuous winds of change" (Bell, 2005: 21).

The evolution of the North Atlantic Treaty Organization (NATO) since the end of the Cold War reflects this shifting geopolitical landscape. At first, many observers felt that NATO would disappear along with the rival Warsaw Pact. The purpose for which NATO was first created—containing Soviet expansionism—no longer was relevant, because the threat no longer existed. However, NATO did not dissolve. It reinvented itself, changing its mission and adding former communist bloc states to reach twenty-eight total members by 2010. Much to the dismay of Russian leaders, who insist they had been promised at the end of the Cold War that former Soviet Republics and Warsaw Pact members would not be brought into NATO, some people have proposed that Georgia and Ukraine be brought under NATO's security umbrella.

Following the 2001 terrorist attacks on the World Trade Center and the Pentagon, NATO invoked its mutual defense principle for the first time, declaring that the attack on the United States was an attack on all members. In 2006, NATO took command of security and reconstruction work throughout most of southern Afghanistan, opening a new chapter in the organization's history. Yet some members wonder how far beyond Europe the alliance should go. In particular, former Warsaw Pact members want NATO's priorities adjusted to focus on protecting their borders against threats that might arise from a resurgent Russia. Critics complain that this could spark a confrontation. A military alliance in Europe rehearsing contingency plans for sending troops and equipment eastward would raise security concerns in Moscow. Supporters assert that this charge is unjustified because NATO's new decision rules, giving every full member a veto over decisions regarding military operations, remove the threat of a preemptive strike against Russia.

Despite its innovative redesign and new decision rules, NATO cohesion has been affected by American military intervention into Iraq as part of its proclaimed war on global terrorism. NATO today is being pulled in two directions. Led by Britain, some members favor a broad interpretation of NATO's strategic role, and advocate creating a small multinational "solidarity" force to assist in crises on the Continent, leaving NATO's Response Force (NRF) to function like an expeditionary force outside of Europe. Led by France, other members prefer a narrow interpretation, therein allowing the European Union to take on more military responsibilities.

Adding to the transatlantic debate over collective defense was the decision by the European Union to create its own rapid deployment force so it could undertake military actions on its own without the approval of the United States. As the European reaction to America's use of its military might demonstrates, the quest for national security in an anarchical world springs from states' uncertainties of the intentions of others. Because the unchecked growth in one country's power makes others insecure, nearly all states continually look for ways to defend themselves. In this sense, the realists' military paths to peace discussed in this chapter are intimately related to the widespread quest for armaments described in Chapter 8. Convinced that a more peaceful world is not on the diplomatic horizon, realists insist that the tragic struggle for security among great powers will continue.

The validity of this interpretation of the global future is still at issue, however. In the next chapter, we will turn our attention away from the balance-of-power politics of realism and examine proposals by liberal and constructivist theorists for using international norms and institutions to create a more peaceful world.

CHAPTER SUMMARY

- The term *balance of power* is used in many ways. At the core of its many meanings is the idea that state security and survival are most likely when there is a rough military parity among rivals.

- In order to function effectively, balance-of-power theory prescribes that national leaders follow certain rules of statecraft. They should be vigilant, forge alliances when they cannot keep pace with the arms increases of competitors, choose alliance partners on the basis of strategic needs rather than cultural or ideological affinity, always oppose those who seek hegemony, and act with moderation toward those who are defeated in battle.

- Balance-of-power theory is criticized for its logical inconsistencies, the lack of a reliable way for national leaders to gauge accurately the distribution of military capabilities, the propensity to foster rapid arms buildups, the assumption that leaders are risk averse, and its inability to prevent destructive wars.

- Great-power concerts attempt to stabilize power balances by creating regular channels of communication among latent rivals. Concerts are fragile, however. Friction often develops when some members come to believe that they have sacrificed more for the common good than others.

- Some realists argue that military parity can be preserved through arms limitation agreements. Whereas arms control refers to restrictions on the growth of weapons inventories, disarmament pertains to the reduction or elimination of weapons. Arms control agreements have tended to be more effective than disarmament agreements, especially when they involve bilateral negotiations.

- Various obstacles stand in the way of reaching effective arms control agreements. Negotiations are generally slow, they rarely cover new weapons systems, and those agreements that are reached pose difficult verification problems and are hard to enforce.

- Throughout the Cold War, the balance of power between the United States and the Soviet Union followed a pattern of direct bipolar opposition, with two counterbalanced blocs facing off against one another.

- After the collapse of the Soviet Union, the structure of the state system moved toward unipolarity, with the United States standing as the world's sole superpower. Unipolarity has never lasted long in modern history. As described in balance-of-power theory, states eventually combine forces to check the power of the dominate state. Currently, many scholars are debating how long the United States will remain in its dominant position. Some scholars predict that American unipolarity will be followed by a return to the pattern of direct bipolar opposition, with a rising China and perhaps several additional states counterbalancing the United States. Other scholars disagree. They foresee a return to the classical balance-of-power pattern of fluid competition, involving the United States, China, Russia, Japan, India, Brazil, and a united Europe.

KEY TERMS

alliance	balancer	extended deterrence
arms control	bandwagoning	hegemonic stability theory
arms race	concert	
balance of power	disarmament	

SUGGESTED READINGS

Burns, Richard Dean. *The Evolution of Arms Control: From Antiquity to the Nuclear Age.* Westport, CT: Praeger, 2009.

Gibler, Douglas M. *International Military Alliances 1648–2008,* 2 vols. Washington, DC: CQ Press, 2008.

Kaufman, Stuart J., Richard Little, and William C. Wohlforth (eds.). *The Balance of Power in World History.* New York: Palgrave Macmillan, 2007.

Little, Richard. *The Balance of Power in International Relations: Metaphors, Myths, and Models.* Cambridge: Cambridge University Press, 2007.

Mandelbaum, Michael. *The Case for Goliath: How America Acts as the World's Government in the Twenty-First Century.* New York: Public Affairs, 2006.

CRITICAL THINKING QUESTIONS

Metaphorical expressions are routinely used by national leaders to explain certain aspects of world politics. For example, they may assert that others should not interfere with geographic areas in their country's "backyard," or that military forces should be engaged somewhere to fill a power "vacuum" but not elsewhere because intervention would be a "slippery slope" (see Shimko, 1995). Balance-of-power theory contains metaphors as well. The most common is an intricate weighing scale (Little, 2007). Statecraft, according to this imagery, is similar to mechanical engineering.

(Continued)

Strategist Terry Deibel (2007: 54–56) proposes two other ways of conceptualizing international political processes. First, rather than seeing these processes as machine-like, he suggests imagining them as being akin to those of a living organism that goes through cycles of growth and decay. A second metaphor comes from chaos theory, where seemingly minor random events can cause dramatic, system-wide changes in a network of interacting entities, as in the flow of information traffic on the Internet. How does adopting a mechanical metaphor to describe international processes shape the way that one thinks about world politics? Are organic metaphors or metaphors based on complex networks better suited for making sense out of world politics? Do they provide useful insights that are not apparent from a mechanistic worldview?

10

International Law and Organization as Alternative Paths to Peace

CHAPTER OUTLINE

I refuse to accept the cynical notion that nation after nation must spiral down a militaristic stairway ... .

MARTIN LUTHER KING, JR.
AMERICAN CIVIL RIGHTS LEADER

Some people left in a caravan of tractors and rusty old cars. Others jammed into trains and cattle trucks. Many more hobbled along on foot. An estimated 740,000 ethnic Albanian refugees streamed out of Kosovo during March 1999. Not since World War II had Europe witnessed such an exodus.

On the eve of this exodus, Kosovo was a province within Serbia, one of the republics that formed Yugoslavia. Roughly 90 percent of Kosovo's 2 million inhabitants were ethnic Albanians. They had the highest birth rate on the Continent and a population largely under the age of thirty, demographic trends that disturbed many Serbs, angered by what they believed were Albanian efforts to gain independence by pressuring the Serb minority into leaving. Slobodan Milosevic, who had risen to the presidency of Yugoslavia in 1997 under a banner of Serb nationalism, insisted that Kosovo, the location of many important cultural and religious sites for Serbs, would never become an independent Albanian state. "Yugoslavia would disintegrate without Kosovo," he told a crowd of supporters on a field near Prestina, where Serbs had fought an epic battle against the Ottoman Empire centuries earlier.

Milosevic proposed to retain control over Kosovo by ridding the province of ethnic Albanians through brute force, a policy known euphemistically as "ethnic cleansing." Friction between Serbs and Kosovo's Albanians had existed long before Milosevic's rise to power. Claiming that discrimination against Albanians had led the per capita income in Kosovo to fall to less than one-third of the national average, some Kosovars had called for the province to be decoupled from Serbia and elevated to the legal status of a full republic within Yugoslavia. Others within Kosovo's Albanian population made more radical demands, insisting on secession from Yugoslavia. The conflict escalated to violence in May 1993, when an ethnic Albanian organization called the Kosovo Liberation Army (KLA) gunned down a group of Serb police officers in Glogovac. Over the next few years, KLA guerrillas launched sporadic raids against Serbs, which prompted harsh reprisals against villages suspected of supporting the KLA. Each KLA attack triggered stronger Serbian retaliation, which radicalized even more ethnic Albanians.

Beginning in the late spring of 1998, intermittent skirmishing gave way to protracted fighting. After weeks of KLA gains, a Serb counteroffensive in mid-July drove the guerrillas into hiding but brutally displaced some 200,000 ethnic Albanians. The violence worsened a year later, unleashing a tidal wave of refugees and prompting the United States and several European countries to summon the Serbs and Kosovar Albanians to peace talks in Rambouillet, a small town about 30 miles from Paris. When efforts to persuade the Serbs to accept a cease-fire, remove their military units from Kosovo, and allow the deployment of a NATO peacekeeping force failed, many observers feared that the situation would deteriorate into a humanitarian catastrophe. In a last-minute attempt to stop further ethnic cleansing, U.S. envoy Richard Holbrooke told Milosevic that NATO would bomb Yugoslavia unless he accepted the Rambouillet proposal.

NATO's air attack began on March 24, 1999, at 8:00 PM local time. By the end of the 78-day war, NATO aircraft had flown more than 37,000 sorties, causing an estimated $60 billion in damage to Serbia's industry and infrastructure.

Within days after Milosevic accepted defeat, hundreds of thousands of ethnic Albanians began returning to Kosovo. By late November, 808,913 refugees had returned and 247,391 people, primarily Serbs intimidated by KLA members bent on revenge, had departed (Judah, 2000: 286–287).

Although Milosevic remained in power when the war ended, he was indicted by the International Criminal Tribunal for the former Yugoslavia (ICTY), a court in The Hague, Netherlands, created by the UN Security Council to prosecute those who committed war crimes, crimes against humanity, and acts of genocide during the armed conflicts that led to the breakup of Yugoslavia. Milosevic, the first sitting head of state to be indicted by an international court for war crimes, had no intention of surrendering to the ICTY. Moreover, his government did not buckle under diplomatic and economic pressure from the Clinton administration. However, his tenure in office came to an end when Vojislav Kostunica, a constitutional lawyer backed by a coalition of eighteen opposition parties, defeated him in the fall 2000 presidential election.

In January 2001, Carla del Ponte, the ICTY chief prosecutor, delivered an arrest warrant for Milosevic to the Kostunica government. Arguing that the ICTY was biased because it had not vigorously prosecuted Kosovar Albanians or NATO members for war crimes, Kostunica hesitated to comply. But when Milosevic was subsequently linked to the theft of state funds, Prime Minister Zoran Djindzic and Justice Minister Vladan Batic pushed for his arrest. After being taken into custody by Yugoslav authorities, he was transferred to The Hague to stand trial.

Milosevic's trial began on February 12, 2002, but ended without a verdict when he died of a heart attack on March 11, 2006. Chief Prosecutor del Ponte expressed regret that his death during the proceedings had deprived the victims of ethnic cleansing of the justice they deserved; nonetheless, she noted that the indictment of an incumbent head of state for war crimes set an important precedent. No longer could national leaders evade legal accountability for their actions by invoking state sovereignty.

Slobodan Milosevic's indictment and trial draw attention to the role of international law and organization in world politics. Whereas liberal theorists place great stock in these approaches to the control of armed conflict, hardboiled realists have long scoffed that without compulsory jurisdiction and a mechanism to ensure compliance with judicial verdicts, these procedures will remain a blind alley rather than a path to peace. The purpose of this chapter is to examine the contributions that international legal norms and institutions make to world order. We will begin by analyzing the nature and functions of international law.

INTERNATIONAL LEGAL NORMS
AND WORLD ORDER

Throughout recorded history, all autonomous, independent political entities engaged in sustained interaction have developed rules that define appropriate behavior for certain situations. Although the rules of modern international law

Boris Grdanoski/AP Photo

NATO's Mission in Kosovo NATO's 1999 intervention in Kosovo marked the first time that alliance used force "out of area." Here a British tank is greeted by ethnic Albanians, thankful that Slobodan Milosevic's policy of "ethnic cleansing" had ended.

private international law law pertaining to routinized transnational intercourse between or among states as well as nonstate actors.

public international law law pertaining to government-to-government relations.

may not be backed by a formal, unified system of sanctions, both state and nonstate actors rely on them to coordinate their behavior and redress grievances. Most of this activity falls within the realm of **private international law**—the regulation of routine transnational activities in such areas as commerce, communications, and travel. This is where the majority of international disputes are regularly settled and where the record of compliance compares favorably with that achieved in domestic legal systems.

In contrast, **public international law** covers relations between governments as well as the interactions of governments with intergovernmental organizations (IGOs) and nongovernmental organizations (NGOs). Most critics of international law focus their attention here rather than on private international law. Their complaints generally emphasize instances where bystanders overlooked the transgressions of aggressive states engaged in illegal activities. As Israeli diplomat Abba Eban once famously lamented, public international law "is that law which the wicked do not obey and the righteous do not enforce." Although public international law has deficiencies, that should not lead to the conclusion that it is irrelevant or useless. No legal system can prevent all of its members from breaking laws. There are miscreants who ignore domestic law just as there are states who flagrantly violate international law. In spite of its shortcomings, states themselves find international law useful and expend considerable effort attempting to shape its development. Because this chapter examines the capacity of public international law to control war, our discussion will address only the laws and institutional machinery created to manage armed conflict between states. That is, it will explore that segment of international law popularly regarded as the most deficient.

Sovereignty and the Rules of International Law

Public international law is the body of general normative principles and specific legal rules that govern the behavior of states in their relations with one another. Rather than being a static code of conduct, it has evolved significantly over the past four centuries, changing in response to transformations in world politics.

No principle of international law is more important than state sovereignty. As discussed in previous chapters, sovereignty means that no authority is legally above the state, except that which the state voluntarily confers on the international organizations it joins. Nearly every legal doctrine supports and extends the principle that states are the primary subjects of international law. As outlined in the Montevideo Convention of 1933 on the Rights and Duties of States, a state must possess a permanent population, a well-defined territory, and a government capable of ruling its citizens and of managing formal diplomatic relations with other states. This last criterion is particularly important because the acquisition of statehood ultimately depends on a political entity's acceptance as such by other states, which are entitled to give or withhold **diplomatic recognition**. In other words, recognition is a political tool, through which approval of a government can be expressed and certain rights granted.

diplomatic recognition
the formal legal acceptance of a state's official status as an independent country. De facto recognition acknowledges the factual existence of another state or government short of full recognition. De jure recognition gives a government formal, legal recognition.

The Rights of States.   Under international law, political entities that meet the criteria of statehood hold certain rights. First, states possess the right of continued national existence, which means the prerogative to use force in self-defense. Second, they have the right of independence, which allows them to manage their domestic affairs without external interference and act as free agents in foreign affairs, negotiating commercial treaties, forming military alliances, and entering into other types of agreements without the supervision of another state. Finally, states also have the right of legal equality. Although unequal in size and strength, states are equal before the law in the sense that they all (1) possess the same privileges and responsibilities, (2) can appeal to the same rules of conduct when defending themselves, and (3) can expect to have these rules applied impartially whenever they consent to have a third party help settle their quarrels. The most common third-party procedures used in international dispute resolution include:

- *Good offices:* A third party offers a location for discussions among disputants but does not participate in the actual negotiations.

- *Conciliation:* A third party assists both sides but does not offer any solution.

- *Mediation:* A third party proposes a nonbinding solution to a conflict between states.

- *Arbitration:* A third party gives a binding decision through an ad hoc forum.

- *Adjudication:* A third party gives a binding decision through a standing court.

By defining states' rights in this manner, international law traditionally held that no state could claim jurisdiction over another, nor could it sit in judgment over the validity of the public acts other states initiated under their own laws. Furthermore, heads of state and diplomatic representatives were immune from prosecution in foreign courts.

The Duties of States.   Besides recognizing the rights of existence, independence, and equality, international law acknowledges certain corresponding duties. A sovereign state has the right to maintain its corporate personality as a state, but it also possesses a corollary duty of **nonintervention**—not meddling in the internal matters of other states. Another duty is carrying out promissory obligations in good faith. A sovereign state possesses the right to act as a free agent when dealing with others, but it also has a duty to honor agreements not signed under duress. As expressed in the norm *pacta sunt servanda* (treaties are binding), promises made voluntarily by parties to international treaties must be upheld. However, some legal scholars claim that a radical change in the circumstances that existed when a commitment was made can be invoked under the norm *rebus sic stantibus* (as matters stand) as a ground for unilaterally terminating an agreement.

nonintervention the legal principle prohibiting one state from interfering in another state's internal affairs.

The Limitations of International Law

Sovereignty and the legal principles derived from it provide the foundation upon which the international legal order rests. But because the international legal order is premised upon the voluntary consent of sovereign states, many people question whether international law is *really* law. From their perspective, international law suffers from the following limitations:

- *The international system lacks a legislative body capable of making binding legal rules.* Whereas in most national legal systems a legislature makes domestic laws, there is no global legislature empowered to make international laws. The UN General Assembly makes recommendations, not statutes. According to Article 38 of the Statute of the International Court of Justice (ICJ), the sources of legal rules are: (1) custom; (2) international treaties and agreements; (3) national and international court decisions; (4) the writings of legal authorities and specialists; and (5) the "general principles" of law recognized since antiquity as part of "natural law" and "right reason." Of these, custom and multilateral treaties signed by a substantial number of states are considered the most important. Critics question the efficacy of these sources, retorting that there can never be a true rule of law among states until everyone is under a common authority (Bork, 1989/1990).

- *The international system lacks a judicial body with compulsory jurisdiction that can identify breaches of legal rules and impose remedies for violations.* The International

Court of Justice differs from national courts primarily in that its jurisdiction is based on the consent of the disputants. Sovereign states cannot be forced to appear before the ICJ when charged with breaking legal rules, and they are hesitant to give unconditional consent given the risk of receiving an unfavorable verdict on an issue of vital importance. John Bolton, a former U.S. ambassador to the United Nations, reflected this hesitancy when he claimed it would be "a big mistake" for anyone "to grant validity to international law." In his opinion, "those who think that international law really means anything are those who want to constrict the United States" (*New Yorker*, March 21, 2005: 23).

■ *The international system lacks an executive body capable of enforcing legal rules.* Unlike in national legal systems, no centralized mechanism exists to apprehend and punish those who violate legal rules. Although the UN Security Council has the power to act when there is a "threat of breach of international peace and security" (Article 39 of UN Charter), it is often paralyzed by vetoes in cases involving serious militarized disputes, and it is not designed to operate like a municipal police force investigating and bringing to justice those who commit other violations of the law. As one skeptic quipped, without meaningful enforcement capability, international law will be "to law as professional wrestling is to wrestling" (*U.S. News & World Report*, September 29, 1993: 8).

■ *In the absence of robust global institutions that can make, interpret, and enforce legal rules, international law serves as an instrument of the powerful, justifying self-help and the competitive pursuit of national advantage without regard to justice.* By accepting unbridled sovereign autonomy, the international legal system is essentially a "horizontal" normative order composed of laws of coordination, not a "vertical" order based on laws of subordination. Within horizontal orders, the behavior of the powerful has a significant impact in establishing how others should behave. When a particular behavior becomes widespread, it tends to be seen as obligatory; rules *of* behavior become rules *for* behavior (Hoffmann, 1971). Yet the legal rules to which the powerful willingly agree are those that serve their interest. The outcome of any legal dispute, assert realists, thus hinges on the relative power of the violator of the law and the victim of the violation (Morgenthau, 1985).

Despite the limitations listed here, most states comply with international law because it communicates the "rules of the game" through which virtually everyone within the international system conducts their relations. By shaping expectations, legal rules reduce uncertainty about the behavior of others and increase predictability in world affairs. Those who consistently play by recognized rules enhance their reputations for trustworthiness; those who opportunistically break them undermine their credibility, which weakens their bargaining positions in future interactions as other states become suspicious about their intentions. National leaders who value their reputations are likely to violate an international legal norm only if it or the situation they face is ambiguous enough to plausibly claim an exemption (V. Shannon, 2000). Leaders with high levels of distrust, a belief that they can control events, and a tendency to see the world in "us versus them" terms are less likely to be constrained by legal norms (Shannon and Keller, 2007).

In summary, compliance with law does not necessarily derive from commands backed by punishment from some central authority. States voluntarily observe international legal rules because their long-term self-interests are served by the order that comes from shared expectations. Legal scholar William Slomanson (2010) likens this process to the behavior of motorists at intersections. Most drivers stop when the traffic light is red and go when it turns green, even when no police officer is present to enforce traffic laws. They comply with the law because of a common interest in proceeding safely, knowing that collisions would occur if people ignored the signals at intersections. Similarly, almost all states follow almost all principles of international law almost all of the time, argues Louis Henkin (1979), because everyone benefits from avoiding the chaos that would otherwise exist.

International Law and the Preservation of Peace

Although rudimentary when compared to national legal systems, international law nonetheless mitigates the most pernicious aspects of an anarchic state system. Among the most important international legal rules that prescribe limits on state behavior are those that pertain to the use of armed force. They delineate when it is legitimate for states to employ force, how it should be used, and against whom it may be applied. Because the content of these rules has been heavily influenced by **just war doctrine**, we begin our analysis of the role of international law in preserving peace by examining this ethical tradition.

just war doctrine   a set of criteria that indicate when it is morally justifiable to wage war and how it should be fought once it begins.

Just War Doctrine.   The term *just war* originated with Aristotle. Attempts to enumerate criteria for determining whether a particular war was just were subsequently undertaken by the Roman writer Cicero, as well as by early Christian thinkers such as Ambrose, Augustine, and Aquinas (see Raymond, 2010). Over the intervening centuries, philosophers and theologians continued to advance contending theories regarding when it would be morally justifiable to use military force as a tool of foreign policy.

The roots of modern just war doctrine lie in the effort of Hugo Grotius to transform these earlier moral theories into a body of international law that would specify those circumstances under which war might be legally initiated and how it should be waged upon its commencement. An eminent Dutch scholar who was outraged by the brutality of the Thirty Years' War, Grotius (1949: 10–11) complained that states "rush to arms" for "trifling pretexts," and then behave "as though by some edict a fury had been let loose to commit every crime." To counteract this deplorable pattern, he drew upon ancient and medieval writers to develop two bodies of rules about warfare, *jus ad bellum* (the justice of a war) and *jus in bello* (justice in a war). The former set the standards by which a political leader could determine whether a war was just. The latter described the military actions that were permissible in fighting a just war.

The rules proposed by Grotius have inspired international lawyers since their publication in 1625 (see CONTROVERSY: Was the War in Iraq Just?). Rather than condemning all warfare as intrinsically evil, just-war theorists submit that recourse to war is permissible when the following conditions are met:

1. *Just cause:* The state contemplating the use of military force must have a morally good objective.

2. *Right intention:* War must be waged for the purpose of correcting a wrong and establishing peace and justice, not for revenge or some other malicious reason.

3. *Last resort:* War should not be undertaken until all other reasonable means of resolving the conflict have been exhausted.

4. *Political proportionality:* The harm caused by the fighting must not outweigh the good toward which the war aims.

5. *Declaration by legitimate authority:* Duly constituted rulers must publicly declare a state of war.

6. *Reasonable chance of success:* States must not engage in futile uses of force.

In addition to elucidating *when* it is morally permissible to fight, just-war theory also stipulates *how* wars should be fought. While numerous rules have been proposed on the right and wrong ways to conduct war, most revolve around the following two principles:

1. *Discrimination:* Noncombatants must be immune from attack; civilians not engaged in their state's war efforts cannot be targeted.

2. *Military proportionality:* Combatants must cause no more destruction than is required to achieve their military objectives.

These *jus ad bellum* and *jus in bello* standards have parallels in non-Western moral thought (see H. Hensel, 2010) and continue to color thinking about the laws of war. However, the advent of weapons of mass destruction raised new questions about the ethics of war and peace, since their use would violate many of the traditional principles of just war doctrine. A high-yield nuclear device, for example, would not only obliterate the target area, but it would also produce enough radioactive fallout to kill vast numbers of people in countries that had no part in the conflict, thereby violating the standards of military proportionality and discrimination. Scholars and policy makers alike are now struggling to rethink just war doctrine in the light of the new strategic realities of contemporary warfare.

In addition to wrestling with questions about how modern technology affects how a just war should be waged, scholars and policy makers have recently considered the propriety of conduct by the victor once a war ends. Battlefield success, regardless of how impressive, does not automatically yield a durable postwar settlement. Nor does military victory, no matter how justly attained,

RUIT HORA

Mierevelt, Michiel Jansz. van. Stedelijk Museum het Prinsenhof, Delft, The Netherlands/Erich Lessing/Art Resource, Inc.

War and the Birth of Modern International Law Revolted by the international violence he witnessed during his lifetime, Dutch reformer Hugo Grotius (1583–1645) wrote *On the Law of War and Peace*, a treatise that specified the legal principles he felt would facilitate cooperation and peaceful intercourse among states. Because of his pioneering work, Grotius is known today as the "father of international law."

guarantee a moral outcome. One school of thought on *jus post bellum* (justice after war) counsels leniency: Victors should be magnanimous in their peace terms to extinguish any desire for revenge by the defeated, and they should recognize their moral responsibility to assist in the rehabilitation of the vanquished (see Evans, 2009). Another school calls for sterner measures: Victors should be exacting to ensure that the enemy's defeat is irreversible. The first approach seeks peace by fostering reconciliation between adversaries; the second, by eliminating an adversary's capacity to mount a future military challenge. Weighing the merits of these contending positions is important because postwar policies heavily influence whether the defeated will accept or reject the peace settlement, and whether its role on the world stage ultimately will be constructive or destructive.

Problems in the Legal Control of Warfare.   As Figure 10.1 shows, the international legal community has increasingly rejected the realist contention that states can use military force to achieve their foreign policy objectives. Influenced by many of the standards contained in just war doctrine, the laws of war have

CONTROVERSY   Was the War in Iraq Just?

On February 5, 2003, U.S. Secretary of State Colin Powell delivered a lengthy address to the United Nations Security Council, charging Iraq with a breach of its disarmament obligations under UN Security Council Resolution 1441. American intelligence agencies, Powell asserted, had evidence that Saddam Hussein's regime possessed weapons of mass destruction. After emphasizing the gravity of the threat these weapons posed, Powell reminded his audience of the Iraqi leader's ruthlessness and warned that he would "stop at nothing until something stops him."

Over the next few weeks, U.S. President George W. Bush and other members of his administration reiterated these accusations. On March 17, Bush claimed that Iraq "continued to possess and conceal some of the most lethal weapons ever devised," and threatened military action if Saddam Hussein did not leave the country within forty-eight hours. When Hussein failed to comply, the United States and its allies launched a series of precision air strikes and swarming ground attacks that quickly overwhelmed Iraqi defenses.

The Bush administration gave three primary justifications for its war against Iraq: (1) Saddam Hussein had weapons of mass destruction; (2) he had close ties with the Al Qaeda terrorist network; and (3) his removal from power would provide an opportunity to transform Iraq into a democratic regime, which would change the political atmosphere throughout the entire Middle East.

Yet, more than three years after the president declared victory on May 1, 2003, from the flight deck of the *USS Abraham Lincoln*, American and allied troops were locked in fierce fighting with Iraqi insurgents. Though expected to be welcomed with rice and rose petals, the coalition forces came to be seen as occupiers rather than liberators. Iraqi public opinion polls sponsored by the U.S. Coalition Provisional Authority showed over 80 percent of those interviewed indicated that they had no confidence in the United States after the Abu Ghraib prison abuse scandal, and wanted Washington to withdraw its troops as soon as possible. Meanwhile, the much-touted Iraqi weapons of mass destruction had not been found, and the commission investigating the September 11 terror attacks on the United States indicated that they failed to discover any collaborative relationship between Saddam Hussein and Al Qaeda.

In response, the Bush administration continued to insist that the war had been just. Vice President Dick Cheney maintained that even if there was just a 1 percent chance of terrorists getting weapons of mass destruction, the United States had to act as if it were a certainty (Suskind, 2006: 62). According to Cheney, absolute proof of an adversary's capabilities and intentions should not be a precondition for American military action; it's too high a threshold in a world where warnings of a catastrophic attack would be limited and confirmation of the perpetrator's identity unattainable in operational time. What do you think? Drawing on the criteria proposed by just-war theorists, would you evaluate the 2003 war against Iraq as a just war? Was it initiated for a just cause and with the right intentions? Was it undertaken as a last resort with the appropriate authorization? Did the good toward which the war aimed outweigh the harm caused by the fighting? Do you agree with Vice President Dick Cheney's claim that the risks of American inaction were far greater than the risks of action?

---

sought to prohibit all uses of force by individual states except in self-defense. Traditionally, the right of self-defense has been understood as allowing states recourse to force when repelling armed attacks and when facing imminent security threats. As articulated by U.S. Secretary of State Daniel Webster in 1837, to exercise this right a state must face an "instant, overwhelming necessity … leaving no choice of means, and no moment for deliberation." In addition, the defensive actions taken must be proportionate to the danger, should not endanger noncombatants to minimize one's own risk, and cannot serve as a **reprisal**. Self-defense is thus restricted to protection, not excessive or punitive measures aimed at redressing injuries.

reprisal   a hostile but legal retaliatory act aimed at punishing another state's prior illegal actions.

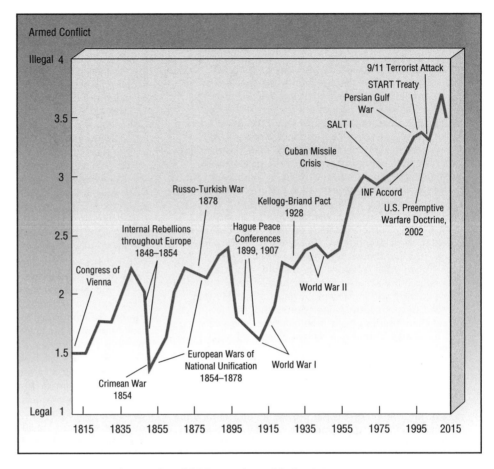

FIGURE 10.1 **The Legal Prohibition against Initiating War**

Legal restraints on the historic right of states to use war as a tool of foreign policy have grown steadily since World War I. After the attacks of September 11, 2001, these prohibitions were questioned by various U.S. policy makers who favored preventive military action against states that supported terrorist movements.

SOURCE: Adapted from data collected by the Transnational Rules Indicators Project, as described in Kegley and Raymond (2007 and 1990).

Following the promulgation of the UN Charter, appeals to this customary right of self-defense became more problematic. The charter addresses self-defense in two places. First, Article 2 (4) declares that "all members shall refrain in their international relations from the threat or use of force against the territorial integrity or political independence of any State, or in any other manner inconsistent with the purposes of the United Nations." Second, Article 51 proclaims that "Nothing in the present Charter shall impair the inherent right of individual or collective self-defense if an armed attack occurs against a Member of the United

Nations, until the Security Council has taken the measures necessary to maintain international peace and security." One school of thought about the Charter interprets Articles 2 (4) and 51 as superseding customary international law, and thus limiting forcible self-defense to cases where the Security Council has not yet responded to an armed attack. A second school of thought disagrees. Highlighting the concept of "inherent right" in Article 51, it argues that pre–charter, customary rules of self-defense continue in place. States, in other words, have a right to use military force so long as the traditional criteria of necessity, proportionality, and protection are met.

The difficulty with the second interpretation of self-defense lies in defining what constitutes an "overwhelming necessity." Appeals to the exigencies of **military necessity** challenge the wrongfulness of an act on the basis that it was the only means of safeguarding an essential interest against a grave peril (Raymond, 1999). According to those who invoke the necessity defense, a state may be absolved from taking military actions that violate the rules of warfare when it faces an absolute strategic imperative that makes it practically impossible to do anything else. Those responsible for national security, they insist, must often make tragic choices among lesser evils. As the former British Secretary of State for War Lord Kitchener once put it: "We must make war as we must; not as we should like" (cited in Howard, 1991: 31).

military necessity a legal doctrine asserting that violation of the rules of war may be excused during periods of extreme emergency.

In addition to the problems that claims of military necessity create for international laws governing the use of force, recent suggestions that the international community has a moral imperative to stop brutal governments from violating the human rights of their citizens raise another set of problems. Allowing the use of coercion by one state to change the political regime in another would significantly change the normative climate of world affairs. As we have seen, the twin principles of sovereignty and nonintervention underpin international law. Traditionally, the only widely accepted exception to the prohibition against interfering in the domestic affairs of other nation-states was military intervention to liberate one's own nationals when they are being held hostage. Yet recently, some states have asserted the right, and even a moral obligation, to use military intervention for humanitarian purposes. As shown in Figure 10.2, the nonintervention principle has begun to erode as a growing proportion of countries has sought a way to stop human rights abuses in a globalized, interconnected world.

The argument claiming it is legally permissible to intervene with armed force in order to end egregious violations of human rights rests on three propositions. The first proposition asserts that human rights are an international entitlement. Article 55 (c) of the UN Charter requires member states to promote "universal respect for, and observance of, human rights." Over the past 50 years, the UN has developed a detailed list of inherent, inalienable rights of all human beings. The most important legal formulation of those rights is expressed in the so-called International Bill of Human Rights, the informal name given to the Universal Declaration of Human Rights (which was passed by a vote of the UN General Assembly in 1948), the International Covenant on Civil and Political Rights, and the International Covenant on Economic, Social, and Cultural

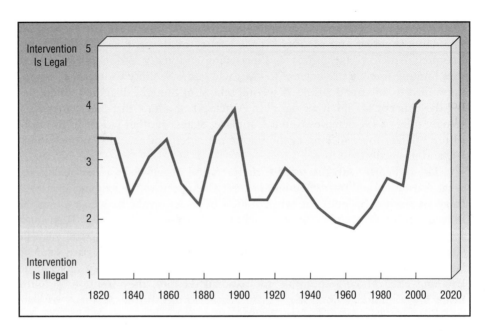

FIGURE 10.2 The Changing Status of the Nonintervention Rule in International Law

Over time, the illegality of intervening in the domestic affairs of sovereign states has changed. Since 1960, international law has adopted an increasingly permissive posture toward such actions for a variety of purposes, including preventing egregious human rights abuses, promoting democracy, and combating global terrorism.

SOURCE: Adapted from data collected by the Transnational Rules Indicators Project, as described in Kegley, Raymond, and Hermann (1998).

Rights (which were both opened for signature in 1966 and entered into force a decade later). For advocates of humanitarian intervention, the legal rules governing these rights are regarded as *jus cogens*—peremptory legal norms that override all other considerations.

The second proposition maintains that governments committing grave violations of human rights lose their legitimacy. Although Article 2 (7) of the UN Charter prevents member states from interfering in one another's domestic affairs, the Charter's legal protection does not extend to genocide, torture, or other horrific acts shocking to the conscience of the international community. Those favoring humanitarian intervention argue that governments involved in these abuses forfeit their protection under international law.

The third proposition asserts that the international community has a responsibility to halt human rights violations. According to the International Court of Justice, there are some obligations that a state has toward the international community as a whole, and all members of that community have a legal interest in their protection. The entitlement for protection against genocide, slavery, and the like gives legal standing to any member of the international community to impose sanctions if these wrongful acts continue. When massive human rights violations occur, intervention from the outside is legally justified and morally required.

The advent of these new justifications for military intervention into the domestic affairs of sovereign states reflects a growing sentiment that sovereignty is no longer sacrosanct. Sovereignty, various commentators now proclaim, cannot shield the perpetrators of grievous crimes against humanity from punishment. Heads of state and military commanders who have been involved in **war crimes** must be held accountable. The international community has a responsibility to protect vulnerable populations from human rights violations (see APPLICATION: The Doctrine of International Community).

To deal with the rising concern about serious violations of international humanitarian law, the UN Security Council set up two *ad hoc* criminal tribunals between 1993 and 1994: the International Criminal Tribunal for the former Yugoslavia, and the International Criminal Tribunal for Rwanda. In 1998, 120 countries meeting in Rome voted to establish a *permanent* International Criminal Court (ICC), so future acts of genocide, crimes against humanity, and war crimes would not go unpunished. The Rome Statute of the ICC also identifies the crime of "aggression," but the signatories disagree on how it should be defined

war crimes acts performed during war that the international community defines as illegal, such as atrocities committed against enemy civilians and prisoners of war.

APPLICATION　**The Doctrine of International Community**

Ever since the Peace of Westphalia ended the Thirty Years' War in 1648, the principles of sovereignty and nonintervention have governed international politics. As the twentieth century drew to a close, however, many legal scholars and human rights activists began arguing that these principles did not apply to national leaders who violated the human rights of their citizens. According to Tony Blair, who served as the prime minister of the United Kingdom from May 1997 to June 2007, the old "rule book of international politics has been torn up." The world is "witnessing the beginnings of a new doctrine of international community." In the following passage, Blair describes the policy implications of this new theoretical doctrine.

> The most pressing foreign policy problem we face is to identify the circumstances in which we should get actively involved in other people's conflicts. Non-interference has long been considered an important principle of international order. And it is not one we would want to jettison too readily. One state should not feel it has the right to change the political system of another … . But the principle of non-interference must be qualified in important respects. Acts of genocide can never be a purely internal matter.

> … So how do we decide when and whether to intervene? I think we need to bear in mind five major considerations.
>
> First, are we sure of our case? War is an imperfect instrument for righting humanitarian distress; but armed force is sometimes the only means of dealing with dictators. Second, have we exhausted all diplomatic options? We should always give peace every chance … . Third, on the basis of a practical assessment of the situation, are there military operations we can sensibly and prudently undertake? Fourth, are we prepared for the long term? In the past we talked too much of exit strategies. But having made a commitment we cannot simply walk away once the fight is over; better to stay with moderate numbers of troops than return for repeat performances with large numbers. And finally, do we have national interests involved? (Blair, 1999)

National interests, Blair would later go on to say, cannot be divorced from national values. Speaking at Georgetown University on May 26, 2006, he noted that in his years as prime minister he had "become more persuaded that the distinction between a foreign policy driven by values and one driven by interests, is obviously wrong." In his opinion, "our values are our guide."

and what specific role the Court should play in dealing with aggression so as not to infringe on the prerogatives of the UN Security Council, which according to the UN Charter has primary responsibility for determining if an act of aggression has occurred (Article 39) and the steps to be taken to maintain peace (Article 24).

The new International Criminal Court differs from the older International Court of Justice (or "World Court"). Whereas the ICC has criminal jurisdiction to prosecute individuals charged with heinous violations of human rights, the ICJ deals with disputes between sovereign states. Founded in the hope that international adjudication would help resolve disputes before they escalated to war, the ICJ languished through much of the Cold War. Powerful countries hesitated to relinquish their military advantage and put issues of importance in the hands of foreign judges that might rule against them. Political realists, depicting the world as a place where states perpetually jockey for relative gains, urge leaders to act in terms of national self-interest, trusting in their own power rather than in international courts. "A statesman who has any other motive," proclaimed one exponent of realism, "would deserve to be hung" (Johannes Haller cited in Niebuhr, 1947: 84).

Despite realist predictions that the World Court would always have more judges than cases, in recent years it has begun to play the kind of role envisioned by its liberal founders. Between 1946 and 1991, the World Court heard only sixty-four contentious cases between states, rendered judgments on fewer than half of these, and handed down only nineteen advisory opinions. Since then, it has

Jacques Collet/AFP/Getty Images

Prosecuting War Criminals In 1999, Swiss criminal lawyer Carla del Ponte was appointed chief prosecutor of the International Criminal Tribunals for Rwanda (ICTR) and the former Yugoslavia (ICTY). As of 2010, the ICTR had rendered judgments on fifty-one people and anticipated completing trials on another twenty-six individuals by the end of 2011, with appellate work scheduled to be completed by the end of 2013. The ICTY estimates that it will close proceedings against 161 indicted people by 2012 and complete appeals by the end of 2013.

expanded its workload and considered cases dealing with many new issues (Raymond, 2004). Since 1992, the ICJ has received fifty-three contentious cases and has become increasingly active in responding to requests for advisory opinions.

Critics assert that the World Court remains ineffective despite its increased caseload, with many states still refusing to submit their most serious disputes. It is instructive, they note, that two-thirds of today's states have never appeared before the ICJ, and those who agree to litigate comply with ICJ judgments only 60 percent of the time. Supporters, however, point to recent high-profile cases that were successfully resolved. For example, in 1992 Honduras and El Salvador accepted the Court's verdict on a border dispute that had been festering for decades. Unconvinced, the ICJ's critics aver that the Court's successes tend to involve litigants who wish to preserve their overall relationship, not bitter foes locked in high-stakes confrontations. They argue that the outcome of Nicaragua's 1984 suit against the United States was more representative of the Court's impact on serious disputes than the case between Honduras and Nicaragua.

In 1979, Nicaraguan dictator Anastasio Somoza was overthrown by a broad-based movement known as the Sandinista National Liberation Front. After ousting Somoza, a Marxist faction within the movement gained power and established ties with Cuba and the Soviet Union. Disturbed by the leftist tilt of the new regime and its support for revolutionary groups elsewhere in Central America, the United States trained antigovernment insurgents, mined three of Nicaragua's harbors, and attacked the country's petroleum facilities in an effort to undermine the Sandinistas. Nicaragua responded by filing suit against the United States on April 9, 1984, in the International Court of Justice.

Nicaragua's suit accused the U.S. Central Intelligence Agency of illegally attempting to destabilize and topple the elected Sandinista government. The Reagan administration replied by refusing to recognize the World Court's jurisdiction and withdrawing from further judicial proceedings. Nevertheless, the ICJ heard Nicaragua's arguments, and on June 27, 1986, ruled against the United States. The verdict had little effect on Washington, however. Neither the World Court nor Nicaragua had any means to enforce the judgment.

As the Nicaragua case demonstrates, international judicial institutions remain a far cry from most domestic courts. Because the ICJ lacks teeth, detractors liken its rulings to sermons, providing gallant rhetoric to encourage the pursuit of wistful ideals (Wedgwood, 2002: 45). For some people, one way to dismantle some of the barriers impeding the development of international law is to strengthen international organizations; hence, we next consider their role in building and maintaining world peace.

INTERNATIONAL INSTITUTIONS AND WORLD ORDER

Critics of realism often recommend creating international institutions as a second political path to peace. To understand this recommendation, we must delve into their beliefs about **collective security** as an alternative to balance-of-power politics.

collective security a security regime guided by the principle that an act of aggression by any state will be met with a unified response from the rest.

The League of Nations and Collective Security

The outbreak of World War I, perhaps more than any other event, discredited the argument that peace was a byproduct of international equilibrium. Citing arms races, secret treaties, and competing alliances as sources of acute tension, many liberals viewed power balancing as a *cause* of war instead of an instrument for its prevention. U.S. President Woodrow Wilson voiced the strongest opposition to balance-of-power politics. He hoped to replace it with a League of Nations, based on a system of world order in which aggression by any state would be met by a united international response.

The Logic of Collective Security.   Long before Wilson and other liberal reformers called for the establishment of a League of Nations, the idea of collective security had been expressed in various peace plans. Between the eleventh and thirteenth centuries, for example, French ecclesiastic councils held in Poitiers (1000), Limoges (1031), and Toulouse (1210) discussed rudimentary versions of collective security. Similar proposals surfaced in the writings of Pierre Dubois (1306), King George Podebrad of Bohemia (1462), the Duc de Sully (1617–1638), and the Abbé de Saint-Pierre (1713). Underlying these plans was the belief that an organized "community" of power would be more effective in preserving peace than shifting alliances aimed at balancing power.

Collective security is based on the creed voiced by Alexandre Dumas' d'Artagnan and his fellow Musketeers: "One for all and all for one!" In order for collective security to function in the rough-and-tumble environment of international politics, its advocates usually translate the Musketeer creed into the following rules of statecraft:

1. *All threats to peace must be a common concern to everyone.* Peace, collective security theory assumes, is indivisible. If aggression anywhere is ignored, it will eventually spread to other countries and become more difficult to stop; hence, an attack on any one state must be regarded as an attack on all states.

2. *Every member of the state system should join the collective security organization.* Instead of maneuvering against one another in rival alliances, states should link up in a single "uniting" alliance. Such a universal collectivity, it is assumed, would possess the international legitimacy and strength to keep the peace.

3. *Members of the organization would pledge to settle their disputes through pacific means.* Collective security is not wedded to the status quo. It assumes that peaceful change is possible when institutions are available to resolve conflicts of interest. In addition to providing a mechanism for mediating disagreements, the collective security organization would also contain a judicial organ authorized to issue binding judgments on contentious disputes.

4. *If a breach of the peace occurs, the organization will apply timely, robust sanctions to punish the aggressor.* A final assumption underpinning the theory holds that members of the collective security organization would be willing and able to

give mutual assistance to any state suffering an attack. Sanctions could range from public condemnation to an economic boycott to military retaliation.

In summary, this approach to world order tries to inhibit national self-help by guaranteeing the territorial integrity and political independence of states through "collective self-regulation." The key to its success is universal participation: To deter war, a potential aggressor would need to be faced by the united opposition of the entire international community (Claude, 1962; K. Thompson, 1953).

Difficulties with Collective Security. As discussed in Chapters 2 and 3, the League of Nations was constructed according to the blueprint of collective security. To the disappointment of its advocates, the League was not endorsed by the United States, the very power that had most championed it in the waning months of the First World War. Other problems for the League arose when its members disagreed over how to define "aggression," and how to share the costs and risks of mounting an organized response to aggressors. In the final analysis, collective security theory's central fallacy was that it expected states to be as anxious to see others protected as they were to protect themselves (see Figure 10.3). That assumption did not prove true in the years preceding World War II; consequently, the League of Nations never became an effective collective security system.

The United Nations and Peacekeeping

Like the League, the United Nations was established to promote international peace and security after a gruesome world war. Article 1 (1) of its Charter directed the organization to take "effective collective measures for the prevention and removal of threats to the peace." In Article 2, all members were called

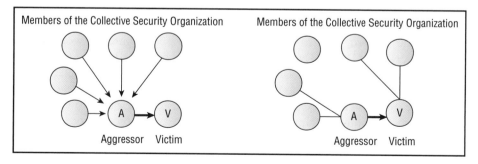

FIGURE 10.3 The Theory and Practice of Collective Security

According to the theory of collective security depicted on the left, all member states would take joint action against an aggressor. However, according to realists, attempts to implement collective security result in the pattern shown on the right. Whereas some members back the victim, others support the aggressor, and still others choose not to become involved.

SOURCE: Adapted from Morgenthau (1985).

on to "refrain in their international relations from the threat or use of force" (paragraph 4) and "settle their international disputes by peaceful means" (paragraph 3).

The architects of the United Nations were painfully aware of the League's disappointing experience with collective security. They hoped a new structure would make the United Nations more effective than the defunct League. Recall from Chapter 6 that the UN Charter established a Security Council of fifteen members, a General Assembly composed of representatives from all member states, and an administrative apparatus (or Secretariat) under the leadership of a secretary-general. While the UN's founders voiced support for collective security, the structure they designed was heavily influenced by the idea of a great-power concert. The UN Charter permitted any of the Security Council's five permanent members (the United States, the Soviet Union, Great Britain, France, and China) to veto and thereby block proposed military actions. Because the Security Council could approve military actions only when the permanent members fully agreed, the United Nations was hamstrung by great-power rivalries, especially between the United States and the Soviet Union.

To further enhance the great powers' authority relative to the UN, the Charter severely restricted the capacity of the General Assembly to mount collective action, authorizing it only to initiate studies of conflict situations, bring perceived hostilities to the attention of the Security Council, and make recommendations for initiatives to keep the peace. Moreover, it restricted the role of the secretary-general to that of chief administrative officer. Article 99 confined the secretary-general to alerting the Security Council to peace-threatening situations and to providing administrative support for the operations that the Security Council approved.

Because the UN's structure limited its ability to function as a collective security organization, the United Nations fell short during the Cold War of many of the ideals its more ambitious founders envisioned, principally because its two most powerful members in the Security Council, the United States and the Soviet Union, did not cooperate. Over 230 Security Council vetoes were cast, stopping action of any type on about one-third of the UN's resolutions. Nevertheless, the United Nations found other ways to contribute to world order. Under Secretary-General Dag Hammarskjöld, **preventive diplomacy** replaced collective security as the organization's primary approach to promoting international peace and security. Recognizing that the United Nations had little leverage in areas where the superpowers were heavily engaged, Hammarskjöld sought to involve the UN in other regions and thus prevent Washington and Moscow from intruding into local disputes. His approach was based on the UN experience in the Middle East crises of 1956 and 1958, the Laos crisis of 1959, and Congo crisis of 1960. In essence, it involved establishing a cease-fire and inserting UN troops as a buffer to separate the belligerents. Ideally, an impartial UN presence would keep the conflict localized, although it did little to resolve the dispute.

The next major innovation in UN peacekeeping efforts began during the 1980s when the organization moved beyond supervising truces and turned its attention to **peacemaking** and **peace-building**. The former involved the UN

preventive diplomacy actions taken in advance of a predictable crisis to prevent superpower involvement and limit violence.

peacemaking peaceful settlement processes such as good offices, conciliation, and mediation, designed to resolve the issues that led to armed conflict.

peace-building post-conflict actions, predominantly diplomatic and economic, that strengthen and rebuild governmental infrastructure and institutions in order to avoid recourse to armed conflict.

in actively working to resolve the underlying dispute between the belligerents; the latter involved it in activities such as monitoring arms control agreements and providing developmental assistance to create the conditions that would make a renewal of the fighting less likely.

The end of the Cold War removed many impediments to the UN's ability to preserve international security by means that the founders of the UN originally envisioned. The potential to play an active security role was demonstrated in 1990 when Iraq invaded Kuwait. The Security Council promptly passed Resolution 678, authorizing member states "to use all necessary means" to dislodge Iraqi forces from Kuwait. Under the authority of this resolution, on January 17, 1991, a U.S.-led coalition launched military actions against Iraq's armed forces, the fourth largest in the world. Forty-three days later, Iraq agreed to a cease-fire and withdrawal from Kuwait.

Bolstered by this success at collective security, optimism about the UN role in promoting peace started to grow. After 1990, the UN launched five times as many peacekeeping missions as it had in its forty previous years of existence. Since then, it has managed on average seventeen operations each year (see Map 10.1). Despite this upsurge in the aftermath of the Cold War, peacekeeping missions have shown mixed results, failing in roughly half of the time and straining the UN's budget (Brooks and Laroia, 2005: 121–122.). For the UN's peacekeeping operations since 1948, expenditures have totaled almost $70 billion, and for the period between July 2009 and June 2010, the cost of supporting over 120,000 UN peacekeeping personnel was $7.9 billion (see Figure 10.4). In view of the costs, the UN has sought to deploy its missions alongside non-UN forces and at other times has requested regional organizations or multiparty state alliances to act as a substitute for the UN. This has raised questions about in whose interest these forces are acting and whether they can be held accountable by the UN.

Regional Security Organizations and Collective Defense

If the UN remains hampered by a lack of resources, perhaps regional organizations, whose members already share many common interests and cultural traditions, offer better prospects for maintaining peace and security. Indeed, some would argue that the kinds of wars raging today do not lend themselves to control by a worldwide body, because these conflicts are now almost entirely civil wars. The UN was designed to manage interstate wars; it was not conceived as an instrument for dealing with battles inside sovereign borders. This, however, is not the case for regional institutions, who see their security interests vitally affected by armed conflicts within countries in their geographic areas. In 2009, no less than 60 peace missions with a total of 187,586 military and civilian personnel were carried out by regional organizations and UN-sanctioned coalitions of states (SIPRI, 2009). Given the rising number of peacekeeping operations in recent years that involve regional security organizations, most observers expect them to play an increasingly larger role in the future.

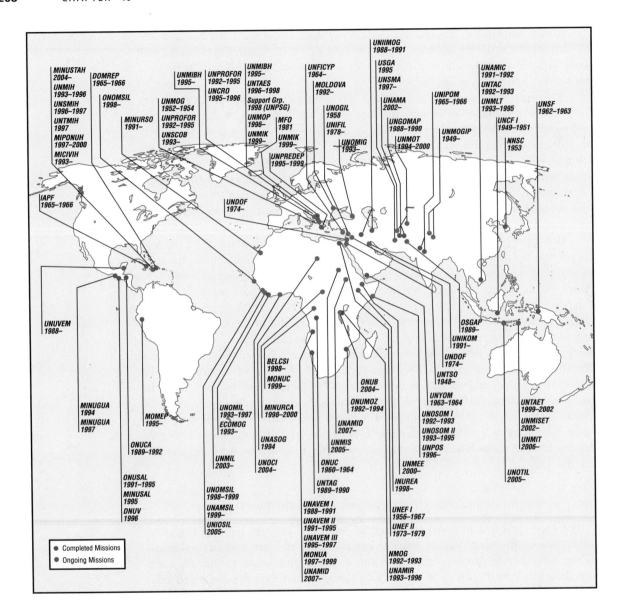

M A P 10.1 UN Peacekeeping Missions since 1948

In its first forty years, only thirteen UN peacekeeping missions were undertaken. As this map shows, the UN has been much more active over the past quarter century, sending peacekeepers to flash points throughout the world. Most of its sixty-three missions have been in operation for at least a decade.

SOURCE: Based on data from the United Nations Department of Public Information.

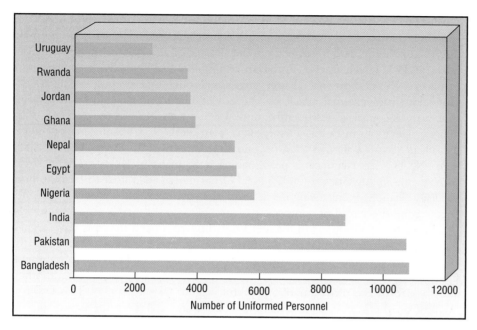

FIGURE 10.4 Major Contributors of Personnel to UN Peacekeeping Operations, 2010

Shown here are the ten countries that have contributed the largest number of uniformed personnel to UN peacekeeping operations in 2010. The top providers of assessed contributions to the UN peacekeeping budget were the United States (27.2%), Japan (12.5%), United Kingdom (8.2%), Germany (8%), France (7.6%), Italy (5.0%), China (3.9%), Canada (3.2%), Spain (3.2%), and the Republic of Korea (2.3%).

SOURCE: United Nations Department of Peacekeeping Operations.

The North Atlantic Treaty Organization (NATO) is the best-known regional security organization. Others include the Organization for Security and Cooperation in Europe (OSCE), the ANZUS pact (Australia, New Zealand, and the United States), and the Southeast Asia Treaty Organization (SEATO). Regional organizations with somewhat broader political mandates beyond defense include the Organization of American States (OAS), the League of Arab States, the Organization of African Unity (OAU), the Nordic Council, the Association of Southeast Asian Nations (ASEAN), and the Gulf Cooperation Council.

Although Article 51 of the UN Charter encourages the creation of regional organizations for collective self-defense, it would be misleading to describe NATO and the other regional organizations as a substitute collective security instrument for the UN. They are not. More accurately, regional **collective defense** systems are designed to deter a potential common threat to the region's peace, one typically identified in advance.

collective defense a military organization within a specific region created to protect its members from external attack.

Many of today's regional security organizations face the challenge of preserving consensus and solidarity without a clearly identifiable external enemy or common threat. Cohesion is hard to maintain in the absence of a clear sense of mission. Consider NATO, which faces a European security setting marked by ethnopolitical conflicts. NATO's original charter envisioned only one purpose—mutual self-protection from external attack by the Soviet Union; it never defined policing civil wars as a goal. Consequently, until 1995, when NATO took charge of all military operations in Bosnia-Herzegovina from the UN, it was uncertain whether the alliance would survive long beyond the demise of the Soviet Union. Since then, NATO has taken on a peacemaking assignment in Kosovo (1999) and a combat role in Afghanistan (2007). NATO has transformed itself to become both a *military* alliance for enhancing the security of its members and a *political* alliance for encouraging the spread of democracy.

From the philosopher Immanuel Kant onward, liberal theorists have argued that democratization enhances the prospects for peace between states. As discussed in earlier chapters, a growing body of research supports their argument. Constitutionally secure democracies rarely (if ever) make war on one another, and they form the most durable, peaceful leagues (Weart, 1994). This lesson is not lost on the leaders of today's democratic states searching for a principle on which to ground their security policies. NATO and the European Union have insisted on democracy as a condition for membership. Major international organizations from the World Bank to the International Monetary Fund have also made the promotion of democracy a policy priority. Since democratic states have a greater propensity than other types of states to employ amicable, legally binding methods of conflict resolution (Dixon, 1994; Raymond, 1994), liberals contend that enlarging the community of democracies will exert a pacifying effect on world politics.

INTERNATIONAL INTEGRATION AND WORLD ORDER

Since antiquity, the world has pursued two primary paths to peace: one road emphasizes military solutions; the other, political solutions. Thus far in this chapter we have examined international law and organization as political approaches to the control of armed conflict. We turn now to consider an approach based on changing the way international actors think about themselves, changing what constructivists would characterize as their identities.

Many theorists who focus on international law and organization see armed conflict as deriving from deeply rooted institutional deficiencies. They believe weak international institutions make humankind's security subservient to the parochial interests of competing, egoistic states. For them, the major security problems of our day simultaneously affect almost everyone. Terrorists with global reach, refugees fleeing horrific civil wars, and the proliferation of weapons of mass destruction exemplify these problems. National borders cannot insulate people from security threats lurking over the horizon. Nor can states manage them unilaterally. According to some theorists, the dangers facing humanity are so grave that they require solutions beyond the nation-state.

World Government

If the anarchic state system is a major obstacle to peace, then one possible solution to the problem of war is a world government. The idea is not new. During the early fourteenth century, for example, the Italian poet Dante responded to incessant fighting among the states of his day by proposing that power be centralized in the hands of a universal monarch. While proposals for a world monarchy are rare today, it is not unusual to hear calls for **world federalism**, that is, incorporating previously sovereign states into a single union, therein reducing the likelihood that the actors on the world stage will have antagonistic identities.

world federalism   a reform movement proposing to combine sovereign states into a single unified federal state.

Federalists reason that if people value humanity's survival in an era of weapons of mass destruction, they will willingly transfer their loyalty to a supranational authority and dismantle the anarchic system of competitive territorial states. Scholars disagree over whether a federal government or a looser combination of supranational institutions would be capable of solving transnational problems ranging from climate change and pandemics to weapons proliferation and terrorism (Baratta, 2005). At the heart of the controversy is a debate about governance without government (see Weiss, 2009). Can effective global governance occur without a single body with the authority and resources to ensure compliance with policy decisions? Alexander Wendt (2003), a leading constructivist, says that a formal world state is inevitable. Just as city-states were superseded by nation-states when advances in military technology undermined their ability to provide their citizens with security, nation-states will someday be amalgamated into a world-state, although some wonder whether a practical first step would be for the world's democracies to combine in a federal union (Yunker, 2007).

The thesis that world government is inevitable remains controversial (see V. Shannon, 2005). In addition to those who believe it is unfeasible, many complain that it is undesirable. For example, ardent nationalists have vehemently attacked the federalist "top-down" peace plan. Because it seeks to abate the national identities associated with the current system of sovereign states, the plan threatens many entrenched interests. Other critics reject the notion that eliminating nation-states will end warfare. Civil wars can erupt under a world government. Still other critics fear that such a global political entity would be unresponsive to the local needs of the diverse indigenous cultures that comprise humanity. A world government need not be a leviathan, respond supporters. Because the threat of external invasion would be nonexistent, it could function as a small, decentralized federal authority without a massive defense establishment (Deudney, 2006).

Although the idea of world government has received increased attention in recent years (see Craig, 2008), aversion to war and concern about climate change and other transnational problems has not mobilized widespread grassroots enthusiasm for creating a universal state. Regional approaches to reforming world politics have attracted far more adherents.

Regional Integration

political integration the processes and activities by which the populations of two or more states transfer their loyalties to a merged political and economic unit.

functionalism a theory of political integration based on the assumption that technical cooperation among different nationalities in economic and social fields will build communities that transcend sovereign states.

spill over the propensity for successful integration across one area of cooperation between states to propel further integration in other areas.

While the merging of sovereign states into a world government is unlikely in the foreseeable future, integration is occurring in certain regions of the world. **Political integration** refers to the process of building new political communities and identities that transcend the nation-state. Advocates of political integration seek reform programs that transform international institutions from instruments *of* states to structures *over* them.

The Functionalist Approach to Integration. In contrast to federalism, **functionalism** is not directed toward creating a world federal government with all its constitutional paraphernalia. Instead, it calls for a "bottom-up," evolutionary strategy based on using specialized technical agencies that solve problems that cross national borders. The Rhine River Commission (1804), the Danube River Commission (1857), the International Telegraphic Union (1865), and the Universal Post Union (1874) were forerunners of these agencies. They were early attempts at crafting administrative units that conformed to the geography of a transnational problem rather than the boundaries of a particular state.

According to functionalists, technical experts, rather than professional diplomats, are the best agents for building collaborative links among people living in separate states. They see diplomats as being overly protective of their country's national interests at the expense of collective human interests. Rather than addressing the immediate sources of national insecurity, the functionalists' peace plan calls for transnational cooperation in technical areas as a first step. Habits of cooperation learned in one technical area (such as transportation), they suggest, will **spill over** into others (such as communication)—especially if the experience is mutually beneficial and demonstrates the potential advantages of further cooperation.

To enhance the probability that cooperative endeavors will prove rewarding, the functionalist plan recommends that less difficult tasks be tackled first. It assumes that successful mastering of a relatively simple problem will encourage working on other more demanding problems collaboratively. If the process continues unabated, the bonds among people living in different countries will multiply, because no government would oppose a web of functional organizations that provide such clear-cut benefits to its citizens (Mitrany, 1966).

Critics charge that as a theory of peace and world order, functionalism does not take into account some important political realities. First, they question its underlying assumption about the causes of war. Functionalism argues that poverty and other socioeconomic woes create frustration, anger, and ultimately war. Critics counter that war may instead cause poverty and other miseries. Addressing issues of poverty may not alleviate war, they also argue, especially if the rapid acquisition of wealth enables dissatisfied states to build armies for war.

Second, functionalism assumes that political differences among countries will be dissolved through the habits of cooperation learned by experts organized transnationally to cope with technical problems such as transportation or telecommunication. The reality, say critics, is that technical cooperation is often more strongly influenced by politics than the other way around. The U.S. withdrawal in the 1980s from the International Labor Organization (ILO) and the UN Educational, Scientific, and Cultural Organization (UNESCO) because Washington felt that those IGOs were too politicized illustrate this charge.

As skeptics conclude, functionalists are naïve to argue that technical (functional) undertakings and political affairs can be separated. If technical cooperation becomes as important to state welfare as the functionalists argue, states will assume an active role in technical developments. Welfare and power cannot be separated, because the solution of economic and social problems cannot be divorced from political considerations. The expansion of transnational institutions' authority and competency at the expense of national governments and state sovereignty is, therefore, unlikely.

These criticisms led to the emergence of a second wave of functionalist theorizing, known as **neofunctionalism**. It argues that growing economic interdependence among states requires closer political coordination, which ultimately will lead to greater political integration. In other words, political integration occurs not simply because of pressures to address common technical problems more efficiently; it comes about when the interests of different pressure groups, political parties, and government officials converge on creating a greater role for supranational institutions.

neofunctionalism a revised functionalist theory asserting that the IGOs states create to manage common problems provide benefits that exert pressures for further political integration.

The Neofunctional Approach to Integration. Europe provides the best example of how a group of independent nation-states can become an integrated political community along the lines suggested by neofunctional thinking. Today, the European Union (EU) is the world's biggest free-trade area, bringing together under a single administrative umbrella over 500 million people in twenty-seven countries (recall Chapter 6).

In order to speak with one voice and act in unison on security issues, the EU adopted a Common Foreign and Security Policy (CFSP), which defined as the EU's objectives safeguarding "the common values, fundamental interests, and independence of the Union," strengthening the EU's security, preserving "world peace and international security [as well as promoting] international cooperation to develop and consolidate democracy and the rule of law, and respect for human rights and fundamental freedoms." To fulfill these goals, at the 2001 Nice Summit, the EU established the European Rapid Reaction Force, seen by its founders as a preliminary step toward becoming a military presence on the world stage capable of unilateral action. According to the officials assembled at Nice, this 60,000-strong military force would enable the EU to reduce its dependence on the United States and NATO.

The political unification of Europe represents an enormous achievement, overturning a past of chronic suspicion and warfare. Constructing a new European identity reinforced by collateral institutions has served as a model for integration in other regions, including Africa, Asia, the Caribbean, and South

America. However, current evidence suggests that the factors promoting successful integration efforts are many and their mixture complex. It is not enough that two or more countries choose to interact cooperatively. Research indicates that chances of political integration wane without geographical proximity, similar political systems, supportive public opinion led by enthusiastic leaders, internal political stability, similar experiences in historical and internal social development, compatible economic systems with supportive business interests, a shared perception of a common external threat, and previous collaborative efforts. While not all of these conditions must be present for integration to occur, the absence of more than a few considerably reduces the chances of success. The integration of two or more societies—let alone entire world regions—is not easily accomplished. Europe's experience indicates that even when conditions are favorable there is no guarantee that integration will proceed automatically.

The substantial difficulty that most regions have experienced in achieving a level of institution building similar to that of the EU suggests the enormity of the obstacles to creating new political communities out of previously divided ones. Even parts of Europe have splintered rather than integrated. In 1991, for example, the Soviet Union shattered into fifteen countries. Since then, six additional states have been created from the former Yugoslavia. Disintegration of many of the world's states could continue. With fewer than twenty-five countries ethnically homogeneous and with 3,000–5,000 indigenous peoples interested in securing sovereign homelands, the prospects are high that the number of independent states will increase in the years ahead.

devolution granting political power to ethnopolitical groups within a state under the expectation that greater autonomy for them in particular regions will curtail their quest for independence.

The division of the globe into more and more smaller states could be slowed if existing states accepted **devolution** (the granting of greater political power to quasi-autonomous regions), as some central governments have done for the purpose of containing separatist revolts. However, in many states where governmental institutions are fragile, the leadership has repressed the minority peoples seeking to share power. About a third of the world's countries contain restless, politically repressed minorities struggling at various levels for human rights and independence. Within such countries, uneven growth rates and vast income inequalities between different groups could easily destabilize the political landscape.

In conclusion, contemporary global affairs are being shaped by centripetal and centrifugal pressures. At the same time that unifying forces are pulling some of the planet's inhabitants together, fragmenting forces are pushing others apart. The paradox of twenty-first-century world politics is that political integration and disintegration are occurring simultaneously. Given this turbulence, many theorists continue to raise concerns about the capacity of independent sovereign states to solve the many shared problems humanity faces. For them, the major issues on the global agenda are ones that cannot be meaningfully managed unilaterally. In the next four chapters, we shall examine these global welfare issues, which transcend political boundaries and resist national solutions.

CHAPTER SUMMARY

- The field of international law is composed of private and public international law. The former pertains to the regulation of transnational activities among individuals and other nongovernmental actors; the latter, to the relations among sovereign states.

- Nearly every legal tenet of public international law supports the principle that sovereign states are the primary actors in world politics. The major rights of states include self-defense, independence, and legal equality. The major duties are nonintervention and upholding the commitments that they voluntarily make.

- Although public international law lacks a central authority for punishing violators, states value international law because it performs an important communication function. By communicating the "rules of the game" in world politics, international law helps shape expectations, reduce uncertainty, and enhance predictability.

- For centuries, philosophers, religious leaders, and legal scholars have debated over when it is morally justifiable to go to war and how wars should be conducted. Just war doctrine emphasizes the need for the cause to be just; for the fighting to be undertaken for the right intention, exhausting all other means of resolving the conflict before issuing a public declaration of war; and for using force in a way that discriminates between legitimate and illegitimate targets, causes no more destruction than necessary, and is not undertaken in a futile effort.

- Collective security is often viewed as an alternative to the balance of power as a method for preserving peace. It calls for all states to join a universal organization, pledge to punish aggressors, and resolve their disagreements through pacific means.

- While the architects of the United Nations voiced support for the ideal of collective security, conflict in the Security Council between the United States and the Soviet Union during the Cold War prevented the UN from attaining many of the ideals envisioned by its founders. As a result, the UN has employed a variety of other means to help promote peace, including preventive diplomacy, peacemaking, and peace-building.

- Because many people see the anarchic structure of the state system as one of the most important causes of war, various theorists have proposed that the political integration of previously sovereign states might dampen the prospects for war. Whereas some have advocated world federalism as a solution to war, most place greater emphasis on regional integration, though they disagree on how to incorporate independent nation-states into a greater political whole. The European Union is the foremost example of regional integration.

KEY TERMS

collective defense	neofunctionalism	public international law
collective security	nonintervention	reprisal
devolution	peace-building	spill over
diplomatic recognition	peacemaking	war crimes
functionalism	political integration	world federalism
just war doctrine	preventive diplomacy	
military necessity	private international law	

SUGGESTED READINGS

Diehl, Paul (ed.). *The Politics of Global Governance: International Organizations in an Interdependent World.* Boulder, CO: Lynne Rienner, 2010.

Hensel, Howard M. (ed.). *The Prism of Just War: Asian and Western Perspectives on the Legitimate Use of Military Force.* Burlington, VT: Ashgate, 2010.

Karns, Margaret P., and Karen A. Mingst. *International Organizations: The Politics and Process of Global Governance,* 2nd ed. Boulder, CO: Lynne Rienner, 2010.

Starkey, Brigid, Mark A. Boyer, and Jonathan Wilkenfeld. *International Negotiation in a Complex World,* 3rd ed. Lanham, MD: Rowman & Littlefield, 2010.

von Glahn, Gerhard, and James Larry Taulbee. *Law Among Nations: An Introduction to Public International Law,* 9th ed. Upper Saddle River, NJ: Prentice-Hall, 2009.

CRITICAL THINKING QUESTIONS

Journalists, scholars, and policy makers frequently use the concepts international "system," "society," and "community" when discussing world politics, sometimes without realizing how each concept frames their discussions in a different way. An international system refers to a set of regularly interacting political actors that are sufficiently interdependent to make the behavior of each influential on the others. When these actors are conscious of common interests and share certain fundamental values, they can be considered members of an international society (Bull, 1977). As pointed out by the so-called "English School" of international relations (see Watson, 1992; Bull and Watson, 1984), the identity of these members is reinforced by criteria of inclusion/exclusion that enumerate what constitutes appropriate behavior for insiders and how it differs from the behavior of outsiders. Finally, if those actors also possess collective feelings of loyalty and solidarity that transcend self-regarding, instrumental interests, they can be thought of as belonging to an international community. As articulated by the ancient Athenian sage Solon, in a community "any wrongs that are done to individuals are resented and redressed by the other members of the community as promptly and as vigorously as if they themselves were personal sufferers."

A number of puzzling questions arise once distinctions are drawn among these concepts. Under what circumstances might states within the international system develop into an international society? What engenders the emergence of an international community? How would norms of behavior and diplomatic practices differ among states belonging to an international system versus an international society or international community? Does an international community exist today? If so, who are its members and what are their moral responsibilities to each other and to outsiders? What are the implications for world politics if an international community cannot be said to exist?

PART IV

The Politics of Global Welfare

What factors most affect the welfare of humanity? World politics may be played out on a large stage, but with the expansion of international communication, transportation, and commerce, a new era of globalization has arisen, knitting the world into a tight web of interdependence. Money, goods, and people travel across national borders at an accelerating pace. To an increasing extent, what happens in one part of the globe influences what happens elsewhere. "We live in a world of transformation," explains British sociologist Anthony Giddens (2003: 6–7). "For better or worse, we are being propelled into a global order that … is making its effects felt upon all of us."

To help make sense out of this new global order, the chapters that follow draw attention to "human security"—the welfare of peoples of the world—and the ways that state-to-state relations have combined with the activities of non-state actors to transform humanity's living standards and future prospects. Part IV of *The Global Future* begins by looking at the ways globalization is transforming everyday life (Chapter 11), and then analyzes how changes in international trade and monetary relations affect world politics (Chapter 12). After exploring the international political economy, the topics of human rights (Chapter 13) and the relationship between population demographics and the earth's ecological system (Chapter 14) are examined.

11

The Globalization
of World Politics

CHAPTER OUTLINE

> The twenty-first century has revealed a world more intertwined
> than at any time in human history.
> BARACK OBAMA
> PRESIDENT OF THE UNITED STATES

In the early summer of 2004, Zilog Incorporated closed its manufacturing facilities in southwestern Idaho after a quarter century of operations. Headquartered in San Jose, California, Zilog concentrates on the micrologic device segment of the semiconductor market, designing and producing devices used in embedded control. Although the firm had design centers in several locations, the Idaho facilities were the firm's only manufacturing plants. With their closure, 150 workers became unemployed. According to company executives, the intention was to convert Zilog into a "fabless" semiconductor company; that is to say, Zilog would continue to design microcontrollers but would contract with firms in Asia to fabricate them (*Idaho Statesman*, June 20, 2004: B2).

Zilog's actions were mirrored over the next few years by several other companies in southwestern Idaho. In the fall of 2007, Micron Technology Inc., which makes dynamic random access memory (DRAM) for computers and flash memory for small digital devices, laid off more than 1,100 workers from various facilities in the Boise Valley. According to its chief executive officer, the company was moving some of its production to China in an effort to lower operating expenses (*Idaho Statesman*, October 20, 2007: B1). A year later, SuperValu, a Minneapolis-based leader in the grocery retailing industry, announced that eighty employees in its Boise finance office would be laid off because the firm's asset management operations were being moved to India (*Idaho Statesman*, June 11, 2008: B1).

The decisions made by Zilog, Micron, and SuperValu are examples of off-shore outsourcing—subcontracting a business function to a foreign supplier. More than 3.3 million U.S. jobs are projected to be lost to outsourcing by 2015, and 14 million (11 percent of the U.S. total) have been identified as at risk of being sent overseas. In addition to affecting manufacturing, offshore outsourcing also has an impact on jobs in the fields of information technology, document management, and customer service. The educational field has recently been affected as well. India, for example, now has a $10 million e-tutoring industry, where companies such as Educomp Solutions (New Delhi), TutorVista (Bangalore), and Growing Stars (Cochin) provide inexpensive online assistance to American college and high school students, primarily in mathematics and science. With a vast pool of English-speaking chemists and engineers, and costs estimated by investment bank Goldman Sachs to be one-eighth of western levels (*Economist*, February 4, 2006: 58), India is also poised to play a larger role in offshore research and development, a market that is expected to grow to $12 billion. Similarly, with numerous attorneys trained at American and British universities, India's legal process outsourcing industry has grown to over 140 firms with revenues projected to reach $1.1 billion in 2014 (*Economist*, June 26, 2010: 69).

Nor is India alone in benefiting from jobs that have moved offshore from high-wage countries. CompuPacific International in Xian, China, processes medical claims, loan applications, and similar documents for American firms. Seagate Technology, which operates a research laboratory in Pittsburgh, uses scientists in Singapore to conduct some of its studies. General Electric plans to produce wind turbine generators in Haiphong, Vietnam, and First Solar, of Tempe, Arizona, will manufacture solar panels in Kulim, Malaysia (*BusinessWeek*, June 8, 2009: 36–37; *New York Times*, April 20, 2008: 5). Furthermore, in what has been called "nearshoring," Estonia, Bulgaria, and other post-communist states, where wages may be half of those paid elsewhere in Europe, provide data processing services and call centers for companies in neighboring countries.

Although American consumers may enjoy lower prices and investors may see increases in the value of the stocks they hold in companies that outsource business functions to foreign suppliers, some people worry that this trend is caus-ing a "race to the bottom" as corporations move more and more operations to countries with lower wages, fewer benefits, and fewer government regulations. Fearing a growth in unemployment (even in high-tech industries once thought immune to competition from low-cost foreign labor), critics of outsourcing vehemently condemn corporate executives for "exporting" American jobs.

Yet at the same time that American jobs are moving abroad, new jobs are arriving as foreign firms outsource some of their jobs to the United States. As the worldwide demand for services increases, the wages of workers in some Global East countries are expected to rise, thereby making offshoring less cost-competitive for companies in the United States and making foreign firms more likely to consider shifting some jobs to America. In 2007, for example, Wipro, an Indian firm, negotiated agreements with several U.S. cities to establish soft-ware development centers.

A related trend is known as "backshoring." Due to the shipping costs associ-ated with manufacturing overseas, some old jobs are returning as fuel becomes more expensive. According to one estimate, by the time Chinese-made machined products arrived at an American port in 2005, they were on average 22 percent cheaper than those made in the United States. By 2009, however, the average price gap had fallen to 5.5 percent. When language barriers and bureau-cratic regulations in the Global South and East are considered, it is more efficient for companies to move certain jobs back to the Global North. By 2010, for instance, one company returned to Germany for every three that moved produc-tion abroad (*Newsweek*, January 11, 2010: 11; *BusinessWeek*, June 15, 2009: 54).

globalization   a set of processes that are widening, deepening, and accelerating the interconnectedness among societies.

What in the world is going on? The answer: **globalization**. Money, goods, people, and information are moving across national borders at an accelerating pace, linking societies in ways that are transforming world politics. This intercon-nectedness creates both possibilities and problems. On the one hand, globaliza-tion is generating unprecedented levels of wealth as many firms streamline their operations and discover new overseas markets for their products. On the other hand, it is producing enormous social strain as displaced workers often cannot replace their lost incomes, even when they retrain in a different industry or move to another location. It is understandable, therefore, that the effects of glob-alization are controversial.

"We were born into a world that will soon cease to exist," proclaims German journalist Gabor Steingart (2008: 4). Due to globalization, the old world of our childhood "is disappearing into the fog of history, while the new one is only beginning to take shape." In this chapter, we will examine the diverse forces driving the process of globalization. In particular, we will look at the growth of worldwide telecommunication, the increased mobility of capital, labor, goods, and services, and the burgeoning number of problems that cross national borders. As we consider these issues, it is important to think about the prospects for the continuation of states as sovereign and independent actors. But before inspecting globalization's consequences, we must first examine its causes.

Richard Vogel/AP Photo

Offshoring Jobs One of the foremost complaints about globalization is that it has led to a shift in labor-intensive jobs from Global North countries to lower-wage countries in the Global East and South. Shown here is one example: workers in Vietnam making sport clothing for sale in European and U.S. markets.

WHAT IS GLOBALIZATION?

Until the fifteenth century, most civilizations remained relatively isolated from one another. Circumscribed by slow, costly, and often dangerous transportation routes, international intercourse tended to occur within self-contained regions of the world. Except for intermittent trade, occasional waves of migrants, and periodic clashes with invaders, contact with distant peoples was rare.

What distinguishes contemporary world politics from earlier eras is its global scope. Various processes are widening, deepening, and accelerating worldwide interconnectedness. Rapid, unrestrained communication is perhaps the most significant of these processes. Indeed, many see it as the foundation of an emerging **global village**—a metaphor used by futurologists to portray a world in which borders vanish and people become a single community.

global village a popular image used to describe the growth of awareness that all people share a common fate, stemming from a view that the world is an integrated and interdependent whole.

The Global Information Age

The decline in the importance of geographic distance as a determinant of the cost of communication has been described as perhaps the single most important economic force shaping societies in the first half of the twenty-first century. It is not only affecting where people live and work, but, as constructivists point out, it has the potential to change the images people have of their own identity and the meaning they attribute to "community."

The wireless technology of smart phones is spreading across the planet, enabling even isolated individuals, who have never before made a phone call, to communicate instantly with others. Text messaging, for example, has empowered political movements, allowing people to organize resistance to policies they oppose and bolster those they support. The rallies that led to the ouster of Philippine President Joseph Estrada in 2001 and challenged the 2009 election of Iranian President Mahmoud Ahmadinejad exemplify what some analysts have called "cellular people power."

Computers are another potent agent of global communication, with ever more people going online to get news, be entertained, or conduct business. In particular, the growth of Internet blogs and podcasting has created an elaborate transnational network with agenda-setting power on issues ranging from environmental matters in Brazil to human rights in Zimbabwe. Furthermore, with the enormous popularity of YouTube, a growing number of people are sharing visual information with others throughout the world. Anyone with access to this technology can bypass traditional news organizations and give their personal perspective on current events to a global audience. By 2010, Facebook had roughly 500 million regular users worldwide; MySpace, 300 million; and Twitter, 124 million (*Economist*, July 24, 2010: 60). The recent conflict over Internet censorship between Google and the Chinese government illustrates the political ramifications of modern information technology.

Although the world is becoming connected, it is happening at different rates: Only one in five Internet users lives in the Global South. As shown in Figure 11.1, use of the Internet is heavily concentrated in the Global North, as is the management of most websites. Thus, the Internet's effects remain uneven, benefiting some countries while putting the rest at a disadvantage. The result is a vast **digital divide**, where many of the world's inhabitants lack access to modern information and communications technology.

digital divide   the division between those states that have a high proportion of Internet users and hosts, and those that do not.

Nevertheless, the communications revolution holds great promise for the Global South, because modern information technology may allow poorer countries to "leap frog" technologies in which the Global North invested heavily as it developed economically. Inexpensive wireless phones, for example, enjoy both popularity and promise in many Global South countries, where the cost of stringing line from pole to pole for traditional wired phones is often prohibitive. In countries where roads are poor, rail lines sparse, and air travel infrequent, mobile broadband service significantly boosts economic development. Farmers can readily find where to get the best prices for their produce, skilled workers can easily advertise their services, and rural villagers can quickly access health information. Several studies have concluded that adding an extra ten mobile phones per 100 people in a typical Global South country increases economic growth in per capita GDP by 0.8 percentage points (*Economist*, September 26, 2009, special issue: 3–7). Driven by these benefits, wireless-phone use in developing countries has more than doubled since 2005 (*Time*, May 31, 2010: 15).

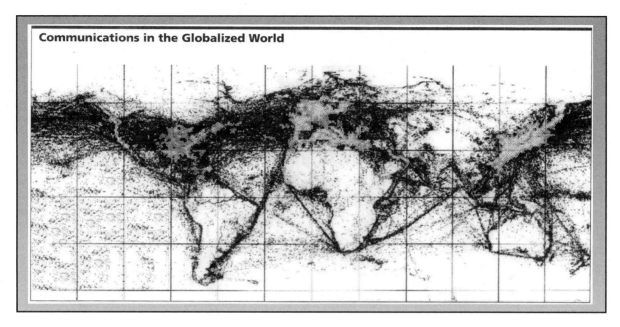

FIGURE 11.1 **The Digital Divide**

This figure, which shows the density of international communications flows throughout the world, reveals the striking division between the technological "haves" in the Global North and East, and the technological "have-nots" in the Global South.

SOURCE: Flanagan, Frost, and Kugler (2001: 24).

Yet, narrowing the digital divide remains difficult. Many cutting-edge technologies require infrastructures that are not widespread throughout the Global South. In countries without reliable electrical grids, for example, computer technology tends not to achieve mass-market scale.

Globalization or Americanization?

Ours is often described as the information age, but a remarkably large portion of the information we receive is controlled by a few huge corporations, notably Time Warner, Disney, General Electric, News Corporation, and Viacom in the United States. Some people worry that as the world's media sources are merged into ever-larger units, an ever-smaller number of corporate executives will control what people hear and see about the world around them. Although thousands of potential sources of information about politics, society, and culture are available, the influence of such media midgets is negligible compared to that of the giants.

The type of power the media wields over international affairs is, in fact, a specific and limited type of power. Scholarship shows that the media influence what people *think about* more than what they *think*. In this way, the media primarily functions to set the agenda of public discussion about current affairs

Visions of America, LLC/Alamy Limited

The World at One's Fingertips Modern technology has made virtually instantaneous communication possible nearly everywhere. Here, in a remote region of northern Kenya, a Samburu warrior makes a call on his cellular telephone.

agenda setting the ability to influence which issues receive attention from governments and international organizations by giving them publicity.

instead of determining public opinion. In the process of **agenda setting**, the media shapes international public policy. For example, many national leaders have grumbled about a "CNN effect," the alleged capacity of round-the-clock news services to highlight certain issues by immediately televising heart-wrenching scenes of famine, atrocities, and other human tragedies to millions of viewers throughout the world. When the CNN effect is combined with the use of email and tweets by grassroots activists to mobilize people rapidly on a particular issue, governments may find that these issues cannot be ignored.

Control of television and other media sources by the United States and a small number of other Global North countries became the focus of a dispute with the Global South beginning in the 1980s. Dissatisfied with the coverage it received from Western news agencies, and wary about the values promoted in foreign programming and advertising, leaders in developing countries complained bitterly about "cultural imperialism." Those who control information, they protested, have clear-cut advantages in framing issues and shaping policy preferences. The popularity of the Al Jazeera network in the Middle East

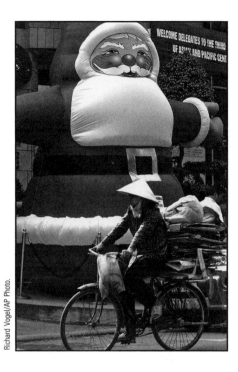

Richard Vogel/AP Photo.

Exporting American Culture? Some people regard globalization as little more than the spread of American values and beliefs. Shown here is one example that fuels this opinion—a large Santa Claus in front of a hotel in Hanoi, Vietnam, a city still subscribing to communist principles that frown on consumer capitalism.

illustrates the interest in the Global South for alternatives to the Western media, which is often seen as giving a biased, inaccurate portrayal of Southern concerns.

Contrary to the claim that globalization imposes an American uniformity on the world, some scholars have argued that cultural influence runs in more than one direction. Not only do various ideas and practices flow from the Global South to the North, but many of the products from the Global North are modified to suit indigenous tastes and needs. Approximately 25 percent of Costco's warehouses operate outside of the United States, where the product mix is tailored to fit foreign markets. Similarly, after committing cultural gaffes in Paris and Hong Kong, Disney theme parks adapted to local conditions. Native cultures, writes William Marling (2006), even put their imprint on McDonald's, arguably one of the most visible symbols of Americanization around the world. Its recipe for chicken, for instance, is far spicier in Indonesia than in the United States. McDonald's franchises outside the United States also sell items that are not on the typical American fast food menu, including beer in Germany, wine in France, salsa in Mexico, and soy flavors in Japan. Local cultures, Marling insists, are more resilient than most people imagine.

Additional evidence weighing against the proposition that globalization is equivalent to Americanization can be found in a growing trend called "reverse innovation." Whereas in the past many companies developed new products in the United States and shipped them abroad, now it is becoming common for them to innovate in Global South countries and send the products to the United

States. Examples include the netbook and handheld electrocardiogram devices (*Newsweek*, February 1, 2010: 10).

THE ECONOMICS OF GLOBALIZATION

When the nation-state emerged in seventeenth-century Europe as the primary actor on the world stage, many national leaders sought to increase their power by acquiring territory. Aside from land that held precious metals or offered access to navigable waterways, the most valuable territory in an age without refrigeration contained cereal grains, an easily transported and stored source of food with sufficient nutrition to sustain farmers as well as people not engaged in agriculture.

With the onset of the Industrial Revolution, physical capital (machinery, equipment, buildings, etc.) increased in value as a factor of production, although the demand for coal, iron ore, and later oil continued to underscore the importance of land. Only after World War II did some states shift their emphasis from territorial expansion through military conquest to international commerce. These "trading states" recognized that exporting manufactured goods could fuel economic growth (Rosecrance, 1986). Soon they realized that exporting was only one path to prosperity; products could be designed at home but made abroad for both foreign and domestic markets. Rather than goods and services being produced by and for people living within a single territorial state, they are now increasingly produced by people working in different regions of the world for a global marketplace. We have entered an era where traditional territorial distinctions are less important than the financial and managerial skills to create products, provide services, and control assets globally (Rosecrance, 1999).

The Globalization of Production

After World War II, the victors in that long, debilitating struggle believed that they could stimulate economic growth by removing barriers to international trade. As we have seen in Chapter 6, under the auspices of the General Agreement on Tariffs and Trade (GATT), the so-called "Geneva Round" of negotiations in 1947 reduced **tariffs** by 35 percent. Successive rounds of negotiations in the 1950s, 1960s (the Kennedy Round), 1970s (Tokyo Round), and the 1980s and 1990s (Uruguay Round) virtually eliminated tariffs on manufactured goods. The World Trade Organization (WTO), which succeeded GATT in 1995, is currently engaged in reducing **nontariff barriers** to international trade.

Examples of global commerce are abundant. In all likelihood, the clothes you wear as well as many of the appliances you use were made in other countries. One way of examining the extent to which commerce has become more global is to look at **trade integration**. It measures the degree to which the growth rate in world trade increases faster than the growth rate of world gross domestic product. As trade integration rises, so does globalization, because interdependence increases when countries' exports account for a larger percentage of

tariffs   taxes imposed by governments on imported goods.

nontariff barriers   governmental restrictions not involving a tax or duty that increase the cost of importing goods into a country.

trade integration   economic globalization measured by the extent to which world trade volume grows faster than the world's combined gross domestic product.

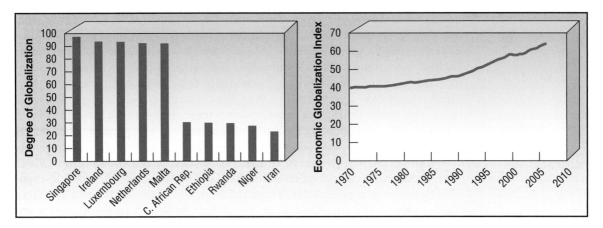

F I G U R E 11.2 Patterns of Economic Globalization

The KOF Swiss Economic Institute releases annual measures of globalization. The graph on the right shows a gradual increase in the extent of economic globalization worldwide over the past four decades. The graph on the left displays the variation in the degree of economic globalization that exists among countries by comparing the five most globalized states with the five least globalized states for which data on the 2010 KOF index were available. Although Singapore heads the list of economically globalized states, twenty of the top twenty-five states are located in Europe. Eighteen of the twenty-five least economically globalized states are located in Africa.

SOURCE: Based on the KOF Index of Globalization 2010, as originally described in Dreher, Gaston, and Martens (2008).

their gross domestic product (GDP). Following the Second World War, countries became more interdependent, and the world increasingly globalized, as evidenced by the twenty-fold expansion of trade versus the six-fold growth in the world economy (Samuelson, 2006). Of course, countries differ in the degree to which their economies have become integrated through trade into the global political economy. As shown in Figure 11.2, the most highly integrated countries tend to be European, although the pace of trade integration has grown in Global South countries, reflecting their mounting share of exports in manufactured products (rising from 10 percent in 1980 to 30 percent in 2009).

A similar pattern may be emerging with regard to trade in services. Because the United States enjoys comparative advantages in this area, it has been a strong advocate of bringing services under the liberalizing rules of the WTO. Trade in services has already expanded more than three-fold since 1980, with the Global North reaping most of the benefits. However, the spread of information technology, the ease with which new business software can be used, and the comparatively lower wage costs in developing economies are among the reasons why the World Bank predicts that developing countries will capture a greater share of world trade in services. Global East countries such as India, with significant numbers of educated, English-speaking citizens, are already operating call centers and consumer assistance hotlines for companies based in the Global North.

Selling products to another country often requires companies to establish a presence abroad, where they can produce goods and offer services. Traditionally, the overseas operations of multinational corporations (MNCs) were "appendages" of a centralized hub. The pattern nowadays is to dismantle the hub by dispersing production facilities worldwide, which was made economically feasible by the revolutions in communication and transportation (including use of the standardized international shipping container). Most large companies now have supply chains that stretch far outside of the countries where they are headquartered. This **globalization of production** is transforming the international political economy. Not only do finished products contain components fabricated in different countries throughout the world, but some countries have begun to specialize in specific steps within the production process of certain industries. MNCs have discovered that to export to another country, it is helpful to locate there. Placing production in an MNC's regional foreign affiliate avoids tariffs and taxes. Today, roughly 40 percent of what we call foreign trade actually involves transactions between MNCs' cross-border affiliates, that is, between a firm and its overseas subsidiaries (Oatley, 2008: 170–173).

globalization of production a manufacturing process in which finished goods are assembled from components produced in multiple countries.

By forming **strategic corporate alliances** with companies in the same industry, and by merging with one another, many MNCs now rival nation-states in financial resources. These corporate networks pursue truly global strategies for financial gain, often through long-term supplier agreements and licensing and franchising contracts. As they funnel large financial flows across national borders, these global corporate conglomerates are integrating national economies into a worldwide market. Since 1970, flows of foreign direct investment have increased almost one hundred-fold, with Global East and South countries increasingly becoming recipients.

strategic corporate alliances cooperation between MNCs and foreign companies in the same industry, driven by the movement of MNC manufacturing overseas.

Among some of the most ardent advocates of globalization, the progressive integration of national economies into a single world marketplace is seen as a panacea for poverty. Such a view is inaccurate, however. Despite evidence that widening and deepening of international trade flows have been associated with economic growth, the distribution of these gains has not been uniform. Globalizing forces have reduced poverty in Global East and South countries that have been able to take advantage of their low labor costs to attract jobs fabricating standardized goods and assembling finished goods from components. But critics of globalization claim that more benefits have accrued to Global North producers of innovative, human-capital-intensive products. Consider the Apple iPod. The 30-gigabyte video model was manufactured in China by Inventec and sold in 2005 for $224 wholesale. According to one study, Apple claimed about $80 in gross profit. The Chinese, who tested and assembled the iPod's 424 parts, accounted for only $3.70 because the research, development, and design, as well as the components, originated elsewhere (*Economist*, November 10, 2007: 8). As the *Human Development Report* of the UN Development Program once put it: "A rising tide of wealth is supposed to lift all boats. But some are more seaworthy than others. The yachts and ocean liners are indeed rising in response to new opportunities, but the rafts and rowboats are taking on water—and some are sinking fast." Trade globalization, in other words, is creating winners and losers both between and within countries. As a result, a backlash against these inequalities is developing among those groups that see themselves as victims of an integrated trade world (Aaronson, 2002: Broad, 2002).

The Globalization of Finance

Finance represents another important aspect of economic globalization. It encompasses capital flows associated with foreign direct investment as well as cross-border portfolio-type transactions, including borrowing and lending, trading currencies and other monetary claims, and the provision of other financial services (B. Cohen, 1996). Evidence of the **globalization of finance** abounds. Since World War II, the volume of cross-border capital flows has increased dramatically, and now greatly exceeds the volume of trade. Similarly, cross-border transactions in bonds and equities have increased at an astonishing rate over the past twenty years. In fact, the global capital market has increased at twice the rate of global GDP, fueled in part by the explosion of hedge-fund trading worldwide that reached $69.8 trillion in 2007 (*Economist*, May 26, 2007: 75).

Further evidence of financial globalization can be seen in recent increases in the daily turnover on the foreign exchange market. On many days, private currency traders may exchange as much as $2 trillion to make profits through **arbitrage** on the basis of minute shifts in the value of states' currencies. Such interconnected markets require more than ever a reliable system of money to conduct business across borders while coping with an array of fluctuating national currencies. The daily turnover on currency markets often is greater now than the global stock of official foreign exchange reserves, and has weakened the capacity of government central banks to influence exchange rates by buying and selling currency in those markets. Globalization has cost states a huge measure of the control that they formerly could exercise over the value of their currencies internationally. The powerlessness of the U.S. government to raise the price of the Chinese yuan against the dollar between July 2008 and June 2010 (to reduce the enormous U.S. balance-of-trade deficit), speaks volumes about the breakdown of governments' ability to modify the rates at which their currencies are exchanged.

As the market value of stock transactions increased five-fold between 1980 and 2008, the rise or fall in the security market of any one state began to immediately cause similar changes in other countries' stock indexes (see APPLICATION: Markets and Economic Interdependence). "Derivatives" are one tool for managing risk by combining speculation in "options" and "futures" to hedge against volatility in financial markets. They are complex financial contracts whose value is determined from the prices or rates of other securities, but they require no actual purchase of stocks or bonds. In the years leading up to the 2008 world financial crisis, derivatives accounted for trillions of dollars in cross-border transactions and were estimated to be the most globalized financial market. Automated online trading for equity sales on the Internet in the emerging digital world economy had lowered the costs and increased the volume of such cross-border exchanges.

globalization of finance   the increasing transnationalization of national markets through the worldwide integration of capital flows.

arbitrage   the selling of one currency (or product) and purchase of another to make a profit on the changing exchange rates; traders ("arbitragers") help to keep states' currencies in balance through their speculative efforts to buy large quantities of devalued currencies and sell them in countries where they are valued more highly.

Anthony Lake served as the national security advisor in the Clinton administration from 1993 to 1996. Whereas early in his tenure policy makers at high-level meetings tended to think along traditional state-centric lines, by the time that he stepped down from his position he noticed that they had come to grips with how globalization was transforming world politics. In the following episode, which refers to an economic crisis in Brazil during 1998, he illustrates how the thinking in Washington had changed.

> During the crisis … I ran into Treasury Secretary Robert Rubin. As we chatted about old times, I recalled how, at our morning senior staff meeting in the White House, we would sometimes ask him what the effect of one event or another might be on the stock market.
>
> As he smiled … at the recollection, an aide rushed up to his side. Secretary Rubin turned to him, and with real concern asked, "How is the market doing?" As the aide replied and they discussed the implication of the news, I realized that he was asking not about the Dow Jones, but about the Brazilian stock market. This is the reality of life in the era of globalization. Secretary Rubin … understood that a strong Brazilian economy is in America's national security interest … [The]

clear corollary is that a weak Brazil could hurt our people at home. How? It could curb American exports, crimping prosperity and chipping at jobs. As Latin America's largest market, with more than half of its people, Brazil is the engine of regional growth. If its economy started to sink, it could pull down its neighbors as well. Not only would we lose our eleventh-largest export market … we would see demand dry up throughout a region that buys 20 percent of American exports. And that could put a lot of our people out of work. A Brazilian setback could also have devastating effects on U.S. private lenders. Both Citibank and BankBoston, for example, have loaned billions of dollars each to Brazil; American enterprises have invested billions more. It could rattle American businesses, some two thousand of which operate in Brazil. Globally, a major panic in Brazil could spark a new contagion … risking a global recession (Lake, 2000: 213–214).

Increasingly, observes Lake, U.S. policy makers realized that globalization complicated their ability to manage America's foreign and domestic affairs. It did so, in his opinion, because national autonomy and state sovereignty gradually were being eroded.

The computerization of financial transactions and contracts occurred at the same time that national deregulation of global investments and capital movements gained acceptance. States relaxed legal controls over their economies and opened their markets to foreign capital. The result was an upsurge in international financial transactions. This largely unregulated flow of capital across borders was seen as contributing to the growth of a single, unified global market, which was not subject to regulation by any one state in particular. However, problems soon appeared. Without parameters circumscribing the behavior of transnational banks, explained Brazilian president Luiz Inácio Lula da Silva, they began leveraging their loans, lending amounts of money that far exceeded their net worth (*BusinessWeek*, October 12, 2009: 13). It wouldn't be long, he lamented, before the international financial system faced an acute crisis.

Financial history, writes British historian Niall Ferguson (2008: 342) "is a roller-coaster ride of ups and downs, bubbles and bursts, manias and panics, shocks and crashes." The lightning speed of capital mobility in the early twenty-first century made national markets extremely volatile and vulnerable to sudden reversals caused by their dependence on foreign capital, which could flee at the first sign of economic trouble. By 2008, capital mobility had reached historically high levels, having tripled since 1990 as a share of world GDP. But when foreign capital began fleeing from the emerging economies of post-communist and Global South states as the global credit market seized up that fall, stock markets in these countries plunged and the value of their currencies dropped.

True, all countries are mutually vulnerable to rapid transfers of capital in an interdependent, globalized financial world. But the globalization of finance does not affect all countries equally. The vast majority of banking, currency, and debt crises during the last four decades have occurred in developing countries. Nevertheless, many economists have called for stricter financial regulations on all countries and the creation of more reliable multilateral mechanisms for policy coordination to manage the massive cross-border flows of capital. One step in this direction was taken in September 2010, when central bank officials and regulators from around the world agreed to the so-called Basel III rules, requiring banks to hold greater capital reserves to cope with potential losses that might emanate from future financial crises.

THE CHALLENGES OF A BORDERLESS WORLD

Thus far, we have seen how technological advances in communication and transportation over the past few decades have fueled a series of far-reaching economic changes. Expanding global production and the torrent of cross-border financial flows that have swept across the world raise the question of whether it is still meaningful to think of the nation-state as a basis for organizing economic activities. As globalization has ruptured one national frontier after the next, questions have also been asked as to whether the nation-state is the most effective problem-solving unit for addressing other challenges that face humanity. Three of the most important involve the impact of globalization on the environment, public health, and migration. In each instance, problems in one part of the world have had consequences for people living elsewhere.

Global Ecopolitics

Ever since the rise of the nation-state, political leaders have claimed sovereign rights over their territorial domain, viewing the use of land, water, and airspace as domestic matters. Although some environmental issues are purely local and can be addressed unilaterally, many span national boundaries and require multilateral action. For example, sulfur oxide emissions from industries in one country may fall as acid rain on neighboring countries. The political world may be a checkerboard of sovereign states, but the natural world is a seamless web. Damage to the ecosystem often transcends national jurisdictions. Yet, as we shall see in Chapter 14, many states remain unwilling to relinquish or pool their sovereignty to forge new global institutions that could offer a more effective response to global environmental problems.

Global Health

Humankind and the threat of infectious disease have always coexisted uneasily. Population growth in the Global South has led many people to move into previously uninhabited regions, exposing them to new sources of disease. Moreover, their ability to travel from one continent to another makes it difficult to contain outbreaks to a single locale. Millions of airline travelers, for example, share cabin-sealed environments with passengers who might be infected with potentially fatal communicable diseases. As the 2003 outbreak of Severe Acute Respiratory Syndrome (SARS) showed, a mobile world population has made the spread of disease across borders rapid, frequent, and hard to control. SARS was initially discovered in Hong Kong, China, in early 2003 but was soon spread by air travelers to Toronto, Canada, where forty people subsequently died from the disease. As a result of fears caused by the SARS epidemic, the Women's World Cup in soccer was moved out of China, Air Canada lost some $400 million Canadian dollars in the second quarter of 2003, and Hong Kong's second quarter economic output dropped 3.7 percent (Kelleher and Klein, 2006: 142).

The AIDS (acquired immune deficiency syndrome) epidemic has become a symbol for the spread of disease in a shrinking world. It is a global problem, with the number of people infected with HIV—the virus that causes AIDS—climbing to over 70 million people by 2009. AIDS strikes most virulently in the impoverished Global South among youthful wage earners who are the foundation of the labor force, but it undermines economic growth everywhere on the planet. The human toll has been most severe in sub-Saharan Africa, where AIDS-related disease is the leading cause of death, cutting life expectancy almost in half. The virus is not confined to any one region, however; it travels throughout the world alongside the more than 2 million people who cross international borders daily.

Adding to the challenge of preventing SARS, AIDS, and other infectious diseases such as deadly strains of influenza like the swine flu (H1N1) is another problem brought on by rising globalization: As a result of underuse of antibiotics in the developing world and overuse in the developed world, viruses are developing stronger strains that are able to overcome standard antibiotics. The World Health Organization reports that almost all infectious diseases are slowly becoming resistant to existing medicines. And humans are not the only victims, as was made evident in 2001 when the contagious hoof-and-mouth disease swept through Europe killing livestock. As national leaders desperately tried to seal their frontiers to a virus that spread with frightening speed, many noted that such epidemics in the European Union were increasingly difficult to contain because borders between countries had all but dissolved and it had been years since anybody needed a passport to travel between most European countries.

Another byproduct of globalization has been the spread of alien animal, plant, and insect species throughout the globe that are causing massive ecological destruction. As the World Conservation Union (an NGO that includes more than 10,000 volunteer scientists from 160 countries) warns, alien species that cross national borders aboard aircraft, ships, or other means of conveyance are doing irreparable damage to thousands of native species and, in the process, creating an enormous problem for the planet's environment and public health. In May 2001, the Union used World Biodiversity Day to heighten awareness of the threat posed by this invasion, which it labeled "among the costliest and least understood aspects of globalization."

Global Migration

The movement of populations across frontiers has reached unprecedented proportions. Each year since 1998, on average more than 12 million people qualified for and received refugee assistance. Porous borders, combined with the ease of modern travel, have made it possible for streams of people to leave their homelands for other countries. Emigration has become routine in the global age, raising a host of political, economic, and social issues. The meaning of citizenship, the composition of the labor force, and the protection of minority rights are just a few of the issues that large flows of migrants raise for host countries. Liberal democracies, in particular, have struggled with the moral inconsistency of defending the right of refugees to emigrate while simultaneously insisting on the right of sovereign states to control their borders.

Far more troubling are the approximately 800,000 people each year that are estimated to be victims of forced migration, which includes the victims of "ethnic cleansing" as well as the trade in humans sold into servitude. The UN estimates that 80 percent of today's slaves are women, with roughly half under the age of eighteen. This criminal activity grosses between $12 and $17 billion annually, ranking as the third largest illicit global business after trafficking in drugs and the arms trade (Obduah, 2006: 241).

National governments are losing their grip on regulating the movement of foreigners across their borders. From American efforts to barricade the southern border of the United States to European attempts to interdict migrants from Africa who are crossing the Mediterranean Sea on makeshift vessels, Global North countries have wrestled with the question of how to cope with people who cross national frontiers furtively to flee discrimination and repression, or to find jobs that will allow them to support family members in their home countries. One in every four workers in Australia was born abroad; one in five in Ireland; and one in six in Spain, Austria, and the United States (*Economist*, July 17, 2010: 97). Every day, legal and illegal migrants living in the Global North send "remittances" (money they have earned while working abroad) back home to their families. By some accounts, these remittances total more than twice the amount of foreign aid given to the Global South. Thus, the worldwide movement of people across national boundaries, like many other aspects of globalization, cannot be understood in isolation from other factors; global migration is intimately linked to global economic as well as humanitarian issues.

These environmental, health, and migration problems are representative of the challenges presented by globalization. Whether nation-states will be able to cope remains uncertain. Our problems are increasingly transnational but our solutions remain steadfastly national.

THE POSSIBILITY OF DEGLOBALIZATION

On April 14, 2010, the eruption of Eyjafjallajökull, a volcano in Iceland, threw an enormous plume of ash 35,000 feet into the atmosphere. Not long ago, few people outside of northern Europe would have noticed. However, in the twenty-first-century world of air freight and global supply chains, the eruption caused more than 100,000 flights to be cancelled, which, in turn, affected merchants in Kenya who couldn't ship fresh flowers to German florists, autoworkers in Japan who didn't receive deliveries of pneumatic sensors from Ireland, and athletes in France who couldn't get to the United States in time to participate in the Boston Marathon. As the Icelandic volcano reminded hundreds of thousands of people worldwide, we live in the most interconnected age in human history.

To say that we live in an age of interconnectedness is not to claim that globalization is immutable. Indeed, the economic crisis that arose in 2008 has led some analysts to predict that we are entering a time of "deglobalization." Pointing to the contraction of world trade and sluggish flows of lending and investment across national frontiers, they forecast a retreat from globalization. Yet, as we have seen, globalization is not a one-dimensional process; it entails social, cultural, and political as well as economic facets. Online social networks, cultural exchanges, and interactions among political activists from disparate countries are as much a part of globalization as trade and capital flows. In the words of one student of world politics, globalization is "such a diverse, broad-based, and potent force that not even today's massive economic crash will … permanently reverse it" (Naím, 2009: 28).

Globalization, driven in large measure by a series of technological revolutions, is likely to continue, albeit at a slower pace. Analysts differ over what to expect next. Some focus on the economic benefits of further globalization; others, on its unevenness and the prospects for marginalizing large numbers of people. Some emphasize the challenge that globalization poses to an international system founded on the sovereign territorial state; others hope cooperation among state and nonstate actors will usher in a new era of global governance (see CONTROVERSY: Does Globalization Mean the End of the Age of Nation-States?). We can expect the controversies about globalization's alleged virtues and vices, benefits and costs, to continue. While the revolutions in communication and transportation have overcome many of the physical barriers separating the world's people, the global village has not proved equally hospitable for everyone.

The key issue raised by this chapter concerns the role of the nation-state in the global future. A world of permeable borders challenges all territorial states, rich and poor alike. Globalization reduces the capacity of states to exercise political power over the territory in which private-sector actors operate. Although some analysts believe this loss of control probably means that the nation-state as a sovereign actor on the world stage will become a thing of the past, most agree that it is not about to disappear. An erosion of sovereignty may be underway, but territorial states will still lay claim as the principal source of security and identity in most people's lives. Nevertheless, they will increasingly find themselves sharing the world stage with powerful nonstate actors. As discussed in Chapter 6, we are moving

CONTROVERSY   **Does Globalization Mean the End of the Age of Nation-States?**

Is globalization an unprecedented, inexorable process that is driving an epochal transformation in world politics? What does it mean for the survival of the nation-state? To some thinkers globalization spells the end of sovereignty as the world's organizing principle.

According to this interpretation of the global future, states are being overwhelmed by globalization, and are losing control over their economies (Boli, Elliot, and Bieri, 2004). Other thinkers remain skeptical. Not only do they question whether globalization is unprecedented historically, they doubt that the term accurately describes the current pattern of international economic interactions. They see a resurrection of the idea of national power (Saul, 2004).

Skeptics maintain that globalization is a new word for an old process. Although the contemporary world economy differs in many ways from that of the late nineteenth and early twentieth centuries, the current level of trade integration is similar to what existed on the eve of World War I. Aside from not being a novel phenomenon, skeptics add that globalization is less significant today than regionalization. The degree of trade integration within the world's geographic regions exceeds the amount of integration between them, although the North American, European, and East Asian regional economies are becoming more interconnected. Contrary to the argument that economic globalization is diminishing the influence of nation-states, the most powerful states have become the "backbone" of world trade: Over three-fourths of total production is traded inside national borders; most corporations are national companies whose assets and ownership are within their own nation-states; and the state is consuming an ever-larger share of the global GDP (Malešević, 2008: 98).

Globalists admit that a homogeneous McWorld (Barber, 1995) doesn't exist, but they contend that the extraordinary advances in telecommunication and transportation technologies have unleashed globalizing forces that are eroding the power of nation-states. Do you agree? Will globalization undermine the Westphalian state system? Is state sovereignty destined to be replaced by some new organizing principles? If so, what principles would guide world politics in a post-Westphalian world order?

away from a world dominated by a single type of actor and toward one composed of many qualitatively different types of actors.

What does this mean for humanity's welfare? We all are now more closely connected than ever before, but the architecture for multilateral cooperation and coordination remains shaky. Liberal theorists, who emphasize the lure of mutual gains, are optimistic about the prospects for pooling sovereignty to deal with global problems. Realists, who are more concerned with relative gains, remain pessimistic. Constructivists aver that globalization will be what state and nonstate actors make of it. Regardless of who is correct, technological innovations will continue to facilitate the flow of production and finance across national boundaries, blurring the distinction between foreign and domestic economic policy. How will this affect trade and monetary relations? The next chapter investigates possible answers to this question.

CHAPTER SUMMARY

- Globalization is a set of processes that are fostering worldwide interconnectedness. Because it is uneven—benefitting some, disadvantaging others—globalization threatens to widen the gulf between the world's rich and poor states.

- Recent advances in telecommunication technology are a major driving force behind globalization. These technologies are changing our conceptions of time and space. With the emergence of a digitized global economy, the boundary between domestic and international transactions is becoming less distinct.

- Technology is reshaping patterns of production and finance. Markets no longer correspond with national boundaries. Rather than goods and services being produced by and for people living within a particular territorial state, they are now increasingly produced by people from several different states who are aiming at a world market. Similarly, a system of financial arrangements is emerging that is not centered on a single state. As a result, international economic flows are not subject to regulation by any single country.

- Globalization has shrunk geographic distances and linked people together in ways that create new challenges for solving environmental, health, and other problems that do not respect territorial boundaries. Owing to their transnational nature, many of these problems cannot be solved unilaterally. However, states are often hesitant to relinquish or pool their sovereignty in order to strengthen global institutions that can better address borderless crises.

- Globalization is a process unlikely to be forestalled, but the consequences are not easily agreed on. Regardless of whether globalization is desirable or despicable, state power will retain its relevance in shaping the global future. Nevertheless, the sovereign, territorial state will not be the only important player on the world stage. What the process of globalization has done in recent years is to disaggregate sovereignty, creating multiple layers of authority that are interlaced in ways that blur distinctions between foreign and domestic, and public and private, entities.

KEY TERMS

agenda setting

arbitrage

digital divide

globalization

globalization of finance

globalization of production

global village

nontariff barriers

strategic corporate alliances

tariffs

trade integration

SUGGESTED READINGS

Agnew, John. *Globalization and Sovereignty*. Lanham, MD: Rowman & Littlefield, 2009.

Chanda, Nayan. *Bound Together: How Traders, Preachers, Adventurers and Warriors Shaped Globalization*. New Haven: Yale University Press, 2007.

Friedman, Thomas L. *The World Is Flat: A Brief History of the Twenty-first Century.* New York: Picador, 2007.

Hebron, Lui, and John F. Stack, Jr. *Globalization: Debunking the Myths*, 2nd ed. Boston: Longman, 2011.

James, Harold. *The Creation and Destruction of Value: The Globalization Cycle.* Cambridge, MA: Harvard University Press, 2009.

CRITICAL THINKING QUESTIONS

As the pace of economic globalization has increased, the ethics of deepening market relations across borders has become a heated topic of debate. The philosopher Peter Singer (2004) sees great benefits in the decline of the doctrine of state sovereignty with its emphasis on crafting policies that try to advance narrow self-interests. Global interdependence, he argues, encourages acting from a moral awareness that there is only "one humanity" and "one economy." In an interdependent world, someone else's problems soon become our own; thus, altruism and a concern for others pay dividends under globalization. The economist Jagdish Bhagwati (2004) submits that this concern should extend to allowing people to move freely, just as under globalization capital moves from country to country in search of higher returns. Until restrictions on migration are lifted, large national differences in pay for similar work will persist. Financial journalist Martin Wolf (2004) disagrees. While condemning restrictions on capital mobility, he accepts them on labor mobility, even if they perpetuate wage differences. Governments, in his opinion, are responsible for the welfare of their citizens; they can rightly limit immigration when it is in their national interest.

What do you think? Does globalization encourage a moral outlook that promotes a worldwide definition of ethical responsibilities? If so, do these responsibilities include liberalizing immigration policies in order to foster a convergence of wage levels among different countries? Or are the responsibilities of national leaders anchored to the interests of the states that they govern, regardless of the impact of their policies on living standards elsewhere?

12

The Political Economy of Trade and Monetary Relations

CHAPTER OUTLINE

Much of politics is economics, and most of economics is politics.
CHARLES E. LINDBLOM
POLICY ANALYST

In November 2001, Qatar, a sheikdom on a small peninsula jutting from Saudi Arabia into the Persian Gulf, hosted the Fourth Ministerial Conference of the World Trade Organization (WTO) in Doha, its capital city. The aim of the conference was to launch a round of negotiations that would result in lower tariffs among WTO members. Although the "Doha Round" of trade negotiations was scheduled to conclude in four years, it dragged on far past the original deadline, requiring Pascal Lamy, the WTO's director-general, to plead in late 2010 for a concerted effort to reach an agreement.

The impasse that plagued the Doha Round puzzled observers on two counts. First, the World Bank had estimated that an agreement would yield significant economic gains by 2015: 32 million people raised from poverty; $125 billion less in tariffs paid by consumers; and $50 to $100 billion in growth for the world economy. Second, the negotiations unfolded in an atmosphere that seemed conducive to liberalizing trade: the world GDP had been averaging roughly 3 percent annual growth since 2001; the volume of global merchandise exports had increased over twice as much; and many governments had already reduced import duties unilaterally (Naím, 2007). Given the anticipated benefits of a successful Doha Round and the apparent momentum behind the negotiations, what went wrong? Why did the negotiators fail to seal an agreement by their original deadline of 2005?

For many analysts, the answer could be found in the politics of international economic relations. Frequently, political complications lurk beneath economic phenomena, as Charles Lindblom suggests in the epigraph of this chapter. The first such complication in the Doha Round pertained to agricultural trade. Led by China and India, a coalition of emerging-market countries within the WTO pushed for the European Union and the United States to cut farm subsidies, and for Japan and several other advanced industrial countries to phase out agricultural import barriers. They also wanted "special safeguard" duties to protect their own farmers from unexpected surges in agricultural imports.

A second complication revolved around demands by Global North countries for Global South and East countries to lower their barriers to nonagricultural imports, strengthen agreements on intellectual property rights, and address a host of issues originally raised during the WTO's 1996 Singapore meetings, including government procurement, competition policy, trade facilitation, and investment. Whereas the European Union desired prompt attention on the Singapore issues, the emerging-market countries were reluctant to proceed until progress occurred on agricultural matters.

Discord persisted through 2010, with negotiators unable to resolve their disagreement over safeguards for protecting farmers in the Global South. China and India favored a low threshold for triggering special duties when agricultural imports surged; the United States and various other developed countries backed a higher threshold. Because under WTO procedures nothing is finalized until an agreement is reached on everything comprising the agenda, the negotiators

regional trade agreements (RTAs)   treaties that integrate the economies of countries within a geographic region by reducing trade barriers among member states.

struggled to conclude the Doha Round. Eying their difficulty, many outside observers feared that the global trade regime would unravel as countries began to question the WTO's usefulness and turned their energies toward creating **regional trade agreements (RTAs)**. If that happened, the world might split into rival trade blocs. The stakes, they warned, were too high to let the Doha Round negotiations drift.

The quest for wealth is an ageless pursuit. Because it provides the means by which many other values can be realized, the successful management of economics lies at the center of how governments define their national interests. The hard bargaining among the Doha negotiators that contributed to the years of stalemate reveals the importance that governments attribute to international economic issues. In view of this importance, we turn now to examine how trade and currency exchanges affect world politics. What practices should governments embrace to regulate commercial and monetary activities within their borders? What should they do to influence economic exchanges with other states? These are among the most important questions we face in an era of accelerating globalization. They form the principal concerns within the field of **international political economy**. To introduce this topic, we will first examine the ways in which the world economic system has evolved. This will allow us to then investigate how trade and monetary activities today are creating new issues in the twenty-first century.

international political economy   the study of the intersection of politics and economics that illuminates the reasons why changes occur in the distribution of states' wealth and power.

CONTENDING ECONOMIC STRATEGIES
FOR AN INTERDEPENDENT WORLD

In today's world, politics and economics are difficult to separate. Although the volume of international commerce contracted 12.2 percent in 2009 after years of exponential growth, trade remains important to countries' economic well-being and still accounts for almost 30 percent of global gross domestic product. While trade is the most visible symbol of globalization, the dynamics of the **international monetary system** are equally important. To comprehend the political debates that are currently raging over trade and monetary issues, we first need to understand the contending economic philosophies of liberalism and mercantilism, which underpin the strategies that different states have adopted in their pursuit of power and wealth.

international monetary system   the financial procedures governing the exchange and conversion of national currencies so that they can be bought and sold for one another to calculate the value of currencies and credits when capital is transferred across borders through trade, investment, and loans.

The Shadow of the Great Depression

In July 1944, forty-four states allied in the Second World War against the Axis powers met in the New Hampshire resort community of Bretton Woods. Their purpose was to devise new rules and institutions to govern international trade and monetary relations after the fighting ended. As the world's preeminent military and economic power, the United States played the leading role. Its proposals were shaped by the perception that the Great Depression of the 1930s created the conditions that gave rise to political extremists in Germany, Italy, and Japan. Operating under the philosophy of **commercial liberalism**, the United States sought free trade, open markets, and monetary stability in the hope that they would foster economic growth. Prosperity, U.S. leaders believed, was the best antidote to political extremism.

The rules established at Bretton Woods, which governed international economic relations for the next twenty-five years, rested on three political bases. First, power was concentrated in the rich Western European and North American countries, which reduced the number of states whose agreement was necessary for effective management of economic relations. Second, the system's operation was facilitated by the dominant states' shared preference for an open international economy with limited government intervention. Third, Bretton Woods worked because the United States assumed the burdens of leadership and others willingly accepted that leadership. The onset of the Cold War helped cement Western unity, because a common external enemy led America's allies to perceive economic cooperation as necessary for both prosperity and military security.

The political bases of the Bretton Woods system crumbled in 1972 when the United States suspended the convertibility of the dollar into gold and abandoned the system of fixed currency exchange rates. Since then, as floating exchange rates and growing capital mobility have made monetary mechanisms unstable, more chaotic processes of international economic relations have materialized. Nonetheless, commercial liberalism's preference for market mechanisms over government intervention and the urge to privatize and otherwise reduce government regulation of markets has spread worldwide. Thus, it is still useful to characterize the contemporary international economic system as a **Liberal International Economic Order (LIEO)**—one based on such free-market principles as openness and nondiscriminatory trade.

Not all states consistently support the liberal tenet that governments should refrain from interfering with trade flows. Commercial liberalism is under attack where political pressure to protect local industries and jobs is growing. States' trade policies are naturally influenced by the desire to increase the domestic benefits of international economic transactions and to lessen their adverse consequences, even if this undermines the expansion of a global capitalist economy propelled by free trade.

commercial liberalism an economic theory advocating free markets and the removal of barriers to the flow of trade and capital.

Liberal International Economic Order (LIEO) the set of regimes created after World War II, designed to promote monetary stability and reduce barriers to the free flow of trade and capital.

The Clash between Liberal and Mercantile Values

How should states behave in the global economy to maximize their gains and minimize their vulnerability? Most controversies in the field of international political economy are ultimately reducible to the competing ideologies of liberalism and **mercantilism**, which represent fundamentally different conceptions of the relationships among society, state, and market. A comparison of the logic behind the two theoretical traditions can help us to appreciate why different national leaders often pursue disparate policies in their international economic relations, with some advocating free trade and others devising ways to protect their countries from foreign competition.

mercantilism the seventeenth-century theory preaching that trading states should increase their wealth and power by expanding exports and protecting their domestic economy from imports.

Commercial Liberalism.   As described in Chapter 2, liberalism begins with the presumption that humankind's natural inclination is to cooperate in order to increase prosperity and enlarge liberty. Commercial liberal theory has many variations, but all liberal thinkers agree that everyone benefits from unfettered exchanges. Open markets and free trade are seen as engines of progress, capable of lifting the poor from poverty and expanding political freedom.

Adam Smith, the eighteenth-century political economist who helped define the precepts of classical liberalism, used the metaphor of the unregulated market's "invisible hand" to show how the public interest can be served by humans' natural tendency to "truck, barter, and exchange" in pursuit of private gain. David Ricardo, a nineteenth-century British political economist, added an important corollary to liberal thought by demonstrating that when all states specialize in the production of those goods in which they enjoy a **comparative advantage** and trade them for goods in which others enjoy an advantage, a net gain in welfare for both states, in the form of higher living standards, will result. The principle of comparative advantage underpins commercial liberalism's advocacy of free trade as a method for capital accumulation. Material progress is realized and mutual gains are achieved, according to this principle, when countries specialize in the production of what they can produce least expensively; are willing to purchase, from other countries, goods that are costly for them to produce; and, in addition, do not restrict the flow of trade across borders (see Table 12.1).

comparative advantage   the concept in liberal economic theory that a state will benefit if it specializes in those goods it can produce comparatively cheaply and acquires through trade goods that it can only produce at a higher cost.

T A B L E   12.1   Comparative Advantage and the Gains from Free Trade

Country	Worker Productivity per Hour		Before Specialization		Specialization, No Trade		Specialization, with Trade	
	Cameras	Computers	Cameras	Computers	Cameras	Computers	Cameras	Computers
Japan	9	3	900	300	990	270	910	300
United States	4	2	400	200	320	240	400	210

Why does free trade produce benefits for trade partners who specialize in the production of goods for which they have comparative advantage? Consider a hypothetical illustration of Japan and the United States, each of which produces cameras and computers but with different worker productivity (output per hour) for each country, as shown in the first column in Table 12.1.

Clearly Japan has an absolute advantage in both products, as Japanese workers are more productive in turning out cameras and computers than American workers are. Does this mean that the two countries cannot benefit by trading with each other? If trade does occur, should each country continue to allocate its resources as in the past? The answer to both questions is no.

Each country should specialize in producing the item for which it has the greatest cost advantage or least cost disadvantage, and trade for others. Because Japan is three times more productive in cameras than computers, it should direct more of its resources into manufacturing cameras. One cost of doing so is lost computer output, but Japan can turn out three additional cameras for every computer given up. The United States, on the other hand, can obtain only two computers. Like their Japanese counterparts, American workers are also more productive in making cameras than computers. Still, U.S. resources should be directed to computers because the United States is at a smaller disadvantage compared with Japan in this area. If the United States specializes in computers and Japan in cameras and they trade with one another, each will benefit. The following scenario shows why.

Begin with 100 workers in each industry without specialization or trade (second column). Next, specialize production by shifting ten Japanese workers from computer to camera production and shifting twenty American workers from camera production to computers (third column). Then permit free trade so that eighty Japanese-manufactured cameras are exported to the United States and thirty U.S. computers are exported to Japan. With specialization and free trade, the benefits to both countries improve.

By shifting Japanese resources into the production of cameras and U.S. resources into computers and allowing trade, the same total allocations will cause camera and computer output to rise ten units each (fourth column). Resources are now being used more efficiently. Both countries realize benefits when each trades some of its additional output for the other's. Japan ends up with more cameras than before specialization and trade and with the same number of computers. The United States finds itself with more computers and the same number of cameras. More output in both countries means higher living standards.

Liberals such as Smith and Ricardo believed that economic processes governing the production, distribution, and consumption of goods and services operate according to certain natural laws; consequently, markets work best when free of government interference. Transferring the logic of **laissez-faire economics** to the international level, commercial liberals suggest that removing trade restrictions among nations promotes more equal access to scarce resources, attracts foreign capital and expertise, and fosters competition—which generates pressure for increasing efficiency to lower production costs. These economic benefits are thought to have positive political consequences. Because war reduces profits by interrupting commerce, high levels of international trade create a material incentive for states to resolve their disputes peacefully. Besides encouraging states to find amicable solutions to their disagreements, trade also makes conflict resolution easier by increasing international communication and eroding parochialism.

There is a fly in this liberal ointment, however. Although commercial liberal theory promises that the "invisible hand" will maximize efficiency so that everyone will gain, it does not promise that everyone will gain equally. This applies at the global level as well: The gains from international trade may be distributed quite unequally, even if the principle of comparative advantage governs. Commercial liberal theory ignores these differences, as it is concerned with *absolute* rather than relative gains. Mercantilists, however, are more concerned with the *relative* distribution of economic rewards.

Mercantilism. In contrast to liberalism, mercantilism advocates government regulation of economic life to increase state power and security. It emerged in Europe as the leading political economy philosophy after the decline of feudalism and helped to stimulate the first wave of Europe's imperialist expansion, which began in the fifteenth century. Accumulating gold and silver was seen by early mercantilists as the route to state power and wealth. Later mercantilists focused on building strong, self-sufficient economies by curbing imports, subsidizing strategically targeted enterprises, and protecting domestic companies from foreign competition.

Today's so-called **neomercantilists** support policies aimed at maintaining a balance-of-trade surplus by reducing imports, stimulating domestic production, and promoting exports. These "new" mercantilists are sometimes called "economic nationalists." In their view, states must compete for position and power, and economic resources are the source of state power. From this, it follows that economic activities should be subordinated to state building and the interests of the state (Gilpin, 2001).

Mercantilism shares much in common with political realism: Realists and mercantilists both see the state as the principal world actor; both view the international system as anarchical; and both dwell on the aggressively competitive drive of people and states for advantage. While commercial liberals emphasize the mutual benefits of cooperative trade agreements, mercantilists are more concerned that the gains realized by one side of the bargain will come at the expense of the other. For mercantilists, relative gains are more important than both parties' absolute gains. An American economic nationalist, for instance, would complain about a trade agreement that promised the United States a 5 percent

laissez-faire economics from a French phrase (meaning literally "let do") that Adam Smith and other commercial liberals in the eighteenth century used to describe the advantages of freewheeling capitalism without government interference in economic affairs.

neomercantilism a contemporary version of classical mercantilism that advocates promoting domestic production and a balance-of-payment surplus by subsidizing exports and using tariffs and nontariff barriers to reduce imports.

growth in income and the Chinese 6 percent. Although the bargain would ensure an eventual increase in U.S. living standards, its position compared with China's would slip. Calculations such as these explain why trade agreements that promise mutual gains often encounter stiff resistance. It also explains why those who fear the loss of domestic manufacturing and high-skilled service jobs to foreign competitors also lobby for mercantilist measures, and why they sometimes succeed against the unorganized interests of consumers who benefit from free trade.

Protectionism is the generic term used to describe a number of mercantilist policies designed to keep foreign goods out of a country and to support the export of domestically produced goods to other countries. These policies include:

- *Quotas.* Two types of quotas are common. **Import quotas** unilaterally specify the quantity of a particular product that can be imported from abroad. **Export quotas** result from negotiated agreements between producers and consumers and restrict the flow of products (for example, shoes or sugar) from the former to the latter. An **orderly market arrangement (OMA)** is a formal agreement in which a country agrees to limit the export of products that might impair workers in the importing country, often under specific rules designed to monitor and manage trade flows. Exporting countries are willing to accept such restrictions in exchange for concessions on other fronts from the importing countries. The Multi-Fiber Arrangement (MFA) is an example of an elaborate OMA that restricts exports of textiles and apparel. It originated in the early 1960s, when the United States formalized earlier, informal **voluntary export restrictions (VERs)** negotiated with Japan and Hong Kong to protect domestic producers from cheap cotton imports. The quota system was later extended to other importing and exporting countries and then, in the 1970s, to other fibers, when it became the MFA. Under both import and export quotas, governments rather than the marketplace regulate the flow of goods between countries.

- *Tariffs.* Instead of using quotas, governments can limit imports by placing a tax on foreign goods. The tax may be a fixed amount imposed on each unit of an item being imported, or it may be based on some percentage of the value of each unit. Under what is known as "strategic trade policy," governments sometimes provide subsidies to a particular industry in order to make its goods more competitive abroad. Two protectionist responses to this practice are **countervailing duties**, the imposition of tariffs to offset alleged subsidies by foreign producers, and **antidumping duties** imposed to counter the alleged sale of products at below the cost of production.

- *Nontariff barriers.* Governments may limit imports without resorting to direct tax levies. Nontariff barriers cover a wide range of creative government regulations designed to shelter particular domestic industries from foreign competition, including elaborate health and safety regulations, strict licensing requirements, and arcane government purchasing procedures.

---

protectionism a policy of creating barriers to foreign trade, such as tariffs and quotas, that protect local industries from competition.

import quotas limits on the quantity of particular products that can be imported.

export quotas barriers to commerce agreed to by two trading states to protect their domestic producers.

orderly market arrangements (OMAs) voluntary export restrictions that involve a government-to-government agreement and often specific rules of management.

voluntary export restrictions (VERs) a protectionist measure popular in the 1980s and early 1990s, in which exporting countries agree to restrict shipments of a particular product to a country to deter it from imposing an even more onerous import quota.

countervailing duties tariffs imposed by a government to offset suspected subsidies provided by foreign governments to their producers.

antidumping duties tariffs imposed to offset another state's alleged selling of a product at below the cost to produce it.

Realist theory helps to account for states' impulse to engage in protectionism. Recall that realism argues that states in an anarchic, self-help environment often shun cooperation because they are suspicious of one another's motives. Uncertainty encourages each state to devote considerable effort to protecting itself against others. Among developing countries whose domestic industrialization goals may be hindered by the absence of protection from the Global North's more efficient firms, the **infant industry** argument is often used to justify mercantilist trade policies. According to this argument, tariffs or other forms of protection are necessary to nurture young industries until they eventually mature and lower production costs to compete effectively in the global marketplace.

> **infant industry** a newly established industry that is not yet strong enough to compete effectively in the global marketplace.

In sum, the insecurity that breeds political competition frequently occurs in international economic relations. Those who see states' power and wealth as inextricably linked conclude that even if states do not worry about physical survival, they fear that a decrease in power will erode their autonomy and lessen their ability to prevail in disputes with others. Thus, many states are "defensively positional actors" that seek not only to promote their domestic well-being but also to defend their rank (or relative standing) in comparison with others (Grieco, 1995; Mastanduno, 1991).

HEGEMONY AND THE MANAGEMENT
OF THE GLOBAL ECONOMY

The relative gains issue speaks to the difficulties of achieving international cooperation under anarchical conditions and explains why some domestic producers vigorously oppose liberal (open) international economies despite the evidence that free trade promotes economic growth. Whereas some people see an unregulated market as the best method for providing the greatest good for the greatest number, others prefer protectionism over the liberalization of trade. According to many scholars, the key to bringing order to this competitive environment lies in the emergence of an all-powerful hegemon.

Hegemony is the ability to shape the rules under which international political and economic relations are conducted. Charles Kindleberger (1973), an international economist, first theorized about the need for a *liberal* hegemon to open and manage the global economy. In his explanation of the 1930s Great Depression, Kindleberger concluded that the international economic system needed a leader to set standards of conduct, to persuade other countries to follow, and to shore up the system during times of adversity. Britain played this role from 1815 until the outbreak of World War I in 1914, and the United States assumed the British mantle in the decades immediately following World War II. During the interwar years, however, Britain was unable to play its previous leadership role, and the United States, although capable of leadership, was unwilling to exercise it. The void, Kindleberger concluded, was a principal cause of the width and depth of the Great Depression in the 1930s.

hegemonic stability theory a school of thought that argues free trade and economic order depend on the existence of an overwhelmingly powerful state willing and able to use its strength to open and organize world markets.

According to what has become known as **hegemonic stability theory**, a preponderant state is able to design and promote rules for the whole global system that also advance its own long-term interests. Liberal hegemons such as the United States (and Britain before it), whose domestic economies are based on capitalist principles, have championed open international economic systems, because their comparatively greater control of technology, capital, and raw materials gives them more opportunities to profit from a system free of protectionist restraints.

Hegemons have also taken on special responsibilities. They have had to manage the international monetary system to enable one state's money to be exchanged for other states' money, make sure that countries facing balance-of-payments deficits (imbalances in their financial inflows and outflows) could find the credits necessary to finance their deficits, and serve as lenders of last resort during financial crises. In the past, when hegemons could not perform these tasks, they often backtracked toward more protected domestic economies, and in doing so undermined the open international system that was previously advantageous to them. This kind of departure historically has made quotas, tariffs, and nontariff barriers to trade more widespread. Thus, hegemonic states not only have had the greatest capacity to make a free-trade regime succeed, but they also have had the greatest responsibility for its effective operation and preservation. To interpret whether hegemonic stability theory is likely to hold in the future, a closer look at the theory's logic is useful.

The Hegemonic Pillars of Open Markets and Free Trade

collective goods goods from which everyone benefits regardless of their individual contributions.

Much of the discussion about the free movement of commodities across national borders centers on the concept of public or **collective goods**—benefits that everyone shares and from which no one can be excluded selectively. National security is one such collective good that governments try to provide for all of their citizens, regardless of the resources that individuals contribute through taxation. In the realm of economic analysis, an open international economy permitting the relatively free movement of commodities is similarly seen as a desirable collective good, inasmuch as it permits economic benefits for all states that would not be available if the global economy were closed to free trade.

free ride to enjoy the benefits of collective goods but pay little or nothing for them.

According to hegemonic stability theory, the collective good of an open global economy needs a single, dominant leader to keep it open. A major way in which the hegemon can exercise leadership is to open its own market to less-expensive imported goods even if other countries **free ride** by not opening their own markets. However, if too many states refuse to forego the short-term gains of free riding and capitulate to domestic protectionist pressures, the entire liberal international economy may collapse.

The analogy of a public park helps us to illustrate this dilemma. If there were no central government to provide for the maintenance of the park, individuals themselves would have to cooperate to keep the park in order (the trees trimmed, the lawn mowed, and so on). But some may try to come and enjoy the benefits of the park without pitching in. If enough people realize that they can get away with this—that they can enjoy a beautiful park without helping with its upkeep—it will not be long before the once-beautiful park looks shabby. Cooperation to provide a collective good is difficult. This is also the case with the collective good of a liberal international economy, because many states that enjoy the collective good of an orderly, open, free-market economy pay little or nothing for it. A hegemon typically tolerates a few free riders, partly because the benefits that the hegemon provides, such as a stable global currency, encourage most other states to accept its rules. But if everyone's benefits seem to come at the hegemon's expense and the costs of leadership multiply, it will become less tolerant of free riding and may gravitate toward more coercive policies. In such a situation, the open global economy could crumble amid a competitive race for individual gain at others' expense.

A Liberal Economic Order without Hegemonic Leadership?

Although hegemonic powers benefit from the liberal economic systems that their power promotes, the very success of liberalism eventually erodes the pillars that support it. Competition fostered by open markets and free trade encourages productive efficiency and economic growth, which affects the international distribution of industrial power. As relative economic strength shifts away from the hegemon toward other states, the capacity of the hegemon to maintain the system decreases. The leading economic power's ability to adapt is critical to maintaining its dominance. Britain was unable to adapt and fell from its top-ranked position. Many wonder if the United States is destined to suffer the same fate, either due to mounting economic problems or a lack of political will to exercise leadership through concerted multilateral action. At the twenty-first century's dawn, the United States stood as an economic superpower; however, the circumstances confronting the United States today are eroding its capacity to continue exercising hegemonic leadership.

At present, the United States possesses the world's largest economy, but few predict that position of dominance will remain indefinitely. The U.S. share of world output has fallen steadily since World War II. In 1947, the United States accounted for nearly 50 percent of the combined gross world product (largely because the war ravaged the territory of its industrial competitors). By 1960, its share had slipped to 28 percent, by 1970 to 25 percent, and by the 1990s to 20 percent—less than what it had been during the Spanish-American War of 1898, when the country first emerged as a world power (D. White, 1998: 42). Another symptom of economic stress is that the U.S. share of world financial reserves has declined. The United States went from being the globe's greatest creditor country in 1980 to the world's largest debtor by 1990, and, with a projected budget deficit for fiscal 2010 of $1.47 trillion, the debt continues to mount. A third symptom lies in the growth of the U.S. trade deficit, which has risen from $31 billion in 1991 to $350 billion in 2009. Finally, alongside these debt burdens and trade imbalances, U.S. investment in education and public infrastructure to stimulate future growth is lower than that of many of its competitors.

These trends suggest that American economic primacy will not continue. The United States is straining under the cost of the wars in Afghanistan and Iraq, a protracted economic recession, and entitlement commitments exceeding $45 trillion in unfunded liabilities. What will happen if the capability and willingness of the United States to lead declines? Have the institutions and rules put into place to govern the liberal economic order in the post–World War II era now taken on a life of their own? Commercial liberals think so, arguing that trade liberalization may be too deeply entrenched for it to collapse. Significant institutional and normative restraints now exist on imposing new trade barriers. The free-trade regime may no longer depend on the existence of an all-powerful hegemon.

To better evaluate this argument and probe the likely future of global economics, let us now inspect how those international trade and monetary rules have evolved since the Second World War.

THE CHANGING FREE-TRADE REGIME

beggar-thy-neighbor policies   the attempt to promote trade surpluses through policies that cause other states to suffer trade deficits.

In the period immediately following World War II, when the United States became the world's dominant political power, it simultaneously became the preeminent voice in international trade affairs. The liberal trading system the United States chose to promote rejected the **beggar-thy-neighbor policies** widely seen as a major cause of the economic depression of the 1930s. Removing barriers to trade became a priority and led to the recurrent rounds of trade negotiations that produced remarkable reductions in tariff rates. As the large U.S. market was opened to foreign producers, other countries' economies grew, and rising trade contributed to a climate that encouraged others to open their markets as well.

The General Agreement on Tariffs and Trade (GATT) became the principal international organization for promoting free trade in the aftermath of World War II. GATT was never intended to be a formal institution with enforcement powers. Instead, a premium was placed on negotiations and reaching consensus to settle disputes among parties to the agreement, which was first and foremost a commercial treaty. As trade disputes multiplied, GATT increasingly became involved in legalistic wrangling. In 1995, GATT was superseded by the World Trade Organization (WTO), a new free-trade IGO with "teeth." The WTO represents a breathtaking step in free-trade management, although it has also provoked violent disagreements over the nature of global capitalism (see CONTROVERSY: Is the World Trade Organization a Friend or Foe?). The WTO extended GATT's coverage to products, sectors, and conditions of trade not previously covered adequately. It also enhanced economic dispute-settlement procedures by making the findings of its arbitration panels binding on the domestic laws of participating states (GATT's findings were not binding). Finally, the WTO dealt with the problem of free riding by being available only to states that belonged to GATT, subscribed to all of the Uruguay Round agreements, and made market access commitments (under the old GATT system, free riding

CONTROVERSY   Is the World Trade Organization a Friend or Foe?

In late November 1999, the then 135-member countries of the World Trade Organization (WTO) and thirty additional observer states made final preparations to stage in Seattle what was billed as the Millennium Round on trade negotiations—the follow-up to the Uruguay Round of trade talks completed in 1993. The mood was optimistic. Everyone expected to celebrate the contributions that lower trade barriers arguably had made to the growth of international exports and, for many members (particularly the United States), their longest and largest peacetime economic expansion in the twentieth century. There appeared to be widespread recognition that a world without walls promotes prosperity and welfare.

A half-century of generally rising prosperity had generated a climate of enthusiasm for the power of free trade. Fears of imports tend to recede in good economic times, and, with the best decade ever, most leaders in the twilight of the twentieth century emphasized the sunnier side of free trade. The delegates to the Seattle meetings shared the liberal conviction that countries, companies, and consumers had much to gain by a globalized economy freed from restraints on the exchange of goods across borders. They expected added benefits from a new trade round that could slash tariffs and other trade barriers in agriculture, manufactured goods, and services.

That mood and the seeming consensus on which it was based was shattered when the Seattle trade talks opened. An estimated 50,000 to 100,000 protesters and grassroots anti-WTO activists, who differed widely in their special interests (the poor, environment, labor, women, indigenous people), joined hands to shout their common opposition to the general idea of globalization and free trade. A plane trailed a banner proclaiming "People Over Profits: Stop WTO" as part of what became known as "The Battle in Seattle." A tirade against open trade ensued, fueled by citizen backlash.

The Seattle conference will be remembered as the moment when the debate over the benefits and costs of the globalized economy rose to the pinnacle of the global agenda. The immediate target of the demonstrations was the WTO; however, the organization itself was simply a convenient symbol of a much larger sea of discontent. The WTO protests (and the failure of

the WTO conference attendees to compromise on tightly held positions and agree on even a minimal accord) exposed the deep divisions about the best ways to open global commerce and adopt new rules at a time of rapid change.

Controversies about globalization, free trade, and global governance are multiple. At the core is the question of whether a globalized economy is inevitable and, if so, is it an antidote to human suffering or a source of new inequities. The debates are explosive, because everyone is affected but in quite different ways. Many people enjoyed the boom years under liberalized trade engineered by the WTO's trade agreements, but the celebration was confined largely to the privileged, powerful, and prosperous. Many others saw themselves as victims of an open global economy, as when a company outsources some of its business functions overseas and workers lose their jobs. Those discontented with globalized free trade include a diverse coalition of protestors, many of whom harbor very specific concerns about wages, the environment, and human rights issues. Labor leaders contend that the WTO is sacrificing worker rights; environmental groups complain that when green values collide with world commerce, environmental standards are left out of trade negotiations; and human rights activists accuse the WTO of serving the preferences of multinational corporations for erasing trade barriers in ways that fail to protect human rights. In addition, enraged trade ministers from the Global South's developing countries see a Global North conspiracy in the WTO's efforts to adopt core labor standards, because the less developed Global South views such high-sounding rules as a method to take away the comparative advantages that Global South developing nations enjoy with lower wage scales.

These, and other issues, are certain to continue as major controversies. What do you think? Is the WTO a valuable tool for improving global governance or a threat to human welfare? Are the WTO and the free trade practices it promotes too strong or too weak? Does the WTO put corporate profits above human rights and environmental protection, as critics charge? Or do you agree with the WTO's claim that "Trade is the ally of working people, not their enemy"?

was possible when some small states were permitted to benefit from trade liberalization without having to make contributions of their own).

The creation of the WTO signaled a victory for multilateralism. It did not end trade squabbles and risks. The seemingly relentless march of trade liberalization since the end of the Second World War exposed more and more industries to fierce international competition. Free trade generated wealth, but it also presented national leaders with complex trade-offs. As Joseph Grieco and John Ikenberry (2003: 103) explain: Open markets stimulate economic growth, but they also create policy dilemmas. States contemplating expanding their participation in the world economy must calculate the trade-offs between the broad-based economic gains that they may acquire through free trade versus the political costs that they may experience in terms of reduced autonomy.

THE CHANGING INTERNATIONAL
MONETARY REGIME

States cannot always trade as they wish. Their exports and imports depend on many factors, especially on changes in the prices for the goods and services that countries' producers sell in the global marketplace. The mechanisms for setting the currency exchange rates by which the value of traded goods are priced heavily influence international trade. Indeed, the monetary system is crucial for international trade, for without a stable and predictable method of calculating the value of sales and foreign investments, those transactions become too risky, causing trade and investment activities to fall. In short, the success of international trade depends on the health of the monetary system.

The Elements of Monetary Policy

Monetary and financial policies are woven into a complex set of relationships between states and the international system, and, because monetary and currency issues have their own specialized technical terminology, they are difficult to understand. However, the essentials are rather basic. "Monetary policy works on two principal economic variables: the aggregate supply of money in circulation and the level of interest rates." Monetarist economic theory assumes that the **money supply** (currency plus commercial bank demand deposits) is related to economic activity. Increases in the supply facilitate economic growth by enabling people to purchase more goods and services, but a supply that grows too fast may lead to inflation. Through controlling the level of the money supply, some monetarists contend, "governments can regulate their nations' economic activity and control inflation" (Todaro, 2000: 657), although others worry that its effects are too unpredictable in the short run to guide policy.

To understand the importance of monetary policies as a determinant of states' trade, growth rates, and wealth consider both why **exchange rates** fluctuate and the impact of these currency fluctuations. Money works in several

money supply   the total amount of currency in circulation in a state, calculated to include demand deposits—such as checking accounts—in commercial banks and time deposits—such as savings accounts and bonds—in savings banks.

exchange rate   the rate at which one state's currency is exchanged for another state's currency in the global marketplace.

ways and serves different purposes. First, money must be widely accepted, so that people earning it can use it to buy goods and services from others. Second, money must serve to store value, so that people will be willing to keep some of their wealth in the form of money. Third, money must act as a standard of deferred payment, so that people will be willing to lend knowing that when the money is repaid in the future, it will still have purchasing power.

Governments attempt to manage their currencies to prevent inflation, which occurs when the government creates too much money in relation to the goods and services produced in the economy. As money becomes more plentiful and thus less acceptable, it cannot serve effectively to store value or to satisfy debts or as a medium of exchange.

Movements in a state's exchange rate occur in part when changes develop in peoples' assessment of the national currency's underlying economic strength or the ability of its government to maintain the value of its money. A deficit in a country's **balance of payments**, for example, would likely cause a decline in the value of its currency relative to that of others. This happens when the supply of the currency is greater than the demand for it. Similarly, when those engaged in international economic transactions change their expectations about a currency's future value, they might reschedule their lending and borrowing. Fluctuations in the exchange rate could follow.

balance of payments a calculation summarizing a country's financial transactions with the external world, determined by the level of credits (export earnings, profits from foreign investment, receipts of foreign aid) minus the country's total international debts (imports, interest payments on international debts, foreign direct investments, and the like).

Speculators—those who buy and sell money in an effort to make a profit—may also affect the international stability of a country's currency. Speculators make money by guessing the future. If, for instance, they believe that the Japanese yen will be worth more in three months than it is now, they can buy yen today and sell them for a profit three months later. Conversely, if they believe that the yen will be worth less in three months, they can sell yen today for a certain number of dollars and then buy back the same yen in three months for fewer dollars, making a profit. The globalization of finance now also encourages managers of investment portfolios to move funds from one currency to another in order to realize gains from differences in states' interest rates and the declining value of other currencies in the global network of exchange rates. Short-term financial flows are now the norm: The International Monetary Fund estimates that more than 80 percent of transactions relate to round-trip operations of a week or less.

In the same way that governments try to protect the value of their currencies at home, they try to protect them internationally by intervening in currency markets. Their willingness to do so is important to importers and exporters, who depend on orderliness and predictability in the value of the currencies they deal in to carry out transnational exchanges. Governments intervene when countries' central banks buy or sell currencies to change the value of their own currencies in relation to those of others. Unlike speculators, however, governments are pledged not to manipulate exchange rates so as to gain unfair advantages, because states' reputations as custodians of monetary stability are valuable. Whether governments can affect their currencies' values in the face of large transnational movements of capital is increasingly questionable. So is the value of any country's currency in relation to any other's (see Figure 12.1).

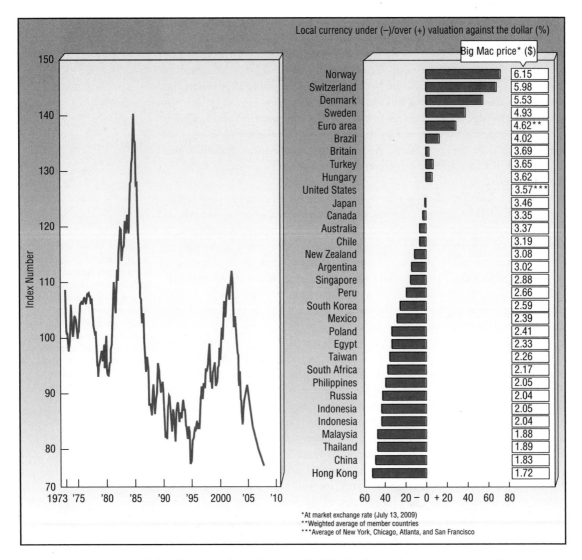

F I G U R E 12.1 **Calculating the Cost of Goods in the World's Confusing Currency Exchange System**

The figure on the left shows the weighted average of the foreign exchange values of the U.S. dollar against a subset of the currencies of a large group of major U.S. trading partners. People from the United States who are traveling abroad use currency exchange rates to convert foreign prices to U.S. dollars. An exchange rate specifies how much one state's currency is worth in terms of another state's currency in the global marketplace. Economists frequently try to predict the future movement of currency exchange rates by examining purchasing power parity (PPP), which holds that in the long run exchange rates should adjust to equalize the cost of an identical basket of goods and services in any two countries. The index in the figure on the right, formulated by the *Economist*, uses a basket with one item—a McDonald's Big Mac, which is produced in approximately 120 countries around the world. This Big Mac PPP is the exchange rate at which hamburgers would cost the same in America as they would anywhere else in the world. A Big Mac could be purchased in China for $1.83 (12.5 yuan at the July 13, 2009 exchange rate), versus an average price of $3.57 in the United States. To make the two prices equal would require an exchange rate of 3.50 yuan to the dollar, rather than the market rate of 6.82, which implies that the yuan was 49 percent "undervalued" against the dollar at that point in time. Conversely, the euro was 29 percent overvalued against the dollar and the Swiss franc was 68 percent overvalued.

SOURCES: Major Currencies Index, U.S. Federal Reserve; Big Mac Index, the *Economist*, July 18, 2009: 74.

The Bretton Woods Monetary System

When the leaders of the world's major capitalist countries met in Bretton Woods, New Hampshire, in 1944, they were acutely aware of the need to create a reliable mechanism for determining the value of countries' currencies in relation to one another, and agreed to a set of concepts to define monetary and currency policy for conducting international trade and finance. Recognizing that a shared system and vocabulary was a necessary precondition for trade, and from it post–World War II economic recovery, the negotiating parties agreed that the postwar monetary regime should be based on **fixed exchange rates**, and they assigned governments primary responsibility for enforcing its rules. In addition, they foresaw the need to create what later became the International Monetary Fund (IMF), to help states maintain equilibrium in their balance of payments and stability in their exchange rates with one another. The International Bank for Reconstruction and Development, known as the World Bank, was also created to aid recovery from the war.

fixed exchange rates a system under which states establish the parity of their currencies and commit to keeping fluctuations in their exchange rates within narrow limits.

Today, the IMF and World Bank are important, if controversial, players in the global monetary and financial systems. Their primary mission is to serve as "lenders of last resort" when member states face financial crises, providing those seeking assistance agree to make often painful domestic reforms to strengthen their economies. In the period immediately after World War II, these institutions commanded little authority and too few resources to cope with the enormous devastation of the war. The United States stepped into the breach.

The U.S. dollar became the key to the hegemonic role that the United States eagerly assumed as manager of the international monetary system. Backed by a vigorous and healthy economy, a fixed relationship between gold and the dollar (pegged at $35 per ounce of gold), and the U.S. commitment to exchange gold for dollars at any time (known as "dollar convertibility"), the dollar became universally recognized as a "parallel currency," accepted in exchange markets as the reserve used by monetary authorities in most countries and by private banks, corporations, and individuals for international trade and capital transactions.

To maintain the value of their currencies, central banks in other countries either bought or sold their own currencies, using the dollar to raise or depress their value. Thus, the Bretton Woods monetary regime was based on fixed exchange rates and ultimately required a measure of government intervention for its preservation.

To get U.S. dollars into the hands of those who needed them most, the Marshall Plan provided Western European states billions of dollars in aid to buy the U.S. goods necessary for rebuilding their war-torn economies. The United States also encouraged deficits in its own balance of payments as a way of providing **international liquidity** in the form of dollars.

international liquidity reserve assets used to settle international accounts.

In addition to providing liquidity, the United States assumed a disproportionate share of the burden of rejuvenating Western Europe and Japan. It supported European and Japanese trade competitiveness, permitted certain forms of protectionism (such as Japanese restrictions on importing U.S. products), and condoned discrimination against the dollar (as in the European Payments

Union, which promoted trade within Europe at the expense of trade with the United States). The United States willingly incurred these leadership costs and others' free riding because subsidizing economic growth in Europe and Japan would widen the U.S. export markets and strengthen the West against communism's possible popular appeal.

Although this system initially worked well with the United States operating as the world's banker, the costs grew as the enormous number of dollars held by others made the U.S. economy increasingly vulnerable to financial shocks from abroad. U.S. leaders found it difficult to devalue the dollar without hurting America's allies, nor could inflationary or deflationary pressures at home be managed without hurting allies abroad. This reduced the United States' ability to use the normal methods available to other states for dealing with the disruption caused by deficits in a country's **balance of trade**, such as adjusting interest and currency exchange rates.

balance of trade a calculation based on the value of merchandise goods and services imported and exported. A deficit occurs when a country buys more from abroad than it sells.

The End of Bretton Woods

As early as 1960, it was clear that the dollar's top currency status could not be sustained. After 1971, U.S. President Nixon abruptly announced—without consulting with allies—that the United States would no longer exchange dollars for gold. With the price of gold no longer fixed and dollar convertibility no longer guaranteed, the Bretton Woods system gave way to a substitute system based on **floating exchange rates**. Market forces, rather than government intervention, were expected to determine currency values. A country experiencing adverse economic conditions now saw the value of its currency fall in response to the choices of traders, bankers, and businesspeople. This was expected to make its exports cheaper and its imports more expensive, which in turn would pull its currency's value back toward equilibrium—all without the need for central bankers to support their currencies. In this way, it was hoped that the politically humiliating devaluations of the past could be avoided.

floating exchange rates an unmanaged process whereby market forces rather than governments influence the relative rate of exchange for currencies between countries.

Those expectations were not met. Beginning in the late 1970s, escalating in the 1980s, and persisting through the 1990s, a rising wave of financial crises, both in currency and banking, occurred. These have been compounded by massive defaults, which occurred when countries were unable to service their debts. About one-third of the world's countries currently have foreign debts in excess of $10 billion, and together the low- and middle-income countries of the Global South have over $4.4 trillion in external debt. This staggering debt load compromises these countries' capabilities to chart their future by themselves and leaves many of them exposed to external economic and political influence.

Financial crises have become increasingly frequent around the world as a result of the inability of states to manage income, debt, and inflation in a monetary system fraught with wild currency exchange-rate gyrations. In the past forty years, more than 100 major episodes of banking insolvency occurred in ninety developing and emerging countries. The financial cost of these crises, in terms of the percentage of GDP lost, has been huge. The disastrous debts generated by banking and currency disruptions forced governments to suffer, on average, costs amounting to as much as 55 percent of GDP (WDI, 2009).

In response to the growing awareness of the extent to which the health of others' economies depended on the value of the U.S. dollar internationally (which in turn depended on the underlying strength of the U.S. economy), a landmark agreement was reached secretly in 1985 at the Plaza Hotel in New York City by the so-called **Group of Five (G-5)**, which pledged to coordinate their economic policies through management of exchange rates internationally and interest rates domestically. An expanded **Group of Seven (G-7)**, and subsequently a **Group of Eight** (**G-8**, with the inclusion of Russia in 1997) sought to continue coordinating global monetary policy. However, beginning with the G-8 summit in Genoa in July 2001, it became clear that these countries were unable to reach consensus about the best way to manage exchange rates, monetary and fiscal policies, and trade relations in order to sustain global economic growth. Additionally, they realized the necessity of broadening the discussions to include China, India, Brazil, South Korea, and other rising economic powers. At a meeting of world leaders in Pittsburgh in September 2009, it was announced that a **Group of Twenty** (or **G-20**) would replace the G-8 as the "premier forum for international economic cooperation." Representing two-thirds of the world's population and 90 percent of the world GDP, the G-20 has sought to play an informal role in strengthening the international financial architecture.

Group of Five (G-5)   a group of advanced industrialized democracies composed of the United States, Britain, France, Japan, and Germany.

Group of Seven (G-7)/ Group of Eight (G-8) the G-5 plus Canada and Italy; after 1997, known as the G-8 with the addition of Russia.

Group of Twenty (G-20) an informal forum that promotes discussion among the world's major and top emerging economic powers on global economic issues.

Plans for Reforming the International Financial Architecture

No institution currently has global responsibility for the arrangement of capital flows, although there does exist a set of principles and rules of relatively universal

The Political Consequences of Economic Austerity Facing an enormous budget deficit and mounting public debt, the Greek government was pressured by the European Union and the International Monetary Fund in 2010 to implement a series of austerity measures. Shown here is a demonstration in Athens protesting proposed pay and pension cuts. Whereas the EU and the IMF worried about how the financial crisis in Greece might affect other euro-zone countries, the demonstrators were apprehensive about how they would make ends meet with lower incomes.

Getty Images

scope. Hardly anyone is happy with the prevailing weak and somewhat haphazard global financial architecture, but it appears that only when severe financial crises occur does sufficient pressure mount to consider new reforms.

Many proposals have been advanced for reforming the international monetary system to help cushion the aftershocks of the rapid movement of investment funds among countries that creates booms and busts, such as the 1980s Latin American debt crisis and the global crisis that followed on the heels of the 1997–1998 flight of capital from Asia. Financial crises swept like an epidemic to fifty-six countries between 1973 and 1997, costing on average 10 percent of each affected state's GNP. The problems that followed—unemployment, rising taxes, crime, and military coups—precipitated numerous calls for reform. Some analysts suggested that a reversion to the pre–World War I gold standard would be preferable to the exchange rates with highly fluctuating currencies. Others recommend something like the Bretton Woods system of fixed but adjustable rates. More recently, Zhou Xiaochuan, governor of China's central bank (the People's Bank of China), has proposed a "supra-sovereign" currency managed by the IMF to replace the U.S. dollar as the world's reserve currency.

What these and other proposals seek is a mechanism for creating the currency stability and flexibility on which prosperity through trade depends and which the current system has failed to achieve. However, there is little agreement on how to bring about reforms. During periods of economic distress, most governments face domestic pressures to sacrifice such goals as exchange rate stability for unemployment reduction, so it seems likely that floating exchange rates, with all their costs and uncertainties, will remain in place for some time to come. Despite a proliferation of schemes for rebuilding the international financial architecture, incremental tinkering is more likely in the years ahead than large-scale restructuring.

THE UNCERTAIN LEGACY OF THE ECONOMIC CRISIS OF 2008

most-favored-nation (MFN) principle
unconditional nondiscriminatory treatment in trade between contracting parties guaranteed by GATT; in 1997, U.S. Senator Daniel Patrick Moynihan introduced legislation to replace the term with "normal trade relations" (NTR) to better reflect its true meaning.

nondiscrimination a principle for trade that proclaims that goods produced at home and abroad are to be treated the same for import and export agreements.

The exponential growth of world trade since 1950 has contributed measurably to the unprecedented rise in global economic prosperity. Many states see advantages in accepting the **most-favored-nation (MFN) principle** (which holds that the tariff preferences granted to one state must be granted to all others exporting the same product) and the **nondiscrimination** rule (goods produced at home and abroad are to be treated the same). However, free trade is attractive only if everyone, developed and developing countries alike, can benefit. Today numerous states seem allured by the prospect of enhancing their domestic well-being through protectionist means. Many of them have retained nontariff barriers to free trade even as tariff walls have come down. "Trade may be global," quip Ramesh Thakur and Steve Lee (2000), but "politics is still local." If neomercantilism spreads, the preservation of the free-trade regime is unlikely throughout the twenty-first century.

Creeping Protectionism and the Fate of Free Trade

Countries differ in their willingness to open their domestic markets. Yet, even in many economically open countries, protectionist pressures are increasing. Job losses during economic recessions usually trigger calls for protectionism. In hard times, people are tempted to build barriers against foreign competitors.

Advocates of free trade frequently cite the U.S. Tariff Act of 1930 (also known as the Smoot-Hawley tariff, after its sponsors, Senator Reed Smoot of Utah and Representative Willis Hawley of Oregon) to illustrate how the combination of economic turmoil at home and vigorous competition from abroad arouses popular support for protectionism. The danger, they warn, is that protectionist policies ignite tit-for-tat retaliation, which can cause export markets to shrivel and economic growth to slow. Whereas the Tariff Act of 1930 sharply increased 890 import duties that affected thousands of items, today the pattern is one of "creeping" protectionism. Subtle, piecemeal measures to restrict imports, such as the "buy local" provisions written into fiscal stimulus packages and government contracts, risk inspiring similar policies from other countries. As former U.S. Federal Reserve chairman Alan Greenspan cautions, protectionist cures harm the patient in the long run. Protectionism, he insists, does "little to create jobs and if foreigners retaliate, we will surely lose jobs."

Besides erecting trade barriers as unemployment rises, governments also can respond to economic distress by subsidizing domestic companies. For many states, **subsidies** have become the preferred form of protectionism. The World Bank estimates that since the onset of the recession, automobile manufacturers around the world have received $48 billion in subsidies. The potentially powerful impact of subsidies on international commerce was highlighted by the WTO in 2010 when it ruled that the European company, Airbus, received government loans at below-market interest rates to design, produce, and sell six models of its

subsidies financial assistance from governments to support enterprises considered important to public welfare.

Alamy Limited

The Politics of Protectionism
Political demands for "Buy American" provisions in government stimulus packages and contracts have become common since the economic crisis of 2008. One study of the steel industry illuminates the policy dilemma surrounding these provisions. Estimates suggest that they would boost U.S. steel production by 0.5 million metric tons each year, which would translate into approximately 1,000 new jobs. But given the magnitude of American steel exports to other countries, a 10 percent loss in that export market due to foreign retaliation would cost the country 65,000 jobs (Zakaria, 2009: 29).

aircraft. Without this financial support, Airbus would have had to shoulder massive debt from commercial lenders and might not have been in a position to overtake its American rival, Boeing, as the world's largest aircraft manufacturer.

Given the seemingly clear-cut economic advantages of free trade, commercial liberals find it difficult to understand why many governments resist open markets. The answer lies in the fact that trade can appear in the eye of the beholder to be inherently unfair. Unions in wealthy Global North states complain that the lower wages of the Global South countries give them "unfair" advantages and, for their part, the less-developed Global South states complain that they cannot "fairly" compete against their more technologically advanced Global North counterparts. Given that many people in both wealthy and poor countries think that they are not competing on a level playing field, the age-old debate between free traders and mercantilists is likely to persist as a global issue.

Emerging Regional Trade Policies

For some time, analysts have worried about the possibility that regional trading arrangements will push the open-trading regime, which is central to the Liberal International Economic Order, toward closure. The United States first experimented with creating trade partnerships within particular regions in 1984, with the Caribbean Basin Initiative to reduce tariffs and provide tax incentives to promote industrialization and trade in Central America and the Caribbean. This was soon followed in 1987 with free-trade agreements with Israel and Canada, and in 1989 with the North American Free Trade Agreement (NAFTA) signed by Canada, Mexico, and the United States in 1993 (see APPLICATION: NAFTA and the Politics of Trade). In addition, at their April 2001 Quebec Summit, the United States and thirty-three Western Hemispheric democracies took a bolder step when they pledged to build a Free Trade Area of the Americas (FTAA), creating the world's largest barrier-free trade zone, from the Arctic to Argentina, linking markets to 800 million people. In December 2005, however, negotiations stalled in response to Venezuela's fiery president Hugo Chávez's opposition to an agreement that he claimed would "permanently extend American political domination of the region to the economic realm."

Efforts to link the countries of the Western Hemisphere in an economic partnership are seen by many as a response to European integration. Since the 1950s, European leaders have tried methodically to build a continent-wide economic union. By 2002, they had established a **regional currency union**, with a single currency (the euro) designed to facilitate economic flows among EU members. Although some EU states (Britain, Denmark, and Sweden) have thus far not adopted the euro, its supporters insist that the euro will strengthen European economic consciousness and transform the continent into a single market for business.

The Mercosur free-trade zone in South America is another example of regionalism. Its full members have expanded trade to $63 billion in 2007 (from only $4.1 billion in 1990). The Southeast Asian Nations (ASEAN) free-trade region represents yet another regional trading bloc. Its intra-bloc trade climbed

regional currency union   the pooling of sovereignty to create a common currency (such as the EU's euro) and single monetary system for members in a region, regulated by a regional central bank within the currency bloc to reduce the likelihood of large-scale liquidity crises.

APPLICATION	NAFTA and the Politics of Trade

For over a century, economics and political science developed as separate academic disciplines: the former largely focusing on the production and consumption of goods and services; the latter, on power and influence in policy making. More recently, however, scholars have begun to look at how economics and politics interact. One area where policy makers wrestle with this interaction is in the creation of regional trade agreements, such as the North American Free Trade Association (NAFTA). In the following passage, James Baker, who served as the U.S. Secretary of State for President George H. W. Bush, discusses the political dynamics that preceded NAFTA's birth.

> From the beginning, we all knew that NAFTA would be no cakewalk. Indeed, some of the President's advisers were initially less than enthusiastic about proceeding. Negotiators would eventually produce a text that ran to five volumes. It would cover trade, investment, the environment, regulation, standards, and mechanisms to resolve disputes. ...
>
> We would also have to sell the agreement politically in the United States. Free-trade agreements always produce losers in some sectors of the economy. But overall, they always generate greater economic activity, which produces more winners than losers. ...
>
> The political problems confronting President [Carlos] Salinas [de Gortari] would be even greater. A free trade agreement would demand accelerated but painful reform of the Mexican economy. Powerful industrial and agricultural interests would fight tooth and nail against opening their markets. Finally, Salinas would have to overcome a hundred-and-fifty-year tradition of anti-American sentiment. ...
>
> Salinas's personal commitment proved critical to negotiating NAFTA. Just weeks after George Bush's election, I had accompanied him to Houston

for the traditional get-together between the American President-elect and his Mexican counterpart. This time the meeting was especially opportune: Salinas himself had just been elected. Between them, the two presidents-elect created the "Spirit of Houston" ... [which] provided the personal foundation for the revolution in bilateral relations that occurred during the next four years.

> For my part, I took the lead in raising the profile of the U.S.-Mexico Binational Commission, a meeting of cabinet members from both nations. ... The American side developed strong working relationships with key Mexican players. These relationships proved decisive when the two sides, joined by Canada, got down to the difficult business of negotiating NAFTA.
>
> ... At State and later the White House ... I always stressed the need for sustained progress, not only to the Mexicans and Canadians, but also to those in our administration who didn't seem to give NAFTA the priority it deserved. Bob Zoellick, my right-hand man on NAFTA, set up an informal channel of communications with José Cordoba de Montoya, Salinas's chief of staff. Through it, the two sides could identify problems and prod our respective bureaucracies (Baker, 1995: 607–608).

According to Baker, even though the U.S. economy was inexorably being bound to those of its neighbors, a regional trade agreement would not have materialized without the political groundwork being carefully prepared by members of each country's administration. Formal talks between the United States and Mexico began in the summer of 1990, with Canada joining in mid-1991. On December 17, 1992, President Bush, President Salinas, and Canadian Prime Minister Brian Mulroney signed the agreement, which was ratified the following year by the legislatures of the three countries.

---

to $376 billion in 2009 from less than $23.7 billion in 1990 (www.aseansec.org/18137.htm).

Many people feel that these types of regional trade agreements (RTAs) are consistent with GATT's rules and see regional regimes as vital pieces in the step toward a free-trade agreement for the entire global economy. Others see the division of the globe into competing trade blocs as a danger, fretting that existing regional free-trade zones actually violate the WTO's nondiscrimination principle

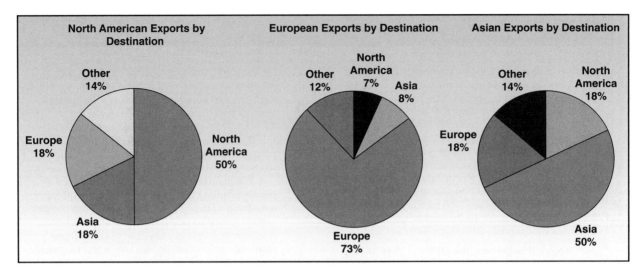

FIGURE 12.2 Trade Blocs and the Regionalization of International Trade

A trend shaping the global economy has been the propensity of trade flows to concentrate within regions instead of between them, with Asia, Europe, and North America forming three distinct trade blocs. As shown in the three pie charts in this figure, intra-bloc exports comprise the majority of the flows in each region. Furthermore, because of the level of economic integration within the European Union, Europe shows the greatest amount of intra-bloc trade.

SOURCE: International Trade Statistics (2009).

by moving away from free trade toward inter-bloc competition. In particular, the critics fear that further development of regionalized markets centered on Asia, Europe, and North America has already split globalized trade into three large, competing trade blocs (see Figure 12.2). Currently, roughly half of exports in Asia go to other Asian countries, half in North America stay within the NAFTA bloc, and over two-thirds of European exports remain within the European Union.

The surge in RTAs has continued unabated since the early 1990s, with 371 having been established as of 2010. The ultimate impact of this trend toward regionalization of the world political economy remains uncertain. Some analysts are concerned about the prospect of a world divided into regional blocs that leave numerous countries outside. Others believe the formation of trade blocs will undermine global free trade and thereby plague world economic growth in the years ahead. If trade-bloc rivalry intensifies, still others warn of a cutthroat mercantile rivalry in which the fear of outsiders may be the only force binding the regional members together.

Yet, contrary to these worries, there are signs that the international trading system may move toward a complex web of commercial ties due to the growth of cross-regional bilateral agreements that create overlapping RTA memberships for many countries. Mexico, for example, is a member of NAFTA and also has bilateral free trade agreements with Australia, New Zealand, and Japan; the European Union has over thirty preferential trade agreements with other states; and the ASEAN countries have individual agreements with China and others are being negotiated with South Korea, Japan, and India. In effect, an intricate network of RTAs and bilateral free-trade agreements currently exists alongside the WTO multilateral trading system.

The Future of Global Economic Governance

Although there are many factors that will define the boundaries within which the global economy is likely to vary in the years ahead, the future will depend heavily on the rules the major economic powers choose to support in trade and monetary policy. Facing the worst financial crisis since the Great Depression, G-20 leaders have been meeting regularly to discuss what rules should guide their policies. Possessing the world's largest economy, the United States continues to play a pivotal role; how it makes economic policy will influence the direction in which others are likely to move. But with the federal government spending a staggering amount to recover from a deep, ongoing recession, can the United States sustain its ability to maintain global economic order?

The architecture of the Liberal International Economic Order constructed at Bretton Woods a half-century ago appeared to depend not only on a consensus about the rules governing the world political economy but also on U.S. leadership. The United States continues to perform many hegemonic functions: It tries to maintain a comparatively open market for others' goods, manage the international monetary system, provide capital to would-be borrowers facing financial stress, and coordinate economic policies among the world's leading economies. Today, however, U.S. willingness to absorb the costs of leadership has waned as Washington increasingly tries to calm economic fears, thaw frozen credit markets, open foreign countries to U.S. exports, and cushion the impact of imports on the domestic economy.

More worrisome still, difficulties facing the Doha Round of global trade talks have raised questions about the future of the WTO as the main forum for crafting rules of world trade. Whereas optimists point to the fits and starts that characterized the earlier Uruguay Round to suggest that current difficulties are merely a temporary interruption within a long-term set of negotiations, pessimists fear that this could spell the end of multilateralism as the organizing principle of global trade. If the Doha Round cannot be salvaged, they warn, the WTO will lose its legitimacy as an umpire in trade disputes and fade into irrelevance.

Clearly, the liberal trading agreements so slowly built up over the past five decades remain fragile. The combination of a lingering recession and financial market volatility could easily bring about a global upsurge in protectionism. Another source of protectionist sentiment comes from worries about the motives driving the investment decisions made by managers of sovereign-wealth funds. Political leaders such as Germany's Angela Merkel and France's Nicolas Sarkozy have voiced suspicions regarding these state-owned funds, the largest of which include the United Arab Emirates' Abu Dhabi Investment Authority and Kuwait's Reserve Fund for Future Generations. Projected to have as much as $12 trillion to invest by 2015, the number of sovereign-wealth funds has multiplied in recent years, often due to windfall profits generated by soaring petroleum prices. Because they generally do not disclose their objectives or the range of their investments, sovereign-wealth funds tend to spark interest in protectionist measures, even though they constitute less than 3 percent of global traded securities. Yet, as former U.S. Federal Reserve chairman Alan Greenspan observes, the protectionist cures advanced to address these concerns will make matters worse rather than better. Protectionism often triggers economic retaliation, which can result in fewer sales abroad and lost jobs at home.

A new wave of mercantilism and trade wars is not preordained. A number of other important developments are also likely to influence the future direction of the world political economy. Commerce has become globalized, and with the development of more free-trade areas and cross-regional trade agreements, the prospects for commercial liberalism to weather calls for protectionism seem promising. But if mercantilists are right, an emerging era of geoeconomic rivalry among competing regional trade blocs will increase the likelihood of political conflict. Meanwhile, national leaders are struggling with how to reconcile domestic political pressures to create and protect jobs with external economic forces over which they have little control. In the tug-of-war between the competing values of trade liberalization and protectionism, they will constantly face trade-offs as they balance policy initiatives seeking to promote growth with those designed to protect autonomy. How they manage these trade-offs will have profound effects on the global future.

CHAPTER SUMMARY

- World politics and economics are inextricably linked. Whether a state's economic system is open or closed, events in the global political economy have domestic consequences. As a result, policymakers play two-level games. The moves they make on the international level affect what they can do on the domestic level, and vice versa.

- Most debates today in the field of international political economy are ultimately reducible to the competing theories of commercial liberalism and mercantilism. Whereas liberals advocate open markets and free trade, mercantilists call for government regulation of economic endeavors to increase state power and security. Although free trade contributes to economic growth, its benefits are not distributed equally.

- Rules governing international commerce evolve according to the wishes of the powerful. The Bretton Woods agreements of 1944 established a Liberal International Economic Order (LIEO), which rested on three political bases: the concentration of power in the hands of a small number of states, the existence of a cluster of interests shared by those states, and the presence of a hegemonic power (the United States) willing to exercise a leadership role.

- The postwar Liberal International Economic Order led to a dramatic upswing in the exchange of goods and services among states, which brought about an increasingly integrated and prosperous global economy.

- The immediate postwar economic system was a dollar-based system, with the United States operating, in effect, as the world's banker. By the early 1970s, however, U.S. leadership was no longer readily accepted by others or willingly exercised by Washington. Power had become more widely dispersed among states. Where hegemony once reigned, various groups of industrialized nations now participated in a series of quasi-official negotiating forums to deal with monetary issues.

- The simultaneous pursuit of liberalism and mercantilism today shows states' determination to reap the benefits of interdependence while minimizing its costs. It also reveals the tension between the promise that everyone will benefit and the fear that the benefits will not be equally distributed. The absence of world government encourages each state to be more concerned with how it fares competitively in relation to other states—its relative gains—than collectively with its absolute gains. These simple yet powerful ideas shed light on the reasons why the United States, the principal advocate of free trade in the post–World War II era, has increasingly engaged in protectionism.

- Economic nationalism and a retreat from multilateral economic cooperation threaten to undermine the overall prospects for world economic growth. Given the growing regionalization of trade and the formation of competitive trade blocs, the rise of regional neomercantilism is a possibility. However, economic globalization is likely to accelerate, and, as competition expands wealth and reduces the costs of both products and labor, the economic fate of the world's 6.8 billion people will be tied closer together, making the welfare of any one important to the welfare of all.

KEY TERMS

antidumping duties

balance of payments

balance of trade

beggar-thy-neighbor policies

collective goods

commercial liberalism

comparative advantage

countervailing duties

exchange rate

export quotas

fixed exchange rates

floating exchange rates

free ride

Group of Eight (G-8)

Group of Five (G-5)

Group of Seven (G-7)

Group of Twenty (G-20)

hegemonic stability theory

import quotas

infant industry

international liquidity

international monetary system

international political economy

laissez-faire economics

Liberal International Economic Order (LIEO)

mercantilism

money supply

most-favored-nation (MFN) principle

neomercantilism

nondiscrimination

orderly market
   arrangements
   (OMAs)

protectionism

regional currency union

regional trade
   agreements (RTAs)

subsidies

voluntary export
   restrictions (VERs)

SUGGESTED READINGS

Bernstein, William J. *A Splendid Exchange: How Trade Shaped the World*. New York: Atlantic Monthly Press, 2008.

Ferguson, Niall. *The Ascent of Money: A Financial History of the World*. New York: Penguin, 2008.

Frieden, Jeffry A., David A. Lake, and J. Lawrence Broz (eds.). *International Political Economy: Perspectives on Global Power and Wealth*, 5th edition. New York: Norton, 2010.

Irwin, Douglas. *Free Trade Under Fire*, 3rd edition. Princeton, NJ: Princeton University Press, 2009.

Oatley, Thomas. *International Political Economy: Interests and Institutions in the Global Economy*, 4th edition. New York: Pearson Longman, 2010.

CRITICAL THINKING QUESTIONS

On July 26, 1956, Egyptian president Gamal Abdel Nasser announced to a jubilant crowd in Alexandria that he would eradicate the last vestige of Egypt's colonial past by nationalizing the Suez Canal, a vital artery of world commerce linking the Mediterranean to the Red Sea. The canal had been operated by the Universal Suez Canal Company, owned primarily by British and French stockholders. Alarmed that Nasser would now control the waterway through which Britain's oil supply flowed, British Prime Minister Anthony Eden desperately sought a way to oust the charismatic Egyptian president and regain the canal.

Britain's concerns about Nasser were echoed in France and Israel. Political leaders in Paris believed he was helping Algerians resist French colonial rule; those in Tel Aviv grumbled that he had closed the Straits of Tiran to Israeli shipping and supported guerrilla attacks against Israel. The United States also found Nasser's behavior deplorable but insisted on finding a negotiated solution to the dispute. U.S. President Dwight Eisenhower was engaged in a reelection campaign, and the Republican Party had emphasized his contributions to international peace. Unable to secure Washington's backing for a military strike against Nasser, Britain, France, and Israel began planning their next moves in secret.

On October 29, the Israelis attacked the Egyptian army in the Sinai Peninsula, and the following day the British and French announced that they would intervene to protect the Suez Canal. British paratroopers landed in Suez and Port Said on November 5, setting off a storm of opposition in the United Nations. Eisenhower was furious with what he saw as British deception on the eve of the American elections. The following day, U.S. Secretary of the Treasury George Humphrey gave the British an ultimatum: Either agree to a cease-fire or the United States would ruin the pound sterling, Britain's currency. Unless the British withdrew, Humphrey threatened to block their drawing rights on the International Monetary Fund, deny credit from the United States Export-Import Bank, and have the American Federal Reserve sell off large quantities of sterling (Neustadt, 1970: 26). Faced with a looming monetary crisis, the British capitulated.

Some analysts worry that the United States may someday face pressure similar to that experienced by Great Britain in the Suez crisis. Although America holds unchallenged military might, its economy depends on foreign capital because the country consumes more than it produces and has to borrow at a rate of $4 billion every day to sustain its enormous current account deficit. Currently, it owes foreign creditors over $13 trillion. This dependence on foreign creditors, these analysts warn, could give other countries leverage over the United States. For example, as 2010 began, China held $797 billion in Treasury securities. "Simply by dumping U.S. Treasury bills and other dollar-denominated assets, China—which holds more federal U.S. debt than any other country—could cause the value of the dollar to plummet, leading to a major crisis for the U.S. economy" (Schwenninger, 2004: 129). Like Great Britain in 1956, the precarious financial position of United States today could undercut its foreign policy.

Are the fears expressed by these analysts warranted? How much leverage does Beijing have over Washington by holding U.S. debt, given that about 70 percent of China's $2.4 trillion in foreign-exchange reserves are denominated in dollars? What would a steep decline in the dollar do to countries that hold dollar-denominated assets? Does the importance of American consumption of Chinese goods for China's economic growth counterbalance any pressure that Beijing could exert on Washington? Is the 1956 Suez analogy helpful in understanding the political economy of U.S.-Chinese relations? What are the key similarities between Great Britain's position in 1956 and that of the United States today? What are the major differences?

13

International Human Rights

CHAPTER OUTLINE

Evaluating the Human Condition

Communitarian and Cosmopolitan Approaches to Human Rights

Human Development and Human Security

CONTROVERSY: What Is Security?

Human Rights and the Protection of People

The Subordinate Status of Women and Its Consequences

The Precarious Life of Indigenous Peoples

The Global Refugee Crisis

Responding to Human Rights Abuses

Internationally Recognized Human Rights

The Challenge of Enforcement

APPLICATION: Human Rights Start in Small Places, Close to Home

All human beings are born free and equal in dignity and rights.

ARTICLE 1

UNIVERSAL DECLARATION OF HUMAN RIGHTS (1948)

O n April 29, 2008, the government of Myanmar (formerly known as Burma) announced that rain showers, accompanied by winds reaching forty-five miles an hour, were approaching the country's southern coast. Three days later, Cyclone Nargis made landfall, inundating the Irrawaddy Delta in 12 feet of water and pounding the region with winds three times more powerful than predicted. Caught off guard, the population suffered horribly. Estimates placed the number of dead at over 100,000, with more than 1 million people left homeless and vulnerable to infectious waterborne diseases.

For several days after the storm, Myanmar's military government scarcely took any actions to assist the survivors. General Than Shwe, the government's leader, rebuffed attempts by UN Secretary-General Ban Ki-moon to persuade him to allow emergency aid into the country. Although Myanmar was on the verge of a humanitarian catastrophe, the government repeatedly turned away rescue teams from foreign nations as well as offers of relief supplies from U.S. and French naval vessels in the Andaman Sea. According to the World Food Program, only 20 percent of desperately needed food aid was getting to cyclone victims.

Frustrated by the military regime's callous behavior, French Foreign Minister Bernard Kouchner suggested that international aid might have to be imposed on Myanmar. Diego Lopez Garrido, Spain's secretary of state for European affairs, complained that the regime's obstructionism was similar to a crime against humanity. David Miliband, Britain's foreign secretary, added that the world community would be morally justified in using all available instruments to open Myanmar's borders to aid under the doctrine of Responsibility to Protect (*Economist*, May 17, 2008: 73).

At the September 2005 UN World Summit in New York, the "responsibility to protect populations from genocide, war crimes, ethnic cleansing, and crimes against humanity" was unanimously adopted by the assembled heads of state (http://www.un.org/summit2005/). Whereas article 2(7) of the UN Charter proclaims that "nothing should authorize intervention in matters essentially within the domestic jurisdiction of any state," the principle of **Responsibility to Protect (R2P)** holds that outside intervention could be undertaken if national authorities were either unable or unwilling to safeguard their populations and peaceful international engagement proved inadequate for addressing the humanitarian emergency. Calls for applying R2P to Myanmar did not trigger a humanitarian intervention, however. In the first place, natural disasters are not included within the scope of the doctrine. In the second place, many Global South countries worried that any effort to widen its application to situations beyond genocide, war crimes, ethnic cleansing, and crimes against humanity would provide a rationale for powerful, disingenuous states to infringe on the domestic affairs of the weak under the guise of a moral imperative to stop human rights violations. R2I ("right to intervene") would be a more accurate name for such an expanded doctrine, complained Nicaraguan diplomat Miguel d'Escoto Bockman (*Economist*, July 25, 2009: 58).

The intransigence of Myanmar's military government in the aftermath of Cyclone Nargis raises several questions about the role of **human rights** in world politics. What are human rights? When a sovereign state violates them, is it legally permissible for others to intervene on behalf of the victims? Does the world community have a moral responsibility to protect those suffering from egregious human rights violations?

Until relatively recently, the theoretical study of world politics neglected human rights. It pictured the plight of the ordinary people as a matter of domestic politics, shielded from outside scrutiny by a state's sovereignty. Human beings were relegated to the status of "subjects" whom rulers could treat as if they were things. Today, this outlook seems strange. Understanding how people think and feel has grown in importance as the world community increasingly recognizes

Responsibility to Protect (R2P) a principle adopted at the 2005 UN World Summit that declares states have a responsibility to protect their citizens from genocide, war crimes, ethnic cleansing, and crimes against humanity, and that they should take appropriate action when others fail to protect their populations from these crimes.

human rights the political and social entitlements recognized by international law as inalienable and valid for individuals in all countries by virtue of their humanity.

the inherent moral status of humans and the concomitant obligation of states to protect that status.

The purpose of this chapter is to examine the human condition and assess its prospects for the global future. There are now 6.8 billion people on the face of the earth, and the world population is growing. Over 2 billion more people will be added to the planet's population between now and 2050. With these numbers comes a concern over how humanity will fare in the decades ahead. To what extent will people around the world have an opportunity to shape their destiny? Will they be empowered to take responsibility for their own lives?

EVALUATING THE HUMAN CONDITION

During an August 2009 interview in Cape Town, South Africa, U.S. Secretary of State Hillary Clinton discussed the importance of human rights as a "central driving force" behind American foreign policy, adding that a broad assessment of the human condition was the proper way to begin examining human rights. Do people have shelter, health care, and educational opportunities as well as political freedom and civil liberties? Clinton asked. If we ignore basic needs for sustaining a life of dignity, she concluded, we are defining human rights too narrowly.

How is humanity faring? Is human dignity adequately protected around the world? As we saw in Chapter 5, despite some people enjoying unprecedented material wealth, daunting levels of poverty exist throughout the world. As measured by the World Bank's standard of $1.25 a day in purchasing power parity (PPP), 1.3 billion people are living in extreme poverty. Yet as tragic as such destitution may be, the World Bank's index only reflects the economic dimension of life. Even people with higher incomes may be deprived in other ways.

According to an analysis of the human condition based on the Multidimensional Poverty Index (MPI), which measures noneconomic aspects of poverty, about 1.7 billion people endure acute deprivation. As shown in Figure 13.1, roughly half of them reside in South Asia and over one-quarter in Sub-Saharan Africa. However, one's chances of living in poverty vary significantly depending on where you live within these two regions. In Kenya, for example, the residents of Nairobi, the capital city, suffer from fewer deprivations than rural Kenyans living in the northeastern part of the country. Ethnicity also matters. Different ethnic groups with similar levels of poverty experience different deprivations. Thirty-nine percent of the Kikuyu in Kenya and 37 percent of the Embu are extremely poor. But whereas malnutrition and child mortality contribute most to Kikuyu poverty, inadequate access to electricity, sanitation facilities, and clean drinking water contribute more heavily to Embu poverty (Alkire and Santos, 2010).

Given the intense deprivations harming so many people, there are ample reasons for humanitarian concern. Crushing poverty is a recipe for hopelessness and desperation. Privation certainly is a serious problem, but is it one that should be viewed through the lens of human rights? Are there fundamental

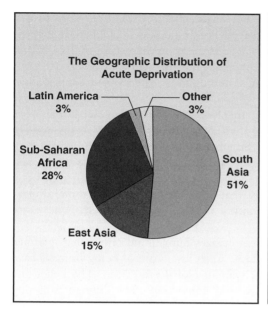

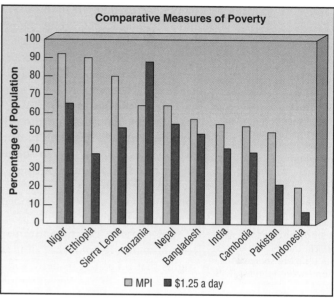

FIGURE 13.1 **Global Poverty**

The Multidimensional Poverty Index (MPI) uses ten indicators to measure three dimensions of poverty: health, educa-tion, and living standard. The graph on the left displays where the world's poor live as measured by the MPI. The graph on the right compares the percentage of people in selected countries that live in poverty as measured by the MPI and by income (under $1.25 a day). This graph reveals that many people who are not income poor may still suffer from serious health, education, or other deprivations.

SOURCE: Multidimensional Poverty Index: 2010 data, available at http://www.ophi.org.uk/policy/multidimensional-poverty-index/.

socioeconomic entitlements of persons that create a moral obligation for other countries to ensure minimal shelter, health care, and educational opportunity out of considerations of human dignity and distributive justice? Or is this only a matter of domestic concern, with national leaders having no obligation to ame-liorate poverty among those who live in other countries?

Communitarian and Cosmopolitan Approaches to Human Rights

Do national leaders have a moral obligation to try to alleviate human suffering no matter where it occurs? Indeed, do they have *any* duties to people outside of their country's borders? These questions have received growing attention since the end of World War II, when the idea of "human rights" was included in the Preamble and in Article 1 of the Charter of the United Nations. Until then, human rights were rarely part of diplomatic discourse.

Rights are entitlements that a person has to something of value. By acknowledging a right, we set limits on the actions of others and empower the right-holder to have nullified any encroachments into what is protected. The idea of human rights has been called "*the* idea of our times," the "principal counter-current to realpolitik values" (Henkin, 1991: 187). Yet, to note that there is wide acceptance of the principle that all individuals have certain inalienable rights is not to say that there is total agreement on the nature of those rights. There are many interpretations of the scope of human rights; however, two contending schools of thought stand out: communitarian theory and cosmopolitan theory (C. Brown, 1992).

communitarianism an ethical theory that places the ultimate source of moral value in political communities.

Communitarianism holds that the leaders of sovereign, territorial states have moral obligations to those living within their borders, not to the welfare of humanity as a whole. Human rights, from this perspective, are a matter of national jurisdiction. Given the diversity of cultures throughout the world, and given that we have no widely accepted basis for choosing among different value systems, communitarian theorists insist that references to universal moral obligations are problematic. A bounded political community, they assert, is necessary for a shared code of morality.

cosmopolitanism an ethical theory that places the ultimate source of moral value in individuals.

In contrast, **cosmopolitanism** emphasizes humankind rather than national communities. It holds that all individuals, solely by virtue of being human, have rights that no state can deny and that warrant global protection. The belief in a transcendent humanitarian imperative—a conviction that human suffering obliges others to respond—has ancient roots. From Zeno (335–263 BCE) and Chrysippus (250–207 BCE) through Seneca (4 BCE–65 CE) and Marcus Aurelius (121–180 CE), Greek and Roman Stoics believed in the equality and unity of humankind. Contemporary cosmopolitans assert that despite the world's division into a welter of separate states, the well-being of people in any one state should not come at the expense of people from different states, because their common humanity entails moral obligations to each other (Linklater, 2002). Some argue further that if one has the power to prevent something bad from happening to those living elsewhere, action should be taken as long as it does not sacrifice anything of comparable moral significance (P. Singer, 1979).

While communitarian theories have their adherents, the process of globalization has led many people to gravitate toward the view that all individuals equally hold certain rights simply by sharing a common humanity. Modern telecommunication highlights these commonalities by making us aware that distant strangers often share our everyday hopes and fears. As discussed in Chapter 11, satellites, broadband links, and the Internet have compressed space and time. Of course, not everyone around the world enjoys the human rights that cosmopolitan theories articulate; consequently, many IGOs and NGOs have made a significant effort in recent years to promote **human security**, which they believe will enhance development and, in turn, respect for human rights (see CONTROVERSY: What Is Security?).

human security a concept that refers to the degree to which the welfare of individuals is protected and advanced, in contrast to national security, which puts the interests of states first.

Human Development and Human Security

The human dimension of development gained attention in the 1970s when analysts realized the importance of focusing on aspects of human welfare not measured by economic indicators that describe a country's wealth. Beyond looking at indicators such as the average income for each person in a particular country,

---

CONTROVERSY   **What Is Security?**

How should *security* be defined? Policy makers disagree. Some see it primarily in military terms; others in human welfare terms. Underlying the disagreement are different conceptions of what is most important on the global agenda. One tradition gives states first priority and assumes that protecting their territorial integrity must be foremost in the minds of national leaders. Others challenge this conception and give primacy to the security of individual people, arguing that social and environmental protection must be seen as a global priority, because all people depend on a clean, healthy environment for survival.

What do you think? To what extent should social and environmental protection be defined as security issues? When reflecting on these questions, take into consideration the realist view that national security entails safeguarding the state from external attack. Realists maintain that protecting one's country from existential threats is a political leader's paramount task. For them, national survival overrides all other concerns; thus, they define security in military terms, focusing on the state's ability to fend off armed aggression.

In contrast, many liberals contend that secure nation-states do not imply secure people. Guarding against foreign attacks may be a necessary condition for the security of individuals, but it is not a sufficient one. Pointing to the devastating floods that inundated Pakistan during the late summer of 2010, proponents of "human security" insist that national leaders should also protect individuals from hunger, disease, and natural disasters, because they kill more people than war. From their perspective, the degradation of vital ecological systems, from fresh water to clean air, would have effects comparable to those associated with traditional national security threats, such as invasion and territorial occupation. Achieving security, therefore, entails more than generating national military power.

Which conception of security is more persuasive to you? Is the concept of human security too broad to be useful in policy making? To what extent is the "national security" approach emphasized by realists and the "human security" approach favored by liberals in competition with one another? Might they instead be mutually reinforcing? Can either type of security be achieved in the absence of the other?

---

analysts began devoting attention to noneconomic factors that contributed to living a long, rewarding life.

Many things affect human development. Among them, political freedom stands out. The degree to which countries rule themselves democratically and protect civil liberties is a potent determinant of human development. Map 13.1 shows the various levels of human development in countries across the globe. One conclusion that the United Nations Development Program has drawn from the data displayed in the map is that human development flourishes where people are free to express their views and participate in the decisions that shape destinies.

For human development goals to be met, prosperity clearly helps. When countries are ranked according to their human development performance, as we might expect, the level of human development is highest in the Global North, where economic prosperity is also highest on average; conversely, it is generally lower in the Global South where per capita economic output is substantially lower. Nevertheless, the link between economic well-being and human development is not automatic. Two countries with similar per capita incomes can have very different levels of human development, because some governments are more effective in converting national wealth into better lives for their people. Costa Rica and South Africa, for example, recently ranked 73 and 78 among the world's countries, respectively, on per capita gross domestic

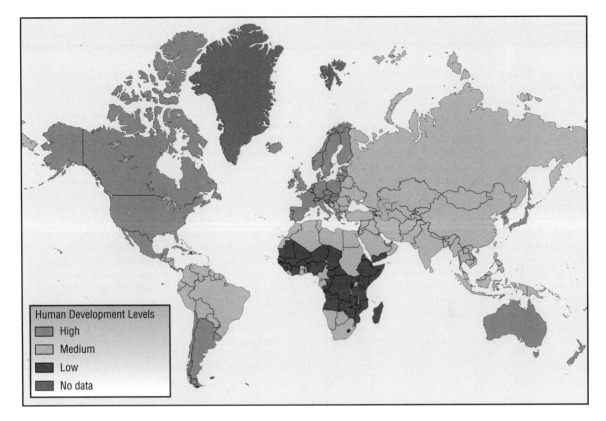

M A P 13.1 The Map of Human Development

This map shows the level of human development in countries of the world, based on the UN Human Development Index (HDI), which uses life expectancy, literacy, average number of years of schooling, and income to assess a country's performance in providing for its people's security and welfare. Although poorer countries have made big gains in the past quarter century, a gap in levels of human development is apparent and parallels to some degree the gap between the Global North and Global South. Note: The high category contains both high (0.80–0.89) and very high (0.90 or higher) HDI scores.

SOURCE: UNDP (2009: 213)

product (GDP), adjusted for purchasing power parity. When compared on the UN Development Program's Human Development Index (a measure that includes life expectancy, literacy, and education), Costa Rica ranked 54 and South Africa 129 (HDR, 2009: 114–117). In short, income alone is not a good predictor of human development. How countries politically organize themselves is a more important factor.

The rapid transfer of capital and investment across borders that is integrating the world's economies has led to widespread speculation that globalization will provide a cure for the chronic poverty facing the majority of humanity. Impressive gains have been made in various countries. Since 1990, the number of people without access to clean water has been cut in half, the number of children dying before the age of five has fallen by one-quarter, and life expectancy in developing countries has increased by two years. "On the whole," concludes the World Bank, "people are healthier and better educated than they were 30 years ago, but progress has been deeply unequal" (WDI, 2010: 60). According to global optimists, these gains suggest that poverty can be eradicated.

However, critics complain that while capital may flow more freely around the world, it flows slowly to places where human suffering is the greatest. The developing countries are a heterogeneous group, and the poorest are not catching up. Although progress in human development has occurred and will likely persist, so will trends that can erode human security, making the early twenty-first century appear to be both the best of times and the worst of times. As a result, some commentators on world politics see progress as possible while others see regress as inevitable.

HUMAN RIGHTS AND THE PROTECTION OF PEOPLE

As we have noted, human rights are entitlements that a person possesses simply because he or she is a human being. As such, they are held equally by all and cannot be lost or forfeited. Unfortunately, not everyone enjoys all of the human rights recognized by international law. Three major areas where this problem exists are the rights of women, indigenous peoples, and refugees.

The Subordinate Status of Women and Its Consequences

Over the past three decades, the status of women has become a major human rights concern (see Table 13.1). Increasingly, people have realized that women have an important influence on human development, and that their treatment is an issue that affects everyone.

As gauged by the UN's Gender Empowerment Measure (GEM), women throughout the world continue to be disadvantaged relative to men in various ways. They have less access to primary education and to advanced training in professional fields, such as science, engineering, law, and business. In addition, within occupational groups, they are almost always in less prestigious jobs, where they receive less pay than men in comparable positions and they face formidable barriers to advancement. Although these and other gender differences have narrowed in recent years, particularly in Scandinavia and the Benelux countries, gender inequalities remain widespread. Women's share of earned income in developing countries is less than a third of men's. Furthermore, their share of administrative and managerial jobs is minuscule. Only 5 percent of top corporate positions worldwide are held by women. Much the same holds true in politics: Since 1900 only 15 percent of the world's countries have had one or more female heads of state, and many of them came to power as widows of male rulers (*Harper's*, January 2008: 15). In 2010, the Inter-Parliamentary Union reported that women accounted for just 19 percent of the seats in parliaments worldwide (www.ipu.org/wmn-e/world.htm).

T A B L E 13.1   International Steps Toward Women's Rights and Gender Empowerment

Year	Conference	Key Action
1975	International Women's Year Conference (Mexico City)	Initiated movement to establish the UN Development Fund for Women; asserts "The human body, whether that of a woman or man, is inviolable, and respect for it is a fundamental element of human dignity and freedom."
1979	Convention on the Elimination of All Forms of Discrimination Against Women (New York)	Article 12 calls on countries to "take all appropriate measures to eliminate discrimination against women in the field of health care in order to ensure, on a basis of equality of men and women, access to health care services, including those related to family planning."
1980	Second World Conference on Women (Copenhagen)	Advocates measures to strengthen women's rights of inheritance and ownership of property.
1985	Third World Conference on Women (Nairobi)	Calls for institutional mechanisms to promote empowerment of women.
1992	United Nations Conference on Environment and Development (Rio de Janeiro)	Agenda 21 calls for "women-centered, women-managed, safe and accessible, responsible planning of family size and service."
1993	United Nations World Conference on Human Rights (Vienna)	The Vienna Declaration includes nine paragraphs on "The Equal Status and Human Rights of Women," and, for the first time, recognizes that "violence against women is a human-rights abuse."
1995	United Nations Fourth World Conference on Women (Beijing)	Sets a wide-ranging, ambitious agenda for promoting human development by addressing gender inequality and women's rights.
2002	World Summit on Sustainable Development (Johannesburg)	Drafts resolutions to combat abject and dehumanizing poverty, stressing the importance of reform to encourage gender equality and the rights of women in order to stimulate sustainable economic growth.
2004	United Nations Conference on the Human Rights Obligations of Multinational Corporations (Geneva)	Opens debate to create a code of human rights and gender equality obligations for businesses.
2005	United Nations World Conference on Women (Beijing)	Launched Platform for Action, which outlines strategies for empowering women.
2010	Commission on the Status of Women (New York)	Assesses implementation of the Platform for Action.

The need to extend women equal rights has been long articulated by feminists and is now generally recognized. Nevertheless, addressing women's rights is difficult because the issues touch deeply entrenched and widely divergent religious and social beliefs. In certain Islamic countries, for example, women must hide their faces with

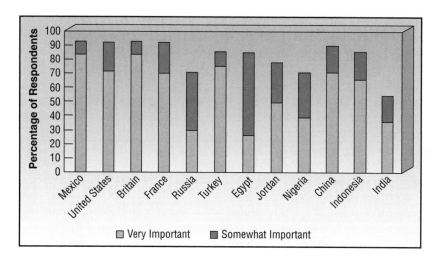

F I G U R E 13.2 Opinions on Importance of Women's Rights

This graph shows the results in 12 countries of public opinion surveys that were conducted between January and October 2008. Each respondent was asked: "How important do you think it is for women to have full equality of rights compared to men?" On average, 86 percent said it was important, with 59 percent saying it was very important. The margin of error in each of the surveys varied between +/- 2 and 4 percent.

SOURCE: WorldPublicOpinion.org.

veils in public, and women and men are often completely separated for various activities. For many in Western countries, these traditions are difficult to understand. On the other hand, various Western ideas about gender roles can be perplexing to people elsewhere. Given these differences, it is interesting to note that a 2008 public opinion poll conducted in 20 countries found a strong consensus across cultures that supported women's rights (see Figure 13.2).

Gender myopia, denying the existence of the barriers that prevent women from having the same rights and opportunities as enjoyed by men, is pervasive. Much of feminist scholarship seeks to rectify this situation under the conviction that only the realization of the full potential of all people can enable true human development to occur.

The Precarious Life of Indigenous Peoples

As noted in Chapter 6, where we first addressed the topic of nonstate actors (NGOs), **indigenous peoples** are members of ethnic groups native to a geographic location now controlled by another state or political group. The planet is populated by an estimated 6,000 separate indigenous "nations," each of which has a unique language, culture, and strong, often spiritual, ties to an ancestral homeland. Estimates suggest there are at least 300 million indigenous peoples comprising more than 5 percent of the world's population living in seventy countries. Recall that this segment of global society is conventionally referred to as the "Fourth World" to heighten awareness of their poverty and lack of self-rule.

Many indigenous peoples feel persecuted because their livelihoods, lands, and cultures are threatened. In part, these fears are inspired by the 130 million indigenous peoples who were slaughtered between 1900 and 1987 by state-

indigenous peoples
the native ethnic and cultural inhabitant populations within countries ruled by a government controlled by others, often referred to as the "Fourth World."

sponsored violence in their own countries (Rummel, 1994). The mass killings of Armenians by Turks, of Jews (and other groups) by Hitler, of Cambodians by the Khmer Rouge, and of the Tutsi of Rwanda by the Hutu exemplify the atrocities committed during the past century. Responding to the tragedy of the Nazi holocaust, Polish jurist Raphael Lemkin coined the word **genocide** from the Greek word *genos* (race, people) and the Latin *caedere* (to kill), and called for it to be singled out as the gravest violation of human rights, a heinous crime the international community would be morally responsible for punishing (Turk, 2001). In his view, genocide has several dimensions, including physical (the annihilation of members of a group), biological (measures taken to reduce the reproductive capacity of a group), and cultural (efforts to eliminate a group's language, literature, art, and other institutions).

genocide the deliberate extermination of an ethnic or minority group.

Various native peoples are now fighting back across the globe against the injustice they perceive states to have perpetrated against them. This is not to suggest that all indigenous groups are bent on using violence to attain power. The members of many such nonstate nations are divided about objectives, and militants who are prepared to fight for independence are usually in a minority. In fact, most Fourth World indigenous movements only seek a greater voice in redirecting the policies and allocation of resources within existing states and are eliciting the support of NGOs and IGOs to pressure states to recognize their claims and protect their rights.

A substantial number of indigenous movements in the last decade have successfully negotiated settlements resulting in devolution—the granting of political power to increase local self-governance. Examples include the Miskitos in Nicaragua, the Gagauz in Moldova, and most regional separatists in Ethiopia and in India's Assam region. Yet, as suggested by the hostilities between the Chechens and the Russian Federation, resolving clashes between aspiring peoples and established states can be extremely difficult.

The goal expressed in the UN Charter of promoting "universal respect for, and observance of, human rights and fundamental freedoms" for everyone is a challenge for many nationally diverse countries, because protecting the human rights and civil liberties of minority populations is inherently difficult. The division of these states along ethnic and cultural lines makes them inherently fragile. Consider the degree to which minority groups compose many states: for example, the share of indigenous populations in Bolivia is 70 percent and Peru, 40 percent. Or consider the number of distinct languages spoken in some countries, with Indonesia's 719 living languages, Nigeria's 514, India's 438, and Brazil's 236 being conspicuous examples (Lewis, 2009).

Racism and intolerance are hothouses for fanaticism and violence. The belief that one's nationality is superior to all others undermines the concept of human rights. Although interethnic competition is a phenomenon that dates back to biblical times, it remains a contemporary plague. According to *The Minorities at Risk Project* (http://www.cidcm.umd.edu/mar), since 1998, 283 politically active minority groups suffering from organized discrimination have mobilized politically to defend themselves. Some analysts predict that conflict within and between ethnically divided states could become a major axis on which twenty-first-century world politics revolves.

The Global Refugee Crisis

Nowhere are the problems of human security more evident than in the refugee crisis that now prevails. **Refugees** are individuals whose religion, ethnicity, political opinions, or membership in a particular social group make them targets of persecution in their homelands and who migrate from their country of origin. According to the UN High Commissioner for Refugees (UNHCR, 2010), the world's refugee population by the beginning of 2010 was approximately 15.2 million, with 10.4 million falling under the mandate of the UNHCR (see Figure 13.3) and another 4.8 million coming under the responsibility of the United Nations Relief and Works Agency for Palestinian Refugees in the Near East (UNRWA). Also of concern are some 15.6 million internally **displaced people** as well as 6.6 million "stateless" people who, like the Bidoun of the Middle East and the Biharis of South Asia, cannot prove their rights to citizenship anywhere and thus belong to no country.

Refugees and displaced persons are often the victims of war. For example, the 1994 genocide in Rwanda drove more than 1.7 million refugees from their homelands, and the armed conflict between 1991 and 1999 that accompanied the breakup of the former Yugoslavia uprooted nearly 3 million people. More recently, the UN estimates that almost 3 million people have been displaced during the war in Afghanistan.

A large proportion of the world's refugees flee their homelands when ethnic and religious conflicts weaken the capacity of governments to maintain domestic law and order. As public authority dissolves amid rising civil strife, some people move because they do not receive police protection, cannot expect the prosecution of anyone who violates their rights, nor will they receive legal redress of their grievances.

People also leave home in search of economic opportunity. Legal migrants—particularly young people in the Global South without productive employment—are among those departing at record rates, mostly to Global North countries, though migration also is occurring *between* developing Global South countries. Nigeria, for example, attracts workers from Ghana; South Africa, from Tanzania and Zimbabwe. Foreign workers from Global South countries make up over 80 percent of the population of the United Arab Emirates.

Some of the people leaving their home states are the best educated and most talented, causing a serious **brain drain**. For instance, Moroccan engineers frequently migrate to France, and numerous Malawian nurses have relocated to Great Britain. However, the majority of migrants take low-wage jobs shunned by local inhabitants. Typically, this means migrants earn less than the citizens of those states but more than they would earn in their homelands when performing the same tasks. Host countries may admit migrants (as Europe did during the 1970s guest worker era) not only because they accept low wages for undesirable jobs, but also because in many places the host pays little if anything for migrants'

refugees   people who flee for safety to another country because of a well-founded fear of persecution.

displaced people   people involuntarily uprooted from their homes but still living in their own countries.

brain drain   the exodus of the most educated people from their homeland to a more prosperous foreign country where the opportunities for high incomes are better, which deprives their homeland of their ability to contribute to its economic development.

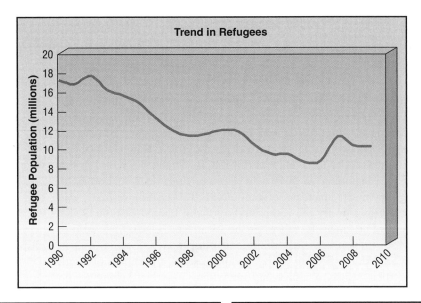

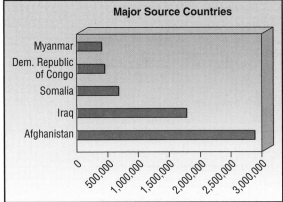

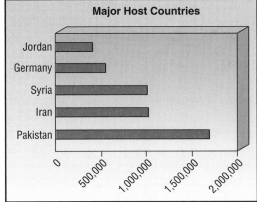

F I G U R E 13.3 Trends and Patterns in Refugees

At the onset of 2010, 10.4 million refugees were under UNHCR responsibility. As shown in the upper graph, the number of refugees has recently increased after declining in the mid-1990s. The lower graphs show the primary source and host countries of the current refugee population. Afghanistan and Iraq are the leading countries of origin. Pakistan and Iran are the primary host countries. Approximately one-third of the world's refugees are lodged in camps.

SOURCE: UNHCR (2010: 4, 6–8)

health, education, and welfare needs. On the other hand, the home (source) countries sometimes encourage people to emigrate as a way of exporting unwanted elements of the population, reducing unemployment, or in the expectation that the emigrants will send much of their income back as remittances to family members in their homeland. In Guinea-Bissau, Eritrea, and Tajikistan, remittances account for over 35 percent of the GDP (*Economist*, January 5, 2008: 11–12).

In summary, a combination of push and pull factors has propelled migration to the forefront of the global humanitarian agenda. War, ethnic and religious conflict, human rights violations, and famine all *push* millions beyond their homelands; but migrants also are *pulled* abroad by the promise of economic opportunity and political freedom elsewhere. However, many refugees are finding the doors to safe havens closing. Tougher policies on **asylum** applicants has reduced the number of those receiving sanctuary in the Global North, turning many people toward Global South countries. One-quarter of the applications for asylum in 2009 were filed in South Africa, with the next three most common destinations (the United States, France, and Malaysia) receiving a sum amounting to only 60 percent of South Africa's total. Security concerns stimulated by terrorist fears are sometimes at work, as in the United States, where many believe the catastrophic terrorist attacks of September 11, 2001, would not have occurred had immigration controls been tighter. Economic concerns may also play a role, as unemployed low and semiskilled citizens express resentment about increased competition for scarce jobs.

asylum   the provision of sanctuary to safeguard refugees escaping from the threat of persecution in the country where they hold citizenship.

Efforts to toughen domestic refugee legislation raise important ethical issues. The UN has become increasingly concerned that difficulty in gaining asylum contributes to "protracted refugee situations," where 25,000 or more people of the same nationality have been in exile for at least five years. The UNHCR estimates that almost two-thirds of the refugees today are in this situation, living in 21 host countries around the world. Where will the homeless, the desperate, the weak, and the poor find sanctuary—a safe place to live where human rights are safeguarded? Will the world act with compassion or respond with indifference? These questions may involve irreconcilable values, and will thus make the global refugee crisis a topic of intense debate for years to come.

RESPONDING TO HUMAN RIGHTS ABUSES

The idea of human rights has advanced over the past few decades from a mere slogan to a program of action. But as the examples of the status of women, indigenous peoples, and refugees illustrate, much work remains to be done on implementing the human rights program.

Internationally Recognized Human Rights

The body of legal rules and norms designed to protect individual human beings is anchored in the ethical requirement that every person should be treated with equal concern and respect. The Universal Declaration of Human Rights, unanimously adopted by the UN General Assembly on December 10, 1948, is the most authoritative statement of these norms. It set forth a wide range of civil and political rights, and proclaimed that they should be protected by the rule of law. These rights have since been codified and extended in a series of treaties, most notably in the International Covenant on Civil and Political Rights, and the International Covenant on Economic, Social, and Cultural Rights (which were both open for signature in 1966 and entered into force a decade later).

There are many ways to classify the rights listed in these treaties. Charles Beitz (2001: 271), an authority on international ethics, groups them into five categories.

1. *Rights of the person:* "Life, liberty, and security of the person; privacy and freedom of movement; ownership of property; freedom of thought, conscience, and religion, including freedom of religious teaching and practice 'in public and private'; and prohibition of slavery, torture, and cruel or degrading punishment."

2. *Rights associated with the rule of law:* "Equal recognition before the law and equal protection of the law; effective legal remedy for violation of legal rights; impartial hearing and trial; presumption of innocence; and prohibition of arbitrary arrest."

3. *Political rights:* "Freedom of expression, assembly, and association; the right to take part in government; and periodic and genuine elections by universal and equal suffrage."

4. *Economic and social rights:* "An adequate standard of living; free choice of employment; protection against unemployment; 'just and favorable remuneration'; the right to join trade unions; 'reasonable limitation of working hours'; free elementary education; social security; and the 'highest attainable standard of physical and mental health.'"

5. *Rights of communities:* "Self-determination and protection of minority cultures."

Although the multilateral treaties enumerating these rights are legally binding on the states ratifying them, many have either not ratified them or have done so with significant reservations. When states specify reservations, they are expressing agreement with the broad declarations of principle contained in these treaties while indicating that they object to certain specific provisions and elect not to be bound by them. The United States, for example, ratified the International Covenant on Civil and Political Rights with reservations in 1992, but has not ratified the International Covenant on Economic, Social, and Cultural Rights. As this example illustrates, countries who agree with the general principle that all human beings possess certain rights that cannot be withheld may still disagree on the scope of these rights, with some countries emphasizing legal and political rights, and others stressing economic and social rights.

The Challenge of Enforcement

Once the content of human rights obligations was enumerated in multilateral treaties, international attention shifted to monitoring their implementation and addressing violations. The policy question now facing the world is what practical steps can be taken to safeguard these rights (see APPLICATION: Human Rights Start in Small Places, Close to Home). Agreement has yet to be reached on the

AFP/Getty Images

What Constitutes a Human Right? How a state treated its own citizens was, until very recently, its own business under the rules of sovereignty in international law. Now the international community has defined humane treatment of people as a fundamental human right, and ninety-five countries have abolished the death penalty because they saw it as a violation of human rights. Other countries do not see capital punishment as a violation of human rights. Shown here are a group of alleged criminals who have been sentenced to death in China. According to Amnesty International, China, Iran, Iraq, Saudi Arabia, the United States, and Yemen accounted for the overwhelming majority of executions in 2009.

means that should be used to assist people suffering due to political turmoil or deliberate government policy. Guidelines on how to halt genocide and mass atrocities remain elusive. The issue is not whether there exists a compelling need to do something about populations suffering egregious violations of human rights, as the principle of Responsibility to Protect prescribes; the issue is about how to craft a just response, when any nonconsensual use of force will interfere in the domestic affairs of a sovereign state.

The rationale for intervening into the internal affairs of other states has been expressed by William Schulz, the executive director of the NGO Amnesty International USA. Political realists, he argues, "regard the pursuit of rights as an unnecessary, sometimes even a dangerous extravagance, often at odds with our national interest. What they seem rarely to garner is that in far more cases than they will allow, defending human rights is a prerequisite to *protecting* that interest." Human rights buttress political and economic freedom "which in turn tends to bring international trade and prosperity. And governments that treat their own people with tolerance and respect tend to treat their neighbors in the same way" (Schulz, 2001: 13–14).

The failure of the international community to take timely, decisive action in 1994 to stop the genocide in Rwanda prompted many people to ask whether states pick which cases they respond to based on cold calculations of national security interest. Those that do not significantly affect the interests of the permanent members of the UN Security Council, they fear, tend to be ignored. In the following passage, Mary Robinson, who served as the president of Ireland (1990–1997) and as UN High Commissioner for Human Rights (1997–2002), points out that the United Nations is more active in responding to alleged human rights abuses than most people realize.

> Since I was appointed United Nations High Commissioner for Human Rights ..., I have been continuously confronted by the challenge of how human rights can best be secured and defended. Most people know about the gross human rights violations that are all too common in our modern world ... but I would like to draw your attention today to less well-known forms of abuse that are all too prevalent. I refer to the countless individual communications received by my Office each day on behalf of people in detention, women who are victims of violence, children who have been abused and tortured, human rights defenders who are harassed, journalists who have been kidnapped, people who have disappeared, migrant workers who have been victimized, people who have been displaced, refugees and indigenous people who have been intimidated.

> These appeals for help not only come in ever-increasing numbers but also from almost all the countries of the world. Most of the communications are dealt with quietly and do not come to public attention. It can be difficult, therefore, for the public to appreciate the extent and geographic spread of human rights abuses ....

> I see my own challenge in this respect as being to ensure that these allegations are effectively investigated, to redress the wrongs suffered by the victims, and to bring the perpetrators to justice ... .

> ... Human rights should not be thought of as something for other people or other countries and not for your own country ... . Human rights are universal, and, unfortunately, so are human rights abuses. Eleanor Roosevelt, one of the chief architects of the Universal Declaration [of Human Rights], reminds us that "human rights start in small places, close to home" (Robinson, 2006: 284–285).

By underscoring the universality of human rights, Robinson counters the argument advanced by former Prime Minister Lee Kuan Yew of Singapore that the prevailing liberal interpretation of rights is not consistent with the culture and political traditions of Asia. Asian values, he contends, emphasize social cohesion and stability over individual freedom and liberty. For Robinson, the yearning for individual rights exists everywhere; it is not a uniquely Western phenomenon.

---

humanitarian intervention   the use of peacekeeping forces by foreign states or international organizations to protect endangered people from gross violations of their human rights.

Whereas the school of thought that Schulz exemplifies believes that timely, decisive international responses are obligatory when flagrant violations of human rights occur, **humanitarian intervention** is controversial. Global South leaders generally see it as a cover used by powerful states to justify unilateral military action. Like humanitarian intervention, the R2P principle has come under political fire for allegedly excusing infringements on the sovereignty of weak states. Recent hostilities between Russia and Georgia have heightened this criticism.

On August 7, 2008, military units of the Republic of Georgia swarmed into South Ossetia, a secessionist region that had been seeking to withdraw from Georgia and align itself with Russia. The following morning, Russian armored forces launched a counterattack, which compelled the Georgians to retreat and put Russia in control of parts of Georgia. Shortly thereafter, the Kremlin recognized the independence of South Ossetia and Abkhazia, another breakaway region of Georgia. In justifying Russia's actions, President Dmitry Medvedev

Pavel Rahman/AP Photo

Child Labor in a Global Market Children are among the most vulnerable members of society, and their human rights are often violated. Many are victims of human trafficking, ending up as soldiers or prostitutes. Many more are forced into hazardous jobs. Although some countries see child labor as exploitative and have laws prohibiting it, others do not. Here children heat and mix rubber in a Bangladesh factory, producing goods for export under dangerous conditions.

explained that Moscow had "privileged interests" in neighboring countries with which it shares "special historical relations." Russia could not idly stand by, added Foreign Minister Sergei Lavrov. The Georgians broke a ceasefire with the South Ossetians and endangered people in the area. Russian intervention, he asserted, was in accord with the principle of Responsibility to Protect.

Although Lavrov's assertion did not gain international traction, the episode illuminated the potential problem of great powers invoking R2P to legitimize coercive interference in the affairs of other states. Supporters of R2P responded to this worry by situating military intervention within a continuum of measures, emphasizing that it was only one of many possible actions that the international community could take to deal with human rights abuses. However, they never resolved the question of whether military force would be the right option (Bellamy, 2010). Because concerns for human rights have gained stature under international law and are being monitored more closely by IGOs and NGOs than ever before, we can expect debates about humanitarian intervention and R2P to continue, as long as states embrace an impermeable conception of sovereignty and people face threats to human rights.

The global community has expanded its legal protection of human rights significantly over the past fifty years. As Table 13.2 shows, a large number of

T A B L E 13.2   Major Conventions in the Development of International Human Rights

1948	Universal Declaration of Human Rights
1949	Convention on the Prevention and the Punishment of the Crime of Genocide
1950	Convention for the Suppression of the Traffic of Persons and the Exploitation of the Prostitution of Others
1951	Convention Relating to the Status of Refugees
1953	Convention on the Political Rights of Women
1959	Declaration of the Rights of the Child
1965	International Convention on the Elimination of All Forms of Racial Discrimination
1966	International Covenant on Civil and Political Rights
1966	International Covenant on Economic, Social, and Cultural Rights
1966	Optional Protocol to the International Covenant on Civil and Political Rights
1967	Declaration of Territorial Asylum
1969	Inter-American Convention on Human Rights
1973	Principles of International Co-Operation in the Punishment of War Crimes and Crimes against Humanity
1977	Protocols on Humanitarian Law for International Armed Conflicts and Noninternational Armed Conflicts
1979	Convention on the Elimination of All Forms of Discrimination Against Women
1981	Declaration on the Elimination of All Forms of Intolerance and of Discrimination Based on Religion or Belief
1984	Convention against Torture and Other Cruel, Inhuman, or Degrading Treatment or Punishment
1989	Second Optional Protocol to the International Covenant on Civil and Political Rights, Aiming at the Abolition of the Death Penalty
1989	Convention on the Rights of the Child
1990	International Convention on the Protection of the Rights of All Migrant Workers and members of Their Families
1991	Convention on the Prevention and Suppression of Genocide
1992	Declaration of Principles of International Law on Compensation to Refugees
1993	Vienna Convention on Human Rights
1993	Declaration on the Rights of Persons Belonging to National or Ethnic, Religious, or Linguistic Minorities
1993	Declaration on the Elimination of Violence against Women
1994	African Convention on Human and Peoples' Rights
2000	Convention Prohibiting Trafficking of Women and Children for Prostitution
2000	International Convention for the Suppression of the Financing of Terrorism
2002	Protocol to the Convention against Torture and Other Cruel, Inhuman or Degrading Treatment or Punishment
2006	Convention on the Rights of Persons with Disabilities

Note: The International Covenant on Civil and Political Rights, the International Covenant on Economic, Social, and Cultural Rights, and the Optional Protocol were all adopted in 1966 and entered into force in 1976.

conventions have been enacted that have steadily endowed individuals with rights—asserting that people must be treated as worthy of the freedom and dignity traditionally granted by international law to states and rulers. Promoting the rights and dignity of ordinary people around the world is a formidable challenge. Eleanor Roosevelt was a modern champion of this cosmopolitan ideal, and the energetic leadership she displayed was largely responsible for global acceptance in 1948 of the Universal Declaration of Human Rights. Her actions show that one person can make a difference in transforming world politics. When thinking about the human condition in the early twenty-first century, we can profit by the inspiration of her nightly prayer: "Save us from ourselves and show us a vision of a world made new."

CHAPTER SUMMARY

- Although some of humanity enjoys an unprecedented standard of living, a daunting amount of poverty and misery is evident throughout the world. The concept of human security expands the traditional notion of protecting the state from military threats to safeguarding individuals from such threats as poverty and environmental degradation.

- Communitarianism and cosmopolitanism hold different interpretations of human rights: the former anchor them in particularistic moral values held by political communities; the latter, in universalistic moral values that one has simply by being human.

- Women throughout the world continue to be disadvantaged relative to men in various ways.

- Roughly five percent of the world's population is composed of indigenous peoples. Many of them feel persecuted because their livelihoods and cultures are threatened by the governments of those states in which they reside; consequently, some have joined separatist movements to pursue self-determination, while others have tried to negotiate a measure of local self-governance.

- A combination of push and pull forces have propelled migration to the forefront of population dynamics. Migrants are pushed out of their homelands by war, famine, and human rights violations. They are pulled abroad by the hope of freedom and economic opportunity.

- Over the past fifty years, the United Nations has developed a detailed list of inherent, inalienable rights of all human beings. They can be grouped into five general categories: rights of the person, rights associated with the rule of law, political rights, economic and social rights, and rights of communities.

- Various international treaties and conventions have sought to protect human rights. However, agreement on the principles that should guide states on when humanitarian intervention is justifiable has proven elusive.

KEY TERMS

asylum

brain drain

communitarianism

cosmopolitanism

displaced people

genocide

human rights

human security

humanitarian
   intervention

indigenous peoples

refugees

Responsibility to
   Protect (R2P)

SUGGESTED READINGS

Amstutz, Mark R. *International Ethics*, 3rd edition. Lanham, MD: Rowman & Littlefield, 2008.

Beitz, Charles R. *The Idea of Human Rights*. New York: Oxford University Press, 2009.

Ishay, Micheline R. *The History of Human Rights: From Ancient Times to the Globalization Era*, 2nd edition. Berkeley: University of California Press, 2008.

Sen, Amartya. *The Idea of Justice*. Cambridge, MA: Belknap, 2009.

Simmons, Beth A. *Mobilizing Human Rights: International Law and Domestic Politics*. New York: Cambridge University Press, 2009.

CRITICAL THINKING QUESTIONS

At 1:00 AM on December 20, 1989, U.S. troops supported by stealth aircraft invaded Panama in what President George H. W. Bush called Operation Just Cause. The purpose of the operation was to capture General Manuel Noriega, a military dictator who had gained control over Panama six years earlier. During his time in power, Noriega repressed opposition movements, manipulated elections, and ordered the murder of dissident political leaders. Up to this point, his ruthless behavior had been overlooked because he had previously assisted the United States in its fight against communism in Central America. By 1987, however, Noriega's human rights abuses as well as his involvement in narcotics trafficking and money laundering led Bush's predecessor, Ronald Reagan, to impose economic sanctions on Panama.

Sanctions did little to weaken Noriega's regime. On December 16, 1989, following the murder of an unarmed U.S. Marine lieutenant by members of the Panama Defense Forces, the wounding of another American serviceman, and the arrest and brutal interrogation of a U.S. naval officer and his wife, Bush decided to remove Noriega by force. U.S. diplomats Thomas R. Pickering, speaking to the United Nations Security Council on December 20, and Luigi R. Einaudi, speaking to the Organization of American States (OAS) on December 22, justified the intervention by emphasizing America's responsibility to protect the Panamanian people from human rights abuses. Noriega, argued Pickering, "repeatedly obstructed the will of the Panamanian people." Panamanians, added Einaudi, were "sick of stolen elections, sick of military dictatorships, sick of narco-strongmen, and sick of the *likes of Manuel Noriega." Both diplomats insisted that Washington was supporting the will of the Panamanian people, not simply acting out of its own interests (*Panama: A Just Cause, *1989: 133).*

Moral appeals, such as those articulated by Pickering and Einaudi, can be powerful in foreign policy argumentation, swinging the weight of presumption in favor of intervention regardless of the real motives behind the decision to use force. Do you think that there was a moral imperative for the United States to take military action against the Noriega regime? Or do you think that the Bush administration masked its narrow political interests as expansive moral duties? Looking beyond this case to the larger question of international humanitarian engagement, who should have the responsibility to protect the victims of egregious human rights abuses? When is that responsibility acquired? What does it involve? How does the international community know when it is being appropriately discharged?

14

Population, Resources, and Global Environmental Politics

CHAPTER OUTLINE

Global Demographic Patterns

The Demographic Divide

World Population Prospects

Environmental Security and Sustainable Development

The Ecopolitics of Energy

APPLICATION: Cartels and Commodity Power

The Ecopolitics of the Atmosphere

The Ecopolitics of Land and Water

Future Environmental Policy Choices

CONTROVERSY: How Should the World's Problems Be Prioritized?

> Throughout history, humans have lived on the Earth's sustainable yield—the interest from its natural endowment. Now, however, we are consuming the endowment itself.
>
> LESTER BROWN
> PRESIDENT, EARTH POLICY INSTITUTE

According to the folk tales of Central Asia, centuries ago an adviser to a powerful king invented an intriguing game. It was played by moving pieces on a board that contained eight columns and eight rows of squares. The king was so delighted with the game that he offered to reward his adviser with gold and jewels. The adviser declined, protesting that he was a humble man with simple tastes. Rather than accept such a lavish reward, he asked that he be given a single grain of rice for the first square of his board game, two grains for the second square, twice that for the third, and so on, until each of the 64 squares had their complement of rice. The king quickly agreed to what he believed was a modest request. When the Master of the Royal Granary counted out the grains, the numbers began small enough (1, 2, 4, 8, 16, 32, 64, …), but before long, he realized the staggering numbers that would soon be involved. For the 64th square alone, 9,223,372,036,854,775,808 grains would be needed to meet the adviser's request. That would amount to roughly 153 billion tons of rice, enough to fill 31 million cargo ships full if each ship held approximately 5,000 tons (Dörner, 1996: 111). Of course, that would be merely the amount of rice on the last square of the board game. The next-to-the-last square would take half as much, only 4,611,686,018,427,387,904 grains, the square before it, 2,305,843,009,213,693,952 grains, and so on.

The story of the king's adviser is a fable that reminds us of the consequences of exponential growth. Under certain conditions, amazing configurations can develop over time. Ever since the Reverend Thomas Malthus proposed in 1798 that when unchecked, population increases in a geometric ratio (for example, 1 to 2, 2 to 4, 4 to 8) while subsistence increases in only an arithmetic ratio (1 to 2, 2 to 3, 3 to 4), demographers have speculated about the long-term consequences of rapid population growth. The Earth's population at the beginning of the twentieth century totaled 1.7 billion people; today, it has reached 6.8 billion. Every two years, it grows roughly by the size of Russia, with over 200,000 people added to the world total every day. Will these kinds of increases in the world's population continue in the decades ahead? If so, what impact would they have on the planet's **carrying capacity**—the Earth's ability to support and sustain life? Will population growth outstrip natural resources? Can enough food be produced to feed the billions who will be born in the future? These concerns have attracted the attention of various scholars and policy makers who are studying how current demographic and environmental trends may affect the global future.

The **tragedy of the commons** is a metaphor that highlights the potential impact of human behavior on the planet's resources and its delicately balanced ecological systems. First articulated in 1833 by English political economist William Foster Lloyd, the metaphor was later popularized by ecologist Garrett Hardin. It depicts a medieval English village, where the village green was common pasture on which all villagers could graze their cattle. Freedom of access to the commons was a cherished value. Sharing the common grazing area worked well as long as usage by individuals (and their cattle) didn't reduce the land's usefulness to everyone else. Assuming the villagers were driven by the profit motive and no laws existed to restrain their greed, herders had an incentive to increase their stock as much as possible. In the short run, the addition of one more animal would produce a personal gain whose feeding costs would be borne by everyone. But if everyone increased their stock of cattle, in the long

carrying capacity the maximum biomass that can be supported by a given territory.

tragedy of the commons a metaphor, widely used to explain the impact of human behavior on ecological systems, that explains how rational self-interested behavior by individuals may have a destructive collective impact.

run the village green would be destroyed by overgrazing. The unrestrained pursuit of individual self-interest, concluded Hardin (1968), yields ruin for all.

This chapter explores the impact of humanity on the natural environment and how it will most likely affect the global future. It opens with an examination of prevailing trends in demography and ecology, and then considers the ways that these trends interact, often creating global environmental problems that can be exacerbated when, as in the tragedy of the commons metaphor, self-interested actors pursue personal, short-run gains without anticipating the side effects and long-term repercussions of their behavior.

GLOBAL DEMOGRAPHIC PATTERNS

How many people can the Earth support? This question is almost as old as recorded history. According to demographer Joel Cohen (2005), cuneiform tablets from three and a half millennia ago show that the Babylonians worried that the world already had too many people. Over the last half-century alone, numerous estimates have been made, with some analysts warning about overpopulation and others concluding that there was little reason to fret about continued population growth. In order to get a better understanding of this issue, it is helpful to trace the global trends in population growth, giving particular attention to changes in fertility and mortality rates (see Figure 14.1).

The story of population growth is told in its statistics: Today, 158 more people are born every minute than die (WPDS, 2010: 2). The annual rate of global population growth has increased from less than 1 percent in 1900 to a peak of 2.2 percent in 1964. It has since decreased to 1.2 percent. Despite this drop in rate, the absolute number of people *added* each year has been significant, growing from 16 million in 1900 to a peak of 88 million in 1988, and thereafter falling to a current increase of about 83 million annually. The Earth is certain to have many more people by the mid-twenty-first century, well beyond the 6.8 billion already on the planet. Yet, the feared "population explosion" once believed certain is now unlikely.

If the probability of explosive population growth overwhelming the planet's carrying capacity has decreased, why then do population issues remain so controversial in world politics? We can begin to answer that question by exploring how population dynamics are affecting countries in the Global North, East, and South in different ways.

The Demographic Divide

Population growth rates are not the same throughout the world. They are much higher in the developing Global South countries than in the emerging economies of the Global East and the wealthy countries in the Global North, a trend that is expected to continue. This "demographic divide," as projected in Figure 14.2, suggests why population dynamics have important political and economic ramifications.

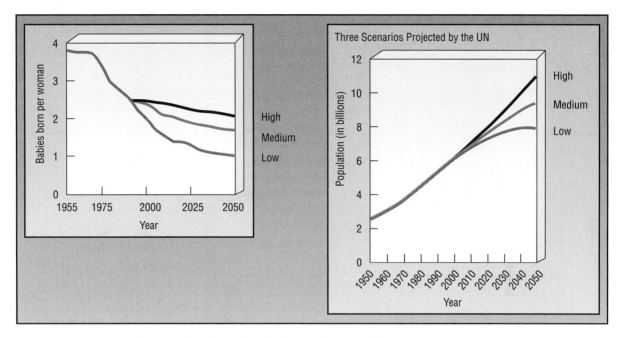

FIGURE 14.1 World Population Growth Projections to the Year 2050

Between 1.2 and 2.4 billion additional people will be living on Earth by the middle of the twenty-first century, depending on how fast fertility rates fall (see figure on the left) and life spans increase. The figure on the right sketches three potential scenarios for the future, showing that by 2050 world population is expected to be between 8 billion (low variant) and 11 billion (high variant), with the medium variant producing 9.3 billion.

SOURCE: United Nations Population Division.

Global population cannot be expected to stabilize until it falls below replacement-level fertility in the developing countries. Today, the worldwide average number of children born to a woman during her lifetime—the total **fertility rate**—is 2.5. However, projections for the entire globe overlook the different rates for rich and poor countries. Roughly 86 percent of population growth worldwide is centered in the developing Global South, already home to eight of every ten people on the planet. It is the result of new births in Africa, Latin America, and parts of Asia, where the fertility rate averaged 3.1 children for each mother (and 4.5 for the least-developed countries). In contrast, the wealthy, developed Global North's fertility rate has actually declined to 1.7 children for each woman, which is below **replacement-level fertility**. Fertility rates around the world must decrease to an average of 2.1 children for each woman in order to fall to replacement level. Yet, throughout much of the Global South, the preferred family size remains far in excess of the replacement level, especially in the poorest countries. Fertility rates in Niger, Mali, and Uganda, for example, are 7.4, 6.6, and 6.5, respectively (WPDS, 2010: 6).

The developing countries' high fertility rates have important economic consequences. Many of the problems in the North–South dispute can be traced to

fertility rate   the average number of children born to women during their reproductive years.

replacement-level fertility   one couple replacing themselves with two children, so that a country's population will remain stable if this rate prevails. The rate is 2.1 rather than 2.0 because some females die before reaching child-bearing years.

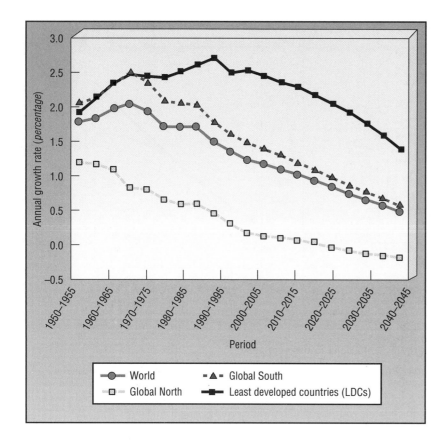

FIGURE   14.2 The North–South Population Divide

The UN projects a slowing of population growth rates that will lead to a reduction in world population. Nearly all the population growth in the twenty-first century will occur in the Global South. Assuming continuing declines in fertility, the population in Global South countries is expected to rise to 8.2 billion in 2050.

SOURCE: United Nations Population Division.

disparities in income and economic growth that are directly linked to differentials in population growth rates. A brief look at these dynamics can help us comprehend the demographic divide between the world's haves and the have-nots.

Population Momentum.   The surge in the Global South's population in the twentieth century is easily explained as a combination of high birthrates and rapidly falling death rates. But to make sense of the population surge projected throughout the twenty-first century—when birthrates throughout the world will decline—we have to understand the force of population momentum, the continued growth of population for decades into the future because of the large number of women now entering their childbearing years. Like the inertia of a descending airliner when it first touches down on the runway, population growth simply cannot be halted even with an immediate, full application of the brakes. Instead, many years of high fertility mean that more women will be entering their reproductive years than in the past. Not until the size of the generation giving birth to children is no larger than the generation among which deaths are occurring will the population growth come to a halt. Because of population momentum, the number of people is expected to triple by 2050 in Niger and Uganda, and more than double in Angola, Burkina Faso, Democratic Republic of Congo, Guinea-Bissau, Liberia, Malawi, and Tanzania.

Sub-Saharan Africa and Western Europe illustrate the force of population momentum. Africa's demographic profile is one of rapid population growth, as each new age group (cohort) contains more people than the one before it. Thus, even if individual African couples choose to have fewer children than their parents, Africa's population will continue to grow because there are now more men and women of childbearing age than ever before. Europe's population profile is the opposite, as recent cohorts have been smaller than preceding ones. In fact, Europe has dropped below replacement-level fertility to become a "declining" population, described by low birthrates and the increased longevity of a growing number of people who survive middle age.

As the Global North generally ages, much of the Global South continues to mirror the Sub-Saharan African profile: Because each cohort is typically larger than the one before it, the number of young men and women entering their reproductive years will also continue to grow. The resulting differences in these demographic momentums will produce quite different population profiles in the developed and the developing worlds. The example of Germany illuminates the contrast. Germany has at present a fertility rate of 1.3 and a large number of people who survive middle age; in the year 2030, people over sixty-five will account for almost half the adult population (compared with one-fifth in 2001). The net result will be that Germany's total population of 82.7 million will shrink to about 70 million, and the number of working-age people will fall about 25 percent. The figures are similar for most other developed countries. Fertility rates in Japan, Switzerland, and the Netherlands are 1.4, 1.5, and 1.7, respectively (WPDS, 2010: 8–9). Thus, the population divide will grow; Global North countries will become older and smaller. By 2050, for example, the size of Japan's population will decline 25 percent, with almost 36 percent of the population composed of people age sixty-five or older, compared to 23 percent in 2009. If the current retirement and demographic trends continue, Japan at mid-century will have only 1.5 workers for every pensioner. The only Global North country that is an exception to this pattern is the United States, with a fertility rate roughly at replacement level.

Together with differentials in fertility rates, population momentum will alter the rank order of the world's most populous states. At the onset of World War I, the number of people living in Europe, the United States, and Canada totaled approximately one-third of the world's inhabitants. By 2050, this figure is expected to fall to 12 percent. China, the most populous country in the twentieth and early twenty-first centuries, currently has a population of 1.3 billion, with 270 million under the age of 15. Over the next few decades, it will drop into second place behind India, which now has 1.2 billion people and 372 million under the age of 15. Even more striking, the number of people earning middle-class incomes in developing countries will be larger than the combined population of Europe, Japan, and the United States (Goldstone, 2009: 32–34).

By the middle of the century, America will be the only Global North country among the world's twenty most-populous states.

The Demographic Transition. High rates of population growth place an enormous burden on a country's economy. The theory of **demographic transition** attempts to explain when population growth in the Global South will slow, easing the economic strain on developing countries.

Based on the historical experience of Europe and North America, the theory proposes that countries pass through a series of stages as they modernize. The first stage, traditional society, is characterized by a combination of high birth and death rates, which produce relatively stable populations. Birth rates are high because children provide labor that contributes to family income; death rates, because disease is unchecked by effective, widespread health programs. As societies modernize, they enter a second stage: Birth rates remain high, but improvements in nutrition, medical techniques, and public health facilities reduce death rates, which lead to increased population growth. Once people begin to live longer lives, couples expect more of their children to reach adulthood, and thus they can achieve their desired number of surviving children with fewer births. In this third stage, birth rates decline along with death rates, yielding little or no population growth. Recent research, however, suggests that at very high levels of economic development, births may begin increasing as women in wealthy countries have children later in life (Myrskyla, Kohler, and Billari, 2009).

Demographic transition is now under way virtually everywhere in the world but at much different rates in different countries and regions. Whereas in the Global North and parts of the Global East, birth and death rates have converged at a low level, in most of the Global South, birth rates have remained high but death rates have declined rapidly due, in part, to more effective public health programs. If these trends continue, Global North and some Global East countries will possess increasingly aged populations.

According to the UN Population Division, the world's median age is 29 today, and is expected to reach 38 by the middle of the century. The number of people over the age of sixty has tripled during the past half century, and, at the present rate, in fifty years the number of people older than sixty will again triple. By 2050, the elderly would comprise a third of humanity, outnumbering the world's youths, with two older persons for every child. Furthermore, those eighty years or over are expected to increase even faster.

This unprecedented graying of the world might create economic problems of crisis proportions. With the percentage of taxpaying workers shrinking, the budgets of national governments could be overwhelmed by attempts to provide retirement and health benefits for the elderly. In addition, dwindling birthrates, lengthening life spans, and early retirements could spell trouble for a worker-hungry Global North in need of immigrants to supply labor. Similar issues face the Global East. The number of pensioners in China is expected to climb from the equivalent of 12 percent of the labor force to 30 percent during the next four decades, giving the country more elderly dependents than children

demographic transition an explanation of population changes that highlights the role of birth and death rates in moving countries from stable to rapidly increasing and finally to declining populations.

(*Economist*, May 9, 2009: 102; June 27, 2009 special report: 14). South Korea is a more extreme case. Although its population is projected to decline by 9 percent in the next thirty years, the number of South Koreans aged 60 and older will likely soar by 150 percent (Goldstone, 2009: 34). All this suggests that the global future will be a mix of aging, slowly declining populations in industrialized countries and young, rapidly growing populations in developing countries.

Urbanization.   When interpreting demographic projections, it is also important to take into account population density. Some states are crowded and others are not. For example, Singapore is one of the most congested, with 18,189 people for each square mile; Mongolia is one of the most wide open, with only 4 people per square mile. This difference represents another kind of demographic divide: urban versus rural (see Map 14.1). Today, five mega-cities have populations over 15 million: Mumbai (21.1 million), Mexico City (19.5 million), New Delhi (17 million), Shanghai (15.8 million), and Calcutta, or Kolkata (15.6 million). Another fifteen mega-cities have between 10 and 15 million inhabitants. By 2050, demographers predict that 70 percent of the world's population will live in cities. Already, 97 percent of Belgians reside in urban areas, as do 93 percent of Venezuelans, and 90 percent of Argentineans. During the next thirty years, more than 80 percent of the planet's urban growth will occur in Africa and Asia, currently home to eighteen of the world's fastest-growing urban areas (*Foreign Policy*, January/February, 2008: 42). This surge in urbanization is likely to aggravate existing environmental problems, straining supplies of energy and

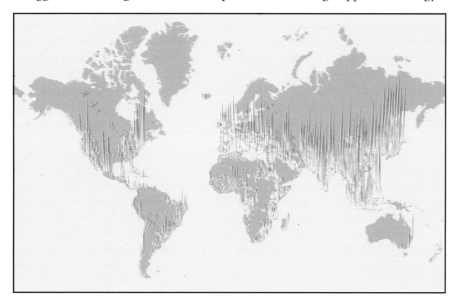

M A P 14.1 Global Population Density

Whereas the share of the world's population living in urban areas was nearly 30 percent in 1950, today it stands above 50 percent. This map shows the clustering of people in the world's urban areas.

SOURCE: *Atlantic Monthly*, October 2005: 48–49.

resources while complicating efforts to control pollution and provide adequate sanitation. It may also magnify crime and civil strife if employment opportunities and social services cannot keep pace with the needs of a swelling urban population.

World Population Prospects

Population projections can be misleading. Natural or human-made events may overturn the conditions that produced today's trends. For example, current projections could be invalidated overnight by a nuclear war or a massive terrorist act with biological weapons. Other threats also could produce a **population implosion**—a severe reduction in world population. We take a brief look at two possible sources of implosion: **pandemics** and famine.

The Threat of Contagious Diseases. On a global level, life expectancy at birth has increased steadily since the beginning of the twentieth century, climbing from around 30 years in 1900 to 69 by 2009, and projected by the UN Population Division to reach 76 by 2050. However, this trend could be reversed if globally transmittable diseases cut into the extension of life spans made possible by improvements in health care, nutrition, water quality, and public sanitation. For example, drug-resistant strains of tuberculosis (TB) have developed recently, and they can be passed from one country to the next by a sneeze on an international flight. Preventing the outbreak of a highly contagious disease within any region of the world is virtually impossible in an age of globalization.

The grim possibility that virulent disease will reduce the world's population is evident from the spread of the human immunodeficiency virus (HIV) that causes AIDS (acquired immune deficiency syndrome). According to data from the World Health Organization, AIDS has killed over 25 million people worldwide since 1981. About 33 million people are now living with HIV and, on average, every day almost 5,500 die of AIDS. Antiretroviral treatment can help manage the disease, but patients in the Global South typically lack access to treatment.

Most health experts agree that at the current rate, some countries could lose one-fifth of their gross domestic product due to the effects of AIDS on their workforce. Sub-Saharan Africa has suffered the most, accounting for two-thirds of all HIV cases, with only 11 percent receiving treatment with antiretroviral drugs. Women in the southern part of the continent have been hit especially hard: The percentage of females between the ages of 15 and 49 with HIV/AIDS in Swaziland, Botswana, and Lesotho are 32.1, 28.9, and 27.1, respectively (WPDS, 2010: 11). Eastern Europe and Central Asia also face serious problems. Because infectious diseases respect no borders, nearly 30 million people worldwide could die from AIDS over the next two decades.

The Threat of Famine. At the same time that medical experts worry that death rates due to tuberculosis, AIDS, Ebola, and other diseases could take a horrific toll on humanity, agricultural specialists shudder at the possibility of food shortages. Famine already haunts some regions of the world, most notably East

---

population implosion a rapid reduction of population that reverses a previous trend toward progressively larger populations.

pandemic a disease that spreads throughout one or more continents.

Africa. If the Earth's population grows to over 9 billion, will food production keep pace? According to some estimates, by 2050 the combination of world population growth and rising incomes in Global East countries will increase demand for agricultural goods by 70 percent (*Economist*, November 21, 2009: 14). Whereas pessimists warn of mass starvation, optimists claim these fears are unwarranted, arguing that wider uses of drip irrigation, no-till farming, and technological breakthroughs in the field of genetic engineering will revolutionize farming and feed future generations.

Genetically engineered crops are created to develop a desired trait, such as herbicide tolerance or increased oil content. Unlike crop varieties developed through traditional plant breeding, **transgenic crops** often contain genes from unrelated species—of plant, animal, bacteria, or other origin—with which the crop could not reproduce naturally. Despite lingering consumer unease, genetically engineered crops are gaining ground. The United States accounts for three-fourths of global production, with Argentina, Brazil, Canada, and China included among the world's major producers. As of 2010, twenty-five countries have planted transgenic crops and another thirty-two have approved importing them for food or animal feed (*Time*, June 28, 2010: 2). Furthermore, as the risk of plant and animal extinction escalates, some scientists have tried to replicate certain species through cloning—an approach that has met with considerable opposition from groups who feel that tampering with life is immoral.

transgenic crops new crops with improved characteristics created artificially through genetic engineering, which combines genes from species that would not naturally interbreed.

Isabelle Rouvillois/Green Peace International

Genetic Engineering in Agriculture A Greenpeace activist in France protests against genetically modified corn. Supporters of genetically modified (GM) foods tout their resistance to disease and their tolerance of drought and cold weather. Opponents criticize their potential to cause allergic reactions, cross-breed with wild populations, and harm beneficial insects.

Geneticists could revolutionize agriculture and transform the capability of the planet to feed the world's growing population. However, the increasing availability of commercially produced and globally marketed, genetically engineered agricultural products is a growing controversy. Should scientists manipulate nature for human needs? Are gene-spliced plants and hormone-treated meat safe? Do crops created through genetic engineering contain allergens that may cause serious allergic reactions and endanger public health?

Mounting a sustained effort to address the consequences of world population growth remains a formidable challenge. An interdependent and rapidly globalizing world promises that none will be immune to population trends, especially those that strain the supply of natural resources on which we depend. Although population dynamics are not the only factor that affect the planet's ecology, demographic variables such as the size, composition, and distribution of the world's population exert a significant impact on the global environment.

ENVIRONMENTAL SECURITY AND SUSTAINABLE DEVELOPMENT

When U.S. astronauts first viewed the Earth from the Apollo spacecraft, they described how the clouds and continents flowed into one another without regard to the political boundaries humans had drawn across the planet. Improvement in space technology since the 1960s has enabled the world to see a different set of images—of atmospheric pollution that encircles the globe, of violent storms pounding coastlines with relentless fury, of massive holes in the ozone shield that protects humans from dangerous ultraviolet rays, and of vanishing forests and widening deserts.

To explore the linkage between population pressures and global environmental challenges, we need to examine *ecopolitics*—how political actors influence perceptions of, and policy responses to, managing the impact of human behavior on their environments. By taking an ecopolitical perspective, we can broaden our conception of security, pushing it to include processes that may imperil our ecological niche on the planet.

sustainable development improving the quality of life by reconciling economic needs with environmental protection.

One of the key concepts embraced by those who look at security from an ecopolitical perspective is **sustainable development**. The level of international attention given to environmental issues increased significantly in 1972, when the United Nations convened the first UN Conference of the Human Environment in Stockholm. Conferences have since been held on a wide range of environmental topics, with scores of treaties negotiated and new international agencies put into place to promote cooperation and monitor environmental developments. The concept of sustainable development entered into popular discourse during the 1980s and today enjoys widespread support among governments and a broad range of NGOs that are active in shaping the global environmental agenda. According to the 1987 report of the World Commission on Environment and Development—popularly known as the "Brundtland Commission" after the Norwegian prime minister who chaired it—a "sustainable society" is one that "meets the needs of the present without compromising the ability of future generations to meet their own needs."

Another milestone in the movement to foster sustainable development was the Earth Summit, which took place in Rio de Janeiro in 1992. Formally known as the UN Conference on Environment and Development, the meeting brought together more than 150 states, 1,400 nongovernmental organizations, and 8,000 journalists. Prior to the Earth Summit, environment and economic development had been treated separately—and often regarded as being in conflict with each other. In Rio, the concept of sustainability galvanized a simultaneous treatment of environmental and development issues, and paved the way for the UN World Summit on Sustainable Development that concluded in early September 2002 in Johannesburg. These and other international conferences have stressed that what happens anywhere ultimately affects conditions everywhere, and therefore protecting the global environment is a security issue.

Sustainability cannot be realized without dramatic changes in the social, economic, and political practices of an increasingly interconnected world. But is that possible? The metaphor of the tragedy of the commons provides little basis for optimism, whether applied to individuals or states. When rational, self-interested actors strive for relative gains in the absence of strong international regulation, everyone's well-being may plummet.

To better understand the multiple tensions that global environmental problems pose in an anarchical world, we turn next to consider three interrelated clusters of issues on the global ecopolitical agenda: (1) oil and energy, (2) climate change and ozone depletion, and (3) biodiversity and deforestation. These issues illustrate the problems and pitfalls that states and nonstate actors (IGOs and NGOs) face as they seek environmental security and sustainable development.

The Ecopolitics of Energy

In April 1990, the average price for a barrel of internationally traded crude oil was less than $15. Five months later—stimulated by Iraq's invasion of the tiny oil sheikdom of Kuwait—it rose to more than $40. For the third time in less than two decades, the world suffered an "oil shock" when the price paid for the most widely used commercial energy source skyrocketed.

The 1990 Persian Gulf War was precipitated by Iraq's attempt to subjugate Kuwait and acquire its oil. Pointing to America's enormous thirst for petroleum, some critics of U.S. President George W. Bush maintained that his decision to go to war against Iraq thirteen years later was influenced by economic considerations involving oil. While the president's supporters vigorously denied this charge, ensuring access to the region's oil is nonetheless critical to the economic fortunes of the Global North, because almost all the oil that is inexpensive to extract lies within the borders of a handful of countries around the Persian Gulf.

Global Patterns of Oil Consumption. The importance of oil to the Global North generally and the United States in particular is evident from their disproportionate share of energy consumption. The average person living in Europe uses more than twice as much energy as someone in the Global South, while the United States uses more than six times as much. China's total energy consumption is now roughly equivalent to that of the United States, although the typical American still uses four and a half times as much energy as the average person in China (*Economist*, June 12, 2010: 106).

Oil consumption has been spiraling upward for decades. The International Energy Agency predicts that by 2030 the world will be using 50 percent more oil than today and warns that $3 trillion will need to be spent over the next two decades to meet the soaring global demand.

The industrialization of many emerging Global South economies has contributed to the growing demand, and the global shift to oil has been propelled by the aggressive production and promotion of a small group of multinational corporations (MNCs). Their operations encompass every aspect of the business, from exploration to the retail sale of products at their gas stations. For decades, their search for, production of, and marketing of low-cost oil was largely unhindered. Concessions from the oil-rich Middle East were easy to obtain, which reduced incentives for developing technologies for alternative energy sources.

cartel an organization of the producers of a commodity that seeks to regulate the pricing and production of that commodity to increase revenue.

Eventually, many of the world's major oil-producing states were able to wrest control from the oil companies, and they formed a **cartel** known as the Organization of Petroleum Exporting Countries (OPEC) in an effort to maximize profits. Because the resources OPEC controls cannot be easily replaced, it has been able to use oil as an instrument of coercive diplomacy (see APPLICATION: Cartels and Commodity Power). By cutting production to limit world supplies, OPEC can trigger sharp price increases to exert pressure on countries that rely on oil as their primary source of energy.

Is Energy Security an Elusive Goal? The question of oil supplies has great importance to world politics, because petroleum is not a renewable resource and for every two barrels pumped out of the ground, the oil companies discover less than one new barrel. Production in the United States peaked thirty years ago, Russia's peaked in 1987, and North Sea production appears to have peaked. Meanwhile, demand for oil keeps rising.

With somewhere between 1.2 and 3.7 trillion barrels of proven reserves that can supply the global market (depending on which estimates one accepts), the era of cheap, abundant oil is ending. One of the major problems the world faces with regard to these reserves is that they are concentrated in a small number of countries, many of which are politically unstable. Because OPEC members, who control approximately half of the world's oil reserves, are drawing down their reserves at below the average global rate, it seems almost inevitable that OPEC's share of the world oil market will grow. This means that OPEC is critical to global oil supply, the Middle East is critical to OPEC, and countries that depend on oil imports from this volatile source are highly vulnerable to disruptions. By 2025, world energy consumption is likely to double, leading petroleum companies to undertake deepwater drilling projects, which can plumb new offshore fields that are not controlled by OPEC countries but pose serious environmental risks, as the calamitous 2010 oil spill in the Gulf of Mexico illustrated.

APPLICATION   Cartels and Commodity Power

Little more than a century ago, fuelwood was the world's primary energy source. As the mechanical revolution altered the nature of transportation, work, and leisure, coal began replacing fuelwood. New technological developments, particularly the internal combustion engine, then spurred the shift away from coal to oil. OPEC's emergence as a successful oil cartel in the 1970s derived from several factors. One was its ability to take control of production and pricing policies from multinational oil companies. A second factor was the growing dependence of much of the world on Middle Eastern oil. The third factor that contributed to OPEC's success was the absence of inexpensive energy alternatives in the face of growing worldwide demand for oil.

As OPEC began to realize the potential leverage that it had over oil-consuming countries, the possibility of using oil as a political weapon to affect the outcome of the unsettled Arab–Israeli dispute intrigued the organization's Arab members. Their common desire to defeat Israel was a principal element uniting them. Thus, when the Yom Kippur War broke out on October 6, 1973, the stage for using the oil weapon was set. In the following passage, Henry Kissinger, who served as secretary of state in the Nixon and Ford administrations, describes how OPEC's use of commodity power had an enormous psychological impact on policy makers in Global North countries.

> No crisis in the second half of the twentieth century fell on a world less prepared than the one triggered by the quadrupling of oil prices in the fall of 1973. Within the space of three months the global political and economic system found itself faced with a series of stark challenges threatening its very foundations.
> ... It was the Middle East War of 1973 that gave the oil-producing countries the pretext for unleashing their new bargaining power to its full extent. On October 16, 1973, OPEC raised the price of oil by 70 percent. ... On October 17 the Arab OPEC oil ministers ... agreed to reduce OPEC production by 5 percent in order to sustain the

> higher oil price. On October 18, Saudi Arabia ... cut its production by 10 percent. On October 20, to protest the American airlift to Israel, Saudi Arabia announced a total embargo of oil exports to the United States and also to the Netherlands, which was deemed too supportive of Israel.
> The combined impact of these decisions precipitated an energy crisis lasting well over a decade. Because the principal Western policymakers lacked sufficient understanding of the oil market, their initial reactions made matters worse. Regulatory blunders at home exacerbated short-term shortages. In addition, the urgency and frequency of ... appeals to remove the embargo probably convinced the oil producers that they had discovered a marvelous new lever for extorting concessions.
> ... Soon other dangers loomed. Spurred by OPEC's success, producers of other commodities began exploring the prospects of organizing cartels of their own. ... Never before had nations so weak militarily ... been able to impose such strains on the international system (Kissinger, 1999: 664, 666–667).

In Kissinger's (1982: 873) opinion, "The true impact of the embargo was psychological." Policy makers in oil-consuming countries feared further production cutbacks were on the horizon, triggering "a wave of panic buying by Europe and Japan, which constricted supplies and drove prices up even more." In the aftermath of this "oil shock," several lessons were drawn about cartels and commodity power. One was that the oil weapon could be used again. The inability of the major multinational oil companies to control the situation, as they had done for decades, was a second. Finally, with American oil production peaking two years before the onset of the Yom Kippur War, the events showed that even the world's foremost power had become vulnerable to foreign economic pressures as it lost energy self-sufficiency and imported over a third of the oil that it consumed.

Owing to the vulnerability of oil-consuming Global North countries to economic pressure from oil-producing states, efforts are underway to transform the global energy system. Humans only became dependent on nonrenewable finite stocks of fossilized fuel when Europeans began mining coal in the seventeenth century. Looking back from a century or so in the future, today's hydrocarbon-based economy may be seen as only a brief interlude in history. The primary energy resources in the years ahead may be solar, wind, geothermal, biomass, and other renewable power sources.

The impact of such a global transformation would be huge, overturning the past 130-year pattern in world energy development and consumption. A number of energy analysts and industry officials suggest that in the process we can expect a gradual shift from petroleum to natural gas, nuclear power, and oil derived from unconventional sources (such as tar sands and shale) before relying heavily on renewable sources of energy. These analysts and officials picture a radically changing twenty-first century. They urge immediate planning for a new global "eco-economy," one that alters how we heat and light our buildings and how we travel and transport our goods. Many people remain skeptical of their vision, but if alternatives to oil become technologically and economically viable, their development would reduce dependence on oil from politically turbulent regions of the world.

In a world in which population growth and industrialization in Global South and East countries means an increasing global demand for energy, how states address their future energy needs will affect the global environment. As biologist E.O. Wilson describes it, we are entering a "bottleneck," a period of time that will put enormous stress on the planet's ecology and natural resources. To illustrate his concerns, let us begin by considering the problem of protecting airsheds and other common-pool resources.

The Ecopolitics of the Atmosphere

For years, scientists have warned that global warming—the gradual rise in world temperature—would cause destructive changes in climatological patterns, resulting in rising sea levels and powerful storms. Evidence of global warming abounds. Consider the world's glaciers: Only 27 glaciers are left of the 150 estimated to have existed in Glacier National Park in the United States; the Himalayan glaciers, which provide water to seven of Asia's major river systems, have been receding at an average rate of 75 feet per year; Andean glacial runoff, which feeds the rivers that provide 70 percent of Peru's hydroelectric power, is expected to fall significantly after 2020; the snowcap on the summit of 19,340-foot Mount Kilimanjaro in Africa is predicted to disappear in just over a decade; and workers now use reflective sheets to cover parts of the Gurschen glacier above the Swiss ski resort of Andermatt to protect it from melting during the summer. The scientific consensus today is that (1) the Earth is warming, (2) human activities are the principal cause, (3) it is affecting the planet's climate, and (4) the impact is substantial and threatening (see Oreskes, 2004). Where climatologists disagree is over how rapidly things are changing and whether the process is now self-sustaining. Concerned that the planet may be approaching a "tipping point," where small increases in temperature could suddenly cause catastrophic effects, many scientists have called on the international community to reduce emissions of carbon dioxide and other gases, which they blame for global warming.

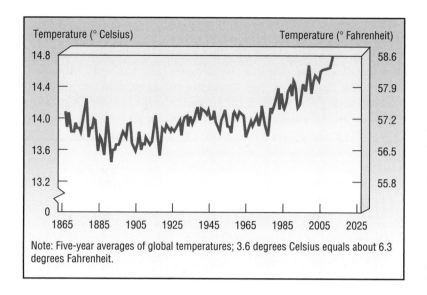

Temperature (° Celsius)   Temperature (° Fahrenheit)

Note: Five-year averages of global temperatures; 3.6 degrees Celsius equals about 6.3 degrees Fahrenheit.

FIGURE 14.3 Rising Average Global Temperatures since 1867

The World Meteorological Organization (WMO) monitors average global surface temperatures at thousands of sites around the world. Their data reveal that temperatures have been rising significantly since the mid-1970s, with the 1996–2009 period being the warmest since measurements began.

SOURCE: Intergovernmental Panel on Climate Change.

Climate Change. Scientists believe that the gradual rise in the Earth's temperature—especially evident since the late eighteenth century when the invention of power-driven machinery produced the Industrial Revolution—is caused by an increase in human-made gases that alter the atmosphere's insulating effects. The gas molecules, primarily carbon dioxide (CO_2) and chlorofluorocarbons (CFCs), trap heat emitted from the Earth that would otherwise escape into outer space. As these gases are released into the atmosphere, they create a **greenhouse effect** that has caused the global temperature to rise. As shown in Figure 14.3, the temperature on the Earth's surface has increased nearly a half degree since 1950. According to the U.S. National Climatic Data Center, March 2010 was the warmest March ever recorded worldwide, fourteen of the hottest years since record-keeping began over a century ago have occurred since 1987, with the six hottest occurring since 1997. NASA scientist Jim Hansen (2006: 12) suggests one way to visualize how the odds of having unusually hot summers have increased in recent years is to imagine a die with some of its six sides colored red to represent blistering weather. Between 1951 and 1980, two sides would have been red to approximate the odds of a very hot summer. Today, four sides would be red.

The Earth's average surface temperature has climbed 1.4 degrees Fahrenheit since the early twentieth century and is projected to increase anywhere from 2.7 to 10.7 degrees Fahrenheit over the next 100 years if preventive action is not taken. Although CO_2 is the principal greenhouse gas, concentrations of methane in the atmosphere are growing more rapidly. Methane gas emissions arise from livestock populations, rice cultivation, and the production and transportation of natural gas. To many scientists' alarm, the largest concentrations of methane are not in the atmosphere, but are locked in ice and permafrost, which raises the probability that warming will cause more methane to be released into the atmosphere, thereby accelerating the process because of methane's strong warming potential.

greenhouse effect the phenomenon producing planetary warming when gases released by burning fossil fuels act as a blanket in the atmosphere, thereby increasing temperatures.

While some people believe that the rise in global temperature is primarily due to cyclical changes that the world has experienced for tens of thousands of years, this view has not been supported by scientific research. Human action, not natural cycles, appears to be the dominant source of global warming. Moreover, global temperature will continue to rise throughout the remainder of this century even if greenhouse gases are curbed tomorrow because the CO_2 being emitted now will stay in the atmosphere long into the future.

Thus, the world has already entered a period of climatic instability likely to cause widespread economic, social, and environmental dislocation over the twenty-first century. The effects of continued temperature rises could be both dramatic and devastating. Africa and Asia are likely to be the hardest-hit, but no continent will be spared.

- Sea levels could rise up to two feet, mostly because of melting glaciers and the expansion of water as it warms up. That will inundate vast areas of low-lying coastal land, including major cities, river deltas, and islands throughout the world. More than 100 million people would be put at risk by rising seas and floods. To highlight the problem, in October 2009, government officials from the Republic of Maldives donned scuba gear and held a cabinet meeting underwater. Their country is composed of over 1,000 islands in the Indian Ocean, 80 percent of which are less than 3.3 feet above sea level.

- Winters will get warmer and warm-weather hot spells more frequent. Droughts and wildfires would be more severe. Because water evaporates more easily in a warmer world, drought-prone regions would become dryer. The International Organization for Migration warns that there will be over 200 million climate-change migrants by 2050.

- As oceans heat, hurricanes, which draw their energy from warm oceans, would become even stronger. For every one degree Celsius rise in Atlantic Ocean surface temperature, rainfall from tropical storms increase 6 to 18 percent and wind speed increases up to 8 percent (*Newsweek*, July 7, 2008: 53).

- Entire ecosystems would vanish from the planet, and a hotter Earth would drive some plants to higher latitudes and altitudes and require farmers to irrigate and change their crops and agriculture practices. Some species, such as polar bears and walruses, could lose their habitat and become extinct. Others, such as the pine beetle, would be able to survive the winter and combine forces with the subsequent generations of beetles to devastate coniferous forests.

- The combination of flooding and droughts would cause tropical diseases such as malaria and dengue fever to flourish in previously temperate regions and at elevations that were formerly too cold for their insect carriers.

- As oceans absorb carbon dioxide, they will become more acidic. By the beginning of the next century, they could be 150 percent more acidic than they were at the onset of the Industrial Revolution, which would endanger plankton and shellfish, thereby reducing the food supply for larger sea creatures.

- Crop production in high-latitude regions would increase as the growing season lengthened. Formerly icebound shipping lanes would become navigable, and previously inaccessible resources beneath the Arctic Ocean would be easier to obtain. With expectations of perhaps one-quarter of the world's remaining oil and gas reserves under the polar icecap, Canada, Russia, Denmark, Norway, and the United States have begun jockeying for position in the region.

Not everyone contributes to global warming at the same rate. As a group, industrialized Global North states are the principal source, accounting for over half of global CO_2 emissions. Individually, the United States and China emit more greenhouse gases into the atmosphere than anyone else, although China's per capita emissions are less than one-fifth of America's (*Economist*, December 5, 2009 special report: 4). The International Energy Agency forecasts that the rise in greenhouse gases from China alone by 2030 will nearly equal the increase from the entire industrial world. India, which currently produces roughly one-quarter of China's emissions, could see its total rise 70 percent.

Coal, which China relies on for three-fourths of its energy, is a major source of atmospheric sulfur and nitrogen oxides. These pollutants return to Earth, typically after traveling long distances, in the form of **acid rain**, which adds to the acidification of lakes, the corrosion of materials and structures, and the impairment of ecosystems. Acid rain is a serious problem in much of China. Because the oxides that cause it are also transboundary pollutants, China's domestic energy policies have become an irritant in its relations with its neighbors, particularly South Korea and Japan. Nonetheless, China plans to increase the amount of coal it burns, and other Asian states are following in its path, including India, which, like China, has sizable coal deposits.

acid rain   precipitation that has been made acidic through contact with sulfur dioxide and nitrogen oxides.

To combat the danger of accelerating global warming, the 1997 Kyoto Protocol to the UN Framework Convention on Climate Change (UNFCCC) called on industrial countries to reduce their greenhouse gas emissions on average 5.2 percent below 1990 levels by the year 2012. Developing countries were not required to reduce emissions. The Protocol entered into force in 2005, making its emissions targets binding on those that ratified it. The United States was the only major industrial power that did not ratify the Protocol. Though signed by the Clinton administration, it was not submitted for ratification because of resistance by various members of the Senate, who complained about the negative impact that achieving the emissions-reduction targets set by the Protocol might have on the U.S. economy.

In December 2007, officials from nearly 190 countries met in Bali, Indonesia, under the auspices of the UNFCCC to launch negotiations on an agreement to supersede the Kyoto Protocol. Little of substance was achieved during the contentious two-week meeting, however. Two years later, representatives from 193 countries attending the 2009 Copenhagen climate summit also failed to agree on legally binding reductions in greenhouse gas emissions, although many of the participating nations put forward voluntary targets. Believing that a smaller group of states might make more progress, some thirty countries responsible for

90 percent of greenhouse gas emissions have explored meeting outside of the UNFCCC structure in what has been called a "minilateralist" approach to negotiating environmental agreements.

Ozone Depletion.   The story of climate change is similar to states' efforts to cope with depletion of the atmosphere's protective **ozone layer**. In this case, however, an international regime has emerged, progressively strengthened by mounting scientific evidence that environmental damage was directly caused by human activity.

ozone layer   the protective layer of the upper atmosphere over the Earth's surface that shields the planet from the sun's harmful impact on living organisms on the planet.

Ozone is a pollutant in the lower atmosphere, but in the upper atmosphere, it provides the Earth with a critical layer of protection against the sun's harmful ultraviolet radiation. Scientists have discovered a marked depletion of the ozone layer—most notably an "ozone hole" over Antarctica that has grown larger than the continental United States, and they have linked the thinning of the layer to chlorofluorocarbons (CFCs). Depletion of the ozone layer exposes humans to health hazards of various sorts, particularly skin cancer, and threatens other forms of marine and terrestrial life.

Scientists began to link CFCs to ozone depletion in the early 1970s. This research motivated the United Nations Environment Program (UNEP) to seek some form of regulatory action. The 1987 landmark Montreal Protocol on Substances That Deplete the Ozone Layer treaty was signed by 146 countries and led to a 90 percent reduction since the late 1980s in global atmospheric concentrations of CFCs. Although production of CFCs in the Global North declined sharply, production in the Global South continued, and increased demand for refrigerators, air conditioners, and other products using CFCs is offsetting the gains realized by stopping production in the Global North. Developed countries agreed to provide aid to help the developing countries adopt CFC alternatives but have failed to provide all of the resources promised. Without this support, many in the Global South may not be able to construct plants to produce CFC alternatives. Meanwhile, an illegal trade in both virgin and recycled CFCs has emerged, threatening to further undermine the positive effects of the ozone regime.

Having clear, persuasive scientific evidence, many believe, is what made the ozone initiative successful. Other factors contributing to its success included precise targets and timetables, verification mechanisms, the existence of economically viable substitutes for CFCs, and a mechanism for financial and technology transfers to assist Global South countries in assuming specific obligations. Can the ozone regime serve as a model for breakthroughs on other global environmental issues? To explore this question, we turn finally to the problems facing the world's biological heritage.

The Ecopolitics of Land and Water

biodiversity   the variety of life on Earth.

Forests are critical in preserving the Earth's **biodiversity** and to protecting the atmosphere and land resources. For these reasons they have been a rising ecological issue on the global agenda. Some rules have emerged to guide international behavior in the preservation of biodiversity, but issues concerning forests have proven much more difficult to address.

Deforestation.   Destruction of the world's forests contributes to climate change through global warming and threatens the planet's biodiversity and genetic heritage. Currently, about 30 percent of Earth's total landmass is classified as forests, with three-fourths located in the Global South. Destruction of tropical rain forests in such places as Brazil, Indonesia, and Malaysia is a matter of special concern, because much of the world's genetic heritage is found there.

The representatives sent to the 1992 Earth Summit hoped to secure an easy victory on a statement of principle for global forest conservation. But opposition quickly developed to the notion that the global interest makes all countries responsible for protecting national forests. The Global South—led by Malaysia, a principal exporter of tropical wood products—objected to the view that the world's forests were a "common heritage of mankind," fearing that accepting this view would enable the Global North to interfere with the local management of their tropical forest resources. In the end, the Earth Summit backed away from the goal of establishing international guidelines for trade in "sustainably managed" forest products. The situation today remains largely unchanged, even though the International Tropical Timber Organization (ITTO) exists as a forum for addressing the issue of trade in timber products and the 2007 Bali conference agreed to establish a program to study how tropical deforestation could be reduced.

Desertification.   Meanwhile, high population growth rates, industrialization, and urbanization increase pressure to clear forests for farming and to divert rivers for irrigating land that might not be well suited for cultivation. This has led to **desertification**, which makes an increasing portion of the Earth's landmass useless for agricultural productivity or wildlife habitats. The Aral Sea in Central Asia exemplifies the problem. Because water from the Amu Darya and Syr Darya Rivers was diverted to irrigate cotton fields, this once-vast body of water has shrunk by 75 percent. Villages that had survived on fishing are now forty miles from the coastline and salt from the exposed seabed has blown across nearby pastures and croplands, causing ecological damage.

desertification the creation of deserts due to soil erosion, over-farming, and deforestation, which converts cropland to non-productive, arid sand.

Freshwater supplies are being depleted across the planet. Only 2.5 percent of Earth's water is fresh, and two-thirds of that is frozen in polar ice caps and glaciers. Water demand is growing rapidly, and groundwater in many aquifers around the world is being depleted faster than the natural recharge rate. Australia is already suffering from its worst drought on record. By 2025, the global demand for water is expected to exceed supply by 56 percent, leaving 1.8 billion people in a condition of severe water scarcity (Kingsolver, 2010: 56; Finnegan, 2002: 44). Twenty-five years later, fully two-thirds of the world's population could be living in regions with chronic, widespread water shortages (Cetron and Davies, 2008: 63–64). The supply of fresh water can be increased through desalination, but it is expensive, takes enormous amounts of energy, and can result in brine discharges that damage the environment. With roughly 40 percent

From Farmland to Dust Bowl
Worldwide, each year some 26 billion tons of topsoil are lost due to erosion with more than 10 million acres of farmland becoming deserts. The 1994 UN Convention to Combat Desertification (CCD) has sought to stop the spread of deserts, which now cover 2 million square miles.

of the world's population depending on water from river systems that are shared by at least two states, access to water will likely become a source of international conflict in the decades ahead. Three billion people rely on water from the Himalayan glaciers that flows through the Ganges, the Indus, the Brahmaputra, the Mekong, the Yellow, and the Yangtze Rivers and their tributaries. Upstream diversion can easily trigger disputes with downstream states. In Africa, the Niger, Nile, Volta, and Zambezi basins are all considered potential flashpoints.

Together with water shortages, soil degradation has removed billions of acres of the Earth's surface from productive farming. Erosion is a problem both in densely populated developing countries and in the more highly developed regions of mechanized industrial agriculture. Human beings employ 35 percent of the planet's land surface for crops and pastures. It is estimated that the addition of another 2 billion people by mid-century will result in as much as 5 million square kilometers of additional land being cleared for food production. Concomitant increases in the use of industrial fertilizers would significantly increase the flows of nitrogen and phosphorus in agricultural runoff, degrading riparian areas, producing toxic algae blooms in coastal waters, and harming aquatic life (Foley, 2010: 55–56).

Biodiversity.   A term that refers to the Earth's variety of life, biodiversity encompasses three basic levels of organization in living systems: genetic diversity, species diversity, and ecosystem diversity. Until recently, public attention has been focused almost exclusively on preserving species diversity, including old-growth forests, tall grass prairies, wetlands, coastal habitats, and coral reefs.

Forests, especially tropical forests, are important to preserving biodiversity because they are home to countless species of animals and plants, many of them still unknown. Scientists believe that the global habitat contains between 8 and 10 million species. Of these, only about 1.5 million have been named, and most of them are in the temperate regions of North America, Europe, Russia, and Australia. Destruction of tropical forests, where two-thirds to three-fourths of all species are believed to live, thus threatens the destruction of much of the world's undiscovered biological diversity and genetic heritage.

Many experts worry that the planet is headed toward accelerating species loss. According to the International Union for Conservation of Nature, more than one-third of the 47,000 plant and animal species they track face extinction. Thirty percent of amphibians, 28 percent of reptiles, 18 percent of mammals, and 10 percent of birds are endangered (Moyer, 2010: 78–79). Three-quarters of all marine fish species are at risk of falling below sustainable levels. Some international efforts to protect spawning and young fish have helped. Iceland, for example, has enjoyed success with scientifically based quotas on commercial species that are strictly enforced. Unfortunately, the ineffective EU common fisheries policy is widely viewed as more typical of international efforts, with quotas that disregard scientific evidence, pervasive cheating, and lax enforcement of violations (*Economist*, January 3, 2009: 9, 13–17).

German Environment Minister Sigmar Gabriel estimates that as many as 150 species become extinct every day. Some are lost due to competition from non-native species entering their habitats through cross-border transportation facilitated by globalization; others die out from poaching, unregulated hunting, and overfishing; and still others become extinct as a result of clearing land for housing, roads, and industries. The latter is particularly troubling given the fact that clearing of tropical rain forests with slash-and-burn techniques to make room for farms and ranches is doubly destructive. On the one hand, fewer trees are able to remove CO_2 from the atmosphere during photosynthesis when forests are cut down, and, on the other, forests are burned for clearing, the amount of CO_2 discharged into the atmosphere increases.

Biodiversity's distributional characteristics exacerbate North–South tensions. In 2006, 80 percent of the fish caught for human consumption came from Global South waters, with the vast majority ultimately arriving on dinner tables in the Global North (Pauly, 2009: 36–37). Moreover, because so much of the Earth's biological heritage is concentrated in the tropics, the Global South has a growing concern about protecting its interest in the face of the recent claims that the genetic character of the many species of plants and animals should be considered a part of the global commons and therefore available for commercial use by all, for their medical benefit. Pharmaceutical companies in particular have tried to lay claim to Global South resources. They actively explore plants, microbes, and other living organisms in tropical forests for possible use in prescription drugs. Ten of the world's twenty-five top-selling drugs are derived from "natural biological sources," and roughly 25 percent of the prescription drugs used in the United States have active ingredients extracted or derived from plants. At the 1992 Earth Summit in Rio de Janeiro, a convention on biodiversity was adopted that called on signatories to protect habitats and preserve endangered species. In 2004, the International Treaty on Plant Genetic Resources for Food and Agriculture went into effect after seven years of negotiations. Among other things, it created the Global Crop Diversity Trust to coordinate the approximately 1,500 gene banks scattered throughout more than 100 countries that together now store over 600,000 genetically distinct seed samples. Still, much more needs to be done. As ecologists Stuart Pimn and Clinton Jenkins (2005: 66) remind us, we do not live in Jurassic Park: Once extinct species are gone, nothing can bring them back.

FUTURE ENVIRONMENTAL POLICY CHOICES

We began our exploration of world politics in Chapter 1 by focusing our attention on the interaction of autonomous, territorial states that have no higher authority governing their behavior. Since the birth of the modern state system some three and a half centuries ago, world population has increased eightfold, fossil fuel consumption has risen from nearly nothing to more than 7 billion metric tons of coal equivalent annually, and the use of nonfuel minerals has skyrocketed. Demographic pressures combined with resource-intensive industrialization have placed enormous stress on the global environment. The Earth's atmosphere and oceans are becoming polluted; its natural resources, depleted.

Some of the world's environmental problems are localized and can be addressed through unilateral action. Yet, as we have seen in this chapter, many others span the boundaries between territorial states and require multilateral solutions. The political world may be a checkerboard of sovereign states, but the natural world is a seamless web.

Recognizing that Earth's ecosystem transcends national jurisdictions, the international community has taken various steps to address many environmental threats. The number of international environmental treaties has grown from 84 in the nineteenth century to a total of 2,869 by the start of 2009; however, many ecologists fear that still not enough is being done. Part of the reason is that states differ over global priorities (see CONTROVERSY: How Should the World's Problems Be Prioritized?). In addition, because damage caused by environmental degradation accumulates slowly, is unequally distributed, and remedies remain expensive, many states hesitate to join environmental-preservation efforts unless they are sure that others will act as well. The Earth's atmosphere and oceans are common-pool resources: They do not belong to any single state, and everyone can benefit from their use regardless of whether they help pay for the costs of their preservation. As a result, various states are tempted to be free riders, negotiating treaties that minimize their responsibilities but maximize the obligations of others.

CONTROVERSY   How Should the World's Problems Be Prioritized?

Many of the world's humanitarian and environmental problems are projected to become more severe in the decades ahead. Yet, even if the international community decides not to follow a business-as-usual course and chooses instead to tackle pressing world problems, which ones should it take on, in what order? Arresting global climate change, preserving biodiversity, combating communicable diseases, providing clean water, alleviating poverty, fighting malnutrition and hunger, and restoring forests, fisheries, and other over-exploited renewable resources are just a few of the challenges that humanity faces.

Whereas there are numerous global problems, financial resources to deal with them are limited. When it is impossible to address every major need at once, priorities must be set. But how should they be established? Faced with multiple competing demands and complicated tradeoffs, how should the international community determine which problems warrant the most attention?

One approach focuses on cost-benefit ratios. Bjørn Lomborg, a Danish political scientist known for his skepticism about many of the ecological threats emphasized by environmental scientists, adopted this method when he convened a panel of eminent economists in Copenhagen and asked them how they would allocate a hypothetical $50 billion to advance global welfare. The exercise resulted in a consensus on spending funds on projects that would yield high benefits for low costs. For example, the panelists strongly supported spending money on such things as promoting condom use to prevent the spread of HIV and AIDS, distributing vitamin and mineral supplements to reduce malnutrition, and providing chemically treated mosquito netting for beds to reduce the incidence of malaria. Conversely, steps to avert climate change, such as carbon taxes and mandatory targets for lowering greenhouse gas emissions, were not given high priorities, allegedly because of their enormous expense relative to distant and uncertain benefits.

This so-called "Copenhagen Consensus" has been criticized on several grounds. First, critics complained that cost-benefit analysis was an inappropriate method for setting global priorities. Although it may be a valuable instrument for making narrow, technical choices between different ways of achieving an agreed-on goal (such as whether to build a road along proposed route A or proposed route B), they denied that it could determine what goal should receive the highest priority (such as whether to spend funds on building a road or hiring more teachers for the local school). Second, by giving the panel members a small sum to allocate, the exercise was biased in favor of low-cost projects, like distributing vitamin A supplements to prevent blindness. Finally, critics charged that the panelists did not receive sufficient background information on the state of scientific knowledge in each problem area they attempted to prioritize, which, in particular, led them to overlook existing, affordable technologies that can help in climate stabilization. Operating from the assumption that curbing global climate change was a costly, uncertain venture, they discounted the planet's ecological future in favor of immediate health and nutrition concerns.

Setting priorities is important. But how should it be done? Does cost-benefit analysis offer the international community a viable method for establishing global funding priorities? Or are there too many difficulties in calculating and comparing costs and benefits for it to be a useful tool for setting priorities among the world's many problems? What do you think? How should we go about prioritizing the world's pressing humanitarian and environmental challenges?

Through numerous forums organized by the United Nations, concern has been repeatedly voiced about the need to protect the environment. However, pledges about safeguarding the planet's ecology in the face of rising world population have not significantly improved the global environment. Despite expressing concern about the global future, many national leaders have failed to make firm commitments to sustainable development that might reconcile the conflicts between economic growth and environmental protection.

Differences between rich and poor countries will continue to spark controversy about such issues as the transfer of resources and technology needed to deal with climate change, biodiversity, and a host of other environmental problems. We stand at a critical juncture. The path humanity takes will affect global welfare far into the future. Yet many people remain complacent; ominous predictions have been made before and have been proven wrong. Moreover, numerous environmental risks are only visible in the long term, while countermeasures are costly in the short term. But evidence of serious ecological problems is getting harder to ignore, and because the stakes are so high, all the pieces in the puzzle—population, natural resources, technology, and preferences in lifestyles—must be worked on simultaneously, through coordinated, multilateral efforts. "All things are connected," Chief Seattle of the Suquamish tribe is said to have told the U.S. government in 1854. "Man did not weave the web of life; he is merely a strand in it. Whatever he does to the web, he does to himself."

CHAPTER SUMMARY

- The global environment is a system of delicately and tightly integrated components that together impose limits on the planet's carrying capacity. If population growth exceeds that carrying capacity, it could result in lost economic opportunities, environmental degradation, and domestic strife. However, analysts disagree over the magnitude of the Earth's carrying capacity.

- The planet has become a demographically divided world, with Global North countries experiencing low or declining growth and Global South countries experiencing high levels of growth. Population growth in the Global South will create pressures toward outward movement, and the aging of the industrial societies of the Global North will encourage them to search for new sources of labor. These forces will place migration at the center of national political agendas.

- As trends in births, deaths, and migration unfold worldwide, they will promote significant change in world politics, aggravating some existing problems as valuable resources become increasingly scarce, and creating new challenges as the natural environment experiences greater strain.

- Rapid increases in the rate of energy usage in general and petroleum in particular are primarily post–World War II phenomena. The impact of oil price and production policies on the international political economy derives from the uneven distribution of the demand and supply of oil.

- International efforts to address the problems of global warming and the depletion of the atmosphere's protective ozone layer have yielded mixed results. Attempts to deal with climate change remain confined to voluntary restraints. In contrast, an international regime has emerged to restrict the use of ozone-depleting chemicals.

- Deforestation is a global phenomenon, but its rate is much higher in the Global South than in the Global North. While some norms have emerged to guide states in preserving biodiversity, the world's forests remain at risk of destruction through commercial exploitation and agricultural expansion.

■ Differences between the countries of the Global North and South over worldwide ecopolitical issues will continue to spark controversy in the global future. The controversy arises in part from clashing views over the responsibility for causing and solving the environmental problems facing the world today.

KEY TERMS

acid rain	fertility rate	replacement-level fertility
biodiversity	greenhouse effect	
carrying capacity	ozone layer	sustainable development
cartel	pandemic	tragedy of the commons
demographic transition	population implosion	transgenic crops
desertification		

SUGGESTED READINGS

Axelrod, Regina S., Stacey D. Vandeven, and David Leonard Downie (eds.). *The Global Environment: Institutions, Law and Policy*, 3rd edition. Washington, DC: CQ Press, 2011.

Chasek, Pamela, David L. Downie, and Janet Welsh Brown, *Global Environmental Politics*, 5th edition. Boulder, CO: Westview, 2010.

Conca, Ken, and Geoffrey D. Dabelko (eds.). *Green Planet Blues: Four Decades of Global Environmental Politics*, 4th edition. Boulder, CO: Westview, 2010.

Klare, Michael T. *Rising Powers, Shrinking Planet: The New Geopolitics of Energy*. New York: Metropolitan Books, 2008.

O'Neill, Kate. *The Environment and International Relations*. New York: Cambridge University Press, 2009.

CRITICAL THINKING QUESTIONS

Many people assume that states with shared preferences will coalesce and readily cooperate to advance their collective interests. Yet, this doesn't always happen in global environmental politics. Virtually all states have expressed a preference to arrest climate change, but many have failed to limit greenhouse gas emissions that contribute to global warming. Among the biggest roadblocks to reaching an agreement on emissions cuts is the principle of "common but differential responsibilities." According to this principle, climate change is a common concern of everyone, but because the industrialization of Global North countries originally caused the problem, they are responsible for making the initial emission cuts. Opponents of this principle claim that it hurts the economies of highly industrialized countries by imposing costs on them while exempting competitors from the developing world (such as China and India) that emit a growing amount of greenhouse gases.

Despite the failure of the 2009 Copenhagen climate summit to achieve a binding follow-on agreement to the 1997 Kyoto Protocol, which obligated industrialized Global North countries to make specific reductions in greenhouse gas emissions, negotiations continue. If you were one of the negotiators trying to forge such an agreement, how would you get the consent of Global North, East, and South countries? How would you deal with the principle of "common but differential responsibilities"? Should industrialized countries shoulder the primary responsibility for making deep emissions cuts? Or should the next round of reductions be tied to the efficiency of a country's industry, or perhaps to the size of its population or economy? Does the 1987 Montreal Protocol on ozone depletion offer any clues on how to overcome the political obstacles to an agreement on combating climate change?

Alternative World Futures

Most conjectures about the global future are based on some extrapolation from earlier events and experiences. We generally speculate about future prospects based on our understanding of prevailing trends. What makes this difficult is the sheer complexity of world politics. Some trends are linear, others change direction; some trends intersect, others diverge over time; some trends amplify one another, others dampen their joint impact. Our challenge in deciphering the meaning of these diverse trends is two-fold: (1) distinguish between those that are transient versus those that are likely to have a significant impact on world politics; and (2) project the configuration of the most salient trends rather than become preoccupied with any single trend in isolation. As U.S. Secretary of State Hillary Clinton explained in a recent interview, "you try to keep your eye on the long-term trend lines because what is neither urgent nor important today might become one or the other by next year or the year after" (*Newsweek*, January 4, 2010: 43).

How will the configuration of major trends in world politics today influence the global future? Will previous efforts to construct world order be relevant in the years ahead, or will the approaches of the past be rejected as new issues arise on the global agenda? When your great-grandchildren look back as adults on what happened during the early twenty-first century, what will they applaud and what will they disparage?

Part V presents a set of thought-provoking questions about the prospects for the twenty-first century. When thinking about the issues raised by these questions, ask yourself how they might be addressed to create a more peaceful and just global future.

15

Prospects for a
New World Order

CHAPTER OUTLINE

The person who does not worry about the future will shortly
have worries about the present.
CHINESE PROVERB

Long before the first Europeans came to North America, the indigenous
nations of the continent were engaged in sustained interaction. Commerce
and cultural exchanges, as well as rivalries and military clashes, had been taking
place for centuries.

When the English, French, and Dutch first traveled through what today is upstate New York, they encountered the Iroquoian-speaking Hodenosaunee, or "People of the Longhouse." Although once mired in internecine warfare, the five Iroquois nations—the Mohawks, Oneidas, Onondagas, Cayugas, and Senecas—put their differences aside and formed the Great League of Peace. Under the terms of this confederation, the individual nations maintained control over their own internal affairs but regularly met in a grand council to reach consensus on policy proposals for dealing with issues of common concern (Calloway, 1999: 44–48). Known as skilled diplomats and formidable warriors, the Hodenosaunee were recognized in a 1987 U.S. Senate resolution "for their demonstrated enlightened, democratic principles of Government and their example of a free association of independent Indian nations."

According to Hodenosaunee Faith Keeper, Chief Oren Lyons, one of the principles that guided decision making within the Great League of Peace was a concern for the "seventh generation yet unborn" (Cornish, 2004: 217). Leaders participating in the League's grand council were expected to be men of vision who made decisions with the future in mind. Because the seventh generation would not arrive for approximately 200 years, no leader would meet its members; nevertheless, council decisions could affect their lives. Consequently, the pressing issues of the day were examined in the light of what impact any action might have on the security and welfare of those people coming ahead.

In contrast to the farsightedness of the Hodenosaunee, the original inhabitants of Easter Island, a remote patch of land 2,300 miles off the coast of Chile, showed little appreciation for the future. Although they once lived among the largest species of palm trees in the world, the Easter Islanders eventually cut down all the palms in what has been described as among the most extreme cases of forest destruction in the world. Without the giant palms, the diet of the islanders suffered: Land birds disappeared, crop yields declined due to soil erosion, wild fruit withered in the hot sun, and fishing became limited to shallow waters because timber was no longer available to build seagoing canoes. Deforestation also meant the loss of fronds for making thatched goods and bark for manufacturing cloth. By overexploiting their natural resources, primarily so chiefs from competitive clans could quarry, transport, and erect larger stone monuments than their rivals, the Easter Islanders bequeathed a legacy of malnutrition and fratricidal conflict to their heirs (Diamond, 2005: 79–119).

The contrasting stories of the Hodenosaunee and the Easter Islanders encourage us to reflect on the conditions that generations yet unborn will inherit as a result of decisions made today. What will our legacy be? Will we bequeath to them a world that we would like to inhabit? Chapter 15 draws on the information presented in earlier chapters about prevailing integrative and disintegrative trends to frame a series of questions about the global future. How these questions ultimately are answered will shape world politics throughout the remainder of the twenty-first century.

THE GLOBAL PREDICAMENT: QUESTIONS
FOR A TURBULENT WORLD

Throughout this book, we have argued that world politics is shaped by recurring patterns. Under certain conditions, certain types of international actors respond the same way to the same kinds of stimuli. Yet, there are exceptions. Sometimes, similar actors in similar situations make different decisions. Thus, despite the existence of regularities in world politics, social scientists cannot draw on a body of uniform, deterministic laws to predict the global future precisely. Instead, they make probabilistic forecasts about what is likely to happen, other things being equal (J.D. Singer, 2000: 12–13).

Another factor that makes predictions difficult is the role of happenstance in world politics. History is replete with what Aristotle called *accidental conjunctions*—situations where things come together by chance. Consider, for example, the outbreak of World War I. Recall from Chapter 4 that one of the proximate causes of the war was Austrian archduke Franz Ferdinand's assassination in Sarajevo on June 28, 1914. Earlier that day, several would-be assassins had failed to find an opportunity to kill the archduke and apparently gave up in frustration. When Franz Ferdinand's motorcade made a wrong turn in route to visit patients in a city hospital, it stopped briefly in front of a café where Gavrilo Princip, one of the frustrated assassins, coincidentally had gone to get something to eat. Astonished to find the archduke's open-air car just five feet away, Princip fired two shots, killing him and his wife. Given the political climate in Europe at the time, if Franz Ferdinand had not been assassinated, something else might have precipitated the war. But as political scientist Stuart Bremer (2000: 35) asks, "Who can say whether a different triggering event, a day, a month, or a year later, would have led to the same chain of events that produced World War I?" Each unique event sets different forces in motion, with consequences that ripple outward in myriad directions.

Numerous possible futures lie ahead: Some are desirable; others, frightening. Although we cannot predict with certainty which one will materialize, we can narrow the range of possibilities by forecasting how current trends will probably develop and how steps might be taken to channel the course of events toward a global future that we prefer. As illustrated by the example of the Hodenosaunee, thinking in the future tense does not demand prophecy or divination; rather, it requires anticipating how today's actions will most likely affect generations yet unborn. In other words, it is an approach to inquiry that uses forecasts of alternative futures to improve policy decisions in the present.

What follows is a series of questions designed to help you think about the future of world politics. Each question is based on information presented in previous chapters. When pondering the long-term implications of these questions, we encourage you to (1) imagine what conceivable global futures are possible, (2) estimate which are the most probable, and (3) consider what policies would be helpful in bringing about the one you find preferable. Although these questions do not exhaust the concerns that are likely to emerge in the years ahead, they provide a way to look over the horizon and construct scenarios about

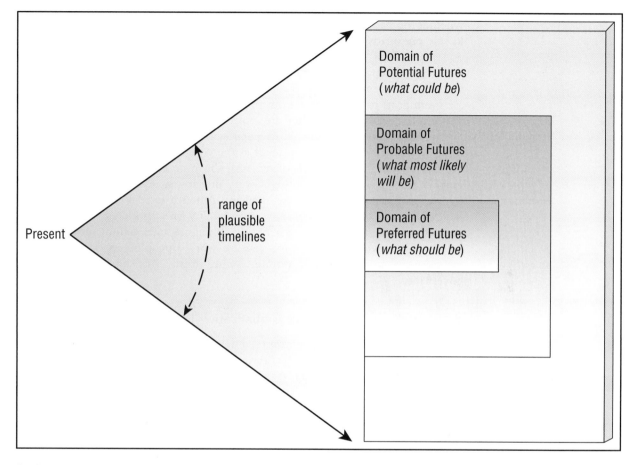

FIGURE 15.1 Forecasting Alternative World Futures

Social scientists frequently construct scenarios that describe what the global future could be, what it is likely to be, and what they believe it should be. These descriptions range from "business-as-usual" scenarios based on simple extrapolations from current conditions to various "wild card" scenarios predicated on sharp discontinuities between the present and the future. Scenario-building helps social scientists clarify their assumptions about global trends and encourages them to consider the long-range consequences of policy decisions made in response to those trends.

alternative global futures. A **scenario** is a logical, compelling story that traces a timeline of events from the present to some point in the future (see Figure 15.1). How you respond to these questions will suggest which scenarios you find germane for exploring the global future.

scenario a narrative description that shows how some hypothetical future state of affairs might evolve out of the present one.

Will the State Remain the Primary Actor in World Politics?

The sovereign, territorial state has been the lead actor on the world stage for nearly four centuries. In some respects, it is still flourishing because many people look to the state as a source of security, welfare, and identity. Yet, numerous states are failing to fulfill these traditional purposes, leading scholars to ask whether the nation-state will remain capable of addressing issues once considered its sole prerogative. With national boundaries becoming increasingly porous and policy problems transcending political frontiers, the managerial capabilities of states have been severely strained, regardless of form of government. Auguste Comte, a nineteenth-century French sociologist, argued that human beings create institutions to deal with serious problems. When they are no longer able to perform this vital function, they are replaced by other institutions. Today, as the Westphalian state seems unable to cope with many transnational problems, is there another unit that will replace it as the central actor on the world stage? Is the nation-state becoming obsolete? Will the pace of international integration quicken outside of Europe as the century progresses, leading to the emergence of "regional states" in Africa, Asia, or Latin America to replace the nation-state? Will grassroots NGOs assume more responsibility for responding to transnational problems through global policy networks. If nation-states cannot meet the challenges of the twenty-first century, can the world's people expect a new global architecture to crystallize around some form of supranational global governance?

Is Economic Globalization Irreversible?

Globalization refers to the increasing interconnectedness among societies. It is not a new phenomenon. Two centuries ago, for example, the German philosopher Johann Gottfried von Herder was amazed by the growth of international interdependence in his day. Inventions like the steam engine seemed to be shrinking the world.

Modern technology has reduced geography's constraints on global interaction even further, allowing people to exchange goods and ideas with speed that would have been unimaginable to those living in the eighteenth century. Although the dramatic decline in worldwide communication and transportation costs has stimulated the economic side of globalization, political globalization lags behind (Stiglitz, 2006). Everyone on the planet is now more closely connected than ever before but on a shaky institutional foundation that remains unprepared to manage the sweeping changes brought on by an expanding global marketplace. As distinctions between what is domestic and what is foreign have become increasingly blurred in the economic arena, multilateral political cooperation among the world's culturally diverse nations has not kept pace. Indeed, some analysts expect political friction to intensify as Asian firms expand in number and reach, giving globalization a non-Western hue.

Can economic globalization be an engine for unity and progress without organized global governance? From one perspective, an awareness of the common destiny of all, alongside the declining ability of many sovereign states to cope with global problems through national means, will energize efforts to put aside political squabbles. Conflict, according to this reasoning, will recede, as states find themselves unable to disentangle themselves from the many economic linkages that bind them together. The emergency financial summit conference held in Washington, D.C., on November 15, 2008, exemplified this vision of the global future. Attended by the leaders of nearly two dozen countries, the meeting culminated with a vow to cooperate closely in reforming international regulatory rules and financial institutions. Drawing attention to how severe financial problems in one part of the world can quickly engulf other regions, Brazilian President Luiz Inácio Lula da Silva warned "No country is safe." Global economic crises require a multilateral response.

From another perspective, however, economic globalization will breed enmity, not amity. Because the world economy is projected to grow unevenly over the next few decades, globalization may generate bitter conflicts between winners and losers. Moreover, as the center of gravity of the world economy shifts from the North Atlantic toward Asia, many of these conflicts could involve the world's most powerful states. Without effective international political institutions to mitigate these wrenching economic changes, analysts from this school of thought expect the intricate but fragile tapestry of global economic ties to unravel (Saul, 2005).

Are Ecopolitical Challenges Reordering the Global Agenda?

What goals should states pursue? In earlier times, the answer was easy: The state should provide for defense against external aggression, preserve the nation's values, and promote the welfare of its citizens. Political leaders followed a largely realist script, putting their national interests ahead of wider global interests. This meant competing with other states for power, position, and prestige. Building multilateral institutions that could address transnational problems was secondary—to be considered only after national security was solidified by acquiring military might and political clout.

Most leaders have similar aims today, but their quest for national self-advantage can carry prohibitively high costs. Many of the troubles they face cannot be solved unilaterally. Climate change, the economic fallout from globalization, and the growth of the world's population have expanded the issues that states confront. In the words of columnist Thomas Friedman (2008), the world is becoming "hot, flat, and crowded," and it will take concerted action to resolve the problems arising from these conditions.

Although important steps have been taken to reduce infant mortality and increase literacy, per capita income, and life expectancy around the world, several ecopolitical challenges cast a shadow over the global future. Even with a decline in fertility rate, the number of inhabitants on Earth will continue to grow due to population momentum, with most of the growth occurring in the poorest countries of the Global South, which least able to cope with a surge in population. The expected 40 percent increase in the world's inhabitants by mid-century will strain the planet's resources as the demand for water, food, energy, and nonfuel minerals soars. Additional demand will come from the rise in economic activity that accompanies the narrowing gap in average incomes between the Global North and the Global East. Without a resolute international response, large sections of the world may become vulnerable to social instability and violence attributable to these pressures.

As economist Jeffrey Sachs (2008) summarizes the situation, humanity shares a "common fate on a crowded planet." Business-as-usual policies will yield calamitous results. Ecopolitical issues must move up on the policy agenda, he concludes, and new, robust forms of global cooperation are required to solve them. "The world has changed in profound ways," laments former UN Secretary-General Kofi Annan, "but I fear our conceptions of national interest have failed to follow suit." We need a higher form of realism, submits political scientist Seyom Brown (2009: 41–43, 50–55), a philosophy of statecraft that recognizes how inextricably bound up each country's national interest has become with the security and well-being of the entire human population. Yet, even if the world's nations embrace a broader definition of interest, how will they set priorities for action on so many interrelated problems, all of which require attention if peace and prosperity with justice is to prevail?

Will Technological Innovation Solve Pressing Global Problems?

The world today faces a series of difficult and potentially unmanageable challenges. The surge in globalization that followed on the heels of late twentieth-century discoveries in microelectronics and information processing has unleashed revolutionary changes. The consequences, however, are not certain. Technological innovations solve some problems but cause others; they can increase productivity and economic output, but they can also displace workers and trigger social unrest.

While acknowledging that there is often a significant time lag between the diffusion of new technology and the adjustment of society to the changes it fosters, some people assert that technological innovation promises humanity a more secure and bountiful future. Indeed, the most optimistic members of this group believe that due to promising developments in such fields as biotechnology and software development, humanity is entering the most innovative period in history. From their perspective, sufficient resources exist to fuel continued progress. With patience, technological solutions eventually will be found to ease the most serious problems facing the world today. Malnutrition and disease, they note as an example, may still exist, but owing to technological advances in agriculture and medicine, many people are alive today who might have perished in previous centuries.

In contrast to those who envision technological innovation as a way to increase economic growth and alleviate social welfare problems, others remain concerned that some proposed technological solutions will compound current problems. Whereas genetically modified crops are seen by members of the former group as a way to reduce famine by developing plants that produce greater yields with more nutrients at lower tillage costs, members of the latter group worry about inadvertent environmental and health consequences, arguing that replacing traditional crops with those that have been genetically modified will reduce genetic diversity and introduce potentially toxic vegetation into the ecosystem. Even the so-called **green revolution** had its drawbacks, they argue. Although fertilizers, pesticides, and herbicides initially increased crop yields in

green revolution the introduction of high-yield seeds, chemical fertilizers, and other agricultural technologies to Global South countries.

Pgiam/istockphoto.com

Technology and the Global Demand for Energy The global economy's need for energy continues to increase. Many analysts believe that new thermal and photonic technologies may make it possible to meet the world's growing demand for energy by harnessing the power of the sun. Shown here is a field of solar panels that convert sunlight into electricity. According to some estimates, covering less than 5 percent of the world's deserts with solar panels could supply the world's total electricity needs.

various Global South countries, they eventually spawned new problems, such as contaminated water supplies. Without wise management, technological advances can have detrimental side effects. Consider the case of the world's fisheries. At first, larger ships and improvements in maritime technology resulted in increases in the amount of fish harvested from the world's oceans. Over time, however, many fisheries were depleted. Applying more technology could not increase catches once the ecosystem had collapsed. As one member of this school of thought has put it: "Many of our new technologies confer upon us new power without automatically giving us new wisdom" (Gore, 2006: 247).

Are Cultural Differences the New Fault Lines on the Geostrategic Landscape?

When communism began collapsing throughout Eastern Europe in 1989, former U.S. State Department analyst Francis Fukuyama (1989) suggested that the world was witnessing the **end of history**. Ideological conflicts were over; democratic

end of history the thesis that the demise of communism marked the triumph of Western market democracy and the end of humanity's ideological evolution.

capitalism had triumphed. But not everyone was so sure. On the one hand, many of the newly emerging democracies were ruled by individuals who, although elected, disregarded constitutional limits on their power and denied citizens basic political freedoms. On the other hand, political movements that drew inspiration from non-Western belief systems began to challenge liberalism. According to political scientist Samuel Huntington (1996), the most prominent of these appealed to Islamic fundamentalism.

clash of civilizations the thesis that future international conflicts will be based on competing cultural values.

Conflict in the future, Huntington proposed, would involve a **clash of civilizations**, collisions between vast cultural entities holding different views on the relationship between God and humankind as well as different interpretations of the relative importance of equality and hierarchy, liberty and authority. From his vantage point, the world was divided into several major civilizations: Western, Slavic-Orthodox, Islamic, Hindu, Confucian, Japanese, Latin American, and African. Just as when violent geological events occur along the boundaries between tectonic plates, Huntington hypothesized that political friction could be expected where civilizations rubbed against one another. The wars in Chechnya and Bosnia have often been cited as examples that support his contention.

Critics, however, point out that no civilization is homogeneous in beliefs or attitudes. By focusing on civilizations as a whole, they insist that Huntington overlooks salient differences within civilizations, such as those between Sunnis and Shiites within the Islamic world, which are more likely to erupt into violence than clashes between civilizations.

For liberals and constructivists, clashes between civilizations are not inevitable: Common moral values and the growth of global civil society make cooperation across cultural fault lines possible, argue the former; over time, mutually beneficial cross-cultural cooperation can lead people to acquire more open, inclusive identities, add the latter. Many realists retort that clashes of civilizations have occurred throughout history and are likely to continue. Human nature has not changed and anarchy remains a key defining property of the international system. As the realist diplomat and strategic thinker George Kennan supposedly remarked, "Whoever thinks the future is going to be easier than the past is certainly mad."

Is the World Preparing for the Wrong Kind of Security Threats?

The conduct of war has undergone several "generational" changes since the Thirty Years' War drew to a close and gave birth to the modern state system. In what has been called the "first generation of modern warfare," which extended from the Peace of Westphalia to the American Civil War, soldiers armed with smooth-bore muskets were normally deployed in tight linear formations to coordinate volleys from relatively inaccurate weapons. Once weapons with greater accuracy and rates of fire became available, line-and-column tactics on open ground lost their effectiveness, which led to a new generation of tactics that emphasized massive firepower to annihilate fixed-fortification defenses.

The second generation of modern land warfare substituted massed artillery for massed infantry. During the First World War, machine guns, barbed wire, minefields, and entrenched defenses strung along continuous fronts stymied the precise, geometric lines of attack typical of early modern warfare. In response, artillery barrages from the rear were used to breach fortified positions, allowing infantry units to overrun crippled defenses.

Although lengthy preparatory barrages could shatter fixed positions, they alerted the other side to where the subsequent infantry assault would occur. By extending defenses in greater depth and maintaining significant reserve forces, defenders could counterattack before advancing foot soldiers were able to break through. However, improvements in transportation and communication technology provided a way to deal with these tactics. Drawing on their country's experience of combining suppressive firepower with movement during the spring offenses of 1918, German officers like Heinz Guderian and Erich von Manstein envisioned a third generation of warfare that accentuated speed and surprise rather than firepower and attrition. Tracked-armored vehicles and tactical air power, they reasoned, enabled an attacker to concentrate mobile forces at a decisive point along the front, penetrate deep into enemy territory, and roll the opposition up from the rear in battles of encirclement.

Whereas third-generation thinking has influenced most countries since the Second World War, today the threat of being attacked by the military forces of another nation-state has receded, particularly in the Global North. Instead, a "fourth generation" of warfare has emerged in which nation-states are pitted against nonstate actors in hostilities that lack front lines and clear distinctions between soldiers and civilians (see Hammes, 2004). Unable to defeat conventional armies on the field of battle, irregular forces using unconventional tactics focus on their adversary's will, using patience, ingenuity, and gruesome acts of violence to compel their opponent to weigh the mounting costs of continuing a long, drawn-out struggle. Some political and military leaders, however, continue to think of warfare in third-generational terms, dismissing this new face of war as an annoyance that detracts from preparations for decisive, large-scale engagements. Do the wars in Afghanistan and Iraq provide a glimpse into the future? Will most military clashes in the early twenty-first century follow their pattern?

Does Diplomatic Engagement with Intransigent Adversaries Promote Peace?

Among the foreign policy issues that candidates for national political office regularly debate during election campaigns around the world is the wisdom of negotiating with obstinate, unsavory foes. Opponents of diplomatic engagement complain that sitting at the bargaining table with such individuals gives them recognition, a propaganda platform, and an opportunity to appear to be seriously negotiating while they are merely stalling. To advance the cause of peace, rigorous preconditions should be met prior to beginning formal talks. Anything less, they maintain, signals weakness to an adversary.

In contrast to this point of view, supporters of diplomatic engagement assert that a prudent foreign policy removes impediments to negotiations. "Talking to our adversaries is no one's idea of fun, and it is not a sure prescription for success in every crisis," explains Nicholas Burns (2008: 40), former U.S. under secretary of state for political affairs. "But it is crude, simplistic and wrong to charge that negotiations reflect weakness or appeasement. More often than not, they are evidence of a strong and self-confident country." According to one student of bargaining behavior, preconditions are appropriate only when the other side is capable of meeting them, and when doing so will not eliminate its leverage in subsequent talks. Otherwise, they become a form of political gamesmanship, invoked to blame an adversary for insincerity and scuttle nascent diplomatic overtures (Malhotra, 2009: 86).

Another way to appraise strategies of engagement is to consider their information value. Because people are prone to ignore or reinterpret information that runs counter to their beliefs, mutual misperceptions exacerbate disputes rooted in competing interests. Although the degree of misperception may not be the same on both sides and one side may cling to its stereotypes with greater tenacity than the other, distrust and suspicion grow as conflicting parties view one another in a negative light. This so-called "mirror image" phenomenon occurred among Russians and Americans during the Cold War. Both countries saw themselves as virtuous and peace-loving while the other side was seen as disingenuous and aggressive. Additionally, both erroneously assumed that their counterparts would interpret policy initiatives as they were intended. Since then, researchers have found stark, black-and-white images held by bitter rivals in other international disputes, including the India–Pakistan and Arab–Israeli conflicts. Under these circumstances conflict resolution is extraordinarily difficult. Not only do opposing sides have different preferences for certain outcomes over others, but their harsh images of one another tend to be self-confirming. When one side expects the other to be hostile, it may treat its opponent in a manner that leads the opponent to take counteractions that confirm the original expectation, therein creating a vicious cycle of deepening hostilities. Of course, clearing up misperceptions will not automatically eradicate truly incompatible aims and conflicts of interest that may divide obdurate foes. Diplomatic engagement "may not always produce accommodation," acknowledges James Dobbins (2010: 161), who served as the Bush administration's special envoy to Afghanistan following the September 11, 2001 attacks. But "it always yields information, which helps to create better policy." For this reason he maintains that "even failed negotiations are better than no negotiation at all."

Should the World Brace for a New Cold War?

In May 2010, a large delegation of American officials led by Secretary of State Hillary Clinton and Secretary of the Treasury Timothy Geithner traveled to China as part of the "Strategic and Economic Dialogue" launched a year earlier between the two countries. The meeting took place in the wake of several public spats that led some observers to speculate that relations between Beijing and Washington were rapidly cooling. Whereas China was annoyed with American arms sales to Taiwan, President Obama's meeting with the Dalai Lama, and U.S. fiscal policy, the United States was frustrated with Chinese behavior at the Copenhagen climate summit, its response to the March 2010 North Korean sinking of a South Korean warship, and China's monetary policy. Historian Niall Ferguson (2009), who popularized the term "Chimerica" to describe the symbiotic relationship between Chinese saving, lending, and exporting, and American spending, borrowing, and importing, mused that the two parties were headed for divorce. Drawing parallels with Anglo-German antagonism in the early twentieth century, he proposed that the many economic ties between China and the United States would not prevent the growth of strategic rivalry and, ultimately, a new cold war.

Foreign policy analysts disagree over the impact of China's economic ascent on its relations with the United States. Some predict that just as China possessed the world's largest economy for most of the last two millennia, it will once again become the center of the planet's economic gravity, dwarfing America's share of global GDP (Fogel, 2010). Others question claims of an inevitable shift of power from West to East, doubting that China will become the hegemon in a budding unipolar system (Pei, 2009).

Inferring from China's rise that the world is about to enter a new cold war is problematic because international politics is a baffling mix of patterned regularities and novel events, deliberate choices and inadvertent accidents. Cognitive psychologists find that we often get blindsided by the way things turn out because of our tendency to imagine that the future can be foreseen simply by extrapolating from the moment. Depicting the global future as a linear extension of the present carries with it the pitfall of focusing on situations, not processes (Dörner, 1996). To make useful forecasts about Chinese-American relations, we must understand the causal processes that are producing friction between the two countries, as well as whether conditions are such that these processes will spawn larger, more serious disputes. Furthermore, we would need to know whether these processes are similar to those that drove other strategic rivalries toward major confrontations in the past. Unraveling complex processes is not easy. Psychological research indicates that most people overlook processes that build slowly; they misjudge the cumulative probability associated with a complicated chain of events; and they underestimate how slow, incremental changes within in a causal chain can give rise to a large, abrupt transformation once some critical threshold is passed. It is for these reasons that Danish physicist and Nobel laureate Niels Bohr reputedly quipped that "prediction is difficult, especially about the future."

HUMAN CHOICE AND THE GLOBAL FUTURE

Anticipating the future has been called an intellectual challenge and a social obligation (Schneider, Gleditsch, and Carey, 2010). We have raised the preceding questions to challenge you to think about what alternative global futures are possible, probable, and preferable, as well as to encourage you to consider the obligations we may have to generations yet unborn. Your answers provide a rough outline for a scenario of how the drama of world politics will progress in the decades ahead.

Although we cannot know exactly what the future will hold, exploring different scenarios is valuable because it sensitizes us to the long-range consequences of the choices we make here and now. As discussed in earlier chapters of this book, our images of the future—what we expect, what we hope for, and what we fear—all exert an influence on the present. "If our image of the future were different," explains policy analyst Willis Harman (1976: 1), "the decisions of today would be different." By acting in a certain manner today, we sculpt the shape of tomorrow.

Thus, the future is not something that just happens; we influence it with our choices. If the scenario that you have formulated depicts an inspiring image of the global future, what choices do you think should be made to support its realization? If the scenario portrays a more disquieting future, what can be done to move the trajectory of international events in a more positive direction? Influencing the global future may be difficult, but we are not hapless victims of fate.

How, then, should we proceed? Futurist David Pearce Snyder (2006) proposes that we heed wisdom that has stood the test of time. Roughly 2,500 years ago, the Greek philosopher Heraclitus of Ephesus observed that nothing about the future is inevitable except change. Not long thereafter, the ancient Chinese general Sun Tzu advised leaders to exploit the inevitable. Their combined message, concludes Snyder, is that wise people take advantage of change. Rather than fearing the global future, we should welcome its opportunities as we strive to build a more peaceful and just world order. Too many of us believe "we are gripped by forces we cannot control," lamented U.S. President John F. Kennedy in a speech delivered at American University following the Cuban missile crisis. But "we need not accept that view," he counseled. "No problem of human destiny is beyond human beings."

CHAPTER SUMMARY

- Social scientists cannot predict the global future with absolute certainty because world politics is a complex mix of chance and human choice.

- The study of the global future entails imagining what is possible, forecasting what is probable, and determining how to attain what is preferable.

- Forecasting what is likely to happen in world politics is difficult because many trends are nonlinear and some display abrupt, discontinuous change. A key task in futures research is to discern which global trends are transient and which will transform the world system.

- Because trends interact, sometimes amplifying and at other times abating one another's impact, it is important to examine the configuration of global trends rather than focus on a single trend in isolation.

KEY TERMS

clash of civilizations   green revolution

end of history   scenario

SUGGESTED READINGS

Bueno de Mesquita, Bruce. *The Predictioneer's Game: Using the Logic of Brazen Self-Interest to See and Shape the Future*. New York: Random House, 2009.

Fukuyama, Francis (ed.). *Blindside*: *How to Anticipate Forcing Events and Wild Cards in Global Politics*. Washington, DC: Brookings, 2008.

Giordano, Eugenio (ed.). *Global Trends 2025: A Transformed World*. Hauppauge, NY: Nova Science Publishers, 2010.

Glenn, Jerome C., Theodore J. Gordon, and Elizabeth Florescu. *State of the Future*. Washington, DC: Millennium Project, 2010.

Smil, Vaclav. *Global Catastrophes and Trends: The Next Fifty Years*. Cambridge, MA: The MIT Press, 2008.

CRITICAL THINKING QUESTIONS

What if the terrorists who hijacked United and American Airlines aircraft on September 11, 2001 had been arrested before they could commandeer those flights? Would that have made the war in Iraq less likely? In the absence of Al Qaeda attacks on New York and Washington, would President George W. Bush have committed the U.S. military to a conflict that involved nation-building operations, which he had criticized while debating Al Gore during the 2000 presidential campaign? Or, given Osama bin Laden's desire to strike the United States, is it probable that some other Al Qaeda attack would have occurred, leading Bush to adopt the doctrine of preemption and topple Saddam Hussein's regime even if 9/11 did not happen?

International relations theorists often use counterfactual reasoning to explore what might have taken place in world politics if some presumed causal factor (X) was changed while all others were held constant. Normally, this entails asking, "If X had not occurred, what would have resulted?" Raising "what if" questions helps theorists evaluate their assumptions about why a particular event transpired the way it did, and gauge the importance of the factor they are negating relative to other hypothesized causes. When used judiciously, counterfactuals can mitigate what psychologists call the hindsight bias—*the tendency to see events that have happened as all but inevitable after they have occurred.*

The challenges of conducting effective counterfactual analyses are considerable. The most persuasive counterfactuals make the case for a different future based on a clear, specific, and plausible change to a single causal factor that is proximate in time to the outcome under investigation. As the sociologist Max Weber once put it, good counterfactual reasoning involves a minimal rewrite of history.

(Continued)

Consider how you could use counterfactual reasoning to explore the global future. Looking back over the last decade, is there some event that you think has moved contemporary history down a particular path, narrowing the probability of certain potential futures while expanding the probability of others? How would the odds of those potential futures change if that event had not occurred? Would a global future that you prefer become more or less likely if something other than that event had happened? Based on what your counterfactual reasoning suggests, are there any foreign policy recommendations that you would make to national leaders about dealing with emerging issues on the international horizon?

Glossary

A

absolute gains conditions in which all participants in exchanges become better off.

acid rain precipitation that has been made acidic through contact with sulfur dioxide and nitrogen oxide.

actor an individual, group, state, or organization that plays a major role in world politics.

agenda setting the ability to influence which issues receive attention from governments and international organizations by giving them publicity.

alliance a formal agreement among sovereign states for the purpose of coordinating their behavior to increase mutual security.

antidumping duties tariffs imposed to offset another state's alleged selling of a product at below the cost to produce it.

appeasement a strategy of making concessions to another state in the hope that, satisfied, it will not make additional claims.

arbitrage the selling of one currency (or product) and purchase of another to make a profit on the changing exchange rates; traders ("arbitragers") help to keep states' currencies in balance through their speculative efforts to buy large quantities of devalued currencies and sell them in countries where they are valued more highly.

arms control bilateral or multilateral agreements to contain arms buildups by setting limits on the number and types of weapons that states are permitted.

arms race an action-reaction process in which rival states rapidly increase their military capabilities in response to one another.

asylum the provision of sanctuary to safeguard refugees escaping from the threat of persecution in the country where they hold citizenship.

asymmetric war an armed conflict between belligerents of vastly unequal military strength, in which the weaker side is often a nonstate actor that relies on unconventional tactics.

autocratic rule a governmental system where unlimited power is concentrated in the hands of a single person.

B

balance of payments a calculation summarizing a country's financial transactions with the external world, determined by the level of credits (export earnings, profits from foreign investment, receipts of foreign aid) minus the country's total international debts (imports, interest payments on international debts, foreign direct investments, and the like).

balance of power the theory that national survival in an anarchic world is most likely when military power is distributed to prevent a single hegemon or bloc from dominating the state system.

balance of trade a calculation based on the value of merchandise goods and services imported and exported. A deficit occurs when a country buys more from abroad than it sells.

balancer an influential global or regional state that throws its support in decisive fashion to the weaker side of the balance of power.

bandwagon the tendency for weak states to seek alliance with the strongest power, regardless of that power's ideology or form of government, in order to increase security.

barter the exchange of one good for another rather than the use of currency to buy and sell items.

beggar-thy-neighbor policies the attempt to promote trade surpluses through policies that cause other states to suffer trade deficits.

behavioralism an approach to the study of world politics that emphasizes the application of the scientific method.

bilateral relationships or agreements between two states.

billiard-ball model a conception of world politics that envisions states as the sole movers of global affairs, explains their behavior as unitary responses to external threats, and attributes little importance to domestic sources of foreign policy.

biodiversity the variety of life on Earth.

bipolar an international system with two dominant power centers.

brain drain the exodus of the most educated people from their homeland to a more prosperous foreign country where the opportunities for high incomes are better, which deprives their homeland of their ability to contribute to its economic development.

brinkmanship intentionally taking enormous risks in bargaining with an adversary in order to compel submission.

bureaucratic politics a description of decision making that sees foreign policy choices as based on bargaining and compromises among government agencies.

Bush Doctrine a policy that singles out states that support terrorist groups and advocates military strikes against them to prevent a future attack on the United States.

C

carrying capacity the maximum biomass that can be supported by a given territory.

cartel an organization of the producers of a commodity that seeks to regulate the pricing and production of that commodity to increase revenue.

civil war armed conflict within a country between the central government and one or more insurgent groups, sometimes referred to as *internal war*.

clash of civilizations the thesis that future international conflicts will be based on competing cultural values.

coercive diplomacy the use of threats or limited armed force to persuade an adversary to alter its foreign and/or domestic policies.

cognitive dissonance the psychological tendency to deny or rationalize away discrepancies between one's preexisting beliefs and new information.

collective defense a military organization within a specific region created to protect its members from external attack.

collective goods goods from which everyone benefits regardless of their individual contributions.

collective security a security regime based on the principle that an act of aggression by any state will be met by a collective response from the rest.

colonialism the rule of a region by an external sovereign power.

commercial liberalism an economic theory advocating free markets and the removal of barriers to the flow of trade and capital.

communitarianism an ethical theory that places the ultimate source of moral value in political communities.

comparative advantage the concept in liberal economic theory that a state will benefit if it specializes in those goods it can produce comparatively cheaply and acquires through trade goods that it can only produce at a higher cost.

compellence a threat of force aimed at making an adversary grant concessions against its will.

complex interdependence a model of world politics based on the assumptions that states are not the only important actors, security is not the dominant national goal, and military force is not the only significant instrument of foreign policy.

concert a cooperative agreement among great powers to jointly manage international relations.

consequentialism an approach to evaluating moral choices on the basis of the results of the action taken.

constitutional democracy a governmental system in which political leaders' power is limited by a body of fundamental principles, and leaders are held accountable to citizens through regular, fair, and competitive elections.

containment a term coined by U.S. policy maker George Kennan for deterring expansion by the Soviet Union, which has since been used to describe a strategy aimed at preventing a state from using force to increase its territory or sphere of influence.

contingent behavior actions that depend on what others are doing.

cosmopolitanism an ethical theory that places the ultimate source of moral value in individuals.

counterforce targeting strategy targeting nuclear weapons on the military capabilities of an opponent.

countervailing duties tariffs imposed by a government to offset suspected subsidies provided by foreign governments to their producers.

countervalue targeting strategy targeting strategic nuclear weapons against an enemy's most valued non-military resources, such as the people and industries located in its cities (sometimes known as *countercity targeting*).

covert operations secret activities undertaken by a state outside its borders through clandestine means to achieve specific political or military goals with respect to another state.

crosscutting cleavages a situation where politically relevant divisions between international actors are contradictory, with their interests pulling them together on some issues and separating them on others.

D

decolonization the achievement of independence by countries that were once colonies of other states.

democratic peace the theory that although democratic states sometimes wage wars against other states, they do not fight each other.

demographic transition an explanation of population changes that highlights the role of birth and death rates in moving countries from stable to rapidly increasing and finally to declining populations.

dependency theory a view of development asserting that the leading capitalist states dominate and exploit the poorer countries on the periphery of the world economy.

dependent development the industrialization of areas outside of the leading capitalist states within the confines set by the dominant capitalist states, which enables the poor to become wealthier without ever catching up to the core Global North countries.

desertification the creation of deserts due to soil erosion, overfarming, and deforestation, which converts cropland to nonproductive, arid sand.

détente a strategy of relaxing tensions between adversaries to reduce the possibility of war.

deterrence a strategy designed to dissuade an adversary from doing what it would otherwise do.

development the processes through which a country increases its capacity to meet its citizens' basic human needs and raise their standard of living.

devolution granting political power to ethnopolitical groups within a state under the expectation that greater autonomy for them in particular regions will curtail their quest for independence.

diasporas the migration of religious or ethnic groups to foreign lands despite their continued affiliation with the land and customs of their origins.

digital divide the division between those states that have a high proportion of Internet users and hosts, and those that do not.

diplomatic recognition the formal legal acceptance of a state's official status as an independent country. *De facto* recognition acknowledges the factual existence of another state or government short of full recognition. *De jure* recognition gives a government formal, legal recognition.

disarmament agreements to reduce or eliminate weapons or other means of attack.

displaced people people involuntarily uprooted from their homes but still living in their own countries.

diversionary theory of war the contention that leaders initiate conflict abroad as a way of steering public opinion at home away from controversial domestic issues.

domino theory a metaphor popular during the Cold War that predicted that if one state fell to communism, its neighbors would also fall in a chain reaction, like a row of falling dominoes.

dualism the existence of a rural, impoverished, and neglected sector of society alongside an urban, developing, or modernizing sector, with little interaction between the two.

E

economic sanctions the punitive use of trade or monetary measures, such as an embargo, to harm the economy of an enemy state in order to exercise influence over its policies.

end of history the thesis that the demise of communism marked the triumph of Western market democracy and the end of humanity's ideological evolution.

ethnopolitical group people whose identity is primarily defined by their sense of sharing common ancestral nationality, language, cultural heritage, and kinship ties.

exchange rate the rate at which one state's currency is exchanged for another state's currency in the global marketplace.

export quotas barriers to commerce agreed to by two trading states to protect their domestic producers.

export-led industrialization a growth strategy that concentrates on developing domestic export industries capable of competing in overseas markets.

extended deterrence the use of military threats by a great power to deter an attack on its allies.

externalities the unintended side effects of choices that reduce the true value of the original decision.

F

failed states countries whose governments have little or no control over their territories and populations.

failing states states in danger of political collapse due to overwhelming internal strife.

fertility rate the average number of children born to a woman during her lifetime.

firebreak the psychological barrier between conventional and nuclear war.

First World the relatively wealthy industrialized countries that share a commitment to varying forms of democratic political institutions and developed market economies.

fixed exchange rates a system under which states establish the parity of their currencies and commit to keeping fluctuations in their exchange rates within narrow limits.

floating exchange rates an unmanaged process whereby market forces rather than governments influence the relative rate of exchange for currencies between countries.

foreign direct investment (FDI) an investment in a country involving a long-term relationship and control of an enterprise by nonresidents and including equity capital, reinvestment of earnings, other long-term capital, and short-term capital as shown in balance of payments.

free riders those who enjoy the benefits of collective goods but pay little or nothing for them.

functionalism a theory of political integration based on the assumption that technical cooperation among different nationalities in economic and social fields will build communities that transcend sovereign states.

G

genocide the deliberate extermination of an ethnic or minority group.

geopolitics a school of thought claiming that states' foreign policies are determined by their locations, natural resources, and physical environments.

Global East the rapidly growing economies of East and South Asia that have made their countries competitors with the traditionally dominant members of the Global North.

Global North a term used to refer to the world's wealthy, industrialized countries located primarily in the Northern Hemisphere.

Global South a term used to designate the less-developed countries located primarily in the Southern Hemisphere.

global village a popular image used to describe the growth of awareness that all people share a common fate, stemming from a view that the world is an integrated and interdependent whole.

globalization a set of processes that are widening, deepening, and accelerating the interconnectedness among societies.

globalization of finance the increasing transnationalization of national markets through the worldwide integration of capital flows.

globalization of production a manufacturing process in which finished goods are assembled from components produced in multiple countries.

green revolution the introduction of high-yield seeds, chemical fertilizers, and other agricultural technologies to Global South countries.

greenhouse effect the phenomenon producing planetary warming when gases released by burning fossil fuels act as a blanket in the atmosphere, thereby increasing temperatures.

Group of 77 (G-77) the coalition of Third World countries that sponsored the 1963 Joint Declaration of Developing Countries calling for reforms to allow greater equity in North-South trade.

Group of Five (G-5) a group of advanced industrial democracies composed of the United States, Britain, France, Japan, and Germany.

Group of Seven (G-7)/Group of Eight (G-8) a group of advanced industrialized democracies composed of the United States, Britain, France, Japan, Germany, Canada, and Italy that meets in regular economic summit conferences; after 1997, known as the G-8 with the addition of Russia.

Group of Twenty (G-20) an informal forum that promotes discussions among the world's major and top emerging economic powers on global economic issues.

groupthink the propensity for members of small, cohesive groups to accept the group's prevailing attitudes in the interest of group harmony, rather than speak out for what they believe.

H

Heavily Indebted Poor Countries (HIPCs) the subset of countries identified by the World Bank's Debtor Reporting System whose ratios of government debt to gross national product are so substantial that they cannot meet their payment obligations without experiencing political instability and economic collapse.

hegemon a single, overwhelmingly powerful state that exercises predominate influence over the global system.

hegemonic stability theory a school of thought that argues free trade and economic order depend on the existence of an overwhelmingly powerful state willing and able to use its strength to open and organize world markets.

heuristics judgmental shortcuts used to compensate for limited information about complicated problems.

high politics the category of global issues related to military and security aspects of relations between governments and peoples.

human rights the political and social entitlements recognized by international law as inalienable and valid for individuals in all countries by virtue of their humanity.

human security a concept that refers to the degree to which the welfare of individuals is protected and advanced, in contrast to national security, which puts the interests of states first.

humanitarian intervention the use of peacekeeping forces by foreign states or international organizations to protect endangered people from gross violations of their human rights.

hypotheses conjectural statements that describe the relationship between an independent variable (the presumed cause) and a dependent variable (the effect).

I

illiquidity an inability to convert assets into cash quickly.

imperial overstretch the historical tendency of hegemons to weaken themselves through costly foreign pursuits that drain their resources.

import quotas limits on the quantity of particular products that can be imported.

import-substitution industrialization a strategy for economic development that involves encouraging domestic entrepreneurs to manufacture products traditionally imported from abroad.

indigenous peoples the native ethnic and cultural inhabitant populations within countries ruled by a government controlled by others, often referred to as the "Fourth World."

individual level of analysis an analytical approach to the study of world politics that emphasizes the psychological factors that motivate people who make foreign policy decisions on behalf of states and other global actors.

inelastic demand a condition under which the quantity demanded of a good does not decrease as its price increases.

infant industry a newly established industry that is not yet strong enough to compete effectively in the global marketplace.

information warfare attacks on an adversary's telecommunications and computer networks to degrade the technological systems vital to its defense and economic well-being.

intergovernmental organizations (IGOs) institutions created and joined by states' governments, which give them authority to make collective decisions to manage particular problem(s) on the global agenda.

international liquidity reserve assets used to settle international accounts.

international monetary system the financial procedures governing the exchange and conversion of national currencies so that they can be bought and sold for one another to calculate the value of currencies and credits when capital is transferred across borders through trade, investment, and loans.

international political economy the study of the intersection of politics and economics that illuminates the reasons why changes occur in the distribution of states' wealth and power.

international regimes sets of principles, norms, rules, and decision-making procedures agreed to by global actors to guide their behavior in particular issue areas.

internationalized civil war an armed conflict between the central government of a country and insurgents with outside intervention by at least one other state in support of the insurgents.

interstate war sustained armed combat between two or more sovereign states.

irredentism efforts by an ethnonational or religious group to regain control of territory by force so that existing state boundaries will no longer separate the group.

isolationism a policy of withdrawing from active participation with other actors in world affairs and instead concentrating state efforts on managing internal affairs.

J

just war doctrine a set of criteria that indicate when it is morally justifiable to wage war and how it should be fought once it begins.

L

laissez-faire economics from a French phrase (meaning literally "let do") that Adam Smith and other commercial liberals in the eighteenth century used to describe the advantages of free-wheeling capitalism without government interference in economic affairs.

least-developed countries (LDCs) the most impoverished states in the Global South.

Liberal International Economic Order (LIEO) the set of regimes created after World War II, designed to promote monetary stability and reduce barriers to the free flow of trade and capital.

long-cycle theory a theory that focuses on the rise and fall of the leading global power as the central political process of the modern world system.

low politics the category of global issues related to the economic, social, and environmental aspects of relations between governments and people.

M

massive retaliation a policy of responding to any act of aggression with the most destructive capabilities available, including nuclear weapons.

mercantilism the seventeenth-century theory that preached that trading states should increase their wealth and power by expanding exports and protecting their domestic economy from imports.

microfinance providing small loans to poor entrepreneurs, usually to help start or expand a small business.

military intervention overt or covert use of force by one or more countries that cross the border of another country in order to affect the target country's government and policies.

military necessity a legal doctrine asserting that violation of the rules of war may be excused during periods of extreme emergency.

military-industrial complex a term coined by U.S. President Eisenhower to describe the coalition among arms manufacturers, military bureaucracies, and top government officials that promotes defense expenditures for its own profit and power.

mirror images the tendency of people in competitive interaction to perceive each other similarly—to see an adversary the same way as an adversary sees them.

modernization a view of development that argues that self-sustaining economic growth is created through technological innovation, efficient production, and investments from capital accumulation.

money supply the total amount of currency in circulation in a state, calculated to include demand deposits—such as checking accounts—in commercial banks and time deposits—such as savings accounts and bonds—in savings banks.

moral hazard a situation in which international institutions create incentives for states to behave recklessly.

most-favored-nation (MFN) principle unconditional nondiscriminatory treatment in trade between contracting parties guaranteed by GATT; in 1997, U.S. Senator Daniel Patrick Moynihan introduced legislation to replace the term with "normal trade relations" (NTR) to better reflect its true meaning.

multinational corporations (MNCs) business enterprises headquartered in one state that invest and operate extensively in other states.

multiple independently targetable reentry vehicles (MIRVs) a technological innovation permitting many nuclear warheads to be delivered from a single missile.

multipolar an international system with more than two dominant power centers.

mutual assured destruction (MAD) a system of deterrence in which both sides possess the ability to survive a first strike and launch a devastating retaliatory attack.

N

nation a group of people who feel a common identity due to a shared language, culture, and history.

nationalism the belief that political loyalty lies with a body of people who share ethnicity, linguistic, or cultural affinity, and perceive themselves to be members of the same group.

nation-state a specific geographic area containing a sovereign polity whose population identifies with that polity.

neofunctionalism a revised functionalist theory asserting that the IGOs states create to manage common problems provide benefits that exert pressures for further political integration.

neomercantilism a contemporary version of classical mercantilism, which advocates promoting domestic production and a balance-of-payment surplus by subsidizing exports and using tariffs and nontariff barriers to reduce imports.

newgroup syndrome the propensity of members of newly formed groups to conform with the opinions expressed by powerful, assertive peers or the group's leader due to a lack of well-developed procedural norms.

New International Economic Order (NIEO) the 1974 policy resolution in the UN that called for a North–South dialogue to open the way for the less-developed countries of the Global South to participate more fully in the making of international economic policy.

newly industrialized countries (NICs) prosperous members of the Global South, which have become important exporters of manufactured goods.

nonalignment a foreign policy posture that rejects participating in military alliances with rival blocs for fear that formal alignment will entangle the state in an unnecessary war.

nondiscrimination a principle for trade that proclaims that goods produced at home and abroad are to be treated the same for import and export agreements.

nongovernmental organizations (NGOs) transnational organizations of private citizens that include foundations, professional associations, multinational corporations, or groups in different countries joined together to work toward common interests.

nonintervention the legal principle prohibiting one state from interfering in another state's internal affairs.

nonstate actors all transnationally active groups other than states, such as international organizations whose members are states (IGOs) and nongovernmental organizations (NGOs) whose members are individuals and private groups from more than one state.

nontariff barrier governmental restrictions not involving a tax or duty that increase the cost of importing goods into a country.

norms generalized standards of behavior that embody collective expectations about appropriate conduct.

Nuclear Nonproliferation Treaty (NPT) an international agreement that seeks to prevent the spread of nuclear weapons by prohibiting further nuclear weapon sales, acquisitions, or production.

nuclear utilization theory (NUTs) a body of strategic thought that claimed deterrent threats would be more credible if nuclear weapons were made more usable.

nuclear winter the expected freeze that would occur in the Earth's climate from the fallout of smoke and dust in the event nuclear weapons were used, blocking out sunlight and destroying plant and animal life that survived the original blast.

O

official development assistance (ODA) grants or loans to countries from other countries, usually channeled through multilateral aid organizations, for the primary purpose of promoting economic development and welfare.

opportunity costs the concept in decision-making theories that when the occasion arises to use resources, what is gained for one purpose is lost for other purposes, so that every choice entails the cost of some lost opportunity.

orderly market arrangements (OMAs) voluntary export restrictions that involve a government-to-government agreement and often specific rules of management.

overlapping cleavages a situation where politically relevant divisions between international actors are complementary; interests pulling them apart on one issue are reinforced by interests that also separate them on other issues.

ozone layer the protective layer of the upper atmosphere over the Earth's surface that shields the planet from the sun's harmful impact on living organisms on the planet.

P

pandemic a disease that spreads throughout one or more continents.

peace-building post-conflict actions, predominantly diplomatic and economic, that strengthen and rebuild governmental infrastructure and institutions in order to avoid recourse to armed conflict.

peaceful coexistence Soviet leader Nikita Khrushchev's 1956 doctrine that war between capitalist and communist states is not inevitable and that interbloc competition could be peaceful.

peacemaking peaceful settlement processes such as good offices, conciliation, and mediation, designed to resolve the issues that led to armed conflict.

polarity the degree to which military and economic capabilities are concentrated among the major powers in the state system.

polarization the degree to which states cluster in alliances around the most powerful members of the state system.

political efficacy the extent to which a policymaker believes in his or her ability to control events politically.

political integration the processes and activities by which the populations of two or more states transfer their loyalties to a merged political and economic unit.

politics the exercise of influence to affect the distribution of values, such as power, prestige, and wealth; to Harold Lasswell, the process that determines "who gets what, when, how, and why."

pooled sovereignty legal authority granted to an IGO by its members to make collective decisions regarding specified aspects of public policy heretofore made exclusively by each sovereign government.

population implosion a rapid reduction of population that reverses a previous trend toward progressively larger populations.

power the ability to make someone continue a course of action, change what he or she is doing, or refrain from acting.

power cycle theory the contention that armed conflict is probable when a state passes through certain critical points along a generalized curve of relative power, and wars of enormous magnitude are likely when several great powers pass through critical points at approximately the same time.

power potential the relative capabilities or resources held by a state that are considered necessary to its asserting influence over others.

power transition theory the contention that war is likely when a dominant great power is threatened by the rapid growth of a rival's capabilities, which reduces the difference in their relative power.

preemption a quick first-strike attack that seeks to defeat an adversary before it can organize a retaliatory response.

preventive diplomacy actions taken in advance of a predictable crisis to prevent superpower involvement and limit violence.

preventive war a war undertaken to preclude an adversary from acquiring the capability to attack sometime in the future.

private international law law pertaining to routinized transnational intercourse between or among states as well as nonstate actors.

procedural rationality a method of decision making based on having perfect information with which all possible courses of action are carefully evaluated.

proliferation the spread of weapon capabilities throughout the state system.

prospect theory a behavioral decision theory that contends that decision makers assess policy options in comparison to a reference point and that they take greater risks to prevent losses than to achieve gains.

protectionism a policy of creating barriers to foreign trade, such as tariffs and quotas, that protects local industries from competition.

proximate causes phenomena occurring close in time to the effects that they produce or help to produce.

public international law law pertaining to government-to-government relations.

purchasing power parity (PPP) a model for calculating the relative purchasing power of different countries' currencies for an equal basket of commodities.

R

rapprochement in diplomacy, a policy seeking to reestablish normal relations between enemies.

rational choice decision-making procedures guided by careful definition of problems, specification of goals, weighing the costs, risks, and benefits of all alternatives, and selection of the optimal alternative.

rational political ambition theory an approach to the study of foreign policy that assumes state leaders want to maintain power and make decisions with that goal in mind.

Reagan Doctrine a pledge of U.S. backing for anti-communist insurgents who sought to overthrow Soviet-supported governments.

refugees people who flee for safety to another country because of a well-founded fear of persecution.

regional currency union the pooling of sovereignty to create a common currency (such as the EU's euro) and single monetary system for members in a region, regulated by a regional central bank within the currency bloc to reduce the likelihood of large-scale liquidity crises.

regional trade agreements (RTAs) treaties that integrate the economies of countries within a geographic region by reducing trade barriers among member states.

relative deprivation people's perception that they are unfairly deprived of the wealth and status in comparison to others who are advantaged but not more deserving.

relative gains a measure of how much one side in an agreement benefits in comparison to the other's side.

remittances the money earned by immigrants working in wealthy countries that they send to family members still living in their home countries.

remote causes phenomena that are removed in time from the effects that they produce or help to produce.

replacement-level fertility one couple replacing themselves with two children, so that a country's population will remain stable if this rate prevails.

reprisal a hostile but legal retaliatory act aimed at punishing another state's prior illegal actions.

Responsibility to Protect (R2P) a principle adopted at the 2005 UN World Summit that declares that states have a responsibility to protect their citizens from genocide, war crimes, ethnic cleansing and crimes against humanity, and that they should take appropriate action when others fail to protect their populations from these crimes.

S

satisficing the tendency for decision makers to choose the first available alternative that meets minimally acceptable standards.

scenario a narrative description showing how some hypothetical future state of affairs might evolve out of the present one.

schematic reasoning the process by which new information is interpreted by comparing it to generic concepts stored in memory about certain stereotypical situations, sequences of events, and characters.

secession the attempt by a religious or ethnic minority to break away from an internationally recognized state.

Second World during the Cold War, the group of countries, including the Soviet Union and its then–Eastern European allies, that shared a commitment to centrally planned economies.

second-strike capability a state's capacity to retaliate after absorbing a first-strike attack with weapons of mass destruction.

security community a group of states whose high level of noninstitutionalized collaboration results in the settlement of disputes by compromise rather than by force.

security dilemma the propensity of armaments undertaken by one state for ostensibly defensive purposes to threaten other states, which arm in reaction, with the result that their national security declines as their arms increase.

self-determination the doctrine that people should be able to determine the government that will manage their affairs.

self-fulfilling prophecies the tendency for one's expectations to evoke behavior that helps to make the expectations become true.

self-help the principle that in anarchy actors must rely on themselves.

smart bombs precision-guided military technology that enables a bomb to search for its target and detonate at the precise time it can do the most damage.

socialization the processes by which people learn the beliefs, values, and behaviors that are acceptable in a given society.

soft power the ability of a country to get what it wants in international affairs through the attractiveness of its culture, political ideals, and policies.

sovereignty under international law, the principle that no higher authority is above the state.

sphere of influence the area dominated by a great power.

spill over the propensity for successful integration across one area of cooperation between states to propel further integration in other areas.

standard operating procedures (SOPs) rules for reaching decisions about particular types of situations.

state an organized political entity with a permanent population, a well-defined territory, and a government.

state level of analysis an analytical approach to the study of world politics that emphasizes how the internal attributes of states influence their foreign policy behavior.

state–sponsored terrorism formal assistance, training, and arming of foreign terrorists by a state in order to achieve foreign policy goals.

strategic corporate alliances cooperation between multinational corporations and foreign companies in the same industry, driven by the movement of MNC manufacturing overseas.

Strategic Defense Initiative (SDI) a plan conceived by the Reagan administration to deploy an antiballistic missile system using space-based lasers that would destroy enemy nuclear missiles.

structural adjustment reforms aimed at reducing the role of the state while increasing the role of the market in Global South countries' economies.

subsidies financial assistance from governments to support enterprises considered important to public welfare.

sunk costs a concept that refers to costs that have already been incurred and cannot be recovered.

sustainable development economic growth that does not deplete the resources needed to maintain growth.

system a set of interconnected parts that function as a unitary whole. In world politics, the parts consist primarily of states that interact on a regular basis.

systemic level of analysis an analytical approach to the study of world politics that emphasizes the impact of international structures and processes on the behavior of global actors.

T

tariff a tax imposed by governments on imported goods.

terrorism the premeditated use or threat of violence perpetrated against noncombatants, usually intended to induce fear in a wider audience.

theory a set of interrelated propositions that explains an observed regularity.

Third World a Cold War term to describe the developing countries of Africa, Asia, and Latin America.

trade integration economic globalization measured by the extent to which world trade volume grows faster than the world's combined gross domestic product.

tragedy of the commons a metaphor, widely used to explain the impact of human behavior on ecological systems, that explains how rational self-interested behavior by individuals may have a destructive collective impact.

transgenic crops new crops with improved characteristics created artificially through genetic engineering, which combines genes from species that would not naturally interbreed.

transnational banks (TNBs) the world's top banking firms, whose financial activities are concentrated in transactions that cross state borders.

transnational relations interactions across state boundaries that involve at least one actor that is not the agent of a government or intergovernmental organization.

triad the combination of ICBMs, SLBMs, and long-range bombers in a second-strike nuclear force.

Truman Doctrine the declaration by President Harry S. Truman that U.S. foreign policy would use intervention to support peoples who allied with the United States against external subjugation.

two–level games a concept that refers to the interaction between international bargaining and domestic politics.

U

ultimatum a demand that contains a time limit for compliance and a threat of punishment for resistance.

unilateral a strategy that relies on independent, self-help behavior in foreign policy.

unipolar an international system with one dominant power center.

unitary actor an agent in world politics (usually a sovereign state) assumed to be internally united, so that changes in its internal circumstances do not influence its foreign policy as much as do the decisions that actor's leaders make to cope with changes in its global environment.

V

voluntary export restrictions (VERs) a protectionist measure popular in the 1980s and early 1990s, in which exporting countries agree to restrict shipments of a particular product to a country to deter it from imposing an even more onerous import quota.

W

war crimes acts performed during war that the international community defines as illegal, such as atrocities committed against enemy civilians and prisoners of war.

Washington consensus the view that Global South countries can best achieve sustained economic growth through democratic governance, fiscal discipline, free markets, a reliance on free enterprise, and trade liberalization.

world federalism a reform movement that proposes to combine sovereign states into a single unified federal state.

X

xenophobia a fear of foreigners.

Z

zero-sum game a situation in which what one side wins, the other side loses.

References

Aaronson, Susan Ariel. (2002) *Taking Trade to the Streets: The Lost History of Public Efforts to Shape Globalization*. Ann Arbor: University of Michigan Press.

Abramowitz, Morton. (2002) "The Bush Team Isn't Coping," *International Herald Tribune* (August 20): 6.

Adichie, Chimanda Ngozi. (2010) Presentation delivered to The Cabin Literary Center, Boise, ID, June 9.

Adler, Emanuel. (2002) "Constructivism and International Relations," pp. 95–118 in Walter Carlsnaes, Thomas Risse, and Beth Simons (eds.), *Handbook of International Relations*. London: Sage.

Albright, Madeleine, with Bill Woodward. (2008) *Memo to the President Elect*. New York: HarperCollins.

Aldonsi, Christian. (2006) *Circle in the Sand: Why We Went Back to Iraq*. New York: Doubleday.

Alkire, Sabina, and Marie Emma Santos. (2010) *Multidimensional Poverty Index: 2010 Data*. Oxford: Oxford Poverty and Human Development Initiative, Oxford Department of International Development, University of Oxford.

Allawi, Ali A. (2007) *The Occupation of Iraq*. New Haven: Yale University Press.

Allison, Graham, and Philip Zelikow. (1999) *Essence of Decision: Explaining the Cuban Missile Crisis*, 2nd ed. New York: Longman.

Alter, Jonathan. (2010) *The Promise: President Obama, Year One*. New York: Simon & Schuster.

Anderson, John Lee. (2008) "Fidel's Heir: The Influence of Hugo Chávez," *The New Yorker* (June 23): 46–57.

Angell, Norman. (1910) *The Great Illusion: A Study of the Relationship of Military Power in Nations to Their Economic and Social Advantage*. London: Weidenfeld & Nicholson.

Applebaum, Anne. (2005) "The Sources of American Conduct," *The American Interest* 1 (Autumn): 14–16.

Ardrey, Robert. (1966) *The Territorial Imperative: A Personal Inquiry into the Animal Origins of Property and Nations*. New York: Atheneum.

Aron, Raymond. (1965) *The Great Debate: Theories of Nuclear Strategy*. Garden City, NY: Doubleday.

Arreguín-Toft, Ivan. (2005) *How the Weak Win Wars: A Theory of Asymmetric Conflict*. Cambridge, UK: Cambridge University Press.

Art, Robert J. (2003) "Coercive Diplomacy: What Do We Know?" pp. 359–420 in Robert J. Art and Patrick M. Cronin (eds.), *The United States and Coercive Diplomacy*. Washington, DC: United States Institute of Peace Press.

Axworthy, Lloyd. (2008) "Canada and Antipersonnel Landmines: Human Security as a Foreign Policy Priority," pp. 229–249 in Steve Smith, Amelia Hadfield, and Tim Dunne (eds.), *Foreign Policy: Theories, Actors, Cases*. Oxford, UK: Oxford University Press.

Baker, James A., III, with Thomas M. DeFrank. (1995) *The Politics of Diplomacy*. New York: G. P. Putnam's Sons.

Baldwin, David A. (ed.). (1993) *Neorealism and Neoliberalism: The Contemporary Debate*. New York: Columbia University Press.

—. (1989) *Paradoxes of Power*. New York: Basil Blackwell.

Baratta, Joseph Preston. (2005) *The Politics of World Federation: From World Federalism to Global Governance*. New York: Praeger.

Barber, Benjamin R. (1995) *Jihad vs. McWorld*. New York: Random House.

Barnet, Michael. (2005) "Social Constructivism," pp. 251–270 in John Baylis and Steve Smith (eds.), *The Globalization of World Politics*, 3rd ed. New York: Oxford University Press.

Barnet, Richard J. (1977) *The Giants: Russia and America*. New York: Simon & Schuster.

Baron, Samuel H., and Carl Pletsch (eds.). (1985) *Introspection in Biography: The Biographer's Quest for Self Awareness*. Hillsdale, NJ: Analytic Press.

Bazerman, Max H., and Michael D. Watkins. (2004) *Predictable Surprises*. Boston: Harvard Business School Press.

Beitz, Charles R. (2001) "Human Rights as a Common Concern," *American Political Science Review* 95 (June): 269–282.

Bell, Coral. (2005) "The Twilight of the Unipolar World," *American Interest* 1 (Winter): 18–29.

Bellamy, Alex J. (2010) "The Responsibility to Protect—Five Years On," *Ethics & International Affairs* 24 (Summer): 143–169.

Berger, Peter, and Thomas Luckmann. (1967) *The Social Construction of Reality*. New York: Anchor.

Bhagwati, Jagdish. (2004) *In Defense of Globalization*. New York: Oxford University Press.

Bhutto, Benazir. (2008) *Reconciliation: Islam, Democracy, and the West*. New York: HarperCollins.

—. (1988) *Daughter of Destiny: An Autobiography*. New York: Harper.

Blair, Tony. (1999) "Doctrine of International Community," speech delivered at the Economic Club, Chicago, Illinois, April 24.

Bloom, Mia. (2005) *Dying to Kill: The Allure of Suicide Terror*. New York: Columbia University Press.

Boli, John, Michael A. Elliot, and Franziska Bieri. (2004) "Globalization," pp. 389–415 in George Ritzer (ed.), *Handbook of Social Problems*. London: Sage.

Bork, Robert. (1989/1990) "The Limits of International Law," *The National Interest* (Winter): 3–10.

Brecke, Peter. (1999) "The Characteristics of Violent Conflict since 1400 A.D.," paper presented at the annual meeting of the International Studies Association, Washington, D.C., February 17–20.

Bremer, Stuart A. (2000) "Who Fights Whom, When, Where, and Why?" pp. 23–36 in John A. Vasquez (ed.), *What Do We Know About War?* Lanham, MD: Rowman & Littlefield.

—. (1992) "Dangerous Dyads: Conditions Affecting the Likelihood of Interstate War, 1816–1965," *Journal of Conflict Resolution* 36 (June): 309–341.

Bremmer, Ian. (2007) *The J Curve: A New Way to Understand Why Nations Rise and Fall*. New York: Simon & Schuster.

Broad, Robin (ed.). (2002) *Global Backlash: Citizen Initiatives for a Just World Economy*. Lanham, MD: Rowman & Littlefield.

Broder, David. (2002) "Senator Brings Vietnam Experiences to Bear on Iraq," *The State* (Columbia, S.C.) (September 18): A15.

Bronfenbrenner, Urie. (1961) "The Mirror Image in Soviet-American Relations," *Journal of Social Issues* 17 (No. 3): 45–56.

Brooks, Doug, and Gaurav Laroia. (2005) "Privatized Peacekeeping," *The National Interest* 80 (Summer): 121–125.

Brown, Archie. (2009) *The Rise and Fall of Communism*. New York: HarperCollins.

Brown, Chris. (1992) *International Relations Theory: New Normative Approaches*. New York: Columbia University Press.

Brown, Seyom. (2009) *Higher Realism: A New Foreign Policy for the United States*. Boulder, CO: Paradigm.

Bueno de Mesquita, Bruce. (1981) "Risk, Power Distributions, and the Likelihood of War," *International Studies Quarterly* 25 (December): 541–568.

Buhaug, Harvard, and Kristian Skrede Gleditsch. (2008) "Contagion or Confusion? Why Conflicts Cluster in Space," *International Studies Quarterly* 52 (June): 215–233.

Bull, Hedley. (1977) *The Anarchical Society: A Study of Order in World Politics*. New York: Columbia University Press.

Bull, Hedley, and Adam Watson (eds.). (1984) *The Expansion of International Society*. Oxford, UK: Oxford University Press.

Bullock, Alan. (1962) *Hitler: A Study in Tyranny*. New York: Harper & Row.

Burns, Nicholas. (2008) "We Should Talk To Our Enemies," *Newsweek* (November 3): 40–41.

Bussmann, Margit, and Gerald Schneider. (2007) "When Globalization Discontent Turns Violent: Foreign Economic Liberalization and Internal War," *International Studies Quarterly* 51 (March): 79–97.

Calloway, Colin G. (1999) *First Peoples: A Documentary Survey of American Indian History*. Boston: Bedford/St. Martin's.

Caporaso, James A. (1993) "Global Political Economy," pp. 451–481 in Ada W. Finifter (ed.), *Political Science: The State of the Discipline II*. Washington, DC: American Political Science Association.

Caprioli, Mary. (2005) "Primed for Violence: The Role of Gender Inequality in Predicting International Conflict," *International Studies Quarterly* 49 (June): 161–178.

Caprioli, Mary, and Mark Boyer. (2001) "Gender, Violence, and International Crisis," *Journal of Conflict Resolution* 45 (4): 503–518.

Cardoso, Fernando Henrique, and Enzo Faletto. (1979) *Dependency and Development in Latin America*. Berkeley: University of California Press.

Carothers, Thomas. (2008) "A League of Their Own," *Foreign Policy* 167 (July/August): 44–49.

Carr, E. H. (1939) *The Twenty-Years' Crisis, 1919–1939*. London: Macmillan.

Cashman, Greg. (2000) *What Causes War?* 2nd ed. Boston: Lexington Books.

Cashman, Greg, and Leonard C. Robinson. (2007) *An Introduction to the Causes of War*. Lanham, MD: Rowman & Littlefield.

Cavoli, Christopher G. (2011) "The Contribution of Counterinsurgency to a Strategy to Combat Global Terrorism," pp. 138–151 in Christopher C. Harmon, Andrew N. Pratt, and Sebastian Gorke (eds.), *Toward a Grand Strategy Against Terrorism*. New York: McGraw-Hill.

Cetron, Martin, and Owen Davies. (2008) *55 Trends Now Shaping the Future*. Carlisle, PA: Proteus.

Chase-Dunn, Christopher. (1989) *Global Formation: Structures of the World-Economy*. Oxford: Basil Blackwell.

Checkel, Jeffrey T. (1998) "The Constructivist Turn in International Relations Theory," *World Politics* 50 (January 1998): 324–348.

Christensen, Thomas J., and Jack Snyder. (1990) "Chain Gangs and Passed Bucks: Predicting Alliance Patterns in Multipolarity," *International Organization* 44 (Spring): 137–168.

Churchill, Winston S. (1948) *The Gathering Storm*. Boston: Houghton Mifflin.

Cincotta, Richard P., and Robert Engelman. (2004) "Conflict Thrives Where Young Men Are Many," *International Herald Tribune* (March): 18.

Claude, Inis L., Jr. (1989) "The Balance of Power Revisited," *Review of International Studies* 15 (January): 77–85.

—. (1971) *Swords into Plowshares*, 4th ed. New York: Random House.

—. (1962) *Power and International Relations*. New York: Random House.

Coggins, Bridget. (2010) "The Pirate Den," *Foreign Policy* 180 (July/August): 86–87.

Cohen, Benjamin J. (1996) "Phoenix Risen: The Resurrection of Global Finance," *World Politics* 48 (January): 268–296.

—. (1973) *The Question of Imperialism*. New York: Basic Books.

Cohen, Eliot A. (1998) "A Revolution in Warfare," pp. 34–46 in Charles W. Kegley, Jr. and Eugene R. Wittkopf (eds.), *The Global Agenda*, 4th ed. New York: McGraw-Hill.

Cohen, Joel E. (2005) "Human Population Grows Up," *Scientific American* 293 (September): 48–55.

—. (1995) *How Many People Can the Earth Support?* New York: Norton.

Cohen, Stephen F. (2009) *Soviet Fates and Lost Alternatives*. New York: Columbia University Press.

Cohn, Theodore E. (2005) *Global Political Economy: Theory and Practice*, 3rd ed. New York: Pearson Longman.

Collier, Paul. (2010) *War, Guns, and Votes: Democracy in Dangerous Places*. New York: HarperCollins.

—. (2005) "The Market for Civil War," pp. 28–32 in Helen E. Purkitt (ed.), *World Politics 04/05*. Dubuque, IA: Dushkin/McGraw-Hill.

Cornish, Edward. (2004) *Futuring: The Exploration of the Future*. Bethesda, MD: World Future Society.

Cortright, David, and George A. Lopez (eds.). (2002) *Smart Sanctions: Targeting Economic Statecraft.* Lanham, MD: Rowman & Littlefield.

—. (1995) "The Sanctions Era: An Alternative to Military Intervention," *Fletcher Forum of World Affairs* 19 (May): 65–85.

Cox, Robert J., with Timothy J. Sinclair. (1996) *Approaches to World Order.* Cambridge: Cambridge University Press.

Craig, Campbell. (2008) "The Resurgent Idea of World Government," *Ethics & International Affairs* 22 (Summer): 133–142.

Dehio, Ludwig. (1962) *The Precarious Balance.* New York: Knopf.

Deibel, Terry. (2007) *Foreign Affairs Strategy: Logic for American Statecraft.* New York: Cambridge University Press.

de Tocqueville, Alexis. (1969 [1835]) *Democracy in America.* New York: Doubleday.

Deudney, Daniel H. (2006) *Bounding Power: Republican Security Theory from the Polis to the Global Village.* Princeton, NJ: Princeton University Press.

Deutsch, Karl W. (1974) *Politics and Government.* Boston: Houghton Mifflin.

Deutsch, Karl W., and J. David Singer. (1964) "Multipolar Power Systems and International Stability," *World Politics* 16 (April): 390–406.

Diamond, Jared. (2005) *Collapse: How Societies Choose to Fail or Succeed.* New York: Viking.

Dickinson, G. Lowes. (1926) *The International Anarchy, 1904–1914.* New York: Century.

Dixon, Jeffrey. (2009) "What Causes Civil Wars? Integrating Quantitative Research Findings," *International Studies Review* 11 (December): 707–735.

Dixon, William J. (1994) "Democracy and the Peaceful Settlement of International Conflict," *American Political Science Review* 88 (March): 14–32.

Dobbins, James. (2010) "Negotiating with Iran: Reflections from Personal Experience," *Washington Quarterly* 33 (January): 149–162.

—. (2007) "Who Lost Iraq? Lessons from the Debacle," *Foreign Affairs* 86 (September/October): 61–74.

Doran, Charles F. (2000) "Confronting the Principles of the Power Cycle: Changing Systems Structure, Expectations, and War," pp. 332–368 in Manus I.

Midlarsky (ed.), *Handbook of War Studies II.* Ann Arbor: University of Michigan Press.

—. (1989) "Power Cycle Theory of Systems Structure and Stability: Commonalities and Complementarities," pp. 83–110 in Manus I. Midlarsky (ed.), *Handbook of War Studies.* New York: Unwin Hyman.

Doran, Charles F., and Wes Parsons. (1980) "War and the Cycle of Relative Power," *American Political Science Review* 74 (December): 947–965.

Dörner, Dietrich. (1996) *The Logic of Failure.* Reading, MA: Addison-Wesley.

Dos Santos, Theotonio. (1970) "The Structure of Dependence," *American Economic Review* 60 (May): 231–236.

Dougherty, James E., and Robert L. Pfaltzgraff, Jr. (2001) *Contending Theories of International Relations,* 5th ed. New York: Longman.

Doyle, Michael W. (1997) *Ways of War and Peace.* New York: Norton.

Dreher, Axel, Noel Gaston, and Pim Martens. (2008) *Measuring Globalization—Gauging Its Consequence.* New York: Springer.

Easterbrook, Gregg. (2002) "Safe Deposit: The Case for Foreign Aid," *New Republic* (July 29): 16–20.

Eck, Kristine. (2009) "From Armed Conflict to War: Ethnic Mobilization and Conflict Intensification," *International Studies Quarterly* 53 (June): 369–388.

Economist Intelligence Unit. (2010) *Global FDI.* London: The Economist.

Emmott, Bill. (2002) "Present at the Creation: A Survey of America's World Role," *The Economist* (June 29): 1–34.

Enloe, Cynthia H. (2004) *The Curious Feminist.* Berkeley: University of California Press.

—. (2000) *Maneuvers: The International Politics of Militarizing Women's Lives.* Berkeley: University of California Press.

Etzioni, Amitai. (2005) *From Empire to Community: A New Approach to International Relations.* London: Palgrave Macmillan.

Evans, Mark. (2009) "Moral Responsibilities and the Conflicting Demands of *Jus Post Bellum*," *Ethics & International Affairs* 23 (Summer): 147–164.

"Failed State Index." (2010) *Foreign Policy* 180 (July/August): 74–79.

Fallows, James. (2002) "The Military-Industrial Complex," *Foreign Policy* 22 (November/December): 46–48.

Ferguson, Niall. (2009) "'Chimerica' Is Headed for Divorce," *Newsweek* (August 14 & 31): 56–57.

—. (2008) *The Ascent of Money: A Financial History of the World*. New York: Penguin.

—. (2004) *Colossus: The Price of America's Empire*. New York: Penguin.

Festinger, Leon. (1957) *A Theory of Cognitive Dissonance*. Evanston, IL: Row, Peterson.

Fieldhouse, D. K. (1973) *Economics and Empire, 1830–1914*. Ithaca, NY: Cornell University Press.

Fields, Lanny B., Russell J. Barber, and Cheryl A. Riggs. (1998) *The Global Past*. Boston: Bedford.

Finnegan, William. (2002) "Leasing the Rain," *The New Yorker* (April 18): 43–53.

Flanagan, Stephen J., Ellen L. Frost, and Richard Kugler. (2001) *Challenges of the Global Century*. Washington, DC: Institute for National Strategic Studies, National Defense University.

Fogel, Robert. (2010) "$123,000,000,000,000," *Foreign Policy* 177 (January/February): 70–75.

Foley, Jonathan. (2010) "Boundaries for a Healthy Planet," *Scientific American* 302 (April): 54–57.

Fortna, Virginia Page. (2008) *Does Peacekeeping Work? Shaping Belligerents' Choices after Civil War*. Princeton, NJ: Princeton University Press.

—. (2004) "Interstate Peacekeeping: Causal Mechanisms and Empirical Effects," *World Politics* 56 (July): 481–519.

Frank, André Gunder. (1969) *Latin America: Underdevelopment or Revolution*. New York: Monthly Review Press.

Freedom House. (2010) *Freedom in the World*. Washington, DC: Freedom House.

Freeland, Jonathan. (2007) "Bush's Amazing Achievement," *New York Review of Books* 54 (June 14): 16–20.

Freud, Sigmund. (1968) "Why War," pp. 71–80 in Leon Bramson and George W. Goethals (eds.), *War*. New York: Basic Books.

Friedman, Thomas L. (2008) *Hot, Flat, and Crowded: Why We Need a Green Revolution– And How It Can Renew America*. New York: Farrar, Straus and Giroux.

—. (2006) "The First Law of Petropolitics," *Foreign Policy* 154 (May/June): 28–36.

Fukuyama, Francis. (1999) *The Great Disruption: Human Nature and the Reconstitution of Social Order*. New York: Free Press.

—. (1989) "The End of History?" *National Interest* 16 (Summer): 3–16.

Gacek, Christopher M. (1994) *The Logic of Force*. New York: Columbia University Press.

Gaddis, John Lewis. (2005) "Grand Strategy in the Second Term," *Foreign Affairs* 84 (January/February): 2–15.

—. (1997) *We Now Know: Rethinking Cold War History*. New York: Oxford University Press.

—. (1982) *Strategies of Containment*. New York: Oxford University Press.

Galbraith, Peter W. (2006) *The End of Iraq*. New York: Simon & Schuster.

Garrison, Jean. (2006) "From Stop to Go in Foreign Policy," *International Studies Review* 9 (June): 291–293.

—. (1999) *Games Advisers Play*. College Station: Texas A&M University Press.

Gartzke, Erik. (2007) "The Capitalist Peace," *American Journal of Political Science* 51 (1): 166–191.

Gazzaniga, Michael S. (2005) *The Ethical Brain*. New York: Dana Press.

Geller, Daniel S. (2000) "Power and International Conflict," pp. 259–277 in John A. Vasquez (ed.), *What Do We Know About War?* Lanham, MD: Rowman & Littlefield.

Geller, Daniel S., and J. David Singer. (1998) *Nations at War: A Scientific Study of International Conflict*. Cambridge: Cambridge University Press.

George, Alexander L. (2006) *On Foreign Policy*. Boulder, CO: Paradigm.

—. (1991) *Forceful Persuasion: Coercive Diplomacy as an Alternative to War*. Washington, DC: United States Institute of Peace Press.

Gerson, Michael. (2006) "The View From the Top," *Newsweek* (August 21): 58–60.

Gibler, Douglas M. (2007) "Bordering on Peace," *International Studies Quarterly* 51 (September): 509–532.

Giddens, Anthony. (2003) *Runaway World*. New York: Routledge.

—. (1984) *The Constitution of Society: Outline of the Theory of Structuration*. Cambridge: Polity.

Gilpin, Robert. (2001) "Three Ideologies of Political Economy," pp. 269–286 in Charles W. Kegley, Jr. and Eugene R. Wittkopf (eds.), *The Global Agenda*, 6th ed. Boston: McGraw-Hill.

Gleditsch, Nils Petter. (2008) "The Liberal Moment Fifteen Years On," *International Studies Quarterly* 52 (December): 691–712.

Glynn, Patrick. (1993) "Letter to the Editor," *Foreign Policy* 90 (Spring): 171–174.

Goldstein, Joshua. (2002) *War and Gender*. Cambridge: Cambridge University Press.

—. (1988) *Long Cycles: Prosperity and War in the Modern Age*. New Haven: Yale University Press.

Goldstone, Jack A. (2009) "The New Population Bomb: The Four Megatrends That Will Change the World," *Foreign Affairs* 89 (January/February): 31–43.

Gore, Al. (2006) *An Inconvenient Truth: The Planetary Emergency and What We Can Do About It*. Emmaus, PA: Rodale.

Greenspan, Alan. (2007) *The Age of Turbulence: Adventures in a New World*. New York: Penguin.

—. (2004) "The Critical Role of Education in the Nation's Economy," speech delivered at the Greater Omaha Chamber of Commerce, February 20. Retrieved at www.federalreserve.gov/boarddocs/speeches/2004/200402202/default.htm.

Gregor, Thomas, and Clayton A. Robarchek. (1996) "Two Paths to Peace: Semai and Mehinaku Nonviolence," pp. 159–188 in Thomas Gregor (ed.), *A Natural History of Peace*. Nashville: Vanderbilt University Press.

Grieco, Joseph M. (1995) "Anarchy and the Limits of Cooperation," pp. 151–171 in Charles W. Kegley, Jr. (ed.), *Controversies in International Relations Theory*. New York: St. Martin's.

Grieco, Joseph M., and John I. Ikenberry. (2003) *State Power and World Markets*. New York: Norton.

Grimmett, Richard F. (2009) *Conventional Arms Transfers to Developing Nations, 2001–2008*. Washington, DC: Congressional Research Service.

Grotius, Hugo. (1949) *The Law of War and Peace*, translated by Louise Loomis. New York: Walter J. Black.

Gulick, Edward V. (1955) *Europe's Classical Balance of Power*. Ithaca, NY: Cornell University Press.

Gurr, Ted Robert. (1970) *Why Men Rebel*. Princeton, NJ: Princeton University Press.

Gvosdev, Nikolas K. (2005) "The Value(s) of Realism," *SAIS Review of International Affairs* 25 (Winter/Spring): 17–25.

Haas, Ernst B. (1953) "The Balance of Power: Prescription, Concept, or Propaganda?" *World Politics* 5 (July): 442–477.

Haass, Richard N. (2009) *War of Necessity, War of Choice*. New York: Simon & Schuster.

—. (2008) "The Age of Nonpolarity," *Foreign Affairs* 87 (May/June): 44–56.

Habermas, Jürgen. (1984) *The Theory of Communicative Action*, 2 vols. Boston: Beacon Press.

Hacking, Ian. (1999) *The Social Construction of What?* Cambridge, MA: Harvard University Press.

Halperin, Morton, and Priscilla Clapp with Arnold Kanter. (2006) *Bureaucratic Politics and Foreign Policy*, 2nd. ed. Washington, DC: Brookings.

Hammes, Thomas X. (2004) *The Sling and the Stone: On War in the 21st Century*. St. Paul, MN: Zenith Press.

Handelman, Howard. (2009) *The Challenge of Third World Development*, 5th ed. Upper Saddle River, NJ: Prentice-Hall.

Hansen, Jim. (2006) "The Threat to the Planet," *New York Review of Books* (July 13): 12–16.

Harbom, Lotta, and Peter Wallersteen. (2009) "Armed Conflict, 1946–2008," *Journal of Peace Research* 46 (5): 577–587.

Hardin, Garrett. (1968) "The Tragedy of the Commons," *Science* 162 (December): 1243–1248.

Harknett, Richard J. (1994) "The Logic of Conventional Deterrence and the End of the Cold War," *Security Studies* 4 (Autumn): 86–114.

Harman, Willis. (1976) *An Incomplete Guide to the Future*. Stanford, CA: Stanford Alumni Association.

Hart, Gary. (2004) *The Fourth Power: A Grand Strategy for the United States in the Twenty-First Century*. New York: Oxford University Press.

Hausmann, Ricardo. (2001) "Prisoners of Geography," *Foreign Policy* 122 (January/February): 45–53.

Haynes, Jeffrey. (2004) "Religion and International Relations," *International Politics* 41 (September): 451–462.

HDI. (2007) *Human Development Indicators*. New York: United Nations Development Programme.

HDR. (2009) *Human Development Report*. New York: United Nations Development Programme.

Hedges, Chris. (2003) "What Every Person Should Know About War," *New York Times* (July 6): www.nytimes.com.

Heilbroner, Robert L. (1960) *The Future as History*. New York: Grove Press.

Henkin, Louis. (1991) "Law and Politics in International Relations," pp. 163–188 in Robert L. Rothstein (ed.), *The Evolution of Theory in International Relations*. Columbia: University of South Carolina Press.

—. (1979) *How Nations Behave: Law and Foreign Policy*. New York: Columbia University Press.

Hensel, Howard M. (ed.). (2010) *The Prism of Just War: Asian and Western Perspectives in the Legitimate Use of Military Force*. Burlington, VT: Ashgate.

Hensel, Paul R. (2000) "Theory and Evidence on Geography and Conflict," pp. 57–84 in John A. Vasquez (ed.), *What Do We Know About War?* Lanham, MD: Rowman & Littlefield.

Hermann, Margaret G. (1988) "The Role of Leaders and Leadership in the Making of American Foreign Policy," pp. 266–284 in Charles W. Kegley, Jr. and Eugene R. Wittkopf (eds.), *The Domestic Sources of Foreign Policy*, New York: St. Martin's Press.

—. (1976) "When Leader Personality Will Affect Foreign Policy: Some Propositions," pp. 326–333 in James N. Rosenau (ed.), *In Search of Global Patterns*. New York: Free Press.

Hermann, Margaret G., and Joe D. Hagan. (2004) "International Decision Making: Leadership Matters," pp. 182–188 in Karen A. Mingst and Jack L. Snyder (eds.), *Essential Readings in World Politics*, 2nd ed. New York: Norton.

Herz, John H. (1951) *Political Realism and Political Idealism*. Chicago: University of Chicago Press.

Hewitt, J. Joseph, Jonathan Wilkenfeld, and Ted Robert Gurr. (2010) *Peace and Conflict, 2010*. Boulder, CO: Paradigm.

Hilsman, Roger, with Laura Gaughran and Patricia A. Weitsman. (1993) *The Politics of Policy Making in Defense and Foreign Affairs*, 3rd ed. Englewood Cliffs, NJ: Prentice-Hall.

Hoffmann, Matthew J. (2009) "Is Constructivist Ethics an Oxymoron?" *International Studies Review* 11 (June): 231–252.

Hoffmann, Stanley. (1971) "International Law and the Control of Force," pp. 34–66 in Karl W. Deutsch and Stanley Hoffmann (eds.), *The Relevance of International Law*. Garden City, NY: Doubleday-Anchor.

Holbrooke, Richard. (1998) *To End a War*. New York: Modern Library.

Hopkins, Terence K., and Immanuel Wallerstein (eds.). (1996) *The Age of Transitions: Trajectory of World Systems 1945–2025*. London: Zed Books.

Horkheimer, Max. (1947) *Eclipse of Reason*. New York: Oxford University Press.

Horn-Phathanothai, Leo. (2010) "The 'China Model' Illusion," presentation delivered at the Carnegie Council for Ethics in International Affairs, New York. Retrieved at http://www.policyinnovations.org/ideas/audio/data/000494.

Howard, Michael E. (1991) "British Grand Strategy in World War I," pp. 31–41 in Paul Kennedy (ed.), *Grand Strategy in War and Peace*. New Haven, CT: Yale University Press.

Hufbauer, Gary Clyde, Jeffrey J. Schott, and Kimberly Ann Elliott. (1990) *Economic Sanctions Reconsidered*, 2nd ed. Washington, DC: Institute for International Economics.

Hume, David. (1817) *Philosophical Essays on Morals, Literature, and Politics*, vol. 1. Washington, DC: Duffy.

Huntington, Samuel P. (1996) *The Clash of Civilizations and the Remaking of World Order*. New York: Simon & Schuster.

—. (1991) *The Third Wave: Democratization in the Late Twentieth Century*. Norman, OK: University of Oklahoma Press.

International Monetary Fund. (2010) *World Economic Outlook*. Washington, DC: International Monetary Fund.

International Trade Statistics. (2009) Geneva: World Trade Organization.

Janis, Irving L. (1989) *Crucial Decisions: Leadership in Policymaking and Crisis Management*. New York: Free Press.

—. (1982) *Groupthink: Psychological Studies of Policy Decisions and Fiascoes*, 2nd ed. Boston: Houghton Mifflin.

Jervis, Robert. (2009) "Unipolarity: A Structural Perspective," *World Politics* 6 (January): 188–213.

—. (2005) *American Foreign Policy in a New Era.* New York: Routledge.

—. (1997) *System Effects: Complexity in Political and Social Life.* Princeton, NJ: Princeton University Press.

—. (1985) "From Balance to Concert: A Study of International Cooperation," *World Politics* 38 (October): 58–79.

—. (1976) *Perception and Misperception in World Politics.* Princeton, NJ: Princeton University Press.

Joffe, Josef. (2009) "The Default Power: The False Prophecy of America's Decline," *Foreign Affairs* 88 (September/October): 21–35.

—. (1995) "Bismarck or Britain? Toward an American Grand Strategy after Bipolarity," *International Security* 19 (Spring): 94–117.

Judah, Tim. (2000) *Kosovo: War and Revenge.* New Haven: Yale University Press.

Juergensmeyer, Mark. (2003) "The Religious Roots of Contemporary Terrorism," pp. 185–193 in Charles W. Kegley, Jr. (ed.), *The New Global Terrorism.* Upper Saddle River, NJ: Prentice Hall.

Kaarbo, Juliet. (2008) "Coalition Cabinet Decision Making: Institutional and Psychological Factors," *International Studies Review* 10 (March): 57–86.

Kagan, Robert. (2008) *The Return of History and the End of Dreams.* New York: Knopf.

Kahneman, Daniel, Paul Slovic, and Amos Tversky. (1982) *Judgment Under Uncertainty: Heuristics and Biases.* New York: Cambridge University Press.

Kaplan, Fred. (2008) *Daydream Believers.* Hoboken, NJ: Wiley.

Kaplan, Morton A. (1957) *System and Process in International Politics.* New York: Wiley.

Keegan, John. (2005) *The Iraq War.* New York: Vintage.

—. (1999) *The First World War.* New York: Knopf.

—. (1993) *A History of Warfare.* New York: Vintage.

Kegley, Charles W., Jr. (1994) "How Did the Cold War Die? Principles for an Autopsy," *Mershon International Studies Review* 38 (April): 11–41.

Kegley, Charles W., Jr., and Gregory A. Raymond. (2007) *After Iraq: The Imperiled American Imperium.* New York: Oxford University Press.

—. (2002) *Exorcising the Ghost of Westphalia: Building World Order in the New Millennium.* Upper Saddle River, NJ: Prentice Hall.

—. (1994) *A Multipolar Peace? Great-Power Politics in the Twenty-First Century.* New York: St. Martin's.

—. (1990) *When Trust Breaks Down: Alliance Norms and World Politics.* Columbia: University of South Carolina Press.

—. (1982) "Alliance Norms and War: A New Piece in an Old Puzzle," *International Studies Quarterly* 26 (December): 572–595.

Kegley, Charles W., Jr., Gregory A. Raymond, and Margaret G. Hermann. (1998) "The Rise and Fall of the Nonintervention Norm," *Fletcher Forum of World Affairs* 22 (Winter/Spring): 81–101.

Kegley, Charles W., Jr., and Eugene R. Wittkopf. (2004) *World Politics: Trend and Transformation*, 9th ed. Belmont, CA: Wadsworth.

Kelleher, Ann, and Laura Klein. (2006) *Global Perspectives*, 2nd ed. Upper Saddle River, NJ: Prentice-Hall.

Kennan, George F. (1991) "Morality and Foreign Policy," pp. 59–76 in Kenneth M. Jensen and Elizabeth P. Faulkner (eds.), *Morality and Foreign Policy: Realpolitik Revisited.* Washington, DC: United States Institute of Peace Press.

—. (1951) *American Diplomacy, 1900–1950.* New York: New American Library.

—. ["X"]. (1947) "The Sources of Soviet Conduct," *Foreign Affairs* 25 (July): 566–582.

Kennedy, Paul. (1987) *The Rise and Fall of the Great Powers.* New York: Random House.

Keohane, Robert O., and Joseph S. Nye. (2001a) *Power and Interdependence*, 3rd ed. New York: Addison Wesley-Longman.

—. (2001b) "Power and Interdependence in the Information Age," pp. 26–36 in Charles W. Kegley, Jr. and Eugene R. Wittkopf (eds.), *The Global Agenda*, 6th ed. Boston: McGraw-Hill.

—. (1977) *Power and Interdependence.* Boston: Little, Brown.

—. (eds.). (1971) *Transnational Relations and World Politics.* Cambridge: Harvard University Press.

Kesgin, Baris, and Juliet Kaarbo. (2010) "When and How Parliaments Influence Foreign Policy: The Case of Turkey's Iraq Decision," *International Studies Perspectives* 11 (February): 19–36.

Kilcullen, David. (2010) *Counterinsurgency*. New York: Oxford University Press.

Kim, Dae Jung, and James D. Wolfensohn. (1999) "Economic Growth Requires Good Governance," *International Herald Tribune* (February 26): 6.

Kim, Woosang. (1989) "Power, Alliance, and Major Wars, 1816–4975," *Journal of Conflict Resolution* 32 (3): 255–273.

Kindleberger, Charles P. (1973) *The World in Depression, 1929–1939*. Berkeley: University of California Press.

Kingsolver, Barbara. (2010) "Water Is Life," *National Geographic* 217 (April): 36–59.

Kissinger, Henry A. (1999) *Years of Renewal*. New York: Simon and Schuster.

—. (1982) *Years of Upheaval*. Boston: Little, Brown.

Klare, Michael T. (2001) "The New Geography of Conflict," *Foreign Affairs* 80 (May/June): 49–61.

—. (1990) "Wars in the 1990s: Growing Firepower in the Third World," *Bulletin of the Atomic Scientists* 46 (May): 9–13.

Klinghoffer, Arthur Jay. (2006) *The Power of Projections: How Maps Reflect Global Politics and History*. Westport, CT: Praeger.

Kose, Ayhan M., Christopher Otrok, and Eswar S. Prasad. (2008) *Global Business Cycles: Convergence or Decoupling?* Working Paper 14292. Cambridge, MA: National Bureau of Economic Research.

Koslowski, Rey, and Friedrich V. Kratochwil. (1994) "Understanding Change in International Politics: The Soviet Empire's Demise in the International System," *International Organization* 48 (Spring): 215–247.

Krauthammer, Charles. (2006) "But Not At the UN," *Time* (October 23): 39.

—. (2004) "Democratic Realism: An American Foreign Policy for a Unipolar World," speech delivered at the American Enterprise Institute, February 10.

—. (1993) "How Doves Become Hawks," *Time* (May 17): 74.

—. (1991) "The Unipolar Moment," *Foreign Affairs* 70 (Winter): 23–33.

Kugler, Jacek, Ronald Tammen, and Brian Efird. (2004) "Integrating Theory and Policy," *International Studies Review* 6 (December): 163–179.

Kupchan, Charles H., and Clifford A. Kupchan. (1992) "A New Concert for Europe," pp. 249–266 in Graham Allison and Gregory F. Treverton (eds.), *Rethinking America's Security: Beyond the Cold War to a New World Order*. New York: Norton.

Lake, Anthony. (2000) *Six Nightmares*. Boston: Little, Brown.

Lamy, Steven L. (2008) "Contemporary Mainstream Approaches: Neo-realism and Neo-liberalism," pp. 124–139 in John Baylis, Steve Smith, and Patricia Owens (eds.), *The Globalization of World Politics*, 4th ed. Oxford, UK: Oxford University Press.

Landes, David S. (1998) *The Wealth and Poverty of Nations: Why Are Some So Rich and Some So Poor?* New York: Norton.

Larson, Deborah Welch. (1994) "The Role of Belief Systems and Schemas in Foreign Policy Decision-Making," *Political Psychology* 15 (March): 17–33.

Lave, Charles A., and James G. March. (1975) *An Introduction to Models in the Social Sciences*. New York: Harper & Row.

Lee, Laura. (2000) *Bad Predictions: 2000 Years of the Best Minds Making the Worst Forecasts*. Roosevelt Hills, MI: Elsewhere Press.

Leffler, Melvyn P. (2007) *For the Soul of Mankind: The United States, the Soviet Union and the Cold War*. New York: Hill and Wang.

Lemke, Douglas. (2003) "Development and War," *International Studies Review* 5 (December): 55–63.

—. (2002) *Regions of War and Peace*. Cambridge, UK: Cambridge University Press.

Levy, Jack S. (2003a) "Applications of Prospect Theory to Political Science," *Syntheses* 135 (May): 215–241.

—. (2003b) "Political Psychology and Foreign Policy," pp. 253–284 in David O. Sears, Leonie Huddy, and Robert Jervis (eds.), *Oxford Handbook of Political Psychology*. New York: Oxford University Press.

—. (2001) "War and Its Causes," pp. 47–56 in Charles W. Kegley, Jr. and Eugene Wittkopf (eds.), *The Global Agenda*, 6th ed. Boston: McGraw-Hill.

—. (1989) "The Diversionary Theory of War: A Critique," pp. 259–288 in Manus I. Midlarsky (ed.), *Handbook of War Studies*. Boston: Unwin Hyman.

—. (1985) "The Polarity of the System and International Stability: An Empirical Analysis," pp. 41–66 in Alan Ned Sabrosky (ed.), *Polarity and War*. Boulder, CO: Westview.

Levy, Jack S., and William R. Thompson. (2010) *Causes of War*. Malden, MA: Wiley-Blackwell.

—. (2005) "Hegemonic Threats and Great-Power Balancing in Europe, 1945–1999," *Security Studies* 14 (January-March): 1–30.

Lewis, M. Paul (ed.). (2009) *Ethnologue: Languages of the World*, 16th ed. Dallas, TX: SIL International.

Lind, Michael. (1993) "Of Arms and the Woman," *New Republic* (November 15): 36–38.

Lindblom, Charles E. (1979) "Still Muddling, Not Yet Through," *Public Administration Review* 39 (November/December): 517–526.

Lindsay, James M. (2009) "The Case for a Concert of Democracies," *Ethics & International Affairs* 23 (Spring): 5–11.

Linklater, Andrew. (2002) "Cosmopolitan Political Communities in International Relations," *International Relations* 16 (1): 135–150.

Lipson, Charles. (1984) "International Cooperation in Economic and Security Affairs," *World Politics* 37 (October): 1–23.

Little, Richard. (2007) *The Balance of Power in International Relations: Metaphors, Myths and Models*. Cambridge, UK: Cambridge University Press.

Lorenz, Konrad. (1963) *On Aggression*. New York: Harcourt, Brace & World.

Machiavelli, Niccolò. (1950) *The Prince*. New York: New American Library.

Mackinder, Sir Halford. (1919) *Democratic Ideals and Reality*. New York: Holt.

Mahan, Alfred Thayer. (1890) *The Influence of Sea Power in History*. Boston: Little, Brown.

Majeed, Akhtar. (1991) "Has the War System Really Become Obsolete?" *Bulletin of Peace Proposals* 22 (December): 419–425.

Maleševi, Sinisa. (2008) "The Sociology of New Wars?" *International Political Sociology* 2 (June): 97–112.

Malhotra, Deepak. (2009) "Without Conditions: The Case for Negotiating with the Enemy," *Foreign Affairs* 88 (September/October): 84–90.

Mansfield, Edward D., and Jack Snyder. (2005) *Electing to Fight*. Cambridge, MA: MIT Press.

Marling, William H. (2006) *How "American" Is Globalization?* Baltimore, MD: Johns Hopkins University Press.

Martin, Lisa L. (2007) "Neoliberalism," pp. 109–126 in Tim Dunne, Milja Kurki, and Steve Smith (eds.), *International Relations Theories*. Oxford, UK: Oxford University Press.

Marx, Karl, and Fredrick Engels. (1948) *Manifesto of the Communist Party*. New York: International Publishers.

Mastanduno, Michael. (1991) "Do Relative Gains Matter?" *International Security* 16 (Summer): 73–113.

Mathews, Jessica T. (1998) "Are Networks Better than Nations?" pp. 8–11 in James M. Lindsay (ed.), *Perspectives: Global Issues*. Boulder, CO: Coursewise Publishing.

Matlock, Jack F., Jr. (2010) *Superpower Illusions*. New Haven, CT: Yale University Press.

Mayer, Jane. (2009) "The Predator War," *The New Yorker* (October 26): 36–45.

Mazumdar, Sudip. (2009) "Man Bites 'Slumdog'," *Newsweek* (March 2): 34–35.

McClelland, Scott. (2008) *What Happened: Inside the Bush White House and Washington's Culture of Deception*. New York: PublicAffairs.

McDonald, Patrick J. (2007) "The Purse Strings of Peace," *American Journal of Political Science* 51 (3): 569–582.

Mearsheimer, John J. (2001) *The Tragedy of Great Power Politics*. New York: Norton.

—. (1994/95) "The False Promise of International Institutions," *International Security* 19 (Winter): 5–49.

Mearsheimer, John J., and Stephen M. Walt. (2003) "An Unnecessary War," *Foreign Policy* 134 (January/February): 50–58.

Melander, Erik. (2005) "Gender Equality and Interstate Armed Conflict," *International Studies Quarterly* 49 (December): 695–714.

Midlarsky, Manus I. (1988) *The Onset of World War*. Boston: Unwin Hyman.

Millennium Development Goals Report. (2010) New York: United Nations Department of Public Information.

Mintz, Alex. (2004) "How Do Leaders Make Decisions? A Poliheuristic Perspective," *Journal of Conflict Resolution* 48 (February): 3–13.

Mitani, John C., David P. Watts, and Sylvia J. Amsler. (2010) "Lethal Intergroup Aggression Leads to Territorial Expansion in Wild Chimpanzees," *Current Biology* 20 (12): 507–508.

Mitchell, David, and Tansa George Massoud. (2009) "Anatomy of Failure: Bush's Decision-Making Process and the Iraq War," *Foreign Policy Analysis* 5 (July): 265–286.

Mitrany, David. (1966) *A Working Peace System.* Chicago: Quadrangle.

Modelski, George, and William R. Thompson. (1999) "The Long and the Short of Global Politics in the Twenty-First Century: An Evolutionary Approach," *International Studies Review*, special issue, edited by Davis B. Bobrow: 109–140.

—. (1996) *Leading Sectors and World Powers.* Columbia: University of South Carolina Press.

Mohan, C. Raja. (2006) "India and the Balance of Power," *Foreign Affairs* 85 (July/August): 17–32.

Morgenthau, Hans J. (1985) *Politics Among Nations,* 6th ed. Revised by Kenneth W. Thompson. New York: Knopf.

—. (1948) *Politics Among Nations.* New York: Knopf.

Mowle, Thomas S., and David H. Sacko. (2007) *The Unipolar World: An Unbalanced Future.* New York: Palgrave Macmillan.

Moyer, Michael. (2010) "How Much Is Left?" *Scientific American* 303 (September): 74–81.

Moyo, Dambisa. (2010) *Dead Aid: Why Aid Is Not Working and How There Is a Better Way for Africa.* New York: Farrar, Straus, and Giroux.

Murdoch, James C., and Todd Sandler. (2004) "Civil Wars and Economic Growth," *American Journal of Political Science* 48 (January): 138–151.

Myers, David. (1990) *Social Psychology,* 3rd ed. New York: McGraw-Hill.

Myrskyla, Mikko, Hans-Peter Kohler, and Francesco C. Billari. (2009) "Advances in Development Reverse Fertility Declines," *Nature* 460 (August 6): 741–743.

Nagl, John A. (2002) *Learning to Eat Soup with a Knife: Counterinsurgency Lessons from Malaya and Vietnam.* Chicago: University of Chicago Press.

Naím, Moisés. (2009) "Globalization," *Foreign Policy* 171 (March/April): 28–34.

—. (2007) "The Free-Trade Paradox," *Foreign Policy* 162 (September/October): 95–96.

National Commission on Terrorist Attacks Upon the United States. (2004) *The 9/11 Commission Report.* New York: Norton.

Natsios, Andrew S. (2008) "Beyond Darfur: Sudan's Slide Toward Civil War," *Foreign Affairs* 87 (May/June): 77–93.

NCTC (National Counter-Terrorism Center). (2009) *Report on Terrorism.* Washington, DC: National Counter-Terrorism Center.

Neustadt, Richard E. (1970) *Alliance Politics.* New York: Columbia University Press.

Niebuhr, Reinhold. (1947) *Moral Man and Immoral Society.* New York: Scribner's.

Norris, Robert S., and Hans M. Kristensen. (2010) "Global Nuclear Weapons Inventories, 1945–2010," *Bulletin of the Atomic Scientists* 66 (July/August): 77–83.

Nuechterlein, Donald E. (2005) *Defiant Superpower.* Washington, DC: Potomac.

Nye, Joseph S., Jr. (2008) "The Costs and Benefits of 'In and Outers'," *International Studies Review* 10 (March): 156–160.

—. (2004) *Soft Power: The Means to Success in World Politics.* New York: Public Affairs Press.

—. (1990) *Bound to Lead: The Changing Nature of American Power.* New York: Basic Books.

Nye, Joseph S., Jr., and David A. Welch. (2011) *Understanding Global Conflict and Cooperation.* Boston: Longman.

Oatley, Thomas. (2008) *International Political Economy,* 3rd ed. New York: Pearson Longman.

Obduah, Emmanuel. (2006) "Combating Global Trafficking in Persons," *International Politics* 43 (April): 241–265.

OECD. (2010) *Perspectives on Global Development: Shifting Wealth.* Paris: Organization for Economic Cooperation and Development.

Onuf, Nicholas. (2002) "Worlds of Our Making: The Strange Career of Constructivism in International

Relations," pp. 119–141 in Donald J. Puchala (ed.), *Visions of International Relations*. Columbia: University of South Carolina Press.

—. (1989) *World of Our Making: Rules and Rule in Social Theory and International Relations*. Columbia: University of South Carolina Press.

Oreskes, Naomi. (2004) "Beyond the Ivory Tower: The Scientific Consensus on Climate Change," *Science* 306 (December): 1686.

Organski, A. F. K. (1968) *World Politics*. New York: Knopf.

Organski, A. F. K., and Jacek Kugler. (1980) *The War Ledger*. Chicago: University of Chicago Press.

Østby, Gudrun, Ragnhild Nordås, and Jan Ketil Rød. (2009) "Regional Inequalities and Civil Conflict in Sub-Saharan Africa," *International Studies Quarterly* 53 (June): 301–324.

Ostrom, Charles W., Jr., and John H. Aldrich. (1978) "The Relationship Between Size and Stability in the Major Power International System," *American Journal of Political Science* 22 (November): 743–771.

O'Sullivan, John. (2005) "In Defense of Nationalism," *The National Interest* 78 (Winter): 22–40.

Owen, John M., IV. (2005) "When Do Ideologies Produce Alliances?" *International Studies Quarterly* 49 (March): 73–99.

Packenham, Robert. (1992) *The Dependency Movement*. Cambridge, MA: Harvard University Press.

Panama: A Just Cause. (1989) Washington, DC: United States Department of State, Bureau of Public Affairs, Current Policy No. 1240.

Pape, Robert A. (2005) *Dying to Win: The Strategic Logic of Suicide Terrorism*. New York: Random House.

—. (1997) "Why Economic Sanctions Do Not Work," *International Security* 22 (Fall): 90–136.

—. (1996) *Bombing to Win: Air Power and Coercion in War*. Ithaca: Cornell University Press.

Paul, T. V., G. John Ikenberry, and John A. Hall (eds.). (2003) *The Nation-State in Question*. Princeton: Princeton University Press.

Pauly, Daniel. (2009) "Sushinomics," *Foreign Policy* 171 (March/April): 36–37.

Pei, Minxin. (2009) "Asia's Rise," *Foreign Policy* 173 (July/August): 32–36.

Perry, Alex. (2010) "Africa's Last Best Opportunity," *Time* (May 31): 4–8.

Peterson, V. Spike, and Anne Sisson Runyan. (2009) *Global Gender Issues in the New Millennium*, 3rd ed. Boulder, CO: Westview Press.

Pethokoukis, James. (2006) "Multinationals 2.0," *U.S. News & World Report* (July 31): 42–47.

Pillar, Paul. (2006) "Intelligence, Policy, and the War in Iraq," *Foreign Affairs* 85 (March/April): 15–27.

Pimn, Stuart L., and Clinton Jenkins. (2005) "Sustaining the Variety of Life," *Scientific American* 293 (September): 66–73.

Powell, Colin L. (2004) "A Strategy of Partnerships," *Foreign Affairs* 83 (January/February): 22–34.

Powell, Colin L., with Joseph E. Persico. (1995) *My American Journey*. New York: Ballantine.

Preston, Thomas. (2007) *From Lambs to Lions: Future Security Relationships in a World of Biological and Nuclear Weapons*. Lanham, MD: Rowman & Littlefield.

—. (2001) *The President and His Inner Circle: Leadership Style and the Advisory Process in Foreign Affairs*. New York: Columbia University Press.

—. (1997) "Following the Leader: The Impact of U.S. Presidential Style Upon Advisory Group Dynamics, Structure, and Decision," pp. 191–248 in Paul t'Hart, Eric K. Stern, and Bengt Sundelius (eds.), *Beyond Groupthink: Political Group Dynamics and Foreign Policy-Making*. Ann Arbor: University of Michigan Press.

Preston, Thomas, and Margaret G. Hermann. (2004) "Presidential Leadership Style and the Foreign Policy Advisory Process," pp. 363–380 in Eugene R. Wittkopf and James M. McCormick (eds.), *The Domestic Sources of Foreign Policy*. Lanham, MD: Rowman & Littlefield.

Prestowitz, Clyde. (2005) *Three Billion New Capitalists*. New York: Basic Books.

—. (2003) *Rogue Nation: American Unilateralism and the Failure of Good Intentions*. New York: Basic Books/Perseus.

Price, Richard, and Christian Reus-Smit. (1998) "Dangerous Liaisons? Critical International Theory and Constructivism," *European Journal of International Relations* 4 (3): 259–294.

Puchala, Donald J. (1994) "Some World Order Options for Our Time," *Peace Forum* 11 (November): 17–30.

Putnam, Robert D. (1988) "Diplomacy and Domestic Politics: The Logic of Two-Level Games," *International Organization* 42 (Summer): 427–460.

Rasler, Karen, and William R. Thompson. (2005) *Puzzles of the Democratic Peace: Theory, Geopolitics, and the Transformation of World Politics.* London: Palgrave Macmillan.

Ray, James Lee. (2008) *American Foreign Policy and Political Ambition.* Washington, DC: CQ Press.

—. (1995) *Democracy and International Conflict: An Evaluation of the Democratic Peace Proposition.* Columbia: University of South Carolina Press.

Raymond, Gregory A. (2010) "The Greco-Roman Roots of the Western Just War Tradition," pp. 7–27 in Howard M. Hensel (ed.), *The Prism of Just War: Asian and Western Perspectives on the Legitimate Use of Military Force.* Burlington, VT: Ashgate.

—. (2004) "International Adjudication and Conflict Management," pp. 221–248 in Howard M. Hensel (ed.), *Sovereignty and the Global Community: The Quest for Order in the International System.* Burlington, VT: Ashgate.

—. (1999) "Necessity in Foreign Policy," *Political Science Quarterly* 113 (Winter): 673–688.

—. (1997) "Problems and Prospects in the Study of International Norms," *Mershon International Studies Review* 41 (November): 205–245.

—. (1994) "Democracies, Disputes, and Third-Party Intermediaries," *Journal of Conflict Resolution* 38 (March): 24–42.

Raymond, Gregory A., and Charles W. Kegley, Jr. (1987) "Long Cycles and Internationalized Civil War," *Journal of Politics* 49 (May): 481–499.

Record, Jeffrey. (2009) *Beating Goliath: Why Insurgencies Win.* Washington, DC: Potomac.

Regan, Patrick M., and Aida Paskevicute. (2003) "Women's Access to Politics and Peaceful States," *Journal of Peace Research* 40 (March): 287–302.

Reiter, Dan, and Allan C. Stam. (2002) *Democracies at War.* Princeton, NJ: Princeton University Press.

Ricks, Thomas E. (2009) *The Gamble: General Petraeus and the American Military Adventure in Iraq, 2006–2008.* New York: Penguin.

—. (2006) *Fiasco: The American Military Adventure in Iraq.* New York: Penguin.

Riker, William H. (1962) *The Theory of Political Coalitions.* New Haven: Yale University Press.

Robinson, Mary, edited by Kevin Boyle. (2006) *A Voice for Human Rights.* Philadelphia: University of Pennsylvania Press.

Rosecrance, Richard. (1999) *The Rise of the Virtual State.* New York: Basic Books.

—. (1986) *The Rise of the Trading State: Commerce and Conquest in the Modern World.* New York: Basic Books.

Rosenau, James N., and Mary Durfee. (1995) *Thinking Theory Thoroughly: Coherent Approaches to an Incoherent World.* Boulder, CO: Westview.

Ross, Dennis. (2007) *Statecraft.* New York: Farrar, Straus and Giroux.

Ross, Michael L. (2001) "Does Oil Hinder Democracy?" *World Politics* 53 (April): 325–361.

Rostow, W.W. (1960) *The Stages of Economic Growth.* Cambridge, UK: Cambridge University Press.

Rousseau, Jean-Jacques. (1971) "The State of War," pp. 53–56 in Arend Lijphard (ed.), *World Politics,* 2nd ed. Boston: Allyn and Bacon.

Rummel, Rudolph J. (1994) *Death by Government.* New Brunswick, NJ: Transaction Books.

Russett, Bruce. (2001) "How Democracy, Interdependence, and International Organizations Create a System for Peace," pp. 232–242 in Charles W. Kegley, Jr. and Eugene Wittkopf (eds.), *The Global Agenda,* 6th ed. Boston: McGraw-Hill.

Russett, Bruce, and John Oneal. (2001) *Triangulating Peace: Democracy, Interdependence, and International Organizations.* New York: Norton.

Sachs, Jeffrey D. (2008) *Common Wealth: Economics for a Crowded Planet.* New York: Penguin Press.

—. (2002) "A New Global Effort to Control Malaria," *Science* 4 (October): 122–124.

Sagan, Carl, and Richard Turco. (1993) "Nuclear Winter in the Post-Cold War Era," *Journal of Peace Research* 30 (November): 369–373.

Samin, Amir. (1976) *Unequal Development.* New York: Monthly Review Press.

Samuelson, Robert J. (2006) "This Year Could Mark the End of Pax Americana," *The State* (Columbia, S.C.) (December 19): A9.

Saul, John Ralston. (2005) *The Collapse of Globalization and the Reinvention of the World.* London: Atlantic.

—. (2004) "The Collapse of Globalism and the Rebirth of Nationalism," *Harper's* 308 (March): 33–43.

Schelling, Thomas C. (1978) *Micromotives and Macrobehavior.* New York: Norton.

—. (1966) *Arms and Influence*. New Haven: Yale University Press.

Schmookler, Andrew Bard. (1984) *The Parable of the Tribes: The Problem of Power in Social Evolution*. Berkeley: University of California Press.

Schneider, Gerald, Nils Petter Gleditsch, and Sabine C. Carey. (2010) "Exploring the Past, Anticipating the Future: A Symposium," *International Studies Review* 12 (March): 1–7.

Schroeder, Paul W. (1989) "The Nineteenth Century System: Balance of Power or Political Equilibrium?" *Review of International Studies* 15 (April): 135–153.

Schulz, William F. (2001) *In Our Own Best Interest: How Defending Human Rights Benefits Us All*. Boston: Beacon Press.

Schweller, Randall L. (2006) *Unanswered Threats: Political Constraints on the Balance of Power*. Princeton, NJ: Princeton University Press.

Schwenninger, Sherle R. (2004) "America's 'Suez Moment,' *The Atlantic* 293 (January/February): 129–130.

Shane, Scott. (2005) "The Beast That Feeds on Boxes: Bureaucracy," *New York Times* (April 10): Section 4, 3.

Shannon, Thomas Richard. (1989) *An Introduction to the World-System Perspective*. Boulder, CO: Westview Press.

Shannon, Vaughn. (2005) "Wendt's Violation of the Constructivist Project: Why a World State Is Not Inevitable," *European Journal of International Relations* 11 (4): 581–587.

—. (2000) "Norms Are What States Make of Them: The Political Psychology of Norm Violation," *International Studies Quarterly* 44 (June): 293–316.

Shannon, Vaughn, and Jonathan W. Keller. (2007) "Leadership Style and International Norm Violation: The Case of the Iraq War," *Foreign Policy Analysis* 3 (January): 79–104.

Shimko, Keith L. (1995) "Foreign Policy Metaphors: Falling 'Dominoes' and Drug 'Wars'," pp. 71–84 in Laura Neack, Jeanne A. K. Hay, and Patrick J. Haney (eds.), *Foreign Policy Analysis*. Englewood Cliffs, NJ: Prentice-Hall.

Simon, Herbert A. (1957) *Models of Man*. New York: Wiley.

Singer, J. David. (2000) "The Etiology of Interstate War," pp. 3–21 in John A. Vasquez (ed.), *What Do We Know About War?* Lanham, MD: Rowman & Littlefield.

—. (1991) "Peace in the Global System," pp. 56–84 in Charles W. Kegley, Jr. (ed.), *The Long Postwar Peace*. New York: HarperCollins.

—. (1968) *Quantitative International Politics: Insights and Evidence*. New York: Free Press.

Singer, Peter. (2004) *One World: The Ethics of Globalization*, 2nd ed. New Haven: Yale University Press.

—. (1979) *Practical Ethics*. Cambridge, UK: Cambridge University Press.

SIPRI (Stockholm International Peace Research Institute). (2010) *SIPRI Yearbook*. New York: Oxford University Press.

—. (2009) *SIPRI Yearbook*. New York: Oxford University Press.

Sivard, Ruth Leger. (1991) *World Military and Social Expenditures 1991*. Washington, DC: World Priorities.

Slomanson, William R. (2010) *Fundamental Perspectives on International Law*, 6th ed. Belmont, CA: Wadsworth.

Small, Melvin, and J. David Singer. (1982) *Resort to Arms: International and Civil Wars, 1816–1980*. Beverly Hills, CA: Sage.

Snyder, David Pearce. (2006) "Five Mega-Trends Changing the World," pp. 13–17 in Robert M. Jackson (ed.), *Global Issues 05/06*. Dubuque, IA: McGraw-Hill/Dushkin.

Snyder, Glenn H. (1971) "'Prisoner's Dilemma' and 'Chicken' Models in International Politics," *International Studies Quarterly* 15 (March): 66–103.

Snyder, Glenn H., and Paul Diesing. (1977) *Conflict Among Nations*. Princeton, NJ: Princeton University Press.

Snyder, Jack. (2004) "One World, Rival Theories," *Foreign Policy* 145 (November/December): 53–62.

—. (1984) "The Security Dilemma in Alliances," *World Politics* 36 (July): 461–495.

Sobek, David. (2005) "Machiavelli's Legacy: Domestic Politics and International Conflict," *International Studies Quarterly* 49 (June): 179–204.

Sorensen, Theodore C. (1963) *Decision Making in the White House*. New York: Columbia University Press.

Sprout, Harold, and Margaret Sprout. (1965) *The Ecological Perspective on Human Affairs*. Princeton, NJ: Princeton University Press.

Spykman, Nicholas. (1944) *Geography of Peace*. New York: Harcourt Brace.

Starr, Harvey. (1978) "'Opportunity' and 'Willingness' as Ordering Concepts in the Study of War," *International Interactions* 4: 363–387.

Steinberg, James B. (2008) "Real Leaders Do Soft Power: Learning the Lessons of Iraq," *Washington Quarterly* 31 (Spring): 155–164.

Steingart, Gabor. (2008) *War for Wealth*. New York: McGraw-Hill.

Stern, Eric K. (1997) "Probing the Plausibility of the Newgroup Syndrome: Kennedy and the Bay of Pigs," pp. 153–189 in Paul 't Hart, Eric K. Stern, and Bengt Sundelius (eds.), *Beyond Groupthink: Political Group Dynamics and Foreign Policy-Making*. Ann Arbor: University of Michigan Press.

Stern, Eric K., and Bengt Sundelius. (1997) "Understanding Small Group Decisions in Foreign Policy: Process Diagnosis and Research Procedure," pp. 123–150 in Paul 't Hart, Eric K. Stern, and Bengt Sundelius (eds.), *Beyond Groupthink: Political Group Dynamics and Foreign Policy-Making*. Ann Arbor: University of Michigan Press.

Stephenson, Carolyn M. (2000) "NGOs and the Principal Organs of the United Nations," pp. 270–294 in Paul Taylor and R. J. Groom (eds.), *The United Nations at the Millennium*. London: Continuum.

Stiglitz, Joseph. (2006) *Making Globalization Work*. New York: Norton.

Stoessinger, John G. (2011) *Why Nations Go To War*, 11th ed. Belmont, CA: Thomson-Wadsworth.

Suskind, Ron. (2006) *The One Percent Doctrine: Deep Inside America's Pursuit of Its Enemies Since 9/11*. New York: Simon & Schuster.

—. (2004) *The Price of Loyalty: George W. Bush, the White House, and the Education of Paul O'Neill*. New York: Simon & Schuster.

Takeyh, Ray, and Nikolas K. Gvosdev. (2009) "Do Terrorist Networks Need a Home?' pp. 79–87 in Russell D. Howard, Reid L. Sawyer, and Natasha E. Bajema (eds.), *Terrorism and Counterterrorism: Understanding the New Security Environment*, 3rd ed. New York: McGraw-Hill.

Talbott, Strobe. (1996) "Democracy and National Interest," *Foreign Affairs* 75 (November/December): 47–63.

Tarrow, Sidney. (2006) *The New Transnational Activism*. New York: Cambridge University Press.

Tessman, Brock, and Steve Chan. (2004) "Power Cycles, Risk Propensity and Great Power Deterrence," *Journal of Conflict Resolution* 48 (April): 131–153.

Tetlock, Philip. (2006) *Expert Political Judgment*. Princeton, NJ: Princeton University Press.

Thakur, Ramesh, and Steve Lee. (2000) "Defining New Goals for Diplomacy in the Twenty-First Century," *International Herald Tribune* (January 19): 8.

't Hart, Paul. (1990) *Groupthink in Government: A Study of Small Groups and Policy Failure*. Amsterdam: Swets & Zeitlinger.

Thatcher, Margaret. (2002) *Statecraft: Strategies for a Changing World*. New York: HarperCollins.

Thomas, Daniel C. (2001) *The Helsinki Effect: International Norms, Human Rights, and the Demise of Communism*. Princeton, NJ: Princeton University Press.

Thompson, Kenneth W. (1953) "Collective Security Reexamined," *American Political Science Review* 47 (September): 753–772.

Thucydides. (1951) *The Peloponnesian War*, translated by Richard Crawley. New York: Modern Library.

Tickner, J. Ann. (2005) "What Is Your Research Program? Some Feminist Answers to International Relations Methodological Questions," *International Studies Quarterly* 49 (March): 1–21.

—. (2002) *Gendering World Politics*. New York: Columbia University Press.

—. (1988) "Hans Morgenthau's Principles of Political Realism: A Feminist Reformulation," *Millennium* 17 (3): 429–440.

Tickner, J. Ann, and Laura Sjoberg (2007) "Feminism," pp. 185–202 in Tim Dunne, Milja Kurki, and Steve Smith (eds.), *International Relations Theories*. Oxford, UK: Oxford University Press.

Timmerman, Kenneth. (1991) *The Death Lobby: How the West Armed Iraq*. Boston: Houghton Mifflin.

Todaro, Michael P. (2000) *Economic Development*, 7th ed. Reading, MA: Addison-Wesley.

Toner, Robin. (2002) "FBI Agent Gives Her Blunt Assessment" *The State* (Columbia, S.C.) (June 7): A5.

Traub, James. (2000) "Holbrooke's Campaign," *New York Times Magazine* (March 26): 41–45, 66, 69, 81.

Tuchman, Barbara W. (1962) *The Guns of August*. New York: Dell.

Turk, Danilo. (2001) "Genocide," p. 316 in Joel Krieger (ed.), *The Oxford Companion to Politics of the World*, 2nd ed. New York: Oxford University Press.

UNDP. (2009) *Human Development Report*. New York: United Nations Development Programme.

UNHCR. (2010) *2009 Global Trends*. Geneva: High Commissioner for Refugees.

United Nations Population Division (UNPD). (2004) *World Population Prospects*. New York: United Nations.

Urdal, Henrik. (2006) "A Clash of Generations? Youth Bulges and Political Violence," *International Studies Quarterly* 20 (September): 607–629.

U.S. Department of State. (2004) *Patterns of Global Terrorism 2004*, rev. ed. Washington, DC: Department of State.

U.S. National Intelligence Council (NIC). (2010) *Global Trends 2025: A Transformed World*. Hauppauge, NY: Nova Science Publishers.

—. (2004) *Mapping the Global Future*. Washington, DC: Government Printing Office.

Van Evera, Stephen. (1997) *Guide to Methods for Students of Political Science*. Ithaca, NY: Cornell University Press.

—. (1994) "Hypotheses on Nationalism and War," *International Security* 18 (Spring): 5–39.

Vasquez, John A. (2000) *What Do We Know About War?* Lanham, MD: Rowman & Littlefield.

—. (1998) *The Power of Power Politics: From Classical Realism to Neotraditionalism*. Cambridge, UK: Cambridge University Press.

—. (1993) *The War Puzzle*. Cambridge, UK: Cambridge University Press.

—. (1986) "Capability, Types of War, and Peace," *Western Political Quarterly* 39 (June): 313–327.

Vasquez, John A., and Colin Elman (eds.). (2003) *Realism and the Balancing of Power: A New Debate*. Upper Saddle River, NJ: Prentice Hall.

Vreeland, James Raymond. (2003) *The IMF and Economic Development*. Cambridge, UK: Cambridge University Press.

Wallace, Michael D. (1973) "Alliance Polarization, Cross-Cutting, and International War, 1815–1964: A Measurement Procedure and Some Preliminary Evidence," *Journal of Conflict Resolution* 17 (December): 575–604.

Wallerstein, Immanuel. (2005) *World-Systems Analysis*. Durham, NC: Duke University Press.

Walt, Stephen M. (2005) *Taming American Power*. New York: Norton.

—. (1987) *The Origins of Alliances*. Ithaca, NY: Cornell University Press.

Waltz, Kenneth N. (1988) "War in Neorealist Theory," pp. 39–52 in Robert I. Rotberg and Theodore K. Rabb (eds.). *The Origin and Prevention of Major Wars*. New York: Cambridge University Press.

—. (1979) *Theory of International Politics*. Reading, MA: Addison-Wesley.

Watson, Adam. (1992) *The Evolution of International Society*. London: Routledge.

Wayman, Frank. (1985) "Bipolarity, Multipolarity, and the Threat of War," pp. 115–144 in Alan Ned Sabrosky (ed.), *Polarity and War*. Boulder, CO: Westview.

WDI. (2010) *World Development Indicators 2010*. Washington, DC: World Bank.

—. (2009) *World Development Indicators 2009*. Washington, DC: World Bank.

WDR. (2010) *World Development Report 2010*. Washington, DC: World Bank.

—. (2009) *World Development Report 2009*. Washington, DC: World Bank.

Weart, Spencer R. (1994) "Peace among Democratic and Oligarchic Republics," *Journal of Peace Research* 31 (August): 299–316.

Weber, Cynthia. (2010) *International Relations Theory: A Critical Introduction*, 3rd ed. London: Routledge.

Wedgwood, Ruth. (2002) "Gallant Delusions," *Foreign Policy* 132 (September/October): 44–46.

Weede, Erich. (2005) *Balance of Power, Globalization and the Capitalist Peace*. Berlin: Liberal.

Weidenbaum, Murray. (2004) "Surveying the Global Marketplace," *USA Today* (January): 26–27.

Weiss, Thomas G. (2009) "What Happened to the Idea of World Government," *International Studies Quarterly* 53 (June): 253–271.

Wendt, Alexander. (2003) "Why a World State Is Inevitable," *European Journal of International Relations* 9 (4): 491–542.

—. (1999) *Social Theory of International Politics*. Cambridge: Cambridge University Press.

—. (1995) "Constructing International Politics," *International Security* 20 (Summer): 71–81.

White, Donald W. (1998) "Mutable Destiny: The End of the American Century?" *Harvard International Review* 20 (Winter): 42–47.

White, Ralph K. (1990) "Why Aggressors Lose," *Political Psychology* 11 (June): 227–242.

Williamson, Samuel R., Jr. (1988) "The Origins of World War I," pp. 225–248 in Robert I. Rotberg and Theodore K. Rabb (eds.), *The Origins and Prevention of Major Wars*. Cambridge: Cambridge University Press.

Wilmer, Franke. (2000) "Women, the State and War: Feminist Incursions into World Politics," pp. 385–395 in Richard W. Mansbach and Edward Rhodes (eds.), *Global Politics in a Changing World*. Boston: Houghton Mifflin.

Wilson, James Q. (1993) *The Moral Sense*. New York: Free Press.

Wilson, Woodrow. (1992) "The Coming Age of Peace," pp. 267–270 in Evan Luard (ed.), *Basic Texts in International Relations*. New York: St. Martin's Press.

Wohlforth, William C. (1999) "The Stability of a Unipolar World," *International Security* 24 (Summer): 5–41.

Wolf, Martin. (2004) "A Matter More Than Economics," *Financial Times* (April 13): Retrieved at yaleglobal.yale.edu/display.article?id=3701.

Wolfers, Arnold, and Laurence W. Martin (eds.). (1956) *The Anglo-American Tradition in Foreign Affairs*. New York: Oxford University Press.

Woodward, Bob. (2004) *Plan of Attack*. New York: Simon & Schuster.

—. (2002) *Bush At War*. New York: Simon & Schuster.

World Factbook. (2009) Washington, DC: Central Intelligence Agency.

World Investment Report. (2010) New York: United Nations Conference on Trade and Development.

WPDS (*World Population Data Sheet*). (2010) Washington, DC: Population Reference Bureau.

Yang, David W. (2005) "In Search of an Effective Democratic Realism," *SAIS Review of International Affairs* 15 (Winter/Spring): 199–205.

Yearbook of International Organizations. (2008–2009) Munich: K.G. Saur and Union of International Associations.

Yunker, James A. (2007) *Political Globalization: A New Vision of Federal World Government*. Lanham, MD: University Press of America.

Zacher, Mark W., and Richard A. Matthew. (1995) "Liberal International Theory: Common Threads, Divergent Strands," pp. 107–149 in Charles W. Kegley, Jr. (ed.), *Controversies in International Relations Theory*. New York: St. Martin's.

Zakaria, Fareed. (2009) "The Trouble with Subsidies," *Newsweek* (March 30): 29.

—. (2003) *The Future of Freedom: Illiberal Democracy at Home and Abroad*. New York: Norton.

—. (2002) "Stop the Babel over Babylon," *Newsweek* (October 16): 34.

Index

Note: Page numbers followed by f indicate figures, those followed by t indicate tables, those followed by m indicate maps.